CHILTON BOOK COMPANY

REPAIR MANUAL

DATSUN/NISSAN F10 · 310 · STANZA · PULSAR 1976-88

All U.S. and Canadian models of F10 • 310 • Stanza • Pulsar

MW00396452

car

plugs		air filter		Oil		
≈ 99,000	7/93	≈ 99,000		102,500	→ 10-30W	
≈ 111,000	12/23/94	≈ 111,000	purolator A34271 12/23/94	105,700	→ 10-40w	
				108,200	→ 10-40w	8/20/94
				111,000	→ 5-30W	12/19/94
				113,000	– Breakdown 10-40w ?	
				117,000	– 30W	11/1/95

Sr. Vice President	Ronald A. Hoxter
Publisher and Editor-In-Chief	Kerry A. Freeman, S.A.E.
Managing Editors	Peter M. Conti, Jr. □ W. Calvin Settle, Jr., S.A.E.
Assistant Managing Editor	Nick D'Andrea
Senior Editors	Richard J. Rivele, S.A.E. □ Ron Webb
Director of Manufacturing	Mike D'Imperio
Manager of Manufacturing	John F. Butler
Editor	Anthony C. Tortorici, A.S.E., S.A.E.

CHILTON BOOK COMPANY

ONE OF THE DIVERSIFIED PUBLISHING COMPANIES,
A PART OF CAPITAL CITIES/ABC, INC.

CONTENTS

1 GENERAL INFORMATION and MAINTENANCE

2 ENGINE PERFORMANCE and TUNE-UP

3 ENGINE and ENGINE OVERHAUL

4 EMISSION CONTROLS

5 FUEL SYSTEM

6 CHASSIS ELECTRICAL

7  DRIVE TRAIN

8  SUSPENSION and STEERING

9  BRAKES

10 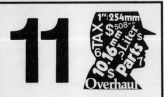 BODY

11 MECHANIC'S DATA

SAFETY NOTICE

Proper service and repair procedures are vital to the safe, reliable operation of all motor vehicles, as well as the personal safety of those performing repairs. This book outlines procedures for servicing and repairing vehicles using safe, effective methods. The procedures contain many NOTES, CAUTIONS and WARNINGS which should be followed along with standard safety procedures to eliminate the possibility of personal injury or improper service which could damage the vehicle or compromise its safety.

It is important to note that repair procedures and techniques, tools and parts for servicing motor vehicles, as well as the skill and experience of the individual performing the work vary widely. It is not possible to anticipate all of the conceivable ways or conditions under which vehicles may be serviced, or to provide cautions as to all of the possible hazards that may result. Standard and accepted safety precautions and equipment should be used during cutting, grinding, chiseling, prying, or any other process that can cause material removal or projectiles.

Some procedures require the use of tools specially designed for a specific purpose. Before substituting another tool or procedure, you must be completely satisfied that neither your personal safety, nor the performance of the vehicle will be endangered.

Although the information in this guide is based on industry sources and is as complete as possible at the time of publication, the possibility exists that the manufacturer made later changes which could not be included here. While striving for total accuracy, Chilton Book Company cannot assume responsibility for any errors, changes, or omissions that may occur in the compilation of this data.

PART NUMBERS

Part numbers listed in this reference are not recommendations by Chilton for any product by brand name. They are references that can be used with interchange manuals and aftermarket supplier catalogs to locate each brand supplier's discrete part number.

SPECIAL TOOLS

Special tools are recommended by the vehicle manufacturer to perform their specific job. Use has been kept to a minimum, but where absolutely necessary, they are referred to in the text by the part number of the tool manufacturer. Datsun special tools referred to in this guide are available through Kent-Moore Corporation, 29784 Little Mack, Roseville, Michigan 48066. For Canada, contact Kent-Moore of Canada, LTD., 2395 Cawthra Mississauga, Ontario, Canada L5A 3Ps., or an equivalent tool can be purchased locally from a tool supplier or parts outlet.

ACKNOWLEDGMENTS

Chilton Book Company expresses appreciation to the Nissan Motor Corporation in the U.S.A., Carson, California 90248 for their generous assistance.

Copyright © 1989 by Chilton Book Company
All Rights Reserved
Published in Radnor, Pennsylvania 19089 by Chilton Book Company

Manufactured in the United States of America
    67890   876543

Chilton's Repair Manual: Datsun/Nissan F-10, 310, Stanza, Pulsar 1976–88
ISBN 0-8019-7853-X pbk.
Library of Congress Catalog Card No. 87-47921

General Information and Maintenance

HOW TO USE THIS BOOK

Chilton's Repair Manual for the Datsun/Nissan F10, 310, Stanza and Pulsar is intended to help you learn more about the inner workings of your vehicle and save you money on its upkeep and operation.

The first two chapters will be the most used, since they contain maintenance and tune-up information and procedures. Studies have shown that a properly tuned and maintained car can get at least 10% better gas mileage than an out-of-tune car. The other chapters deal with the more complex systems of your car. Operating systems from engine through brakes are covered to the extent that the average do-it-yourselfer becomes mechanically involved. This book will not explain such things as rebuilding the differential for the simple reason that the expertise required and the investment in special tools make this task uneconomical. It will give you detailed instructions to help you change your own brake pads and shoes, replace spark plugs, and do many more jobs that will save you money, give you personal satisfaction, and help you avoid expensive problems.

A secondary purpose of this book is a reference for owners who want to understand their car and/or their mechanics better. In this case, no tools at all are required.

Before removing any bolts, read through the entire procedure. This will give you the overall view of what tools and supplies will be required. There is nothing more frustrating than having to walk to the bus stop on Monday morning because you were short one bolt on Sunday afternoon. So read ahead and plan ahead. Each operation should be approached logically and all procedures thoroughly understood before attempting any work.

All chapters contain adjustments, maintenance, removal and installation procedures, and repair or overhaul procedures. When repair is not considered practical, we tell you how to remove the part and then how to install the new or rebuilt replacement. In this way, you at least save the labor costs. Backyard repair of such components as the alternator is just not practical.

Two basic mechanic's rules should be mentioned here. One, whenever the left side of the car or engine is referred to, it is meant to specify the driver's side of the car. Conversely, the right side of the car means the passenger's side. Secondly, most screws and bolt are removed by turning counterclockwise, and tightened by turning clockwise.

Safety is always the most important rule. Constantly be aware of the dangers involved in working on an automobile and take the proper precautions. (See the section in this chapter Servicing Your Vehicle Safely and the SAFETY NOTICE on the acknowledgment page.)

Pay attention to the instructions provided. There are 3 common mistakes in mechanical work:

1. Incorrect order of assembly, disassembly or adjustment. When taking something apart or putting it together, doing things in the wrong order usually just costs you extra time; however, it CAN break something. Read the entire procedure before beginning disassembly. Do everything in the order in which the instructions say you should do it, even if you can't immediately see a reason for it. When you're taking apart something that is very intricate (for example, a carburetor), you might want to draw a picture of how it looks when assembled at one point in order to make sure you get everything back in its proper position. (We will supply exploded views whenever possible). When making adjustments, especially tune-up adjustments, do them in order; often, one adjustment affects another, and you cannot expect even satisfac-

tory results unless each adjustment is made only when it cannot be changed by any order.

2. Overtorquing (or undertorquing). While it is more common for over-torquing to cause damage, undertorquing can cause a fastener to vibrate loose causing serious damage. Especially when dealing with aluminum parts, pay attention to torque specifications and utilize a torque wrench in assembly. If a torque figure is not available, remember that if you are using the right tool to do the job, you will probably not have to strain yourself to get a fastener tight enough. The pitch of most threads is so slight that the tension you put on the wrench will be multiplied many, many times in actual force on what you are tightening. A good example of how critical torque is can be seen in the case of spark plug installation, especially where you are putting the plug into an aluminum cylinder head. Too little torque can fail to crush the gasket, causing leakage of combustion gases and consequent overheating of the plug and engine parts. Too much torque can damage the threads, or distort the plug which changes the spark gap.

There are many commercial products available for ensuring that fasteners won't come loose, even if they are not torqued just right (a very common brand is Loctite®). If you're worried about getting something together tight enough to hold, but loose enough to avoid mechanical damage during assembly, one of these products might offer substantial insurance. Read the label on the package and make sure the products is compatible with the materials, fluids, etc. involved before choosing one.

3. Crossthreading. This occurs when a part such as a bolt is screwed into a nut or casting at the wrong angle and forced. Cross threading is more likely to occur if access is difficult. It helps to clean and lubricate fasteners, and to start threading with the part to be installed going straight in. Then, start the bolt, spark plug, etc. with your fingers. If you encounter resistance, unscrew the part and start over again at a different angle until it can be inserted and turned several turns without much effort. Keep in mind that many parts, especially spark plugs, used tapered threads so that gentle turning will automatically bring the part you're treading to the proper angle if you don't force it or resist a change in angle. Don't put a wrench on the part until its's been turned a couple of turns by hand. If you suddenly encounter resistance, and the part has not seated fully, don't force it. Pull it back out and make sure it's clean and threading properly.

Always take your time and be patient; once you have some experience, working on your car will become an enjoyable hobby.

TOOLS AND EQUIPMENT

The service procedures in this book presuppose a familiarity with hand tools and their proper use. However, it is possible that you may have a limited amount of experience with the sort of equipment needed to work on an automobile. This section is designed to help you assemble a basic set of tools that will handle most of the jobs you may undertake.

In addition to the normal assortment of screwdrivers and pliers, automotive service work requires an investment in wrenches, sockets and the handles needed to drive them, plus various measuring tools such as torque wrenches and feeler gauges.

You will find that virtually every nut and bolt on your vehicle is metric. Therefore, despite a few close size similarities, standard inch-size tools will not fit and must not be used. You will need a set of metric wrenches as your most basic tool kit, ranging from about 6-17mm in size. High quality forged wrenches are available in three styles: open end, box end and combination open/box end. The combination tools are generally the most desirable as a starter set; the wrenches shown in the accompanying illustration are of the combination type.

The other set of tools inevitably required is a ratchet handle and socket set. This set should have the same size range as your wrench set. The ratchet, extensions and flex drives for the sockets are available in many sizes; it is advisable to choose a ⅜″ drive set initially. One break in the inch/metric sizing war is that metric sized sockets sold in the U.S. have inch-sized drive (¼″, ⅜″, ½″ and etc.). Thus, if you already have an inch-sized socket set, you need only buy new metric sockets in the sizes needed. Sockets are available in 6- and 12-point versions; six point types are stronger and are a good choice for a first set. The choice of a drive handle for the sockets should be made with some care. If this is your first set, take the plunge and invest in a flex-head ratchet; it will get into many places otherwise accessible only through a long chain of universal joints, extensions and adapters. An alternative is a flex handle, which lacks the ratcheting feature but has a head which pivots 180°; such a tool is shown below the ratchet handle in the illustration. In addition to the range of sockets mentioned, a rubber lined spark plug socket should be purchased. The correct size for the plugs in your vehicle's engine is $^{13}/_{16}″$.

The most important thing to consider when purchasing hand tools is quality. Don't be misled by the low cost of bargain tools. Forged wrenches, tempered screwdriver blades and fine tooth ratchets are much better investments than their less expensive counterparts. The skinned knuckles and frustration inflicted by poor quality tools make any job an unhappy chore. Another consideration is that quality tools come with an unbeatable replacement guarantee; if the tool breaks, you get a new one, no questions asked.

Most jobs can be accomplished using the tools on the accompanying lists. There will be an occasional need for a special tool, such as snap ring pliers; that need will be mentioned in the text. It would not be wise to buy a large assortment of tools on the premise that someday they will be needed. Instead, the tools should be acquired one at a time, each for a specific job, both to avoid unnecessary expense and to be certain that you have the right tool.

The tools needed for basic maintenance jobs, in addition to the wrenches and sockets mentioned, include:

1. Jackstands, for support.
2. Oil filter wrench.
3. Oil filter spout or funnel.
4. Grease gun.
5. Battery post and clamp cleaner.
6. Container for draining oil.
7. Many rags for the inevitable spills.

In addition to these items there are several others which are not absolutely necessary but handy to have around. These include a transmission funnel and filler tube, a drop (trouble) light on a long cord, an adjustable (crescent) wrench and slip joint pliers.

A more advanced list of tools, suitable for tune-up work, can be drawn up easily. While the tools are slightly more sophisticated, they need not be outrageously expensive. The key to these purchases is to make them with an eye towards adaptability and wide range. A basic list of tune-up tools could include:

1. Tachometer/dwell meter.
2. Spark plug gauge and gapping tool.
3. Feeler gauges for valve adjustment.
4. Timing light.

Note that if your vehicle has electronic ignition, you will have no need for a dwell meter and of course a tachometer is provided on the instrument panel of the vehicle. You will need both the wire type (spark plugs) and the flat type (valves) feeler gauges. The choice of a timing light should be made carefully. A light which works on the DC current supplied by the vehicle battery is the best choice; it should have a xenon tube for brightness. Since most of the vehicles have electronic ignition or will have it in the future, the light should have an inductive pickup which clamps around the No. 1 spark plug cable (the timing light illustrated has one of these pickups).

In addition to these basic tools, there are several other tools and gauges which you may find useful. These include:

1. A compression gauge. The screw-in type is slower to use but eliminates the possibility of faulty reading due to escaping pressure.
2. A manifold vacuum gauge.
3. A test light.
4. A combination volt/ohmmeter.
5. An induction meter, used to determine whether or not there is current flowing in a wire, an extremely helpful tool for electrical troubleshooting.

Finally, you will find a torque wrench necessary for all but the most basic of work. The beam type models are perfectly adequate. The newer click type (breakaway) torque wrenches are more accurate but are much more expensive and must be periodically recalibrated.

Special Tools

Special tools are available from:
Kent-Moore Corporation
29784 Little Mack
Roseville, Michigan 48066

In Canada:
Kent-Moore of Canada, Ltd.,
2395 Cawthra
Mississauga, Ontario
Canada L5A 3P2

SERVICING YOUR CAR SAFELY

It is virtually impossible to anticipate all of the hazards involved with automotive maintenance and service, but care and common sense will prevent most accidents.

The rules of safety for mechanics range from "don't smoke around gasoline," to "use the proper tool(s) for the job." The trick to avoiding injuries is to develop safe work habits and take every possible precaution.

Do's

● Do keep a fire extinguisher and first aid kit within easy reach.

● Do wear safety glasses or goggles when cutting, drilling, grinding or prying, even if you have 20–20 vision. If you wear glasses for the sake of vision, they should be made of hardened glass that can serve also as safety glasses or wear safety goggles over your regular glasses.

● Do shield your eyes whenever you work around the battery. Batteries contain sulphuric acid. In case of contact with the eyes or skin, flush the area with water or a mixture of water/ baking soda and get medical attention immediately.

● Do use safety stands for any undercar ser-

This basic collection of hand tools will handle most service needs

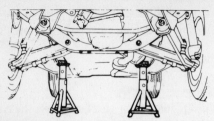

Always use jackstands or ramps when working under your car

vice. Jacks are for raising vehicles; safety stands are for making sure the vehicle stays raised until you want to come down. Whenever the car is raised, block the wheels remaining on the ground and set the parking brake.

• Do use adequate ventilation when working with any chemicals or hazardous materials. Like carbon monoxide, the asbestos dust resulting from break lining wear can be poisonous in sufficient quantities.

• Do disconnect the negative battery cable when working on the electrical system. The secondary ignition system can contain up to 40,000 volts.

• Do follow manufacturer's directions whenever working with potentially hazardous materials. Both brake fluid and antifreeze are poisonous if taken internally.

• Do properly maintain your tools. Loose hammerheads, mushroomed punches and chisels, frayed or poorly grounded electrical cords, excessively worn screwdrivers, spread wrenches (open end), cracked sockets, slipping ratchets or faulty droplight sockets can cause accidents.

• Do use the proper size and type of tool for the job being done.

• Do, when possible, pull on a wrench handle rather than push on it and adjust your stance to prevent a fall.

• Do be sure the adjustable wrenches are tightly closed on the nut or bolt and pulled so that the face is on the side of the fixed jaw.

• Do select a wrench or socket that fits the nut or bolt. The wrench or socket should sit straight, not cocked.

• Do strike squarely with a hammer; avoid glancing blows.

• Do set the parking brake and block the drive wheels if the work requires the engine running.

Don'ts

• Don't run an engine in a garage or anywhere else without proper ventilation–EVER! Carbon monoxide is poisonous; it takes a long time to leave the human body and you can build up a deadly supply of it in your system by simply breathing in a little every day. You may not realize you are slowly poisoning yourself. Always use power vents, windows, fans or open the garage doors.

• Don't work around moving parts while wearing a necktie or other loose clothing. Short sleeves are much safer than long, loose sleeves; hard-toed shoes with neoprene soles protect your toes and give a better grip on slippery surfaces. Jewelry such as watches, fancy belt buckles, beads or body adornment of any kind is not safe working around a car. Long hair should be hidden under a hat or cap.

• Don't use pockets for toolboxes. A fall or bump can drive a screwdriver deep into your body. Even a wiping cloth hanging from the back pocket can wrap around a spinning shaft or fan.

• Don't smoke when working around gasoline, cleaning solvent or other flammable material.

• Don't smoke when working around the battery. When the battery is being charged, it gives off explosive hydrogen gas.

• Don't use gasoline to wash your hands; there are excellent soaps available. Gasoline may contain lead, which can enter the body through a cut, accumulating in the body until you are very ill. Gasoline also removes all the natural oils from the skin so that bone dry hands will suck up oil and grease.

• Don't service the air conditioning system unless you are equipped with the necessary tools and training. The refrigerant (R-12) is under pressure; when released into the air, it will instantly freeze any surface it contacts, including your eyes. Although the refrigerant is normally non-toxic, R-12 becomes a deadly poisonous gas in the presence of an open flame. One good whiff of the vapors from burning refrigerant can be fatal.

HISTORY

In 1976, Datsun introduced the F10 model, equipped with an A14 engine. In 1979, the vehicle was changed to a 310 model, still equipped with the A14 engine. In 1981, the 310 model became equipped with an A15 engine, which is 5.0 cu. in. larger than the A14 engine. In 1982, the 310 model A15 engine was converted from the conventional point-type distributor to an electronic design; the newly converted engine is known as the E15 engine.

In 1982, Datsun Corporation merged with Nissan Corporation to become known as the Datsun/Nissan Corporation and in 1984, the Datsun name was dropped and the new company emerged as Nissan Corporation. The newly formed company dropped the 310 model in 1983. The Stanza model was introduced in 1982 with a CA20 engine. In 1984 the Stanza engine was redesigned into the CA20E (Electronic Fuel Injection) engine as is used to the present day. The Canadian version which was known as the CA20S engine was carbureted in 1984 up till 1986 and then dropped. In 1986, the Stanza wagon was introduce in a 2 wheel drive and 4 wheel drive models, using only the CA20E engine.

In 1983, a new sport model was introduced; known as the Pulsar, it uses an E16 or E16S carbureted engine, which is larger than the E15 engine. Only during 1984 did Nissan introduce into Canada the E15ET (EFI) engine, which is the turbo-charged version of the E15 engine. In 1987 the Pulsar E16i (fuel injected version of the E16S) and CA16DE were introduced. The CA16DE (1.6L) is a dual overhead camshaft, 16 valve engine. In 1988 the CA18DE (1.8L) replaced the CA16DE which is basically the same engine but larger.

SERIAL NUMBER IDENTIFICATION

Chassis

The chassis number is on the firewall under the hood on all models. All vehicles also have the chassis number (also known as the vehicle identification number) on a plate attached to the top of the instrument panel on the driver's side, visible through the windshield. The chassis serial number is preceded by the model designation. All models have an Emission Control information label on the firewall or on the underside of the hood.

Vehicle Identification Plate

The vehicle identification plate is attached to the right-side of the firewall. This plate gives the vehicle type, identification number, model, body color code, trim color code, engine model and displacement, transaxle model and axle model.

Engine

The engine number is stamped on the right-side top edge of the cylinder block on all models. The engine serial number is preceded by the engine model code.

Transaxle

The transaxle number is stamped on the front upper face of the transaxle case (1976–81 manual and 1982–88 automatic) or attached to the clutch withdrawal lever (1982–88 manual).

ROUTINE MAINTENANCE

Air Cleaner

REMOVAL AND INSTALLATION

All vehicles covered in this guide are equipped with a disposable paper cartridge air cleaner element. At every tune-up or sooner, if the car is operated in a dusty area, remove the housing cover and remove the element. Check the element by holding a drop light or equivalent up to the filter if light can be seen through the filter then filter should be OK. Replace the filter if it is extremely dirty. Loose dust can sometimes be removed by striking the filter against a hard surface several times or by blowing through it with compressed air from the inside out. The filter should be replaced every 30,000 miles or 24 months. Before installing either the original or a replacement filter, wipe out the inside of the air cleaner housing with a clean rag or paper towel. Install the paper air cleaner filter, seat the top cover on the bottom housing and tighten the cover.

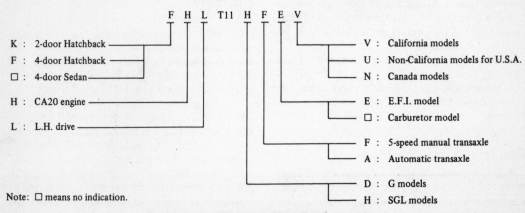

F H L T11 H F E V

K : 2-door Hatchback	V : California models
F : 4-door Hatchback	U : Non-California models for U.S.A.
□ : 4-door Sedan	N : Canada models
H : CA20 engine	E : E.F.I. model
L : L.H. drive	□ : Carburetor model
	F : 5-speed manual transaxle
	A : Automatic transaxle
	D : G models
	H : SGL models

Note: □ means no indication.

Description of the vehicle identification number

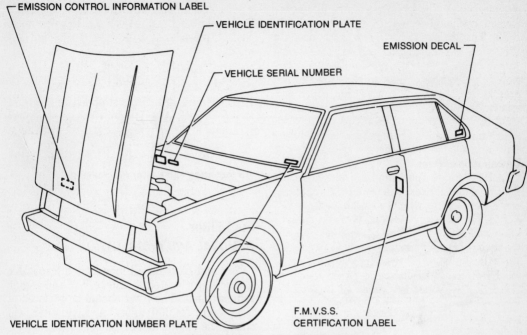

Locations of various identification plates

NISSAN MOTOR CO., LTD. JAPAN

型 式	TYPE TIPO	⚠

CHASSIS NO.
NO. DE CHASIS ⚠
MODEL
MODELO

○ カラ−COLOR TRIM
トリム COLOR GUARNICION ⚠ ⚠   ○

エン ENGINE
ジン MOTOR ⚠ ⚠   cc

ミッション TRANS, AXLE
アクスル TRANS, EJE ⚠ ⚠

工場 PLANT
PLANTA

日産自動車株式会社

1. Type
2. Vehicle identification number
   (chassis number)
3. Model
4. Body color code
5. Trim color code
6. Engine model
7. Engine displacement
8. Transaxle model
9. Axle model

View of the identification plate

NOTE: *The Stanza (1984 and later) and the Pulsar (1984 Turbo), use flat-rectangular cartridge type air cleaner elements, which have the word "UP" printed on them; be sure the side with "UP" on it, faces upward.*

Air Induction Valve Filter
REMOVAL AND INSTALLATION

This filter is located in the air cleaner on both fuel injected and carburetor models. To replace

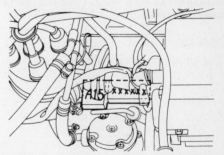

Engine ID number for 1976–81, other models are similar

it, remove the screws and the valve filter case. Install the new filter, paying attention to which direction the valve is facing so that exhaust gases will not flow backwards through the system.

NOTE: *Not all years and models use this filter.*

Transaxle ID number for 1976–81, other models are similar

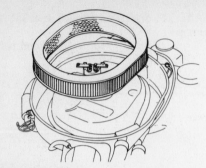

Air filter replacement

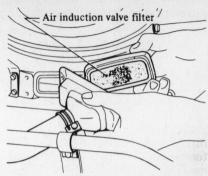

Air induction valve filter replacement

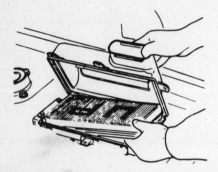

Replacing the air filter; Stanza (1984 and later) and Pulsar (1984 Turbo)

Fuel Filter

REMOVAL AND INSTALLATION

The fuel filter on all models is a disposable plastic unit; located at the rear of the engine compartment. The filter should be replaced at least every 24,000 miles. A dirty filter will starve the engine and cause poor running.

CAUTION: *If equipped with an Electronic Fuel Injected (EFI) engine, refer to the Fuel Pressure Release Procedure in this section*

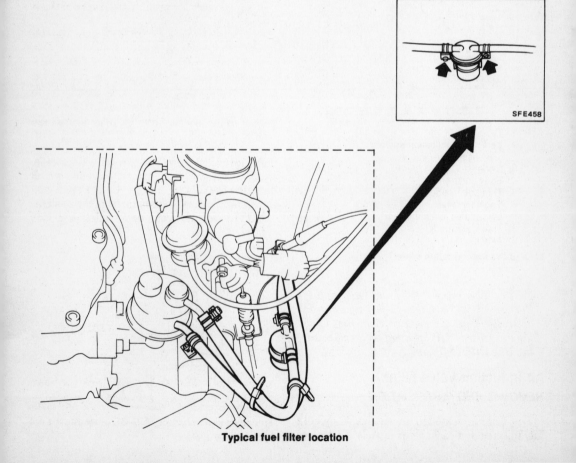

SFE458

Typical fuel filter location

and release the fuel pressure before removing filter.

1. Locate fuel filter on right-side of the engine compartment and place a container under the filter to catch the excess fuel.

NOTE: *On the Stanza 4 × 4 wagon, the fuel filter is found in-line, under the floor, near the fuel pump.*

2. Disconnect the inlet and outlet hoses from the fuel filter. Make certain that the inlet hose (bottom) doesn't fall below the fuel tank level or the gasoline will drain out.

3. Pry the fuel filter from its clip and replace the assembly.

4. Replace the inlet and outlet lines. Always replace the hose clamps. Tighten hose clamp so that clamp end is 3mm from the hose end.

NOTE: *Ensure that the screw does not contact adjacent parts.*

5. Start the engine and check for leaks.

FUEL PRESSURE RELEASE PROCEDURE

1. Start the engine.

2. On non-turbocharged engines, disconnect the (black) electrical harness connector, located under the passenger seat. On the turbocharged engines, disconnect the (green) electrical connector from the fuel pump relay, located on the fender at the front-left of the engine compartment.

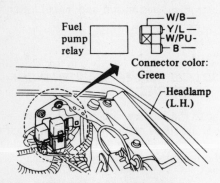

Location of the turbo fuel pump relay

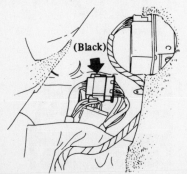

Location of the nonturbo fuel pump electrical connector

3. After the engine has stalled, crank it over 2–3 times.

4. Turn **OFF** the ignition switch and reconnect the electrical connector.

NOTE: *On all Pulsar and Stanza models that are fuel injected if the fuse box is equipped with a fuse for fuel pump, this fuse can be removed instead of disconnecting the electrical connector from the fuel pump or relay.*

Positive Crankcase Ventilation (PCV) Valve

REMOVAL AND INSTALLATION

This valve feeds crankcase blow-by gases into the intake manifold to be burned with the normal air/fuel mixture. The PCV valve should be replaced every 24,000 miles. Make sure that all PCV connections are tight. Check that the connecting hoses are clear and not clogged. Replace any brittle or broken hoses.

To replace the valve, which is located in the intake manifold:

1. Squeeze the hose clamp with pliers and remove the hose.

2. Using a wrench, unscrew the PCV valve and remove the valve.

3. Disconnect the ventilation hoses and flush with solvent.

4. Install the new PCV valve, then replace the hoses and clamp.

NOTE: *On all Pulsar models except turbocharged engine E15ET and on all Stanza models with a carburetor CA20 and CA20S engines a PCV filter is used. To replace this filter just remove the wing nut from the air cleaner lid and remove lid, gently lift out the*

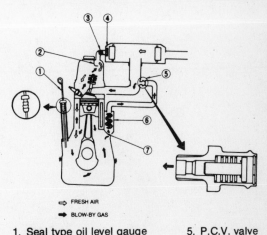

⇨ FRESH AIR
➡ BLOW-BY GAS

1. Seal type oil level gauge
2. Baffle plate
3. Flame arrester
4. Filter
5. P.C.V. valve
6. Steel net
7. Baffle plate

Typical PCV system

*filter which is mounted on the side of the air
cleaner. This filter is usually about 4" long.*

Evaporative Canister
SERVICING

A carbon filled canister stores fuel vapors until the engine is started and the vapors are
drawn into the combustion chambers and
burned. To check the operation of the carbon
canister purge control valve, disconnect the
rubber hose between the canister control valve
and the T-fitting, at the T-fitting. Apply vacuum to the hose leading to the control valve. The
vacuum condition should be maintained indefinitely. If the control valve leaks, remove the top
cover of the valve and check for a dislocated or
cracked diaphragm. If the diaphragm is damaged, a repair kit containing a new diaphragm,
retainer and spring is available and should be
installed.

The carbon canister has an air filter in the
bottom of the canister. The filter element

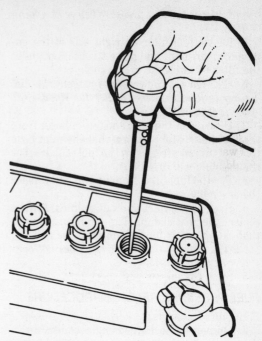

**Specific gravity can be checked with an hydro-
meter**

should be checked once a year or every 12,000
miles; more frequently if the car is operated in
dust areas. Replace the filter by pulling it out of
the bottom of the canister and installing a new
one.

Battery
FLUID LEVEL (EXCEPT MAINTENANCE FREE BATTERIES)

Check the battery electrolyte level at least
once a month, or more often in hot weather or
during periods of extended car operation. The
level can be checked through the case on trans-

1. Cover
2. Diaphragm
3. Retainer
4. Diaphragm spring

Typical vapor canister

INDICATOR

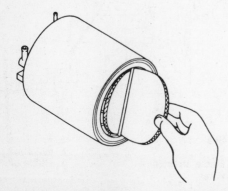

Canister filter replacement

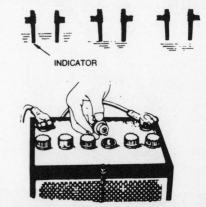

**Make sure the battery electrolite is at the bottom
of the filler holes**

lucent polypropylene batteries; the cell caps must be removed on other models. The electrolyte level in each cell should be kept filled to the split ring inside, or the line marked on the outside of the case.

If the level is low, add only distilled water, or colorless, odorless drinking water, through the opening until the level is correct. Each cell is completely separate from the others, so each must be checked and filled individually.

If water is added in freezing weather, the car should be driven several miles to allow the water to mix with the electrolyte. Otherwise, the battery could freeze.

SPECIFIC GRAVITY (EXCEPT "MAINTENANCE FREE" BATTERIES)

At least once a year, check the specific gravity of the battery. It should be between 1.20–1.26 at room temperature.

The specific gravity can be checked with an hydrometer, an inexpensive instrument available from many sources, including auto parts stores. The hydrometer has a squeeze bulb at one end and a nozzle at the other. Battery electrolyte is sucked into the hydrometer until the float is lifted from its seat. The specific gravity is then read by noting the position of the float. Generally, if after charging, the specific gravity between any 2 cells varies more than 50 points (0.050), the battery is bad and should be replaced.

It is not possible to check the specific gravity (in this manner) on sealed , maintenance free batteries. Instead, the indicator built into the top of the case must be relied on to display any signs of battery deterioration. If the indicator is dark, the battery can be assumed to be OK. If

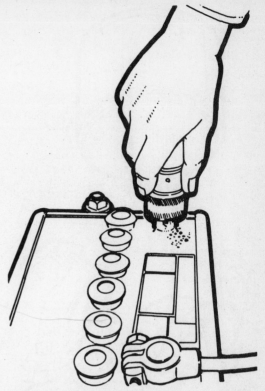

Clean the posts with a wire brush or a terminal cleaner made for the purpose (shown)

Clean the inside of the clamps with wire brush or the special tool

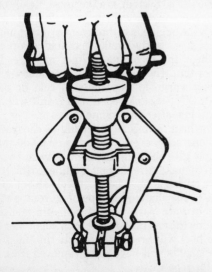

Removing the cable clamp with a special puller

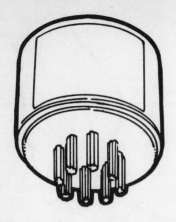

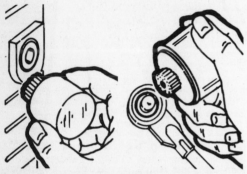

Special tools are also available for cleaning the posts and clamps on side terminal batteries

the indicator is light, the specific gravity is low and the battery should be charged or replaced.

CABLES AND CLAMPS

Once a year the battery terminals and the cable clamps should be cleaned. Loosen the clamps and remove the cables, the negative cable first. On top post batteries, a special puller is used to remove the cable clamps; these are inexpensive and are available from the auto parts stores. The side terminal battery cables are secured with a bolt.

Clean the cable clamps and the battery terminal with wire brush, until corrosion, grease and etc. are removed and the metal is shiny. It is especially important to clean the inside of the clamp thoroughly, since a small deposit of foreign material or oxidation will prevent electrical flow. Special tools are available for cleaning these parts, one type for conventional batteries and another type for side terminal batteries.

Before installing the cables, loosen the battery hold-down clamp or strap, remove the battery and check the battery tray. Clear it of any debris and check it for soundness. Rust should be wire brushed away and the metal given a coat of anti-rust paint. Replace the battery and tighten the hold-down clamp or strap securely,

but be careful not to overtighten, which will crack the battery case.

After the clamps and the terminals are clean, reinstall the cables, negative cable last; do not hammer on the clamps to install. Tighten the clamps securely but do not distort them. Give the clamps and the terminals a thin coat of petroleum jelly or equivalent after installation, to retard corrosion.

Check the cables at the same time that the terminals are cleaned. If the cable insulation is cracked, broken or if the ends are frayed, the cable should be replaced with a new cable of the same length and gauge.

CAUTION: *Keep flames or sparks away from the battery; it gives off explosive hydrogen gas. The electrolyte contains sulphuric acid. If you should splash any on your skin or in your eyes, flush the affected area with plenty of fresh water; if it gets into your eyes, get medical help immediately.*

REPLACEMENT

When it becomes necessary to replace the battery, select one with a rating equal to or greater than the original. Deterioration, embrittlement or just plain aging of the battery cables, starter motor and associated wiring makes the batteries job harder in successive years. The slow increase in electrical resistance over time makes it prudent to install a new battery with a greater capacity than the old. Details on battery removal and installation are covered in Chapter 3.

Heat Control Valve
SERVICING

The heat control valve or Early Fuel Evaporative (EFE) System, is a thermostatically operated valve in the exhaust manifold. It closes when the engine is warming up to direct hot exhaust gases to the intake manifold, in order to pre-heat the incoming air/fuel mixture. If it sticks shut, the result will be frequent stalling during warm–up, especially in cold or damp weather. If it sticks open, the result will be a rough idle after the engine is warm.

The heat control valve should be checked for free operation every 6 months or 6,000 miles. Simply give the counterweight a twist (engine cold) to make sure that no binding exists. If the valve sticks, apply a heat control solvent to the ends of the shaft. This type of solvent is available in auto parts stores. Sometimes lightly rapping the end of the shaft with a hammer (engine hot) will break it loose. If this fails, the components will have to be removed from the car for repair.

NOTE: *The 1980 and later engines do not*

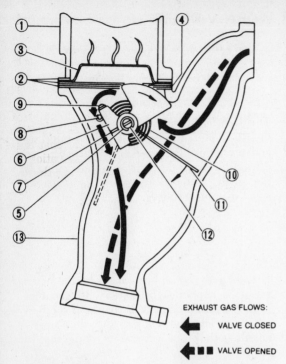

EXHAUST GAS FLOWS:

← VALVE CLOSED

←■■ VALVE OPENED

1. Intake manifold
2. Stove gasket
3. Manifold stove
4. Heat shield plate
5. Snap ring
6. Counterweight
7. Key
8. Stopper pin
9. Screw
10. Thermostat spring
11. Heat control valve
12. Control valve shaft
13. Exhaust manifold
14. Cap
15. Bushing
16. Coil spring

Heat riser used on earlier models with A series engines

use the heat control valve. Instead, these engines warm the fuel mixture by a coolant passage under the carburetor. No maintenance is required.

Belts

INSPECTION

Check the drive belts for cracks, fraying, wear and tension every 6,000 miles. It is recommended that the belts be replaced every 24 months or 24,000 miles. Belt deflection at the midpoint of the longest span between pulleys should not be more than $7/16''$ with 22 lbs. of pressure applied to the belt when engine is cold.

ADJUSTING

NOTE: *An overtight belt will wear out the pulley bearings on the assorted components.*

To adjust the tension on all components except the air conditioning compressor and power steering pump, loosen the pivot and mounting bolts of the component which the belt is driv-

ing, then, using a wooden lever or equivalent pry the component toward or away from the engine until the proper tension is achieved. Tighten the component mounting bolts securely. If a new belt is installed, recheck the tension after driving about 1,000 miles.

Belt tension adjustments for the factory installed air conditioning compressor are made at the idler pulley. The idler pulley is the smallest of the 3 pulleys. At the top of the slotted bracket holding the idler pulley there is a bolt which is used to either raise or lower the pulley. To free the bolt for adjustment, it is necessary to loosen the lock nut in the face of the idler pulley. After adjusting the belt tension, tighten the lock nut in the face of the idler pulley.

Belt tension adjustments for the power steering oil pump are made at the pump. Loosen the power steering oil pump adjusting lock bolt and its securing bolt. Adjust the adjusting bolt until the belt deflection is correct. Tighten the adjusting bolt lock bolt and oil pump securing bolt securely.

REMOVAL AND INSTALLATION

To replace a drive belt loosen the pivot and mounting bolts of the component which the belt is driving, then, using a wooden lever or equivalent pry the component inward to relieve the tension on the drive belt, always be careful where you locate the pry bar not to damage the component. Slip the belt off the component pulley, match up the new belt with the old belt for length and width, these measurement must be the same or problems will occur when you go to adjust the new belt. After new belt is installed correctly adjust the tension of the new belt.

NOTE: *When replacing more than one belt it is a good idea, to make note or mark what belt goes around what pulley. This will make installation fast and easy.*

On air conditioning compressor and power steering pump belt replacements loosen the lock bolt for the adjusting bolt on idler pulley or power steering pump and then loosen the adjusting bolt. Pry pulley or pump inward to relieve the tension on the drive belt, always be careful where you locate the pry bar not to damage the component or pulley.

Hoses

REMOVAL AND INSTALLATION

After engine is cold, remove the radiator cap and drain the radiator into a clean pan if you are going to reuse the old coolant. Remove the hose clamps and remove the hose by either cutting it off or twisting it to break its seal on the

HOW TO SPOT WORN V-BELTS

V-Belts are vital to efficient engine operation—they drive the fan, water pump and other accessories. They require little maintenance (occasional tightening) but they will not last forever. Slipping or failure of the V-belt will lead to overheating. If your V-belt looks like any of these, it should be replaced.

Cracking or weathering

This belt has deep cracks, which cause it to flex. Too much flexing leads to heat build-up and premature failure. These cracks can be caused by using the belt on a pulley that is too small. Notched belts are available for small diameter pulleys.

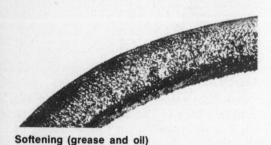

Softening (grease and oil)

Oil and grease on a belt can cause the belt's rubber compounds to soften and separate from the reinforcing cords that hold the belt together. The belt will first slip, then finally fail altogether.

Glazing

Glazing is caused by a belt that is slipping. A slipping belt can cause a run-down battery, erratic power steering, overheating or poor accessory performance. The more the belt slips, the more glazing will be built up on the surface of the belt. The more the belt is glazed, the more it will slip. If the glazing is light, tighten the belt.

Worn cover

The cover of this belt is worn off and is peeling away. The reinforcing cords will begin to wear and the belt will shortly break. When the belt cover wears in spots or has a rough jagged appearance, check the pulley grooves for roughness.

Separation

This belt is on the verge of breaking and leaving you stranded. The layers of the belt are separating and the reinforcing cords are exposed. It's just a matter of time before it breaks completely.

HOW TO SPOT BAD HOSES

Both the upper and lower radiator hoses are called upon to perform difficult jobs in an inhospitable environment. They are subject to nearly 18 psi at under hood temperatures often over 280°F., and must circulate nearly 7500 gallons of coolant an hour—3 good reasons to have good hoses.

Swollen hose

A good test for any hose is to feel it for soft or spongy spots. Frequently these will appear as swollen areas of the hose. The most likely cause is oil soaking. This hose could burst at any time, when hot or under pressure.

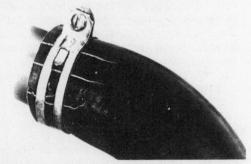

Cracked hose

Cracked hoses can usually be seen but feel the hoses to be sure they have not hardened; a prime cause of cracking. This hose has cracked down to the reinforcing cords and could split at any of the cracks.

Frayed hose end (due to weak clamp)

Weakened clamps frequently are the cause of hose and cooling system failure. The connection between the pipe and hose has deteriorated enough to allow coolant to escape when the engine is hot.

Debris in cooling system

Debris, rust and scale in the cooling system can cause the inside of a hose to weaken. This can usually be felt on the outside of the hose as soft or thinner areas.

radiator and engine coolant inlets. When installing the new hose, do not overtighten the hose clamps or you might cut the hose or destroy the neck of the radiator. Refill the radiator with coolant, run the engine with the radiator cap on and then recheck the coolant level after engine has reached operating temperature which is about 5 minutes.

NOTE: *It always is good idea, to replace hose clamps when replacing radiator hoses.*

Air Conditioning
SAFTEY WARNINGS

Because of the importance of the necessary safety precautions that must be exercised when working with air conditioning systems and R-12 refrigerant, a recap of the safety precautions are outlined.

1. Avoid contact with a charged refrigeration system, even when working on another part of the air conditioning system or vehicle. If a heavy tool comes into contact with a section of copper tubing or a heat exchanger, it can easily cause the relatively soft material to rupture.

2. When it is necessary to apply force to a fitting which contains refrigerant, as when checking that all system couplings are securely tightened, use a wrench on both parts of the fitting involved, if possible. This will avoid putting torque on refrigerant tubing. (It is advisable, when possible, to use tube or line wrenches when tightening these flare nut fittings.)

3. Do not attempt to discharge the system by merely loosening a fitting, or removing the service valve caps and cracking these valves. Precise control is possibly only when using the service gauges. Place a rag under the open end of the center charging hose while discharging the system to catch any drops of liquid that might escape. Wear protective gloves when connecting or disconnecting service gauge hoses.

4. Discharge the system only in a well ventilated area, as high concentrations of the gas can exclude oxygen and act as an anesthesia. When leak testing or soldering, this is particularly important, as toxic gas is formed when R-12 contacts any flame.

5. Never start a system without first verifying that both service valves are backseated, if equipped, and that all fittings are throughout the system are snugly connected.

6. Avoid applying heat to any refrigerant line or storage vessel. Charging may be aided by using water heated to less than +125°F (+51°C) to warm the refrigerant container. Never allow a refrigerant storage container to sit out in the sun, or near any other source of heat, such as a radiator.

7. Always wear goggles when working on a system to protect the eyes. If refrigerant contacts the eye, it is advisable in all cases to see a physician as soon as possible.

8. Frostbite from liquid refrigerant should be treated by first gradually warming the area with cool water, and then gently applying petroleum jelly. A physician should be consulted.

9. Always keep refrigerant can fittings capped when not in use. Avoid sudden shock to the can which might occur from dropping it, or from banging a heavy tool against it. Never carry a can in the passenger compartment of a car.

10. Always completely discharge the system before painting the vehicle (if the paint is to be baked on), or before welding anywhere near the refrigerant lines.

SYSTEM INSPECTION

CAUTION: *The compressed refrigerant used in the air conditioning system expands into the atmosphere at a temperature of −2°F or lower. This will freeze any surface, including your eyes, that it contacts. In addition, the refrigerant decomposes into a poisonous gas in the presence of a flame. Do not open or disconnect any part of the air conditioning system.*

Sight Glass Check

You can safely make a few simple checks to determine if your air conditioning system needs service. The tests work best if the temperature is warm (about 70°F).

NOTE: *If your vehicle is equipped with an after-market air conditioner, the following system check may not apply. You should contact the manufacturer of the unit for instructions on systems checks.*

1. Place the automatic transmission in **PARK** or the manual transaxle in **NEUTRAL**. Set the parking brake.

2. Run the engine at a fast idle (about 1,500 rpm) either with the help of a friend or by temporarily readjusting the idle speed screw.

3. Set the controls for maximum cold with the blower on High.

4. Locate the sight glass in one of the system lines. Usually it is on the left alongside the top of the radiator.

5. If you see bubbles, the system must be recharged. Very likely there is a leak at some point. If it is determined that the system has a leak, it should be corrected as soon as possible. Leaks may allow moisture to enter and cause a very expensive rust problem.

6. If there are no bubbles, there is either no refrigerant at all or the system is fully charged. Feel the 2 hoses going to the belt-driven compressor. If they are both at the same tempera-

ture, the system is empty and must be recharged.

7. If one hose (high-pressure) is warm and the other (low-pressure) is cold, the system may be all right. However, you are probably making these tests because you think there is something wrong, so proceed to the next step.

8. Have an assistant in the car, turn the fan control on and off to operate the compressor clutch. Watch the sight glass.

9. If bubbles appear when the clutch is disengaged and disappear when it is engaged, the system is properly charged.

10. If the refrigerant takes more than 45 seconds to bubble when the clutch is disengaged, the system is overcharged. This usually causes poor cooling at low speeds.

NOTE: *Run the air conditioner for a few minutes, every 2 weeks or so, during the cold months. This avoids the possibility of the compressor seals drying out from lack of lubrication.*

GAUGE SETS

Most of the service work performed in air conditioning requires the use of a set of 2 gauges, one for the high (head) pressure side of the system, the other for the low (suction) side.

The low side gauge records both pressure and vacuum. Vacuum readings are calibrated from 0 to 30 inches Hg and the pressure graduations read from 0 to no less than 60 psi.

The high side gauge measures pressure from 0 to at last 600 psi.

Both gauges are threaded into a manifold that contains two hand shut-off valves. Proper manipulation of these valves and the use of the attached test hoses allow the user to perform the following services:

1. Test high and low side pressures.
2. Remove air, moisture, and contaminated refrigerant.
3. Purge the system (of refrigerant).
4. Charge the system (with refrigerant).

The manifold valves are designed so that they have no direct effect on gauge readings, but serve only to provide for, or cut off, flow of refrigerant through the manifold. During all testing and hook-up operations, the valves are kept in a close position to avoid disturbing the refrigeration system. The valves are opened only to purge the system or refrigerant or to charge it.

DISCHARGING THE SYSTEM

1. Close the high and low pressure valves of the manifold gauge fully.
2. Connect the 2 charging hoses of the manifold gauge to their respective service valves.
3. Open both manifold gauge valves and discharge the refrigerant from the system.

NOTE: *Do not allow the refrigerant to rush out. Otherwise, compressor oil will be discharged along with the refrigerant.*

EVACUATING THE SYSTEM

NOTE: *This procedure requires the use of a vacuum pump.*

1. Connect the manifold gauge set.
2. Discharge the system.
3. Connect the center service hose to the inlet fitting of the vacuum pump.
4. Turn both gauge set valves to the wide open position.
5. Start the pump and note the low side gauge reading.
6. Operate the pump for a minimum of 30 minutes after the lowest observed gauge reading.
7. Leak test the system. Close both gauge set valves. Turn off the pump and note the low side gauge reading. The needle should remain stationary at the point at which the pump was turned off. If the needle drops to 0 rapidly, there is a leak in the system which must be repaired.
8. If the needle remains stationary for 3 to 5 minutes, open the gauge set valves and run the pump for at least 30 minutes more.
9. Close both gauge set valves, stop the pump and disconnect the gauge set. The system is now ready for charging.

CHARGING THE SYSTEM

1. Close (clockwise) both gauge set valves.
2. Connect the gauge set.
3. Connect the center hose to the refrigerant can opener valve.
4. Make sure the can opener valve is closed, that is, the needle is raised, and connect the valve to the can. Open the valve, puncturing the can with the needle.
5. Loosen the center hose fitting at the pressure gauge, allowing refrigerant to purge the hose of air.
6. Open the low side gauge set valve and the can valve.
7. Start the engine and turn the air conditioner to the maximum cooling mode. The compressor will operate and pull refrigerant gas into the system.

NOTE: *To help speed the process, the can may be placed, upright, in a pan of warm water, not exceeding +125°F (+51°C).*

8. If more than one can of refrigerant is needed, close the can valve and gauge set low side valve when the can is empty and connect a new can to the opener. Repeat the charging process until the sight glass indicates a full charge.
9. When the charging process has been completed, close the gauge set valve and can valve.

Troubleshooting Basic Air Conditioning Problems

Problem	Cause	Solution
There's little or no air coming from the vents (and you're sure it's on)	• The A/C fuse is blown • Broken or loose wires or connections • The on/off switch is defective	• Check and/or replace fuse • Check and/or repair connections • Replace switch
The air coming from the vents is not cool enough	• Windows and air vent wings open • The compressor belt is slipping • Heater is on • Condenser is clogged with debris • Refrigerant has escaped through a leak in the system • Receiver/drier is plugged	• Close windows and vent wings • Tighten or replace compressor belt • Shut heater off • Clean the condenser • Check system • Service system
The air has an odor	• Vacuum system is disrupted • Odor producing substances on the evaporator case • Condensation has collected in the bottom of the evaporator housing	• Have the system checked/repaired • Clean the evaporator case • Clean the evaporator housing drains
System is noisy or vibrating	• Compressor belt or mountings loose • Air in the system	• Tighten or replace belt; tighten mounting bolts • Have the system serviced

Sight glass condition
  Constant bubbles, foam or oil streaks
  Clear sight glass, but no cold air
  Clear sight glass, but air is cold
  Clouded with milky fluid
	
	• Undercharged system
	
	• No refrigerant at all
	• System is OK
	• Receiver drier is leaking dessicant
		
		• Charge the system
		
		• Check and charge the system
		
		• Have system checked

Large difference in temperature of lines	• System undercharged	• Charge and leak test the system
Compressor noise	• Broken valves • Overcharged • Incorrect oil level • Piston slap • Broken rings • Drive belt pulley bolts are loose	• Replace the valve plate • Discharge, evacuate and install the correct charge • Isolate the compressor and check the oil level. Correct as necessary. • Replace the compressor • Replace the compressor • Tighten with the correct torque specification
Excessive vibration	• Incorrect belt tension • Clutch loose • Overcharged • Pulley is misaligned	• Adjust the belt tension • Tighten the clutch • Discharge, evacuate and install the correct charge • Align the pulley
Condensation dripping in the passenger compartment	• Drain hose plugged or improperly positioned • Insulation removed or improperly installed	• Clean the drain hose and check for proper installation • Replace the insulation on the expansion valve and hoses
Frozen evaporator coil	• Faulty thermostat • Thermostat capillary tube improperly installed • Thermostat not adjusted properly	• Replace the thermostat • Install the capillary tube correctly • Adjust the thermostat
Low side low—high side low	• System refrigerant is low • Expansion valve is restricted	• Evacuate, leak test and charge the system • Replace the expansion valve
Low side high—high side low	• Internal leak in the compressor— worn	• Remove the compressor cylinder head and inspect the compressor. Replace the valve plate assembly if necessary. If the compressor pistons, rings or

Troubleshooting Basic Air Conditioning Problems (cont.)

Problem	Cause	Solution
Low side high—high side low (cont.)		cylinders are excessively worn or scored replace the compressor
	• Cylinder head gasket is leaking	• Install a replacement cylinder head gasket
	• Expansion valve is defective	• Replace the expansion valve
	• Drive belt slipping	• Adjust the belt tension
Low side high—high side high	• Condenser fins obstructed	• Clean the condenser fins
	• Air in the system	• Evacuate, leak test and charge the system
	• Expansion valve is defective	• Replace the expansion valve
	• Loose or worn fan belts	• Adjust or replace the belts as necessary
Low side low—high side high	• Expansion valve is defective	• Replace the expansion valve
	• Restriction in the refrigerant hose	• Check the hose for kinks—replace if necessary
	• Restriction in the receiver/drier	• Replace the receiver/drier
	• Restriction in the condenser	• Replace the condenser
Low side and high side normal (inadequate cooling)	• Air in the system	• Evacuate, leak test and charge the system
	• Moisture in the system	• Evacuate, leak test and charge the system

Run the system for at least 5 minutes to allow it to normalize.

10. Loosen both service hoses at the gauges to allow any refrigerant to escape. Remove the gauge set and install the dust caps on the service valves.

NOTE: *Multi-can dispensers are available which allow a simultaneous hook-up of up to four 1 lb. cans of R-12.*

CAUTION: *Never exceed the recommended maximum charge for the system. The maximum charge for systems is 3 lbs.*

Windshield Wipers

For maximum effectiveness and longest element life, the windshield and wiper blades should be kept clean. Dirt, tree sap, road tar and so on will cause streaking, smearing and blade deterioration if left on the windshield. It is advisable to wash the windshield carefully with a commercial glass cleaner at least once a month. Wipe off the rubber blades with a wet rag afterwards. Do not attempt to move the wipers back and forth by hand; damage to the motor and drive mechanism will result.

If the blades are found to be cracked, broken or torn they should be replaced immediately. Replacement intervals will vary with usage, although ozone deterioration usually limits blade life to about 1 year. If the wiper pattern is smeared or streaked, or if the blade chatters across the glass, the blades should be replaced. It is easiest and most sensible to replace them in pairs.

There are basically 3 different types of wiper blade refills, which differ in their method of replacement. One type has 2 release buttons, approximately ⅓ of the way up from the ends of the blade frame. Pushing the buttons down releases a lock and allows the rubber blade to be removed from the frame. The new blade slides back into the frame and locks in place.

The second type of refill has 2 metal tabs which are unlocked by squeezing them together. The rubber blade can then be withdrawn from the frame jaws. A new one is installed by inserting it into the front frame jaws and sliding it rearward to engage the remaining frame jaws. There are usually 4 jaws; be certain when installing that the refill is engaged in all of them. At the end of its travel, the tabs will lock into place on the front jaws of the wiper blade frame.

The third type is a refill made from polycarbonate. The refill has a simple locking device at one end which flexes downward out of the groove into which the jaws of the holder fit, allowing easy release. By sliding the new refill through all the jaws and pushing through the slight resistance when it reaches the end of its travel, the refill will lock into position.

Regardless of the type of refill used, make sure that all of the frame jaws are engaged as the refill is pushed into place and locked. The

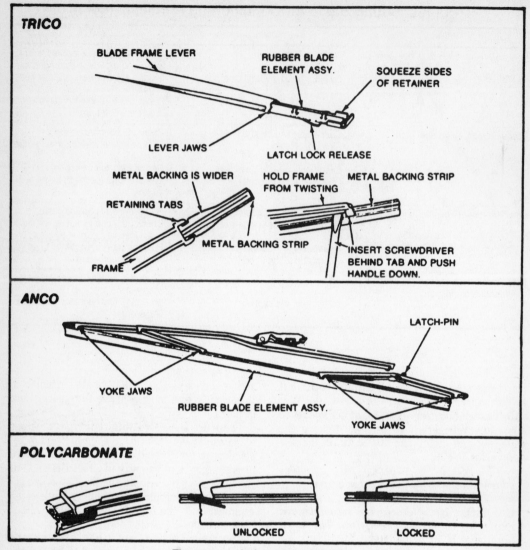

Three types of wiper blade retention

metal blade holder and frame will scratch the glass if allowed to touch it.

Tire and Wheels

TIRE ROTATION

Tires should be rotated periodically to get the maximum tread lift available. A good time to do this is when changing over from regular tires to snow tires, or about once per year. If front end problems are suspected have them corrected before rotating the tires. Torque the lug nuts to 58–72 ft. lbs. on all models up to 1986. Starting in 1987, torque lug nuts to 72–87 ft. lbs.

NOTE: *Mark the wheel position or direction of rotation on radial, or studded snow tires before removing them.*

Avoid overtightening the lug nuts to prevent damage to the brake disc or drum. Alloy wheels can also be cracked by overtightening. Use of a torque wrench is highly recommended. Tighten the lug nuts in a criss-cross sequence.

TIRE DESIGN

All 4 tires should be of the same construction type. Radial, bias, or bias-belted tires should not be mixed. The wheels must be the correct width for the tire. Tire dealers have charts of tire and rim compatibility. A mismatch can cause sloppy handling and rapid tire wear. The tread width should match the rim width (inside bead to inside bead) within an inch. For radial tires, the rim width should be 80% or less of the tire (not tread) width. The height (mounted diameter) of the new tires can greatly change speedometer accuracy, engine speed at a given

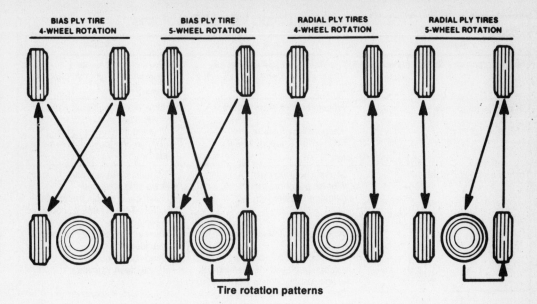

| BIAS PLY TIRE 4-WHEEL ROTATION | BIAS PLY TIRE 5-WHEEL ROTATION | RADIAL PLY TIRES 4-WHEEL ROTATION | RADIAL PLY TIRES 5-WHEEL ROTATION |

Tire rotation patterns

road speed, fuel mileage, acceleration, and ground clearance. Tire manufacturers furnish full measurement specifications.

TIRE INFLATION

The tires should be checked frequently for proper air pressure. Make sure that the tires are cool, as you will get a false reading when the tires are heated because air pressure increases with temperature. A chart in the glove compartment or on the driver's door pillar gives the recommended inflation pressure. Maximum fuel economy and tire life will result if pressure is maintained at the highest figure given on chart. When checking pressures, do

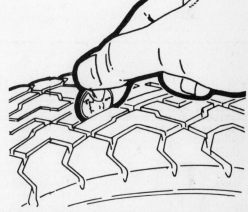

A Lincoln penny can be used to approximate tread depth. If the top of Lincoln's head is visible in two adjacent grooves, replace the tire

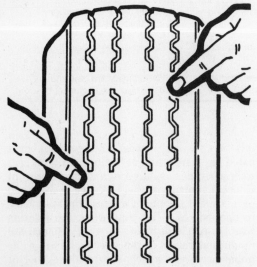

Tread wear indicators will appear when the tire is worn out

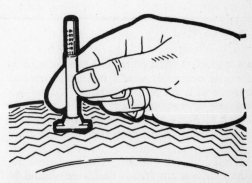

Check the tread depth with an inexpensive depth gauge

Troubleshooting Basic Wheel Problems

Problem	Cause	Solution
The car's front end vibrates at high speed	• The wheels are out of balance • Wheels are out of alignment	• Have wheels balanced • Have wheel alignment checked/adjusted
Car pulls to either side	• Wheels are out of alignment • Unequal tire pressure • Different size tires or wheels	• Have wheel alignment checked/adjusted • Check/adjust tire pressure • Change tires or wheels to same size
The car's wheel(s) wobbles	• Loose wheel lug nuts • Wheels out of balance • Damaged wheel • Wheels are out of alignment • Worn or damaged ball joint • Excessive play in the steering linkage (usually due to worn parts) • Defective shock absorber	• Tighten wheel lug nuts • Have tires balanced • Raise car and spin the wheel. If the wheel is bent, it should be replaced • Have wheel alignment checked/adjusted • Check ball joints • Check steering linkage • Check shock absorbers
Tires wear unevenly or prematurely	• Incorrect wheel size • Wheels are out of balance • Wheels are out of alignment	• Check if wheel and tire size are compatible • Have wheels balanced • Have wheel alignment checked/adjusted

Troubleshooting Basic Tire Problems

Problem	Cause	Solution
The car's front end vibrates at high speeds and the steering wheel shakes	• Wheels out of balance • Front end needs aligning	• Have wheels balanced • Have front end alignment checked
The car pulls to one side while cruising	• Unequal tire pressure (car will usually pull to the low side) • Mismatched tires • Front end needs aligning	• Check/adjust tire pressure • Be sure tires are of the same type and size • Have front end alignment checked
Abnormal, excessive or uneven tire wear	• Infrequent tire rotation • Improper tire pressure • Sudden stops/starts or high speed on curves	• Rotate tires more frequently to equalize wear • Check/adjust pressure • Correct driving habits
Tire squeals	• Improper tire pressure • Front end needs aligning	• Check/adjust tire pressure • Have front end alignment checked

not neglect the spare tire. The tires should be checked before driving since pressure can increase as much as 6 pounds per square inch (psi) due to heat buildup.

NOTE: *Some spare tires require pressures considerably higher than those used in other tires.*

While you are checking the tire pressure, take a look at the tread. The tread should be wearing evenly across the tire. Excessive wear in the center of the tread could indicate over-inflation. Excessive wear on the outer edges could indicate underinflation. An irregular wear pattern is usually a sign of incorrect front wheel alignment or wheel balance. A front end that is out of alignment will usually pull the car to one side of a flat road when the steering wheel is released. Incorrect wheel balance will produce vibration in the steering wheel, while unbalanced rear wheels will result in floor or trunk vibration.

It is a good idea to have your own accurate

Tire Size Comparison Chart

"Letter" sizes			Inch Sizes	Metric-inch Sizes		
"60 Series"	"70 Series"	"78 Series"	1976–77	"60 Series"	"70 Series"	"80 Series"
			5.50-12, 5.60-12	165/60-12	165/70-12	155-12
		Y78-12	6.00-12			
		W78-13	5.20-13	165/60-13	145/70-13	135-13
		Y78-13	5.60-13	175/60-13	155/70-13	145-13
			6.15-13	185/60-13	165/70-13	155-13, P155/80-13
A60-13	A70-13	A78-13	6.40-13	195/60-13	175/70-13	165-13
B60-13	B70-13	B78-13	6.70-13	205/60-13	185/70-13	175-13
			6.90-13			
C60-13	C70-13	C78-13	7.00-13	215/60-13	195/70-13	185-13
D60-13	D70-13	D78-13	7.25-13			
E60-13	E70-13	E78-13	7.75-13			195-13
			5.20-14	165/60-14	145/70-14	135-14
			5.60-14	175/60-14	155/70-14	145-14
			5.90-14			
A60-14	A70-14	A78-14	6.15-14	185/60-14	165/70-14	155-14
	B70-14	B78-14	6.45-14	195/60-14	175/70-14	165-14
	C70-14	C78-14	6.95-14	205/60-14	185/70-14	175-14
D60-14	D70-14	D78-14				
E60-14	E70-14	E78-14	7.35-14	215/60-14	195/70-14	185-14
F60-14	F70-14	F78-14, F83-14	7.75-14	225/60-14	200/70-14	195-14
G60-14	G70-14	G77-14, G78-14	8.25-14	235/60-14	205/70-14	205-14
H60-14	H70-14	H78-14	8.55-14	245/60-14	215/70-14	215-14
J60-14	J70-14	J78-14	8.85-14	255/60-14	225/70-14	225-14
L60-14	L70-14		9.15-14	265/60-14	235/70-14	
	A70-15	A78-15	5.60-15	185/60-15	165/70-15	155-15
B60-15	B70-15	B78-15	6.35-15	195/60-15	175/70-15	165-15
C60-15	C70-15	C78-15	6.85-15	205/60-15	185/70-15	175-15
	D70-15	D78-15				
E60-15	E70-15	E78-15	7.35-15	215/60-15	195/70-15	185-15
F60-15	F70-15	F78-15	7.75-15	225/60-15	205/70-15	195-15
G60-15	G70-15	G78-15	8.15-15/8.25-15	235/60-15	215/70-15	205-15
H60-15	H70-15	H78-15	8.45-15/8.55-15	245/60-15	225/70-15	215-15
J60-15	J70-15	J78-15	8.85-15/8.90-15	255/60-15	235/70-15	225-15
	K70-15		9.00-15	265/60-15	245/70-15	230-15
L60-15	L70-15	L78-15, L84-15	9.15-15			235-15
	M70-15	M78-15				255-15
		N78-15				

Note: Every size tire is not listed and many size comparisons are approximate, based on load ratings. Wider tires than those supplied new with the vehicle, should always be checked for clearance.

gauge, and to check pressures weekly. Not all gauges on service station air pumps can be trusted.

Tires should be replaced when a tread wear indicator appears as a solid band across the tread.

CARE OF SPECIAL WHEELS

Aluminum wheels should be cleaned and waxed regularly. Do not use abrasive cleaners, as they could damage the protective coating. Inspect wheel rims regularly for dents or corrosion, which may cause loss of pressure, damage the tire bead, or sudden wheel failure.

FLUIDS AND LUBRICANTS

Fuel Recommendations

All engines covered in this book have been designed to run on unleaded fuel. The minimum octane requirement is 91 RON (Research Octane Nunber) or 87 AKI (Anti-Knock Index); all unleaded fuels sold in the U.S. are required to meet this minimum octane rating.

The use of a fuel too low in octane (a measurement of anti-knock quality) will result in spark knock. Since many factors such as altitude, terrain, air temperature and humidity af-

Capacities

Year	Model	Engine Crankcase (qts)		Transaxle (pts)			Fuel Tank (gal)	Cooling System (qts)	
		with Filter	w/o Filter	4-sp	5-sp	Auto.		with Heater	w/o Heater
1976–78	F10	3.5	3.0	4.9	4.9	—	10.6①	7.0	6.4
1979–81	310	3.4	2.8	4.9	4.9	—	13.25	6.2	5.6
1982	310	4.1	3.6	4.9	5.75	12.75	13.25	6.5	5.5
1982–83	Stanza	4.1	3.75	—	5.75	12.75	14.25	7.75	6.9
1984	Stanza	4.0	3.75	—	5.75	12.75	14.25	7.1②	6.1②
1985–88	Stanza	3.6	3.25	—	5.75	12.75	14.25	7.1②	6.1②
1983–84	Pulsar	4.1	3.6	—	5.75	12.75	13.25	5.0③	4.4③
1985–88	Pulsar	3.5	3.1	—	5.75	12.75	13.25	5.0③	4.4③

① Wagon 9.1 gal.
② For A/T, add ⅜ qts.
③ For A/T, add ⅝ qts.

fect the operating efficiency, knocking may result even though the recommended fuel is being used. If persistent knocking occurs, it may be necessary to switch to a higher grade of fuel. Continuous or heavy knocking may result in engine damage.

NOTE: *Your engine's fuel requirement can change with time, mainly due to carbon buildup, which will in turn change the compression ratio. If your engine pings, knocks or runs on, switch to a higher grade of fuel. Sometimes just changing brands will cure the problem. If it becomes necessary to retard the timing from the specifications, don't change it more than a few degrees. Retarded timing will reduce power output and fuel mileage, in addition to increasing the engine temperature.*

Engine Oil Recommendations

Oil must be selected with regard to the anticipated temperatures during the period before the next oil change. Using the chart, select the oil viscosity for the lowest expected temperature and you will be assured of easy cold starting and sufficient engine protection. The oil you pour into your engine should have the designation "SE or SE/SF" marked on the top of its container.

SYNTHETIC OIL

There are many excellent synthetic and fuel-efficient oils currently available that can provide better gas mileage, longer service life, and in some cases better engine protection. These benefits do not come without a few hitches, however — the main one being the price of synthetic oils, which is 3 or 4 times the price per quart of conventional oil.

Synthetic oil is not for every car and every type of driving, so you should consider your engine's condition and your type of driving. Also, check your car's warranty guidelines at the dealership that you purchased the car from, regarding the use of synthetic oils and your powertrain and or extended warranty.

Both brand new engines and older, high mileage engines are the wrong candidates for synthetic oil. The synthetic oils are so slippery that they can prevent the proper break-in of new engines; most manufacturers recommend that you wait until the engine is properly broken in (5,000 miles) until using synthetic oil. Older engines with wear have a different problem with synthetics: they use (consume during opera-

Oil Viscosity Selection Chart

	Anticipated Temperature Range	SAE Viscosity
Multi-grade	Above 32°F	10W—40 10W—50 20W—40 20W—50 10W—30
	May be used as low as −10°F	10W—30 10W—40
	Consistently below 10°F	5W—20 5W—30
Single-grade	Above 32°F	30
	Temperature between +32°F and −10°F	10W

tion) more oil as they age. Slippery synthetic oils get past these worn parts easily. If your engine is using conventional oil, it will use synthetics much faster. Also, if your car is leaking oil past old seals you'll have a much greater leak problem with synthetics.

Cars used under harder circumstances, such as stop-and-go, city type driving, short trips, or extended idling, should be serviced more frequently. For the engines in these cars, the much greater cost of synthetic or fuel-efficient oils may not be worth the investment. Internal wear increases much quicker on these cars, causing greater oil consumption and leakage.

NOTE: *The mixing of conventional and synthetic oils is not recommended. If you are using synthetic oil, it might be wise to carry 2 or 3 quarts with you no matter where you drive, as not all service stations carry this type of lubricant.*

OIL LEVEL CHECK

The best time to check the engine oil is before operating the engine or after it has been sitting for at least 10 minutes in order to gain an accurate reading. This will allow the oil to drain back in the crankcase. To check the engine oil level, make sure that the vehicle is resting on a level surface, remove the oil dipstick, wipe it clean and reinsert the stick firmly for an accurate reading. The oil dipstick has two marks to indicate high and low oil level. If the oil is at or below the "low level" mark on the dipstick, oil should be added as necessary. The oil level should be maintained in the safety margin, neither going above the "high level" mark or below the "low level" mark.

OIL AND FILTER CHANGE

NOTE: *Datsun/Nissan factory maintenance intervals (every 7,500 miles) specify changing the oil filter at every second oil change after the initial service. We recommend replacing the oil filter with every oil change. For the small price of an oil filter, it's cheap insurance to replace the filter at every oil change.*

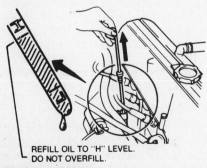

REFILL OIL TO "H" LEVEL.
DO NOT OVERFILL.

Oil dipstick markings

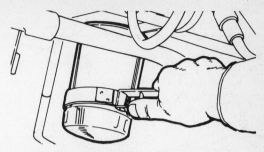

Removing the oil filter with a strap wrench

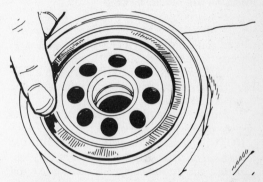

Apply a light coat of oil to the filter gasket before installation

One of the larger filter manufacturers points out in its advertisements that not changing the filter leaves 1 quart of dirty oil in the engine. This claim is true and should be kept in mind when changing your oil.

1. Run the engine until it reaches normal operating temperature.

2. Jack up the front of the car and support it on safety stands if necessary to gain access to the filter.

3. Slide a drain pan of at least 6 quarts capacity under the oil pan.

4. Loosen the drain plug. Turn the plug out by hand. By keeping an inward pressure on the plug as you unscrew it, oil won't escape past the threads and you can remove it without being burned by hot oil.

5. Allow the oil to drain completely and then install the drain plug. Don't overtighten the

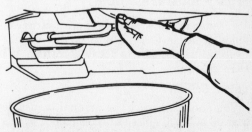

By keeping inward pressure on the plug as you unscrew it, oil won't escape past the threads

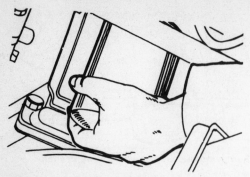

Install the new oil filter by hand

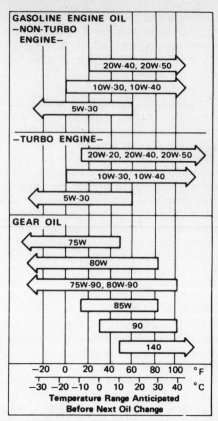

Manual transaxle and engine oil recommendations; automatic transaxle uses Dexron automatic transmission fluid.

plug or you'll be buying a new pan or a trick replacement plug for damaged threads.

6. Using a strap wrench, remove the oil filter. Keep in mind that it's holding about one quart of dirty, hot oil.

7. Empty the old filter into the drain pan and dispose of the filter and old oil.

NOTE: *One ecologically desirable solution to the used oil disposal problem is to find a cooperative gas station owner who will allow you to dump your used oil into his tank or take the oil to a reclamation center (often at garages and gas stations.*

8. Using a clean rag, wipe off the filter adapter on the engine block. Be sure that the rag doesn't leave any lint which could clog an oil passage.

9. Coat the rubber gasket on the filter with fresh oil. Spin it onto the engine *by hand*; when the gasket touches the adapter surface give it another ½-¾ turn. No more or you'll squash the gasket and it will leak.

10. Refill the engine with the correct amount of fresh oil. See the Capacities chart.

11. Crank the engine over several times and then start it. If the oil pressure indicator light doesn't go out or the pressure gauge shows zero, shut the engine down and find out what's wrong.

12. If the oil pressure is OK and there are no leaks, shut the engine off and lower the car.

Manual Transaxle

FLUID RECOMMENDATION

For manual transaxles, there are a variety of fluids available (depending upon the outside temperature); be sure to use fluid with an API GL-4 rating.

LEVEL CHECK

You should inspect the manual transaxle gear oil at 3,000 miles or once a month at this point you should correct the level or replace the oil as necessary. The lubricant level should be

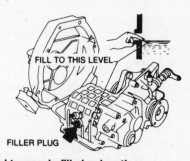

Manual transaxle fill plug location

even with the bottom of the filler hole. Hold in on the filler plug when unscrewing it. When you are sure that all of the threads of the plug are free of the transaxle case, move the plug away from the case slightly. If lubricant begins to flow out of the transaxle, then you know it is full. If not, add gear oil as necessary

DRAIN AND REFILL

NOTE: *It is recommended that the manual transaxle fluid be changed every 30,000 miles. If the vehicle is normally used in severe service, the interval should be halved. You*

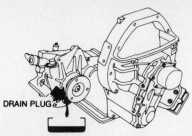

Manual transaxle drain plug

DRAIN PLUG

may also want to change it if you have bought your car used or if it has been driven in water deep enough to reach the transaxle case.

1. Run the engine until it reaches normal operating temperature then turn key to the **OFF** position.

2. Jack up the front of the car and support it on safety stands if necessary to gain access.

3. Remove the filler plug from the left-side of the transaxle to provide a vent.

4. The drain plug is located on the bottom of the transaxle case. Place a pan under the drain plug and remove it.

CAUTION: *The oil will be HOT. Push up against the threads as you unscrew the plug to prevent leakage.*

5. Allow the oil to drain completely. Clean off the plug and replace it. DO NOT OVERTIGHTEN PLUG.

6. Fill the transaxle with gear oil through the filler plug hole. Use API service GL-4 gear oil of the proper viscosity (see the ''Viscosity Chart''). This oil usually comes in a squeeze bottle with a long nozzle. If yours isn't, use a plastic squeeze bottle (the type used in the kitchen). Refer to the ''Capacities'' chart for the amount of oil needed.

7. The oil level should come up to the edge of the filler hole. You can stick your finger in to verify this. Watch out for sharp threads.

8. Replace the filler plug. Lower the vehicle, dispose of the old oil in the same manner as old engine oil. Take a drive in the vehicle, stop and check for leaks.

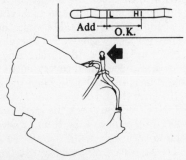

Automatic transaxle dipstick

Automatic Transaxle
FLUID RECOMMENDATION

All automatic transaxle, use Dexron®II ATF (automatic transaxle fluid)

LEVEL CHECK

You should inspect the automatic transaxle gear oil at 3,000 miles or once a month, at this point you should correct the level or replace the oil as necessary. There is a dipstick at the right rear of the engine. It has a scale on each side, one for **COLD** and the other for **HOT**. The transmission is considered hot after 15 miles of highway driving. Park the car on a level surface with the engine running. If the transaxle is not hot, shift into Drive, Low, then Park. Set the handbrake and block the wheels.

NOTE: *The fluid level should be checked when the engine is at normal operating temperature and engine running. The COLD range is used for reference only.*

Remove the dipstick, wipe it clean, then reinsert it firmly. Remove the dipstick and check the fluid level on the appropriate scale. The level should be at the Full mark. If the level is below the Full mark, add Dexron®II AFT (automatic transaxle fluid) as necessary, with the engine running, through the dipstick tube. Do not overfill, as this may cause the transaxle to malfunction and damage itself.

DRAIN AND REFILL

NOTE: *It is recommended that the automatic transaxle fluid be changed every 30,000 miles. If the vehicle is normally used in severe service, the interval should be halved. You may also want to change it if you have bought your car used or if it has been driven in water deep enough to reach the transaxle case.*

1. Run the engine until it reaches normal operating temperature then turn the key to the **OFF** position.

2. Jack up the front of the car and support it on safety stands if necessary to gain access.

3. If There is no drain plug, the fluid pan must be removed. On newer models, there is a hexagon drain plug near the oil pan, if so equipped remove the plug and then drain the transaxle, refill and road test.

4. If not partially remove the pan screws until the pan can be pulled down at one corner. Place a container under the transaxle, lower a rear corner of the pan and allow the fluid to drain.

5. After draining, remove the pan screws completely, then the pan and gasket.

6. Clean the pan thoroughly and allow it to air dry. If you wipe it out with a rag, be sure

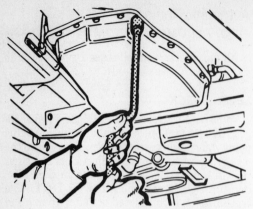

Removing the pan to drain the automatic transaxle

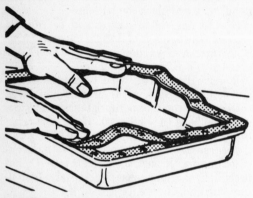

Installing a new pan gasket

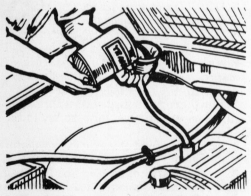

Adding fluid through the transaxle dipstick tube

there is no lint left behind to clog the oil passages.

NOTE: *It is very important to clean the old gasket from the oil pan, to prevent leaks upon installation, a razor blade does a excellent job at this.*

7. Install the pan using a new gasket and a small bead of RTV sealant; be sure to apply sealant around the outside of the pan bolt

holes. Tighten the pan screws evenly in rotation from the center outwards, to 3–5 ft. lbs., then lower the vehicle.

8. It is a good idea to measure the amount of fluid drained to determine how much fresh fluid to add. This is because some part of the transaxle, such as the torque converter, will not drain completely and using the dry refill amount specified in the Capacities chart may lead to overfilling. Fluid is added through the dipstick tube. Make sure that the funnel, hose or whatever your are using is completely clean and dry before pouring transaxle fluid through it. Use Dexron®II automatic transaxle fluid.

9. Replace the dipstick after filling. Start the engine and allow it to idle. DO NOT race the engine.

10. After the engine has idled for a few minutes, shift the transaxle slowly through the gears, then return the lever to **PARK**. With the engine idling, check the fluid level on the dip stick. It should be between the "H" and "L" marks. If below "L", add sufficient fluid to raise the level to between the marks.

11. Drive the car until the transaxle is at operating temperature. The fluid should be at the "H" mark. If not, add sufficient fluid until this is the case. Be careful not to overfill; overfilling causes slippage, overheating and seal damage.

NOTE: *If the drained fluid is discolored (brown or black), thick or smells burnt, serious transaxle problems due to overheating should be suspected. Your car's transaxle should be inspected by a transaxle specialist to determine the cause.*

Cooling System

FLUID RECOMMENDATION

The cooling fluid or antifreeze, should be changed every 30,000 miles or 24 months. When replacing the fluid, use a mixture of 50% water and 50% ethylene glycol antifreeze.

LEVEL CHECK

Check the coolant level every 3,000 miles or once a month. In hot weather operation, it may be a good idea to check the level once a week. Check for loose connections and signs of deterioration of the coolant hoses. Maintain the coolant level 3/4-1 1/4" below the level of the filler neck when the engine is cold. If the engine is equipped with a coolant recovery bottle check the coolant level in the bottle when the engine is cold, the level should be up to the MAX mark. If the bottle is empty, check the level in the radiator and refill as necessary, then fill the bottle up to the MAX level.

CAUTION: *Never remove the radiator cap when the vehicle is hot or overheated. Wait*

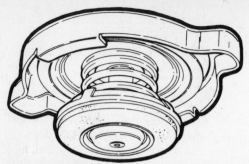

Always check the gasket in the radiator cap when checking coolant level

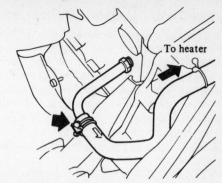

Removing the inlet hose from connector pipe

until it has cooled. Place a thick cloth over the radiator cap to shield yourself from the heat and turn the radiator cap, SLIGHTLY, until the sound of escaping pressure can be heard. DO NOT turn any more; allow the pressure to release gradually. When no more pressure can be heard escaping, remove the cap with the heavy cloth, CAUTIOUSLY.

NOTE: *Never add cold water to an overheated engine while the engine is not running.*

After filling the radiator, run the engine until it reaches normal operating temperature, to make sure that the thermostat has opened and all the air is bled from the system.

DRAIN AND REFILL

To drain the cooling system, allow the engine to cool down **BEFORE ATTEMPTING TO REMOVE THE RADIATOR CAP.** Then turn the cap until it hisses. Wait until all pressure is off the cap before removing it completely.

CAUTION: *To avoid burns and scalding, always handle a warm radiator cap with a heavy rag.*

1. At the dash, set the heater TEMP control lever to the fully HOT position.

2. With the radiator cap removed, drain the radiator by loosening the petcock at the bottom of the radiator.

NOTE: *On the Stanza models, remove the heater inlet hose from the connector pipe at the left rear of the cylinder block to drain completely. After draining, reconnect the hose to the pipe.*

3. Close the petcock, then refill the system with a 50/50 mix of ethylene glycol antifreeze; fill the system to ¾-1¼" from the bottom of the filler neck. Reinstall the radiator cap.

NOTE: *If equipped with a fluid reservoir tank, fill it up to the MAX level.*

4. Operate the engine at 2,000 rpm for a few minutes and check the system for signs of leaks.

NOTE: *If you have replaced or repaired any cooling system component on the Stanza models (1983 and later), the system must be*

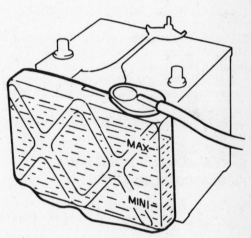

Fill the reservoir up to the MAX level

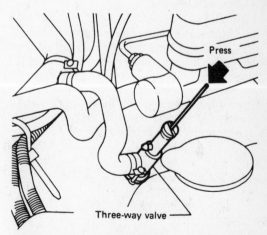

Using the 3-way valve to bleed the cooling system

bled. Insert a 3mm pin into the 3-way valve, located at the firewall, and push it in as far as it will go. While pushing in on the pin, fill the radiator up to the filler opening. Replace the radiator cap and fill the reservoir.

FLUSHING AND CLEANING THE SYSTEM

To flush the system you must first, drain the cooling system but do not close the petcock valve on the bottom of the radiator. You can insert a garden hose, in the filler neck, turn the water pressure on moderately then start the engine. After about 10 minutes or less the water coming out of the bottom of the radiator should be clear. Shut off the engine and water supply, allow the radiator to drain then refill and bleed the system as necessary.

NOTE: *DO NOT allow the engine to overheat. The supply of water going in the top must be equal in amount to the water draining from the bottom, this way the radiator will always be full when the engine us running.*

Usually flushing the radiator using water is all that is necessary to maintain the proper condition in the cooling system.

Radiator flush is the only cleaning agent that can be used to clean the internal portion of the radiator. Radiator flush can be purchased at any auto supply store. Follow the directions on the label.

Brake and Clutch Master Cylinder
FLUID RECOMMENDATION

When adding or changing the fluid in the systems, use a quality brake fluid of the DOT 3 specifications.

NOTE: *Never reuse old brake fluid.*

LEVEL CHECK

Check the levels of brake fluid in the brake and clutch master cylinder reservoirs every 3,000 miles or once a month. The fluid level should be maintained to a level not below the bottom line on the reservoirs and not above the top line. Any sudden decrease in the level in either of the 3 reservoirs (2 for the brakes and 1 for the clutch) indicates a leak in that particular system and should be checked out.

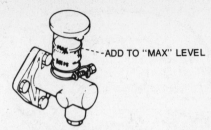

----ADD TO "MAX" LEVEL

Typical clutch master cylinder

Power Steering System
FLUID RECOMMENDATION

When adding or changing the power steering fluid, use Dexron®II ATF (Automatic Transmission Fluid); the system uses approximately 1⅛ qts. of fluid.

LEVEL CHECK

NOTE: *Like all other general maintenance items, check every 3,000 miles or once a month.*

Check the oil level in the reservoir by checking the side of the dipstick marked "HOT" after running the vehicle or the side marked "COLD" when the car has not been used. In each case, the fluid should reach the appropriate full line. See Chapter 8, "Suspension and Steering" for system bleeding procedures if necessary.

Chassis Greasing

The manufacturer doesn't install lubrication fittings in lube points on the steering linkage or suspension. You can buy metric threaded fittings to grease these points or use a pointed, rubber tip end on your grease gun. Lubricate all joints equipped with a plug, every 15,000 miles

ADD TO "MAX" LEVEL

MAX
MIN

Typical brake master cylinder reservoir

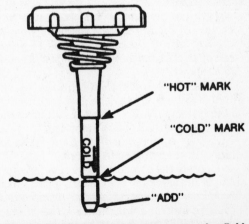

"HOT" MARK

"COLD" MARK

"ADD"

Use the dipstick to check the power steering fluid

or once a year with NLGI No. 2 (Lithium base) grease. Replace the plugs after lubrication.

Rear Wheel Bearings

For front wheel bearings, refer to the procedures in Chapter 8.

REMOVAL, REPACKING, INSTALLATION, ADJUSTMENT

Before handling the bearings, there are a few things that you should remember to do and not to do.

Remember to DO the following:
- Remove all outside dirt from the housing before exposing the bearing.
- Treat a used bearing as gently as you would a new one.
- Work with clean tools in clean surroundings.
- Use clean, dry canvas gloves, or at least clean, dry hands.
- Clean solvents and flushing fluids are a must.
- Use clean paper when laying out the bearings to dry.
- Protect disassembled bearings from rust and dirt. Cover them up.
- Use clean rags to wipe bearings.
- Keep the bearings in oil-proof paper when they are to be stored or are not in use.

- Clean the inside of the housing before replacing the bearing.

Do NOT do the following:
- Don't work in dirty surroundings.
- Don't use dirty, chipped or damaged tools.
- Try not to work on wooden work benches or use wooden mallets.
- Don't handle bearings with dirty or moist hands.
- Do not use gasoline for cleaning; use a safe solvent.
- Do not spin-dry bearings with compressed air. They will be damaged.
- Do not spin dirty bearings.
- Avoid using cotton waste or dirty cloths to wipe bearings.
- Try not to scratch or nick bearing surfaces.
- Do not allow the bearing to come in contact with dirt or rust at any time.

REMOVAL AND INSTALLATION

F10 and 310
Pulsar and Stanza (2WD)

1. Raise and support the vehicle safely.
2. Remove the rear wheels.
3. Work off center hub cap by using thin tool. If necessary tap around it with a soft hammer while removing.
4. Pry off cotter pin and take out adjusting cap and wheel bearing lock nut.

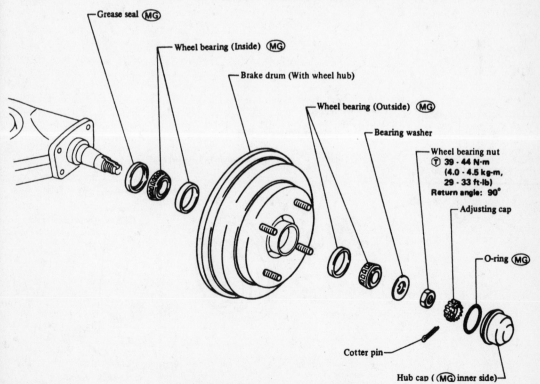

Wheel bearing installation—Pulsar (1983–86)

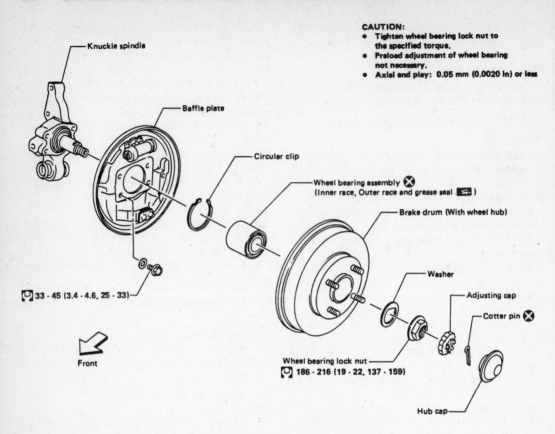

CAUTION:
- Tighten wheel bearing lock nut to the specified torque.
- Preload adjustment of wheel bearing not necessary.
- Axial end play: 0.05 mm (0.0020 in) or less

Wheel bearing installation—Pulsar (1987–88)

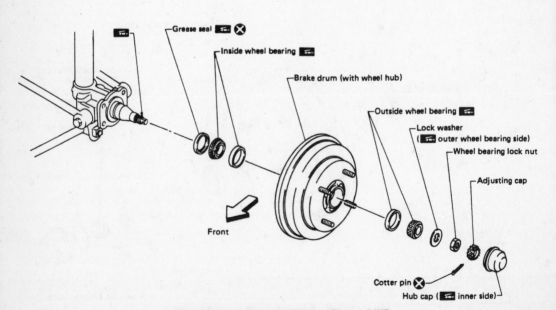

Rear wheel bearing installation—Stanza 2 WD

NOTE: *During removal, be careful to avoid damaging O ring in dust cap on 310 model.*

5. Remove drum with bearing inside.

NOTE: *On Pulsar models, a circular clip holds inner wheel bearing in brake hub.*

6. Remove bearing from drum using long brass drift pin or equivalent.

7. Install the inner bearing assembly in the brake drum and install the drum on the vehicle.

NOTE: *The rear wheel bearings must be adjusted after installation, if one piece bearing is used just the torque wheel bearing lock nut.*

8. Install the outer bearing assembly, wheel bearing lock nut, adjusting cap and cotter pin.

9. Install the center cap and the wheel assembly. To remove the wheel bearing races knock them out of the brake drum using a suitable brass punch.

ADJUSTMENT

1. Raise the rear of the vehicle and support it on jackstands.

2. Remove the wheel/tire assembly.

3. Remove the bearing dust cap with a pair of channel locks pliers.

4. Remove the cotter pin and retaining nut cap (if equipped), dispose of the cotter pin.

5. Tighten the wheel bearing nut to 18–22 ft.lb. (F10) or to 29–33 ft.lb. (all other models).

6. Rotate the drum back and forth a few revolutions to snug down the bearing.

7. On the F10, loosen the nut until it can be turned by hand, then tighten it with a hand held socket as far as it will go.

8. On the 310, Pulsar and Stanza, after turning the wheel, recheck the torque of the nut, then loosen it 90° from its position.

9. Install the retaining nut cap (if equipped). Align the cotter pin holes in the nut or nut cap with the hole in the spindle by turning the nut clockwise on the F10. On the 310, Pulsar and Stanza tighten the nut no more than 15° to align the holes.

10. Install the cotter pin, bend up its ends and install the dust cap.

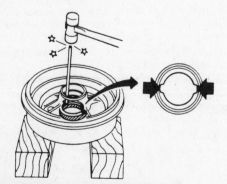

Removing wheel bearing race from drum

Packing wheel bearing

Stanza (4WD)

1. Raise and support the vehicle safely.

2. Remove wheel bearing lock nut while depressing brake pedal.

3. Disconnect brake hydraulic line and parking brake cable.

4. Separate drive shaft from knuckle by slightly tapping it with suitable tool. Cover axle boots with waste cloth so as not to damage them when removing drive shaft.

5. Remove all knuckle retaining bolts and nuts. Make a match mark before removing adjusting pin.

6. Remove knuckle and inner and outer circular clips. Remove wheel bearings.

NOTE: *To remove the wheel bearing races knock them out of the knuckle using a suitable brass punch.*

7. Install the knuckle with wheel bearings to the drive shaft.

8. Connect brake hydraulic line and parking brake cable.

9. Install the wheel bearing lock nut.

10. Bleed brakes.

PUSHING AND TOWING

All manual transaxle vehicles, non-California and Canadian can be push started; automatic transaxles may not be push started. Check to make sure that the bumpers of both vehicles are aligned so neither will be damaged. Be sure that all electrical system components are turned OFF (headlights, heater blower and etc.). Turn on the ignition switch. Place the shift lever in 3rd or 4th gear and push in the clutch pedal. At about 15 mph, signal the driver of the pushing vehicle to fall back, depress the accelerator pedal and release the clutch pedal slowly. The engine should start.

The manufacturer advises against trying to tow-start your vehicle for fear of ramming the tow vehicle when the engine starts.

Both types of transaxles may be towed for short distances and at speeds of no more than 20 mph (automatic) or 50 mph (manual). If the car must be towed a great distance, it should be done with the drive wheels off the ground.

JUMP STARTING

Jump starting is the favored method of starting a car with a dead battery. Make sure that the cables are properly connected, negative-to-negative and positive-to-positive or you stand a chance of damaging the electrical systems of both vehicles.

JACKING

Never use the tire changing jack for anything other than that. If you intend to use this tool to perform your own maintenance, a good scissors or small hydraulic jack and 2 sturdy jackstands would be a wise purchase. Always chock the wheels when changing a tire or working beneath the vehicle. It cannot be over-emphasized, **CLIMBING UNDER A CAR SUPPORTED BY JUST THE JACK IS EXTREMELY DANGEROUS!**

TRAILER TOWING

General Recommendations

Your car was primarily designed to carry passengers and cargo. It is important to remember that towing a trailer will place additional loads on your vehicle's engine, drive train, steering, braking and other systems. However, if you find it necessary to tow a trailer, using the proper equipment is a must.

Local laws may require specific equipment such as trailer brakes or fender mounted mirrors. Check your local laws.

NOTE: *A trailering brochure with information on trailer towing, special equipment required and optional equipment available can be obtained from your Datsun dealer*

Trailer Weight

The weight of the trailer is the most important factor. A good weight-to-horsepower ratio is about 35:1, 35 lbs. of GCW (Gross Combined Weight) for every horsepower your engine develops. Multiply the engine's rated horsepower by 35 and subtract the weight of the car passengers and luggage. The result is the approximate ideal maximum weight you should tow, although a a numerically higher axle ratio can help compensate for heavier weight.

Hitch Weight

Figure the hitch weight to select a proper hitch. Hitch weight is usually 9-11% of the trailer gross weight and should be measured with the trailer loaded. Hitches fall into three types: those that mount on the frame and rear bumper or the bolt-on or weld-on distribution type used for larger trailers. Axle mounted or clamp-on bumper hitches should never be used.

Check the gross weight rating of your trailer. Tongue weight is usually figured as 10% of gross trailer weight. Therefore, a trailer with a maximum gross weight of 2,000 lb. will have a maximum tongue weight of 200 lb. Class I trailers fall into this category. Class II trailers are those with a gross weight rating of 2,000-3,500 lb., while Class III trailers fall into the 3,500-6,000 lb. category. Class IV trailers are those over 6,000 lb. and are for use with fifth wheel trucks, only.

When you've determined the hitch that you'll need, follow the manufacturer's installation instructions, exactly, especially when it comes to fastener torques. The hitch will subjected to a lot of stress and good hitches come with hardened bolts. Never substitute an inferior bolt for a hardened bolt.

Cooling
ENGINE

One of the most common, if not THE most common, problems associated with trailer towing is engine overheating.

If you have a standard cooling system, without an expansion tank, you'll definitely need to get an aftermarket expansion tank kit, preferably one with at least a 2 quart capacity. These kits are easily installed on the radiator's overflow hose, and come with a pressure cap designed for expansion tanks.

Another helpful accessory is a Flex Fan. These fan are large diameter units are designed to provide more airflow at low speeds, with blades that have deeply cupped surfaces. The blades then flex, or flatten out, at high speed, when less cooling air is needed. These fans are far lighter in weight than stock fans, requiring less horsepower to drive them. Also, they are far quieter than stock fans.

If you do decide to replace your stock fan with a flex fan, note that if your car has a fan clutch, a spacer between the flex fan and water pump hub will be needed.

Aftermarket engine oil coolers are helpful for prolonging engine oil life and reducing overall engine temperatures. Both of these factors increase engine life.

While not absolutely necessary in towing Class I and some Class II trailers, they are recommended for heavier Class II and all Class III towing.

Engine oil cooler systems consist of an adapt-

JUMP STARTING A DEAD BATTERY

The chemical reaction in a battery produces explosive hydrogen gas. This is the safe way to jump start a dead battery, reducing the chances of an accidental spark that could cause an explosion.

Jump Starting Precautions

1. Be sure both batteries are of the same voltage.
2. Be sure both batteries are of the same polarity (have the same grounded terminal).
3. Be sure the vehicles are not touching.
4. Be sure the vent cap holes are not obstructed.
5. Do not smoke or allow sparks around the battery.
6. In cold weather, check for frozen electrolyte in the battery. Do not jump start a frozen battery.
7. Do not allow electrolyte on your skin or clothing.
8. Be sure the electrolyte is not frozen.
CAUTION: *Make certain that the ignition key, in the vehicle with the dead battery, is in the OFF position. Connecting cables to vehicles with on-board computers will result in computer destruction if the key is not in the OFF position.*

Jump Starting Procedure

1. Determine voltages of the two batteries; they must be the same.
2. Bring the starting vehicle close (they must not touch) so that the batteries can be reached easily.
3. Turn off all accessories and both engines. Put both cars in Neutral or Park and set the handbrake.
4. Cover the cell caps with a rag—do not cover terminals.
5. If the terminals on the run-down battery are heavily corroded, clean them.
6. Identify the positive and negative posts on both batteries and connect the cables in the order shown.
7. Start the engine of the starting vehicle and run it at fast idle. Try to start the car with the dead battery. Crank it for no more than 10 seconds at a time and let it cool off for 20 seconds in between tries.
8. If it doesn't start in 3 tries, there is something else wrong.
9. Disconnect the cables in the reverse order.
10. Replace the cell covers and dispose of the rags.

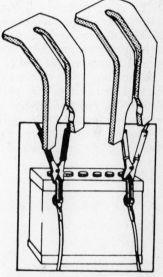

Side terminal batteries occasionally pose a problem when connecting jumper cables. There frequently isn't enough room to clamp the cables without touching sheet metal. Side terminal adaptors are available to alleviate this problem and should be removed after use.

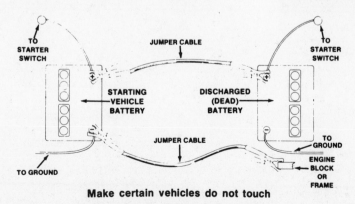

TO STARTER SWITCH   JUMPER CABLE   TO STARTER SWITCH

STARTING VEHICLE BATTERY   DISCHARGED (DEAD) BATTERY

TO GROUND   JUMPER CABLE   TO GROUND

ENGINE BLOCK OR FRAME

Make certain vehicles do not touch

This hook-up for negative ground cars only

er, screwed on in place of the oil filter, a remote filter mounting and a multi-tube, finned heat exchanger, which is mounted in front of the radiator or air conditioning condenser.

TRANSMISSION

An automatic transmission is usually recommended for trailer towing. Modern automatics have proven reliable and, of course, easy to operate, in trailer towing.

The increased load of a trailer, however, causes an increase in the temperature of the automatic transmission fluid. Heat is the worst enemy of an automatic transmission. As the temperature of the fluid increases, the life of the fluid decreases.

It is essential, therefore, that you install an automatic transmission cooler.

The cooler, which consists of a multi-tube, finned heat exchanger, is usually installed in front of the radiator or air conditioning compressor, and hooked inline with the transmission cooler tank inlet line. Follow the cooler manufacturer's installation instructions.

Select a cooler of at least adequate capacity, based upon the combined gross weights of the car and trailer.

Cooler manufacturers recommend that you use an aftermarket cooler in addition to, and not instead of, the present cooling tank in your radiator. If you do want to use it in place of the radiator cooling tank, get a cooler at least two sizes larger than normally necessary.

NOTE: *A transmission cooler can, sometimes, cause slow or harsh shifting in the transmission during cold weather, until the fluid has a chance to come up to normal operating temperature. Some coolers can be purchased with or retrofitted with a temperature bypass valve which will allow fluid flow through the cooler only when the fluid has reached operating temperature, or above.*

Handling A Trailer

Towing a trailer with ease and safety requires a certain amount of experience. It's a good idea to learn the feel of a trailer by practicing turning, stopping and backing in an open area such as an empty parking lot.

Engine Performance and Tune-Up

2

TUNE-UP PROCEDURES

The following procedures will show you exactly how to tune your vehicle. For 1976-79 models, the manufacturer recommends a tune-up, including distributor points (unless equipped with electronic ignition) and spark plugs every 12,000 miles.

The 1980 through 1988 vehicles, use a more durable spark plug in all models. The manufacturer recommends that the new plugs be replaced every 30,000 miles or 24 months, which ever comes first. On the Pulsar engines CA16DE and CA18DE, platinum-tipped spark plugs are original equipment and should be replaced at 60,000 miles or 48 months, which ever comes first. If conventional spark plugs are used (after first change) these should be replaced at 30,000 miles or 24 months. Certain 1980 Canadian vehicles still use the conventional 12 month, 12,000 mile spark plugs. All later models have electronic ignition systems, so there are no breaker points and condenser to replace.

Even though the manufacturer suggests a 30,000 mile, 24 month spark plug replacement span for 1980 and later models, it would be wise to remove the plugs and inspect them every 12,000 miles or once a year.

It might be noted that the tune-up is a good time to take a look around the engine compartment for problems in the making, such as oil and fuel leaks, deteriorating radiator or heater hoses, loose and/or frayed fan belts and etc.

Spark Plugs

NOTE: *Blue rings on the ceramic portion indicate that the plugs are platinum-tipped type. Do not check and adjust the plug gap.*

A typical spark plug consists of a metal shell surrounding a ceramic insulator. A metal electrode extends downward through the center of the insulator and protrudes a small distance. Located at the end of the plug and attached to the side of the outer metal shell is the side electrode. The side electrode bends in at a 90° angle, so that its tip is even with and parallel to, the tip of the center electrode. The distance between these two electrodes (measured in thousandths of an inch) is called the spark plug gap. The spark plug in no way produces a spark but merely provides a gap across which the current can arc. The coil produces anywhere from 20,000-40,000 volts, which travels to the distributor where it is distributed through the spark plug wire to the spark plugs. The current passes along the center electrode, then jumps the gap to the side electrode and ignites the air/fuel mixture in the combustion chamber.

Spark plug life and efficiency depend upon the condition of the engine and the temperatures to which the plug is exposed. Combustion chamber temperatures are affected by many factors such as compression ratio of the engine, air/fuel mixtures, exhaust emission equipment and the type of driving you do. Spark plugs are designed and classified by number according to the heat range at which they will operate most efficiently.

NOTE: *A few of the most common reasons for plug fouling and a description of the plug's appearance, are listed in the Color Insert Section, which also offers solutions to the problem.*

HEAT RANGE

While the spark plug heat range has always seemed to be somewhat of a mystical subject for many people, in reality, the entire subject is quite simple. Basically, it boils down to this; the amount of heat the plug absorbs is determined by the length of the lower insulator. The longer the insulator (or the further it extends into the engine), the hotter the plug will operate; the shorter the insulator the cooler it will operate.

Troubleshooting Engine Performance

Problem	Cause	Solution
Hard starting (engine cranks normally)	• Binding linkage, choke valve or choke piston	• Repair as necessary
	• Restricted choke vacuum diaphragm	• Clean passages
	• Improper fuel level	• Adjust float level
	• Dirty, worn or faulty needle valve and seat	• Repair as necessary
	• Float sticking	• Repair as necessary
	• Faulty fuel pump	• Replace fuel pump
	• Incorrect choke cover adjustment	• Adjust choke cover
	• Inadequate choke unloader adjustment	• Adjust choke unloader
	• Faulty ignition coil	• Test and replace as necessary
	• Improper spark plug gap	• Adjust gap
	• Incorrect ignition timing	• Adjust timing
	• Incorrect valve timing	• Check valve timing; repair as necessary
Rough idle or stalling	• Incorrect curb or fast idle speed	• Adjust curb or fast idle speed
	• Incorrect ignition timing	• Adjust timing to specification
	• Improper fast idle cam adjustment	• Adjust fast idle cam
	• Faulty EGR valve operation	• Test EGR system and replace as necessary
	• Faulty PCV valve air flow	• Test PCV valve and replace as necessary
	• Choke binding	• Locate and eliminate binding condition
	• Air leak into manifold vacuum	• Inspect manifold vacuum connections and repair as necessary
	• Improper fuel level	• Adjust fuel level
	• Faulty distributor rotor or cap	• Replace rotor or cap
	• Improperly seated valves	• Test cylinder compression, repair as necessary
	• Incorrect ignition wiring	• Inspect wiring and correct as necessary
	• Faulty ignition coil	• Test coil and replace as necessary
	• Restricted air vent or idle passages	• Clean passages
	• Restricted air cleaner	• Clean or replace air cleaner filler element
	• Faulty choke vacuum diaphragm	• Repair as necessary
Faulty low-speed operation	• Restricted idle transfer slots	• Clean transfer slots
	• Restricted idle air vents and passages	• Clean air vents and passages
	• Restricted air cleaner	• Clean or replace air cleaner filter element
	• Improper fuel level	• Adjust fuel level
	• Faulty spark plugs	• Clean or replace spark plugs
	• Dirty, corroded, or loose ignition secondary circuit wire connections	• Clean or tighten secondary circuit wire connections
	• Faulty ignition coil high voltage wire	• Replace ignition coil high voltage wire
	• Faulty distributor cap	• Replace cap
Faulty acceleration	• Improper accelerator pump stroke	• Adjust accelerator pump stroke
	• Incorrect ignition timing	• Adjust timing
	• Inoperative pump discharge check ball or needle	• Clean or replace as necessary
	• Worn or damaged pump diaphragm or piston	• Replace diaphragm or piston

Troubleshooting Engine Performance (cont.)

Problem	Cause	Solution
Faulty acceleration (cont.)	• Leaking carburetor main body cover gasket	• Replace gasket
	• Engine cold and choke set too lean	• Adjust choke cover
	• Faulty spark plug(s)	• Clean or replace spark plug(s)
	• Improperly seated valves	• Test cylinder compression, repair as necessary
	• Faulty ignition coil	• Test coil and replace as necessary
	• Improper feedback system operation	• Refer to Chapter 4
Faulty high speed operation	• Incorrect ignition timing	• Adjust timing
	• Faulty distributor centrifugal advance mechanism	• Check centrifugal advance mechanism and repair as necessary
	• Faulty distributor vacuum advance mechanism	• Check vacuum advance mechanism and repair as necessary
	• Low fuel pump volume	• Replace fuel pump
	• Wrong spark plug air gap or wrong plug	• Adjust air gap or install correct plug
	• Faulty choke operation	• Adjust choke cover
	• Partially restricted exhaust manifold, exhaust pipe, catalytic converter, muffler, or tailpipe	• Eliminate restriction
	• Restricted vacuum passages	• Clean passages
	• Improper size or restricted main jet	• Clean or replace as necessary
	• Restricted air cleaner	• Clean or replace filter element as necessary
	• Faulty distributor rotor or cap	• Replace rotor or cap
	• Faulty ignition coil	• Test coil and replace as necessary
	• Improperly seated valve(s)	• Test cylinder compression, repair as necessary
	• Faulty valve spring(s)	• Inspect and test valve spring tension, replace as necessary
	• Incorrect valve timing	• Check valve timing and repair as necessary
	• Intake manifold restricted	• Remove restriction or replace manifold
	• Worn distributor shaft	• Replace shaft
Misfire at all speeds	• Faulty spark plug(s)	• Clean or replace spark plug(s)
	• Faulty spark plug wire(s)	• Replace as necessary
	• Faulty distributor cap or rotor	• Replace cap or rotor
	• Faulty ignition coil	• Test coil and replace as necessary
	• Primary ignition circuit shorted or open intermittently	• Troubleshoot primary circuit and repair as necessary
	• Improperly seated valve(s)	• Test cylinder compression, repair as necessary
	• Faulty hydraulic tappet(s)	• Clean or replace tappet(s)
	• Faulty valve spring(s)	• Inspect and test valve spring tension, repair as necessary
	• Worn camshaft lobes	• Replace camshaft
	• Air leak into manifold	• Check manifold vacuum and repair as necessary
	• Improper carburetor adjustment	• Adjust carburetor
	• Fuel pump volume or pressure low	• Replace fuel pump
	• Blown cylinder head gasket	• Replace gasket
	• Intake or exhaust manifold passage(s) restricted	• Pass chain through passage(s) and repair as necessary
	• Incorrect trigger wheel installed in distributor	• Install correct trigger wheel

Troubleshooting Engine Performance (cont.)

Problem	Cause	Solution
Power not up to normal	• Incorrect ignition timing	• Adjust timing
	• Faulty distributor rotor	• Replace rotor
	• Trigger wheel loose on shaft	• Reposition or replace trigger wheel
	• Incorrect spark plug gap	• Adjust gap
	• Faulty fuel pump	• Replace fuel pump
	• Incorrect valve timing	• Check valve timing and repair as necessary
	• Faulty ignition coil	• Test coil and replace as necessary
	• Faulty ignition wires	• Test wires and replace as necessary
	• Improperly seated valves	• Test cylinder compression and repair as necessary
	• Blown cylinder head gasket	• Replace gasket
	• Leaking piston rings	• Test compression and repair as necessary
	• Worn distributor shaft	• Replace shaft
Intake backfire	• Improper ignition timing	• Adjust timing
	• Faulty accelerator pump discharge	• Repair as necessary
	• Lean air/fuel mixture	• Check float level or manifold vacuum for air leak. Remove sediment from bowl
Exhaust backfire	• Air leak into manifold vacuum	• Check manifold vacuum and repair as necessary
	• Exhaust leak	• Locate and eliminate leak
Ping or spark knock	• Incorrect ignition timing	• Adjust timing
	• Distributor centrifugal or vacuum advance malfunction	• Inspect advance mechanism and repair as necessary
	• Excessive combustion chamber deposits	• Remove with combustion chamber cleaner
	• Air leak into manifold vacuum	• Check manifold vacuum and repair as necessary
	• Excessively high compression	• Test compression and repair as necessary
	• Fuel octane rating excessively low	• Try alternate fuel source
	• EGR valve not functioning properly	• Test EGR system and replace as necessary
Surging (at cruising to top speeds)	• Low carburetor fuel level	• Adjust fuel level
	• Low fuel pump pressure or volume	• Replace fuel pump
	• Improper PCV valve air flow	• Test PCV valve and replace as necessary
	• Air leak into manifold vacuum	• Check manifold vacuum and repair as necessary
	• Incorrect spark advance	• Test and replace as necessary
	• Restricted main jet(s)	• Clean main jet(s)
	• Undersize main jet(s)	• Replace main jet(s)
	• Restricted air vents	• Clean air vents
	• Restricted fuel filter	• Replace fuel filter
	• Restricted air cleaner	• Clean or replace air cleaner filter element
	• EGR valve not functioning properly	• Test EGR system and replace as necessary

A plug that absorbs little heat and remains too cool will quickly accumulate deposits of oil and carbon since it is not hot enough to burn them off. This leads to plug fouling and consequently to misfiring. A plug that absorbs too much heat will have no deposits but due to the excessive heat, the electrodes will burn away quickly and in some instances, preignition may result. Pre-ignition takes place when plug tips get so hot that they glow sufficiently to ignite the fuel/air mixture before the actual spark occurs. This early ignition will usually cause a pinging during low speeds and heavy loads. In severe cases, the heat may become high enough to start the fuel/air mixture burning throughout the combustion chamber rather than just to the front of

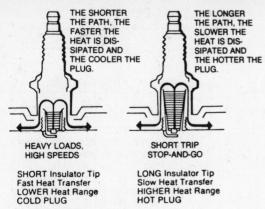

THE SHORTER THE PATH, THE FASTER THE HEAT IS DISSIPATED AND THE COOLER THE PLUG.

THE LONGER THE PATH, THE SLOWER THE HEAT IS DISSIPATED AND THE HOTTER THE PLUG.

HEAVY LOADS, HIGH SPEEDS

SHORT TRIP STOP-AND-GO

SHORT Insulator Tip
Fast Heat Transfer
LOWER Heat Range
COLD PLUG

LONG Insulator Tip
Slow Heat Transfer
HIGHER Heat Range
HOT PLUG

Spark plug heat ranges

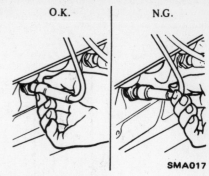

O.K.   N.G.

SMA017

Spark plug wire removal

the plug as in normal operation. At this time, the piston is rising in the cylinder making its compression stroke. The burning mass is compressed and an explosion results, forcing the piston back down in the cylinder while it is still trying to go up. Obviously, something must go and it does: pistons are often damaged.

The general rule of thumb for choosing the correct heat range when picking a spark plug is: if most of your driving is long distance, high speed travel, use a colder plug; if most of your driving is stop and go, use a hotter plug. Factory installed plugs are, of course, compromise plugs, since the factory has no way of knowing what sort of driving you do. It should be noted that most people never have the need to change their plugs from the factory recommended heat range.

REMOVAL AND INSTALLATION

NOTE: *The Stanza has 2 spark plugs in each cylinder; the plugs are of different heat ranges; the exhaust side uses the colder plug. All 8 plugs should be replaced at every tune-up for maximum fuel efficiency and power. Always mark the spark plug wires, in the order of removal for easy installation. On Pulsar engines, CA16DE and CA18DE the oranament cover (8 screws) must be removed to gain access to the spark plugs.*

1. Grasp the spark plug boot and pull it straight out. Don't pull on the wire. If the boot(s) are cracked, replace them.

2. Place the spark plug socket firmly on the plug. Turn the spark plug out of the cylinder head in a counterclockwise direction.

NOTE: *The cylinder head is aluminum, which is easily stripped. Remove the plugs ONLY when the engine is cold. If removal is difficult, loosen the plug only slightly and drip penetrating oil onto the threads. Allow the oil time enough to work and then unscrew*

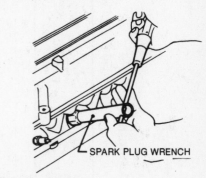

SPARK PLUG WRENCH

Spark plug removal

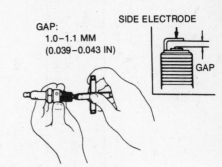

GAP:
1.0–1.1 MM
(0.039–0.043 IN)

SIDE ELECTRODE

GAP

Spark plug gap adjustment

the plug. Proceeding in this manner will prevent damaging the cylinder head threads. Be sure to keep the socket straight to avoid breaking the ceramic insulator.

3. Continue to remove the remaining spark plugs.

4. Inspect the plugs using the Color Insert section illustrations and then clean or discard them according to condition.

New spark plugs come pre-gapped but double check the setting. The recommended spark plug gap is listed in the Tune-Up Specifications chart. On platinum-tipped plugs do not check or adjust the plug gap. Use a spark plug wire gauge for checking the gap. The wire should pass through the electrode with just a slight

Tune-Up Specifications

When analyzing compression test results, look for uniformity among cylinders, rather than specific pressures.

| Year | Model | Spark Plug | | Distributor | | Ignition Timing (deg) | | Fuel Pump Pressure (psi) | Idle Speed (rpm) | | Valve Clearance | |
		Type	Gap (in.)	Point Dwell (deg)	Point Gap (in.)	MT	AT		MT	AT ①	In	Ex
1976	F10	BP-5ES	.031–.035	49–55	.018–.022	10B	—	3.8	700	—	.014 Hot	.014 Hot
	F10 Calif.	BP-5ES	.031–.035	Electronic	②	10B	—	3.8	700	—	.014 Hot	.014 Hot
1977	F10	BP5ES-11	.039–.043	49–55	.018–.022	10B	—	3.8	700	—	.014 Hot	.014 Hot
	F10 Calif.	BPR5ES	.031–.035	Electronic	②	10B	—	3.8	700	—	.014 Hot	.014 Hot
1978	F10	BP5ES-11	.039–.043	Electronic	②	10B	—	3.8	700	—	.014 Hot	.014 Hot
1979	310	BP5ES-11 ④	.039–.043	Electronic	⑧	10B ③	—	3.8	700	—	.014 Hot	.014 Hot
1980	310	BPR5ES-11 ④	.039–.043	Electronic	⑧	8B	—	3.8	750	—	.014 Hot	.014 Hot
1981	310	BPR5ES-11 ④	.039–.043	Electronic	⑧	5B	—	3.8	750	—	.014 Hot	.014 Hot
1982	310	BPR5ES-11 ④	.039–.043	Electronic	⑧	2A ⑤	2A ⑤	3.8	750	750 ⑥	.011 Hot	.011 Hot
	Stanza	⑦	.039–.043	Electronic	⑧	0	—	3.8	650	—	.012 Hot	.012 Hot
1983	Stanza	⑦	.039–.043	Electronic	⑧	0	0 ①	3.8	650	650	.012 Hot	.012 Hot
	Pulsar	BPR5ES-11 ④	.039–.043	Electronic	⑧	5A	5A	3.8	750	650	.011 Hot	.011 Hot
1984	Stanza	⑦	.039–.043	Electronic	⑧	0	0	3.8 ㉓	750 ⑨	700 ⑨	.012 Hot	.012 Hot
	Pulsar	BPR5ES-11 ④⑩	.039–.043	Electronic	⑧	15B ⑪⑭	8B ⑪⑭	3.8 ㉒	800 ⑫⑮⑳	650 ⑬⑯㉑	.011 Hot	.011 Hot

Year	Model	Spark Plug Type	Gap	Ignition		Ignition Timing MT	Ignition Timing AT	Compression	Idle Speed MT	Idle Speed AT	Valve Clearance Intake	Valve Clearance Exhaust
1985–86	Stanza	[17][18]	.039–.043	Electronic	[8]	4B [19]	0 [19]	3.8 [23]	750 [9]	700 [9]	.012 Hot	.012 Hot
	Pulsar	BPR5ES-11	.039–.043	Electronic	[8]	15B [11][27]	8B [11][27]	3.8	800 [12][20]	650 [13][21]	.011 Hot	.011 Hot
1987–88	Stanza	[17][18]	.039–.043	Electronic	[8]	15B	15B	37 [29]	750	700	.012 Hot [24]	.012 Hot [24]
	Pulsar	BPR5ES-11 [25][26]	.039–.043	Electronic	[8]	7B [28]	7B [28]	50 [30]	800	650	.011 Hot [31]	.011 Hot [31]

① In Drive
② Reluctor gap: .008–.016
③ Calif.: 5B
④ Canada: BPR-5ES; gap .031–.035
⑤ Canada: 4A
⑥ Canada: AT 650
⑦ Intake side: BPR-6-ES-11
   Exhaust side: BPR-5ES-11
⑧ Reluctor gap: .012–.020
⑨ Canada: 650
⑩ E15ET engine (Canada): BPR6ES-11
⑪ Calif and Canada: 5A
⑫ Calif and Canada: 750
⑬ Calif and Canada: 650
⑭ E15ET engine (Canada): 15B
⑮ E15ET engine (Canada): 750
⑯ E15ET engine (Canada): 650
⑰ Intake side: BCPR6ES-11
   Exhaust side: BCPR5ES-11
⑱ (Canada) intake side: BPR6ES-11
   exhaust side: BPR5ES-11
⑲ Canada: 0

⑳ VCM valve OFF: 700
㉑ VCM valve OFF: 550
㉒ At idle 30 psi—E15ET (turbo)
㉓ On fuel injected engine 37 psi—CA20E
㉔ Stanza models (1982–86) and station wagons only from (1986–88). Stanza models (1987–88) have hydraulic lash adjusters—no adjustment possible.
㉕ 1987—CA16DE PFR6A-11 (do not check or adjust plug gap.)
㉖ 1988—CA18DE PFR6A-11 (do not check or adjust plug gap.)
㉗ 1986—non-California model 10° BTDC
㉘ 15 BTDC on M/T and 15 BTDC on A/T CA16DE and CA18DE
㉙ 1988—43.4 psi on CA20E engine
㉚ 14 psi—E16i engine
   28 psi—CA16DE engine
   36 psi—CA18DE engine
㉛ CA16DE and CA18DE engines
   No adjustment (hyd.)

drag. Using the electrode bending tool on the end of the gauge, bend the side electrode to adjust the gap. Never attempt to adjust the center electrode. Lightly oil the threads of the replacement plug and install it hand-tight. It is a good practice to use a torque wrench to tighten the spark plugs on any vehicle, especially the aluminum head type. Torque the spark plugs to 14-22 ft. lbs. Install the ignition wire boots firmly on the spark plugs.

NOTE: *Always start threading the spark plugs by hand. Never use a tool to start threading a spark plug. Be careful not to crossthread the spark plug.*

Spark Plug Wires

Visually inspect the spark plug cables for burns, cuts or breaks in the insulation. Check the spark plug boots and the nipples on the distributor cap and coil. Replace any damaged wiring. If no physical damage is obvious, the wires can be checked with an ohmmeter for excessive resistance. Remove the distributor cap and leave the wires connected to the cap. Connect one lead of the ohmmeter to the corresponding electrode inside the cap and the other lead to the spark plug terminal (remove it from the spark plug for the test). Replace any wire which shows over 50,000Ω. Generally speaking, however, resistance should run between 35,000-50,000Ω. Test the coil wire by connecting the ohmmeter between the center contact in the cap and either of the primary terminals at the coil. If the total resistance of the coil and the cable is more than 25,000Ω, remove the cable from the coil and check the resistance of the cable. If the resistance is higher than 15,000Ω, replace the cable. It should be remembered that wire resistance is a function of length and that the longer the cable, the greater the resistance. Thus, if the cables on your car are longer than the factory originals, resistance will be higher and quite possibly outside of these limits.

When installing a new set of spark plug cables, replace the cables one at a time so that you can match up the length of each old plug wire

with the new ones and there will be no mix-up. Start by replacing the longest cable first. Install the boot firmly over the spark plug. Route the wire exactly the same as the original. Insert the nipple firmly into the tower on the distributor cap. Repeat the process for each cable.

NOTE: *On the Pulsar engines, CA16DE and CA18DE no spark plug wires are used.*

Firing Orders

NOTE: *To avoid confusion, remove and tag the wires one at a time, for replacement.*

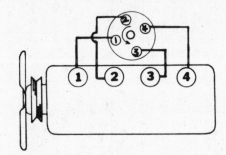

A-series engines—firing order: 1-3-4-2

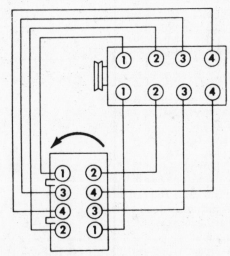

CA20 engine—firing order: 1-3-4-2

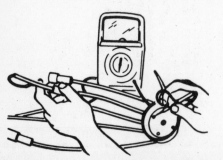

Checking plug wire resistance with an ohmmeter

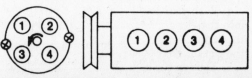

E15, E16 engine—firing order: 1-3-4-2

Breaker Points and Condenser

NOTE: *Certain 1976-1977 and virtually all 1978 and later models are equipped with electronic, breakerless ignition systems. See the following section for maintenance procedures.*

REMOVAL AND INSTALLATION

1. Remove the coil's high tension wire from the top of the distributor cap. Remove the distributor cap and place it out of the way. Remove the rotor from the distributor shaft by pulling up.

2. Remove the points assembly attaching screws, the condenser and the points.

NOTE: *A magnetic screwdriver or one with a holding mechanism will come in handy here, so that you don't drop a screw into the distributor and have to remove the entire distributor to retrieve it.*

3. After the points are removed, wipe off the cam and apply new cam lubricant. If you don't the points will wear out in a few thousand miles.

4. Slip the new set of points onto the locating dowel and install the screws that hold the assembly onto the plate. Don't tighten them all the way yet, since you'll only have to loosen them to set the point gap.

5. Install the new condenser and attach the condenser lead to the points.

6. Set the point gap and dwell (see the following sections).

DWELL ADJUSTMWENT WITH FEELER GAUGE

1. If the contact points of the assembly are not parallel, bend the stationary contact so that they make contact across the entire surface of the contacts. Bend only the stationary bracket part of the point assembly; not the movable contact.

2. Turn the engine until the rubbing block of the points is on one of the high points of the distributor cam. You can do this by either turning the ignition switch to the **START** position and releasing it quickly (bumping the engine) or by using a wrench on the crankshaft pulley bolt.

3. Place the correct size feeler gauge between the contacts (see the Tune-Up Chart). Make sure that it is parallel with the contact surfaces.

NOTE: *When adjusting the points, there should be a slight drag felt when the feeler gauge passes through the contact points.*

4. With your free hand, insert a screwdriver into the eccentric adjusting screw, then twist the screwdriver to either increase or decrease the gap to the proper setting.

5. Tighten the adjustment lockscrew and recheck the contact gap to make sure that it

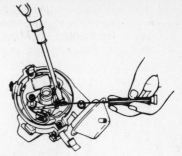

Adjusting point gap

didn't change when the lockscrew was tightened.

6. Replace the rotor, the distributor cap and the high tension wire from the top of the distributor to the coil. Make sure that the rotor is firmly seated all the way onto the distributor shaft and that the tab of the rotor is aligned with notch in the shaft. Align the tab in the base of the distributor cap with the notch in the distributor body. Make sure that the cap is firmly seated on the distributor and that the retainer clips are in place. Make sure that the end of the high tension wire is firmly installed in the top of the distributor and the coil.

DWELL ADJUSTMWENT WITH DWELL METER

1. Adjust the points with a feeler gauge as previously described.

2. Connect the dwell meter to the ignition circuit as according to the manufacturer's instructions.

NOTE: *To hook up the Dwell/Tach meter, connect one lead of the meter (usually the black one) to a good ground on the engine and the other lead (red lead) to the negative side of the coil. This terminal is easy to find, look for the terminal which has the small wire that leads to the distributor.*

3. If the dwell meter has a set line on it, adjust the meter to zero the indicator.

4. Start the engine.

NOTE: *Be careful when working on any vehicle while the engine is running. Make sure that the transaxle is in NEUTRAL and that the parking brake is applied. Keep hands, clothing, tools and the wires of the test instruments clear of the rotating fan blades.*

5. Observe the reading on the dwell meter. If the reading is within the specified range, turn off the engine and remove the dwell meter.

NOTE: *If the meter does not have a scale for 4 cylinder engines, multiply the 8 cylinder reading by 2.*

6. If the reading is above the specified range, the breaker point gap is too small. If the reading

is below the specified range, the gap is too large. In either case, the engine must be stopped and the gap adjusted in the manner previously covered. After making the adjustment, start the engine and check the reading on the dwell meter. When the correct reading is obtained, disconnect the dwell meter.

7. Check and/or adjust the ignition timing.

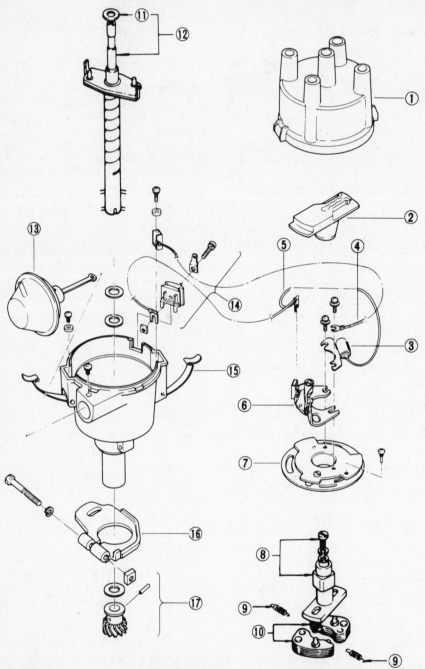

1. Cap	7. Breaker plate	13. Vacuum control assembly
2. Rotor	8. Cam assembly	14. Terminal assembly
3. Condenser	9. Governor spring	15. Clamp
4. Ground wire	10. Governor weight	16. Retaining plate
5. Lead wire	11. Thrust washer	17. Gear set
6. Breaker points	12. Shaft assembly	

Point type distributor

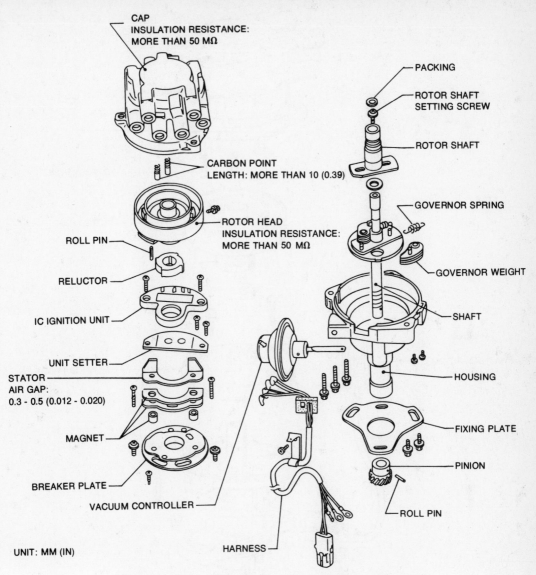

CAP
INSULATION RESISTANCE:
MORE THAN 50 MΩ

PACKING

ROTOR SHAFT
SETTING SCREW

ROTOR SHAFT

CARBON POINT
LENGTH: MORE THAN 10 (0.39)

GOVERNOR SPRING

ROTOR HEAD
INSULATION RESISTANCE:
MORE THAN 50 MΩ

ROLL PIN

RELUCTOR

GOVERNOR WEIGHT

IC IGNITION UNIT

SHAFT

UNIT SETTER

STATOR
AIR GAP:
0.3 - 0.5 (0.012 - 0.020)

HOUSING

MAGNET

FIXING PLATE

BREAKER PLATE

PINION

VACUUM CONTROLLER

ROLL PIN

UNIT: MM (IN)

HARNESS

Stanza distributor (1982–86)—IC ignition unit without pick-up coil

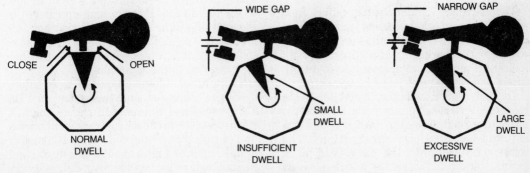

WIDE GAP

NARROW GAP

CLOSE   OPEN

SMALL
DWELL

LARGE
DWELL

NORMAL
DWELL

INSUFFICIENT
DWELL

EXCESSIVE
DWELL

Dwell angle adjustment

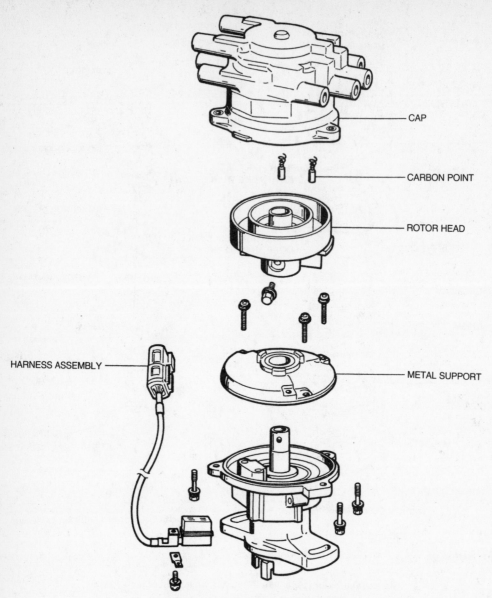

CAP

CARBON POINT

ROTOR HEAD

HARNESS ASSEMBLY

METAL SUPPORT

Stanza distributor 1987—88 (crankangle sensor)

Electronic Ignition

The electronic ignition system differs from the conventional breaker points system in form only; its function is exactly the same: to supply a spark to the spark plugs at precisely the right moment to ignite the compressed gas in the cylinders and create mechanical movement.

Located in the distributor, in addition to the rotor cap, is a spoked reluctor which fits on the distributor shaft where the breaker points cam is found on non-electronic ignitions. The reluctor revolves with the rotor head, as it passes a pickup coil inside the distributor body it breaks a high flux field, which occurs in the space between the reluctor and the pickup coil. The breaking of the field allows current to flow to the pickup coil. Primary ignition current is then cut off by the electronic ignition unit, allowing the magnetic field in the ignition coil to collapse, creating the spark which the distributor passes on to the spark plug.

There are 4 different types of distributors used with electronic ignition systems on F10, 310, Stanza and Pulsar (E16 engine only). A single post pickup coil with a transistor ignition unit, a ring type pickup coil with a IC ignition unit, IC ignition unit without a pick up coil and a crankangle sensor are the main differences in the distributors used for these systems.

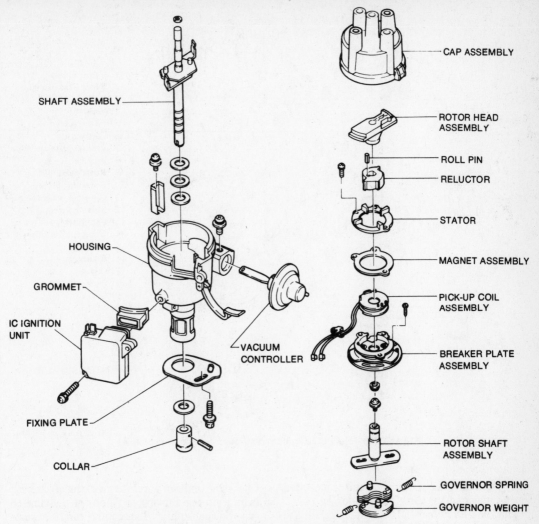

F10 and 310 distributor—IC ignition unit and ring type pick-up coil

The 1976-78 Datsun/Nissan models used a single post pickup coil and a transistor type ignition unit which is located on the right hand or left hand dash side panel in the passenger compartment.

The 1979-81 Datsun/Nissan models used a ring type pickup coil which surrounds the reluctor instead of the single post type pickup coil. The IC ignition unit on these models is mounted on the outside of the distributor housing.

The 1982 310 model and the 1982-86 Stanza models used no pickup coil and the IC ignition unit is mounted on the inside of the distributor. The dual spark plug ignition system is used on the 1982-88 Stanza models only. There are 2 ignition coils and each cylinder has 2 spark plugs which fire simultaneously. In this manner the engine is able to consume large quantities of re-

circulated exhaust gas which would cause a single spark plug cylinder to misfire and idle roughly.

The 1987-88 Stanza models uses a dual spark plug system and a crankangle sensor. This sensor monitors engine speed and piston position and sends to the computer signals on which the controls of the fuel injection, ignition timing and other functions are based. No maintenance is required but inspect and replace, if necessary, the spark plug wires, rotor head and the distributor cap every 2 years.

The 1983 Pulsar for the 49 states and the California and Canada models used no pickup coil for the electronic ignition system and the IC ignition unit is mounted on the inside of the distributor. The 1984-86 Pulsar for California and Canada models without a turbocharged engine uses no pickup coil for the electronic igni-

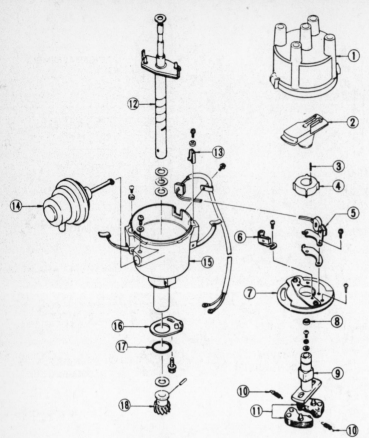

1	Cap assembly
2	Rotor head assembly
3	Roll pin
4	Reluctor
5	Pick-up coil
6	Contactor
7	Breaker plate assembly
8	Packing
9	Rotor shaft
10	Governor spring
11	Governor weight
12	Shaft assembly
13	Cap setter
14	Vacuum controller
15	Housing
16	Fixing plate
17	O-ring
18	Pinion

F10 and 310—electronic ignition distributor (single post pickup)

tion system and the IC ignition unit is mounted on the inside of the distributor housing.

The 1984-88 Pulsar (E16 engine only) for the 49 states, the 1987-88 California and Canada models (E16 engine only) and the turbocharged version of the Pulsar use a crankangle sensor. This sensor monitors engine speed and piston position and sends to the computer signals on which the controls of the fuel injection, ignition timing and other functions are based.

Since no points or condenser are used on electronic ignition system and the dwell is determined by the electronic unit, no adjustments are necessary. The ignition timing is checked in the usual way; unless the distributor is disturbed, it is not likely to ever change very much.

The Pulsar CA16DE and CA18DE engines do not utilize a conventional distributor and high tension wires. Instead they use 4 small ignition coils fitted directly to each spark plug and a crankangle sensor mounted in the front timing belt cover.

Service on electronic ignition systems consist of inspection of the distributor cap, rotor and ignition wires replacing them when necessary.

Check the ignition wires for cracking of exterior insulation and for proper fit on the distributor cap and spark plugs. These parts can be expected to last for at least 40,000 miles but you should inspect these parts every 2 years or 30,000 miles. In addition, the reluctor air gap

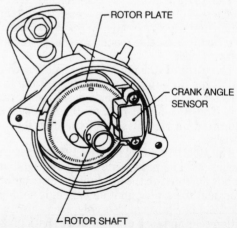

Pulsar distributor—49 states 1984–88—Calif. and Canada 1987–88 (crankangle sensor)

should be checked periodically if the system has no crankangle sensor.

AIR GAP ADJUSTMENT

1. The distributor cap is held on by 2 spring clips. Release them with a screwdriver and lift the cap straight up and off, with the wires attached.

2. Pull the rotor head (not the spoked reluctor) straight up to remove it.

3. Check the reluctor air gap by using a non-magnetic feeler gauge. Rotate the engine until a reluctor spoke is aligned with the single post pickup coil or stator depending on the type used on the vehicle. Bump the engine around with the starter or turn it with a wrench on the

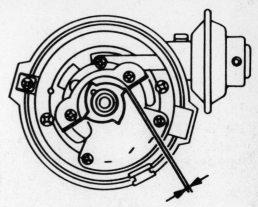

Checking the air gap (1982 and later)

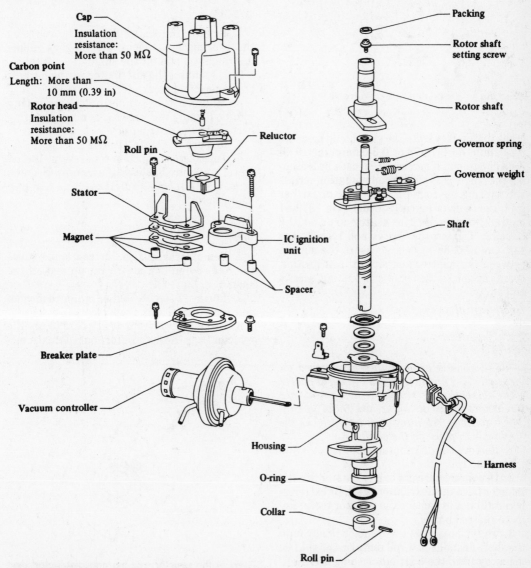

Pulsar distributor (1983 all models and 1984–86 Calif. and Canada)—IC ignition unit without pick-up coil

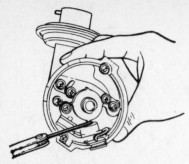

Checking air gap on single post pickup coil

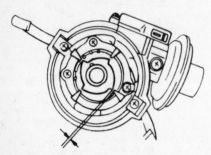

Checking air gap on ring type pickup coil

crankshaft pulley bolt. The gap should measure 0.2-0.4mm for 1976-78 or 0.3-0.5mm for 1979-86. Adjustment, if necessary, is made by loosening the single post pickup coil mounting screws and shifting the coil either closer to or farther from the reluctor on early models. On 1979-81 models, centering the stator around the reluctor. Tighten the screws and recheck the gap. On 1982-86 models, measure the air gap between the reluctor and stator. If not within specifications, loosen stator retaining screws and adjust.

PARTS REPLACEMENT

Reluctor
1976-78

NOTE: *The reluctor cannot be removed on early 1976-77 models. It is an integral part of the distributor shaft. Non-removable reluctors can be distinguished by the absence of a roll pin (retaining pin) which locks the reluctor in place on the shaft.*

1. Remove the distributor cap, the rotor and the pickup coil.
2. Use 2 screwdrivers or pry bars to pry the reluctor from the distributor shaft. Be extremely careful not to damage the reluctor teeth. Remove the roll pin.
3. To replace, press the reluctor firmly onto the shaft. Install a new roll pin with the slit facing away from the distributor shaft; DO NOT reuse the old roll pin.

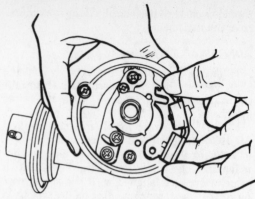

Removing the pickup coil (1976–78)

Single Post pickup Coil
1976-78

1. Remove the distributor cap by releasing the 2 spring clips. Remove the rotor by pulling it straight up and off the shaft.
2. Disconnect the distributor wiring harness at the terminal block.
3. Remove the 2 pickup coil mounting screws. Remove the screws retaining the wiring harness to the distributor.
4. Remove the pickup coil.
5. To replace the pickup coil, reverse the removal procedure but leave the mounting screws slightly loose to facilitate the air gap adjustment.

Reluctor
1979-81

1. Remove the distributor cap and remove the rotor by pulling it straight up and off the shaft.
2. Remove 3 screws holding stator to magnet and remove both parts.
3. Use 2 screwdrivers or pry bars to pry the reluctor from the distributor shaft. Be extreme-

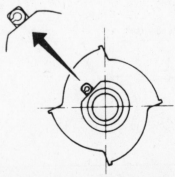

View of the reluctor, roll pin and distributor shaft (1979–81)

ly careful not to damage the reluctor teeth. Remove the roll pin.

4. To replace, press the reluctor firmly onto the shaft. Install a new roll pin with the slit facing away from the distributor shaft; DO NOT reuse the old roll pin

Ring Type Pickup Coil

1979-81

1. Remove the distributor cap and remove the rotor by pulling it straight up and off the shaft.

2. Remove 3 screws holding stator to magnet and remove both parts.

3. Use 2 screwdrivers or pry bars to pry the reluctor from the distributor shaft. Be extremely careful not to damage the reluctor teeth. Remove the roll pin.

4. Remove pickup coil assembly from the distributor.

5. To install place the pickup coil assembly on rotor shaft assembly.

6. Press the reluctor firmly onto the shaft. Install a new roll pin with the slit facing away from the distributor shaft; DO NOT reuse the old roll pin.

7. Install the stator and magnet but do not tighten the hold down screws on the stator all the way as the air gap adjustment has to be made.

8. Bump the engine around with the starter or turn it with a wrench on the crankshaft pulley bolt to align the reluctor with the stator and adjust the air gap.

9. Install the rotor head and distributor cap.

Reluctor and IC Ignition Unit

1982-86

NOTE: *The engines of this period are equipped with a slightly different ignition system and do not utilize a pickup coil.*

1. Remove the distributor cap and pull the rotor from the distributor shaft.

NOTE: *The rotor on the Stanza is held to the*

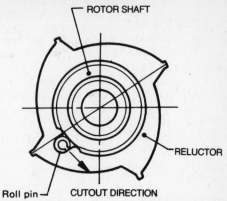
View of the reluctor, roll pin and distributor shaft (1982 and later)

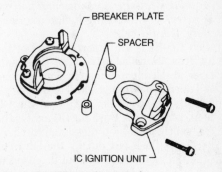
Pulsar—IC ignition unit removal

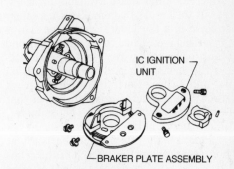
Stanza—IC ignition unit removal

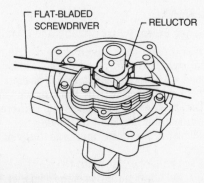
Removing reluctor from rotor shaft

distributor shaft by a retaining screw, which must be removed.

2. Remove the wiring harness and the vacuum controller from the housing.

3. Using 2 flat bladed screwdrivers, place one on each side of the reluctor and pry it from the distributor shaft.

NOTE: *When removing the reluctor, be careful not to damage or distort the teeth.*

4. Remove the roll pin from the reluctor.

NOTE: *If it is necessary to remove the IC unit, mark and remove the breaker plate assembly and separate the IC unit from it. Be careful not to loose the spacers when you remove the IC unit.*

5. To install, reverse the removal procedures. When you install the roll pin into the reluctor position the cutout direction of the roll pin in parallel with the notch in the reluctor. Make sure that the harness to the IC ignition unit is tightly secured, then adjust the air gap between the reluctor and the stator. On Pulsar, position the cutout of the rotor so it aligns with the keyway on the rotor shaft before installing the rotor.

Ignition Timing

CAUTION: *When performing this or any other operation with the engine running, be very careful of the alternator belt and pulleys. Make sure that your timing light wires don't interfere with the belt.*

Ignition timing is an important part of the tune-up. It is always adjusted after the points are gapped (dwell angle changed), since altering the dwell affects the timing. The 3 basic types of timing lights are available, the neon, the DC and the AC powered. Of the 3 the DC light is the most frequently used by professional mechanics. The bright flash put out by the DC light makes the timing marks stand out on even the brightest of days. Another advantage of the DC light is that you don't need to be near an electrical outlet. Neon lights are available for a few dollars but their weak flash makes it necessary to use them in a fairly dark work area. The 1 neon light lead is attached to the spark plug and the other to the plug wire. The DC light attaches to the spark plug and the wire with an adapter and 2 clips attach to the battery posts for power. The AC unit is similar, except that the power cable is plugged into a house outlet.

Ignition timing is the measurement, in degrees of crankshaft rotation, of the point at which the spark plugs fire in each of the cylinders. It is measured in degrees before or after Top Dead Center (TDC) of the compression stroke. Ignition timing is controlled by turning the distributor body in the engine.

Ideally, the air/fuel mixture in the cylinder will be ignited by the spark plug just as the piston passes TDC of the compression stroke. If this happens, the piston will be beginning its downward motion of the power stroke just as the compressed and ignited air/fuel mixture starts to expand. The expansion of the air/fuel mixture then forces the piston down on the power stroke and turns the crankshaft.

Because it takes a fraction of a second for the spark plug to ignite the mixture in the cylinder, the spark plug must fire a little before the piston reaches TDC. Otherwise, the mixture will not be completely ignited as the piston passes TDC and the full power of the explosion will not be used by the engine.

The timing measurement is given in degrees of crankshaft rotation before or after the piston reaches TDC (ATDC) (BTDC). If the setting for the ignition timing is 5° BTDC, the spark plug must fire 5° before each piston reaches TDC. This only holds true, however, when the engine is at idle speed.

As the engine speed increases, the pistons go faster. The spark plugs have to ignite the fuel even sooner, if it is to be completely ignited when the piston reaches TDC. To do this, the distributor has a means to advance the timing of the spark as the engine speed increases. This is accomplished by centrifugal weights within the distributor and a vacuum diaphragm, mounted on the side of the distributor. It is necessary to disconnect the vacuum line from the diaphragm when the ignition timing is being set.

The timing is best checked with a timing light. This device is connected in series with the No. 1 spark plug. The current which fires the spark plug also causes the timing light to flash. The timing marks consist of a notch or cut out line on the crankshaft pulley and a numbered plate showing crankshaft rotation attached to the front cover. When the engine is running, the timing light is aimed at the marks on the crankshaft pulley and the pointer.

On 1987-88 Pulsar (E16) and Stanza (CA20E) models the E.C.C.S. system controls the timing there is no mechanical or vacumm advance used in the distributor. Different sensors send signals to the E.C.U. (E.C.C.S. control unit) which controls the timing.

On the Pulsar CA16DE for 1987 and the CA18DE for 1988 these engines do not utilize a conventional distributor and spark plug wires. Instead they use 4 small ignition coils fitted directly to each spark plug and a crankangle sensor mounted in the front timing belt like the E16 engine available the E.C.C.S. system controls the timing.

ADJUSTMENT

All Engines Except Pulsar CA16DE And CA18DE

1. If equipped with a point type distributor, set the dwell to the proper specification. If equipped with electronic ignition type distributor, check and/or adjust the reluctor air gap.

2. Locate the timing marks on the crankshaft pulley and the front of the engine.

3. Clean off the timing marks so that you can see them.

4. Use chalk or white paint to color the mark on the crankshaft pulley and the mark on the scale which will indicate the correct timing

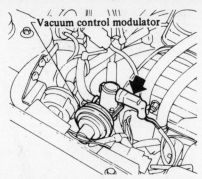

Location of the vacuum control module, E16 engine

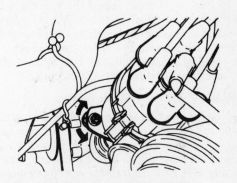

Location of the throttle and the idle adjusting screws—all engines, except E15ET

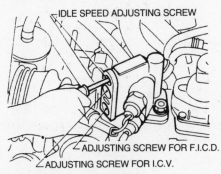

Idle control valve—Pulsar E15ET

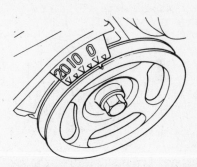

Loosen the distributor lockbolt and turn the distributor slightly to advance (upper arrow) or retard (lower arrow) the timing

when aligned with the notch on the crankshaft pulley.

5. Attach a tachometer and a timing light to the engine, according to the manufacturer's instructions.

6. Disconnect and plug the vacuum line at the distributor vacuum diaphragm if so equipped. Distributors with a crankangle sensor do not have a vacuum diaphragm. If you have a distributor with a crankangle sensor go to Step 7. The 1984-88 Pulsar (E16 engine only) for the 49 states, the 1987-88 California and Canada models (E16 engine only) and the turbocharged version of the Pulsar use a crankangle sensor.

NOTE: *On the A14 (1976-79) leave the vacuum line connected to the distributor vacuum diaphragm. On the Pulsar, E15ET (1984, Canadian Turbo) engines, disconnect the Idle Control (ICV) valve harness connector. On the Pulsar, E16 (1984 and later, except Calif. and Canada) engines, disconnect the Vacuum Control Modulator (VCM) valve harness connector to adjust the idle speed, then reconnect the harness and make sure that the idle speed is within the proper range.*

7. Check to make sure that all of the wires clear the fan and then start the engine. Allow the engine to reach normal operating temperature.

View of the timing marks at the front of the engine

CAUTION: *Be sure to block the wheels and set the parking brake; if equipped with an automatic transaxle, place the shift selector in the DRIVE position.*

8. Adjust the idle to the correct setting.

NOTE: *Before checking and/or adjusting the timing, make sure the electrical switches, such as: the headlights, the radiator cooling fan, the heater blower and the air conditioning are turned OFF; if equipped with power steering, make sure that the wheels are faced straight ahead.*

9. Aim the timing light at the timing marks at the front of the engine cover. If the timing marks are aligned when the light flashes, the

timing is correct. Turn off the engine, then remove the tachometer and the timing light.

10. If the timing marks are not aligned, proceed with the following steps:

a. Turn off the engine.

b. Loosen the distributor lockbolt, just enough, so that the distributor can be turned with a little effort.

c. Start the engine. Keep the wires of the timing light clear of the fan.

d. With the timing light aimed at the crankshaft pulley and the timing plate on the engine, turn the distributor in the direction of rotor rotation to retard the spark and in the opposite direction to advance the spark. Align the marks on the pulley and the engine scale with the flashes of the timing light.

e. Tighten the holddown bolt. Remove the tachometer and the timing light.

Pulsar CA16DE And CA18DE Engines

NOTE: *The CA16DE and CA18DE engines do not utilize a conventional distributor and high tension wires. Instead they use 4 small ignition coils fitted directly to each spark plug. The ECU controls the coils by means of a crankangle sensor. The crank angle sensor can be found attached to the upper front timing belt cover.*

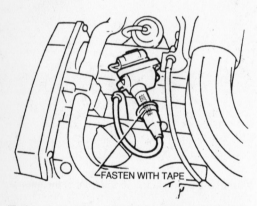

Timing connections—Pulsar CA16DE and CA18DE

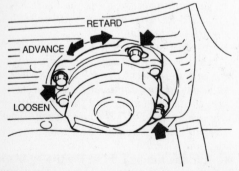

Adjust timing with crankangle sensor (1987–88) CA16DE and CA18DE

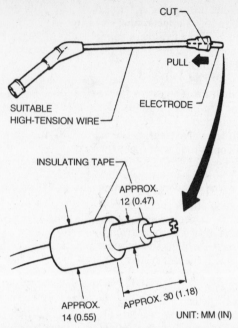

Suitable wire for checking timing—Pulsar CA16DE and CA18DE

1. Run the engine until it reaches normal operating temperature.

2. Check that the idle speed is at specifications.

3. Disconnect the air duct and both air hoses at the throttle chamber.

4. Remove the ornament cover between the camshaft covers. It has 8 screws and says "Twin Cam".

5. Remove the ignition coil at the No. 1 cylinder.

6. Connect the No. 1 ignition coil to the No. 1 spark plug with a suitable high tension wire.

7. Use an inductive pick-up type timing light and clamp it to the wire connected in Step 6.

8. Reconnect the air duct and hoses and then start the engine.

9. Check the ignition timing. If not to specifications, turn off the engine and loosen the crank angle sensor mounting bolts slightly.

10. Restart the engine and adjust the timing by turning the sensor body slightly until the timing comes into specifications.

Valve Lash

Valve adjustment determines how far the valves enter the cylinder and how long they stay open and closed.

If the valve clearance is too large, part of the lift of the camshaft will be used in removing the excessive clearance. Consequently, the valve will not be opening as far as it should. This condition has 2 effects:

  a. The valve train components will emit a tapping sound as they take up the excessive clearance.

  b. The engine will perform poorly for the valves will not open fully and allow the proper amount of gases to flow through the cylinders.

If the valve clearance is too small, the valves will open too far and not fully seat in the cylinder head when they close. When a valve seats itself in the cylinder head, it does 2 things:

  a. It seals the combustion chamber so that none of the gases in the cylinder escape.

  b. It cools itself by transferring some of the heat it absorbs from the combustion process, through the cylinder head into the engine's cooling system.

If the valve clearance is too small, the engine will run poorly because of the gases escaping from the combustion chamber. The valves will also become overheated and warped, since they cannot transfer heat unless they are touching the valve seat in the cylinder head.

NOTE: *While all valve adjustments must be made as accurately as possible, it is better to have the valve adjustment slightly loose than slightly tight, as a burned valve may result from overly tight adjustments.*

VALVE ADJUSTMENT

NOTE: *On all Stanza models from 1987-88 except station wagons no routine valve adjustment is necessary or possible these models are equipped with hydraulic lash adjusters, which continually take up excess clearance in the valve train. On Pulsar CA16DE and CA18DE engines hydraulic lifter are used no valve adjustment is necessary or possible. Datsun/Nissan recommends that valve adjustment all other models should be done every 12 months or 15,000 miles.*

1. Run the engine until it reaches normal operating temperature. Oil temperature, not water temperature, is critical to valve adjustment. With this in mind, make sure the engine is fully warmed up since this is the only way to make sure the parts have reached their full expansion. Generally speaking, this takes around 15 minutes. After the engine has reached normal operating temperature, shut it off.

2. Purchase a new valve cover gasket before removing the valve cover. The new silicone gasket sealers are just as good or better if you can't find a gasket.

3. Note the location of any hoses or wires which may interfere with valve cover removal, disconnect and move them aside. Remove the bolts which hold the valve cover in place.

**A series
Valve adjustment—**

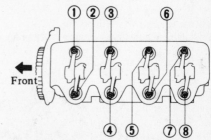

310 E-series and Pulsar valve adjustment

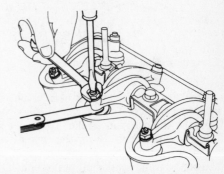

Typical valve adjustment with a feeler gauge

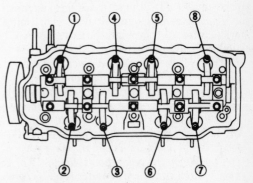

CA20 valve sequence—Stanza model

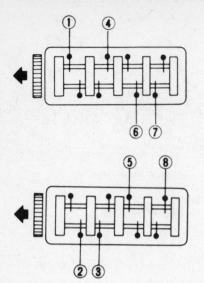

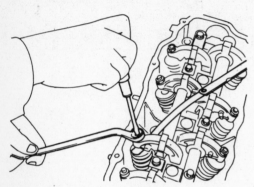

Valve adjustment sequence—Stanza (1982 only)

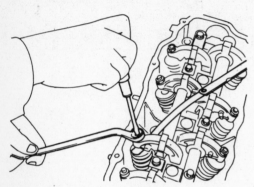

Adjusting the valves—Stanza model

4. After the valve cover has been removed, the next step is to get the number one piston at TDC on the compression stroke. There are at least two ways to do this: Bump the engine over with the starter or turn it over by using a wrench on the front crankshaft pulley bolt. The easiest way to find TDC is to turn the engine over slowly with a wrench (after first removing No. 1 plug) until the piston is at the top of its stroke and the TDC timing mark on the crankshaft pulley is in alignment with the timing mark pointer. At this point, the valves for No. 1 cylinder should be closed.

NOTE: *Make sure both valves are closed with the valve springs up as high as they will go. An easy way to find the compression stroke is to remove the distributor cap and observe which spark plug lead the rotor is pointing to. If the rotor points to No. 1 spark plug lead, No. 1 cylinder is on its compression stroke. When the rotor points to the No. 2 spark plug lead, No. 2 cylinder is on its compression stroke.*

5. Set the No. 1 piston at TDC of the compression stroke, then check and/or adjust the valve clearance on the F10 and 310 (1976-81), Nos. 1, 2, 3 and 5; on the 310 (1982), Nos. 1, 2, 3 and 6; on the Pulsar E16 engine (1983-88), Nos. 1, 2, 3 and 6; on the Stanza (1982), Nos. 1, 4, 6 and 7; on the Stanza (1983-86 and 1986-88 Stanza wagon), Nos. 1, 2, 4 and 6.

6. To adjust the clearance, loosen the locknut with a wrench and turn the adjuster with a screwdriver while holding the locknut. The correct size feeler gauge should pass with a slight drag between the rocker arm and the valve stem.

7. Turn the crankshaft one full revolution to position the No. 4 piston at TDC of the compression stroke. Check and/or adjust the valves (counting from the front to the rear) on the F10 and 310 (1976-81), Nos. 4, 6, 7 and 8; on 310 (1982), Nos. 4, 5, 7 and 8; on the Stanza (1982), Nos. 2, 3, 5 and 8; on the Stanza (1983-86 and 1986-88 Stanza wagon), Nos. 3, 5, 7 and 8; on the Pulsar E16 (1983-88), Nos. 4, 5, 7 and 8.

8. Replace the valve cover and torque the bolts on the valve cover down evenly.

Idle Speed and Mixture Adjustment
CARBURETOR

CAUTION: *When checking the idle speed, set the parking brake and block the drive wheels.*

NOTE: *The 1980 and later models require a CO Meter to adjust their mixture ratios, therefore, no procedures concerning this adjustment are given. Also, many California models have a plug over their mixture control screw. It is suggested that in both of these cases, mixture adjustment to be left to a qualified technician.*

Make sure that all of the electrical equipment is turned OFF, including: The headlights, the heater blower and the air conditioning.

F10 Models (1976-78)

1. Connect a tachometer to the engine according the manufacturer's instructions.

2. Start the engine and operate it until it reaches operating temperatures.

3. Operate it at 2,000 rpm for 5 minutes under no load, then idle for 10 minutes.

NOTE: *If the cooling fan is operating, wait until it stops.*

4. For U.S.A. models, disconnect and plug the air hose from the air check valve. For Canada models, disconnect and plug the air induction pipe at the air cleaner.

5. Race the engine to 1,500-2,000 rpm a few

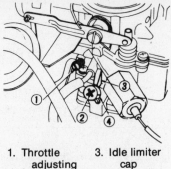

1. Throttle
   adjusting
   screw
2. Idle adjust-
   ing screw
3. Idle limiter
   cap
4. Stopper

Carburetor adjusting screws (1976–81)

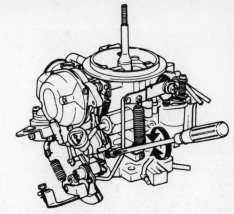

Adjusting idle speed—Stanza models

times under no-load, then run it for 1 minute at idle.

6. If the idle speed is not correct, adjust the throttle adjusting screw at the carburetor.

7. When the idle speed is correct, stop the engine, reconnect the removed hose and disconnect the tachometer.

310 Models (1979-82)

1. Connect a tachometer to the engine according the manufacturer's instructions.

2. Start the engine and run it until it reaches normal operating temperatures.

3. For Canadian models, stop the engine, then disconnect and plug the air induction hose at the air filter. Start the engine and run it at idle speed for 2 minutes.

4. Operate it at 2,000 rpm for 2 minutes under no load, then idle for 1 minute.

NOTE: *If the cooling fan is operating, wait until it stops.*

5. If equipped with a manual transaxle, place the shift selector in **NEUTRAL**; if equipped with an automatic transaxle, place the shift selector in **DRIVE**.

6. If the idle speed is not correct, adjust the throttle adjusting screw at the carburetor.

7. When the idle speed is correct, stop the engine and disconnect the tachometer, then reconnect the air induction hose (if removed).

Stanza Models 49 States (1982-83)
Stanza Models Canada (1984-85)

1. Connect a tachometer to the engine according the manufacturer's instructions.

2. Start the engine and run it until it reaches normal operating temperatures.

3. Operate it at 2,000 rpm for 2 minutes under no load, then idle for 1 minute.

NOTE: *If the cooling fan is operating, wait until it stops.*

4. If equipped with a manual transaxle, place

the shift selector in **NEUTRAL**; if equipped with an automatic transaxle, place the shift selector in **DRIVE**.

5. If the idle speed is not correct, adjust the throttle adjusting screw at the carburetor.

6. When the idle speed is correct, stop the engine and disconnect the tachometer.

Pulsar w/E16 Engine (1983-86)

1. Connect a tachometer to the engine according the manufacturer's instructions.

2. Start the engine and run it until it reaches normal operating temperatures.

3. Operate it at idle for 2 minutes under no-load, then race to 2,000-3,000 a few times and allow it to return to idle speed.

4. Turn **OFF** the engine.

NOTE: *For U.S.A. models, disconnect the vacuum control modulator harness connector. For Canada models, disconnect and plug the air induction hose at the air filter; also, for Canada models (1984-86), disconnect and plug the throttle opener control valve vacuum hose at the throttle opener control valve side.*

5. Start the engine and check the idle speed.

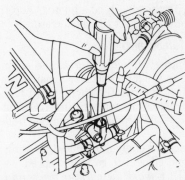

Adjusting the idle speed by turning the idle speed adjusting screw

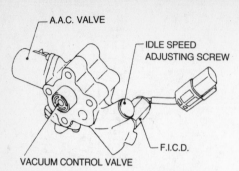

Idle Air Adjusting (I.A.A) unit—Stanza (1984–88)

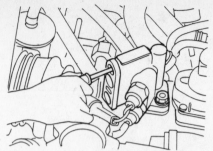

Adjusting the E15ET engine throttle adjusting screw

NOTE: *If the cooling fan is operating, wait until it stops.*

6. If equipped with a manual transaxle, place the shift selector in **NEUTRAL**; if equipped with an automatic transaxle, place the shift selector in **DRIVE**.

7. If the idle speed is not correct, adjust the throttle adjusting screw at the carburetor.

8. When the idle speed is correct, stop the engine, reconnect the vacuum control modulator and the throttle opener control valve vacuum hose (if equipped), then disconnect the tachometer.

THROTTLE BODY

Stanza (1984-88)

1. Connect a tachometer to the engine, according to the manufacturer's instructions.

2. Start and operate the engine until it reaches normal operating temperatures. Operate the engine for 5 minutes under no load.

NOTE: *Engage the parking brake and block the drive wheels. If equipped with a manual transaxle, place the shift selector in the NEUTRAL position. If equipped with an automatic transaxle, place the shift selector in the DRIVE position.*

3. Check and/or adjust the engine speed. If necessary to adjust, turn the idle speed adjusting screw on the I.A.A. (Idle Air Adjusting) unit.

4. With the idle speed adjusted, stop the engine and disconnect the tachometer.

Pulsar Turbo (1984)

1. Connect a tachometer to the engine, according to the manufacturer's instructions.

2. Start and run the engine until it reaches normal operating temperatures. Operate the engine at 2,000 rpm, for 2 minutes under no-load.

3. Race the engine to 2,000-3,000 rpm a few times and allow it to go to idle speed.

NOTE: *Engage the parking brake and block the drive wheels. If equipped with a manual transaxle, place the shift selector in the NEU-*

TRAL position. If equipped with an automatic transaxle, place the shift selector in the DRIVE position.

4. Check and/or adjust the engine speed. If necessary to adjust, turn the throttle adjusting screw in the idle control valve.

5. With the idle speed adjusted, stop the engine and disconnect the tachometer.

Pulsar E16i (1987-88)

NOTE: *To adjust the idle speed on the fuel injected Pulsar the special tool number EG11170000 adapter harness connector is needed to hookup a tachometer to the engine.*

1. Set shift lever in **NEUTRAL** position for the manual transaxle and **N** or **P** for the automatic transaxle models.

2. Set the parking brake and block both front and rear wheels.

3. Turn all the accessories off and keep the front wheels straight ahead at all times.

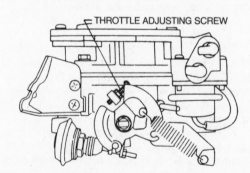

Idle speed adjusting screw—Pulsar E16i

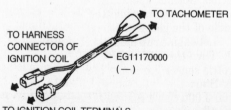

Special tool adapter harness connector—Pulsar E16i

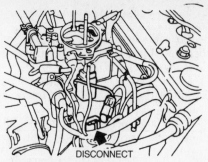

Disconnecting the throttle sensor connector—Pulsar E16i

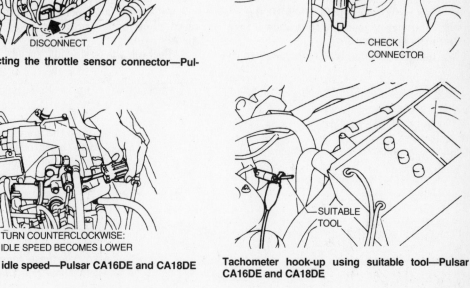

CHECK CONNECTOR

SUITABLE TOOL

Tachometer hook-up using suitable tool—Pulsar CA16DE and CA18DE

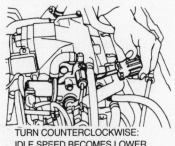

TURN COUNTERCLOCKWISE: IDLE SPEED BECOMES LOWER

Adjusting idle speed—Pulsar CA16DE and CA18DE

F.I.C.D. SOLENOID VALVE

IDLE ADJUST SCREW

TO AIR REGULATOR VALVE

TO AIR DUCT

TO INTAKE MANIFOLD

A.A.C. VALVE

Idle Air Adjusting (I.A.A) unit—Pulsar CA16DE and CA18DE

4. Attach the special tool (adapter harness) between the ignition coil primary winding terminals and the harness connector. Then connect your tachometer to the adapter harness.

5. Start the engine and warm the engine so it reaches normal operating temperature. The water temperature indicator should be in the middle of the gauge.

6. Let engine run at idle speed for 2 minutes.

7. Turn the engine OFF and disconnect the throttle sensor harness connector.

8. Start the engine and race the engine to 2,000-3,000 rpm a few times under no load and then allow it to return to the idle speed.

CAUTION: *The automatic transmission*

equipped model should be shifted into DRIVE for the idle speed check. When in DRIVE the parking brake must be fully applied and both the front and the rear wheels chocked. After all the adjustments are made, shift the car to the PARK position and remove the wheel chocks.

9. Check the idle speed on the manual transaxle model in NEUTRAL and on the automatic transaxle model check in DRIVE.

10. If necessary, adjust the idle speed by turning the throttle adjusting screw on the throttle body.

11. Turn the engine OFF and connect the throttle sensor harness connector.

12. Start the engine and race the engine to 2,000-3,000 rpm a few times under no load and then allow it to return to idle speed.

13. Recheck the idle speed on the manual transaxle model check in NEUTRAL and on the automatic transaxle model check in DRIVE.

Pulsar CA16DE (1987)
Pulsar CA18DE (1988)

1. Before adjusting the idle speed on these engines you must visually check the following items first: air cleaner for being clogged, hoses and ducts for leaks, EGR valve for proper oper-

ation, all electrical connectors, gaskets and the throttle valve, throttle valve switch on the CA16DE engine and idle switch on the CA18DE engine.

2. Start the engine and warm the engine so it reaches normal operating temperature. The water temperature indicator should be in the middle of the gauge.

3. Then race the engine to 2,000-3,000 rpm a few times under no load and then allow it to return to the idle speed.

4. Connect a voltage type tachometer to the engine by using a suitable type tool in the check connector for a lead outlet.

5. Check the idle speed on the manual transaxle model in **NEUTRAL** and on the automatic transaxle model check in **DRIVE**.

6. If the idle speed has to be adjusted you must disconnect the A.A.C. valve harness connector (Auxiliary Air Control).

7. Adjust the idle speed by turning the idle speed adjusting screw on the I.A.A. unit (Idle Air Adjusting).

8. Recheck the engine idle speed.

Engine and Engine Overhaul

3

ENGINE ELECTRICAL

Understanding the Engine Electrical System

The engine electrical system can be broken down into three separate and distinct systems:
1. The starting system.
2. The charging system.
3. The ignition system.

BATTERY AND STARTING SYSTEM

Basic Operating Principles

The battery is the first link in the chain of mechanisms which work together to provide cranking of the automobile engine. In most modern cars, the battery is a lead/acid electrochemical device consisting of six 2v subsections connected in series so the unit is capable of producing approximately 12v of electrical pressure. Each subsection, or cell, consists of a series of positive and negative plates held a short distance apart in a solution of sulfuric acid and water. The two types of plates are of dissimilar metals. This causes a chemical reaction to be set up, and it is this reaction which produces current flow from the battery when its positive and negative terminals are connected to an electrical appliance such as a lamp or motor. The continued transfer of electrons would eventually convert the sulfuric acid in the electrolyte to water, and make the two plates identical in chemical composition. As electrical energy is removed from the battery, its voltage output tends to drop. Thus, measuring battery voltage and battery electrolyte composition are two ways of checking the ability of the unit to supply power. During the starting of the engine, electrical energy is removed from the battery. However, if the charging circuit is in good condition and the operating conditions are normal, the power removed from the battery will be replaced by the generator (or alternator) which will force electrons back through the battery, reversing the normal flow, and restoring the battery to its original chemical state.

The battery and starting motor are linked by very heavy electrical cables designed to minimize resistance to the flow of current. Generally, the major power supply cable that leaves the battery goes directly to the starter, while other electrical system needs are supplied by a smaller cable. During starter operation, power flows from the battery to the starter and is grounded through the car's frame and the battery's negative ground strap.

The starting motor is a specially designed, direct current electric motor capable of producing a very great amount of power for its size. One thing that allows the motor to produce a great deal of power is its tremendous rotating speed. It drives the engine through a tiny pinion gear (attached to the starter's armature), which drives the very large flywheel ring gear at a greatly reduced speed. Another factor allowing it to produce so much power is that only intermittent operation is required of it. This, little allowance for air circulation is required, and the windings can be built into a very small space.

The starter solenoid is a magnetic device which employs the small current supplied by the starting switch circuit of the ignition switch. This magnetic action moves a plunger which mechanically engages the starter and electrically closes the heavy switch which connects it to the battery. The starting switch circuit consists of the starting switch contained within the ignition switch, a transmission neutral safety switch or clutch pedal switch, and the wiring necessary to connect these in series with the starter solenoid or relay.

A pinion, which is a small gear, is mounted to a one-way drive clutch. This clutch is splined to the starter armature shaft. When the ignition switch is moved to the **start** position, the solenoid plunger slides the pinion toward the fly-wheel ring gear via a collar and spring. If the teeth on the pinion and flywheel match proper-ly, the pinion will engage the flywheel immedi-ately. If the gear teeth butt one another, the spring will be compressed and will force the gears to mesh as soon as the starter turns far enough to allow them to do so. As the solenoid plunger reaches the end of its travel, it closes the contacts that connect the battery and start-er and then the engine is cranked.

As soon as the engine starts, the flywheel ring gear begins turning fast enough to drive the pinion at an extremely high rate of speed. At this point, the one-way clutch begins allow-ing the pinion to spin faster than the starter shaft so that the starter will not operate at ex-cessive speed. When the ignition switch is re-leased from the starter position, the solenoid is de-energized, and a spring contained within the solenoid assembly pulls the gear out of mesh and interrupts the current flow to the starter.

Some starter employ a separate relay, mount-ed away from the starter, to switch the motor and solenoid current on and off. The relay thus replaces the solenoid electrical switch, buy does not eliminate the need for a solenoid mounted on the starter used to mechanically engage the starter drive gears. The relay is used to reduce the amount of current the starting switch must carry.

THE CHARGING SYSTEM

Basic Operating Principles

The automobile charging system provides electrical power for operation of the vehicle's ig-nition and starting systems and all the electri-cal accessories. The battery services as an elec-trical surge or storage tank, storing (in chemi-cal form) the energy originally produced by the engine driven generator. The system also pro-vides a means of regulating generator output to protect the battery from being overcharged and to avoid excessive voltage to the accessories.

The storage battery is a chemical device in-corporating parallel lead plates in a tank con-taining a sulfuric acid/water solution. Adjacent plates are slightly dissimilar, and the chemical reaction of the two dissimilar plates produces electrical energy when the battery is connected to a load such as the starter motor. The chemi-cal reaction is reversible, so that when the gen-erator is producing a voltage (electrical pres-sure) greater than that produced by the bat-tery, electricity is forced into the battery, and the battery is returned to its fully charged state.

The vehicle's generator is driven mechanical-ly, through V-belts, by the engine crankshaft. It consists of two coils of fine wire, one stationary (the stator), and one movable (the rotor). The rotor may also be known as the armature, and consists of fine wire wrapped around an iron core which is mounted on a shaft. The electric-ity which flows through the two coils of wire (provided initially by the battery in some cases) creates an intense magnetic field around both rotor and stator, and the interaction between the two fields creates voltage, allowing the gen-erator to power the accessories and charge the battery.

There are two types of generators: the earlier is the direct current (DC) type. The current produced by the DC generator is generated in the armature and carried off the spinning ar-mature by stationary brushes contacting the commutator. The commutator is a series of smooth metal contact plates on the end of the armature. The commutator is a series of smooth metal contact plates on the end of the armature. The commutator plates, which are separated from one another by a very short gap, are connected to the armature circuits so that current will flow in one directions only in the wires carrying the generator output. The gen-erator stator consists of two stationary coils of wire which draw some of the output current of the generator to form a powerful magnetic field and create the interaction of fields which gener-ates the voltage. The generator field is wired in series with the regulator.

Newer automobiles use alternating current generators or alternators, because they are more efficient, can be rotated at higher speeds, and have fewer brush problems. In an alterna-tor, the field rotates while all the current pro-duced passes only through the stator winding. The brushes bear against continuous slip rings rather than a commutator. This causes the cur-rent produced to periodically reverse the direc-tion of its flow. Diodes (electrical one-way switches) block the flow of current from travel-ing in the wrong direction. A series of diodes is wired together to permit the alternating flow of the stator to be converted to a pulsating, but unidirectional flow at the alternator output. The alternator's field is wired in series with the voltage regulator.

The regulator consists of several circuits. Each circuit has a core, or magnetic coil of wire, which operates a switch. Each switch is con-nected to ground through one or more resis-tors. The coil of wire responds directly to sys-tem voltage. When the voltage reaches the re-quired level, the magnetic field created by the winding of wire closes the switch and inserts a resistance into the generator field circuit, thus reducing the output. The contacts of the switch cycle open and close many times each second to precisely control voltage.

While alternators are self-limiting as far as maximum current is concerned, DC generators employ a current regulating circuit which responds directly to the total amount of current flowing through the generator circuit rather than to the output voltage. The current regulator is similar to the voltage regulator except that all system current must flow through the energizing coil on its way to the various accessories.

ENGINE ELECTRICAL

Ignition Coil
TESTING
Primary Resistance Check

On the 1976-77 models, disconnect the distributor harness wires from the ignition coil ballast resistor, leaving the ballast resistor-to-coil wires attached. On the 1978 and all later models, disconnect the ignition coil wires at the coil. Connect the leads of an ohmmeter to the ballast resistor outside terminals (at each end) for 1976-77 and to the two coil (side) terminals for 1978 and later.

With the ohmmeter set on the X1 range, the reading should be 0.84-1.02Ω for the Stanza models from 1982-86. On the Stanza models from 1987-88 a Mold type coil is used, first remove the coil wire then connect the leads of an ohmmeter to the positive (+) and negative (−) terminals at the the bottom of the coil assembly the reading should 0.8-1.0Ω for this type coil.

The readings should be 1.08-1.32Ω, for F10 model (1976-78), except the 1978 USA model which should be 0.84-1.02Ω and the 1976 California model which should read 0.45-0.55Ω. The 1979-81 310 model should read 0.84-1.02Ω and the 310 model (1982) and the Pulsar (1983 all models and the 1984-86 California and Canada models) should read 1.04-1.27Ω and for the 1984-86 49 states Pulsar the reading is 0.84-1.02Ω if the reading is more than specified, replace the ignition coil assembly.

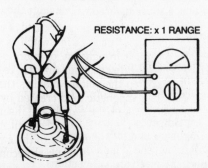

Checking the primary circuit of the ignition coil

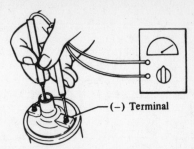

Checking the secondary circuit of the ignition coil

Secondary Resistance Check

Turn the ignition key **OFF**, then remove the high tension and a primary coil wire from the coil using an ohmmeter, set it on the X1000 scale. Touch one lead to a primary terminal and the other lead to the center terminal. The resistance should be 8,200-12,400Ω, except F10 (1978, USA), 310 (1982) and Puslar (1983 and later); 7,300-11,000, for 310 (1982) and Pulsar (1983 all models and the 1984-86 California and Canada models); and 17,000-23,000Ω, for F10 (1978, USA); if not, replace the ignition coil.

Note: *On the Pulsar E16 1984-86 (49 states models), Pulsar E16 1987-88 (all models) and Stanza 1987-88 (all models) a power transistor is used with the ignition coil. The ignition signal from the E.C.U. is amplified by the power transistor, which turns the ignition coil primary circuit on and off, inducing the proper high voltage in the secondary circuit. On these models the the ignition coil is a small molded type. Checking the ignition coils on the 1987-88 Pulsar (CA16DE and CA18DE) involves complicated diagnostic procedures.*

REMOVAL AND INSTALLATION

On all models with the exception of the Pulsar CA16DE and CA18DE engines the coil is either mounted to the wall of the engine compartment or the engine. To remove disconnect and mark all electrical connections then transfer coil mounting bracket if so equipped to the new coil. When installing the new coil make sure that the coil wire and all other electrical connections are properly installed.

On the Pulsar CA16DE and CA18DE engines 4 small ignition coil fit directly to each spark plug. The ECU controls the coils by means of a crankangle sensor. To remove disconnect the air duct and the air hoses then remove the ornamemt cover. Remove the holding down screws and careful remove the ignition coil from the spark plug.

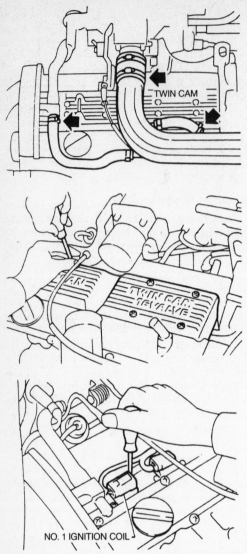

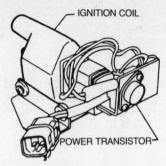

Molded ignition coil—Pulsar E16—Stanza similar

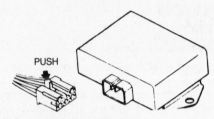

Ignition module/unit (1976–78)

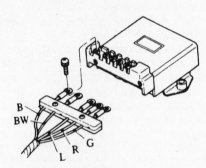

Ignition module/unit (1976–78)

Removing ignition coils—Pulsar CA16DE and CA18DE

Ignition Module
REMOVAL AND INSTALLATION
1976-78

NOTE: *These models used a transistor type ignition unit which is located on the right hand or left hand dash side panel in the passenger compartment.*

LEFT SIDE

1. Disconnect the battery terminals.
2. Disconnect the ignition unit connector from the unit. To remove the ignition unit connector, push latch of connector and pull the connector out.
3. Remove 2 setscrews and remove the unit.
4. To install, reverse the order of removal.

RIGHT SIDE

1. Disconnect the battery terminals.
2. Remove the package tray.
3. Disconnect and tag the wiring harness from the unit.
4. Remove 2 setscrews and remove the unit.
5. To install, reverse the order of removal. Be sure to connect wiring harness to their proper positions. Failure to do so will damage the unit.

1979-81

NOTE: *The IC ignition unit on these models is mounted on the outside of the distributor housing.*

1. Disconnect the battery terminals.
2. Remove the distributor cap by releasing the 2 spring clips. Remove the rotor by pulling it straight up and off the shaft.
3. Remove the 2 hold down screws and disconnect the electrical connections.
4. To install, reverse the order of removal.

1982 310
1982-86 Stanza
1983 Pulsar(All models)
1984-86 Pulsar (California and Canada models without a turbocharged engine)

NOTE: *The IC ignition unit is mounted on the inside of the distributor.*

1. Remove the distributor cap and pull the rotor from the distributor shaft.

NOTE: *The rotor on the Stanza is held to the distributor shaft by a retaining screw, which must be removed.*

2. Remove the wiring harness and the vacuum controller from the housing.

3. Using 2 flat bladed screwdrivers, place one on each side of the reluctor and pry it from the distributor shaft.

NOTE: *When removing the reluctor, be careful not to damage or distort the teeth.*

4. Remove the roll pin from the reluctor.

5. Mark and remove the breaker plate assembly and separate the IC unit from it Becareful not to loose the spacers when you re move the IC unit.

6. To install, reverse the removal procedures. When you install the roll pin into the reluctor position the cutout direction of the roll pin in parallel with the notch in the reluctor. Make sure that the harness to the IC ignition unit is tightly secured, then adjust the air gap between the reluctor and the stator. On Pulsar, position the cutout of the rotor so it aligns with the keyway on the rotor shaft before installing the rotor.

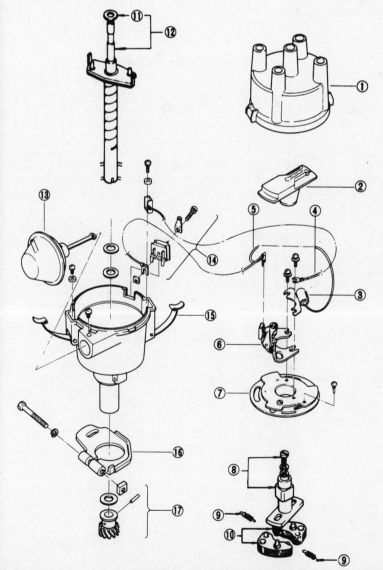

1. Cap
2. Rotor
3. Condenser
4. Ground wire
5. Lead wire
6. Breaker points
7. Breaker plate
8. Cam assembly
9. Governor spring
10. Governor weight
11. Thrust washer
12. Shaft assembly
13. Vacuum control assembly
14. Terminal assembly
15. Clamp
16. Retaining plate
17. Gear set

Exploded view of the single point distributor—F10 1976–77

Distributor

REMOVAL

NOTE: *These procedures are for distributors with out a crankangle sensor. The Pulsar CA16DE and CA18DE engines do not utilize a conventional distributor.*

1. Unfasten the retaining clips and lift the distributor cap straight up. It will be easier to install the distributor if the wiring is not disconnected from the cap. If the wires must be removed from the cap, mark their positions to aid in installations.

2. Disconnect the distributor wiring harness.

3. Disconnect the vacuum lines.

4. Note the position of the rotor in relation to the base. Scribe a mark on the base of the distributor and on the engine block to facilitate reinstallation. Align the marks with the direction the metal tip of the rotor is pointing.

5. Remove the bolt which hold the distributor to the engine.

6. Pull the distributor assembly from the engine.

INSTALLATION

1. Insert the distributor shaft and assembly into the engine. Line up the mark on the distributor and the one on the engine with the metal tip of the rotor. Make sure that the vacuum advance diaphragm is pointed in the same direction as it was pointed originally. This will be done automatically if the marks on the engine and the distributor are lined up with the rotor.

2. Install the distributor holddown bolt and clamp. Leave the screw loose so that you can move the distributor with heavy hand pressure.

3. Connect the primary wire to the coil. Install the distributor cap on the distributor housing. Secure the distributor cap with the spring clips.

4. Install the spark plug wires if removed. Make sure that the wires are pressed all the way into the top of the distributor cap and firmly onto the spark plug.

5. Adjust the point dwell (non-electronic) and set the ignition timing.

NOTE: *If the crankshaft has been turned or the engine disturbed in any manner (disassembled and/or rebuilt) while the distributor was removed or if the marks were not drawn, it will be necessary to initially time the engine. Follow the procedure given below.*

INSTALLATION—ENGINE DISTURBED

1. It is necessary to place the No. 1 cylinder in the firing position to correctly install the distributor. To locate this position, the ignition timing marks on the crankshaft front pulley are used.

2. Remove the No. 1 cylinder spark plug. Turn the crankshaft until the piston in the No. 1 cylinder is moving up on the compression stroke. This can be determined by placing your

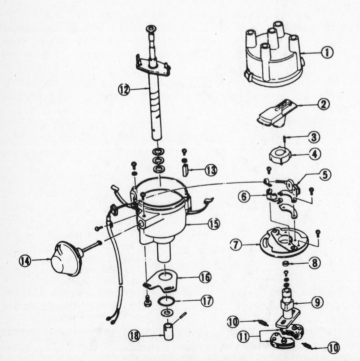

1. Cap assembly
2. Rotor head assembly
3. Roll pin
4. Reluctor
5. Pick-up coil
6. Contactor
7. Breaker plate assembly
8. Packing
9. Rotor shaft
10. Governor spring
11. Governor weight
12. Shaft assembly
13. Cap setter
14. Vacuum controller
15. Housing
16. Fixing plate
17. O-ring
18. Collar

Exploded view of electronic distributor—F10 1976–78

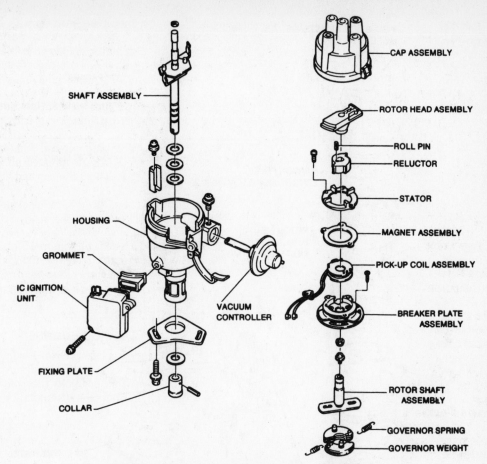

SHAFT ASSEMBLY

HOUSING

GROMMET

IC IGNITION
UNIT

VACUUM
CONTROLLER

FIXING PLATE

COLLAR

CAP ASSEMBLY

ROTOR HEAD ASEMBLY

ROLL PIN

RELUCTOR

STATOR

MAGNET ASSEMBLY

PICK-UP COIL ASSEMBLY

BREAKER PLATE
ASSEMBLY

ROTOR SHAFT
ASSEMBLY

GOVERNOR SPRING

GOVERNOR WEIGHT

Exploded view of electronic distributor—310 1979–81

thumb over the spark plug hole and feeling the air being forced out of the cylinder. Stop turning the crankshaft when the timing marks that are used to time the engine are aligned.

3. Oil the distributor housing lightly where the distributor bears on the cylinder block.

4. Install the distributor with the rotor, which is mounted on the shaft, pointing toward the No. 1 spark plug terminal on the distributor cap. Of course you won't be able to see the direction in which the rotor is pointing if the cap is on the distributor.

NOTE: *Lay the cap on top of the distributor and make a mark on the side of the distributor housing just below the No. 1 spark plug terminal. Make sure that the rotor points toward that mark when you install the distributor.*

5. When the distributor shaft has reached the bottom of the hole, move the rotor back and forth slightly until the driving lug on the end of the shaft enters the slots cut in the end of the oil pump shaft and the distributor assembly slides down into place.

6. When the distributor is correctly installed,

the breaker points (non-electronic) should be in such a position that they are just ready to break contact. This is accomplished by rotating the distributor body after it has been installed in the engine. Once again, line up the marks that you made before the distributor was removed from the engine.

7. Install the distributor holddown bolt.

8. Install the spark plug and continue from Step 3 of the proceeding distributor installation procedure.

If your engine has a distributor with a crankangle sensor set up read the above section and then you will be able to remove and install the distributor.

Basically, you have to remove the distributor cap, mark or tag all the spark plug wires and electrical connections then remove them. Next, mark the postion of the base of the distributor with relation to the engine mounting location and the rotor position as opposed to the the base of the distributor.

When installing the distributor, line up your marks and gently install the distributor and reconnect all spark wires and electrical connec-

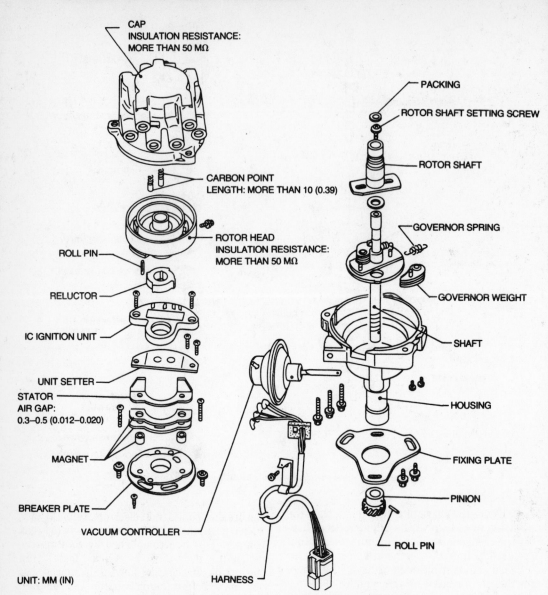

CAP
INSULATION RESISTANCE:
MORE THAN 50 MΩ

PACKING

ROTOR SHAFT SETTING SCREW

ROTOR SHAFT

CARBON POINT
LENGTH: MORE THAN 10 (0.39)

GOVERNOR SPRING

ROTOR HEAD
INSULATION RESISTANCE:
MORE THAN 50 MΩ

ROLL PIN

GOVERNOR WEIGHT

RELUCTOR

IC IGNITION UNIT

SHAFT

UNIT SETTER

STATOR
AIR GAP:
0.3–0.5 (0.012–0.020)

HOUSING

MAGNET

FIXING PLATE

PINION

BREAKER PLATE

VACUUM CONTROLLER

ROLL PIN

UNIT: MM (IN)

HARNESS

Exploded view of electronic distributor—Stanza (1982–86)

tions. If you disturb the engine while the distributior is removed you will have to set inital timing refer to the section "INSTALLATION—ENGINE DISTURBED".

Alternator

The alternator charging system is a negative (–) ground system which consists of an alternator, a regulator, a charge indicator, a storage battery and wiring connecting the components, and fuse link wire.

The alternator is belt-driven from the engine. Energy is supplied from the alternator/regulator system to the rotating field through two brushes to two slip-rings. The slip-rings are mounted on the rotor shaft and are connected to the field coil. This energy supplied to the rotating field from the battery is called excitation current and is used to initially energize the field to begin the generation of electricity. Once the alternator starts to generate electricity, the excitation current comes from its own output rather than the battery.

The alternator produces power in the form of alternating current. The alternating current is rectified by 6 diodes into direct current. The direct current is used to charge the battery and power the rest of the electrical system.

When the ignition key is turned on, current flows from the battery, through the charging system indicator light on the instrument panel,

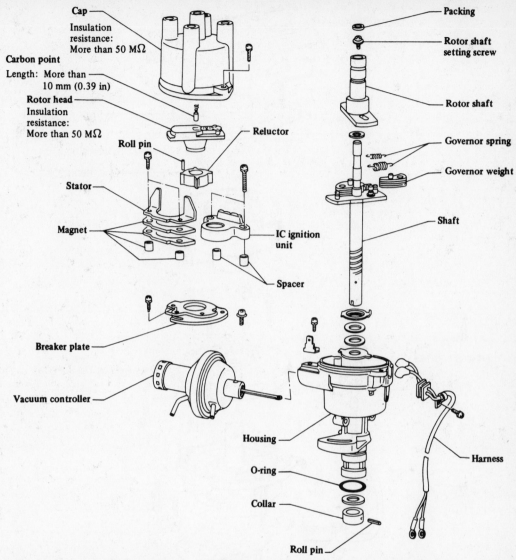

Cap
Insulation resistance: More than 50 MΩ

Carbon point
Length: More than 10 mm (0.39 in)

Rotor head
Insulation resistance: More than 50 MΩ

Roll pin

Reluctor

Stator

Magnet

IC ignition unit

Spacer

Breaker plate

Vacuum controller

Packing

Rotor shaft setting screw

Rotor shaft

Governor spring

Governor weight

Shaft

Housing

O-ring

Collar

Roll pin

Harness

Exploded view of electronic distributor—310 (1982) and Pulsar (1983) all models (1984–86) Calif. and Canada

to the voltage regulator, and to the alternator. Since the alternator is not producing any current, the alternator warning light comes on. When the engine is started, the alternator begins to produce current and turns the alternator light off. As the alternator turns and produces current, the current is divided in two ways: part to the battery to charge the battery and power the electrical components of the vehicle, and part is returned to the alternator to enable it to increase its output. In this situation, the alternator is receiving current from the battery and from itself. A voltage regulator is wired into the current supply to the alternator to prevent it from receiving too much current which would cause it to put out too much current. Conversely, if the voltage regulator does not allow the alternator to receive enough current, the battery will not be fully charged and will eventually go dead.

The battery is connected to the alternator at all times, whether the ignition key is turned on or not. If the battery were shorted to ground, the alternator would also be shorted. This would damage the alternator. To prevent this, a fuse link is installed in the wiring between the battery and the alternator. If the battery is shorted, the fuse link is melted, protecting the alternator.

ALTERNATOR PRECAUTIONS

To prevent damage to the alternator and regulator, the following precautionary measures

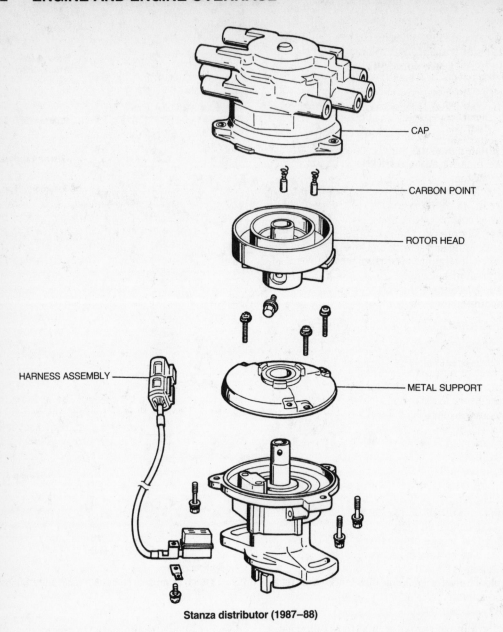

CAP

CARBON POINT

ROTOR HEAD

HARNESS ASSEMBLY

METAL SUPPORT

Stanza distributor (1987—88)

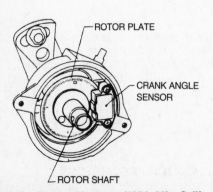

ROTOR PLATE

CRANK ANGLE SENSOR

ROTOR SHAFT

Pulsar distributor—49 states (1984—88)—Calif. and Canada (1987—88)

must be taken when working with the electrical system.

1. Never reverse the battery connections.

2. Booster batteries for starting must be connected properly: positive-to-positive and negative-to-ground.

3. Disconnect the battery cables before using a fast charger; the charger has a tendency to force current through the diodes in the opposite direction for which they were designed. This burns out the diodes.

4. Never use a fast charger as a booster for starting the vehicle.

5. Never disconnect the voltage regulator while the engine is running.

6. Avoid long soldering times when replacing diodes or transistors. Prolonged heat is damaging to AC generators.

7. Do not use test lamps of more than 12 volts (V) for checking diode continuity.

8. Do not short across or ground any of the terminals on the AC generator.

9. The polarity of the battery, generator, and regulator must be matched and considered before making any electrical connections within the system.

10. Never operate the alternator on an open circuit. make sure that all connections within the circuit are clean and tight.

11. Disconnect the battery terminals when performing any service on the electrical system. This will eliminate the possibility of accidental reversal of polarity.

12. Disconnect the battery ground cable if arc welding is to be done on any part of the car.

CHARGING SYSTEM TROUBLESHOOTING

There are many possible ways in which the charging system can malfunction. Often the source of a problem is difficult to diagnose, requiring special equipment and a good deal of experience. This is usually not the case, however, where the charging system fails completely and causes the dash board warning light to come on or the battery to become dead. To troubleshoot a complete system failure only two pieces of equipment are needed: a test light, to determine that current is reaching a certain point; and a current indicator (ammeter), to determine the direction of the current flow and its measurement in amps.

This test works under three assumptions:

1. The battery is known to be good and fully charged.

2. The alternator belt is in good condition and adjusted to the proper tension.

3. All connections in the system are clean and tight.

NOTE: *In order for the current indicator to give a valid reading, the car must be equipped with battery cables which are of the same gauge size and quality as original equipment battery cables.*

1. Turn off all electrical components on the car. Make sure the doors of the car are closed. If the car is equipped with a clock, disconnect the clock by removing the lead wire from the rear of the clock. Disconnect the positive battery cable from the battery and connect the ground wire on a test light to the disconnected positive battery cable. Touch the probe end of the test light to the positive battery post. The test light should not light. If the test light does light, there is a short or open circuit on the car.

2. Disconnect the voltage regulator wiring harness connector at the voltage regulator. Turn on the ignition key. Connect the wire on a test light to a good ground (engine bolt). Touch the probe end of a test light to the ignition wire connector into the voltage regulator wiring connector. This wire corresponds to the **I** terminal on the regulator. If the test light goes on, the charging system warning light circuit is complete. If the test light does not come on and the warning light on the instrument panel is on, either the resistor wire, which is parallel with the warning light, or the wiring to the voltage regulator, is defective. If the test light does not come on and the warning light is not on, either the bulb is defective or the power supply wire form the battery through the ignition switch to the bulb has an open circuit. Connect the wiring harness to the regulator.

3. Examine the fuse link wire in the wiring harness from the starter relay to the alternator. If the insulation on the wire is cracked or split, the fuse link may be melted. Connect a test light to the fuse link by attaching the ground wire on the test light to an engine bolt and touching the probe end of the light to the bottom of the fuse link wire where it splices into the alternator output wire. If the bulb in the test light does not light, the fuse link is melted.

4. Start the engine and place a current indicator on the positive battery cable. Turn off all electrical accessories and make sure the doors are closed. If the charging system is working properly, the gauge will show a draw of less than 5 amps. If the system is not working properly, the gauge will show a draw of more than 5 amps. A charge moves the needle toward the battery, a draw moves the needle away from battery. Turn the engine off.

5. Disconnect the wiring harness from the voltage regulator at the regulator at the regulator connector. Connect a male spade terminal (solderless connector) to each end of a jumper wire. Insert one end of the wire into the wiring harness connector which corresponds to the **A** terminal on the regulator. Insert the other end of the wire into the wiring harness connector which corresponds to the **F** terminal on the regulator. Position the connector with the jumper wire installed so that it cannot contact any metal surface under the hood. Position a current indicator gauge on the positive battery cable. Have an assistant start the engine. Observe the reading on the current indicator. Have your assistant slowly raise the speed of the engine to about 2,000 rpm or until the current indicator needle stops moving, whichever comes first. Do not run the engine for more than a short period of time in this condition. If the wiring harness connector or jumper wire becomes excessively hot during this test, turn off the engine and

check for a grounded wire in the regulator wiring harness. If the current indicator shows a charge of about three amps less than the output of the alternator, the alternator is working properly. If the previous tests showed a draw, the voltage regulator is defective. If the gauge does not show the proper charging rate, the alternator is defective.

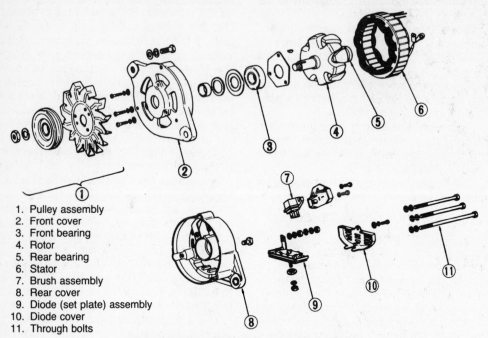

1. Pulley assembly
2. Front cover
3. Front bearing
4. Rotor
5. Rear bearing
6. Stator
7. Brush assembly
8. Rear cover
9. Diode (set plate) assembly
10. Diode cover
11. Through bolts

Exploded view of the alternator—F10 1976–77

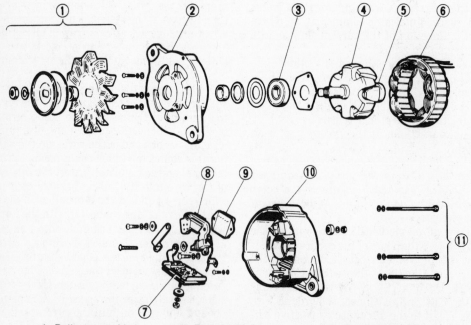

1. Pulley assembly	5. Rear bearing	8. Brush assembly
2. Front cover	6. Stator	9. IC voltage regulator
3. Front bearing	7. Diode (Set plate)	10. Rear cover
4. Rotor	assembly	11. Through bolt

Integral regulator type alternator

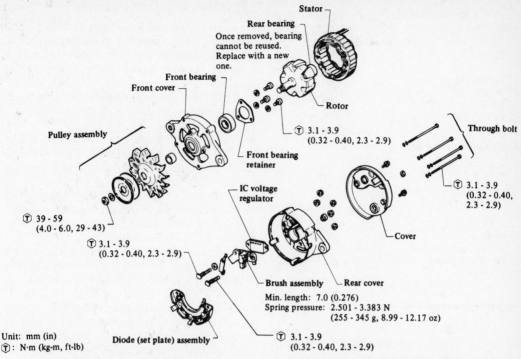

Caption: **Exploded view of the alternator—310 1982, Stanza 1982 and later, Pulsar 1983 and later**

Labels within the exploded view:

Stator

Rear bearing
Once removed, bearing cannot be reused. Replace with a new one.

Front bearing
Front cover

Rotor

Pulley assembly

Through bolt

⟨T⟩ 3.1 - 3.9
(0.32 - 0.40, 2.3 - 2.9)

⟨T⟩ 3.1 - 3.9
(0.32 - 0.40, 2.3 - 2.9)

Front bearing retainer

IC voltage regulator

⟨T⟩ 39 - 59
(4.0 - 6.0, 29 - 43)

⟨T⟩ 3.1 - 3.9
(0.32 - 0.40, 2.3 - 2.9)

Cover

Brush assembly
Min. length: 7.0 (0.276)
Spring pressure: 2.501 - 3.383 N
(255 - 345 g, 8.99 - 12.17 oz)

Rear cover

Unit: mm (in)
⟨T⟩: N·m (kg-m, ft-lb)

Diode (set plate) assembly

⟨T⟩ 3.1 - 3.9
(0.32 - 0.40, 2.3 - 2.9)

REMOVAL AND INSTALLATION

NOTE: *The alternators for Pulsar and Stanza have not changed much over the years. The 1987-88 alternators for Pulsar and Stanza have a different internal diode assembly.*

1. Disconnect the negative battery terminal.
2. Disconnect the 2 lead wires and connector from the alternator.
3. Loosen the drive belt adjusting bolt and remove the belt.
4. Unscrew the alternator attaching bolts and remove the alternator from the vehicle.
5. Install the alternator in the reverse order of removal.

Regulator

REMOVAL AND INSTALLATION

NOTE: *The 1978-88 models are equipped with internal voltage regulator. Since the regulator is part of the alternator, no adjustments are possible or necessary.*

1. Disconnect the negative battery terminal.
2. Disconnect the electrical lead connector of the regulator.
3. Remove the 2 mounting screws and remove the regulator from the vehicle.
4. Install the regulator in the reverse order of removal.

ADJUSTMENT

1. Adjust the voltage regulator core gap by loosening the screw which is used to secure the contact set on the yoke and move the contact up or down as necessary. Retighten the screw. The gap should be 0.60-1.00mm.
2. Adjust the point gap of the voltage regulator coil by loosening the screw used to secure the upper contact and move the upper contact up or down. The point gap is 0.35-0.45mm.
3. The core gap and point gap on the charge relay coil is or are adjusted in the same manner as previously outlined for the voltage regulator coil. The core gap is to be set at 0.79-1.00mm and the point gap adjusted to 0.30-0.40mm.
4. The regulated voltage is adjusted by loos-

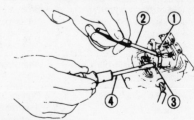

1. Contact set
2. Thickness gauge
3. 4 mm (0.157 in) dia. screw
4. Phillips screwdriver

Adjusting the core gap

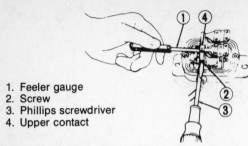

1. Feeler gauge
2. Screw
3. Phillips screwdriver
4. Upper contact

Adjusting the point gap

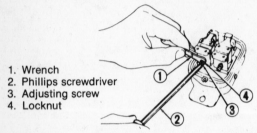

1. Wrench
2. Phillips screwdriver
3. Adjusting screw
4. Locknut

Adjusting the regulated voltage

ening the locknut and turning the adjusting screw clockwise to increase or counterclockwise to decrease the regulated voltage. The voltage should be between 14.3-15.3 volts at 68°F.

Battery

Refer to Chapter One for details on battery maintenance.

REMOVAL AND INSTALLATION

1. Disconnect the negative (ground) cable from the terminal and then the positive cable. Special pullers are available to remove the cable clamps. To avoid sparks, always disconnect the ground cable first and connect it last.

2. Remove the battery holddown clamp.

3. Remove the battery, being careful not to spill the acid.

NOTE: *Spilled acid can be neutralized with a baking soda/water solution. If you somehow get acid into your eyes, flush it out with lots of water and get to a doctor.*

4. Clean the battery posts thoroughly before reinstalling or when installing a new battery.

5. Clean the cable clamps, using a wire brush, both inside and out.

6. Install the battery and the holddown clamp or strap. Connect the positive, and then the negative cable. DO NOT hammer them in place.

NOTE: *The terminals should be coated lightly (externally) with vasoline to prevent corrosion. There are also felt washers impregnated with an anti-corrosion substance which are slipped over the battery posts before installing the cables; these are available in auto parts stores. Make absolutely sure that the battery is connected properly before you turn on the ignition switch. Reversed polarity can burn out your alternator and regulator within a matter of seconds.*

Troubleshooting Basic Charging System Problems

Problem	Cause	Solution
Noisy alternator	• Loose mountings • Loose drive pulley • Worn bearings • Brush noise • Internal circuits shorted (High pitched whine)	• Tighten mounting bolts • Tighten pulley • Replace alternator • Replace alternator • Replace alternator
Squeal when starting engine or accelerating	• Glazed or loose belt	• Replace or adjust belt
Indicator light remains on or ammeter indicates discharge (engine running)	• Broken fan belt • Broken or disconnected wires • Internal alternator problems • Defective voltage regulator	• Install belt • Repair or connect wiring • Replace alternator • Replace voltage regulator
Car light bulbs continually burn out— battery needs water continually	• Alternator/regulator overcharging	• Replace voltage regulator/alternator
Car lights flare on acceleration	• Battery low • Internal alternator/regulator problems	• Charge or replace battery • Replace alternator/regulator
Low voltage output (alternator light flickers continually or ammeter needle wanders)	• Loose or worn belt • Dirty or corroded connections • Internal alternator/regulator problems	• Replace or adjust belt • Clean or replace connections • Replace alternator or regulator

Alternator and Regulator Specifications

Model	Year	Alternator Identification Number	Rated Output @ 5000 RPM	Output @ 2500 RPM (not less than)	Brush Length (in.)	Brush Spring Tension (oz.)	Regulated Voltage
F-10	1976–77	LT150-26 ①	50	37.5	0.295	9.0–12.2	14.3–15.3
	1978	LR150-36	50	40	0.295	8.99–12.7	14.3–15.3
		LR160-46 ②	60	45	0.295	8.99–12.17	14.4–15.0
310 U.S.A.	1979–80	LR160-46	60	40	0.295	8.99–12.17	14.4–15.0
310 Canada	1979–80	LR150-36	50	40	0.295	8.99–12.17	14.4–15.0
310 U.S.A.	1981–82	LR160-125	50	42	0.295	8.99–12.17	14.4–15.0
310 Canada	1981–82	LR150-99	50	40	0.295	8.99–12.17	14.4–15.0
Stanza	1982–86	LR160-104	60	50	0.295	8.99–12.17	14.4–15.1
	1985–86	LR170-14	70	50	0.295	8.99–12.17	14.4–15.0
Pulsar	1983–86	LR150-125B	50	42	0.295	8.99–12.17	14.4–15.0
	1984	LR160-121	60	50	0.295	8.99–12.17	14.4–15.0
Stanza	1987–88	A2T48298	70	50	0.31	10.93–15.17	14.1–14.7
		LR170-716	67	50	0.28	9.88–14.11	14.1–14.7
Pulsar	1987–88	A2T48292 ③	70	50	0.31	10.93–15.17	14.1–14.7
		A2T48298 ④	70	50	0.31	10.93–15.17	14.1–14.7
		A5T41592 ⑤	60	50	0.31	10.93–15.17	14.1–14.7

① Uses external voltage regulator
② With air conditioning
③ CA16DE–CA18DE engine without A/C
④ CA16DE–CA18DE engine with A/C
⑤ E16i engine

Starter

REMOVAL AND INSTALLATION

In 1978, a gear reduction starter was introduced on some Canadian and United States models. The differences between the gear reduction and conventional starters are: the gear reduction starter has a set of ratio reduction gears while the conventional starter does not. The extra gears on the gear reduction starter make the starter pinion gear turn at about half the speed of the starter, giving the starter twice the turning power of a conventional starter.

1. Disconnect the negative battery cable from the battery.

2. Disconnect the starter wiring at the starter, taking note of the positions for correct reinstallation.

3. Remove the bolts attaching the starter to the engine and remove the starter from the vehicle.

4. Install the starter in the reverse order of removal.

SOLENOID REPLACEMENT

All Models

NOTE: *The starter solenoid is also know as the magnetic switch assembly.*

1. Remove the starter from the engine as outlined above.

2. Place the starter in a vise or equivalent to hold the starter in place while you are working on the solenoid. DO NOT tighten the vise to tight around the case of the starter. The case will crack if you tighten the vise to much.

3. Loosen the locknut and remove the connection from the starter motor going to the **M** terminal of the solenoid or bottom terminal of the solenoid.

4. Remove the securing screws and remove the solenoid.

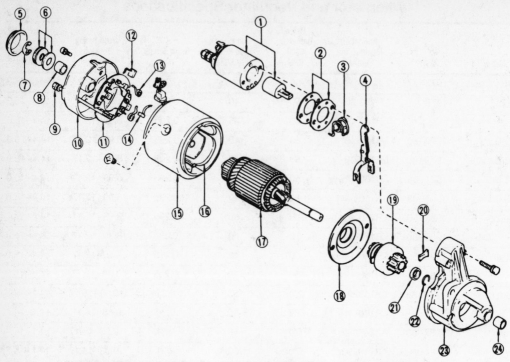

1. Magnetic switch assembly
2. Dust cover
   (Adjusting washer)
3. Torsion spring
4. Shift lever
5. Dust cover
6. Thrust washer
7. E-ring
8. Rear cover metal
9. Through bolt
10. Rear cover
11. Brush holder
12. Brush (−)
13. Brush spring
14. Brush (+)
15. Yoke
16. Field coil
17. Armature
18. Center bracket
19. Pinion assembly
20. Dust cover
21. Pinion stopper
22. Stopper clip
23. Gear case
24. Gear case metal

Exploded view of the non-reduction gear starter for F10 (1976–78) and 310 (1979–81)

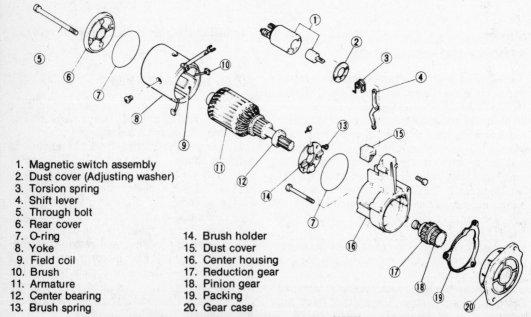

1. Magnetic switch assembly
2. Dust cover (Adjusting washer)
3. Torsion spring
4. Shift lever
5. Through bolt
6. Rear cover
7. O-ring
8. Yoke
9. Field coil
10. Brush
11. Armature
12. Center bearing
13. Brush spring
14. Brush holder
15. Dust cover
16. Center housing
17. Reduction gear
18. Pinion gear
19. Packing
20. Gear case

Exploded view of the reduction gear starter for F10 (1978) and 310 (1979–81)

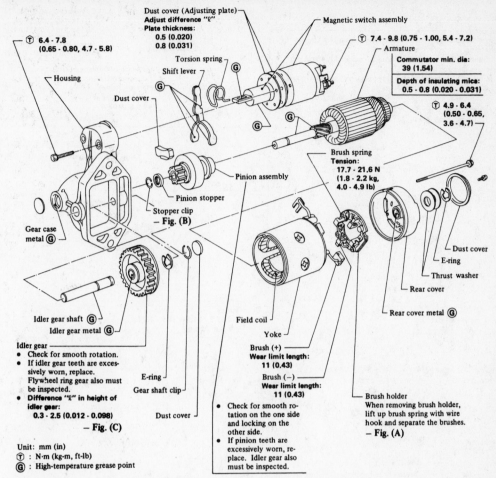

Dust cover (Adjusting plate)
Adjust difference "ℓ"
Plate thickness:
0.5 (0.020)
0.8 (0.031)

Magnetic switch assembly

Ⓣ 6.4 - 7.8
(0.65 - 0.80, 4.7 - 5.8)

Ⓣ 7.4 - 9.8 (0.75 - 1.00, 5.4 - 7.2)

Armature

Commutator min. dia:
39 (1.54)

Depth of insulating mica:
0.5 - 0.8 (0.020 - 0.031)

Torsion spring

Shift lever

Housing

Dust cover

Ⓣ 4.9 - 6.4
(0.50 - 0.65,
3.6 - 4.7)

Brush spring
Tension:
17.7 - 21.6 N
(1.8 - 2.2 kg,
4.0 - 4.9 lb)

Pinion assembly

Pinion stopper

Stopper clip
— Fig. (B)

Gear case
metal Ⓖ

Dust cover
E-ring
Thrust washer
Rear cover
Rear cover metal Ⓖ

Idler gear shaft Ⓖ
Idler gear metal Ⓖ

Field coil

Yoke

Idler gear
- Check for smooth rotation.
- If idler gear teeth are excessively worn, replace.
  Flywheel ring gear also must be inspected.
- Difference "ℓ" in height of idler gear:
  0.3 - 2.5 (0.012 - 0.098)
  — Fig. (C)

Brush (+)
Wear limit length:
11 (0.43)

Brush (−)
Wear limit length:
11 (0.43)

E-ring

Gear shaft clip

Dust cover

- Check for smooth rotation on the one side and locking on the other side.
- If pinion teeth are excessively worn, replace. Idler gear also must be inspected.

Brush holder
When removing brush holder, lift up brush spring with wire hook and separate the brushes.
— Fig. (A)

Unit: mm (in)
Ⓣ : N·m (kg-m, ft-lb)
Ⓖ : High-temperature grease point

Exploded view reduction gear starter—310 (1982) and Pulsar (1983–85)—automatic transaxle models

5. To install, reverse the removal procedures.

OVERHAUL
Brush Replacement
NON-REDUCTION GEAR TYPE

1. With the starter out of the vehicle, remove the bolts holding the solenoid to the top of the starter and remove the solenoid.

2. To remove the brushes, remove the 2 through-bolts, the 2 rear cover attaching screws (some models) and the rear cover.

NOTE: *Remove the dust cover, E-ring and thrust washers from the armature shaft before the rear cover.*

3. Using a wire hook, lift the brush springs to separate the brushes from the commutator.

4. Install the brushes in the reverse order of removal and reasssemble the rear cover to the starter.

REDUCTION GEAR TYPE

1. Remove the starter, then the solenoid or magentic switch.

2. Remove the dust cover, E-ring and thrust washers.

3. Remove the starter through-bolts and brush holder setscrews.

4. Remove the rear cover. The rear cover can be pried off with a screwdriver, be careful not to damage the O-ring or gasket if equipped.

5. Remove the starter housing, armature and brush holder from the center housing. They can be removed as an assembly.

6. Using a wire hook on the spring, lift the spring then remove the positive side brush from its holder. The positive brush is insulated from the brush holder and its lead wire is connected to the field coil.

7. Using a wire hook on the spring, lift the spring and remove the negative brush from the holder.

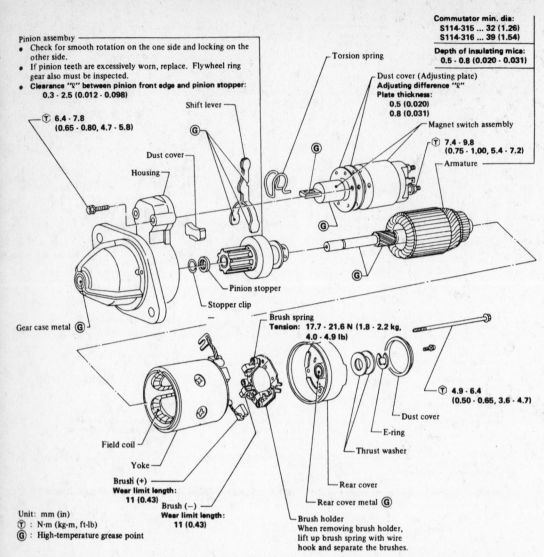

Pinion assembly
• Check for smooth rotation on the one side and locking on the other side.
• If pinion teeth are excessively worn, replace. Flywheel ring gear also must be inspected.
• Clearance "ℓ" between pinion front edge and pinion stopper: 0.3 - 2.5 (0.012 - 0.098)

Commutator min. dia:
S114-315 ... 32 (1.26)
S114-316 ... 39 (1.54)
Depth of insulating mica:
0.5 - 0.8 (0.020 - 0.031)

Torsion spring

Dust cover (Adjusting plate)
Adjusting difference "ℓ"
Plate thickness:
0.5 (0.020)
0.8 (0.031)

Magnet switch assembly

Ⓣ 6.4 - 7.8 (0.65 - 0.80, 4.7 - 5.8)

Shift lever

Ⓣ 7.4 - 9.8 (0.75 - 1.00, 5.4 - 7.2)

Armature

Dust cover

Housing

Pinion stopper

Stopper clip

Gear case metal Ⓖ

Brush spring
Tension: 17.7 - 21.6 N (1.8 - 2.2 kg, 4.0 - 4.9 lb)

Ⓣ 4.9 - 6.4 (0.50 - 0.65, 3.6 - 4.7)

Dust cover

E-ring

Thrust washer

Field coil

Yoke

Brush (+)
Wear limit length: 11 (0.43)

Brush (−)
Wear limit length: 11 (0.43)

Rear cover

Rear cover metal Ⓖ

Brush holder
When removing brush holder, lift up brush spring with wire hook and separate the brushes.

Unit: mm (in)
Ⓣ : N·m (kg-m, ft-lb)
Ⓖ : High-temperature grease point

Exploded view non-reduction gear starter—310 (1982)—Pulsar (1983–85)—manual transaxle models

8. Replace all the brushes in the starter assembly.
9. Insert the new brushes in the brush holder.
10. Install the starter housing, armature and brush holder to the center housing.
11. Install the brush holder setscrews, rear cover and starter through-bolts.
12. Install the thrust washers, E-ring and dust cover.
13. Install the solenoid or magnetic switch.

Starter Drive Replacement
NON-REDUCTION GEAR TYPE

1. With the starter motor removed from the vehicle, remove the solenoid from the starter.
2. Remove the 2 through-bolts at the rear cover but do not disassemble the entire starter. Mark the front gear cover with relationship to the yoke housing.
3. Separate the front gear case from the yoke housing, then the shift lever from the armature, without removing the armature from starter assembly.
4. Push the pinion stopper toward the rear cover, then remove the pinion stopper clip and the pinion stopper.
5. Slide the starter drive from the armature shaft.
6. Install the starter drive on the armature shaft.
7. Install pinion stopper and stopper clip.
8. Reassemble the front gear case to the yoke and the shift lever to the armature.
9. Install the rear cover through-bolts.

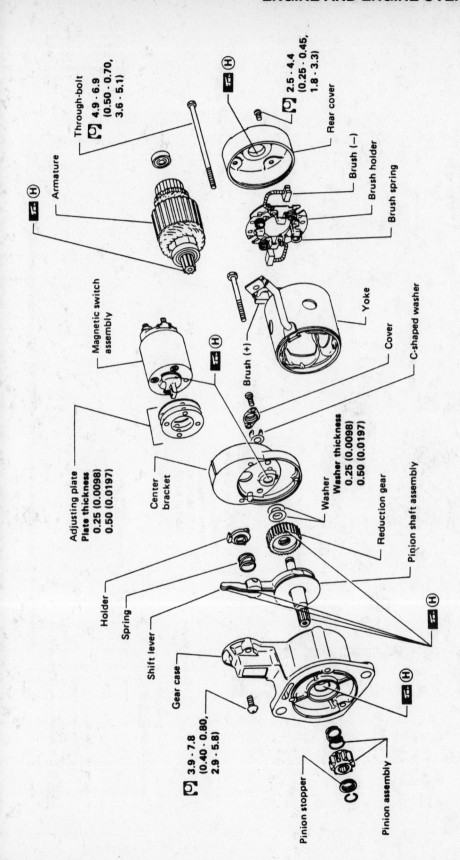

Through-bolt
4.9 - 6.9 (0.50 - 0.70, 3.6 - 5.1)

2.5 - 4.4 (0.25 - 0.45, 1.8 - 3.3)

Rear cover

Armature

Brush (−)

Brush holder

Brush spring

Magnetic switch assembly

Yoke

Brush (+)

Cover

C-shaped washer

Adjusting plate
Plate thickness
0.25 (0.0098)
0.50 (0.0197)

Washer

Washer thickness
0.25 (0.0098)
0.50 (0.0197)

Center bracket

Reduction gear

Pinion shaft assembly

Holder

Spring

Shift lever

Gear case

3.9 - 7.8 (0.40 - 0.80, 2.9 - 5.8)

Pinion stopper

Pinion assembly

Unit: mm (in)
N·m (kg-m, ft-lb)
H : High-temperature grease points

Exploded view of reduction gear starter—Pulsar E16i (1987–88)—Stanza (1987–88)—manual transaxle

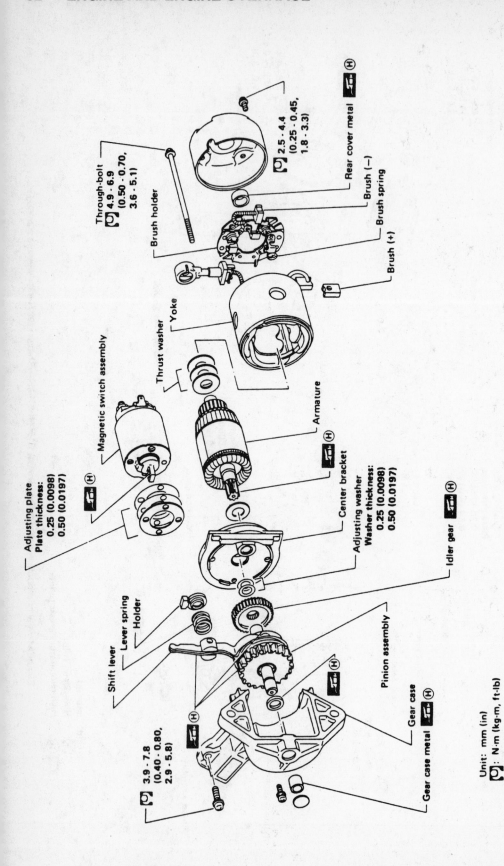

Through-bolt
4.9 - 6.9
(0.50 - 0.70,
3.6 - 5.1)

Brush holder

2.5 - 4.4
(0.25 - 0.45,
1.8 - 3.3)

Rear cover metal (H)

Brush (−)

Brush spring

Brush (+)

Thrust washer

Yoke

Armature (H)

Magnetic switch assembly

Center bracket

Adjusting plate
Plate thickness:
0.25 (0.0098)
0.50 (0.0197) (H)

Adjusting washer
Washer thickness:
0.25 (0.0098)
0.50 (0.0197)

Idler gear (H)

Shift lever

Lever spring

Holder

Pinion assembly

Gear case (H)

3.9 - 7.8
(0.40 - 0.80,
2.9 - 5.8)

Gear case metal (H)

Unit: mm (in)
: N·m (kg-m, ft-lb)
(H) : High-temperature grease point

Exploded view of reduction gear starter—Pulsar E16i (1986—88)—automatic transaxle

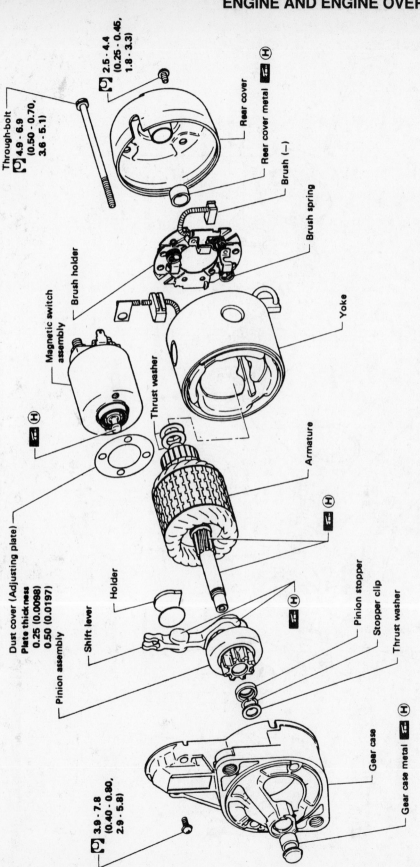

Through-bolt
$\boxed{\text{Ⓣ}}$ 4.9 - 6.9
(0.50 - 0.70,
3.6 - 5.1)

$\boxed{\text{Ⓣ}}$ 2.5 - 4.4
(0.25 - 0.45,
1.8 - 3.3) Ⓗ

Rear cover

Rear cover metal 🔧

Brush (−)

Brush spring

Brush holder

Magnetic switch assembly

Yoke

Thrust washer

Ⓗ 🔧

Armature

Ⓗ 🔧

Dust cover (Adjusting plate)
Plate thickness
0.25 (0.0098)
0.50 (0.0197)

Holder

Shift lever

Pinion assembly

Pinion stopper

Stopper clip

Thrust washer

Ⓗ 🔧

Gear case

Gear case metal 🔧 Ⓗ

$\boxed{\text{Ⓣ}}$ 3.9 - 7.8
(0.40 - 0.80,
2.9 - 5.8)

Unit: mm (in)
$\boxed{\text{Ⓣ}}$: N·m (kg-m, ft-lb)
🔧 Ⓗ : High-temperature grease points

Exploded view of non-reduction gear starter—Pulsar E16i (1988 Calif. only)—manual transaxle

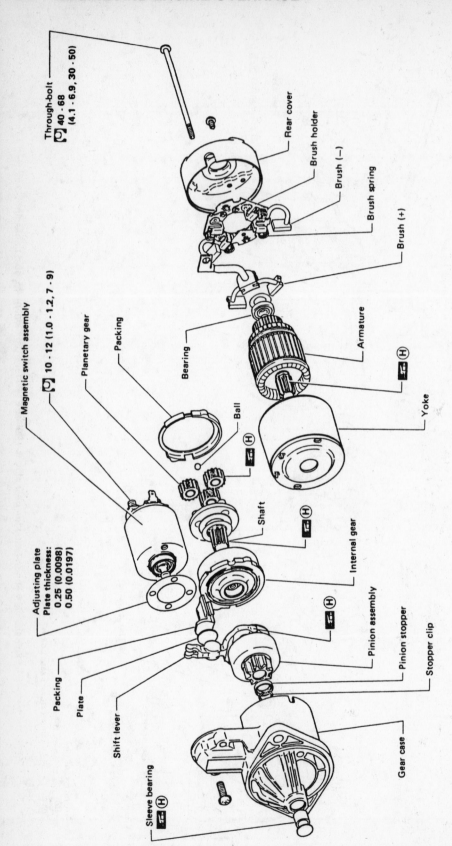

Through-bolt
🔧 40 - 68
(4.1 - 6.9, 30 - 50)

Rear cover

Brush holder

Brush (−)

Brush spring

Brush (+)

Magnetic switch assembly

🔧 10 - 12 (1.0 - 1.2, 7 - 9)

Planetary gear

Packing

Bearing

Ball

Armature

Yoke

Shaft

Internal gear

Adjusting plate
Plate thickness:
0.25 (0.0098)
0.50 (0.0197)

Packing

Plate

Shift lever

Sleeve bearing

Pinion assembly

Pinion stopper

Stopper clip

Gear case

Unit: mm (in)
🔧 : N·m (kg·m, ft-lb)
(H) : High-temperature grease point

Exploded view of reduction gear starter—Pulsar CA16DE/CA18DE—Stanza 4WD (1987–88)

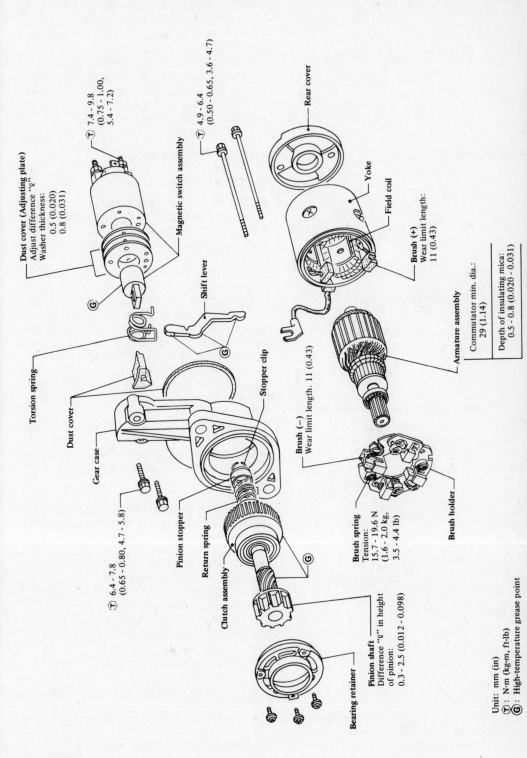

Dust cover (Adjusting plate)
Adjust difference "ℓ"
Washer thickness:
0.5 (0.020)
0.8 (0.031)

Ⓣ 7.4 - 9.8
(0.75 - 1.00,
5.4 - 7.2)

Ⓣ 4.9 - 6.4
(0.50 - 0.65, 3.6 - 4.7)

Rear cover

Magnetic switch assembly

Yoke

Field coil

Brush (+)
Wear limit length:
11 (0.43)

Shift lever

Ⓖ

Torsion spring

Dust cover

Gear case

Ⓖ

Stopper clip

Brush (–)
Wear limit length: 11 (0.43)

Armature assembly

Commutator min. dia.:
29 (1.14)

Depth of insulating mica:
0.5 - 0.8 (0.020 - 0.031)

Ⓣ 6.4 - 7.8
(0.65 - 0.80, 4.7 - 5.8)

Pinion stopper

Return spring

Clutch assembly

Brush spring
Tension:
15.7 - 19.6 N
(1.6 - 2.0 kg,
3.5 - 4.4 lb)

Brush holder

Ⓖ

Pinion shaft
Difference "ℓ" in height
of pinion:
0.3 - 2.5 (0.012 - 0.098)

Bearing retainer

Unit: mm (in)
Ⓣ : N·m (kg-m, ft-lb)
Ⓖ : High-temperature grease point

Exploded view reduction gear starter—Stanza (1982–86) and Stanza 2wd wagon (1987–88)—Pulsar (1986)—manual transaxle models

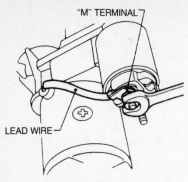

"M" TERMINAL

LEAD WIRE

Removing solenoid from starter

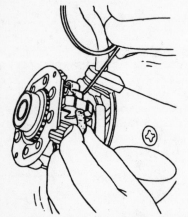

Lift brush spring with a wire hook and remove brush

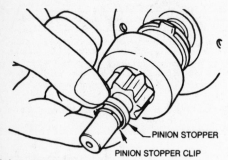

PINION STOPPER

PINION STOPPER CLIP

Pinion stopper removal

10. Install the solenoid or the magnetic switch.

REDUCTION GEAR TYPE

1. Remove the starter.
2. Remove the solenoid and the torsion spring. Mark the front housing with relationship to the center housing.
3. Remove the center housing-to-front housing bolts, then separate the front housing from the center housing . Do not disassemble the entire starter.

4. Remove the pinion/reduction gear assembly from the armature shaft.
NOTE: *It may be necessary to remove the shift lever pivot pin, to disconnect the pinion/ reduction gear assembly from the armature shaft.*
5. Installation is the reverse of the removal procedures. The best idea is to try not to disassemble the entire starter when removing the pinion/reduction gear. Do not disturb the brush assembly in the rear cover.

ENGINE MECHANICAL

Engine Overhaul Tips

Most engine overhaul procedures are fairly standard. In addition to specific parts replacement procedures and complete specifications for your individual engine, this chapter also is a guide to accept rebuilding procedures. Examples of standard rebuilding practice are shown and should be used along with specific details concerning your particular engine.

Competent and accurate machine shop services will ensure maximum performance, reliability and engine life.

In most instances it is more profitable for the do-it-yourself mechanic to remove, clean and inspect the component, buy the necessary parts and deliver these to a shop for actual machine work.

On the other hand, much of the rebuilding work (crankshaft, block, bearings, piston rods, and other components) is well within the scope of the do-it-yourself mechanic.

TOOLS

The tools required for an engine overhaul or parts replacement will depend on the depth of your involvement. With a few exceptions, they will be the tools found in a mechanic's tool kit (see Chapter 1). More in-depth work will require any or all of the following:
• a dial indicator (reading in thousandths) mounted on a universal base
  • micrometers and telescope gauges
  • jaw and screw-type pullers
  • scraper
  • valve spring compressor
  • ring groove cleaner
  • piston ring expander and compressor
  • ridge reamer
  • cylinder hone or glaze breaker
  • Plastigage®
  • engine stand
The use of most of these tools is illustrated in this chapter. Many can be rented for a one-time use from a local parts jobber or tool supply house specializing in automotive work.

Troubleshooting Basic Starting System Problems

Problem	Cause	Solution
Starter motor rotates engine slowly	• Battery charge low or battery defective • Defective circuit between battery and starter motor • Low load current • High load current	• Charge or replace battery • Clean and tighten, or replace cables • Bench-test starter motor. Inspect for worn brushes and weak brush springs. • Bench-test starter motor. Check engine for friction, drag or coolant in cylinders. Check ring gear-to-pinion gear clearance.
Starter motor will not rotate engine	• Battery charge low or battery defective • Faulty solenoid • Damage drive pinion gear or ring gear • Starter motor engagement weak • Starter motor rotates slowly with high load current • Engine seized	• Charge or replace battery • Check solenoid ground. Repair or replace as necessary. • Replace damaged gear(s) • Bench-test starter motor • Inspect drive yoke pull-down and point gap, check for worn end bushings, check ring gear clearance • Repair engine
Starter motor drive will not engage (solenoid known to be good)	• Defective contact point assembly • Inadequate contact point assembly ground • Defective hold-in coil	• Repair or replace contact point assembly • Repair connection at ground screw • Replace field winding assembly
Starter motor drive will not disengage	• Starter motor loose on flywheel housing • Worn drive end busing • Damaged ring gear teeth • Drive yoke return spring broken or missing	• Tighten mounting bolts • Replace bushing • Replace ring gear or driveplate • Replace spring
Starter motor drive disengages prematurely	• Weak drive assembly thrust spring • Hold-in coil defective	• Replace drive mechanism • Replace field winding assembly
Low load current	• Worn brushes • Weak brush springs	• Replace brushes • Replace springs

Battery and Starter Specifications

All cars use 12 volt, negative ground electrical systems

Year	Model	Battery Amp Hour Capacity	Starter			Brush Spring Tension (oz)	Min Brush Length (in)
			No Load Test				
			Amps	Volts	RPM		
1976–78	F10	60	60	12	7,000 U.S.A.	49–64	0.47
1978	F10 Canada	100	100 RG	12	4,300 Canada	49–64	0.43
1979–81	310	60 100 RG	60 100	11.5 11	7,000 U.S.A. 3,900 Canada	50–64 56–70	0.47 0.43
1982	310	60 U.S.A.	60	11.5	7,000	64–78	0.43
		60 Canada ①	60	11.5	7,000	64–78	0.43
		60 Canada ②	60	11.5	6,000	64–78	0.43

Battery and Starter Specifications (cont.)

All cars use 12 volt, negative ground electrical systems

| | | Battery Amp Hour Capacity | Starter | | | | |
| | | | No Load Test | | | Brush Spring Tension (oz) | Min Brush Length (in) |
Year	Model		Amps	Volts	RPM		
1982–86	Stanza	60 100 RG	60 U.S.A. 100 Canada (U.S. option)	11.5 11	7,000 U.S.A. 3,900 Canada	64–78 56–70	0.43 0.43
1983–86	Pulsar	60 ①	60	11.5	7,000	64–78	0.43
1983	Pulsar	60 ②	60 U.S.A.	11.5	7,000	64–78	0.43
1983	Pulsar	60 ②	60 Canada	11.5	2,000	64–78	0.43
1984	Pulsar	60 ①	60 Canada	11.5	2,350	64–78	0.43
1987	Pulsar	60 ③	50–75	11–11.5	2,500	50–90	0.45–0.47
	Stanza	60 ③	50–75	11.0	3,000	56–70	0.43–0.47
1988	Pulsar	60 ③	50–75	12.0	3,000–4,000	50–91	0.45–0.47
	Stanza	60 ③	Less than 100	11.5	2,700–3,000	59–78	0.43–0.47

RG: Reduction Gear type starter
① Manual Transmission
② Auto. Transmission
③ 65 amp hours Canada, optional
  For U.S.A. models

Occasionally, the use of special tools is called for. See the information on Special Tools and Safety Notice in the front of this book before substituting another tool.

INSPECTION TECHNIQUES

Procedures and specifications are given in this chapter for inspecting, cleaning and assessing the wear limits of most major components. Other procedures such as Magnaflux® and Zyglo® can be used to locate material flaws and stress cracks. Magnaflux® is a magnetic process applicable only to ferrous materials. The Zyglo® process coats the material with a fluorescent dye penetrant and can be used on any material Check for suspected surface cracks can be more readily made using spot check dye. The dye is sprayed onto the suspected area, wiped off and the area sprayed with a developer. Cracks will show up brightly.

OVERHAUL TIPS

Aluminum has become extremely popular for use in engines, due to its low weight. Observe the following precautions when handling aluminum parts:
• Never hot tank aluminum parts (the caustic hot tank solution will eat the aluminum.
• Remove all aluminum parts (identification tag, etc.) from engine parts prior to the tanking.
• Always coat threads lightly with engine oil or anti-seize compounds before installation, to prevent seizure.
• Never overtorque bolts or spark plugs especially in aluminum threads.

Stripped threads in any component can be repaired using any of several commercial repair kits (Heli-Coil®, Microdot®, Keenserts®, etc.).

When assembling the engine, any parts that will be frictional contact must be prelubed to provide lubrication at initial start-up. Any product specifically formulated for this purpose can be used, but engine oil is not recommended as a prelube.

When semi-permanent (locked, but removable) installation of bolts or nuts is desired, threads should be cleaned and coated with Loctite® or other similar, commercial non-hardening sealant.

REPAIRING DAMAGED THREADS

Several methods of repairing damaged threads are available. Heli-Coil® (shown here), Keenserts® and Microdot® are among the most widely used. All involve basically the same principle – drilling out stripped threads, tapping the hole and installing a prewound insert – making welding, plugging and oversize fasteners unnecessary.

Two types of thread repair inserts are usually supplied: a standard type for most Inch Coarse, Inch Fine, Metric Course and Metric Fine thread sizes and a spark lug type to fit most spark plug port sizes. Consult the individual manufacturer's catalog to determine exact applications. Typical thread repair kits will contain a selection of prewound threaded inserts, a tap (corresponding to the outside diameter threads of the insert) and an installation tool. Spark plug inserts usually differ because they require a tap equipped with pilot threads and a combined reamer/tap section. Most manufacturers also supply blister-packed thread repair inserts separately in addition to a master kit containing a variety of taps and inserts plus installation tools.

Before effecting a repair to a threaded hole, remove any snapped, broken or damaged bolts or studs. Penetrating oil can be used to free frozen threads. The offending item can be removed with locking pliers or with a screw or stud extractor. After the hole is clear, the thread can be repaired, as shown in the series of accompanying illustrations.

Checking Engine Compression

A noticeable lack of engine power, excessive oil consumption and/or poor fuel mileage measured over an extended period are all indicators of internal engine war. Worn piston rings, scored or worn cylinder bores, blown head gaskets, sticking or burnt valves and worn valve seats are all possible culprits here. A check of each cylinder's compression will help you locate the problems.

As mentioned in the Tools and Equipment section of Chapter 1, a screw-in type compression gauge is more accurate that the type you simply hold against the spark plug hole, although it takes slightly longer to use. It's worth it to obtain a more accurate reading. Follow the procedures below.

Gasoline Engines

1. Warm up the engine to normal operating temperature.

2. Remove all the spark plugs.

3. Disconnect the high tension lead from the ignition coil.

4. On fully open the throttle either by operating the carburetor throttle linkage by hand or by having an assistant floor the accelerator pedal.

5. Screw the compression gauge into the no.1 spark plug hole until the fitting is snug.

WARNING: *Be careful not to crossthread the plug hole. On aluminum cylinder heads use extra care, as the threads in these heads are easily ruined.*

6. Ask an assistant to depress the accelerator pedal fully on both carbureted and fuel injected vehicles. Then, while you read the compression

gauge, ask the assistant to crank the engine four in short bursts using the ignition switch.

7. Read the compression gauge at the end of each series of cranks, and record the highest of these readings. Repeat this procedure for each of the engine's cylinders. Compare the highest reading of each cylinder to the compression pressure specification in the Tune-Up Specifications chart in Chapter 2. The specs in this chart are maximum values.

A cylinder's compression pressure is usually acceptable if it is not less than 80% of maximum. The difference between any two cylinders should be no more than 12-14 pounds.

8. If a cylinder is unusually low, pour a tablespoon of clean engine oil into the cylinder through the spark plug hole and repeat the compression test. If the compression comes up after adding the oil, it appears that the cylinder's piston rings or bore are damaged or worn. If the pressure remains low, the valves may not be seating properly (a valve job is needed), or the head gasket may be blown near that cylinder. If compression in any two adjacent cylinders is low, and if the addition of oil doesn't help the compression, there is leakage past the head gasket. Oil and coolant water in the combustion chamber can result from this problem. There may be evidence of water droplets on the engine dipstick when a head gasket has blown.

Engine

REMOVAL AND INSTALLATION

CAUTION: *On EFI equipped models, release the fuel pressure in the system before disconnecting the fuel lines. Situate the vehicle on as flat and solid a surface as possible. Place chocks or equivalent at front and rear of rear wheels to stop vehicle from rolling.*

NOTE: *The engine and transaxle must be removed as a single unit. The engine and transaxle is removed from the top of the vehicle.*

1. Mark the location of the hinges on the hood. Remove the hood by holding at both sides and unscrewing bolts. This requires 2 people.

2. Disconnect the battery cables and remove the battery.

3. Drain the coolant from the radiator, then remove the radiator and the heater hoses.

CAUTION: *When draining the coolant, keep in mind that cats and dogs are attracted by the ethylene glycol antifreeze, and are quite likely to drink any that is left in an uncovered container or in puddles on the ground. This will prove fatal in sufficient quantity. Always drain the coolant into a sealable container. Coolant should be reused unless it is contaminated or several years old.*

Troubleshooting Engine Mechanical Problems

Problem	Cause	Solution
External oil leaks	• Fuel pump gasket broken or improperly seated	• Replace gasket
	• Cylinder head cover RTV sealant broken or improperly seated	• Replace sealant; inspect cylinder head cover sealant flange and cylinder head sealant surface for distortion and cracks
	• Oil filler cap leaking or missing	• Replace cap
	• Oil filter gasket broken or improperly seated	• Replace oil filter
	• Oil pan side gasket broken, improperly seated or opening in RTV sealant	• Replace gasket or repair opening in sealant; inspect oil pan gasket flange for distortion
	• Oil pan front oil seal broken or improperly seated	• Replace seal; inspect timing case cover and oil pan seal flange for distortion
	• Oil pan rear oil seal broken or improperly seated	• Replace seal; inspect oil pan rear oil seal flange; inspect rear main bearing cap for cracks, plugged oil return channels, or distortion in seal groove
	• Timing case cover oil seal broken or improperly seated	• Replace seal
	• Excess oil pressure because of restricted PCV valve	• Replace PCV valve
	• Oil pan drain plug loose or has stripped threads	• Repair as necessary and tighten
	• Rear oil gallery plug loose	• Use appropriate sealant on gallery plug and tighten
	• Rear camshaft plug loose or improperly seated	• Seat camshaft plug or replace and seal, as necessary
	• Distributor base gasket damaged	• Replace gasket
Excessive oil consumption	• Oil level too high	• Drain oil to specified level
	• Oil with wrong viscosity being used	• Replace with specified oil
	• PCV valve stuck closed	• Replace PCV valve
	• Valve stem oil deflectors (or seals) are damaged, missing, or incorrect type	• Replace valve stem oil deflectors
	• Valve stems or valve guides worn	• Measure stem-to-guide clearance and repair as necessary
	• Poorly fitted or missing valve cover baffles	• Replace valve cover
	• Piston rings broken or missing	• Replace broken or missing rings
	• Scuffed piston	• Replace piston
	• Incorrect piston ring gap	• Measure ring gap, repair as necessary
	• Piston rings sticking or excessively loose in grooves	• Measure ring side clearance, repair as necessary
	• Compression rings installed upside down	• Repair as necessary
	• Cylinder walls worn, scored, or glazed	• Repair as necessary
	• Piston ring gaps not properly staggered	• Repair as necessary
	• Excessive main or connecting rod bearing clearance	• Measure bearing clearance, repair as necessary
No oil pressure	• Low oil level	• Add oil to correct level
	• Oil pressure gauge, warning lamp or sending unit inaccurate	• Replace oil pressure gauge or warning lamp
	• Oil pump malfunction	• Replace oil pump
	• Oil pressure relief valve sticking	• Remove and inspect oil pressure relief valve assembly
	• Oil passages on pressure side of pump obstructed	• Inspect oil passages for obstruction

Troubleshooting Engine Mechanical Problems (cont.)

Problem	Cause	Solution
No oil pressure (cont.)	• Oil pickup screen or tube obstructed	• Inspect oil pickup for obstruction
	• Loose oil inlet tube	• Tighten or seal inlet tube
Low oil pressure	• Low oil level	• Add oil to correct level
	• Inaccurate gauge, warning lamp or sending unit	• Replace oil pressure gauge or warning lamp
	• Oil excessively thin because of dilution, poor quality, or improper grade	• Drain and refill crankcase with recommended oil
	• Excessive oil temperature	• Correct cause of overheating engine
	• Oil pressure relief spring weak or sticking	• Remove and inspect oil pressure relief valve assembly
	• Oil inlet tube and screen assembly has restriction or air leak	• Remove and inspect oil inlet tube and screen assembly. (Fill inlet tube with lacquer thinner to locate leaks.)
	• Excessive oil pump clearance	• Measure clearances
	• Excessive main, rod, or camshaft bearing clearance	• Measure bearing clearances, repair as necessary
High oil pressure	• Improper oil viscosity	• Drain and refill crankcase with correct viscosity oil
	• Oil pressure gauge or sending unit inaccurate	• Replace oil pressure gauge
	• Oil pressure relief valve sticking closed	• Remove and inspect oil pressure relief valve assembly
Main bearing noise	• Insufficient oil supply	• Inspect for low oil level and low oil pressure
	• Main bearing clearance excessive	• Measure main bearing clearance, repair as necessary
	• Bearing insert missing	• Replace missing insert
	• Crankshaft end play excessive	• Measure end play, repair as necessary
	• Improperly tightened main bearing cap bolts	• Tighten bolts with specified torque
	• Loose flywheel or drive plate	• Tighten flywheel or drive plate attaching bolts
	• Loose or damaged vibration damper	• Repair as necessary
Connecting rod bearing noise	• Insufficient oil supply	• Inspect for low oil level and low oil pressure
	• Carbon build-up on piston	• Remove carbon from piston crown
	• Bearing clearance excessive or bearing missing	• Measure clearance, repair as necessary
	• Crankshaft connecting rod journal out-of-round	• Measure journal dimensions, repair or replace as necessary
	• Misaligned connecting rod or cap	• Repair as necessary
	• Connecting rod bolts tightened improperly	• Tighten bolts with specified torque
Piston noise	• Piston-to-cylinder wall clearance excessive (scuffed piston)	• Measure clearance and examine piston
	• Cylinder walls excessively tapered or out-of-round	• Measure cylinder wall dimensions, rebore cylinder
	• Piston ring broken	• Replace all rings on piston
	• Loose or seized piston pin	• Measure piston-to-pin clearance, repair as necessary
	• Connecting rods misaligned	• Measure rod alignment, straighten or replace
	• Piston ring side clearance excessively loose or tight	• Measure ring side clearance, repair as necessary
	• Carbon build-up on piston is excessive	• Remove carbon from piston

Troubleshooting Engine Mechanical Problems (cont.)

Problem	Cause	Solution
Valve actuating component noise	• Insufficient oil supply	• Check for: (a) Low oil level (b) Low oil pressure (c) Plugged push rods (d) Wrong hydraulic tappets (e) Restricted oil gallery (f) Excessive tappet to bore clearance
	• Push rods worn or bent	• Replace worn or bent push rods
	• Rocker arms or pivots worn	• Replace worn rocker arms or pivots
	• Foreign objects or chips in hydraulic tappets	• Clean tappets
	• Excessive tappet leak-down	• Replace valve tappet
	• Tappet face worn	• Replace tappet; inspect corresponding cam lobe for wear
	• Broken or cocked valve springs	• Properly seat cocked springs; replace broken springs
	• Stem-to-guide clearance excessive	• Measure stem-to-guide clearance, repair as required
	• Valve bent	• Replace valve
	• Loose rocker arms	• Tighten bolts with specified torque
	• Valve seat runout excessive	• Regrind valve seat/valves
	• Missing valve lock	• Install valve lock
	• Push rod rubbing or contacting cylinder head	• Remove cylinder head and remove obstruction in head
	• Excessive engine oil (four-cylinder engine)	• Correct oil level

Troubleshooting the Cooling System

Problem	Cause	Solution
High temperature gauge indication—overheating	• Coolant level low	• Replenish coolant
	• Fan belt loose	• Adjust fan belt tension
	• Radiator hose(s) collapsed	• Replace hose(s)
	• Radiator airflow blocked	• Remove restriction (bug screen, fog lamps, etc.)
	• Faulty radiator cap	• Replace radiator cap
	• Ignition timing incorrect	• Adjust ignition timing
	• Idle speed low	• Adjust idle speed
	• Air trapped in cooling system	• Purge air
	• Heavy traffic driving	• Operate at fast idle in neutral intermittently to cool engine
	• Incorrect cooling system component(s) installed	• Install proper component(s)
	• Faulty thermostat	• Replace thermostat
	• Water pump shaft broken or impeller loose	• Replace water pump
	• Radiator tubes clogged	• Flush radiator
	• Cooling system clogged	• Flush system
	• Casting flash in cooling passages	• Repair or replace as necessary. Flash may be visible by removing cooling system components or removing core plugs.
	• Brakes dragging	• Repair brakes
	• Excessive engine friction	• Repair engine
	• Antifreeze concentration over 68%	• Lower antifreeze concentration percentage
	• Missing air seals	• Replace air seals
	• Faulty gauge or sending unit	• Repair or replace faulty component

Troubleshooting the Cooling System (cont.)

Problem	Cause	Solution
High temperature gauge indication— overheating (cont.)	• Loss of coolant flow caused by leakage or foaming • Viscous fan drive failed	• Repair or replace leaking component, replace coolant • Replace unit
Low temperature indication— undercooling	• Thermostat stuck open • Faulty gauge or sending unit	• Replace thermostat • Repair or replace faulty component
Coolant loss—boilover	• Overfilled cooling system • Quick shutdown after hard (hot) run • Air in system resulting in occasional "burping" of coolant • Insufficient antifreeze allowing coolant boiling point to be too low • Antifreeze deteriorated because of age or contamination • Leaks due to loose hose clamps, loose nuts, bolts, drain plugs, faulty hoses, or defective radiator • Faulty head gasket • Cracked head, manifold, or block • Faulty radiator cap	• Reduce coolant level to proper specification • Allow engine to run at fast idle prior to shutdown • Purge system • Add antifreeze to raise boiling point • Replace coolant • Pressure test system to locate source of leak(s) then repair as necessary • Replace head gasket • Replace as necessary • Replace cap
Coolant entry into crankcase or cylinder(s)	• Faulty head gasket • Crack in head, manifold or block	• Replace head gasket • Replace as necessary
Coolant recovery system inoperative	• Coolant level low • Leak in system • Pressure cap not tight or seal missing, or leaking • Pressure cap defective • Overflow tube clogged or leaking • Recovery bottle vent restricted	• Replenish coolant to FULL mark • Pressure test to isolate leak and repair as necessary • Repair as necessary • Replace cap • Repair as necessary • Remove restriction
Noise	• Fan contacting shroud • Loose water pump impeller • Glazed fan belt • Loose fan belt • Rough surface on drive pulley • Water pump bearing worn • Belt alignment	• Reposition shroud and inspect engine mounts • Replace pump • Apply silicone or replace belt • Adjust fan belt tension • Replace pulley • Remove belt to isolate. Replace pump. • Check pulley alignment. Repair as necessary.
No coolant flow through heater core	• Restricted return inlet in water pump • Heater hose collapsed or restricted • Restricted heater core • Restricted outlet in thermostat housing • Intake manifold bypass hole in cylinder head restricted • Faulty heater control valve • Intake manifold coolant passage restricted	• Remove restriction • Remove restriction or replace hose • Remove restriction or replace core • Remove flash or restriction • Remove restriction • Replace valve • Remove restriction or replace intake manifold

NOTE: *Immediately after shutdown, the engine enters a condition known as heat soak. This is caused by the cooling system being inoperative while engine temperature is still high. If coolant temperature rises above boiling point, expansion and pressure may push some coolant out of the radiator overflow tube. If this does not occur frequently it is considered normal.*

General Engine Specifications

Year	Model	Type (model)	Engine Displacement Cu In. (cc)	Carburetor Type	Horsepower (SAE) @ rpm	Torque @ rpm (ft. lbs.)	Bore x Stroke (in.)	Compression Ratio	Normal Oil Pressure (psi)
1976–78	F10	OHV 4 (A14)	85.2 (1397)	Dual throat downdraft	80 @ 6,000	83 @ 3,600	2.99 x 3.03	8.5:1	43–50
1979–80	310	OHV 4 (A14)	85.2 (1397)	Dual throat downdraft	65 @ 5,600	75 @ 3,600	2.99 x 3.03	8.9:1	43–50
1981	310	OHV 4 (A15)	90.8 (1488)	Dual throat downdraft	65 @ 5200	82 @ 2800	2.992 x 3.228	8.9:1	43–50
1982	310	OHC 4 (E15)	90.8 (1488)	Dual throat downdraft	67 @ 5200	85 @ 3200	2.92 x 3.228	9.0:1	50–57
1982–83	Stanza	OHC 4 (CA20)	120.4 (1974)	Dual throat downdraft	88 @ 5200	112 @ 2800	3.33 x 3.46	8.5:1	50–60
1984–86	Stanza (U.S.A.)	OHC 4 (CA20E)	120.4 (1974)	EFI	97 @ 5200	116 @ 3200	3.33 x 3.46	8.5:1	57 @ 4000
	Stanza (Canada)	OHC 4 (CA20S)	120.4 (1974)	Dual throat downdraft	88 @ 5200	112 @ 2800	3.33 x 3.46	8.5:1	57 @ 4000
1984	Pulsar Turbo (Canada)	OHC 4 (E15ET)	90.8 (1488)	EFI	100 @ 5200	152 @ 3200	2.99 x 3.23	8.0:1	50–57
1983–86	Pulsar	OHC 4 (E16)	97.4 (1597)	Dual throat downdraft	69 @ 5200	92 @ 3200	2.99 x 3.46	9.4:1	50–57
1987	Pulsar	OHC 4 (E16i)	97.4 (1597)	EFI	70 @ 5000	94 @ 2800	2.99 x 3.46	9.4:1	43 @ 1700 RPM
		DOHC (CA160E)	97.5 (1598)	EFI	113 @ 6400	99 @ 4800	3.07 x 3.29	10.0:1	67 @ 2000 RPM
	Stanza	OHC4 (CA20E)	120.4 (1974)	EFI	97 @ 5200	114 @ 3200	3.33 x 3.46	8.5:1	43 @ 2000 RPM
1988	Pulsar	OHC 4 (E16i)	97.4 (1597)	EFI	70 @ 5000	94 @ 2800	2.99 x 3.46	9.4:1	64 @ 3000 RPM
		DOHC (CA18DE)	110.3 (1809)	EFI	125 @ 6400	115 @ 4800	3.27 x 3.29	10.0:1	67 @ 2000 RPM
	Stanza	OHC 4 (CA20E)	120.4 (1974)	EFI	97 @ 5200	114 @ 2800	3.33 x 3.46	8.5:1	58 @ 3000 RPM

Valve Specifications

Year	Model	Seat Angle (deg)	Spring Test Pressure lbs. @ in.	Free Length (in.)	Stem-to-Guide Clearance (in.)		Stem Diameter (in.)	
					Intake	Exhaust	Intake	Exhaust
1976–78	A14	44°	52.7 @ 1.189	1.83	0.0006–0.0018	0.0016–0.0028	0.3138–0.3144	0.3128–0.3134
1979–81	A14, A15	44°	52.7 @ 1.19	1.83	0.0006–0.0018	0.0016–0.0028	0.3138–0.3144	0.3128–0.3134
1982	E15	44°30′	128 @ 1.189	1.839	0.0008–0.0020	0.0018–0.0030	0.2744–0.2750	0.2734–0.2740
1982–86	CA20, CA20E, CA20S	44°30′	①	②	0.0008–0.0021	0.0016–0.0029	0.2742–0.2748	0.2734–0.2740
1983–86	E16	44°30′	51.66 @ 1.543	1.839	0.0008–0.0020	0.0018–0.0030	0.2744–0.2750	0.2734–0.2740
1984	E15ET	44°30′	51.66 @ 1.543	1.839	0.0008–0.0020	0.0018–0.0030	0.2744–0.2750	0.2734–0.2740
1987	E16i	44°30′	—	1.839	0.0008–0.0020	0.0018–0.0030	0.2744–0.2750	0.2734–0.2740
	CA16DE	44°30′	—	1.697	0.0008–0.0021	0.0016–0.0021	0.2348–0.2354	0.2341–0.2346
	CA20E	44°30′	108 @ 1.16 ③	1.575 ④	0.0008–0.0021	0.0016–0.0029	0.2742–0.2748	0.2734–0.2740
1988	E16i	45°	—	1.839	0.0008–0.0020	0.0018–0.0030	0.2744–0.2750	0.2734–0.2740
	CA18DE	45°	⑤	1.697	0.0008–0.0021	0.0016–0.0029	0.2348–0.2354	0.2341–0.2346
	CA20E	45°	129.9 @ 2.32 ⑥	1.959 ⑦	0.0008–0.0021	0.0016–0.0029	0.2742–0.2748	0.3136–0.3138

① Inner: 24 @ 1.38
  Outer: 47 @ 1.58
② Inner: 1.7362
  Outer: 1.9677
③ Outer; Inner: 57 @ 0.98

④ Outer; Inner: 1.378
⑤ 0.650 (in.) at 121 lbs. of load
⑥ Outer; Inner 66.6 @ 1.19
⑦ Outer; Inner: 1.736

4. Remove the air cleaner-to-rocker cover hose and the air cleaner cover, then place a clean rag in the carburetor or throttle body opening to keep out the dirt or any foreign object.

NOTE: *Disconnect and label all the necessary vacuum hoses and electrical connectors, for reinstallation purposes. A good rule of thumb when disconnecting the rather complex engine wiring of today's cars is to put a piece of masking tape on the wire and on the connection you removed the wire from, then mark both pieces of tape 1, 2, 3, etc. When replacing wiring, simply match the pieces of tape.*

5. If equipped, disconnect the air pump cleaner and remove the carbon canister.

6. Remove the auxiliary fan, the washer tank and the radiator grille. Remove the radiator together with the fan motor assembly as a unit.

7. On 1976-81 models, remove the slave cylinder from the clutch housing; on 1982 and lat-

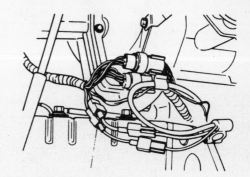

F10 engine harness connector

er models, remove the clutch control wire or cable from the transaxle. Remove the right and the left buffer rods but do not alter the length of these rods. Disconnect the speedometer cable from the transaxle and plug the hole with a clean rag.

NOTE: *On the Stanza (1982 and later), re-*

Camshaft Specifications

Year	Eng. Displacement Cu. In. (cc)	Journal Diameter					Lobe Lift		Bearing Clearance	Camshaft End Play
		1	2	3	4	5	In.	Ex.		
1976–80	85.2 (1397)	1.7237– 1.7242	1.7041– 1.7046	1.6844– 1.6849	1.6647– 1.6652	1.6224– 1.6229	N/A	N/A	①	0.0004– 0.0020
1981–82	90.8 (1488)	1.6515– 1.6522	1.6498– 1.6505	1.6515– 1.6522	1.6498– 1.6505	1.6515– 1.6522	N/A	N/A	0.0014– 0.0030 ②	0.0160
1982–88	120.4 (1974)	1.8085– 1.8092	1.8085– 1.8092	1.8085– 1.8092	1.8085– 1.8092	1.8077– 1.8085	0.354	0.354	0.0040 ③	0.0028– 0.0055
1983–88	97.4 (1597)	1.6515– 1.6522	1.6498– 1.6505	1.6515– 1.6522	1.6498– 1.6505	1.6515– 1.6522	N/A	N/A	0.0014– 0.0030 ②	0.0059– 0.0114
1984	90.8 (1488) Turbo	1.6515– 1.6522	1.6498– 1.6505	1.6515– 1.6522	1.6498– 1.6505	1.6515– 1.6522	N/A	N/A	0.0014– 0.0030 ②	0.0160
1987	97.5 (1598)	1.0998– 1.1006	1.0998– 1.1006	1.0998– 1.1006	1.0998– 1.1006	1.0998– 1.1006	0.335	0.335	0.0018– 0.0035	0.0028– 0.0059
1988	110.3 (1809)	1.0998– 1.1006	1.0998– 1.1006	1.0998– 1.1006	1.0998– 1.1006	1.0998– 1.1006	0.335	0.335	0.0018– 0.0035	0.0028– 0.0059

N/A Not available
① No. 1 & 5: 0.0015–0.0024
No. 2 & 4: 0.0011–0.0020
No. 3: 0.0016–0.0025

② Journals No. 1, 3, & 5
No. 2 & 4: 0.0031–0.0047
③ Clearance limit

Crankshaft and Connecting Rod Specifications

All measurements given in inches

Year	Engine Model	Crankshaft				Connecting Rod Bearings		
		Main Brg Journal Dia	Main Brg Oil Clearance	Shaft End-Play	Thrust on No.	Journal Dia	Oil Clearance	Side Clearance
1976–78	A14	1.966– 1.967	0.0008– 0.002	0.002– 0.006	3	1.7701– 1.7706	0.0008– 0.002	0.008– 0.012
1979–81	A14, A15	1.9666– 1.9671	0.001– 0.0035	0.002– 0.0059	3	1.7701– 1.7706	0.0012– 0.0031	0.004– 0.008
1982	E15	1.9663– 1.9671	①	0.002– 0.007	3	1.5730– 1.5738	0.0012– 0.0024	0.004– 0.0146
1982–88	CA20, CA20S, CA20E	2.0847– 2.0852	0.0016– 0.0024	0.002– 0.007	3	1.7701– 1.7706	0.0008– 0.0024	0.008– 0.012
1983–86	E16	1.9663– 1.9671	①	0.0020– 0.0071	3	1.5730– 1.5738	0.0012– 0.0024	0.0040– 0.0146
1984	E15ET	1.9663– 1.9671	②	0.0020– 0.0071	3	1.5730– 1.5738	0.0006– 0.0023	0.0040– 0.0146
1987	E16i	1.9661– 1.9671	③	0.002– 0.007	3	1.5730– 1.5738	0.0004– 0.0017	0.0040– 0.0146
	CA16DE	2.0847– 2.0856	0.0008– 0.0019	0.0120	3	1.7698– 1.7706	0.0007– 0.0018	0.0007– 0.0018
1988	E16i	1.9661– 1.9671	④	0.002– 0.006	3	1.5733– 1.5738	0.0004– 0.0017	0.0040– 0.0146
	CA18DE	2.0847– 2.0856	0.0008– 0.0019	0.0020– 0.0091	3	1.7698– 1.7706	0.0007– 0.0018	0.0079– 0.0138

① #1 & 5: 0.0012–0.0030
#2, 3, 4: 0.0012–0.0036
② #1 & 5: 0.0012–0.0030
#2 & 4: 0.0011–0.0035
#3: 0.0012–0.0036

③ #1 & 5: 0.0012–0.0022
#2, 3, 4: 0.0012–0.0036
④ #1, 3 & 5: 0.0012–0.0022
#2 & 4: 0.0012–0.0036

Piston and Ring Specifications

All measurements in inches

Year	Engine Model	Piston Clearance	Ring Gap			Ring Side Clearance		
			Top Compression	Bottom Compression	Oil Control	Top Compression	Bottom Compression	Oil Control
1976–78	A14	0.0009–0.002	0.008–0.014	0.006–0.012	0.012–0.035	0.002–0.003	0.001–0.002	Combined ring
1979–80	A14	0.0010–0.0018	0.008–0.014	0.006–0.012	0.012–0.035	0.002–0.003	0.001–0.002	0.0039 ②
1981	A15	0.0010–0.0018	0.0079–0.0138	0.0059–0.0118	0.0118–0.0354	0.0016–0.0028	0.0012–0.0024	0.0039 ②
1982	E15	0.0009–0.0017	0.0079–0.0138	0.0059–0.0018	0.0118–0.0354	0.0016–0.0029	0.0012–0.0025	0.0020–0.0057
1982–84	CA20, CA20E, CA20S	0.0010–0.0018	0.0098–0.0157	0.0059–0.0118	0.0118–0.0354	0.0016–0.0029	0.0012–0.0025	0.0020–0.0057
1985–86	CA20E CA20S	0.0010–0.0018	0.0098–0.0138	0.0059–0.0098	0.0080–0.0240	0.0016–0.0029	0.0012–0.0025	0.0020–0.0057
1983–86	E16	0.0009–0.0017	0.0079–0.0138	0.0059–0.0118	0.0118–0.0354	0.0016–0.0029	0.0012–0.0025	0.0020–0.0057
1984	E15ET	0.0016–0.0024	①	0.0059–0.0098	0.0079–0.0236	0.0016–0.0029	0.0012–0.0025	0.0020–0.0049
1987	E16i	0.0009–0.0017	③	④	0.0079–0.0236	0.0016–0.0029	0.0012–0.0025	⑤
	CA20E	0.0010–0.0018	0.0098–0.0201	0.0059–0.0122	0.0079–0.0299	0.0016–0.0029	0.0012–0.0025	—
	CA16DE	0.0006–0.0014	0.0087–0.0154	0.0075–0.0177	0.0079–0.0299	0.0016–0.0029	0.0012–0.0025	0.0010–0.0033
1988	E16i	0.0009–0.0017	③	④	0.0079–0.0236	0.0016–0.0029	0.0012–0.0025	⑥
	CA20E	0.0010–0.0018	0.0098–0.0201	0.0059–0.0122	0.0079–0.0299	0.0016–0.0029	0.0012–0.0025	—
	CA18DE	0.0006–0.0014	0.0087–0.0154	0.0075–0.0177	0.0079–0.0299	0.0016–0.0029	0.0012–0.0025	0.0010–0.0033

① Grade 1 & 2: 0.0079–0.0102 (Yellow)
Grade 3, 4 & 5: 0.0055–0.0079
② Limit
③ Type 1: 0.0055–0.0102
Type 2: 0.0079–0.0118
④ Type 2: 0.0110–0.0146
Type 2: 0.0059–0.0098

⑤ Type 1: 0.0026–0.0055
Type 2: 0.0002–0.0069
⑥ Type 1: 0.0026–0.0055
Type 2: 0.0002–0.0069

move the EGR vacuum control valve with the bracket from the body.

8. If equipped with air conditioning, loosen the idler pulley nut and the adjusting bolt, then remove the compressor belt. Remove the compressor to one side and suspend on a wire. Remove the condenser and the receiver drier and place them on the right fender.

NOTE: *If equipped with AC, DO NOT ATTEMPT TO UNFASTEN ANY OF THE REFRIGERANT HOSES. See Chapter 1 for additional warnings. If equipped with power steering, loosen the idler pulley nut and adjusting bolt, then remove the drive belt and the power steering pulley.*

9. If equipped with a manual transaxle, disconnect the transaxle shifting rods by removing the spring pins (1976-81) or the securing bolts (1982 and later). If equipped with an automatic transaxle, disconnect the mounting bracket and the control wire from the transaxle.

10. Attach the engine sling, tool Nos. 10005M4900 and 10006M4900 (1976-81), 1000501M00 and 1000623M00 (310, 1982 and Pulsar, 1983 and later) or 10005D0100 and 10007D0100 (Stanza, 1982 and later) at each end of the engine block. Connect a chain or cable to the engine slingers.

11. Unbolt the exhaust pipe from the exhaust manifold. There are 3 bolts which attach the

Torque Specifications
All readings in ft. lbs.

Year	Engine Model	Cylinder Head Bolts	Main Bearing Bolts	Rod Bearing Bolts	Crankshaft Pulley Bolts	Flywheel to Crankshaft Bolts	Manifolds Intake	Manifolds Exhaust
1976–78	A14	51–54	36–43	23–27	108–145	54–61	11–14	11–14
1979–81	A14, A15	51–54	36–43	23–27	108–145	58–65	11–14	11–14
1982	E15	51–54	36–43	23–27	83–108	58–65	11–14	11–14
1982	CA20	51–58	33–40	22–27	90–98	72–80	13–16	13–17
1983	CA20	58–65	33–40	22–27	90–98	72–80	13–16	13–17
1984–86	CA20E CA20S	①	33–40	24–27	90–98	72–80	14–19	14–22
1983–86	E-16	②	36–43	23–27	83–108	58–65	12–15	12–15
1984	E15ET	②	36–43	23–27	83–108	58–65	12–15	12–15
1987	E16i	51–54 ②	36–43	23–27	80–94	58–65	12–15	12–15
	CA16DE	76 ③	33–40	30–33	105–112	61–69	14–19	27–35
	CA20E	④	33–40	24–27	90–98	72–80	14–19	14–22
1988	E16i	⑤	36–43	23–27	80–94	58–65	12–15	12–15
	CA18DE	76 ③	33–40	⑥	105–112	61–69	14–19	27–35
	CA20E	⑦	33–40	24–27	90–98	72–80	14–19	14–22

① a. Torque to 22 ft. lbs.
   b. Torque to 58 ft. lbs.
   c. Loosen all bolts
   d. Torque to 22 ft. lbs.
   e. Torque to 54–61 ft. lbs.
② 1st step: 29–33
   2nd step: 51–54
③ Tighten in 2 steps: 1st—22 ft. lbs.; 2nd—76 ft. lbs. Then loosen all bolts completely. Final torque in 2 steps: 1st—22 ft. lbs.; 2nd—76 ft. lbs. (If angle torquing, tighten all bolts to 85–90 degrees clockwise.)
④ Tighten in two steps: 1st—22 ft. lbs.; 2nd—58 ft. lbs. Then loosen all bolts completely. Final torque is in two steps: 1st—22 ft. lbs.; 2nd—54–61 ft. lbs. If angle torquing, turn all bolts 90–95 degrees clockwise.
⑤ Tighten in 2 steps: 1st—22 ft. lbs., 2nd—51 ft. lbs. Then loosen all bolts completely. Final torque in two steps: 1st—22 ft. lbs.; 2nd—51–54 ft. lbs.
⑥ Tighten in 2 steps: 1st—10–12 ft. lbs.; 2nd—28–33 ft. lbs. (If angle torquing, tighten bolts to 60–65 degrees clockwise.)
⑦ Tighten in two steps: 1st—22 ft. lbs.; 2nd—58 ft. lbs. Then loosen all bolts completely. Final torque is in 2 steps: 1st—22 ft. lbs.; 2nd—54–61 ft. lbs. (If angle torquing, tighten bolt 8 to 83–88 degrees and all other bolts to 75–80 degrees clockwise.) NOTE: No. 8 bolt is the longest bolt.

pipe to the manifold and bolts which attach the pipe support to the engine.

NOTE: *On the Stanza and Pulsar, remove the tie rod ends and the lower ball joints. Disconnect the right and left side drive shafts from their side flanges and remove the bolt holding the radius link support. When drawing out the halfshafts, it is necessary to loosen the strut head bolts also becareful not to damage the grease seals.*

12. On 1976–81 models, unbolt the axle shafts from the transaxle flanges; on the 1982 and later models, refer to Chapter 7, for the axle shaft, removal and installation procedures, then remove the axle shafts.

13. Remove the radius link support bolt, then lower the transaxle shift selector rods.

14. Unbolt the engine from the engine and the transaxle mounts.

15. Using an overhead lifting device, attach it to the engine lifting sling and slowly remove the engine and transaxle assembly from the vehicle.

NOTE: *When removing the engine, be careful not to knock it against the adjacent parts.*

16. Separate the engine from the transaxle if necessary. Install all the necessary parts on the engine before lowering it into the vehicle, such as, spark plugs, water pump etc.

17. Lower the engine and transaxle as an as-

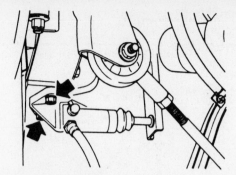

F10, 310 slave cylinder

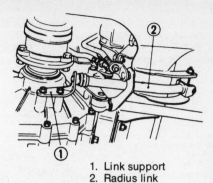

1. Link support
2. Radius link

F10 radius link support

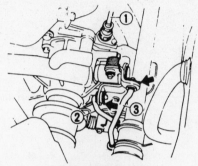

1. Speedometer cable
2. Shift rod
3. Select rod

F10 and 310 (1979–81) speedometer cable and shift rod removal

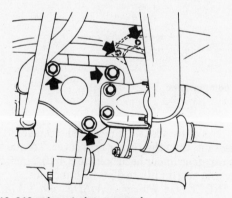

F10, 310 exhaust pipe removal

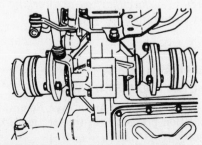

F10 and 310 (1979–81) axle shaft removal

sembly into the car and onto the frame, make sure to keep it as level as possible.

18. Check the clearance between the frame and clutch housing and make sure that the engine mount bolts are seated in the groove of the mounting bracket.

19. Install the motor mounts, remove the engine sling and install the buffer rods, tighten the engine mount bolts first, then apply a load to the mounting insulators before tightening the buffer rod and sub-mounting bolts.

20. If the buffer rod length has not been altered, they should still be correct. Shims are placed under the engine mounts, be sure to replace the exact ones in the correct places.

21. Install the transaxle shift selector rods or cable and attaching parts.

22. Install the axle shafts and the attaching parts.

23. Install the exhaust pipe to the manifold, it is a good idea to replace the gasket for the exhaust pipe at this time.

24. Install slave cylinder, clutch cable if so equipped and speedometer cable.

25. Install the condenser, receiver drier, air conditioning compressor, power steering pump and all drive belts.

26. Install the radiator with fan motor attached as assembly, radiator grille, washer tank and the auxiliary fan.

27. Install air pump cleaner, if so equipped and the carbon canister.

28. Install all other attaching parts such as brackets etc. and the air cleaner that were removed and connect all the vacuum hoses and the electrical connectors.

29. Connect the radiator and heater hoses and refill the system with the correct amount of antifreeze.

30. Install the battery and reconnect the battery cables.

31. Install the hood in the same location as you removed it from.

32. Fill and check all fluids, start engine, let it warm up and check for leaks.

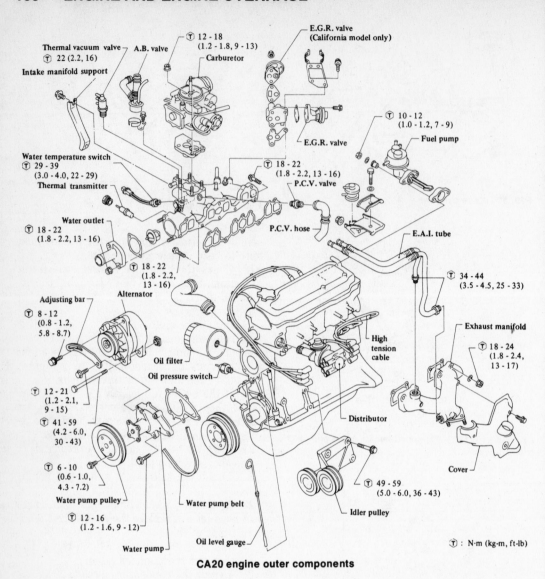

Thermal vacuum valve
ⓣ 22 (2.2, 16)

Intake manifold support

A.B. valve

ⓣ 12 - 18
(1.2 - 1.8, 9 - 13)

Carburetor

E.G.R. valve
(California model only)

ⓣ 10 - 12
(1.0 - 1.2, 7 - 9)

Fuel pump

E.G.R. valve

Water temperature switch
ⓣ 29 - 39
(3.0 - 4.0, 22 - 29)

Thermal transmitter

ⓣ 18 - 22
(1.8 - 2.2, 13 - 16)

P.C.V. valve

Water outlet
ⓣ 18 - 22
(1.8 - 2.2, 13 - 16)

ⓣ 18 - 22
(1.8 - 2.2,
13 - 16)

P.C.V. hose

E.A.I. tube

ⓣ 34 - 44
(3.5 - 4.5, 25 - 33)

Adjusting bar

ⓣ 8 - 12
(0.8 - 1.2,
5.8 - 8.7)

Alternator

High
tension
cable

Exhaust manifold

ⓣ 18 - 24
(1.8 - 2.4,
13 - 17)

Oil filter

Oil pressure switch

ⓣ 12 - 21
(1.2 - 2.1,
9 - 15)

ⓣ 41 - 59
(4.2 - 6.0,
30 - 43)

ⓣ 6 - 10
(0.6 - 1.0,
4.3 - 7.2)

Distributor

Cover

ⓣ 49 - 59
(5.0 - 6.0, 36 - 43)

Water pump pulley

ⓣ 12 - 16
(1.2 - 1.6, 9 - 12)

Water pump belt

Idler pulley

Oil level gauge

Water pump

ⓣ : N·m (kg-m, ft-lb)

CA20 engine outer components

33. Road test vehicle after you are sure there are no leaks.

Rocker Arm Cover
REMOVAL AND INSTALLATION

1. Remove or disconnect any electrical lines, hoses or tubes which may interfere with the removal procedures.
   NOTE: *It may be necessary to remove the air cleaner (carburetor models) or the air duct (EFI and turbo models).*
2. Remove the rocker arm cover-to-cylinder head acorn nuts (310, 1982 and Pulsar, 1983 and later) or mounting screws (all others), then lift the cover from the cylinder head.
3. Using a putty knife, clean the gasket mounting surfaces.

4. To install, use a new gasket and/or RTV sealant, then the rocker arm cover. Torque the cover-to-cylinder head bolts to 8.4-13.2 inch lbs. or the acorn nuts to 35.0-69.6 inch lbs.
   NOTE: *On Pulsar, CA16DE and CA18DE engines there are 2 valve covers. When using RTV sealant apply a even bead and make sure the surface that you are working on is very clean before applying sealer.*

Rocker Arm Shaft
REMOVAL AND INSTALLATION

1. Refer the Rocker Arm Cover, Removal and Installation procedure in this section and remove the cover.
   NOTE: *The CA20 engine uses 2 rocker arm*

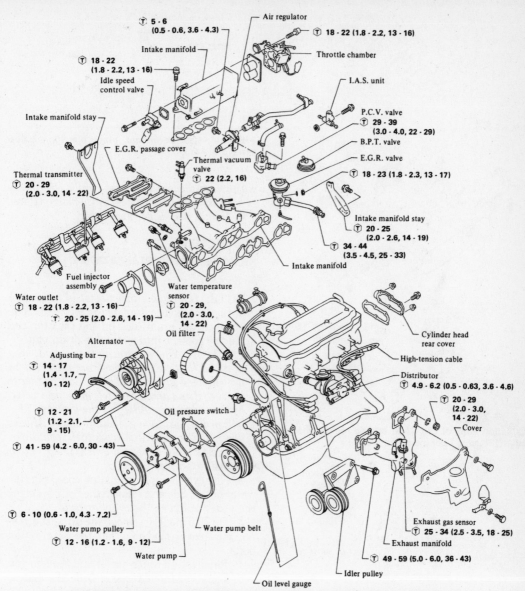

Ⓣ 5 - 6
(0.5 - 0.6, 3.6 - 4.3)

Air regulator

Ⓣ 18 - 22 (1.8 - 2.2, 13 - 16)

Intake manifold

Throttle chamber

Ⓣ 18 - 22
(1.8 - 2.2, 13 - 16)

Idle speed
control valve

I.A.S. unit

Intake manifold stay

P.C.V. valve
Ⓣ 29 - 39
(3.0 - 4.0, 22 - 29)

E.G.R. passage cover

Thermal vacuum
valve
Ⓣ 22 (2.2, 16)

B.P.T. valve

E.G.R. valve

Thermal transmitter
Ⓣ 20 - 29
(2.0 - 3.0, 14 - 22)

Ⓣ 18 - 23 (1.8 - 2.3, 13 - 17)

Intake manifold stay
Ⓣ 20 - 25
(2.0 - 2.6, 14 - 19)

Ⓣ 34 - 44
(3.5 - 4.5, 25 - 33)

Fuel injector
assembly

Intake manifold

Water outlet
Ⓣ 18 - 22 (1.8 - 2.2, 13 - 16)

Water temperature
sensor
Ⓣ 20 - 29
(2.0 - 3.0,
14 - 22)

Ⓣ 20 - 25 (2.0 - 2.6, 14 - 19)

Oil filter

Cylinder head
rear cover

Alternator

High-tension cable

Adjusting bar
Ⓣ 14 - 17
(1.4 - 1.7,
10 - 12)

Distributor
Ⓣ 4.9 - 6.2 (0.5 - 0.63, 3.6 - 4.6)

Ⓣ 20 - 29
(2.0 - 3.0,
14 - 22)

Ⓣ 12 - 21
(1.2 - 2.1,
9 - 15)

Oil pressure switch

Cover

Ⓣ 41 - 59 (4.2 - 6.0, 30 - 43)

Ⓣ 6 - 10 (0.6 - 1.0, 4.3 - 7.2)

Water pump pulley

Water pump belt

Exhaust gas sensor
Ⓣ 25 - 34 (2.5 - 3.5, 18 - 25)

Ⓣ 12 - 16 (1.2 - 1.6, 9 - 12)

Water pump

Exhaust manifold

Ⓣ 49 - 59 (5.0 - 6.0, 36 - 43)

Oil level gauge

Idler pulley

Exploded view of the CA20 EFI engine outer components—1984 and later

shafts. The CA16DE and the CA18DE engines do not use rocker arm shafts.

2. Loosen the valve rocker adjusting nuts, then turn the adjusting screws to separate them from the push rods.

3. Evenly, loosen the rocker shaft bolts, then remove the bolts and lift the rocker shafts from the cylinder head.

NOTE: *If it is necessary to remove the rocker arms from the shafts, perform the following procedures: on 1976-81 models, remove the rocker arm shaft mounting bolts, then slide the shaft mounts, the rocker arms and the springs; on 1982 and later models, remove the shaft bolts and the spring clips, then slide*

the rocker arms from the shaft. Be sure to keep the parts in order for reassembly purposes.

4. To install, position the rocker arm shaft and brackets in the correct place and hand tighten the bolts. Torque the rocker arm shaft, from the center working to the end, bracket bolts to 14-18 ft. lbs. (A-series engines), 12-15 ft. lbs. (E-series engines) and 13-16 ft. lbs. (CA20 engine). Adjust the valve clearance.

5. To adjust the valve clearance, refer to the Valve Adjustment procedures in this section. On all Stanza models, from 1987-88 except station wagons no routine valve adjustment is necessary or possible these models are equipped

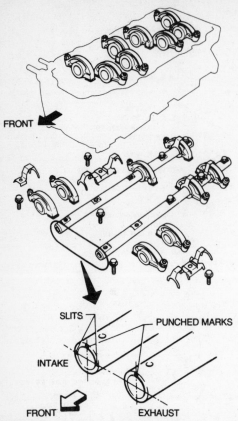

SLITS

PUNCHED MARKS

INTAKE

FRONT

EXHAUST

Exploded view of the CA20 engine rocker shafts, other 1982 and later models are similar

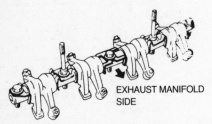

EXHAUST MANIFOLD SIDE

Installation rocker arm shaft—Pulsar E16

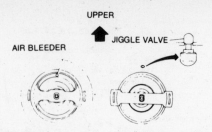

UPPER

AIR BLEEDER

JIGGLE VALVE

1980 and later thermostat: place the jiggle valve toward the top

with hydraulic lash adjusters, which continually take up excess clearance in the valve train.

6. Install the rocker arm cover.

Thermostat

REMOVAL AND INSTALLATION

All Engines

NOTE: *The engine thermostat is housed in the water outlet casting on the cylinder head.*

1. Open the drain cock on the radiator and drain the coolant into a suitable drain pan.

CAUTION: *When draining the coolant, keep in mind that cats and dogs are attracted by the ethylene glycol antifreeze, and are quite likely to drink any that is left in an uncovered container or in puddles on the ground. This will prove fatal in sufficient quantity. Always drain the coolant into a sealable container. Coolant should be reused unless it is contaminated or several years old.*

2. Remove the upper radiator hose from the water outlet side and remove the bolts securing the water outlet to the cylinder head.

3. On E16 models, remove the exhaust air induction tube clamp bolts, then the water outlet bolts.

4. Remove the water outlet and thermostat.

5. Clean off the old gasket from the mating surfaces with a razor blade or equivalent.

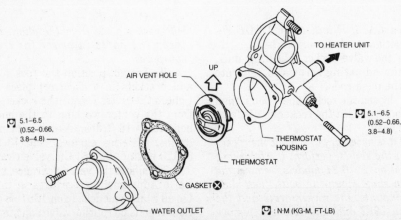

TO HEATER UNIT

AIR VENT HOLE

UP

5.1–6.5 (0.52–0.66, 3.8–4.8)

5.1–6.5 (0.52–0.66, 3.8–4.8)

THERMOSTAT HOUSING

THERMOSTAT

GASKET

WATER OUTLET

: N·M (KG-M, FT-LB)

Thermostat and housing installation—Pulsar E16—others similar

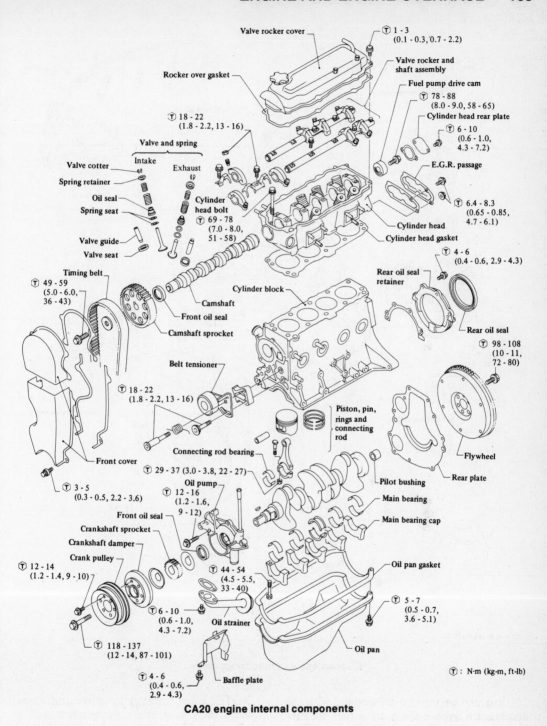

Valve rocker cover

Rocker over gasket

T 1 - 3
(0.1 - 0.3, 0.7 - 2.2)

Valve rocker and
shaft assembly

Fuel pump drive cam

T 78 - 88
(8.0 - 9.0, 58 - 65)

Cylinder head rear plate

T 6 - 10
(0.6 - 1.0,
4.3 - 7.2)

E.G.R. passage

T 18 - 22
(1.8 - 2.2, 13 - 16)

Valve and spring

Intake   Exhaust

Valve cotter

Spring retainer

Oil seal

Spring seat

Valve guide

Valve seat

Cylinder head
bolt
T 69 - 78
(7.0 - 8.0,
51 - 58)

T 6.4 - 8.3
(0.65 - 0.85,
4.7 - 6.1)

Cylinder head

Cylinder head gasket

T 4 - 6
(0.4 - 0.6, 2.9 - 4.3)

Timing belt

T 49 - 59
(5.0 - 6.0,
36 - 43)

Rear oil seal
retainer

Camshaft

Cylinder block

Front oil seal

Camshaft sprocket

Rear oil seal

T 98 - 108
(10 - 11,
72 - 80)

Belt tensioner

T 18 - 22
(1.8 - 2.2, 13 - 16)

Piston, pin,
rings and
connecting
rod

Flywheel

Rear plate

Connecting rod bearing

T 29 - 37 (3.0 - 3.8, 22 - 27)

Front cover

Oil pump
T 12 - 16
(1.2 - 1.6,
9 - 12)

Pilot bushing

Main bearing

T 3 - 5
(0.3 - 0.5, 2.2 - 3.6)

Front oil seal

Crankshaft sprocket

Crankshaft damper

Crank pulley

Main bearing cap

T 12 - 14
(1.2 - 1.4, 9 - 10)

T 44 - 54
(4.5 - 5.5,
33 - 40)

Oil pan gasket

T 5 - 7
(0.5 - 0.7,
3.6 - 5.1)

T 6 - 10
(0.6 - 1.0,
4.3 - 7.2)

Oil strainer

T 118 - 137
(12 - 14, 87 - 101)

Oil pan

T 4 - 6
(0.4 - 0.6,
2.9 - 4.3)

Baffle plate

T : N·m (kg-m, ft-lb)

CA20 engine internal components

6. When installing the thermostat, be sure to install a new gasket and be sure the air bleed hole in the thermostat is facing the left side (or upward) of the engine and that the spring is toward the inside of the engine. Also make sure that the new thermostat to be installed is equipped with a air bleed hole.

COOLING SYSTEM BLEEDING

1. Fill the radiator with the proper type of coolant.

2. With the radiator cap off, start the engine and allow it to run and reach normal operating temperature.

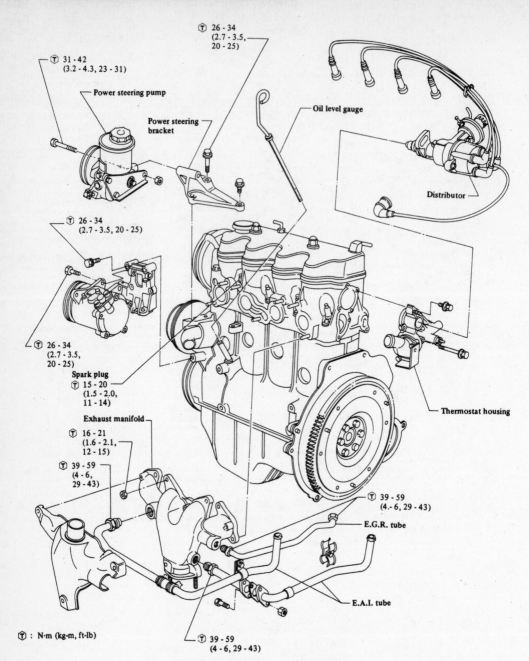

Ⓣ 26 - 34
(2.7 - 3.5,
20 - 25)

Ⓣ 31 - 42
(3.2 - 4.3, 23 - 31)

Oil level gauge

Power steering pump

Power steering bracket

Distributor

Ⓣ 26 - 34
(2.7 - 3.5, 20 - 25)

Ⓣ 26 - 34
(2.7 - 3.5,
20 - 25)

Spark plug
Ⓣ 15 - 20
(1.5 - 2.0,
11 - 14)

Thermostat housing

Exhaust manifold

Ⓣ 16 - 21
(1.6 - 2.1,
12 - 15)

Ⓣ 39 - 59
(4 - 6,
29 - 43)

Ⓣ 39 - 59
(4 - 6, 29 - 43)

E.G.R. tube

E.A.I. tube

Ⓣ : N·m (kg-m, ft-lb)

Ⓣ 39 - 59
(4 - 6, 29 - 43)

E series engine outer components

3. Run the heater at full force and with the temperature lever in the hot position. Be sure that the heater control valve is functioning.

4. Shut the engine off and recheck the coolant level, refill as necessary.

Intake Manifold

REMOVAL AND INSTALLATION

Carbureted E-Series and CA20 Engines

1. Remove the air cleaner assembly together with all of the hoses.

NOTE: *When unplugging wires and hoses, mark each hose and its connection with a piece of masking tape, then match code the 2 pieces of tape with the numbers 1, 2, 3, etc. When assembling, simply match up the pieces of tape.*

2. Disconnect and label the throttle linkage, the fuel and the vacuum lines from the carburetor and the intake manifold components.

NOTE: *The carburetor can be removed from the manifold at this point or can be removed as an assembly with the intake manifold.*

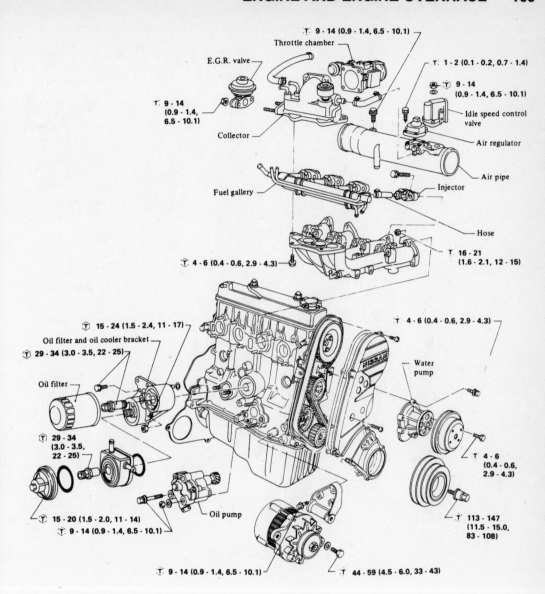

T : N·m (kg-m, ft-lb)

Exploded view of the E15ET engine outer components—1984 turbocharged

3. Remove the intake manifold bolts or nuts and the manifold from the engine.

4. Using a putty knife, clean the gasket mounting surfaces.

5. Install the intake manifold and gasket on the engine. Always use a new gasket. Tighten the mounting bolts from the, center working to the end, in two or three stages. Torque the intake manifold bolts to 14-19 ft. lbs. (CA20 engine) or the nuts 12-15 ft. lbs. (E-series engine).

6. Install throttle linkage, fuel and vacuum lines and the air cleaner assembly.

7. Start engine and check for leaks.

1984 and Later Fuel Injected CA20 Engine

NOTE: *Refer to the Fuel Release Procedure in Chapter 5 and release the fuel pressure in the system.*

1. Remove the air duct between the air flow meter and the throttle body. Remove the throttle linkage.

2. Disconnect the fuel line(s) from the fuel injector assembly.

3. Disconnect and label all of the electrical connectors and the vacuum hoses to the throt-

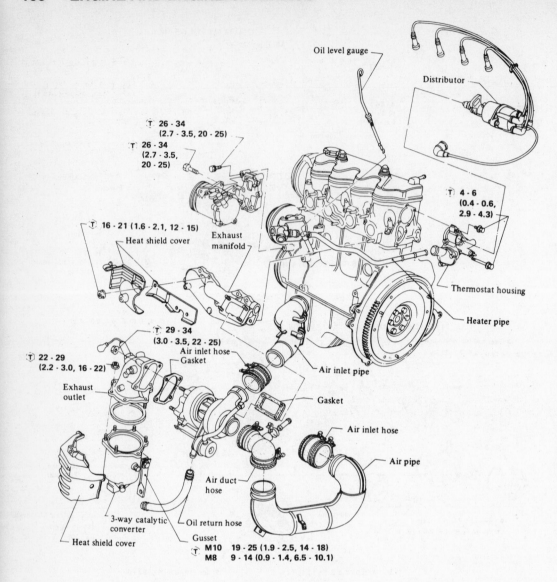

Oil level gauge

Distributor

Ⓣ 26 - 34
(2.7 - 3.5, 20 - 25)

Ⓣ 26 - 34
(2.7 - 3.5,
20 - 25)

Ⓣ 4 - 6
(0.4 - 0.6,
2.9 - 4.3)

Ⓣ 16 - 21 (1.6 - 2.1, 12 - 15)

Heat shield cover

Exhaust
manifold

Thermostat housing

Heater pipe

Ⓣ 29 - 34
(3.0 - 3.5, 22 - 25)
Air inlet hose
Gasket

Ⓣ 22 - 29
(2.2 - 3.0, 16 - 22)

Air inlet pipe

Exhaust
outlet

Gasket

Air inlet hose

Air pipe

Air duct
hose

3-way catalytic
converter

Oil return hose

Gusset

Heat shield cover

Ⓣ M10   19 - 25 (1.9 - 2.5, 14 - 18)
Ⓣ M8   9 - 14 (0.9 - 1.4, 6.5 - 10.1)

Ⓣ : N·m (kg-m, ft-lb)

Exploded view of the E15ET engine outer components—1984 turbocharged

tle, the intake manifold assembly and the related components. Remove the high tension wires from the spark plugs.

4. Disconnect the EGR valve tube from the exhaust manifold. Remove the intake manifold mounting brackets.

5. Remove the mounting bolts and separate the intake manifold from the cylinder head.

6. Using a putty knife, clean the gasket mounting surfaces.

7. Install the intake manifold and gasket on the engine. Always use a new gasket. Tighten the mounting bolts from the, center working to the end, in two or three stages. Torque the intake manifold mounting bolts to 14-19 ft. lbs.

8. Install intake manifold mounting brackets

and reconnect the EGR valve tube to the exhaust manifold.

9. Install the spark plug wires, electrical connectors and the vacuum hoses to the throttle, the intake manifold assembly and the related components.

10. Reconnect the fuel line(s) to the fuel injector assembly.

11. Install the air duct between the air flow meter and the throttle body. Connect the throttle linkage.

12. Start engine and check for leaks.

1984 Turbocharged E15ET Engine

NOTE: *Refer to the Fuel Release Procedure in Chapter 5 and release the fuel pressure.*

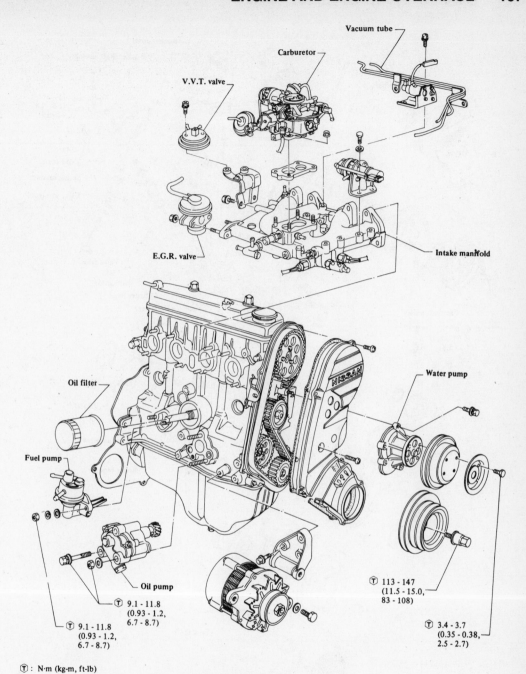

E-series engine outer components

1. Disconnect the air intake duct between the air filter and the air pipe, then the air intake duct between the air pipe and the turbocharger. Remove the air inlet duct between the turbocharger and the throttle body. Remove the air pipe.

2. Disconnect and label all of the electrical connectors and the vacuum hoses to the throttle, the intake manifold assembly and the related components. Remove the high tension wires from the spark plugs.

3. Disconnect the EGR valve tube from the exhaust manifold and the fuel line(s) from the fuel injector assembly.

NOTE: *For clearance purposes, it may be necessary to remove the throttle body and the*

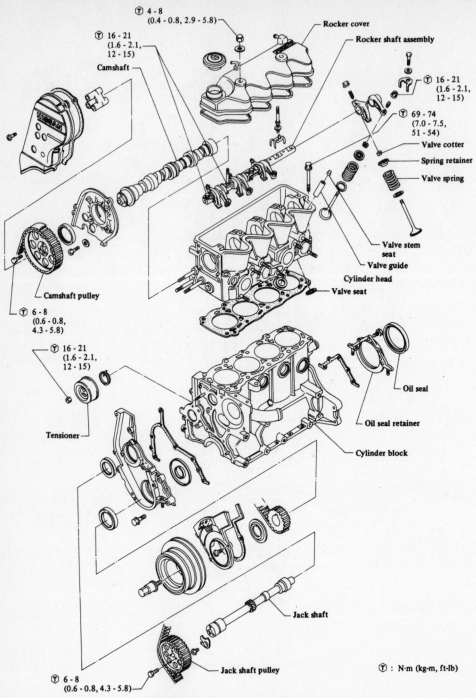

Ⓣ 4 - 8
(0.4 - 0.8, 2.9 - 5.8)

Ⓣ 16 - 21
(1.6 - 2.1,
12 - 15)

Camshaft

Rocker cover

Rocker shaft assembly

Ⓣ 16 - 21
(1.6 - 2.1,
12 - 15)

Ⓣ 69 - 74
(7.0 - 7.5,
51 - 54)

Valve cotter

Spring retainer

Valve spring

Valve stem
seat

Valve guide

Cylinder head

Valve seat

Camshaft pulley

Ⓣ 6 - 8
(0.6 - 0.8,
4.3 - 5.8)

Ⓣ 16 - 21
(1.6 - 2.1,
12 - 15)

Tensioner

Oil seal

Oil seal retainer

Cylinder block

Jack shaft

Jack shaft pulley

Ⓣ : N·m (kg-m, ft-lb)

Ⓣ 6 - 8
(0.6 - 0.8, 4.3 - 5.8)

E series engine internal components

*collector chamber from the intake manifold;
if the fuel injector assembly is in the way, remove it.*

4. Remove the intake manifold mounting
nuts and the intake manifold.

5. Using a putty knife, clean the gasket
mounting surfaces.

6. Install the intake manifold and gasket on

the engine. Always use a new gasket. Tighten
the mounting bolts from the, center working to
the end, in two or three stages. Torque the intake manifold-to-cylinder head nuts to 12-15 ft.
lbs., the intake manifold-to-collector chamber
bolts to 2.9-4.3 ft. lbs. and the air pipe bolt(s) to
6.5-10.1 ft. lbs.

7. Install the throttle body and the collector

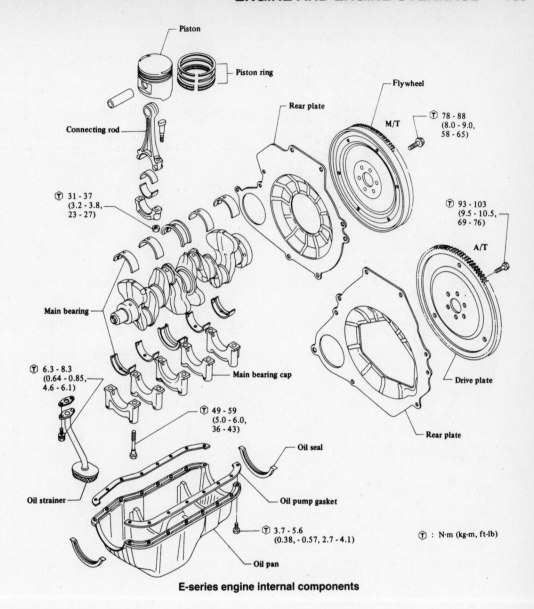

E-series engine internal components

chamber on the intake manifold if it was removed.

8. Connect the EGR valve tube to the exhaust manifold and the fuel line(s) to the fuel injector assembly.

9. Install the spark plug wires, electrical connectors and the vacuum hoses to the throttle, the intake manifold assembly and the related components.

10. Connect the air intake duct between the air filter and the air pipe, then connect the air intake duct between the air pipe and the turbocharger. Install the air inlet duct between the turbocharger and the throttle body. Connect the air pipe.

11. Start engine and check for leaks.

1987 and Later Fuel Injected E16i, CA16DE and CA18DE Engines

NOTE: *Refer to the Fuel Release Procedure in Chapter 5 and release the fuel pressure in the system.*

1. Remove the air cleaner assembly together with all of the attending hoses.

2. Disconnect the throttle linkage and fuel and vacuum lines from the throttle body on the engines).

3. The throttle body can be removed from the manifold at this point or can be removed as an assembly with the intake manifold.

4. Remove the manifold support stay on the CA16DE and CA18DE.

5. Remove the EGR valve assembly, air regu-

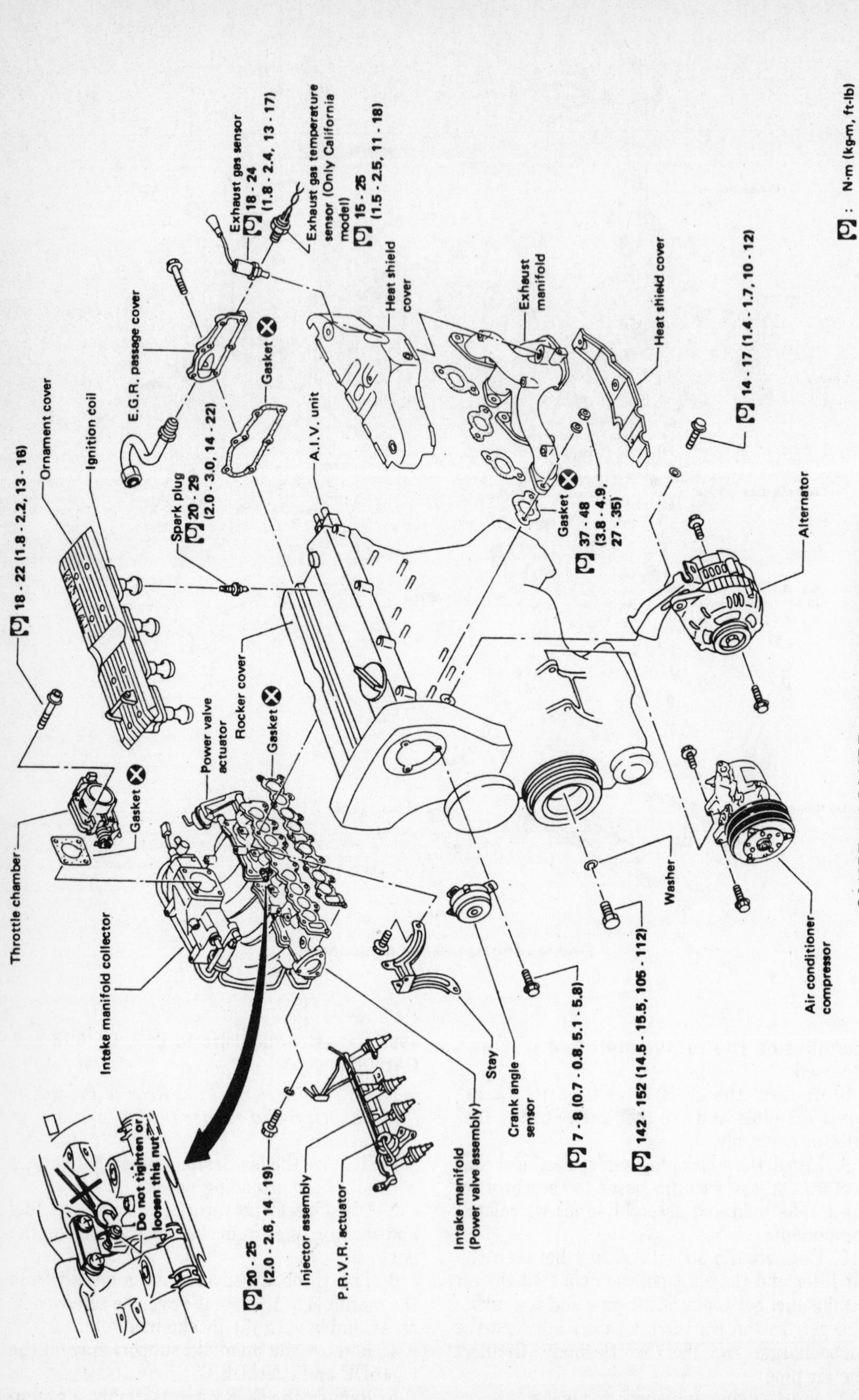

Exhaust gas sensor
⟨T⟩ 18 - 24 (1.8 - 2.4, 13 - 17)

Exhaust gas temperature sensor (Only California model)
⟨T⟩ 15 - 25 (1.5 - 2.5, 11 - 18)

Heat shield cover

Exhaust manifold

Heat shield cover

⟨T⟩ 14 - 17 (1.4 - 1.7, 10 - 12)

E.G.R. passage cover

Gasket ⊗

Ornament cover

Ignition coil

Spark plug
⟨T⟩ 20 - 29
(2.0 - 3.0, 14 - 22)

A.I.V. unit

Gasket ⊗
⟨T⟩ 37 - 48
(3.8 - 4.9,
27 - 35)

Alternator

⟨T⟩ 18 - 22 (1.8 - 2.2, 13 - 16)

Throttle chamber

Gasket ⊗

Power valve actuator

Rocker cover

Gasket ⊗

Intake manifold collector

Air conditioner compressor

Washer

Stay

Crank angle sensor

⟨T⟩ 7 - 8 (0.7 - 0.8, 5.1 - 5.8)

⟨T⟩ 142 - 152 (14.5 - 15.5, 105 - 112)

Do not tighten or loosen this nut

⟨T⟩ 20 - 25
(2.0 - 2.6, 14 - 19)

Injector assembly

P.R.V.R. actuator

Intake manifold
(Power valve assembly)

⟨T⟩ : N·m (kg-m, ft-lb)

CA16DE and CA18DE engine outer components

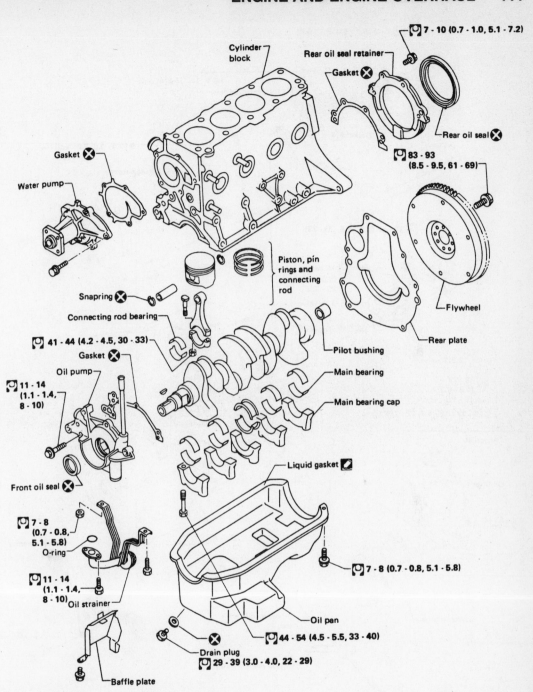

7 - 10 (0.7 - 1.0, 5.1 - 7.2)

Cylinder block

Rear oil seal retainer

Gasket ✖

Rear oil seal ✖

83 - 93 (8.5 - 9.5, 61 - 69)

Gasket ✖

Water pump

Flywheel

Rear plate

Piston, pin rings and connecting rod

Snapring ✖

Connecting rod bearing

Pilot bushing

41 - 44 (4.2 - 4.5, 30 - 33)

Gasket ✖

Main bearing

Oil pump

Main bearing cap

11 - 14 (1.1 - 1.4, 8 - 10)

Liquid gasket ✎

Front oil seal ✖

7 - 8 (0.7 - 0.8, 5.1 - 5.8)

O-ring

7 - 8 (0.7 - 0.8, 5.1 - 5.8)

11 - 14 (1.1 - 1.4, 8 - 10)

Oil strainer

Oil pan

44 - 54 (4.5 - 5.5, 33 - 40)

Drain plug

29 - 39 (3.0 - 4.0, 22 - 29)

Baffle plate

When installing sliding parts such as bearings, be sure to apply engine oil on the sliding surfaces.

: N·m (kg-m, ft-lb)

CA16DE and CA18DE engine internal components

lator and F.I.C.D valve from the manifold on the CA16DE and CA18DE.

6. Loosen the intake manifold attaching nuts, working from the two ends toward the center, and then remove them.

NOTE: *NEVER tighten or loosen the power*

valve adjusting screw on the CA16DE or CA18DE engines.

7. Remove the intake manifold from the engine.

8. Install the intake manifold and gasket on the engine. Always use a new gasket. Tighten

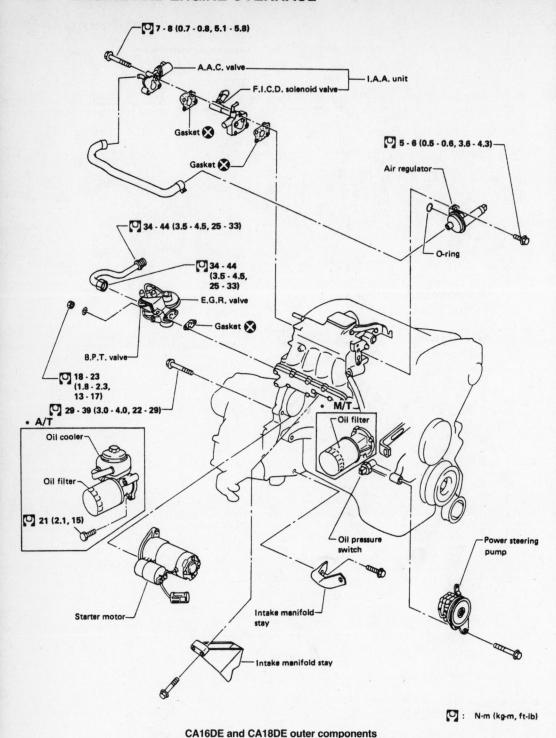

CA16DE and CA18DE outer components

the intake manifold attaching nuts, working from the center toward the ends, in two or three stages. Torque the intake manifold to 12-15 ft. lbs. on the E16i engine and 14-19 ft. lbs. on the CA16DE and CA18DE engines.

9. Install the EGR valve assembly, air regulator and F.I.C.D valve on the manifold on the CA16DE and CA18DE.

10. Connect the manifold support stay on the CA16DE and CA18DE.

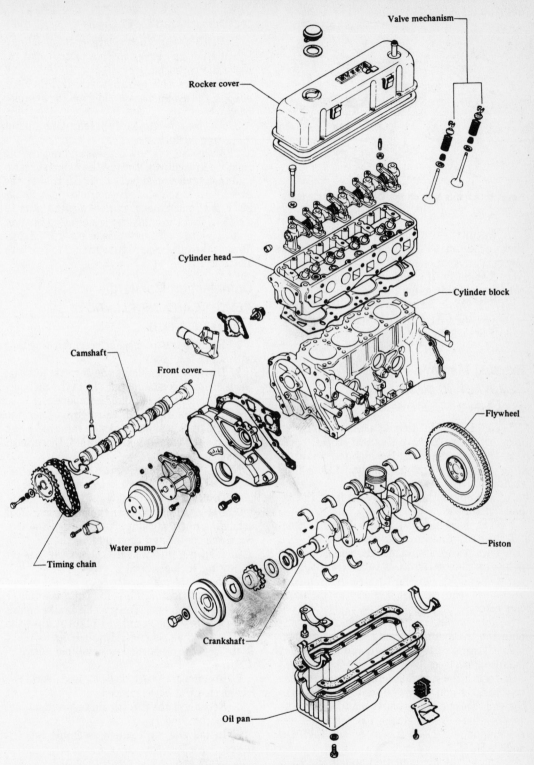

Valve mechanism

Rocker cover

Cylinder head

Cylinder block

Camshaft

Front cover

Flywheel

Water pump

Piston

Timing chain

Crankshaft

Oil pan

A-series engine internal components

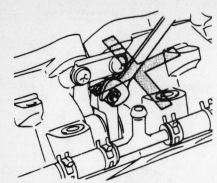

Never touch this bolt on the CA16DE and CA18DE

11. Install the throttle body if it was removed, then reconnect all fuel and vacuum lines and any related components.

12. Reconnect the throttle linkage and air cleaner assembly and all hoses.

NOTE: *Don't forget to install the support stay on the CA16DE and CA18DE engines.*

13. Start engine and check for leaks.

Exhaust Manifold
REMOVAL AND INSTALLATION
All Engines

1. Remove the air cleaner assembly, if necessary for access. Remove the heat shield.

2. Disconnect and tag the high tension wires from the spark plugs on the exhaust side of the engine.

3. Disconnect the exhaust pipe from the exhaust manifold.

NOTE: *Soak exhaust pipe bolts with penetrating oil if necessary to loosen them.*

4. On the carbureted models, remove the air induction and/or the EGR tubes from the exhaust manifold. On the throttle body model, disconnect the exhaust gas sensor electrical connector.

5. Remove the exhaust manifold mounting nuts and the manifold from the cylinder head.

6. Using a putty knife, clean the gasket mounting surfaces.

7. Install the manifold onto the engine, use new gaskets and from the, center working to the end. Torque the exhaust manifold nuts to 14-22 ft. lbs. CA20 engine or 12-15 ft. lbs. E-series engine and 27-35 ft. lbs. on the CA16DE and CA18DE.

8. Install the air induction and/or the EGR tubes from the exhaust manifold or the exhaust gas sensor electrical connector.

9. Reconnect exhaust pipe.

10. Connect spark plug wires and air cleaner and any related hoses.

11. Start engine and check for leaks.

1984 Turbocharged E15ET Engine

1. Refer to the Turbocharger, Removal and Installation procedure in this section and remove the turbocharger.

2. Remove the exhaust manifold's heat shields, the exhaust manifold from the cylinder head.

3. Using a putty knife, clean the gasket mounting surfaces.

4. To install, use new gaskets and reverse the removal procedures. Torque the exhaust manifold-to-cylinder head bolts to 12-15 ft. lbs., the turbocharger-to-exhaust manifold nuts to 22-25 ft. lbs., the exhaust outlet-to-turbo nuts to 22-25 ft. lbs., the converter's mounting bracket bolt to 14-18 ft. lbs. (10mm) or 6.5-10.1 ft. lbs. (8mm), the oil pressure tube fitting-to-turbo to 14-22 ft. lbs.

Combination Manifold
REMOVAL AND INSTALLATION
A-Series (1976-1981)

1. Remove the air cleaner assembly together with all of the hoses.

2. Disconnect and label the throttle linkage, the fuel and the vacuum lines from the carburetor and the intake manifold components.

3. The carburetor can be removed from the manifold at this point or can be removed as an assembly with the intake manifold. Disconnect the exhaust pipe.

NOTE: *Soak exhaust pipe bolts with penetrating oil if necessary to loosen them.*

4. Disconnect the intake and exhaust manifold as an assembly. Loosen the intake manifold attaching nuts, working from the two ends toward the center and then remove them.

5. Using a putty knife, clean the gasket mounting surfaces.

6. Install the manifold to the engine, use new gaskets and tighten the bolts, from the center working to the end. Torque the intake manifold-to-cylinder head nuts to 11-14 ft. lbs., the intake-to-exhaust manifold nuts/bolts to 11-14 ft. lbs. and the carburetor-to-manifold nuts 2.9-4.3 ft. lbs.

7. Reconnect the exhaust pipe and install the carburetor if it was removed.

8. Reconnect the throttle linkage and all fuel and vacuum lines.

9. Install the air cleaner assembly and all hoses.

10. Start engine and check for leaks.

NOTE: *It is important to replace the gasket whenever either manifold is removed. Because the manifolds share a common gasket, it is necessary to remove both manifolds for access to the gasket. Be sure to get the correct replacement gasket for the car.*

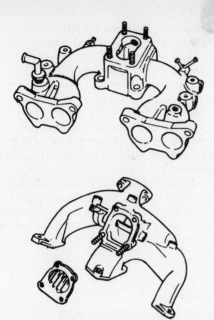

Combination manifold—A series engine

Turbocharger

REMOVAL AND INSTALLATION

1984 Pulsar w/E15ET Engine

1. Disconnect the air inlet and the outlet pipes from the turbocharger.

2. Disconnect the oil pressure tube and the oil return hose from the turbocharger. Discon-nect and mark the high tension wires from the spark plugs.

3. Remove the catalytic converter heat shield, then the converter's mounting bracket. NOTE: *Soak the exhaust pipe outlet bolts with penetrating oil if necessary to loosen them.*

4. Remove the exhaust outlet-to-turbocharger mounting nuts and separate the outlet from the turbocharger.

5. Remove the turbocharger-to-exhaust manifold mounting nuts and lift the turbocharger from the exhaust manifold.

6. Using a putty knife, clean the gasket mounting surfaces.

7. Install the turbocharger to the exhaust manifold, using a new gasket. Torque the turbocharger-to-exhaust manifold nuts to 22-25 ft. lbs., the exhaust outlet-to-turbo nuts to 22-25 ft. lbs. make sure you replace the gasket, the converter's mounting bracket bolt to 14-18 ft. lbs. (10mm) or 6.5-10.1 ft. lbs. (8mm), the oil pressure tube fitting-to-turbo to 14-22 ft. lbs.

8. Connect the air inlet and the outlet pipes from the turbocharger connect the high tension wires for the spark plugs.

9. Check fluid levels, start engine and check for leaks.

Air Conditioning Compressor

Refer to Chapter 1 for Charging and Discharging procedures.

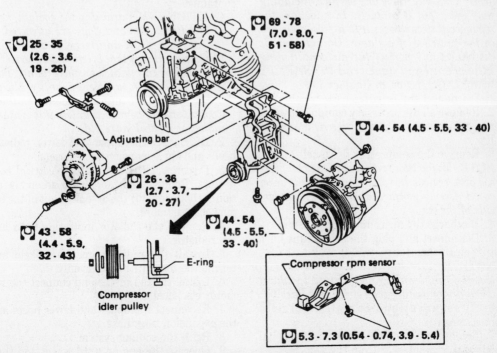

Compressor mounting—Stanza (typical)

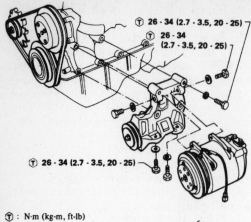

ⓣ 26 - 34 (2.7 - 3.5, 20 - 25)

ⓣ 26 - 34 (2.7 - 3.5, 20 - 25)

ⓣ 26 - 34 (2.7 - 3.5, 20 - 25)

ⓣ : N·m (kg-m, ft-lb)

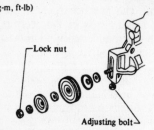

Lock nut

Adjusting bolt

Compressor mounting—Pulsar (typical)

REMOVAL AND INSTALLATION

All Models

CAUTION: *The compressed refrigerant used in the air conditioning system expands into the atmosphere at a temperature of −2°F or lower. This will freeze any surface, including your eyes, that it contacts. In addition, the refrigerant decomposes into a poisonous gas in the presence of a flame. Do not open or disconnect any part of the air conditioning system until you have read the SAFETY WARNINGS section in Chapter 1.*

1. Disconnect the negative battery cables.
2. Remove all the necessary equipment in order to gain access to the compressor mounting bolts.
3. Remove the compressor drive belt.
NOTE: *To facilitate removal of the compressor belt, remove the idler pulley and bracket as an assembly beforehand from the underside of the car.*
4. Discharge the air conditioning system.
5. Disconnect and plug the refrigerant lines with a clean shop towel.
NOTE: *Be sure to use 2 wrenches (one to loosen fitting—one to hold fitting in place) when disconnecting the refrigerant lines.*
6. Disconnect and tag all electrical connections.
7. Remove the compressor mounting bolts. Remove the compressor from the vehicle.
8. Install the compressor on the engine and

evenly torque all the mounting bolts the same.
9. Connect all the electrical connections and unplug and reconnect all refrigerant lines.
10. Install all the necessary equipment in order to gain access to the compressor mounting bolts.
11. Install and adjust the drive belt.
12. Connect the negative battery cable.
13. Evacuate and charge the system as required. Make sure the oil level is correct for the compressor.
NOTE: *Do not attempt to the leave the compressor on its side or upside down for more than a couple minutes, as the oil in the compressor will enter the low pressure chambers. Be sure to always replace the O-rings.*

Radiator

REMOVAL AND INSTALLATION

A-Series Engines

NOTE: *On some models, it may be necessary to remove the front grille to remove the radiator. The cooling system can be drained from opening the drain cock at the bottom of the radiator or by removing the bottom hose at the radiator. Be careful not to damage the fins or core tubes when removing and installing the radiator from the vehicle. NEVER OPEN THE RADIATOR CAP WHEN HOT!*

1. Drain the engine coolant into a clean container.
CAUTION: *When draining the coolant, keep in mind that cats and dogs are attracted by the ethylene glycol antifreeze, and are quite likely to drink any that is left in an uncovered container or in puddles on the ground. This will prove fatal in sufficient quantity. Always drain the coolant into a sealable container. Coolant should be reused unless it is contaminated or several years old.*
2. Disconnect the upper and lower radiator hoses and the expansion tank hose.
3. Disconnect the fan motor electrical connectors. Remove the fan motor assembly retaining bolts and lift the assembly out of the engine compartment.
4. Remove the radiator mounting bolts and the radiator.
5. Install the radiator on the vehicle and torque the mounting bolts evenly.
6. Install the fan motor and connect the fan motor electrical connectors.
7. Reconnect the upper and lower hoses and the expansion tank hose.
8. Refill the cooling system.
9. Operate the engine until warm and then check the water level and for leaks.

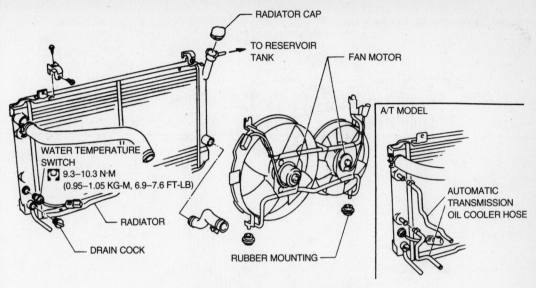

Radiator mounting—Pulsar E16i engine

E16 Series Engines
E15ET Engine
CA16DE Engine
C18DE Engine

1. Drain the cooling system.
CAUTION: *When draining the coolant, keep in mind that cats and dogs are attracted by the ethylene glycol antifreeze, and are quite likely to drink any that is left in an uncovered container or in puddles on the ground. This will prove fatal in sufficient quantity. Always drain the coolant into a sealable container. Coolant should be reused unless it is contaminated or several years old.*

2. Unbolt and set aside the power steering pump if necessary to gain access. DO NOT disconnect the power steering pressure hoses or drain the system.

3. Disconnect the upper and lower radiator hoses, reservoir hose.

4. If equipped with an automatic transaxle, disconnect and cap the cooling lines at the radi-

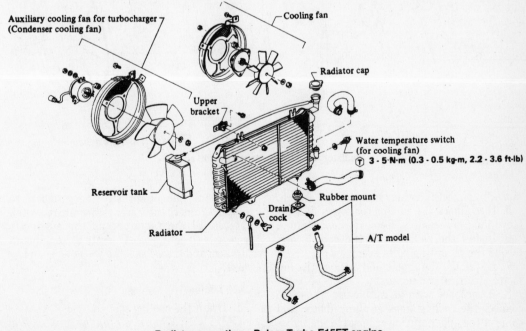

Radiator mounting—Pulsar Turbo E15ET engine

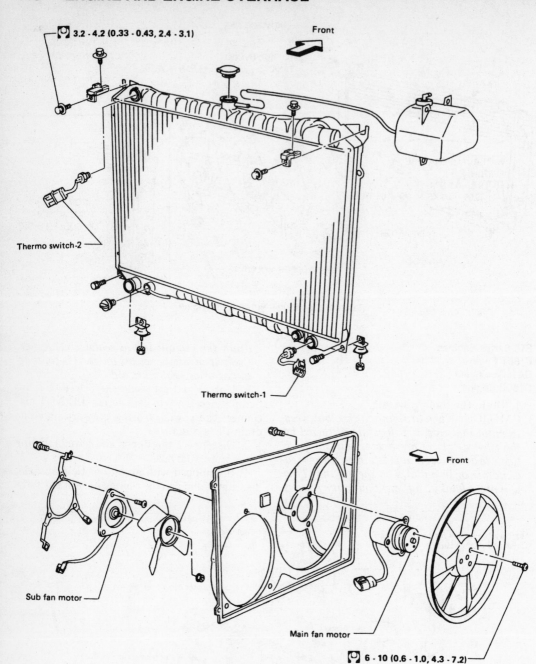

3.2 - 4.2 (0.33 - 0.43, 2.4 - 3.1)

Front

Thermo switch-2

Thermo switch-1

Sub fan motor

Main fan motor

Front

6 - 10 (0.6 - 1.0, 4.3 - 7.2)

Radiator mounting—Stanza CA20E engine

ator. Disconnect the water temperature switch.

5. Disconnect the fan motor wires and re-move the fan assembly. Remove the radiator.

6. Install the radiator on the vehicle and torque the mounting bolts evenly.

7. Install the fan motor and connect the fan motor electrical connectors.

8. If equipped with an automatic transaxle, connect the cooling lines at the radiator and connect the upper and lower hoses to the radia-tor and the reservoir hose.

9. Install the power steering pump if re-moved. Connect the water temperature switch.

10. Refill the radiator and the automatic transaxle (if equipped). Operate the engine un-til warm and then check the water level and for leaks.

CA20 Engine

1. Drain the cooling system.

CAUTION: *When draining the coolant, keep in mind that cats and dogs are attracted by the ethylene glycol antifreeze, and are quite likely to drink any that is left in an uncovered container or in puddles on the ground. This will prove fatal in sufficient quantity. Always drain the coolant into a sealable container. Coolant should be reused unless it is contaminated or several years old.*

2. Disconnect the upper and lower radiator hoses and the coolant reserve tank hose.

3. Disconnect the water temperature switch connector and the fan wiring. Disconnect the fan assembly and remove it from the engine compartment.

4. If equipped with an automatic transaxle, disconnect and cap the cooling lines at the radiator.

5. Remove the radiator.

6. Install the radiator on the vehicle and torque the mounting bolts evenly.

7. Install the fan motor and connect the fan motor electrical connectors.

8. If equipped with an automatic transa. connect the cooling lines at the radiator.

9. Install the fan assembly and reconnect the water temperature switch.

10. Connect the upper and lower hoses and the coolant reserve tank hose.

11. Refill the cooling system and automatic transaxle if necessary, operate the engine until warm and then check the water level and for leaks.

Condenser

Refer to Chapter 1 for Charging and Discharging procedures.

REMOVAL AND INSTALLATION

All Models

CAUTION: *The compressed refrigerant used in the air conditioning system expands into the atmosphere at a temperature of −2°F or*

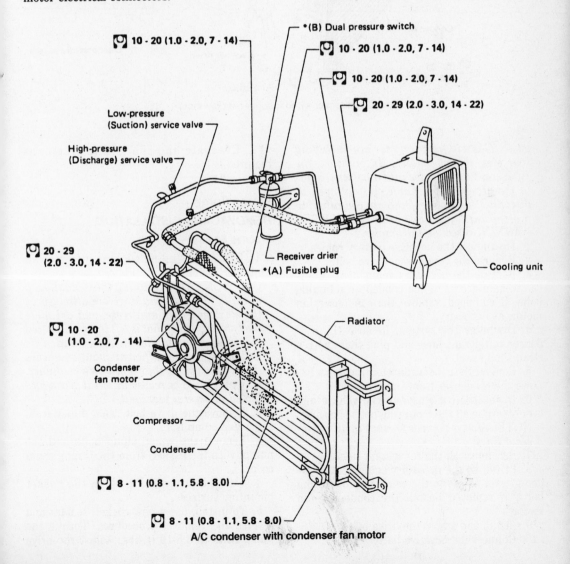

A/C condenser with condenser fan motor

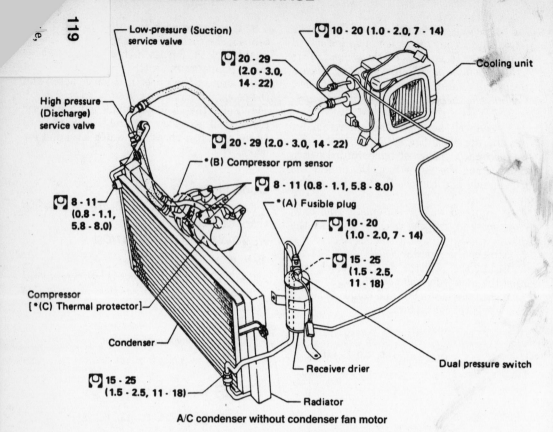

A/C condenser without condenser fan motor

lower. *This will freeze any surface, including your eyes, that it contacts. In addition, the refrigerant decomposes into a poisonous gas in the presence of a flame. Do not open or disconnect any part of the air conditioning system until you have read the SAFTEY WARNINGS section in Chapter 1.*

1. Disconnect the negative battery cables.
2. Remove the compressor drive belt.
3. Remove the necessary components in order to gain access to the condenser retaining bolts. If equipped, remove the condenser fan motor, as necessary.
4. Discharge the system. Remove the condenser refrigerant lines and plug them with a clean shop towel.
5. Remove the condenser retaining bolts. Remove the condenser from the vehicle.
6. Install the condenser in the vehicle and evenly torque all the mounting bolts the same.
NOTE: *Always use new O-rings in all refrigerant lines.*
7. Reconnect all the refrigerant lines.
8. Install all the necessary equipment in order to gain access to the condenser mounting bolts. If removed, install the condenser fan motor.
9. Install and adjust the drive belt.
10. Connect the negative battery cable.

11. Evacuate and charge the system as required.

Water Pump
REMOVAL AND INSTALLATION
A-Series Engines

1. Drain the engine coolant into a clean container.
CAUTION: *When draining the coolant, keep in mind that cats and dogs are attracted by the ethylene glycol antifreeze, and are quite likely to drink any that is left in an uncovered container or in puddles on the ground. This will prove fatal in sufficient quantity. Always drain the coolant into a sealable container. Coolant should be reused unless it is contaminated or several years old.*
2. Remove the drive belt, then pulley from the water pump hub.
3. Remove the water pump bolts and the pump (with the gasket) from the timing chain cover.
4. Using a putty knife, clean the gasket mounting surfaces.
5. To install, use a new gasket, sealant and reverse the removal procedures. Torque the pump bolts to 6.5-10 ft. lbs. Adjust the drive

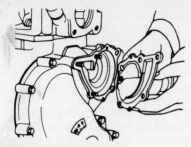

A series water pump removal

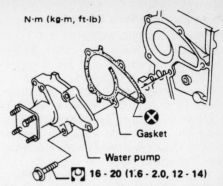

N·m (kg-m, ft-lb)

Gasket

Water pump

16 - 20 (1.6 - 2.0, 12 - 14)

Water pump mounting—CA20E and CA16DE/CA18DE engines

belt and refill the cooling system. Start the engine and check for leaks.

E-Series Engines

1. Drain the cooling system.
CAUTION: *When draining the coolant, keep in mind that cats and dogs are attracted by the ethylene glycol antifreeze, and are quite likely to drink any that is left in an uncovered container or in puddles on the ground. This will prove fatal in sufficient quantity. Always drain the coolant into a sealable container. Coolant should be reused unless it is contaminated or several years old.*
2. Remove the power steering drive belt and the power steering pump.
NOTE: *When removing the power steering pump, do not disconnect the pressure hoses or drain the system.*
3. Remove the water pump/alternator drive belt.
4. Remove the alternator mounting bolts and move it aside.
5. Remove the water pump pulley, then the water pump and the gasket.
6. Using a putty knife, clean the gasket mounting surfaces.
7. Install the water pump on the engine, with a new gasket. Torque the water pump bolts evenly, to 6.5-10 ft. lbs.
8. Install the water pump pulley, alternator and the power steering pump.

E series water pump removal

9. Adjust the drive belts and refill the cooling system. Start the engine and check for leaks.

CA20 Engine
CA16DE Engine
CA18DE Engine

1. Drain the engine coolant.
CAUTION: *When draining the coolant, keep in mind that cats and dogs are attracted by the ethylene glycol antifreeze, and are quite likely to drink any that is left in an uncovered container or in puddles on the ground. This will prove fatal in sufficient quantity. Always drain the coolant into a sealable container. Coolant should be reused unless it is contaminated or several years old.*
2. Loosen the bolts retaining the fan shroud to the radiator and remove the shroud.
3. Loosen the belt, then remove the fan and pulley from the water pump hub.
4. Remove the bolts retaining the pump and remove the pump together with the gasket from the front cover.
5. Remove all traces of gasket material and install the pump in the reverse order. Use a new gasket and sealer. Tighten the bolts uniformly and torque to 12-14 ft. lbs..
6. Install the pulley and fan onto the water pump hub.
7. Install and adjust the drive belt and radiator shroud.
8. Refill the cooling system and start the engine and check for leaks.
NOTE: *The water pump cannot be disassembled and must be replaced as a unit. Be careful not to get coolant on the timing belt*

Cylinder Head

REMOVAL AND INSTALLATION

NOTE: *To prevent distortion or warping of the cylinder head, allow the engine to cool completely before removing the head bolts.*

A-Series (Overhead Valve Engines)

1. Drain the engine coolant.

CAUTION: *When draining the coolant, keep in mind that cats and dogs are attracted by the ethylene glycol antifreeze, and are quite likely to drink any that is left in an uncovered container or in puddles on the ground. This will prove fatal in sufficient quantity. Always drain the coolant into a sealable container. Coolant should be reused unless it is contaminated or several years old.*

2. Disconnect the battery ground cable.

3. Remove the upper radiator hose. Remove the water outlet elbow and the thermostat.

4. Remove the air cleaner, carburetor, rocker arm cover, and both manifolds.

5. Remove the spark plugs.

6. Disconnect the temperature gauge connection.

7. Loosen the rocker arm adjusting nuts and turn the adjusting screws out to disengage the pushrods. Loosen the rocker shaft bolts evenly and remove the rocker shaft assembly. Remove the pushrods, keeping them in the same order for reassembly.

8. Remove the head bolts and remove the head. Carefully tap the head with a rubber mallet to loosen it from the block. Remove it and discard the gasket.

To install:

9. Make sure that the cylinder head and block mating surfaces are clean. Check the cylinder head surface with a straightedge and a feeler gauge for flatness. If the head is warped more than 0.08mm, it must be trued or replace. If this is not done, there will probably be a leak. The block surface should also be checked in the same way. If the block is warped more than 0.08mm, it must be trued (machined flat) or replaced.

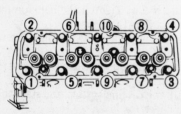

A series head bolt loosening sequence

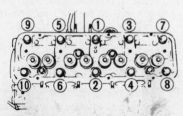

A series head bolt tightening sequence

10. Install a new head gasket. Most gaskets have a **TOP** marking. Make sure that the proper head gasket is used so that no water passages are blocked off.

11. Install the cylinder head. Install the pushrods in their original locations. Install the rocker arm assembly. Loosen the rocker arm adjusting screws to prevent bending the pushrods when tightening the head bolts. Tighten the head bolts finger tight. The single bolt marked **T** must go in the No. 1 position on the center right side of the engine.

NOTE: *The No.1, right side center, head bolt is smaller in diameter than the others. It acts as an oil passageway for the rocker components, it must be inserted in the correct hole or the valve train will seize after a few hundred miles.*

12. Refer to the "Torque Specifications" chart for the correct head bolt torque. Tighten the bolts to one third of the specified torque in the order shown in the head bolt tightening sequence illustration. Torque the rocker arm mounting bolts to 15-18 ft. lbs.

13. Tighten the bolts to $\frac{2}{3}$ of the specified torque in sequence.

14. Tighten the bolts to the full specified torque in sequence.

15. Adjust the valves. If no cold setting is given, adjust the valves to the normal hot setting.

16. Reassemble the engine. Intake and exhaust manifold bolt torque is 11-14 ft. lbs. Fill the cooling system. Start the engine and run it until normal temperature is reached. Remove the rocker arm cover. Torque the bolts in sequence once more. Check the valve clearances.

17. Retorque the head bolts after 600 miles of driving. Check the valve clearances after torquing, as this may disturb the settings.

E-Series Single Overhead Camshaft Engines

NOTE: *If the engine mounting bracket must be removed. Support the engine by placing a jack or equivalent, with a wooden block on top, under the oil pan away from the oil drain plug.*

1. Crank the engine until the No. 1 piston is at Top Dead Center on its compression stroke and disconnect the negative battery cable. Drain the cooling system and remove the air cleaner assembly.

CAUTION: *When draining the coolant, keep in mind that cats and dogs are attracted by the ethylene glycol antifreeze, and are quite likely to drink any that is left in an uncovered container or in puddles on the ground. This will prove fatal in sufficient quantity. Always drain the coolant into a sealable container. Coolant should be reused unless it is contaminated or several years old.*

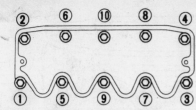

E series head bolt loosening sequence

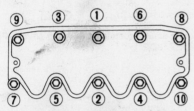

E series head bolt tightening sequence

2. Remove the alternator and all drive belts.

3. Number all spark plug wires as to their respective cylinders, mark and remove the distributor, with all wires attached.

4. Remove the EAI pipes bracket and EGR tube at the right (EGR valve) side. Disconnect the same pipes on the front (exhaust manifold) side from the manifold.

5. Remove the exhaust manifold cover and the exhaust manifold, taking note that the center manifold nut has a different diameter than the other nuts.

6. Remove the air conditioning compressor bracket and the power steering pump bracket (if equipped).

7. Label and disconnect the carburetor throttle linkage, fuel line, and all vacuum and electrical connections.

8. Remove the intake manifold with carburetor or throttle body.

9. Remove water pump pulley and the crankshaft pulley.

10. Remove the rocker (valve) cover.

11. Remove upper and lower dust cover on the camshaft timing belt shroud.

12. With the shroud removed, the cam sprocket, crankshaft sprocket, jackshaft sprocket, tensioner pulley, and toothed rubber timing belt are exposed.

13. Mark the relationship of the camshaft sprocket to the timing belt and the crankshaft sprocket to the timing belt with paint or a grease pencil. This will make setting everything up during reassembly much easier if the engine is disturbed during disassembly.

14. Remove the belt tensioner pulley.

15. Mark an arrow on the timing belt showing direction of engine rotation, because the belt wears a certain way and should be installed the way it was removed. Slide the belt off the sprockets.

16. Carefully remove the cylinder head from the block, pulling the head up evenly from both ends. If the head seems stuck, DO NOT pry it off. Tap lightly around the lower perimeter of the head with a rubber mallet to help break the seal. Label all head bolts with tape, as they must go back in their original positions. On some engines bolts are different size.

To install:

17. Thoroughly clean both the cylinder block and head mating surfaces. Avoid scratching either.

18. Turn the crankshaft and set the No. 1 cylinder at TDC on its compression stroke. This causes the crankshaft timing sprocket mark to be aligned with the cylinder block cover mark.

19. Align the camshaft sprocket mark with the cylinder head cover mark. This causes the valves for No. 1 cylinder to position at TDC on the compression stroke.

20. Place a new gasket on the cylinder block. NOTE: *If cupped washers are used for installation, always make sure that the flat side of the washer is facing downward before tightening the cylinder head bolts.*

21. Install the cylinder head on the block and tighten the bolts in stages: first tighten all bolts to 22 ft. lbs., then retighten them all to 51 ft. lbs. Next, loosen all bolts completely, and then retighten them again to 22 ft. lbs. Tighten all bolts to a final torque of 51-54 ft. lbs.

22. Install the timing belt, tensioner, upper and lower dust cover. Make sure all timing marks are in proper alignment. Connect the engine mount bracket.

23. Install the valve cover, water pump drive belt and pulley. Install the crankshaft pulley.

24. Install the intake manifold with carburetor or throttle body.

25. Connect the carburetor throttle linkage, fuel line, and all vacuum and electrical connections.

26. Install the air conditioning compressor bracket and the power steering pump bracket (if equipped).

27. Install the exhaust manifold and the exhaust manifold cover.

28. Connect all emission pipes and brackets and any other interfering parts that were removed.

29. Install distributor and spark plug wires.

30. Install the alternator, drive belts and the air cleaner assembly.

31. Refill cooling system, adjust the drive belts, start engine, check timing and for coolant or oil leaks.

32. Road test the vehicle.

CA16DE and CA18DE Double Overhead Camshaft Engines

1. Crank the engine until the No. 1 piston is at Top Dead Center on its compression stroke and disconnect the negative battery cable. Drain the cooling system and remove the air cleaner assembly and upper radiator hose.

CAUTION: *When draining the coolant, keep in mind that cats and dogs are attracted by the ethylene glycol antifreeze, and are quite likely to drink any that is left in an uncovered container or in puddles on the ground. This will prove fatal in sufficient quantity. Always drain the coolant into a sealable container. Coolant should be reused unless it is contaminated or several years old.*

2. Loosen the alternator and remove all drive belts. Remove the alternator. If necessary remove the right side under cover.

3. Disconect the air duct at the throttle chamber.

4. Tag and disconnect all lines, hoses and wires which may interfere with cylinder head removal.

5. Remove the 8 screws and lift off the ornament cover.

6. Disconnect the O_2 sensor.

7. Remove the 2 exhaust heat shield covers.

8. Unbolt the exhaust manifold and wire the entire assembly out of the way.

9. Disconnect the EGR tube at the passage cover and then remove the passage cover and its gasket.

10. Disconnect and remove the crank angle sensor from the upper front cover.

NOTE: *Put aligning mark on crank angle sensor and timing belt cover.*

11. Remove the support stay from under the intake manifold assembly.

12. Unbolt the intake manifold and remove it along with the collector and throttle chamber.

13. Disconnect and remove the fuel injectors as an assembly.

14. Remove the upper and lower front covers.

NOTE: *Remove engine mount bracket but support engine under oil pan with wooden blocks or equivalent. Do not position the support near the drain plug.*

15. Remove the timing belt and camshaft sprockets.

NOTE: *When the timing belt has been removed, NEVER rotate the crankshaft and camshaft separately because the valves will hit the pistons!*

16. Remove the camshaft cover.

17. Remove the breather separator.

18. Gradually loosen the cylinder head bolts in several stages, in the sequence illustrated.

19. Carefully remove the cylinder head from

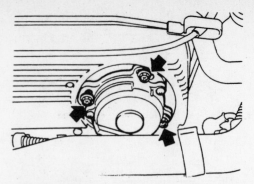

Crankangle sensor location on timing cover—Pulsar CA16DE/CA18DE

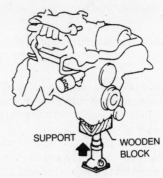

SUPPORT   WOODEN BLOCK

Support under engine—Pulsar CA16DE/CA18DE

CYLINDER HEAD BOLT WASHER DIRECTION

CYLINDER HEAD SIDE

Cupped washer installation—Pulsar CA16DE/CA18DE

the block, pulling the head up evenly from both ends. If the head seems stuck, DO NOT pry it off. Tap lightly around the lower perimeter of the head with a rubber mallet to help break the seal. Label all head bolts with tape or magic marker, as they must go back in their original positions.

To install:

20. Thoroughly clean both the cylinder block and head mating surfaces. Avoid scratching either.

21. Install the cylinder head with bolts on the block. When installing the bolts tighten the two center bolts temporarily to 15 ft. lbs. and install the head bolts loosely. After the timing belt and front cover have been installed, torque all the head bolts in the torque sequence. Tighten all bolts to 22 ft. lbs. Re-tighten all bolts to 76 ft.

LOOSENING ORDER

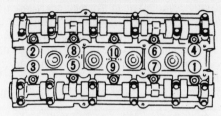

TIGHTENING ORDER

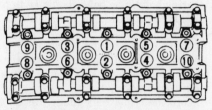

Removal and installation bolt torque sequence—Pulsar CA16DE/CA18DE

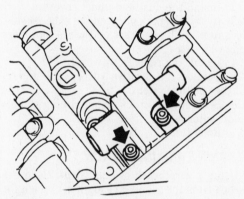

Breather separator mounting—Pulsar CA16DE/ CA18DE

lbs. Loosen all bolts completely and then retighten them once again to 22 ft. lbs. Tighten all bolts to a final torque of 76 ft. lbs.

NOTE: *If cupped washers are used for installation, always make sure that the flat side of the washer is facing downward before tightening the cylinder head bolts.*

22. Install the camshaft sprocket, timing belt and front covers.

23. Reconnect the engine mount support.

24. Install the fuel injectors, intake manifold assembly with collector and throttle chamber attached.

25. Connect the support stay to the intake manifold.

26. Install the crankangle sensor. Align the sensor with mark that was made before removal.

27. Connect EGR tube and passage cover with a new gasket.

28. Install the exhaust manifold assembly and heat shields.

29. Reconnect the O_2 sensor and orament cover.

30. Reconnect the air duct at the throttle chamber. Connect all lines, hoses and wires that were removed.

31. Install the alternator and adjust all the drive belts.

32. Install the air cleaner assembly.

33. Refill cooling system, start engine, check timing and for coolant or oil leaks.

34. Road test the vehicle.

CA20 Series Single Overhead Camshaft Engines

1. Disconnect the negative battery cable and drain the cooling system.

CAUTION: *When draining the coolant, keep in mind that cats and dogs are attracted by the ethylene glycol antifreeze, and are quite likely to drink any that is left in an uncovered container or in puddles on the ground. This will prove fatal in sufficient quantity. Always drain the coolant into a sealable container. Coolant should be reused unless it is contaminated or several years old.*

2. Support vehicle safely, remove the right front wheel.

3. Remove all spark plugs on exhaust side. Tag and disconnect all lines, hoses and wires which may interfere with cylinder removal.

4. Position the No. 1 cylinder at TDC of the compression stroke and remove the dust cover and the under cover.

5. Remove the alternator drive belt, power steering pump drive belt and air conditioning compressor drive belt if so equipped.

6. Remove the crankshaft pulley.

7. Support engine and remove right side engine insulator and mounting bracket.

8. Remove front upper and lower timing belt covers.

9. Loosen timing belt tensioner and return spring, then remove the timing belt.

NOTE: *When the timing belt has been removed, do not rotate the crankshaft and the camshaft separately, because the valves will hit the piston heads.*

10. Remove rocker shafts with rocker arms and securing bolts. The bolts should be loosened in two or three stages.

11. Remove camshaft sprocket.

12. Disconnect exhaust tube from the exhaust manifold.

13. Remove cylinder head together with manifolds as an assembly. The bolts should be loosened in two or three stages.

14. Thoroughly clean both the cylinder block and head mating surfaces. Avoid scratching either.

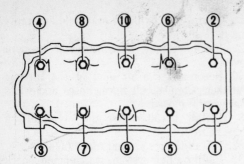

Loosen in numerical order.

• Tightening order

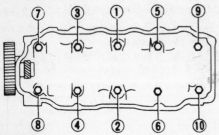

This bolt is
the longest.

Removal and installation bolt torque sequence—
Stanza CA20 series

15. Install a new head gasket on the block and the cylinder head with manifolds attached as an assembly. When installing the bolts tighten the two center bolts temporarily to 15 ft. lbs. and install the head bolts loosely. After the timing belt and front cover have been installed, torque all the head bolts in the torque sequence. Tighten all bolts to 22 ft. lbs. Retighten all bolts to 58 ft. lb. Loosen all bolts completely and then retighten them once again to 22 ft. lbs. Tighten all bolts to a final torque of 54-61 ft. lbs.
NOTE: *Newer models utilize cupped wash-ers, always make sure that the flat side of the washer is facing downward before tightening the cylinder head bolts. Before installing the timing belt, be certain that the crankshaft pulley key is near the top and that the camshaft knock pin or sprocket aligning mark is at the top.*

16. Reconnect exhaust tube to exhaust manifold.

17. Install the camshaft sprocket.

18. Install the rocker shafts with rocker arms and securing bolts. The bolts should be tighten in two or three stages from the center to the ends.

19. Install timing belt and tensioner.

20. Install the front upper and lower timing belt covers and the right side engine insulator and mounting bracket.

21. Install the crankshaft pulley. Install and adjust, the alternator drive belt, power steering pump drive belt and air conditioning compressor drive belt if so equipped.

22. Install the dust and under covers.

23. Install all spark plugs on the exhaust side. Reconnect all lines, hoses and wires that were removed.

24. Install the right front wheel.

25. Connect the negative battery cable and refill the cooling system.

26. Start engine, check engine timing and for oil or water leaks.

27. Road test.

CLEANING AND INSPECTION

Using a wire brush or equivalent, clean the carbon from the cylinder head, then check it for cracks and flaws. Make sure that the cylinder head and the block surfaces are clean. Check the cylinder head surface for flatness, using a straightedge and a feeler gauge. If the cylinder head and/or the block are warped more than

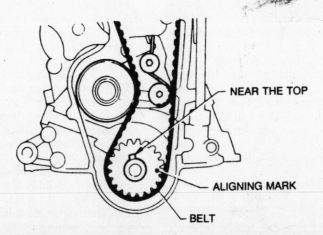

NEAR THE TOP

ALIGNING MARK

BELT

Make sure the crankshaft pulley key is near the top—C-Series engines

0.08mm, it must be trued by a machine shop; if this is not done, there will probably be a compression or water leak.

RESURFACING

Cylinder head resurfacing should be done only by a competent machine shop. If warpage exceeds the manufacturer's tolerance, the cylinder head must be replaced.

Valves and Springs

REMOVAL AND INSTALLATION

1. Refer to the Cylinder Head, Removal and Installation procedures in this section and remove the cylinder head.

2. Loosen and back off the rocker arm adjusting screws, then remove the rocker arm assembly.

NOTE: *After removing the rocker arm assembly (CA20 and E-series), remove the spring retainers and the rocker arms from the shaft(s) (be sure to keep the parts in order), then reinstall the rocker arm shaft.*

3. Using the spring compression tool No. ST12070000 (A-series), No. KV101092S0 (CA20) or No. KV101072S0 (E-series), compress the valve springs. Remove the valve keeper, then relieve the spring pressure. Remove the springs, the valve seals and the valves.

4. To install, use new oil seals and reverse the removal procedures. Tighten the rocker shaft bolts to 14-18 ft. lbs. on the A-series en-

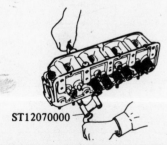

ST12070000

Compressing the valve spring—A-series engine

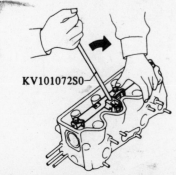

KV101072S0

Compressing the valve spring—E-series engine

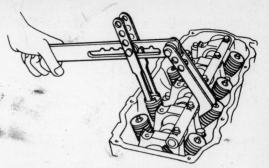

Compressing the valve spring—CA20 engine

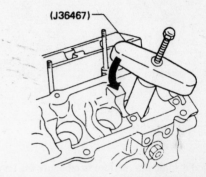

(J36467)

Removing valve oil seal—Pulsar CA16DE/CA18DE

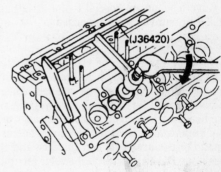

(J36420)

Disassemble valve mechanism—Pulsar CA16DE/CA18DE

gines; 13-16 ft. lbs. on CA20 engines; 13-15 ft. lbs. on E-series engines, in a circular sequence. Adjust the valves.

NOTE: *The intake/exhaust valve springs are the uneven pitch type. That is, the springs have narrow coils at the bottom and wide coils at the top. The narrow coils (painted white) must be the side making contact on the cylinder head surface.*

After the cylinder head is removed from the engine, on the Pulsar CA16DE and CA18DE engines, remove the camshaft sprockets, tensioner pulley and rear cover. Then remove the camshaft mounting bracket bolts gradually in two or three stages. Remove the front oil seals, camshafts and hydraulic lifters. To diassemble

Measuring the valve stem diameter

Using a dial indicator (inside) to measure the valve guide inner diameter

the valve machanism special tool J-36420 and J-36467 or equivalents are needed.

INSPECTION

Before the valves can be properly inspected, the stem, the lower end of the stem, the entire valve face and head must be cleaned. An old valve works well for chipping carbon from the valve head, a wire brush, a gasket scraper or a putty knife can be used for cleaning the valve face and/or the area between the face and the lower stem. DO NOT scratch the valve face during cleaning. Clean the entire stem with a rag soaked in thinners to remove all of the varnish and gum.

Thorough inspection of the valves requires the use of a micrometer and a dial indicator. If these instruments are not available, the parts should be taken to a reputable machine shop for inspection. Refer to the Valve Specifications chart, for the valve stem and stem-to-guide specifications.

Using a dial indicator, measure the inside diameter of the valve guides at their bottom, midpoint and top positions, at 90° apart. Subtract the valve stem measurement; if the clearance exceeds that listed in the specifications chart under Stem-to-Guide Clearance, replace the valve(s).

Check the top of each valve for pitting and unusual wear due to improper rocker adjustment, etc. The stem tip can be ground flat if it is

worn but no more that 0.50mm can be removed; if this limit must be exceeded to make the tip flat and square, then the valve must be replaced. If the valve stem tips are ground, make sure that the valve is fixed securely into the jig, so that the tip contacts the grinding wheel squarely at exactly 90°.

REFACING

Valve refacing should only be handled by a reputable machine shop, as the experience and equipment needed to do the job are beyond that of the average owner/mechanic. During the course of a normal valve job, refacing is necessary when simply lapping the valves into their seats will not correct the seat and face wear. When the valves are reground (resurfaced), the valve seats must also be recut, again requiring special equipment and experience.

Valve Springs

INSPECTION

1. Place the valve spring on a flat, clean surface, next to a square.
2. Measure the height of the spring and rotate it against the edge of the square to measure the distortion (out-of-roundness). If the spring height between springs varies or the distortion exceeds more than 1.6mm, replace the spring(s). The valve spring squareness should not exceed: 2.20mm (outer) or 1.90mm (inner)

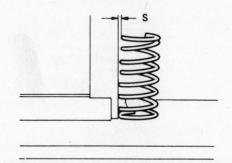

Measuring the spring height and squareness. Make sure the closed coils face downward

Testing the spring pressure

Lapping the valve seat and the valve

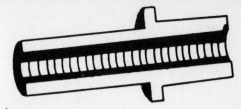

Cross-section view of a knurled valve guide

3. A valve spring tester is needed to test the spring pressure. Compare the tested pressure with the pressures listed in the Valve Specifications chart in this section.

Valve Seats

REMOVAL AND INSTALLATION

NOTE: *To prevent damaging the other cylinder head components, completely disassemble the head.*

1. The old valve seat can be removed by machining it from the head or by heating the head in an 302-320°F (150-160°C) oil bath, then driving it from the head with a punch.

NOTE: *When removing the valve insert, be careful not to damage the cylinder head surface.*

2. Select a valve insert replacement and check the outside diameter, then ream the cylinder head recess at room temperature.

3. Heat the cylinder head to 302-320°F (150-160°C) in an oil bath, then press in the new valve seat, until it seats in the recess.

CUTTING THE SEATS

1. Allow the cylinder head to cool to room temperature. Using a valve seating tool kit, cut a new valve contact surface on the valve seat.

NOTE: *When repairing the valve seat, make sure that the valve and the guide are in good condition; if wear is evident, replace the valve and/or the guide, then correct the valve seat.*

2. To complete the operation, use valve grinding compound and lap the valve to the seat.

3. To install the removed components, reverse the removal procedures.

Valve Guides

REMOVAL AND INSTALLATION

1. Using a 2-ton press or a hammer and a suitable driving tool, drive the old valve guide from the cylinder head, in the rocker cover to combustion chamber direction.

NOTE: *Heating the cylinder head to 302-392°F (150-200°C) will facilitate the operation.*

2. Using the Valve Guide Reamer tool KV11081000 (F10) or ST11081000 (all other models, ream the valve guide hole.

3. Using a new valve guide, press it into the cylinder head and ream the guide hole with the proper size reamer.

4. Using a valve seating tool kit, cut a new valve contact on the valve seat.

5. To install the removed components, reverse the removal procedures.

KNURLING

Valve guides which are not excessively worn or distorted may in some cases, be knurled rather than reamed. Knurling is a process in which metal inside the valve guide bores is displaced and raised (forming a very fine cross-hatch pattern), thereby reducing clearance. Knurling also provides for excellent oil control. The possibility of knurling rather than reaming the guides should be discussed with a machinist.

Oil Pan

REMOVAL AND INSTALLATION

All Models except 1987-88 Pulsar

1. If the engine is in the vehicle, attach a lift, support the engine, and remove the engine mounting bolts.

2. Raise the engine slightly, watching to make sure that no hoses or wires are damaged.

3. Drain the engine oil.

CAUTION: *The EPA warns that prolonged contact with used engine oil may cause a number of skin disorders, including cancer! You should make every effort to minimize your exposure to used engine oil. Protective gloves should be worn when changing the oil. Wash your hands and any other exposed skin areas as soon as possible after exposure to used engine oil. Soap and water, or waterless hand cleaner should be used.*

4. Remove the oil pan bolts and slide the pan out to the rear.

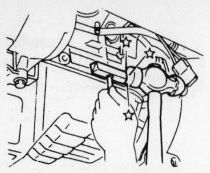

Using a seal cutter on the oil pan

To install the pan:

5. Use a new gasket, coated on both sides with sealer.

6. Apply a thin bead of silicone seal to the engine block at the junction of the block and front cover, and the junction of the block and rear main bearing cap. Then apply a thin coat of silicone seal to the new oil pan gasket, install the gasket to the block and install the pan.

7. Tighten the pan bolts in a circular pattern from the center to the ends, to 4-7 ft. lbs. Overtightening will distort the pan lip, causing leakage.

8. Reinstall the engine mounting bolts.

9. Refill the oil pan to the specified level.

1987-88 Pulsar

1. Drain the engine oil.

CAUTION: *The EPA warns that prolonged contact with used engine oil may cause a number of skin disorders, including cancer! You should make every effort to minimize your exposure to used engine oil. Protective gloves should be worn when changing the oil. Wash your hands and any other exposed skin areas as soon as possible after exposure to used engine oil. Soap and water, or waterless hand cleaner should be used.*

2. Raise the vehicle and support it with safety stands.

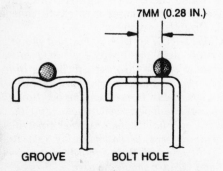

7MM (0.28 IN.)

GROOVE   BOLT HOLE

Apply sealer on the inside of the bolt holes

3. Remove the right side splash cover. Remove the right side under cover.

4. Remove the center member.

5. Remove the forward section of the exhaust pipe.

6. Remove the front buffer rod and its bracket.

7. Remove the engine gussets.

8. Insert a seal cutter (SST KV10111100) between the oil pan and the cylinder block.

NOTE: *DO NOT use a screwdriver!*

9. Tapping the cutter with a hammer, slide it around the oil pan.

10. Remove the oil pan.

11. Remove all old liquid gasket from the pan and block mating surfaces.

12. Apply a continuous bead (3.5-4.5mm) of liquid gasket around the oil pan. Apply the sealer to the *inner* surface around the bolt holes where there is no groove.

13. Wait 5 minutes and then install the pan. Tighten the pan bolts in a circular pattern from the center to the ends, to 4-7 ft. lbs. Overtightening will distort the pan lip, causing leakage.

14. Install the engine gussets, buffer rod, exhaust pipe and center member.

15. Install the right side splash cover and the right side under cover.

16. Refill the oil pan to the specified level. Start engine and check for oil leaks.

Oil Pump
REMOVAL AND INSTALLATION
A-Series Engines

1. Raise and support the vehicle on jackstands.

NOTE: *The oil pump is mounted to the lower right side of the cylinder block. If necessary to have more space, remove the filter from the oil pump.*

2. Remove the oil pump-to-engine mounting bolts, then pull the pump assembly from the engine block.

3. Using a putty knife, clean the gasket mounting surfaces.

4. Pack the pump housing with petroleum jelly.

5. Install the oil pump in the engine, always use a new gasket for the oil pump mounting. Torque the oil pump mounting bolts to 6.5-10 ft. lbs. Start the engine and check for oil leaks.

E-Series Engine

1. Drain the engine oil.

CAUTION: *The EPA warns that prolonged contact with used engine oil may cause a number of skin disorders, including cancer!*

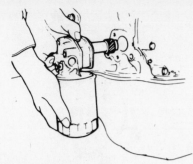

A series oil pump removal

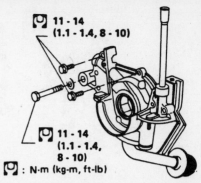

11 - 14
(1.1 - 1.4, 8 - 10)

11 - 14
(1.1 - 1.4,
8 - 10)

: N·m (kg-m, ft-lb)

Oil pump—CA20 and CA16DE/CA18DE engines

You should make every effort to minimize your exposure to used engine oil. Protective gloves should be worn when changing the oil. Wash your hands and any other exposed skin areas as soon as possible after exposure to used engine oil. Soap and water, or waterless hand cleaner should be used.

2. Loosen the alternator lower bolts.

3. Remove the alternator belt and adjusting bar bolt.

4. Move the alternator out of the way and support it safely.

5. Disconnect the oil pressure gauge harness.

6. Remove the oil filter.

7. Remove the pump assembly.

8. For installation, fill the pump with clean engine oil and rotate it several times or pack the pump housing with petroleum jelly.

9. Install the pump on the engine using a new gasket. Torque the pump mounting bolts to 7-9 ft. lbs.

10. Install the oil filter and the oil pressure gauge harness connections.

11. Install the alternator, belt and bracket.

12. Start the engine and check for leaks.

CA20 Engines
CA16DE Engine
CA18DE Engine

1. Disconnect the negative battery cable. Remove all accessory drive belts and the alternator.

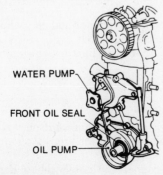

WATER PUMP

FRONT OIL SEAL

OIL PUMP

CA20 oil pump installed

2. Remove the timing (cam) belt covers and remove the timing belt.

3. On the Stanza wagon, unbolt the engine from its mounts and lift or jack the engine up from the unibody. On the Stanza (exc. wagon) and Pulsar, remove the center member from the body.

4. Remove the oil pan.

5. Remove the oil pump assembly along with the oil strainer.

6. If installing a new or rebuilt oil pump, first pack the pump cavity full of petroleum jelly to prevent the pump from cavitating when the engine is started. Apply RTV sealer to the front oil seal end of the pan prior to installation. Install the pump and the strainer as an assembly, torque the mounting bolts to 9-12 ft. lbs.

NOTE: *Always use a new O-ring when installing the strainer to the pump body.*

7. Install the oil pan and bolt the engine in place.

8. Install the center member if it was removed.

9. Install the timing belt and covers.

10. Install the alternator and all drive belts. Reconnect the negative battery cable.

11. Start engine and check for leaks.

Timing Chain/Belt Cover
REMOVAL AND INSTALLATION

A-Series Engines

NOTE: *It may be necessary to raise the vehicle, then remove the wheel assembly and the splash shield.*

1. Disconnect the negative battery cable. Drain the cooling system.

CAUTION: *When draining the coolant, keep in mind that cats and dogs are attracted by the ethylene glycol antifreeze, and are quite likely to drink any that is left in an uncovered container or in puddles on the ground. This will prove fatal in sufficient quantity. Always*

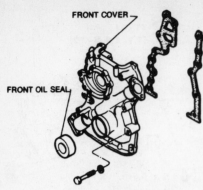

Front cover—A-series engines

Bolt location on timing belt covers—E series engines

drain the coolant into a sealable container. Coolant should be reused unless it is contaminated or several years old.

2. Loosen the alternator adjustment and remove the drive belt.

NOTE: *It may be necessary to remove the alternator and the mounting bracket(s). If equipped with air conditioning, an air pump or power steering, loosen the adjustment(s) and remove the drive belt(s).*

3. Using a socket and a long handle, remove the crankshaft pulley nut, the washer and the pulley.

NOTE: *On certain models, it is recommended that the oil pan be removed or loosened before the front cover is removed.*

4. Remove the water pump pulley and the water pump. Remove the timing chain cover.

5. Replace the crankshaft oil seal in the cover. Most models use a felt seal.

6. Using a putty knife, clean the gasket mounting surfaces.

7. Install the timing chain cover with a new seal on the engine, use new gaskets and sealant. Torque the timing chain cover bolts to 4-5 ft. lbs., the water pump bolts to 7-10 ft. lbs., the oil pan bolts to 11-14 ft. lbs. and the crankshaft pulley bolt to 108-145 ft. lbs.

8. Install the alternator and all the drive belts that were removed. Adjust all drive belts.

9. Install the wheel assembly and splash shield if it was removed.

10. Connect the negative battery cable. Refill the cooling sustem.

11. Start engine and check for leaks.

E-Series Engines

NOTE: *The front crankshaft oil seal can only be replaced when the crankshaft sprocket is removed.*

1. Disconnect the battery, drain the cooling system, and remove the radiator together with the upper and lower radiator hoses.

CAUTION: *When draining the coolant, keep*

in mind that cats and dogs are attracted by the ethylene glycol antifreeze, and are quite likely to drink any that is left in an uncovered container or in puddles on the ground. This will prove fatal in sufficient quantity. Always drain the coolant into a sealable container. Coolant should be reused unless it is contaminated or several years old.

2. Loosen the air conditioning belt and remove.

3. Loosen the alternator adjusting bolt, and remove the alternator belt. Unbolt the alternator mounting bracket and remove the alternator.

4. Remove the power steering belt (if equipped) by loosening the steering pump adjusting bolt.

5. Remove the water pump pulley.

6. Remove crankshaft pulley. Support the engine and remove the right side engine mount bracket.

7. Loosen and remove the 8 torx head bolts securing the timing covers and remove the upper and lower covers.

8. Install the timing belt covers and torque the belt cover bolts to 2.7-3.7 ft. lbs. and reconnect the engine mounting bracket.

9. Install the crankshaft pulley in place and torque the crank pulley bolt to 83-108 ft. lbs.

10. Install the water pump pulley.

11. Install the alternator and all the drive belts.

12. Install the radiator and all cooling hoses. Refill the cooling system.

13. Connect the battery cable and start engine.

CA20 Engines

NOTE: *The front crankshaft oil seal can only be replaced when the crankshaft sprocket is removed.*

1. Disconnect the battery cables. Remove the upper and lower alternator securing bolts until

the alternator can be moved enough to remove the drive belt from the pulley.

2. Loosen the idler pulley locknut and turn the adjusting bolt until the air conditioner compressor belt can be removed.

3. Unbolt and remove the crankshaft pulley, removing the alternator belt along with it. Remove the crankshaft damper.

4. Unbolt and remove the water pump pulley.

5. Remove the upper and lower timing belt covers and their gaskets. If the gaskets are in good condition after removal, they can be reused; if they are in way damaged or broken, replace them.

6. Install the timing belt covers in place. Torque the front cover bolts evenly to 2.2-3.6 ft. lbs; torque the crank pulley damper bolt to 90-98 ft. lbs.; torque the crank pulley bolt to 9-10 ft. lbs.; torque the water pump pulley bolts to 4.3-7 ft. lbs.

7. Install and adjust all drive belts.

8. Connect the battery cables and start engine.

CA16DE and CA18DE Engines

For removal and installation of the timing belt upper and lower covers refer to the timing belt procedures.

Timing Belt and/or Chain
REMOVAL AND INSTALLATION

A-Series w/Overhead Valve Engines

It is recommended that this operation be done with the engine removed from the vehicle.

1. Refer to the Timing Chain Cover, Removal and Installation procedures in this section and remove the cover.

2. Remove the oil throw and the chain tensioner.

3. Turn the crankshaft so that the dowel pin hole in the camshaft sprocket is facing the crankshaft sprocket and the crankshaft sprocket is facing directly away from the camshaft sprocket (see illustration).

4. Remove the camshaft sprocket retaining bolt.

5. Pull off the camshaft sprocket with the timing chain, if necessary, ease off the crankshaft sprocket.

NOTE: *If possible, remove both sprockets and the timing chain as an assembly. Be careful not to lose the shims from behind the crankshaft sprocket.*

6. Using a putty knife, clean the gasket mounting surface.

7. To install, insert the sprockets temporarily and make sure that they are parallel; adjust by shimming under the crankshaft sprocket.

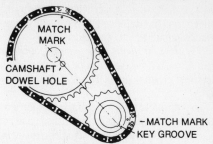

A series engine timing mark alignment

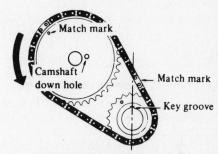

Timing chain sprocket positions with the No. 1 piston at TDC—A-series engine

Correct projection "L":
**Less than
15 mm (0.59 in)**

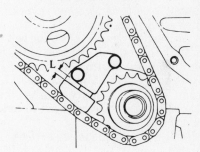

Measuring the chain tensioner gap—A-series engine

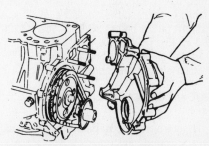

Installing the A-series timing chain cover. Note slinger on end of crankshaft

8. Assemble the sprockets with the chain, aligning them.

9. Turn the crankshaft counterclockwise until the crankshaft keyway and the No. 1 piston

are at the TDC (see illustration); the engine is timed correctly. Replaced the oil slinger with the concave surface to the front.

NOTE: *If installation is correct, the camshaft sprocket marks must be aligned between the shaft centers when the No. 1 piston is at TDC.*

10. To complete the installation, use a new gasket, sealant and install the timing case cover but first, torque the camshaft sprocket retaining bolt to 29-35 ft. lbs., the chain tensioner bolt to 4-6 ft. lbs. and the timing cover to 4-5 ft. lbs.

NOTE: *If the timing chain tensioner adjusting gap L, is greater than 15mm, replace the timing chain.*

11. Start the engine and check the timing.

CA20 and E-Series Overhead Camshaft Engines

1. Refer to the Timing Belt Cover, Removal and Installation procedures, in this section and remove the timing cover.

2. If necessary, remove the spark plug, then turn the crankshaft to position the No. 1 piston at TDC of the compression stroke.

NOTE: *Note the position of the timing marks on the camshaft sprocket, the timing belt and the crankshaft sprocket (see illustrations). Most CA20 engine, camshaft sprockets are similiar in design to the E-series engine; if necessary, install the camshaft sprocket exactly as the E-series engine.*

3. Loosen and/or remove the timing belt tensioner. Mark the rotation direction of the timing belt, then remove it from the sprockets.

4. To remove the front oil seal, pull off the crankshaft sprocket, then pry out the oil seal with a small pry bar (be careful not to scratch the crankshaft).

5. Clean the oil seal mounting surface.

6. Install a new oil seal, the timing belt and tensioner. Torque the tensioner pulley bolts to 13-16 ft. lbs. (CA20) or 12-15 ft. lbs. (E-series), the timing cover bolts to 2.5-4 ft. lbs., the crankshaft pulley bolt to 90-98 ft. lbs. (CA20) or 83-108 ft. lbs. (E-series).

7. Install the timing belt covers.

8. Start engine and check timing.

CA16DE and CA18DE Double Overhead Camshaft Engines

1. Disconnect the negative battery cable. Drain the cooling system.

CAUTION: *When draining the coolant, keep in mind that cats and dogs are attracted by the ethylene glycol antifreeze, and are quite likely to drink any that is left in an uncovered container or in puddles on the ground. This will prove fatal in sufficient quantity. Always drain the coolant into a sealable container.*

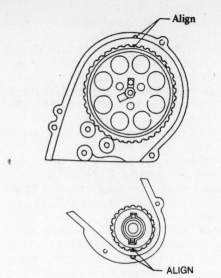

E series engine valve timing mark alignment

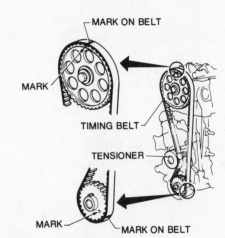

CA20 valve timing mark alignment

Coolant should be reused unless it is contaminated or several years old.

2. Disconnect the upper radiator hose at the elbow and then position it out of the way.

3. Remove the right side engine undercover.

4. Loosen the power steering pump and the air conditioning compressor and then remove the drive belts.

5. Remove the water pump pulley.

6. Matchmark the crank angle sensor to the upper front cover and the remove it. Carefully position it out of the way.

7. Position a floor jack under the engine and raise it just enough to support the engine.

8. Remove the upper engine mount bracket at the right side of the upper front cover.

9. Remove the upper front cover.

10. Align the timing marks on the camshaft pulley sprockets and then remove the crankshaft pulley.

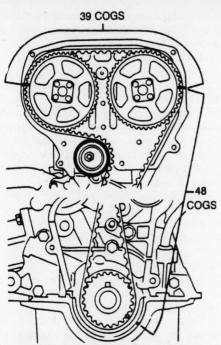

39 COGS

48 COGS

Timing belt timing mark alignment— CA16DE and CA18DE

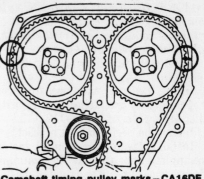

Camshaft timing pulley marks—CA16DE and CA18DE

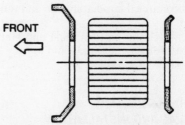

FRONT

FRONT SPROCKET PLATE   REAR SPROCKET PLATE

Crankshaft sprocket plate installation— CA16DE and CA18DE

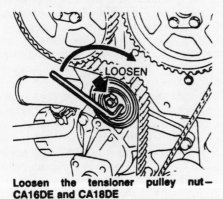

LOOSEN

Loosen the tensioner pulley nut— CA16DE and CA18DE

NOTE: *The crankshaft pulley may be reached by removing the side cover from inside the righthand wheel opening.*

11. Remove the lower front cover.

12. Loosen the tensioner pulley nut to slacken the timing belt and then slide off the belt.

To install:

NOTE: *Do not bend or twist the timing belt. NEVER rotate the crankshaft and camshaft separately with the timing belt removed. Be sure the timing belt is free of any oil, water or debris.*

13. Install the crankshaft sprocket with the sprocket plates.

14. Before installing the timing belt, ensure that the No. 1 piston is at TDC of the compres-

sion stroke (all sprocket timing marks will be in alignment with the marks on the case).

When the timing belt is on and in position, there should be 39 cogs between the timing mark on each of the camshaft sprocket and 48 cogs between the mark on the right camshaft sprocket and the mark on the crankshaft sprocket.

15. Loosen the timing belt tensioner pulley nut.

16. Temporarily install the crankshaft pulley bolt and then rotate the engine two complete revolutions.

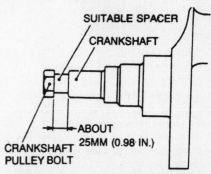

SUITABLE SPACER

CRANKSHAFT

ABOUT 25MM (0.98 IN.)

CRANKSHAFT PULLEY BOLT

A spacer must be installed between the crankshaft and pulley bolt head before rotating the engine—CA16DE and CA18DE

NOTE: *Fabricate and install a suitable 25mm thick spacer between the end of the crankshaft and the head of the crankshaft pulley bolt to prevent bolt damage.*

17. Tighten the tensioner pulley bolt to 16-22 ft. lbs.

18. Install the upper and lower front covers.

19. Install the crankshaft pulley with its washer and tighten it to 105-112 ft. lbs.

20. Install the engine mount bracket.

21. Install the water pump pulley. Install the crankangle sensor so that the matchmarks made previously line up and tighten the bolts to 5.1-5.8 ft. lbs.

22. Install all drive belts and adjust.

23. Install the right side engine undercover.

24. Reconnect the radiator hose and refill the radiator.

25. Connect the battery cable and start the engine. Check engine timing and for any leaks. Road test.

Camshaft Sprocket

REMOVAL AND INSTALLATION

1. Refer to the "Timing Belt/Chain, Removal and Installation" procedures, in this section and remove the timing chain/belt.

2. Remove the sprocket retaining bolt and remove the sprocket from the camshaft. On engines with a timing chain the chain and sprocket are removed at the same time.

3. To install, use new gaskets and reverse the removal procedures.

Camshaft and Bearings

REMOVAL AND INSTALLATION

For the following procedure, the engine should be removed from the vehicle and installed on an engine stand. Remove the right side engine mount and install the Engine Attachment tool No. KV10102500 (all engines), plus No. KV10107110 (E-series) to the attaching studs.

A-Series

1. Refer to the Timing Belt and/or Chain, Removal and Installation procedures in this section and remove the timing chain.

2. Disconnect the high tension wires from the spark plugs, then remove the distributor assembly from the engine.

3. Remove the rocker arm cover, the rocker arm shaft assembly and the push rods (keep the rods in order).

NOTE: *Before removing the rocker arm assembly, loosen and back off the valve adjusters.*

4. Drain the engine oil. Remove the oil pump and the filter assembly, then invert the engine and remove the oil pan.

CAUTION: *The EPA warns that prolonged contact with used engine oil may cause a number of skin disorders, including cancer! You should make every effort to minimize your exposure to used engine oil. Protective gloves should be worn when changing the oil. Wash your hands and any other exposed skin areas as soon as possible after exposure to used engine oil. Soap and water, or waterless hand cleaner should be used.*

5. Remove the clutch and the flywheel assembly from the crankshaft.

6. Disconnect the connecting rods from the crankshaft (DO NOT remove the piston assemblies from the engine) and the crankshaft from the engine block.

NOTE: *When removing the connecting rod and the crankshaft bearings, be certain to keep the parts in order.*

7. Remove the camshaft sprocket bolt, then separate the sprocket from the camshaft. Remove the camshaft thrust plate, then pull the camshaft out through the front of the engine.

8. If necessary to replace the camshaft bearings, use a hammer and the Camshaft Bearing Drift tool No. ST16110000, to drive out and install the bearings in the cylinder block.

NOTE: *After replacing the camshaft bearings, finish the bearing inner diameters by line boring. Using sealant install a new welch plug into the cylinder block.*

9. Install the camshaft in the engine block, use new gaskets. Torque the camshaft sprocket bolt to 29-35 ft. lbs., the timing chain cover bolts to 3.5-5 ft. lbs., the camshaft locating plate to 3-4 ft. lbs., the crankshaft pulley bolt to 108-145 ft. lbs., the main bearing cap bolts to 36-43 ft. lbs., the connecting rod cap bolts to 23-27 ft. lbs. and the rocker shaft bracket bolts to 14-18 ft. lbs. With the camshaft mounted correctly in the cylinder block, mount a dial indicator on the sprocket bolt and check the end play; if it exceeds 0.010mm, replace the locating plate.

10. Install the distributor assembly, spark plugs and wires.

11. Install the engine in the vehicle. Adjust the valves and the drive belts, then refill the cooling and the lubrication systems. Start the engine, then check and/or adjust the timing.

CA16DE and CA18DE Engines

NOTE: *Since these engines DO NOT use replaceable camshaft bearings, overhaul is performed by replacement of the camshaft or the cylinder head. Check the camshaft bearing surfaces (in the cylinder head) with an inter-*

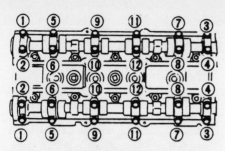

Loosen the camshaft bearing cap bolts in this order—CA16DE and CA18DE

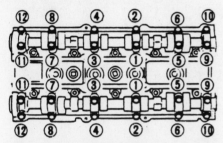

Tighten the camshaft bearing caps in this order—CA16DE and CA18DE

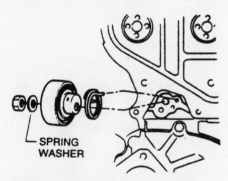

Timing belt tensioner installation—CA16DE and CA18DE

nal micrometer and the bearing surfaces (of the camshaft) with a micrometer.

1. Remove the timing belt.
2. Remove the camshaft cover.
3. Remove the breather separater.
4. Remove the cylinder head.
5. While holding the camshaft sprockets, remove the 4 mounting bolts and then remove the sprockets themselves.
6. Remove the timing belt tensioner pulley. Remove the rear timing belt cover.
7. Loosen the camshaft bearing caps in several stages, in the order shown. Remove the bearing caps, but be sure to keep them in order.
8. Remove the front oil seals and then lift out the camshafts.
9. Check the camshaft runout, endplay, wear

and journal clearance. Refer to the camshaft specification chart.

To install:

10. Position the camshafts in the cylinder head so the knockpin on each is on the outboard side.

NOTE: *The exhaust side camshaft has splines to accept the crank angle sensor.*

11. Position the camshaft bearing caps and finger tighten them. Each cap has an ID mark and a directional arrow stamped into its top surface.

12. Coat a NEW oil seal with engine oil (on the lip) and install it on each camshaft end.

13. Tighten the camshaft bearing cap bolts to 7-9 ft. lbs. in the order shown.

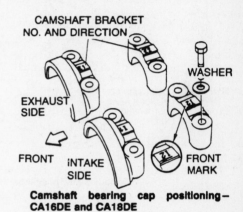

Camshaft bearing cap positioning—CA16DE and CA18DE

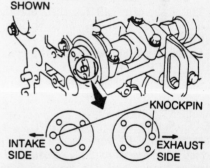

Install the camshaft as shown—CA16DE and CA18DE

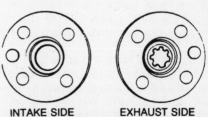

The exhaust side camshaft is splined—CA16DE and CA18DE

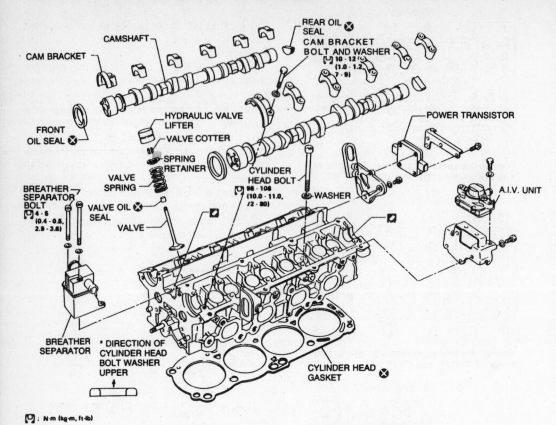

CAMSHAFT

CAM BRACKET

REAR OIL ⊗ SEAL

CAM BRACKET BOLT AND WASHER
〔U〕 10 - 12 (V)
(1.0 - 1.2,
7 - 9)

POWER TRANSISTOR

HYDRAULIC VALVE LIFTER

VALVE COTTER

FRONT OIL SEAL ⊗

SPRING RETAINER

VALVE SPRING

CYLINDER HEAD BOLT
〔U〕 98 - 108
(10.0 - 11.0,
/2 - 80)

WASHER

A.I.V. UNIT

BREATHER SEPARATOR BOLT
〔U〕 4 - 5
(0.4 - 0.5,
2.9 - 3.6)

VALVE OIL ⊗ SEAL

VALVE

BREATHER SEPARATOR

• DIRECTION OF CYLINDER HEAD BOLT WASHER UPPER

CYLINDER HEAD GASKET ⊗

〔U〕 : N·m (kg-m, ft-lb)

Exploded view of cylinder head—CA16DE/CA18DE engines

14. Install the rear timing cover.

15. Install the timing belt tensioner and tighten it to 16-22 ft. lbs.

16. Install the camshaft sprockets and tighten the bolts to 10-14 ft. lbs. while holding the camshaft in place.

17. Install the timing belt and the cylinder head.

18. Start engine, check timing and road test.

CA20 Series Engine

NOTE: *Since these engines DO NOT use replaceable camshaft bearings, overhaul is performed by replacement of the camshaft or the cylinder head. Check the camshaft bearing surfaces (in the cylinder head) with an internal micrometer and the bearing surfaces (of the camshaft) with a micrometer.*

1. Set the No. 1 piston to TDC of the compression stroke and then remove the timing belt.

2. Remove the valve rocker cover.

3. Fully loosen all rocker arm adjusting screws (the valve adjusting screws). Loosen the rocker shaft mounting bolts in two or three stages and then remove the rocker shafts as an assembly. Keep all components in the correct order for reassembly.

4. Hold the camshaft pulley and remove the pulley mounting bolt. Remove the pulley.

5. Carefully pry the camshaft oil seal out of the front of the cylinder head.

6. Slide the camshaft out the front of the cylinder head, taking extreme care not to score any of the journals.

To install:

7. Coat the camshaft with clean engine oil.

8. Carefully slide the camshaft into the cylinder head, coat the end with oil and install a NEW oil seal.

9. Lubricate the rocker shafts lightly and in-

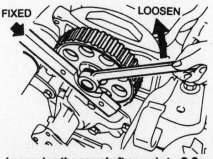

FIXED   LOOSEN

Loosening the camshaft sprocket—C-Series engines

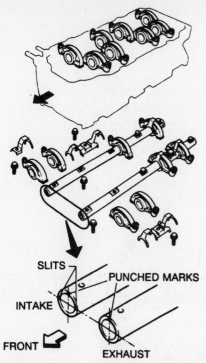

Rocker shaft assembly—C-Series engines

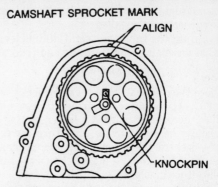

CAMSHAFT SPROCKET MARK
ALIGN
KNOCKPIN

Camshaft sprocket alignment—E-Series engines

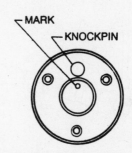

MARK
KNOCKPIN

Camshaft positioning—E-Series engines

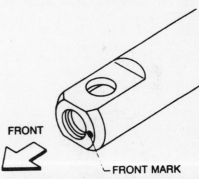

FRONT
FRONT MARK

The punch mark on the rocker shaft should face forward—E-Series engines

stall them, with the rocker arms, into the head. Both shafts have punchmarks on their leading edges, while the intake shaft is also marked with two slits on its leading edge.

NOTE: *To prevent the rocker shaft springs from slipping out of the shaft, insert the bracket bolts into the shaft prior to installation.*

10. Tighten the rocker shaft bolts gradually, in two or three stages.

11. Install the camshaft pulley and then install the timing belt.

12. Adjust the valves and install the cylinder head cover.

13. Start engine, check timing and road test.

E-Series Engines

1. Remove the cylinder head.

2. Remove the rocker shaft along with the rocker arms. Loosen the bolts gradually, in two or three stages.

3. Carefully slide the camshaft out the front of the cylinder head.

4. Check the camshaft runout, endplay, wear and journal clearance. Refer to the camshaft specifications chart.

To install:

5. Slide the camshaft into the cylinder head carefully and then install a NEW oil seal.

6. Install the cylinder head and rear timing belt cover.

7. Set the camshaft so that the knockpin faces upward and then install the camshaft sprocket so its timing mark aligns with the one on the rear timing cover.

8. Install the timing belt.

9. Coat the rocker shaft and the interior of the rocker arm with engine oil. Install them so the punchmark on the shaft faces forward and the oil holes in the shaft face down. The cut-out in the center retainer on the shaft should face the exhaust manifold side of the engine.

10. Make sure tha valve adjusting screws are loosened and then tighten the shaft bolts to 13-15 ft. lbs. in several stages, from the center out.

The first and last mounting bolts should have a new bolt stopper installed.

11. Adjust the valves and refill all fluid levels.

12. Start engine, check timing and road test.

CHECKING CAMSHAFT

Place the camshaft on a set of V-blocks, supported by the outermost bearing surfaces. Place a dial micrometer, with it's finger resting on the center bearing surface, then turn the camshaft to check the runout; the runout should not exceed 0.010mm, if it does exceed the limit, replace the camshaft.

Check the camshaft bearing surfaces (in the

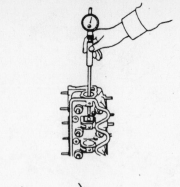

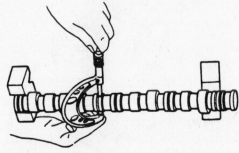

Checking camshaft journal clearance (inside and outside measurement)

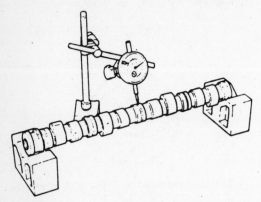

Checking the camshaft runout using a dail micrometer

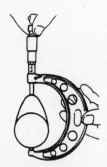

Checking camshaft height

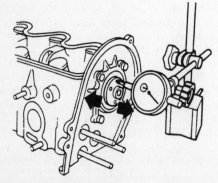

Checking camshaft end play

engine) with an internal micrometer and the bearing surfaces (of the camshaft) with a micrometer.

Jack Shaft — E-Series Engine

REMOVAL AND INSTALLATION

1. Refer to the Timing Belt and/or Chain, Removal and Installation procedures in this section and remove the timing belt.

2. Pull the crankshaft sprocket from the crankshaft. Remove the jackshaft sprocket bolts, then separate the sprocket from the jackshaft.

3. Remove the lower locating plate from the cylinder block. Remove the jackshaft and the crankshaft oil seals from the locating plate.

4. Remove the jackshaft retaining plate, then pull the shaft out through the front of the cylinder block.

5. Check the jackshaft bearing diameters (in the cylinder block) with an internal micrometer and the bearing diameters (of the jackshaft) with a micrometer; the clearance should not exceed 0.15mm, if it does exceed the limit, replace the jackshaft bearings.

6. Use a hammer and a brass drift, to remove and install the jackshaft bearings in the cylinder block.

NOTE: *Be sure to align the oil hole in the bearing with the hole in the cylinder block. After installation, check the bearing clear-*

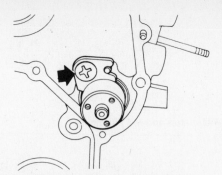

Removing the jackshaft retaining plate

USE A SHORT
PIECE OF 3/8"
HOSE AS A
GUIDE

Use lengths of vacuum hose or rubber tubing to protect the crankshaft journals and cylinder walls during piston installation

ances. Using sealant, install a new welch plug into the cylinder block.

7. Install the jackshaft in the cylinder block with the retaining plate. Torque the jackshaft sprocket bolts to 6.5-9 ft. lbs., the oil pump bolts to 5.8-7.2 ft. lbs., the tensioner pulley bolts to 12-15 ft. lbs., the timing cover bolts to 2.5-4 ft. lbs., the crankshaft pulley bolt to 83-108 ft. lbs.

8. Install the lower locating plate on cylinder block with oil new seals.

9. Install both sprockets and the timing belt.

10. Start engine, check timing and road test.

Pistons and Connecting Rods

REMOVAL AND INSTALLATION

It is recommended that the engine be removed from the vehicle and mount it on an engine stand, before removing the pistons and connecting rods from the engine.

1. Refer to the Cylinder Head, Removal and Installation procedures in this section and remove the cylinder head.

2. Using a ridge reamer tool, remove the carbon buildup from the top of the cylinder wall.

3. Drain the lubricant from the engine. Invert the engine on the stand, then remove the oil pan, the oil strainer and the pickup tube.

CAUTION: *The EPA warns that prolonged contact with used engine oil may cause a number of skin disorders, including cancer! You should make every effort to minimize your exposure to used engine oil. Protective gloves should be worn when changing the oil. Wash your hands and any other exposed skin areas as soon as possible after exposure to used engine oil. Soap and water, or waterless hand cleaner should be used.*

4. Position the piston to be removed at the bottom of its stroke, so that the connecting rod bearing cap can be easily reached.

5. Remove the connecting rod bearing cap nuts and the cap and the lower half of the bearing. Cover the rod bolts with lengths of rubber

tubing or hose to protect the cylinder walls when the rod and piston assembly is driven out.

6. Push the piston/connecting rod assembly, out through the top of the cylinder block with a length of wood or a wooden hammer handle.

NOTE: *When removing the piston/connect-*

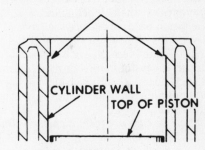

CYLINDER WALL
TOP OF PISTON

Ridge caused by cylinder wear

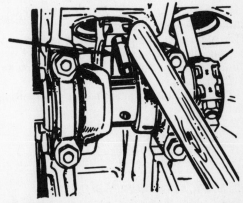

Driving out the piston assemblies with a wooden hammer handle. Note the tubing covering the rod bolts (arrow)

RING COMPRESSOR

Lubricate the components, compress the rings and drive the piston into the bore

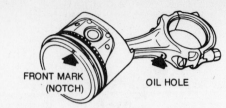

FRONT MARK (NOTCH)   OIL HOLE

CA20 piston and rod alignment

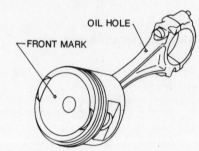

OIL HOLE

FRONT MARK

E series engine piston and rod alignment

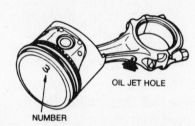

OIL JET HOLE

NUMBER

A series engine piston and rod alignment

ing rod assembly, be careful not to scratch the cylinder wall with the connecting rod.

7. Keep all of the components from each cylinder together and install them in the cylinder from which they were removed.

8. Lubricate all of the piston/connecting rod components with engine oil, including the bearing face of the connecting rod and the outer face of the pistons with engine oil.

NOTE: See the illustrations for the correct positioning of the piston rings.

9. Turn the crankshaft until the rod journal of the particular cylinder you are working on is brought to the TDC position.

10. Clamp the piston/ring assembly into a ring compressor, the notched mark or number (on the piston head) must face the front of the engine and the oil hole (on the side of the connecting rod) must face the right side of the engine; push the piston/connecting rod assembly into the cylinder bore until the big bearing end of the connecting rod seats on the rod journal of the crankshaft.

NOTE: Use care not to scratch the cylinder wall with the connecting rod.

11. Push down on the piston/connecting rod assembly, while turning the crankshaft (the connecting rod rides around on the crankshaft rod journal), until the crankshaft rod journal is at the BDC (bottom dead center).

12. Align the mark on the connecting rod bearing cap with that on the connecting rod and torque the connecting rod bearing cap bolts to 24-27 ft. lbs.

13. Install the oil strainer, pickup tube and oil pan.

14. Install the cylinder head.

15. Install engine assembly in vehicle.

16. Check all fluid levels and road test.

IDENTIFICATION AND POSITIONING

The pistons are marked with a notch or a number stamped on the piston head. When installed in the engine the notch or number

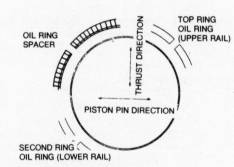

OIL RING SPACER

THRUST DIRECTION

TOP RING
OIL RING (UPPER RAIL)

PISTON PIN DIRECTION

SECOND RING
OIL RING (LOWER RAIL)

A-series piston ring arrangement

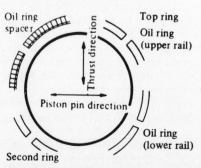

Oil ring spacer

Thrust direction

Top ring
Oil ring (upper rail)

Piston pin direction

Oil ring (lower rail)

Second ring

E-series—piston ring positioning

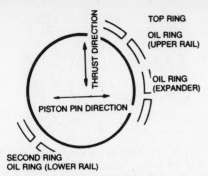

CA20 engine—piston ring positioning

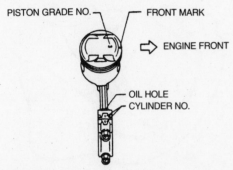

CA16DE/CA18DE engine—piston and rod alignment

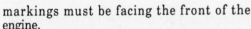

Removing the piston rings with a ring expander

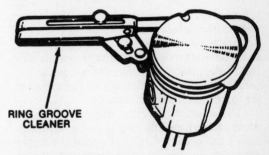

Using a ring groove cleaning tool to properly clean the ring grooves

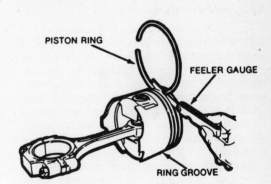

Measuring the piston-to-ring side clearance

markings must be facing the front of the engine.

The connecting rods are installed in the engine with the oil hole facing the right side of the engine.

NOTE: *It is advisable to number the pistons, connecting rods and bearing caps in some manner so that they can be reinstalled in the same cylinder, facing in the same direction from which they are removed.*

CLEANING AND INSPECTION

Clean the piston after removing the rings (Refer to Piston Ring Replacement), by scraping the carbon from the top of the piston (DO NOT scratch the piston surface). Use a broken piston ring or a ring cleaning tool, to clean out the ring grooves. Clean the entire piston and connecting rod with solvent and a brush (NOT a wire brush).

With the piston thoroughly cleaned, place both compression rings on each piston. Using a feeler gauge, check the side clearance of the piston rings. If the side clearance is too large, replace the piston; if the side clearance is too small, cut the land areas a little larger.

Using a feeler gauge to check the ring end gap, lubricate the cylinder wall, then (using an inverted piston) drive the new ring(s) approximately 1-2 inches below the top of the cylinder

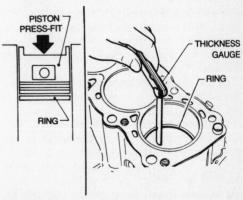

Measuring the piston-to-bore and the piston ring end gap

bore. If the ring gap is too small, carefully remove the rings and file the ends until the proper gap is required.

PISTON PIN REPLACEMENT

The piston pin, the piston and the connecting rod are held together as an assembly, by pressing piston pin into the connecting rod. An arbor press and a special pin removing stand tool No. ST13040000 (F10), KV10105300 (310, 1979-81), KV101070S0 (Stanza) or KV10107400 (310, 1982 and Pulsar), are used for removing and installing the piston pin.

PISTON RING REPLACEMENT

A piston ring expander is necessary for removing and installing the piston rings (to avoid damaging them). When the rings are removed, clean the ring grooves using an appropriate ring groove cleaning tool, using care not to cut too deeply. Use solvent to thoroughly remove all of the carbon and varnish deposits.

When installing the rings, make sure that the stamped mark on the ring is facing upwards. Install the bottom rings first, then the upper ones last. Be sure to use a ring expander, to keep from breaking the rings.

ROD BEARING REPLACEMENT

The connecting rod side clearance and the big-end bearing inspection should be performed while the rods are still installed in the engine. Determine the clearance between the connecting rod sides and the crankshaft, using a feeler gauge. If the side clearance is below the minimum tolerance, have a machine shop correct the tolerance; if the clearance is excessive, substitute an unworn rod and recheck the clearance.

To check the connecting rod big-end bearing clearances, remove the rod bearing caps one at a time. Using a clean, dry shop rag, thoroughly clean all of the oil from the crank journal and the bearing insert in the cap.

NOTE: *The Plastigage® gauging material you will be using to check the clearances with, is soluble in oil; therefore any oil on the journal or bearing could result in an incorrect reading.*

Lay a strip of Plastigage® across the bearing insert. Reinsert the bearing cap and retorque to specifications.

Remove the rod cap and determine the bearing clearance by comparing the width of the now flattened Plastigage® to the scale on the Plastigage® envelope. The journal taper is determined by comparing the width of the strip near its ends. Rotate the crankshaft 90° and retest, to determine the journal eccentricity.

NOTE: *DO NOT rotate the crankshaft with*

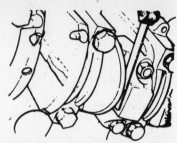

Checking the connecting rod side clearance. Make sure that the feeler gauge is between the shoulder of the crankshaft journal and the side of the rod.

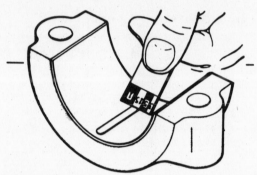

Checking the connecting rod bearing with Plastigage®

Plastigage® installed, for an incorrect reading will result.

If the clearances are not within the tolerances, the bearing inserts must be replaced with ones of the correct oversize or undersize and/or the crankshaft must be ground. If installing new bearing inserts, make sure that the tabs fit correctly into the notch of the bearing cap and rod. Lubricate the face of each insert before installing them onto the crankshaft.

Rear Main Oil Seal
REMOVAL AND INSTALLATION

1. Remove the engine and transaxle assembly from the vehicle.
2. Remove the transaxle from the engine.
3. Remove the clutch/flywheel assembly (manual transmission) or the driveplate (automatic transmission) from the crankshaft.
4. Using a small pry bar, pry the rear main oil seal from around the crankshaft.
5. Apply lithium grease around the sealing lip of the oil seal and install the seal by driving it into the cylinder block using an oil seal installation tool.
6. Install the flywheel or driveplate.
7. Install the transaxle to engine.
8. Install engine and transaxle assembly in the vehicle.

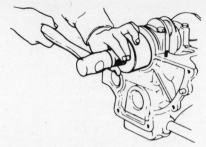

Installing rear main seal

Crankshaft and Main Bearing
REMOVAL AND INSTALLATION

1. Refer to the Piston and Connecting Rod, Removal and Installation procedures, in this section and remove the connecting rod bearings from the crankshaft.

NOTE: *It may not be necessary to remove the piston/connecting rod assemblies from the cylinder block.*

2. On the A-series engine, remove the timing chain and the flywheel from the engine. On the CA20 engine, remove the oil pump from the front of the engine block, then the clutch/flywheel assembly (manual transmission) or driveplate (automatic transmission), the rear oil seal retainer and the rear plate. On the E-series engine, remove the jackshaft sprocket, the crankshaft sprocket, the front side rear timing plate, then the clutch/flywheel assembly (manual transmission) or driveplate (automatic transmission), the rear oil seal retainer and the rear plate. On the CA16DE and CA18DE engines, remove the water pump.

3. Check the crankshaft thrust clearance (end play) before removing the crankshaft from the engine block. Using a pry bar, pry the crankshaft forward to the extent of its travel and measure the clearance at the No. 3 main bearing. Pry the crankshaft rearward to the extent of its travel and measure the clearance on the other side of the bearing.

NOTE: *If the clearance is greater than specified, the thrust bearing must be replaced.*

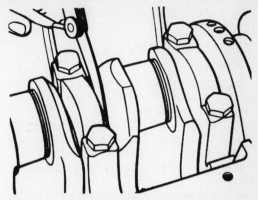

Checking the end-play of the crankshaft with a feeler gauge

When removing the crankshaft bearing caps, be sure to keep the bearing together with the caps, unless new bearings are going to be installed.

4. Remove the crankshaft bearing caps, the cap bearings and the crankshaft from the engine.

5. To install, check the clearances with the Plastigage® method, then replace the bearings if necessary. Torque the crankshaft bearing cap bolts to specifications.

6. Reassemble the engine.

NOTE: *When torquing the main bearing caps, start with the center bearing and work towards both ends at the same time.*

CLEANING AND INSPECTION

The crankshaft inspection and servicing should be handled exclusively by a reputable machinist, for most necessary procedures require a dial indicator, fixing jigs and a large micrometer; also machine tools, such as: crankshaft grinder. The crankshaft should be throughly cleaned (especially the oil passages), Magnafluxed (to check for cracks) and the following checks made: Main journal diameter, crank pin (connecting rod journal) diameter, taper, out-of-round and run-out. Wear, beyond the specification limits, in any of these areas

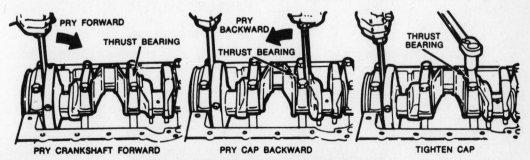

Checking the crankshaft thrust bearing clearance

means the crankshaft must be reground or replaced.

MAIN BEARING CLEARANCE CHECK AND REPLACEMENT

Checking the main bearing clearances is done in the same manner as checking the connecting rod big-end clearances.

1. With the crankshaft installed, remove the main bearing cap. Clean all of the oil from the bearing insert (in the cap and the crankshaft journal), for the Plastigage® material is oil-soluble.

2. Lay a strip of Plastigage® across the full width of the bearing cap and install the bearing cap, then torque the cap to specifications.

NOTE: *DO NOT rotate the crankshaft with the Plastigage® installed.*

3. Remove the bearing cap and compare the scale on the Plastigage® envelope with the flattened Plastigage® material in the bearing. The journal taper is determined by comparing the width of both ends of the Plastigage® material. Rotate the crankshaft 90° and retest, to determine eccentricity.

4. Repeat the procedure for the remaining bearings. If the bearing journal and insert appear to be in good shape (with no unusual wear visible) and are within tolerances, no further main bearing service is required. If unusual wear is evident and/or the clearances are outside specifications, the bearings must be replaced and the cause of their wear determined.

Flywheel and Ring Gear

REMOVAL AND INSTALLATION

F10 and 310 (1979-82)

NOTE: *The clutch cover and the pressure plate are balanced as an assembly; if replacement of either part becomes necessary, replace both parts as an assembly.*

1. Refer to the Clutch, Removal and Installation procedures in Chapter 7 and remove the clutch cover assembly.

2. Remove the flywheel-to-crankshaft bolts and the flywheel.

NOTE: *If necessary the clutch disc should be inspected and/or replaced at this time; the clutch lining wear limit is 0.30mm above the rivet heads.*

3. To install, reverse the removal procedures. Torque the flywheel-to-crankshaft bolts to 58-65 ft. lbs., the clutch cover-to-flywheel bolts and the bearing housing-to-clutch housing bolts to 4.3-7.2 ft. lbs.

Stanza and Pulsar

1. If equipped with a manual transaxle, refer to the Clutch, Removal and Installation proce-

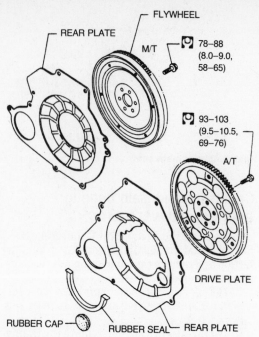

Flywheel and driveplate installation—E16i—others similar

dures in Chapter 7, then remove the transaxle and the clutch assembly. If equipped with an automatic transaxle, refer to the Automatic Transaxle, Removal and Installation procedures in Chapter 7, then remove the transaxle and the torque converter.

2. For manual transaxles, remove the flywheel-to-crankshaft bolts and the flywheel. For automatic transaxles, remove the drive plate-to-crankshaft bolts and the drive plate.

3. To install, reverse the removal procedures. Torque the flywheel-to-crankshaft bolts to 72-80 ft. lbs. (Stanza) or 58-65 ft. lbs. (Pulsar); torque the drive plate-to-crankshaft bolts to 72-80 ft. lbs. (Stanza) or 69-76 ft. lbs. (Pulsar).

NOTE: *On Pulsar CA16DE and CA18DE engines, torque the flywheel-to-crankshaft bolts to 61-69 ft. lbs.*

EXHAUST SYSTEM

Safety Precautions

For a number of reasons, exhaust system work can be dangerous. Always observe the following precautions:

1. Support the vehicle securely by using jackstands or equivalent under the frame of the vehicle.

2. Wear safety goggles to protect your eyes from metal chips that may fly free while working on the exhaust system.

3. If you are using a torch be careful not to come close to any fuel lines.

4. Always use the proper tool for the job.

Special Tools

A number of special exhaust tools can be rented or bought from a local auto parts store. It may also be quite helpful to use solvents designed to loosen rusted nuts or bolts. Remember that these products are often flammable, apply only to parts after they are cool.

Front Pipe

REMOVAL AND INSTALLATION

1. Support the vehicle securely by using jackstands or equivalent under the frame of the vehicle.

2. Remove the exhaust pipe clamps and any front exhaust pipe shield.

3. Soak the exhaust manifold or catalytic converter front pipe mounting studs with penetrating oil. Remove attaching nuts and gasket from the manifold or converter. Pulsar models have 2 catalytic converters.

NOTE: *If these studs snap off, while removing the front pipe the manifold or catalytic converter will have to be removed and the*

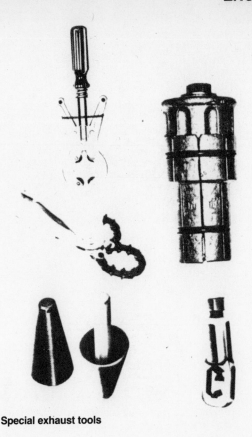

Special exhaust tools

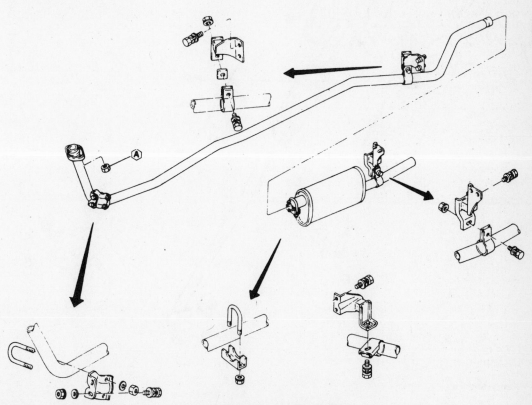

Exhaust system—F10 (Non-Calif.)

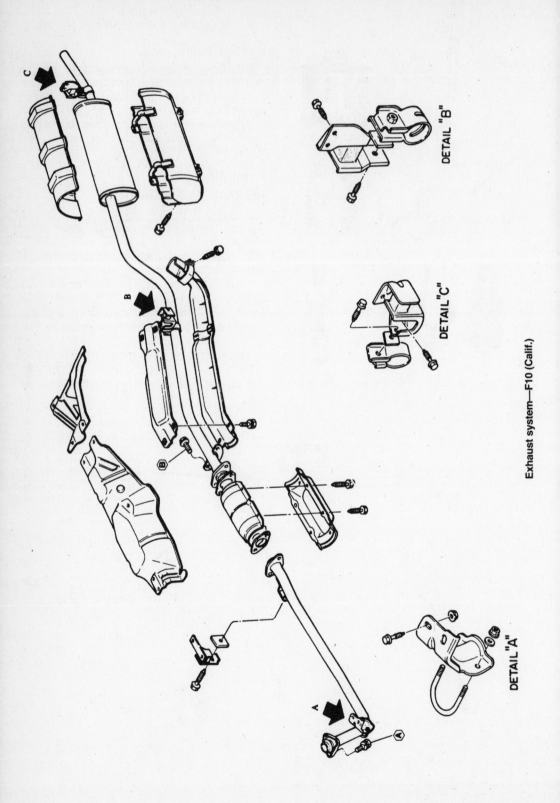

DETAIL "B"

DETAIL "C"

DETAIL "A"

Exhaust system—F10 (Calif.)

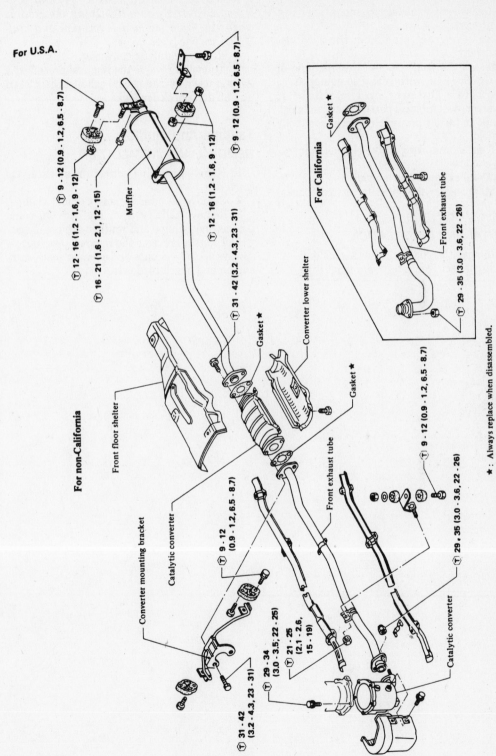

For U.S.A.

Ⓣ 9 - 12 (0.9 - 1.2, 6.5 - 8.7)

Ⓣ 9 - 12 (0.9 - 1.2, 6.5 - 8.7)

Ⓣ 12 - 16 (1.2 - 1.6, 9 - 12)

Muffler

Ⓣ 16 - 21 (1.6 - 2.1, 12 - 15)

Ⓣ 12 - 16 (1.2 - 1.6, 9 - 12)

Ⓣ 31 - 42 (3.2 - 4.3, 23 - 31)

Gasket ★

Converter lower shelter

For non-California

Front floor shelter

Gasket ★

Converter mounting bracket

Catalytic converter

Ⓣ 9 - 12
(0.9 - 1.2, 6.5 - 8.7)

Front exhaust tube

Ⓣ 9 - 12 (0.9 - 1.2, 6.5 - 8.7)

Ⓣ 29 - 34
(3.0 - 3.5, 22 - 25)

Ⓣ 21 - 25
(2.1 - 2.6,
15 - 19)

Ⓣ 29 - 35 (3.0 - 3.6, 22 - 26)

Catalytic converter

Ⓣ 31 - 42
(3.2 - 4.3, 23 - 31)

For California

Gasket ★

Front exhaust tube

Ⓣ 29 - 35 (3.0 - 3.6, 22 - 26)

★ : Always replace when disassembled.

Ⓣ : N·m (kg-m, ft-lb)

Exhaust system—Pulsar—Stanza similar

stud will have to be drill out and the hole tapped.

4. Remove any exhaust pipe mounting hanger or bracket.

5. Remove front pipe from the catalytic connverter.

6. Install the front pipe on the manifold or catalytic converter with seal if so equipped.

7. Install the pipe on the catalytic connverter. Assemble all parts loosely and position pipe to insure proper clearance from body of vehicle.

8. Tighten mounting studs, bracket bolts exhaust clamps.

9. Install exhaust pipe shield.

10. Start engine and check for exhaust leaks.

Catalytic Converter
REMOVAL AND INSTALLATION

1. Remove the converter lower shield.

2. Disconnect converter from front pipe.

3. Disconnect converter from tailpipe.

NOTE: *Assemble all parts loosely and position converter before tightening the exhaust clamps. On some models tail pipe and muffler are one piece.*

4. Remove catalytic converter.

5. To install reverse the removal procedures. Always use new clamps and exhaust seals, start engine and check for leaks.

Tailpipe And Muffler
REMOVAL AND INSTALLATION

1. Remove tailpipe conection at catalytic converter.

2. Remove all brackets and exhaust clamps.

3. Remove tailpipe from muffler. On some models the tailpipe and muffler are one piece.

4. To install reverse the removal procedures. Always use new clamps and exhaust seals, start engine and check for leaks.

Emission Controls

EMISSION CONTROLS

There are three types of automotive pollutants: crankcase fumes, exhaust gases and gasoline evaporation. The equipment that is used to limit these pollutants is commonly called emission control equipment.

Crankcase Ventilation System

The crankcase emission control equipment consists of a positive crankcase ventilation valve (PCV), an oil filler cap (sealed) and hoses (connected to the equipment). The CA20, CA16DE and CA18DE engines use an external oil separator (in the PCV line) to keep excess oil in the crankcase, away from the PCV valve.

OPERATION

When the engine is running, a small portion of the gases which are formed in the combustion chamber during combustion, leak by the piston rings and enter the crankcase. Since these gases are under pressure they tend to escape from the crankcase and enter into the atmosphere. If these gases were allowed to remain in the crankcase for any length of time, they would contaminate the engine oil and cause sludge to build up. If the gases are allowed to escape into the atmosphere, they would pollute the air, for they contain unburned hydrocarbons. The crankcase emission control equipment recycles these gases back into the engine combustion chamber where they are burned.

Crankcase gases are recycled in the following manner: when the engine is running, clean filtered air (from the carburetor air filter) is drawn into the crankcase or the rocker cover, through a hose. As the air passes through the crankcase it mixes with combustion gases, then carries them (out of the crankcase) through the PCV valve and into the intake manifold. After they enter the intake manifold they are drawn into the combustion chamber and burned.

The most critical component in the system is the PCV valve. This vacuum controlled valve regulates the amount of gases which are recycled into the combustion chamber. At low engine speeds, the valve is partially closed, limiting the flow of gases into the intake manifold. At increased engine speeds, the valve opens to admit greater quantities of the gases into the intake manifold. If the valve should become blocked or plugged, the gases will be prevented from escaping from the crankcase by the normal route. Since these gases are under pressure, they will find their own way out of the crankcase. This alternate route is usually a weak oil seal or gasket in the engine. As the gas escapes by the gasket, it also creates an oil leak. Besides causing oil leaks, a clogged PCV valve also allows these gases to remain in the crankcase for an extended period of time, promoting the formation of sludge in the engine.

TESTING AND SERVICE

To check the PCV system, inspect the PCV valve, the air filter(s), the hoses, the connections and the oil separator (CA20, CA16DE and CA18DE engines); check for leaks, plugged valve(s) and/or filters, then replace or tighten, as necessary.

To check the PCV valve, remove it and blow through both of its ends. When blowing from the intake manifold side, very little air should pass through it. When blowing from the crankcase or valve cover side, air should pass through freely.

NOTE: *If the valve fails to function as outlined, replace it with a new one; DO NOT attempt to clean or adjust it.*

To check the hoses, use compressed air to free them or replace them. If the air filters are dirty, replace them.

REMOVAL AND INSTALLATION

To remove the PCV valve, simply loosen the hose clamp and remove the valve from the manifold-to-crankcase hose and intake manifold. Install the PCV valve in the reverse order of removal.

Evaporative Emission Controls

The system consists of sealed fuel tank, vapor/liquid separator (certain models only), vapor vent line, carbon canister, vacuum signal line, a canister purge line and a float bowl vent line (E-series, 1982 and later).

OPERATION

In operation, fuel vapors and/or liquid are routed to the liquid/vapor separator or check valve, where liquid fuel is directed back into the fuel tank as fuel vapors flow into the charcoal filled canister. The charcoal absorbs and stores the fuel vapors when the engine is not running or at idle. When the throttle valves are opened, vacuum from above the throttle valves is routed through a vacuum signal line to the purge control valve on the canister. The control valve opens, the fuel vapors move from the canister through a purge line, into the intake manifold and the combustion chambers.

INSPECTION AND SERVICE

Check the hoses for proper connections and damage. Replace as necessary. Check the vapor separator tank for fuel leaks, distortion and dents, then replace as necessary.

Carbon Canister and Purge Control Valve

To check the operation of the carbon canister purge control valve, disconnect the rubber hose between the canister control valve and the T-fitting, at the T-fitting. Apply vacuum to the hose leading to the control valve. The vacuum condition should be maintained indefinitely. If the control valve leaks, remove the top cover of the valve and check for a dislocated or cracked diaphragm. If the diaphragm is damaged, a repair kit containing a new diaphragm, retainer and spring is available, replace it.

The carbon canister has an air filter in the bottom of the canister. The filter element should be checked once a year or every 12,000 miles; more frequently if the car is operated in dusty areas. Replace the filter by pulling it out of the bottom of the canister and installing a new one.

REMOVAL AND INSTALLATION

Removal and installation of the various evaporative emission control system components consists of disconnecting the hoses, loosening retaining screws and removing the part which is to be replaced or checked. Install in the reverse order. When replacing hose, make sure that it is fuel and vapor resistant.

Spark Plug Switching Control System — CA20 Engine

The system consists of an ignition control unit (installed in the distributor), a vacuum switch (connected to the intake manifold), a clutch switch and a neutral switch (manual transmission) or an inhibitor switch (automatic transmission).

The system is designed to change the ignition system from a 2 plug ignition system to a 1 plug system, during heavy load driving conditions, to reduce engine noise; it also advances the ignition timing by a specified value, during the 1 plug operation.

INSPECTION

1. Disconnect the inhibitor switch connector (automatic transmission) or the clutch switch connector (manual transmission).

2. Disconnect the vacuum hose from the vacuum switch, then connect a vacuum source and gauge to the switch.

3. Connect a timing light to the high tension cable of the exhaust side.

4. Apply 5.91 in. Hg vacuum to the switch and start the engine.

5. Reduce the vacuum gradually, make sure that the timing light does not brighten or dim when the vacuum reaches 3.15 in. Hg or less. If necessary, check and replace each component.

6. Stop the engine and move the timing light to the high tension cable of the intake side, then set the vacuum to 5.91 in.Hg, start the engine and make sure that the timing advances.

Early Fuel Evaporation System

The system's purpose is to heat the air/fuel mixture when the engine is below normal operating temperature. The A-series engines use an exhaust manifold heat riser, the CA20 engines use a coolant water style heater and the E-series use an electric grid style heater. The only adjustment necessary (A-series) is to occasionally lubricate the counterweight, otherwise, the system should be trouble-free; the other systems are trouble-free.

Throttle Opener Control System (TOCS)/Boost Control Deceleration Device (BCDD)

The Throttle Opener Control System (TOCS) is used on A-series (except 1980 and later, Calif.) and the E-series engines; the Boost Con-

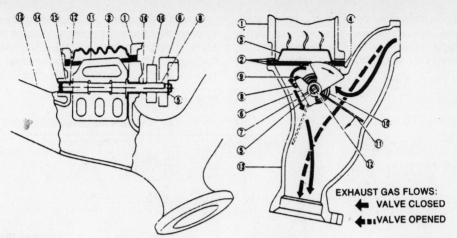

EXHAUST GAS FLOWS:
← VALVE CLOSED
←■▪ VALVE OPENED

1. Intake manifold
2. Stove gasket
3. Manifold stove
4. Heat shield plate
5. Snap ring
6. Counterweight
7. Key
8. Stopper pin
9. Screw
10. Thermostat spring
11. Heat control valve
12. Control valve shaft
13. Exhaust manifold
14. Cap
15. Bushing
16. Coil spring

A-series heat riser type fuel heater

trol Deceleration Device (BCDD) is used on the CA20 engines. The purpose of both systems is to reduce hydrocarbon emissions during coasting conditions.

OPERATIONS

High manifold vacuum during coasting prevents the complete combustion of the air/fuel mixture because of the reduced amount of air. This condition will result in a large amount of HC emission. Enriching the air/fuel mixture for a short time (during the high vacuum condition) will reduce the emission of the HC.

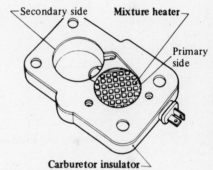

E-series electrical-grid fuel heater

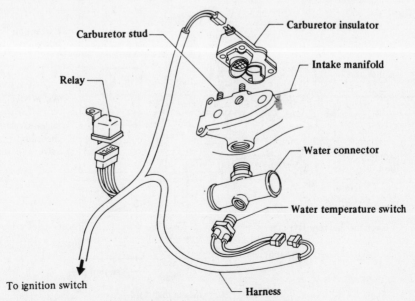

CA20 coolant water heated fuel heater

However, enriching the air/fuel mixture with only the mixture adjusting screw will cause poor engine idle or invite an increase in the carbon monoxide (CO) content of the exhaust gases.

The TOCS system (BCDD system is similar) consists of a servo diaphragm, vacuum control valve, throttle opener solenoid valve, speed detecting switch and amplifier on manual transmission models. Automatic transmission mod-

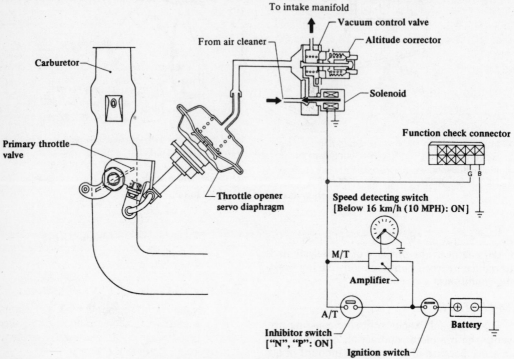

A-series and E-series throttle opener control system

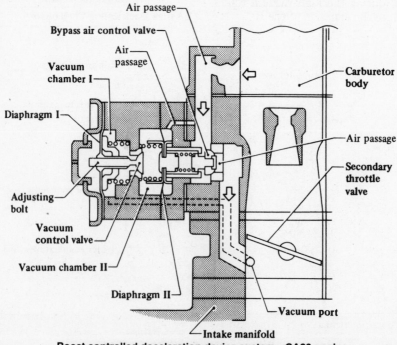

Boost controlled deceleration device system—CA20 engine

els use an inhibitor and inhibitor relay in place of the speed detecting switch and amplifier. At the moment when the manifold vacuum increases, as during deceleration, the vacuum control valve opens to transfer the manifold vacuum to the servo diaphragm chamber and the carburetor throttle valve opens slightly. Under this condition, the proper amount of fresh air is sucked into the combustion chamber. As a result, a more thorough ignition takes place, burning much of the HC in the exhaust gases.

Automatic Temperature Controlled Air Cleaner

The rate of fuel atomization varies with the temperature of the air that the fuel is being mixed with. The air/fuel ratio cannot be held constant for efficient fuel combustion with a wide range of air temperatures. Cold air being drawn into the engine causes a denser and richer air/fuel mixture, inefficient fuel atomization, thus, more hydrocarbons in the exhaust gas. Hot air being drawn into the engine causes a leaner air/fuel mixture and more efficient atomization and combustion for less hydrocarbons in the exhaust gases.

The automatic temperature controlled air cleaner is designed so that the temperature of the ambient air being drawn into the engine is automatically controlled, to hold temperature, consequently, the fuel/air ratio at a constant rate for efficient fuel combustion.

A temperature sensing vacuum switch controls the vacuum applied to a vacuum motor, operating a valve in the intake snorkle of the air cleaner. When the engine is cold or the air being drawn into the engine is cold, the vacuum motor opens the valve, allowing air heated by the exhaust manifold to be drawn into the engine. As the engine warms up, the temperature sensing unit shuts off the vacuum applied to the vacuum motor which allows the valve to close, shutting off the heated air and allowing cooler, outside (under hood) air to be drawn into the engine.

TESTING

When the air around the temperature sensor of the unit mounted inside the air cleaner housing reaches 100°F, the sensor should block the flow of vacuum to the air control valve vacuum motor. When the temperature around the temperature sensor is below 100°F, the sensor should allow vacuum to pass onto the air valve vacuum motor thus blocking off the air cleaner snorkle to under hood (unheated) air.

When the temperature around the sensor is above 118°F, the air control valve should be completely open to under hood air.

If the air cleaner fails to operate correctly, check for loose or broken vacuum hoses. If the hoses are not the cause, replace the vacuum motor in the air cleaner.

Exhaust Gas Recirculation System

The system is used on all models. Exhaust gas recirculation is used to reduce combustion temperatures in the engine, thereby reducing the oxides of nitrogen emissions.

An EGR valve is mounted on the center of the intake manifold. The recycled exhaust gas is drawn into the intake manifold through the exhaust manifold heat stove and EGR valve. A vacuum diaphragm is connected to a timed signal port at the carburetor flange.

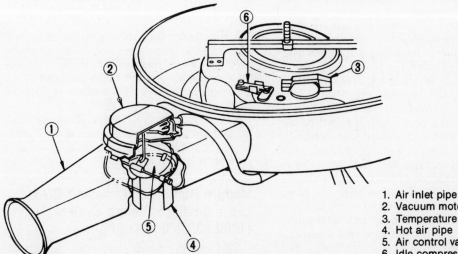

1. Air inlet pipe
2. Vacuum motor ass'y
3. Temperature sensor ass'y
4. Hot air pipe
5. Air control valve
6. Idle compresator

Automatic temperature controlled air cleaner

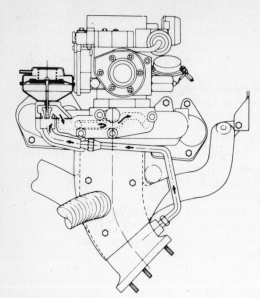

Typical EGR system

OPERATIONS

As the throttle valve is opened, vacuum is applied to the EGR valve vacuum diaphragm. When the vacuum reaches about 2 in.Hg, the diaphragm moves against spring pressure and is in a fully up position at 8 in.Hg of vacuum. As the diaphragm moves up, it opens the exhaust gas metering valve which allows exhaust gas to be pulled into the engine intake manifold. The system does not operate when the engine is idling because the exhaust gas recirculation would cause a rough idle.

A thermal vacuum valve inserted in the engine thermostat housing controls the application of the vacuum to the EGR valve. When the engine coolant reaches a predetermined temperature, the thermal vacuum valve opens and allows vacuum to be routed to the EGR valve. Below the predetermined temperature, the thermal vacuum valve closes and blocks vacuum to the EGR valve.

Some models have a Back Pressure Transducer (BPT) valve installed between the EGR valve and the thermal vacuum valve. The BPT valve has a diaphragm which is raised or lowered by exhaust back pressure. The diaphragm opens or closes an air bleed, which is connected into the EGR vacuum line. High pressure results in higher levels of EGR, because the diaphragm is raised, closing off the air bleed, which allows more vacuum to reach and open the EGR valve. Thus, the amount of recirculated exhaust gas varies with exhaust pressure.

Some models use a Venturi Vacuum Transducer (VVT) valve. The VVT valve monitors exhaust pressure and carburetor vacuum in order to activate the diaphragm which controls the

throttle vacuum applied to the EGR control valve. This system expands the operating range of the EGR unit, as well as increasing the EGR flow rate.

Many vehicles are equipped with an EGR warning system which signals via a light in the dashboard that the EGR system may need service. The EGR warning light should come on every time the starter is engaged as a test to make sure the bulb is not blown. The system uses a counter which works in conjunction with the odometer and lights the warning signal after the vehicle has traveled a predetermined number of miles.

To reset the counter, which is mounted in the engine compartment, remove the grommet installed in the side of the counter, insert the tip of a small screwdriver into the hole and press down on the knob inside the hole, then reinstall the grommet.

TESTING

1. Remove the EGR valve and apply enough vacuum to the diaphragm to open the valve.

2. The valve should remain open for over 30 seconds after the vacuum is removed.

3. Check the valve for damage, such as warpage, cracks and excessive wear around the valve and seat.

4. Clean the seat with a brush and compressed air, then remove any deposits from around the valve and port (seat).

5. To check the operation of the thermal vacuum valve, remove the valve from the engine and apply vacuum to the valve ports; it should not allow vacuum to pass.

6. Place the valve in a container of water with a thermometer and heat the water. When the temperature of the water reaches 134-145°F, remove the valve and apply vacuum to the ports; the valve should allow vacuum to pass.

7. To test the BPT valve, disconnect the two vacuum hoses from the valve. Plug one of the ports. While applying pressure to the bottom of the valve, apply vacuum to the unplugged port and check for leakage. If any exists, replace the valve.

8. To check the VVT valve, disconnect the top and bottom center hoses and apply a vacuum to the top hose. Check for leaks. If a leak is present, replace the valve.

Mixture Ratio Rich/Lean and EGR Large/Small Exchange System (1980-82 California Engines)

This system controls the air/fuel mixture ratio and the amount of recirculated exhaust gas (manual transmission models only) in accordance with the engine coolant temperature and car speed. The system consists of a vacuum switching valve, a power valve, a speed detecting switch located in the speedometer, a speed detecting switch amplifier and a water temperature switch.

When the coolant temperature is above 122°F and the car is traveling at least 40 mph, the vacuum switching valve is on and acts to lean down the fuel mixture; a small amount of EGR is being burned. When the coolant temperature is above 122°F but the vehicle is traveling less than 40 mph, the vacuum switching valve is off and allows the mixture to enrichen; a large amount of EGR is being burned. When coolant temperature is below 122°F, the vacuum switching valve is always on and acts to lean down the fuel mixture.

TESTING

Warm up the engine and raise the drive wheels off the ground; support the raised end of the vehicle with jack stands and block the wheels still on the ground. Start the engine, shift the transmission into TOP speed and maintain a speedometer speed higher than 50 MPH. Pinch off the vacuum switching valve-to-air cleaner hose, then see if the engine speed decreases and operates erratically. Shift the transmission into 3rd speed and run the vehicle at a speed lower than 30 MPH. Disconnect the vacuum switching valve-to-power valve hose, at the power valve and plug the open end with your finger. The engine should operate erratically. If the expected engine reaction in both of these tests does not happen, check all of the wiring connections and hoses for breaks and/or blockage.

Air Injection Reactor System 1976-80

It is difficult to completely burn the air/fuel mixture through normal combustion in the combustion chambers. Under certain operating conditions, unburned fuel is exhausted into the atmosphere.

The air injection reactor system is designed so that ambient air, pressurized by the air pump, is injected through the injection nozzles into the exhaust ports near each exhaust valve. The exhaust gases are at high temperatures and ignite when brought into contact with the oxygen. Unburned fuel is then burned in the exhaust ports and manifold.

The 1976 California models utilized a secondary system consisting of an air control valve, which limits the injection of secondary air and an emergency relief valve, which controls the supply of secondary air. This system protects the catalytic converter from overheating. In

1977, the function of both valves was combined in the Combined Air Control (CAC) valve.

All engines with an air pump system have a series of minor alterations to accommodate the system. These are:

1. Special close tolerance carburetor. Most engines require a slightly rich idle mixture adjustment.
2. Distributor with special advance curve. Ignition timing is retarded about 10° at idle in most cases.
3. Cooling system changes such as: a larger fan, a higher fan speed and a thermostatic fan clutch; this is required to offset the increase in temperature caused by retarded timing at idle.
4. Faster idle speed.
5. Heated air intake on some engines.
NOTE: *The only periodic maintenance required on the air pump system is replacement of the air filter element and adjustment of the drive belt.*

TESTING

Air Pump

If the air pump makes an abnormal noise and cannot be corrected without removing the pump from the vehicle, check the following in sequence:

1. Turn the pulley ¾ of a turn in the clockwise direction and ¼ of a turn in the counterclockwise direction. If the pulley is binding and if rotation is not smooth, a defective bearing is indicated.
2. Check the inner wall of the pump body, vanes and rotor for wear. If the rotor has abnormal wear, replace the air pump.
3. Check the needle roller bearing for wear and damage. If the bearings are defective, the air pump should be replaced.
4. Check and replace the rear side seal if abnormal wear or damage is noticed.
5. Check and replace the carbon shoes holding the vanes if they are found to be worn or damaged.
6. A deposit of carbon particles on the inner wall of the pump body and vanes is normal, but should be removed with compressed air before reassembling the air pump.

Check Valve

Remove the check valve from the air pump discharge line. Test it for leakage by blowing air into the valve from the air pump side and from the air manifold side. Air should only pass through the valve from the air pump side if the valve is functioning normally. A small amount of air leakage from the manifold side can be overlooked. Replace the check valve if it is found to be defective.

Anti-Backfire Valve

Disconnect the rubber hose connecting the mixture control valve with the intake manifold and plug the hose. If the mixture control valve is operating correctly, air will continue to blow out the mixture control valve for a few seconds after the accelerator pedal is fully depressed (engine running) and released quickly. If air continues to blow out for more than five seconds, replace the mixture control valve.

Air Pump Relief Valve

Disconnect the air pump discharge hose leading to the exhaust manifold. With the engine running, restrict the air flow coming from the pump. The air pump relief valve should vent the pressurized air to the atmosphere if it is working properly.

NOTE: *When performing this test do not completely block the discharge line of the air pump as damage may result if the relief valve fails to function properly.*

Air Injection Nozzles

Check around the air manifold for air leakage with the engine running at 2,000 rpm. If air is leaking from the eye joint bolt, retighten or replace the gasket. Check the air nozzles for restrictions by blowing air into the nozzles.

Hoses

Check and replace hoses if they are found to be weakened or cracked. Check all hose connections and clips. Be sure that the hoses are not in contact with other parts of the engine.

Emergency Air Relief Valve

1. Warm up the engine.
2. Check all hoses for leaks, kinks, improper connections and etc.
3. Run the engine up to 2000 rpm, under no load; no air should be discharged from the valve.
4. Disconnect the intake manifold-to-air relief valve hose. Run the engine to 2,000 rpm; air should be discharged from the valve, if not, replace it.

Combined Air Control Valve

1. Check all hoses for leaks, kinks and improper connections.
2. Thoroughly warm the engine.
3. With the engine idling, check for air discharge from the relief opening in the air cleaner case.
4. Disconnect and plug the vacuum hose from the valve; air should be discharged from the valve with the engine idling. If the disconnected vacuum hose is not plugged, the engine will stumble.

5. Connect a hand-operated vacuum pump to the vacuum fitting on the valve and apply 7.8-9.8 in.Hg of vacuum. Run the engine speed to 3000 rpm; no air should be discharged from the valve.
6. Disconnect and plug the air hose at the check valve, with the conditions as in the preceding step. This should cause the valve to discharge air. If not, or if any of the conditions in this procedure are not met, replace the valve.

Air Induction System (1981 And Later)

The air induction system is used to send fresh secondary air to the exhaust manifold by utilizing vacuum created by the exhaust pulsation in the manifold. The system consists of a dual or single set of reed valves connected to the air filter housing, with tube(s) leading to the exhaust manifold.

NOTE: *The air induction system is used on the carburetor models ONLY.*

OPERATION

The exhaust pressure usually pulsates in response to the opening and closing of the exhaust valve and it periodically decreases below atmospheric pressure. If a secondary air intake pipe is opened to the atmosphere under a vacuum condition, secondary air can then be drawn into the exhaust manifold in proportion of the vacuum. Because of this, the air induction system is able to reduce the CO and HC content in the exhaust gases. The system consists of two air induction valves, a filter, hoses and EAI tubes.

TESTING

Disconnect the air induction tube from the tube leading to the exhaust manifold. Place the tube to your mouth, then suck on the tube (air should move freely through the valve); try to blow through the tube (air should not flow through it). If the valve does not respond correctly, replace it.

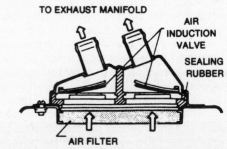

TO EXHAUST MANIFOLD

AIR INDUCTION VALVE

SEALING RUBBER

AIR FILTER

Cross-sectional view of the air induction valve

Fuel Shut-Off System

On the 1980-81, carburetor models, a fuel shut-off system was introduced. The system consist of: a vacuum switch, a speed detecting switch, clutch switch, transaxle neutral switch, neutral relay and a fuel shut-off relay.

NOTE: *The 1982 and later, carburetor models, utilize the Electronic Control Unit (ECU) to control the operation of the anti-dieseling solenoid.*

OPERATION

The system is operated by an anti-dieseling solenoid valve in the carburetor which is controlled by a vacuum switch. When the intake manifold vacuum increases to an extremely high level (which it does during deceleration), the fuel flow of the slow system is shut off by the anti-dieseling solenoid valve. When the intake manifold vacuum drops to a low level, the fuel flow of the slow system is resupplied.

The fuel shut-off system is further controlled by the clutch switch and gear position switches such as the neutral switch (manual transmission) and the inhibitor switch (automatic transmission) to ensure that fuel cannot be shut off even it the manifold vacuum is high enough to trigger the normal fuel shut-off operation.

Electric Choke

The purpose of the electric choke, is to shorten the time the choke is in operation after the engine is started, thus shortening the time of high HC output.

An electric heater warms the bimetal spring which controls the opening and closing of the choke valve. The heater starts to heat as soon as the engine starts.

Catalytic Converter

This system is used on all 1976-78 California models and all 1979 and later models. The catalytic converter is a muffler-like container built into the exhaust system. The catalyst element consists of individual pellets or a honeycomb monolithic substrate coated with a noble metal such as platinum, palladium, rhodium or a combination. When the exhaust gases come into contact with the catalyst, it changes residual HC, CO and NOx in the exhaust gas into CO_2, H_2O and N, before the exhaust gas is discharged into the atmosphere.

All models equipped with an air pump use an emergency air relief valve as a catalyst protection device. When the temperature of the catalyst goes above maximum operating temperature, the temperature sensor signals the switching module to activate the emergency air relief valve. This stops air injection into the exhaust manifold and lowers the temperature of the catalyst.

Certain 1976-78 catalyst equipped models have a floor temperature warning system which emits a warning, if the catalytic converter or engine becomes overly hot or malfunctions, causing floor temperature to rise. The system consists of: a relay (located under the passenger seat) and a light (installed on the instrument panel). The lamp illuminates when the floor temperatures become abnormally high, due to converter or engine malfunction. The light also comes on when the ignition switch is turned to Start, to check its operation. The 1979 and later models, do not have the warning system.

All models with the 3-way converter have an oxygen sensor warning light on the dashboard, which illuminates at the first 30,000 mile internal signaling the need for oxygen sensor replacement. The oxygen sensor is part of the Mixture Ration Feedback System.

No regular maintenance is required for the catalytic converter system, except for periodic replacement of the Air Induction System filter (if equipped). The Air Induction System is used to supply the converter with fresh air; oxygen present in the air is used in the oxidation process.

Precautions

1. Use ONLY unleaded fuel.
2. Avoid prolonged idling; the engine should run no longer than 20 min. at curb idle and not longer than 10 min. at fast idle.
3. Do not disconnect any of the spark plug leads while the engine is running.
4. Make engine compression checks as quickly as possible.

Mixture Ratio Feedback System

The need for better fuel economy coupled to increasingly strict emission control regulations dictates a more exact control of the engine air/fuel mixture. The manufacturer has developed this system which is installed on all 1984 and later models.

The principle of the system is to control the air/fuel mixture exactly, so that a more complete combustion can occur in the engine and more thorough oxidation and reduction of the exhaust gases can occur in the catalytic converter. The object is to maintain a stoichiometric air/fuel mixture, which is chemically correct for theoretically complete combustion.

The components used in the system include an oxygen sensor, installed in the exhaust manifold upstream of the converter, a catalytic converter, an electronic control unit and the fuel injection system.

It should be noted that proper operation of the system is entirely dependent on the oxygen sensor. Thus, if the sensor is not replaced at the correct interval or if the sensor fails during normal operation, the engine fuel mixture will be incorrect, resulting in poor fuel economy, starting problems or stumbling and stalling of the engine when warm.

Maintenance Reminder Lights

RESETTING

Most Datsun/Nissan models utilize an oxygen sensor. After 30,000 miles of operation, the sensor light in the dash will come on. This light indicates that the sensor should be inspected or replaced.

On models with a sensor relay, reset the relay by pushing or inserting a small screwdriver into the reset hole. Reset relay at 30,000 and 60,000 miles. At 90,000 miles, locate and disconnect warning light wire connector.

On models without sensor light relay locate and disconnect the single warning light harness connector. The reminder light will no longer function.

NOTE: *On the Stanza wagons the warning lamp relay is located under the passenger seat.*

SENSOR LIGHT CONNECTOR LOCATIONS

1. 1983-86 Pulsar – LIGHT GREEN/ BLACK-LIGHT GREEN, above fuse box
2. 1987 Pulsar – RED/BLACK-RED/BLUE, above fuse box
3. 1984-86 Stanza – YELLOW-YELLOW/ GREEN, behind left kick panel
4. 1987 Stanza – GREEN-BROWN, above fuse box
5. 1986-87 Stanza Wagon – RED-YELLOW OR RED/BLUE, behind instrument panel

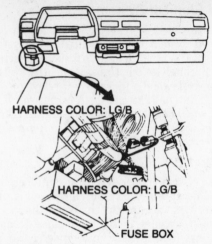

HARNESS COLOR: LG/B

HARNESS COLOR: LG/B

FUSE BOX

Disconnecting the oxygen sensor warning lamp—Pulsar 1983–87

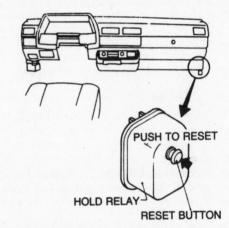

PUSH TO RESET

HOLD RELAY

RESET BUTTON

Resetting oxygen sensor warning lamp—Pulsar 1985–86 (U.S. models)

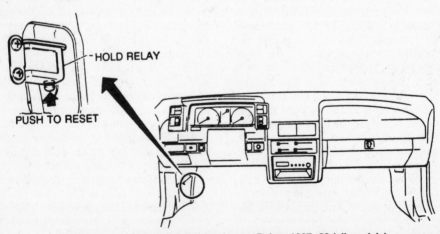

HOLD RELAY

PUSH TO RESET

Resetting oxygen sensor warning lamp—Pulsar 1987–88 (all models)

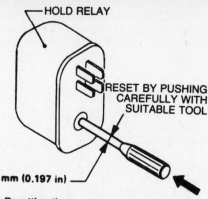

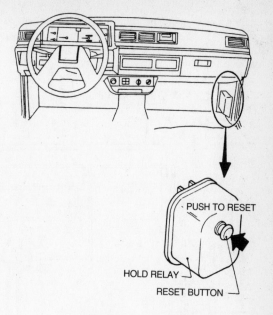

mm (0.197 in)

Resetting the oxygen sensor warning light

PUSH TO RESET

HOLD RELAY

RESET BUTTON

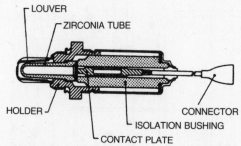

- LOUVER
- ZIRCONIA TUBE
- HOLDER
- CONTACT PLATE
- ISOLATION BUSHING
- CONNECTOR

Oxygen sensor (Zirconia type)

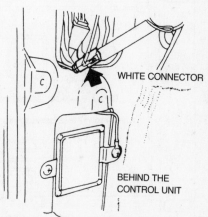

WHITE CONNECTOR

BEHIND THE
CONTROL UNIT

Disconnecting and resetting the oxygen sensor warning lamp—Stanza 1984–87 (exc. wagon)

Oxygen Sensor

The oxygen sensor monitors the density of the oxygen in the exhaust gas. The sensor consists of a closed-end tube made of ceramic zirconia and other components. Porous platinum electrodes cover the tubes inner and outer surfaces. The tubes outer surface is exposed to the exhaust gases in the exhaust manifold, while its inner surface is exposed to normal air.

REMOVAL AND INSTALLATION

The oxygen sensor is installed in the exhaust manifold and is removed in the same manner as a spark plug. Always remove electrical connection before trying to remove the sensor. Exercise care when handling the sensor do not drop or handle the sensor roughly; the electrical connector and louvered end must be kept free of grease and dirt. If a anti-seize compound is used in installation, make sure to coat just the threads of the sensor and care should be used not to get compound on the sensor itself. You should disconnect the negative battery cable when servicing the oxygen sensor and torque the sensor to 13-17 ft. lbs.

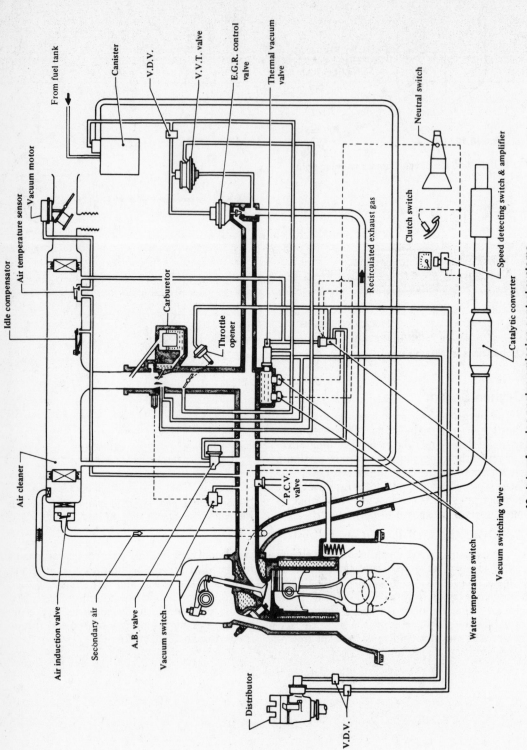

49 states A series engine emission control systems

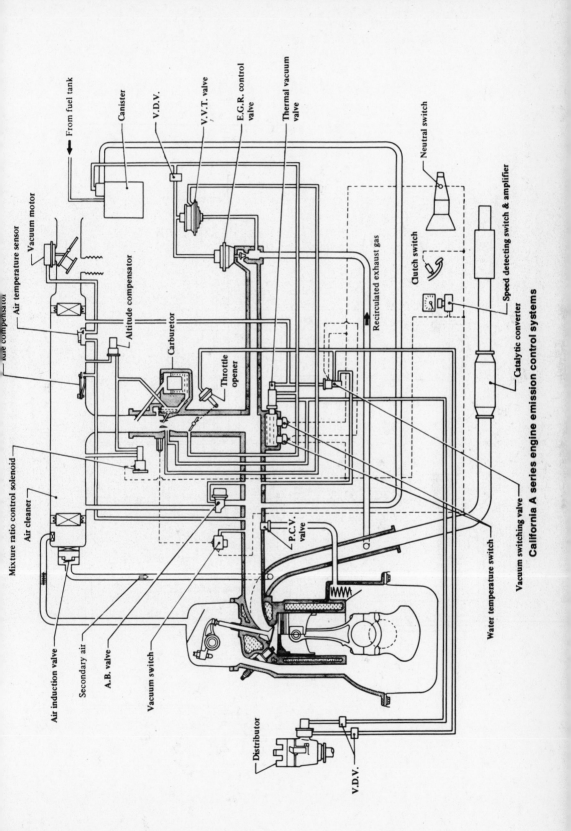

California A series engine emission control systems

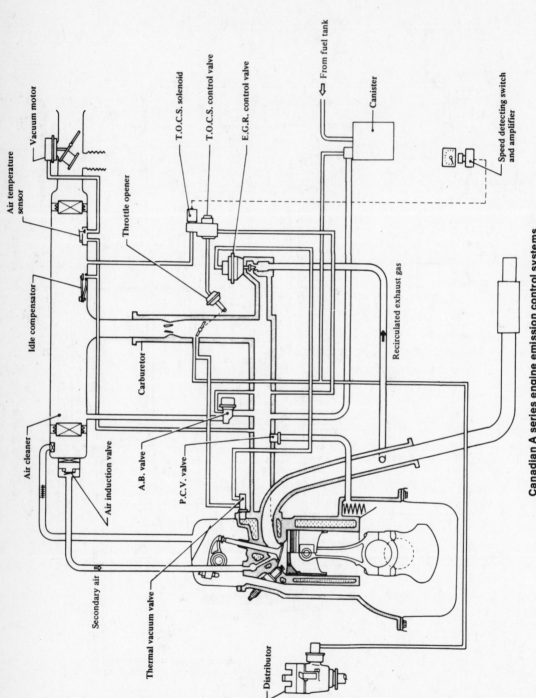

Canadian A series engine emission control systems

Vacuum motor

Air temperature sensor

Idle compensator

Air cleaner

Secondary air

T.O.C.S. solenoid

T.O.C.S. control valve

E.G.R. control valve

Throttle opener

Carburetor

A.B. valve

P.C.V. valve

Air induction valve

Thermal vacuum valve

Distributor

From fuel tank

Canister

Speed detecting switch and amplifier

Recirculated exhaust gas

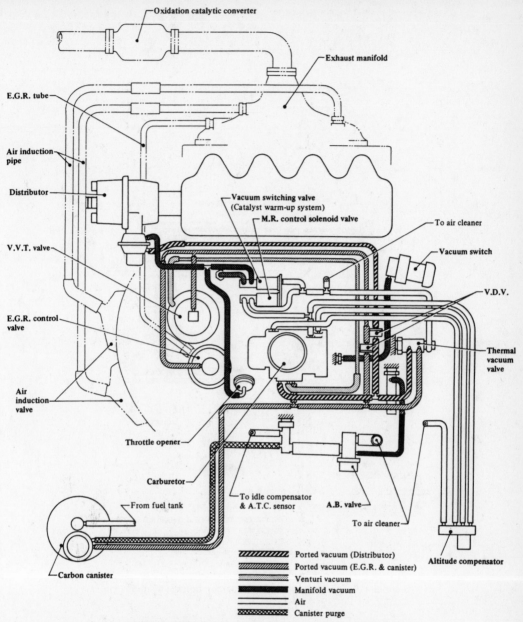

Oxidation catalytic converter

Exhaust manifold

E.G.R. tube

Air induction pipe

Distributor

Vacuum switching valve (Catalyst warm-up system)

M.R. control solenoid valve

To air cleaner

Vacuum switch

V.V.T. valve

V.D.V.

E.G.R. control valve

Thermal vacuum valve

Air induction valve

Throttle opener

Carburetor

To idle compensator & A.T.C. sensor

A.B. valve

From fuel tank

To air cleaner

Carbon canister

Altitude compensator

▨▨▨▨▨	Ported vacuum (Distributor)
▨▨▨▨▨	Ported vacuum (E.G.R. & canister)
▨▨▨▨▨	Venturi vacuum
▬▬▬▬▬	Manifold vacuum
══════	Air
▧▧▧▧▧	Canister purge

E-series (1982, Calif.) engine emission control systems

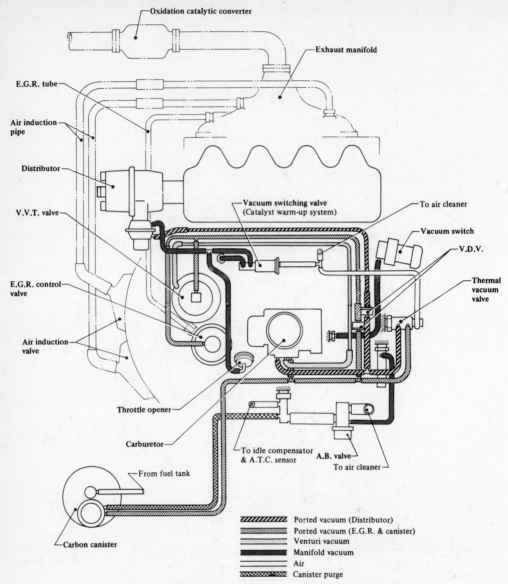

Oxidation catalytic converter

Exhaust manifold

E.G.R. tube

Air induction pipe

Distributor

V.V.T. valve

Vacuum switching valve (Catalyst warm-up system)

To air cleaner

Vacuum switch

V.D.V.

E.G.R. control valve

Thermal vacuum valve

Air induction valve

Throttle opener

Carburetor

To idle compensator & A.T.C. sensor

A.B. valve

To air cleaner

From fuel tank

Carbon canister

/////	Ported vacuum (Distributor)
/////	Ported vacuum (E.G.R. & canister)
≡≡≡	Venturi vacuum
▬▬▬	Manifold vacuum
—	Air
▓▓▓	Canister purge

E-series (1982, 49 states) engine emission control systems

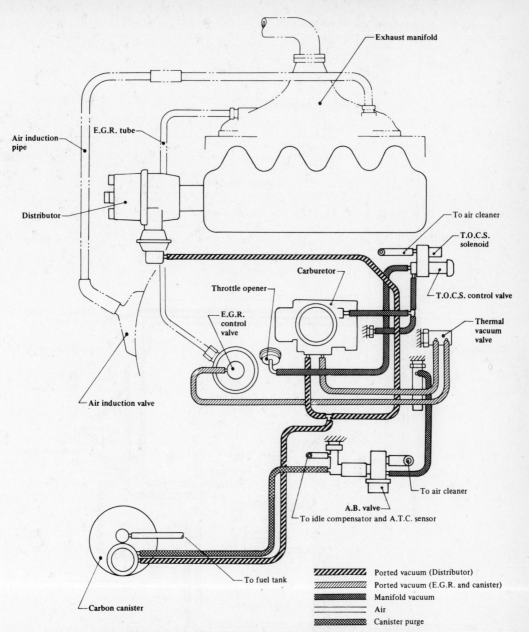

E-series (1982 and later, Canada) engine emission control systems

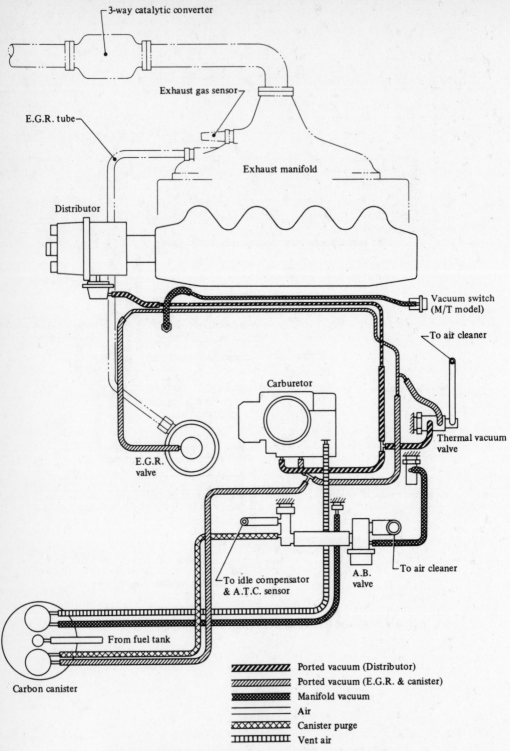

3-way catalytic converter

Exhaust gas sensor

E.G.R. tube

Exhaust manifold

Distributor

Vacuum switch
(M/T model)

To air cleaner

Thermal vacuum
valve

Carburetor

E.G.R.
valve

To idle compensator
& A.T.C. sensor

A.B.
valve

To air cleaner

From fuel tank

Carbon canister

/////////	Ported vacuum (Distributor)
/////////	Ported vacuum (E.G.R. & canister)
▓▓▓▓▓	Manifold vacuum
———	Air
XXXXXXX	Canister purge
IIIIIIIII	Vent air

California E-series (1983 and later) emission control system

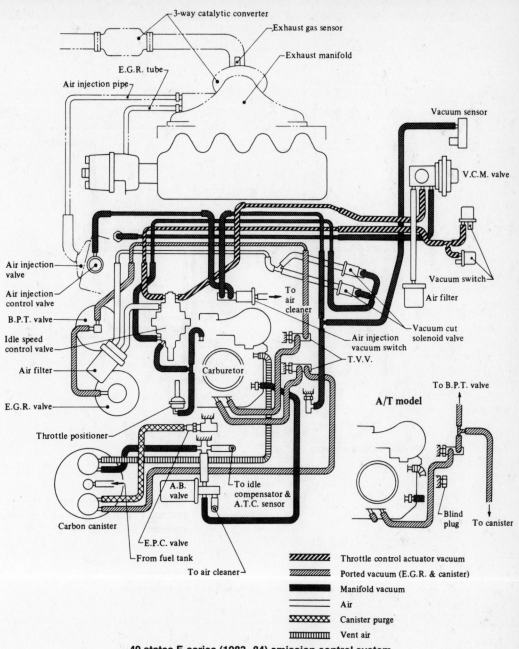

3-way catalytic converter

Exhaust gas sensor

Exhaust manifold

E.G.R. tube

Air injection pipe

Vacuum sensor

V.C.M. valve

Air injection valve

Air injection control valve

B.P.T. valve

Idle speed control valve

Air filter

E.G.R. valve

Throttle positioner

Carburetor

To air cleaner

Air injection vacuum switch

T.V.V.

Vacuum switch

Air filter

Vacuum cut solenoid valve

A/T model

To B.P.T. valve

Blind plug

To canister

Carbon canister

A.B. valve

To idle compensator & A.T.C. sensor

E.P.C. valve

From fuel tank

To air cleaner

/////////	Throttle control actuator vacuum
/////////	Ported vacuum (E.G.R. & canister)
▬▬▬▬▬	Manifold vacuum
─────	Air
XXXXXXX	Canister purge
|||||||||||	Vent air

49 states E-series (1983–84) emission control system

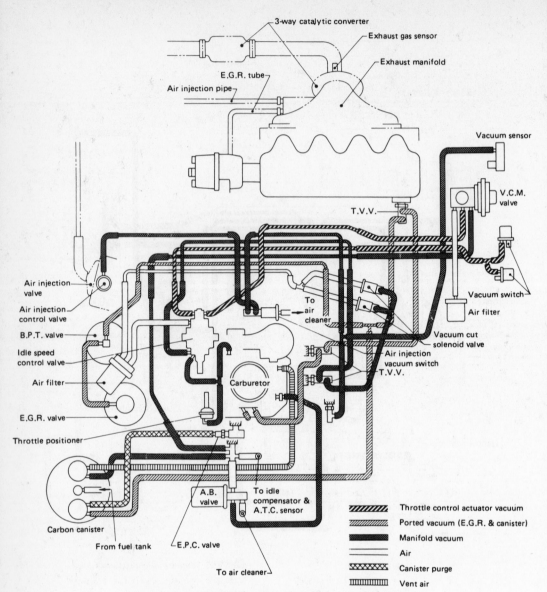

49 states E-series (1985 and later) emission control system

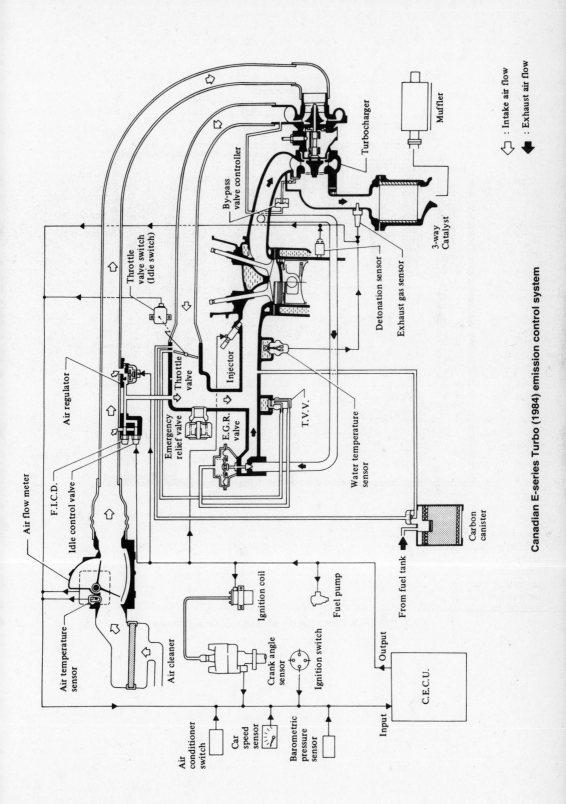

Canadian E-series Turbo (1984) emission control system

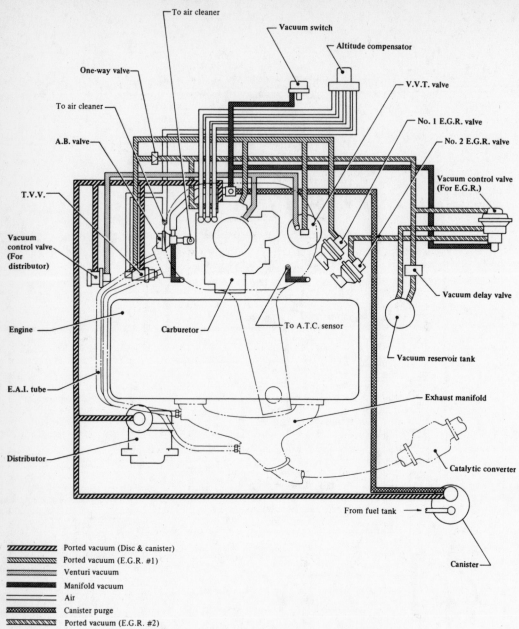

CA20 (1982–83, Calif.) engine emission control systems

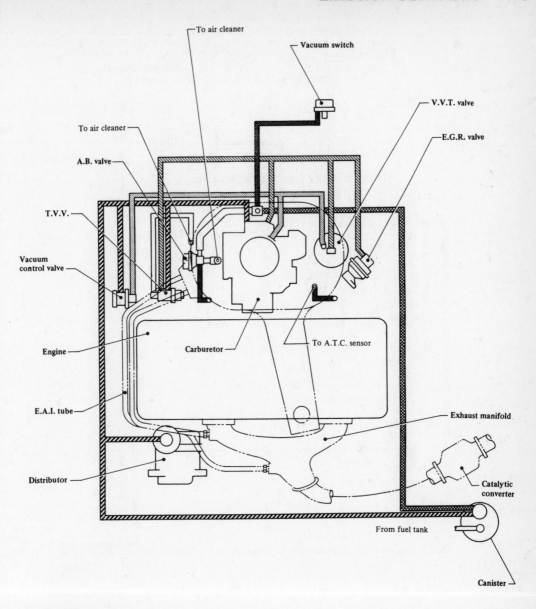

To air cleaner

Vacuum switch

V.V.T. valve

E.G.R. valve

To air cleaner

A.B. valve

T.V.V.

Vacuum
control valve

Engine

Carburetor

To A.T.C. sensor

E.A.I. tube

Exhaust manifold

Distributor

Catalytic
converter

From fuel tank

Canister

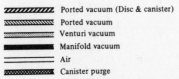

Ported vacuum (Disc & canister)
Ported vacuum
Venturi vacuum
Manifold vacuum
Air
Canister purge

CA20 (1982 and later, 49 states) engine emission control systems

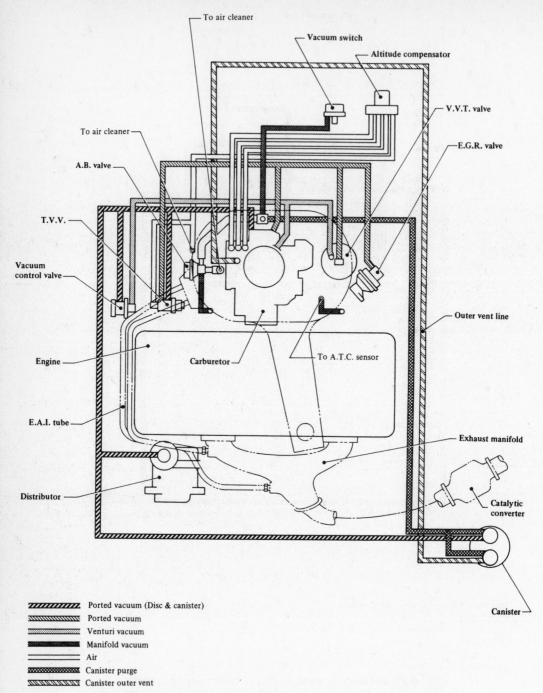

To air cleaner	
Vacuum switch	
Altitude compensator	
V.V.T. valve	
E.G.R. valve	
To air cleaner	
A.B. valve	
T.V.V.	
Vacuum control valve	
Engine	
Carburetor	
To A.T.C. sensor	
Outer vent line	
E.A.I. tube	
Exhaust manifold	
Distributor	
Catalytic converter	
Canister	

▨▨▨	Ported vacuum (Disc & canister)
▨▨▨	Ported vacuum
▨▨▨	Venturi vacuum
██	Manifold vacuum
—	Air
▨▨▨	Canister purge
▨▨▨	Canister outer vent

CA20 (1982–83, 49 states high altitude) engine emission control systems

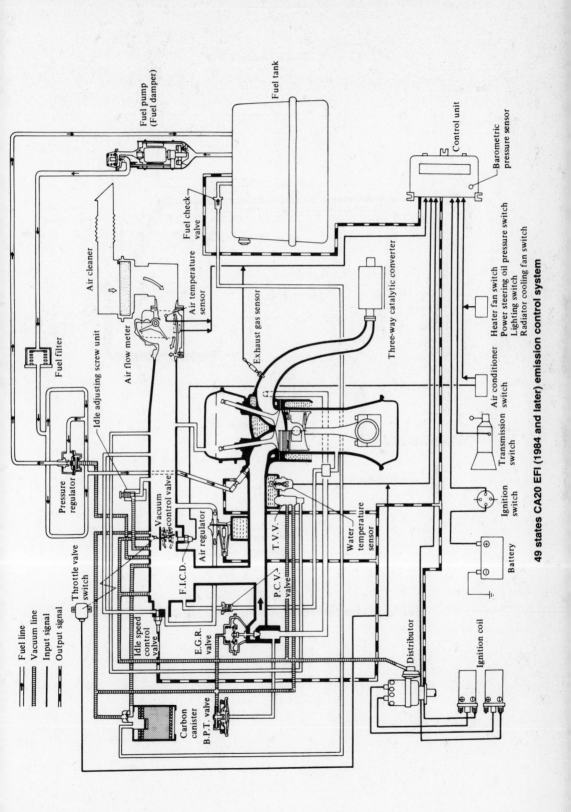

49 states CA20 EFI (1984 and later) emission control system

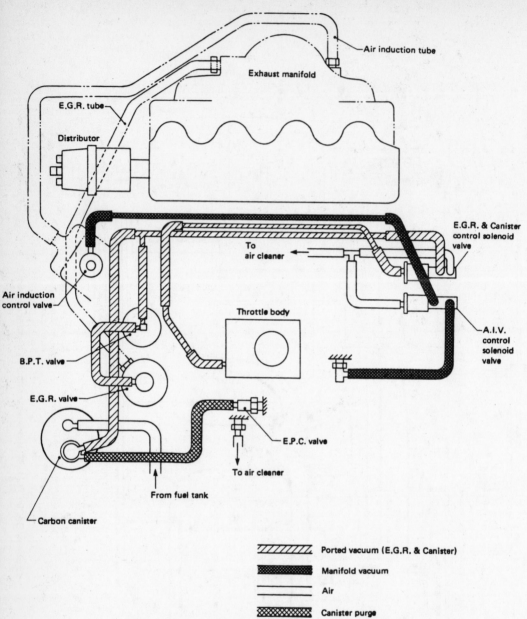

Air induction tube

Exhaust manifold

E.G.R. tube

Distributor

E.G.R. & Canister
control solenoid
valve

To
air cleaner

Air induction
control valve

Throttle body

A.I.V.
control
solenoid
valve

B.P.T. valve

E.G.R. valve

E.P.C. valve

To air cleaner

From fuel tank

Carbon canister

/////////	Ported vacuum (E.G.R. & Canister)
▓▓▓▓▓	Manifold vacuum
═══	Air
▒▒▒▒▒	Canister purge

E-series fuel injected engine emission control system

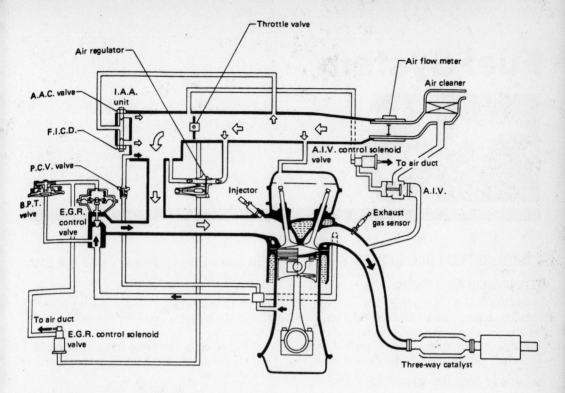

- ⇨ : Intake air flow
- ➡ : Exhaust gas flow

CA16DE/CA18DE engine emission control system

Fuel System

CARBURETED FUEL SYSTEMS

Mechanical Fuel Pump

The fuel pump is a mechanically operated, diaphragm type driven by the fuel pump eccentric on the camshaft. The pump is located on the lower right side (A-series and E-series), on the right rear side of the cylinder head (CA20).

REMOVAL AND INSTALLATION

CAUTION: *Never smoke when working around gasoline! Avoid all sources of sparks* or ignition. *Gasoline vapors are EXTREMELY volatile!*

1. Disconnect the fuel lines from the fuel pump. Be sure to keep the line leading from the fuel tank up high to prevent the excess loss of fuel.

2. Remove the two fuel pump mounting nuts and the fuel pump assembly from the right side of the engine.

3. To install, use a new gasket, sealant and reverse the removal procedures. Torque the fuel pump bolts to 7-9 ft. lbs.

Troubleshooting Basic Fuel System Problems

Problem	Cause	Solution
Engine cranks, but won't start (or is hard to start) when cold	• Empty fuel tank • Incorrect starting procedure • Defective fuel pump • No fuel in carburetor • Clogged fuel filter • Engine flooded • Defective choke	• Check for fuel in tank • Follow correct procedure • Check pump output • Check for fuel in the carburetor • Replace fuel filter • Wait 15 minutes; try again • Check choke plate
Engine cranks, but is hard to start (or does not start) when hot—(presence of fuel is assumed)	• Defective choke	• Check choke plate
Rough idle or engine runs rough	• Dirt or moisture in fuel • Clogged air filter • Faulty fuel pump	• Replace fuel filter • Replace air filter • Check fuel pump output
Engine stalls or hesitates on acceleration	• Dirt or moisture in the fuel • Dirty carburetor • Defective fuel pump • Incorrect float level, defective accelerator pump	• Replace fuel filter • Clean the carburetor • Check fuel pump output • Check carburetor
Poor gas mileage	• Clogged air filter • Dirty carburetor • Defective choke, faulty carburetor adjustment	• Replace air filter • Clean carburetor • Check carburetor
Engine is flooded (won't start accompanied by smell of raw fuel)	• Improperly adjusted choke or carburetor	• Wait 15 minutes and try again, without pumping gas pedal • If it won't start, check carburetor

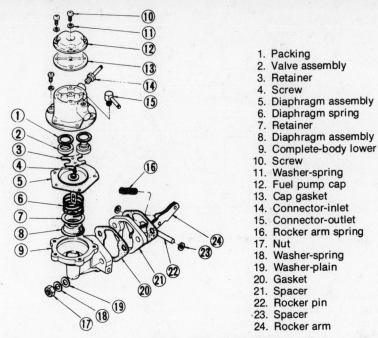

1. Packing
2. Valve assembly
3. Retainer
4. Screw
5. Diaphragm assembly
6. Diaphragm spring
7. Retainer
8. Diaphragm assembly
9. Complete-body lower
10. Screw
11. Washer-spring
12. Fuel pump cap
13. Cap gasket
14. Connector-inlet
15. Connector-outlet
16. Rocker arm spring
17. Nut
18. Washer-spring
19. Washer-plain
20. Gasket
21. Spacer
22. Rocker pin
23. Spacer
24. Rocker arm

A series engine fuel pump

TESTING

Static Pressure

CAUTION: *Never smoke when working around gasoline! Avoid all sources of sparks or ignition. Gasoline vapors are EXTREMELY volatile!*

1. Disconnect the fuel line at the carburetor. Using a T-connector, connect two rubber hoses to the connector, then install it between the fuel line and the carburetor fitting.

NOTE: *When disconnecting the fuel line, be sure to place a container under the line to* catch the excess fuel which will be present.

2. Connect a fuel pump pressure gauge to the T-connector and secure it with a clamp.

3. Start the engine and check the pressure at various speeds. The pressure should be 3.0-3.8 psi (1976-83) or 2.8-3.8 psi (1984 and later). There is usually enough gas in the float bowl to perform this test.

4. If the pressure is OK, perform a capacity test. Remove the gauge and the T-connector assembly, then reinstall the fuel line to the carburetor.

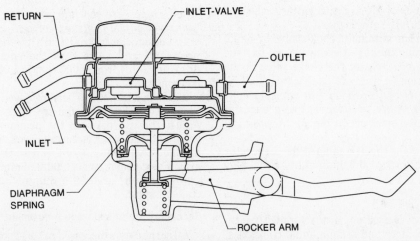

CA20 engine fuel pump

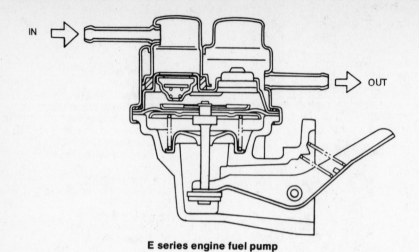

E series engine fuel pump

Capacity Test

1. Disconnect the fuel line from the carburetor and place the line in a graduated container.
2. Fill the carburetor float bowl with gas.
3. Start the engine and run it for one minute at about 1,000 rpm (A-series and CA20) or 600 rpm (E-series). The pump should deliver 0.5L per minute (A-series), 1.5L per minute (CA20) or 0.5L per minute (E-series).

Carburetor

The carburetor used is a 2-barrel down-draft type with a low speed (primary) side and a high speed (secondary) side.

All models have an electrically operated anti-dieseling solenoid. As the ignition switch is turned off, the valve is energized and shuts off the supply of fuel to the idle circuit of the carburetor.

ADJUSTMENTS

Throttle Linkage Adjustment

1. Disconnect the negative battery cable.
2. Remove the air cleaner.
3. Open the automatic choke valve by hand, while turning the throttle valve by pulling the throttle lever, then set the choke valve in the open position.
NOTE: *If equipped with a vacuum controlled throttle positioner, use a vacuum hand pump to retract the the throttle positioner rod.*
4. Adjust the throttle cable at the carburetor bracket, so that a 1.0-2.0mm of free pedal play exists.

Dashpot Adjustment

A dashpot is used on carburetors with automatic transaxles and some manual transaxles. The dashpot slowly closes the throttle on auto-

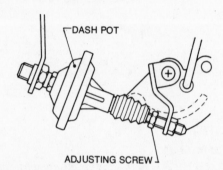

Dashpot adjustment

matic transmissions to prevent stalling and serves as an emission control device on all late model vehicles.

The dashpot should be adjusted to contact the throttle lever on deceleration at approximately 2,000-2,300 rpm (A-series), 1,400-1,600 rpm (CA20), 2,300-2,500 rpm (E15) engines, 1,900-2,100 rpm (E16, automatic transmission) or 2,250-2,450 (E16, manual transmission).
NOTE: *Before attempting to adjust the dashpot, make sure the idle speed, timing and mixture adjustments are correct.*
1. Loosen the locknut (turn the dashpot, if necessary) and make sure the engine speed drops smoothly from 2,000 rpm to 1,000 rpm in 3 seconds.
2. If the dashpot has been removed from the carburetor, it must be adjusted when installed. Adjust the gap between the primary throttle valve and the inner carburetor wall, when the dashpot stem comes in contact with the throttle arm. The dashpot gap is 0.66-0.86mm (manual transmission) or 0.49-0.69mm (automatic transmission).

Secondary Throttle Linkage Adjustment

All carburetors discussed in this book are two stage type carburetors. On this type of carbure-

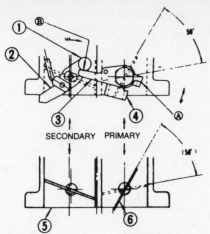

1. Roller
2. Connecting lever
3. Return plate
4. Adjust plate
5. Throttle chamber
6. Throttle valve

Secondary throttle linkage adjustment

tor, the engine runs on the primary barrel most of the time, with the secondary barrel being used for acceleration purposes. When the throttle valve on the primary side opens to an angle of approximately 50° (from its fully closed position), the secondary throttle valve is pulled open by the connecting linkage. The 50° angle of throttle valve opening works out to a clearance measurement of 6mm (F10 model), 5.5-6.0mm (310 model, 1979-80), 5.6-6.4mm (310 model, 1981-82), 7.4-8.4mm (Stanza) or 5.7-6.9mm (Pulsar, Calif.) between the throttle valve and the carburetor body. The easiest way to measure this is to use a drill bit. Drill bits from sizes H to P (standard letter size drill bits) should fit. Check the appendix in the back of the book for the exact size of the various drill bits. If an adjustment is necessary, bend the connecting link between the two linkage assemblies.

NOTE: *The Pulsar carburetor is equipped with a tang on the adjusting link, bend the tang to adjust the clearance.*

Float Level Adjustment

The fuel level is normal if it is within the lines on the window glass of the float chamber (or the sight glass) when the vehicle is resting on level ground and the engine is off.

If the fuel level is outside the lines, remove the float housing cover. Have an absorbent cloth under the cover to catch the fuel from the fuel bowl. Adjust the float level by bending the needle seat on the float.

The needle valve should have an effective stroke of about 1.5mm. When necessary, the needle valve stroke can be adjusted by bending the float stopper.

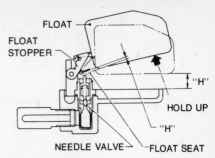

Float level adjustment

NOTE: *Be careful not to bend the needle valve rod when installing the float and baffle plate, if removed.*

Fast Idle Adjustment

EXCEPT STANZA

NOTE: *On the Stanza models, the fast idle cam lever is located next to the fast idle cam screw, so the choke cover does not have to be removed. On the 1985 Stanza, disconnect the Fast Idle Breaker harness at the carburetor.*
1. Remove the carburetor from the vehicle.
CAUTION: *Never smoke when working around gasoline! Avoid all sources of sparks or ignition. Gasoline vapors are EXTREMELY volatile!*
NOTE: *On the Pulsar (1984 Calif.), disconnect the harness cover from the automatic choke heater cover, the vacuum hose from the vacuum break diaphragm (install a plug after pushing the vacuum break stem toward the diaphragm), then move the throttle lever counterclockwise (fully). Go to Step No. 4.*
2. Remove the choke cover, then place the fast idle arm on the 2nd step of the fast idle cam. Using the correct wire gauge, measure the clearance A between the throttle valve and the wall of the throttle valve chamber (at the center of the throttle valve). Check it against the following specifications:

- 1976 F10: 0.80-0.88mm
- 1977-78 F10: 0.73-0.87mm
- 1979-80 310: 0.72-0.89mm
- 1981 310: 0.73-0.87mm
- 1982 310:
  - 0.73-0.87mm MT
  - 1.00-1.14mm AT
- 1982-86 Stanza:
  - 0.66-0.80mm MT
  - 0.81-0.95mm AT
- 1983 Pulsar:
  - 0.79-0.93mm USA MT
  - 1.08-1.22mm USA AT
  - 0.65-0.79mm Canada MT
  - 0.93-1.07mm Canada AT

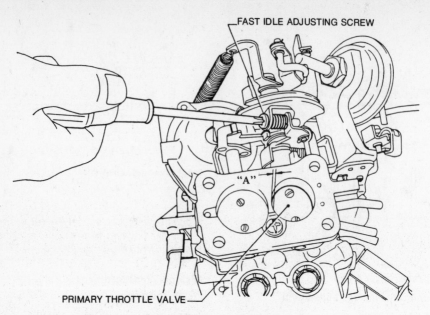

FAST IDLE ADJUSTING SCREW

"A"

PRIMARY THROTTLE VALVE

E series fast idle adjustment

- 1984-86 Pulsar:
    0.76-0.96mm USA MT
    1.05-1.25mm USA AT
    0.54-0.82mm Canada MT
    0.90-1.10mm Canada AT

NOTE: *The first step of the fast idle adjustment procedure is not absolutely necessary.*

3. Install the carburetor on the engine.

4. Start the engine, warm it to operating temperatures and check the fast idle rpm. The cam should be at the 2nd step.

- 1976 F10: 2,450-2,650 rpm
- 1977-78 F10: 1,900-2,700 rpm
- 1979-81 310:
    49 states 2,400-3,200 rpm
    Calif. 2,300-3100 rpm
    Canada 1,900-2,700 rpm

- 1982 310:
    49 states 2,400-3,200 rpm
    Calif. 2,300-3,100 rpm
    Canada 1,900-2,700 rpm MT
    Canada 2,400-3,200 rpm AT
- 1985-86 Stanza:
    2,400-2,700 rpm MT
    2,800-3,100 rpm AT
- 1983 Pulsar:
    49 states 2,400-3,200 rpm MT
    49 states 2,700-3,500 rpm AT
    Calif. 2,600-3,400 rpm MT
    Calif. 2,900-3,700 rpm AT
    Canada 1,900-2,700 rpm MT
    Canada 2,400-3,200 rpm AT
- 1984-86 Pulsar:
    Calif. 2,600-3,400 rpm MT
    Calif. 2,900-3,700 rpm AT
    Canada 1,900-2,700 rpm MT
    Canada 2,400-3,200 rpm AT

5. To adjust the fast idle speed, turn the fast idle adjusting screw counterclockwise to increase the fast idle speed and clockwise to decrease the fast idle speed.

Fast Idle Breaker Adjustment

STANZA (1985-86)

1. Start the engine and warm it to operating temperatures without racing it.

2. Check the engine speed and the breaker operation, it should be high revolution at the start, then idle speed when warm.

3. Disconnect the fast idle breaker harness connector at the carburetor. Using an ohmmeter, check the fast idle breaker for continuity;

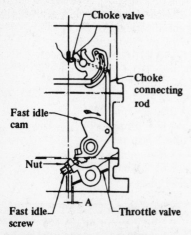

Choke valve

Choke connecting rod

Fast idle cam

Nut

A

Fast idle screw

Throttle valve

Adjusting the fast idle cam—Stanza

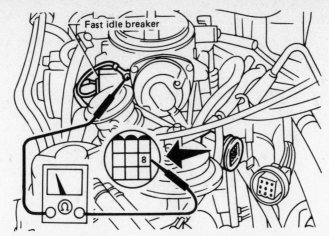

Checking the continuity of the fast idle breaker—Stanza 1985 and later

place one lead on the breaker's ground wire and the other lead on the No. 8 pin of the harness connector.

NOTE: *Checking is performed when the breaker is cold (less than 68°F) and the choke plate closed.*

4. If there is no continuity, replace the breaker.

5. If an ohmmeter is not available, check the breaker with the engine running (harness connector installed), if the breaker does not warm up, replace it.

Cam Follow Lever Adjustment

STANZA

Hold the choke plate closed, turn the adjusting screw until there is no clearance between the cam follow lever and the fast idle cam.

Automatic Choke Adjustment

1. With the engine cold, make sure the choke is fully closed (press the accelerator pedal all the way to the floor and release).

2. Check the choke linkage for binding. The choke plate should be easily opened and closed with your finger. If the choke sticks or binds, it can usually be freed with a liberal application of a carburetor cleaner made for the purpose. A couple of quick squirts of the right stuff normally does the trick; if not, the carburetor will have to be disassembled for repairs.

3. The choke is correctly adjusted when the index mark on the choke housing (notch) aligns with the center mark on the carburetor body. If the setting is incorrect, loosen the three screws clamping the choke body in place and rotate the choke cover left or right until the marks align. Tighten the screws carefully to avoid cracking the housing.

Choke Unloader Adjustment

NOTE: *The choke must be cold for this adjustment.*

1. Close the choke valve completely.

2. Hold the choke valve closed by stretching a rubber band between the choke piston lever and a stationary part of the carburetor.

3. Open the throttle lever fully.

NOTE: *On all vehicles (except Stanza), the unloader cam is located next to the choke plate adjusting lever. On the Stanza, the unloader adjusting lever is connected to the primary throttle plate shaft, an intermediate cam is connected to the choke lever by a choke rod.*

4. Adjustment is made by bending the unloader tongue. Gauge the gap between the choke plate and the carburetor body to:
- 1976-77 F10: 2.00mm
- 1987 F10 and 310: 2.4mm
- Pulsar: 2.96mm
- Stanza: 2.05-2.85mm

Vacuum Break Adjustment

1. With the engine cold, close the choke completely.

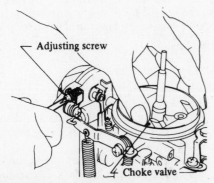

Adjusting the cam follow lever—Stanza

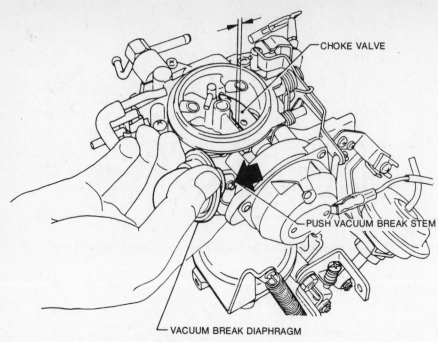

CHOKE VALVE

PUSH VACUUM BREAK STEM

VACUUM BREAK DIAPHRAGM

Vacuum break adjustment

2. Pull the vacuum break stem straight up as far as it will go.

3. Check the clearance between the choke plate and the carburetor wall.
Clearance should be:
- 1976-77 F10: 1.44-1.56mm
- 1978 F10 and 1979-80 310: 1.80-2.00mm
- 1981-82 310:
  1.60-1.80mm USA
  1.40-1.58mm Canada
- 1982-86 Stanza:
  3.12-3.72mm (above 68°F)
  1.65-2.25mm (below 41°F)
- 1983-86 Pulsar:
  1.33-1.73mm (below 63°F)
  2.40-2.80mm (above 75°F)

4. On the F10 and the 310 (1979-80), the adjustment is made by bending the connecting rod. Adjustment is made on Canadian models by bending the connecting rod; on USA 310 (1981-82) models by removing the plastic plug from the adjusting screw hole and turning the adjusting screw. On the Pulsar and the Stanza models, adjustment is made by bending the tang at the choke plate lever assembly.
NOTE: *On the Pulsar and the Stanza models, remove the choke cover, then connect a rubber band to the choke lever to hold it shut.*

Accelerator Pump Adjustment

If a smooth constant stream of fuel is not injected into the carburetor bore when the throt-

tle is opened, the accelerator pump needs adjustment.
NOTE: *The Stanza accelerator pump is of a different design and is not adjustable; if it is not operating correctly, replace it.*

1. Remove the carburetor from the engine.
2. Check the gap between the primary throttle valve and the inner wall of the carburetor when the pump lever comes in contact with the piston pin. This is the stroke limiter gap. It should be 1.3mm. If not, bend the stroke limiter.
3. Fill the carburetor bowl with fuel.
4. Fully open the choke.
5. Place a calibrated container under the throttle bore. Slowly open and close the throttle (full open to full closed) ten times keeping the throttle open 3 seconds each time. Measure the amount of fuel in the container. The amount should be 0.3-0.5 ml. If not, and the stroke limiter gap is correct, replace the accelerator pump unit.

Anti-Dieseling Solenoid

Check this valve if the engine continues to run after the key has been turned off.

1. Run the engine at idle speed and disconnect the lead wire at the anti-dieseling solenoid. The engine should stop.
2. If the engine does not stop, check the harness for current at the solenoid. If current is present, replace the solenoid. Installation

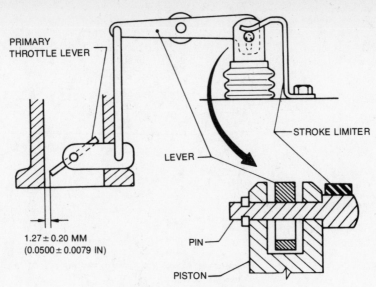

PRIMARY
THROTTLE LEVER

STROKE LIMITER

LEVER

PIN

PISTON

1.27 ± 0.20 MM
(0.0500 ± 0.0079 IN)

Accelerator pump adjustment

torque for the solenoid is 13-25 ft. lbs. for CA20 engines and 13-16 ft. lbs. for all other engines.

REMOVAL AND INSTALLATION

1. Remove the air cleaner.
2. Disconnect the electrical connector(s), the fuel and the vacuum hoses from the carburetor.
3. Remove the throttle lever.
4. Remove the four nuts and washers retaining the carburetor to the manifold.
5. Lift the carburetor from the manifold.
6. Remove and discard the gasket used between the carburetor and the manifold.
7. Install carburetor on the manifold, use a new base gasket and torque the carburetor mounting nuts to 9-13 ft. lbs.
8. Install the throttle lever.
9. Connect the electrical connector(s), the fuel and the vacuum hoses to the carburetor.
10. Install the air cleaner.
11. Start engine, warm engine and adjust as necessary.

OVERHAUL

CAUTION: *Never smoke when working around gasoline! Avoid all sources of sparks or ignition. Gasoline vapors are EXTREMELY volatile!*

Efficient carburetion depends greatly on careful cleaning and inspection during overhaul, since dirt, gum, water and/or varnish in or on the carburetor parts are often responsible for poor performance.

Overhaul your carburetor in a clean, dust free area. Carefully disassemble the carburetor, referring often to the exploded views. Keep all similar and look-alike parts segregated during disassembly and cleaning to avoid accidental interchange during assembly. Make a note of all jet sizes.

When the carburetor is disassembled, wash all the parts (except diaphragms, electric choke units, pump plunger and any other plastic, leather, fiber or rubber parts) in clean carburetor solvent. Do not leave parts in the solvent any longer than is necessary to sufficiently loosen the deposits. Excessive cleaning may remove the special finish from the float bowl and choke valve bodies, leaving these parts unfit for service. Rinse all parts in clean solvent and blow them dry with compressed air to allow them to air dry. Wipe clean all cork, plastic, leather and fiber parts with a clean, lint-free cloth.

Blow out all passages and jets with compressed air, be sure that there are no restrictions or blockages. Never use wire or similar tools for cleaning purposes; clean the jets and valves separately, to avoid accidental interchange.

Check all the parts for wear or damage. If wear or damage is found, replace the defective parts. Especially check the following:

1. Check the float needle and seat for wear. If wear is found, replace the complete assembly.
2. Check the float hinge pin for wear and the float(s) for dents or distortion. Replace the float if fuel has leaked into it.
3. Check the throttle and choke shaft bores for wear or an out-of-round condition. Damage or wear to the throttle arm, shaft or shaft bore will often require replacement of the throttle body. These parts require a close tolerance of fit; wear may allow air leakage, which could affect starting and idling.

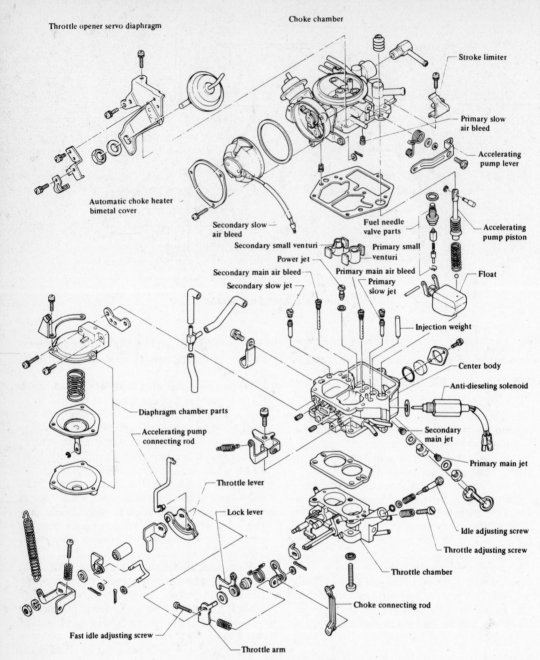

Throttle opener servo diaphragm

Choke chamber

Stroke limiter

Primary slow air bleed

Accelerating pump lever

Automatic choke heater bimetal cover

Secondary slow air bleed

Fuel needle valve parts

Accelerating pump piston

Secondary small venturi

Power jet

Primary small venturi

Secondary main air bleed

Primary main air bleed

Float

Secondary slow jet

Primary slow jet

Primary slow jet

Injection weight

Center body

Diaphragm chamber parts

Anti-dieseling solenoid

Accelerating pump connecting rod

Secondary main jet

Throttle lever

Primary main jet

Lock lever

Idle adjusting screw

Throttle adjusting screw

Throttle chamber

Choke connecting rod

Fast idle adjusting screw

Throttle arm

A series engine carburetor

NOTE: *Throttle shafts and bushings are not included in overhaul kits. They can be purchased separately.*

4. Inspect the idle mixture adjusting needles for burrs or grooves. Any such condition requires replacement of the needle, since you will not be able to obtain a satisfactory idle.

5. Test the accelerator pump check valves. They should pass air one way but not the other. Test for proper seating by blowing and sucking on the valve. Replace the valve if necessary. If the valve is satisfactory, wash the valve again to remove breath moisture.

6. Check the bowl cover for warped surfaces with a straightedge.

7. Closely inspect the valves and seats for wear and/or damage, replacing as necessary.

8. After the carburetor is assembled, check the choke valve for freedom of operation.

Carburetor overhaul kits are recommended for each overhaul. These kits contain all gaskets and new parts to replace those that deteri-

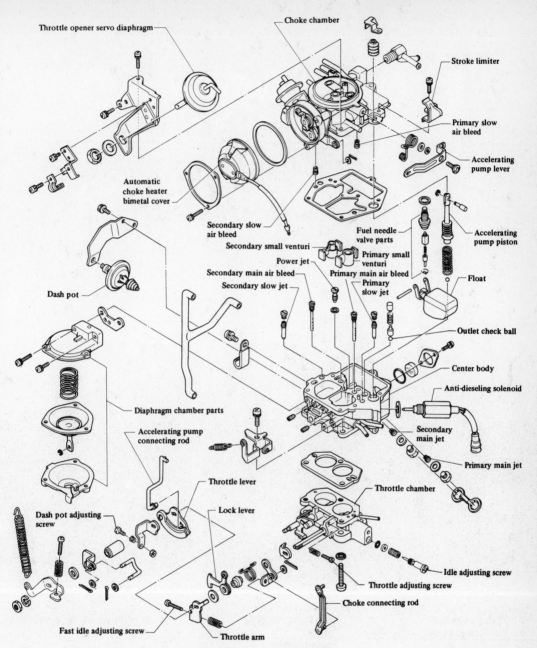

E series engine carburetor

orate most rapidly. Failure to replace all parts supplied with the kit (especially gaskets) can result in poor performance later.

Some carburetor manufacturers supply overhaul kits of three basic types: minor repair, major repair and gasket kits. Basically, they contain the following:

Minor Repair Kits:
- All gaskets
- Float needle valve
- Volume control screw
- All diaphragms

- Spring for the pump diaphragm

Major Repair Kits:
- All jets and gaskets
- All diaphragms
- Float needle valve
- Volume control screw
- Pump ball valve
- Main jet carrier
- Float

Gasket Kits:
- All gaskets

After cleaning and checking all components,

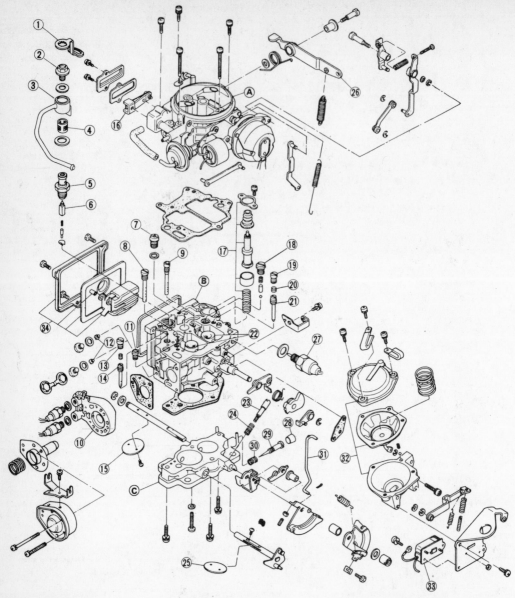

A. Choke chamber
B. Carburetor body
C. Throttle chamber
1. Lock lever
2. Filter set screw
3. Fuel nipple
4. Fuel filter
5. Needle valve body
6. Needle valve
7. Power valve
8. Secondary main air bleed
9. Primary main air bleed
10. B.C.D.D.
11. Secondary slow air bleed

12. Secondary main jet
13. Plug
14. Secondary slow jet
15. Primary throttle valve
16. Idle compensator
17. Accelerating pump parts
18. Plug for accelerating
    mechanism
19. Plug
20. Spring
21. Primary slow jet
22. Primary and secondary small
    venturi
23. Throttle adjusting screw

24. Throttle adjusting screw
    spring
25. Secondary throttle valve
26. Accelerating pump lever
27. Anti-dieseling solenoid valve
28. Blind plug
29. Idle adjusting screw
30. Idle adjusting screw spring
31. Choke connecting rod
32. Diaphragm chamber parts
33. Throttle valve switch
34. Float

CA20 engine carburetor

CHILTON'S
FUEL ECONOMY
& TUNE-UP TIPS

Tune-up • Spark Plug Diagnosis • Emission Controls

Fuel System • Cooling System • Tires and Wheels

General Maintenance

CHILTON'S FUEL ECONOMY & TUNE-UP TIPS

Fuel economy is important to everyone, no matter what kind of vehicle you drive. The maintenance-minded motorist can save both money and fuel using these tips and the periodic maintenance and tune-up procedures in this Repair and Tune-Up Guide.

There are more than 130,000,000 cars and trucks registered for private use in the United States. Each travels an average of 10-12,000 miles per year, and, and in total they consume close to 70 billion gallons of fuel each year. This represents nearly ⅔ of the oil imported by the United States each year. The Federal government's goal is to reduce consumption 10% by 1985. A variety of methods are either already in use or under serious consideration, and they all affect you driving and the cars you will drive. In addition to "down-sizing", the auto industry is using or investigating the use of electronic fuel delivery, electronic engine controls and alternative engines for use in smaller and lighter vehicles, among other alternatives to meet the federally mandated Corporate Average Fuel Economy (CAFE) of 27.5 mpg by 1985. The government, for its part, is considering rationing, mandatory driving curtailments and tax increases on motor vehicle fuel in an effort to reduce consumption. The government's goal of a 10% reduction could be realized — and further government regulation avoided — if every private vehicle could use just 1 less gallon of fuel per week.

How Much Can You Save?

Tests have proven that almost anyone can make at least a 10% reduction in fuel consumption through regular maintenance and tune-ups. When a major manufacturer of spark plugs sur-

TUNE-UP

1. Check the cylinder compression to be sure the engine will really benefit from a tune-up and that it is capable of producing good fuel economy. A tune-up will be wasted on an engine in poor mechanical condition.

2. Replace spark plugs regularly. New spark plugs alone can increase fuel economy 3%.

3. Be sure the spark plugs are the correct type (heat range) for your vehicle. See the Tune-Up Specifications.

Heat range refers to the spark plug's ability to conduct heat away from the firing end. It must conduct the heat away in an even pattern to avoid becoming a source of pre-ignition, yet it must also operate hot enough to burn off conductive deposits that could cause misfiring.

The heat range is usually indicated by a number on the spark plug, part of the manufacturer's designation for each individual spark plug. The numbers in bold-face indicate the heat range in each manufacturer's identification system.

Manufacturer	Typical Designation
AC	R 45 TS
Bosch (old)	WA **145** T30
Bosch (new)	HR **8** Y
Champion	RBL **15** Y
Fram/Autolite	415
Mopar	P-**62** PR
Motorcraft	BRF-**42**
NGK	BP **5** ES-15
Nippondenso	W **16** EP
Prestolite	14GR **5** 2A

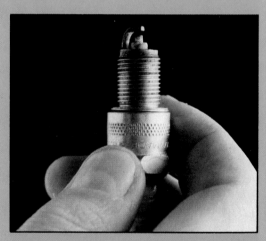

Periodically, check the spark plugs to be sure they are firing efficiently. They are excellent indicators of the internal condition of your engine.

On AC, Bosch (new), Champion, Fram/Autolite, Mopar, Motorcraft and Prestolite, a higher number indicates a hotter plug. On Bosch (old), NGK and Nippondenso, a higher number indicates a colder plug.

4. Make sure the spark plugs are properly gapped. See the Tune-Up Specifications in this book.

5. Be sure the spark plugs are firing efficiently. The illustrations on the next 2 pages show you how to "read" the firing end of the spark plug.

6. Check the ignition timing and set it to specifications. Tests show that almost all cars have incorrect ignition timing by more than 2°.

veyed over 6,000 cars nationwide, they found that a tune-up, on cars that needed one, increased fuel economy over 11%. Replacing worn plugs alone, accounted for a 3% increase. The same test also revealed that 8 out of every 10 vehicles will have some maintenance deficiency that will directly affect fuel economy, emissions or performance. Most of this mileage-robbing neglect could be prevented with regular maintenance.

Modern engines require that all of the functioning systems operate properly for maximum efficiency. A malfunction anywhere wastes fuel. You can keep your vehicle running as efficiently and economically as possible, by being aware of your vehicle's operating and performance characteristics. If your vehicle suddenly develops performance or fuel economy problems it could be due to one or more of the following:

PROBLEM	POSSIBLE CAUSE
Engine Idles Rough	Ignition timing, idle mixture, vacuum leak or something amiss in the emission control system.
Hesitates on Acceleration	Dirty carburetor or fuel filter, improper accelerator pump setting, ignition timing or fouled spark plugs.
Starts Hard or Fails to Start	Worn spark plugs, improperly set automatic choke, ice (or water) in fuel system.
Stalls Frequently	Automatic choke improperly adjusted and possible dirty air filter or fuel filter.
Performs Sluggishly	Worn spark plugs, dirty fuel or air filter, ignition timing or automatic choke out of adjustment.

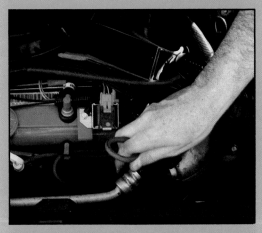

Check spark plug wires on conventional point type ignition for cracks by bending them in a loop around your finger.

Be sure that spark plug wires leading to adjacent cylinders do not run too close together. (Photo courtesy Champion Spark Plug Co.)

7. If your vehicle does not have electronic ignition, check the points, rotor and cap as specified.

8. Check the spark plug wires (used with conventional point-type ignitions) for cracks and burned or broken insulation by bending them in a loop around your finger. Cracked wires decrease fuel efficiency by failing to deliver full voltage to the spark plugs. One misfiring spark plug can cost you as much as 2 mpg.

9. Check the routing of the plug wires. Misfiring can be the result of spark plug leads to adjacent cylinders running parallel to each other and too close together. One wire tends to

pick up voltage from the other causing it to fire "out of time".

10. Check all electrical and ignition circuits for voltage drop and resistance.

11. Check the distributor mechanical and/or vacuum advance mechanisms for proper functioning. The vacuum advance can be checked by twisting the distributor plate in the opposite direction of rotation. It should spring back when released.

12. Check and adjust the valve clearance on engines with mechanical lifters. The clearance should be slightly loose rather than too tight.

SPARK PLUG DIAGNOSIS

Normal

APPEARANCE: This plug is typical of one operating normally. The insulator nose varies from a light tan to grayish color with slight electrode wear. The presence of slight deposits is normal on used plugs and will have no adverse effect on engine performance. The spark plug heat range is correct for the engine and the engine is running normally.

CAUSE: Properly running engine.

RECOMMENDATION: Before reinstalling this plug, the electrodes should be cleaned and filed square. Set the gap to specifications. If the plug has been in service for more than 10-12,000 miles, the entire set should probably be replaced with a fresh set of the same heat range.

Oil Deposits

APPEARANCE: The firing end of the plug is covered with a wet, oily coating.

CAUSE: The problem is poor oil control. On high mileage engines, oil is leaking past the rings or valve guides into the combustion chamber. A common cause is also a plugged PCV valve, and a ruptured fuel pump diaphragm can also cause this condition. Oil fouled plugs such as these are often found in new or recently overhauled engines, before normal oil control is achieved, and can be cleaned and reinstalled.

RECOMMENDATION: A hotter spark plug may temporarily relieve the problem, but the engine is probably in need of work.

Incorrect Heat Range

APPEARANCE: The effects of high temperature on a spark plug are indicated by clean white, often blistered insulator. This can also be accompanied by excessive wear of the electrode, and the absence of deposits.

CAUSE: Check for the correct spark plug heat range. A plug which is too hot for the engine can result in overheating. A car operated mostly at high speeds can require a colder plug. Also check ignition timing, cooling system level, fuel mixture and leaking intake manifold.

RECOMMENDATION: If all ignition and engine adjustments are known to be correct, and no other malfunction exists, install spark plugs one heat range colder.

Carbon Deposits

APPEARANCE: Carbon fouling is easily identified by the presence of dry, soft, black, sooty deposits.

CAUSE: Changing the heat range can often lead to carbon fouling, as can prolonged slow, stop-and-start driving. If the heat range is correct, carbon fouling can be attributed to a rich fuel mixture, sticking choke, clogged air cleaner, worn breaker points, retarded timing or low compression. If only one or two plugs are carbon fouled, check for corroded or cracked wires on the affected plugs. Also look for cracks in the distributor cap between the towers of affected cylinders.

RECOMMENDATION: After the problem is corrected, these plugs can be cleaned and reinstalled if not worn severely.

Photos Courtesy Fram Corporation

MMT Fouled

APPEARANCE: Spark plugs fouled by MMT (Methycyclopentadienyl Maganese Tricarbonyl) have reddish, rusty appearance on the insulator and side electrode.

CAUSE: MMT is an anti-knock additive in gasoline used to replace lead. During the combustion process, the MMT leaves a reddish deposit on the insulator and side electrode.

RECOMMENDATION: No engine malfunction is indicated and the deposits will not affect plug performance any more than lead deposits (see Ash Deposits). MMT fouled plugs can be cleaned, regapped and reinstalled.

High Speed Glazing

APPEARANCE: Glazing appears as shiny coating on the plug, either yellow or tan in color.

CAUSE: During hard, fast acceleration, plug temperatures rise suddenly. Deposits from normal combustion have no chance to fluff-off; instead, they melt on the insulator forming an electrically conductive coating which causes misfiring.

RECOMMENDATION: Glazed plugs are not easily cleaned. They should be replaced with a fresh set of plugs of the correct heat range. If the condition recurs, using plugs with a heat range one step colder may cure the problem.

Ash (Lead) Deposits

APPEARANCE: Ash deposits are characterized by light brown or white colored deposits crusted on the side or center electrodes. In some cases it may give the plug a rusty appearance.

CAUSE: Ash deposits are normally derived from oil or fuel additives burned during normal combustion. Normally they are harmless, though excessive amounts can cause misfiring. If deposits are excessive in short mileage, the valve guides may be worn.

RECOMMENDATION: Ash-fouled plugs can be cleaned, gapped and reinstalled.

Detonation

APPEARANCE: Detonation is usually characterized by a broken plug insulator.

CAUSE: A portion of the fuel charge will begin to burn spontaneously, from the increased heat following ignition. The explosion that results applies extreme pressure to engine components, frequently damaging spark plugs and pistons.

Detonation can result by over-advanced ignition timing, inferior gasoline (low octane) lean air/fuel mixture, poor carburetion, engine lugging or an increase in compression ratio due to combustion chamber deposits or engine modification.

RECOMMENDATION: Replace the plugs after correcting the problem.

Photos Courtesy Champion Spark Plug Co.

EMISSION CONTROLS

13. Be aware of the general condition of the emission control system. It contributes to reduced pollution and should be serviced regularly to maintain efficient engine operation.

14. Check all vacuum lines for dried, cracked or brittle conditions. Something as simple as a leaking vacuum hose can cause poor performance and loss of economy.

15. Avoid tampering with the emission control system. Attempting to improve fuel econ-

FUEL SYSTEM

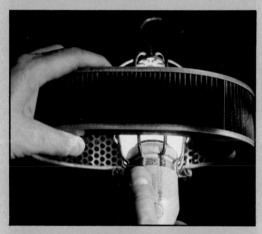

Check the air filter with a light behind it. If you can see light through the filter it can be reused.

Extremely clogged filters should be discarded and replaced with a new one.

18. Replace the air filter regularly. A dirty air filter richens the air/fuel mixture and can increase fuel consumption as much as 10%. Tests show that ⅓ of all vehicles have air filters in need of replacement.

19. Replace the fuel filter at least as often as recommended.

20. Set the idle speed and carburetor mixture to specifications.

21. Check the automatic choke. A sticking or malfunctioning choke wastes gas.

22. During the summer months, adjust the automatic choke for a leaner mixture which will produce faster engine warm-ups.

COOLING SYSTEM

29. Be sure all accessory drive belts are in good condition. Check for cracks or wear.

30. Adjust all accessory drive belts to proper tension.

31. Check all hoses for swollen areas, worn spots, or loose clamps.

32. Check coolant level in the radiator or ex- pansion tank.

33. Be sure the thermostat is operating properly. A stuck thermostat delays engine warm-up and a cold engine uses nearly twice as much fuel as a warm engine.

34. Drain and replace the engine coolant at least as often as recommended. Rust and scale

TIRES & WHEELS

38. Check the tire pressure often with a pencil type gauge. Tests by a major tire manufacturer show that 90% of all vehicles have at least 1 tire improperly inflated. Better mileage can be achieved by over-inflating tires, but never exceed the maximum inflation pressure on the side of the tire.

39. If possible, install radial tires. Radial tires deliver as much as ½ mpg more than bias belted tires.

40. Avoid installing super-wide tires. They only create extra rolling resistance and decrease fuel mileage. Stick to the manufacturer's recommendations.

41. Have the wheels properly balanced.

omy by tampering with emission controls is more likely to worsen fuel economy than improve it. Emission control changes on modern engines are not readily reversible.

16. Clean (or replace) the EGR valve and lines as recommended.

17. Be sure that all vacuum lines and hoses are reconnected properly after working under the hood. An unconnected or misrouted vacuum line can wreak havoc with engine performance.

23. Check for fuel leaks at the carburetor, fuel pump, fuel lines and fuel tank. Be sure all lines and connections are tight.

24. Periodically check the tightness of the carburetor and intake manifold attaching nuts and bolts. These are a common place for vacuum leaks to occur.

25. Clean the carburetor periodically and lubricate the linkage.

26. The condition of the tailpipe can be an excellent indicator of proper engine combustion. After a long drive at highway speeds, the inside of the tailpipe should be a light grey in color. Black or soot on the insides indicates an overly rich mixture.

27. Check the fuel pump pressure. The fuel pump may be supplying more fuel than the engine needs.

28. Use the proper grade of gasoline for your engine. Don't try to compensate for knocking or "pinging" by advancing the ignition timing. This practice will only increase plug temperature and the chances of detonation or pre-ignition with relatively little performance gain.

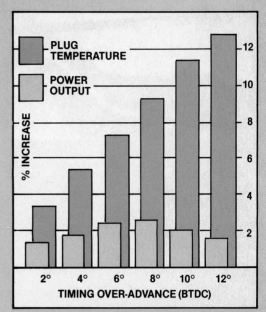

Increasing ignition timing past the specified setting results in a drastic increase in spark plug temperature with increased chance of detonation or preignition. Performance increase is considerably less. (Photo courtesy Champion Spark Plug Co.)

that form in the engine should be flushed out to allow the engine to operate at peak efficiency.

35. Clean the radiator of debris that can decrease cooling efficiency.

36. Install a flex-type or electric cooling fan, if you don't have a clutch type fan. Flex fans use curved plastic blades to push more air at low speeds when more cooling is needed; at high speeds the blades flatten out for less resistance. Electric fans only run when the engine temperature reaches a predetermined level.

37. Check the radiator cap for a worn or cracked gasket. If the cap does not seal properly, the cooling system will not function properly.

42. Be sure the front end is correctly aligned. A misaligned front end actually has wheels going in differed directions. The increased drag can reduce fuel economy by .3 mpg.

43. Correctly adjust the wheel bearings. Wheel bearings that are adjusted too tight increase rolling resistance.

Check tire pressures regularly with a reliable pocket type gauge. Be sure to check the pressure on a cold tire.

GENERAL MAINTENANCE

Check the fluid levels (particularly engine oil) on a regular basis. Be sure to check the oil for grit, water or other contamination.

A vacuum gauge is another excellent indicator of internal engine condition and can also be installed in the dash as a mileage indicator.

44. Periodically check the fluid levels in the engine, power steering pump, master cylinder, automatic transmission and drive axle.

45. Change the oil at the recommended interval and change the filter at every oil change. Dirty oil is thick and causes extra friction between moving parts, cutting efficiency and increasing wear. A worn engine requires more frequent tune-ups and gets progressively worse fuel economy. In general, use the lightest viscosity oil for the driving conditions you will encounter.

46. Use the recommended viscosity fluids in the transmission and axle.

47. Be sure the battery is fully charged for fast starts. A slow starting engine wastes fuel.

48. Be sure battery terminals are clean and tight.

49. Check the battery electrolyte level and add distilled water if necessary.

50. Check the exhaust system for crushed pipes, blockages and leaks.

51. Adjust the brakes. Dragging brakes or brakes that are not releasing create increased drag on the engine.

52. Install a vacuum gauge or miles-per-gallon gauge. These gauges visually indicate engine vacuum in the intake manifold. High vacuum = good mileage and low vacuum = poorer mileage. The gauge can also be an excellent indicator of internal engine conditions.

53. Be sure the clutch is properly adjusted. A slipping clutch wastes fuel.

54. Check and periodically lubricate the heat control valve in the exhaust manifold. A sticking or inoperative valve prevents engine warm-up and wastes gas.

55. Keep accurate records to check fuel economy over a period of time. A sudden drop in fuel economy may signal a need for tune-up or other maintenance.

FUEL SYSTEM   189

Carburetor Specifications

Year	Engine	Vehicle Model	Carb Model	Main Jet # Primary	Main Jet # Secondary	Main Air Bleed # Primary	Main Air Bleed # Secondary	Slow Jet # Primary	Slow Jet # Secondary	Float Level (in.)	Power Jet #
1976	A14 California	F10	DCH306-17	105	145	95	80	45	50	0.75	40
	A14 (Federal)	F10	DCH306-16	103	145	95	80	45	50	0.75	40
1977	A14 California	F10	DCH306-17A	106	145	95	80	45	50	0.75	40
	A14 (Federal)	F10	DCH306-16A	105	145	95	80	45	50	0.75	40
1978	A14 (California)	F10	DCH306-65	106	145	95	80	45	50	0.75	40
	A14 (Federal)	F10	DCH306-64	105	145	95	80	45	50	0.75	40
1979	A14 (California)	310	DCH306-75	107	145	95	80	45	50	0.75	43
	A14 (Federal)	310	DCH306-76	105	145	110	80	45	50	0.75	40
1980	A14 (California)	310	DCH306-112	107	145	80	80	45	50	0.75	38
	A14 (Federal)	310	DCH306-102	107	143	65	60	45	50	0.75	43
1981	A15 (Federal)	310	DCR306-103	114	125	80	80	45	50	0.75	35
	A15 (California)	310	DCR306-113	113	125	60	80	45	50	0.75	35
	A15 (Canada)	310	DCR306-123	100	145	70	80	43	70	0.75	40

Carburetor Specifications (continued)

Year	Engine	Vehicle Model	Carb Model	Main Jet #		Main Air Bleed #		Slow Jet #		Float Level (in.)	Power Jet #
				Primary	Secondary	Primary	Secondary	Primary	Secondary		
1982	E15 (Federal)	310	DCR306-130	116	125	80	80	45	50	0.47	38
	E15 (California)	310	DCR306-140	114	125	60	80	45	50	0.47	38
	E15 (Canada)	310	DCR306-150MT	100	120	70	60	43	80	0.47	40
	E15 (Canada)	310	DCR306-151AT	100	120	70	60	43	80	0.47	40
	CA20 (Fed. & Canada)	Stanza	DCR342-33	111	160	90	60	47	100	0.91	45
	CA20 (California)	Stanza	DCR342-31	113	160	90	60	47	100	0.91	45
1983	CA20 ① (Federal)	Stanza	DCR342-25	111	160	95	60	47	100	0.91	45
	CA20 (Calif.)	Stanza	DCR342-37 ① DCR342-38 ②	113	160	95	60	47	100	0.91	45
	CA20 ② (Canada)	Stanza	DCR342-36	113	160	95	60	47	100	0.91	40
	E16 (Calif.)	Pulsar	DFC328-1 ① DFC328-2 ②	91	130	105	60	43	70	0.47	—
	E16 (Federal)	Pulsar	DCZ328-1 ① DCZ328-2 ②	106	133	100	60	43	55	0.47	35
	E16 (Canada)	Pulsar	DCZ328-11 ① DCZ328-12 ②	100	135	110	60	43	65	0.47	35

Carburetor Specifications (continued)

Year	Engine	Vehicle Model	Carb Model	Main Jet # Primary	Main Jet # Secondary	Main Air Bleed # Primary	Main Air Bleed # Secondary	Slow Jet # Primary	Slow Jet # Secondary	Float Level (in.)	Power Jet #
1984	CA20S (Canada)	Stanza	DCR342-35① DCR342-36②	111	155	95	60	47	100	0.91	45① 40②
	E16 (Federal)	Pulsar	DFE2832-1①	90	105	80	70	43	65	0.47	—
			DFE2832-2②	82	105	110	70	45	65	0.47	—
	E16 (Calif.)	Pulsar	DFC328-1F② DFC328-2F②	91	130	110	60	43	65	0.47	—
	E16 (Canada)	Pulsar	DCZ328-11F① DCZ328-12F②	100	135	110	60	43	65	0.47	35
1985–86	CA20S (Canada)	Stanza	DCR342-35① DCR342-36②	111	155	95	60	47	100	③	45① 40②
	E16 (Federal)	Pulsar	DFE2832-5①	90	105	80	70	43	65	0.47	—
			DFE2832-6②	82	105	110	70	45	65	0.47	—
	E16 (Calif.)	Pulsar	DFC328-1F② DFC328-2F②	91	130	110	60	43	65	0.47	—
	E16 (Canada)	Pulsar	DCZ328-11G① DCZ328-12G②	100	135	110	60	43	65	0.47	35

① Manual Transmission
② Automatic Transmission
③ Use the sight adjusting glass on the side of the float bowl

reassemble the carburetor, using new parts and referring to the exploded view. When reassembling, make sure that all screws and jets are tight in their seats but do not overtighten as the tips will be distorted. Tighten all screws gradually in rotation. Do not tighten needle valves into their seats; uneven jetting will result. Always use new gaskets. Be sure to adjust the float level when reassembling.

FUEL INJECTED SYSTEM

NOTE: *This book contains basic testing and service procedures for your car's fuel injection system. More comprehensive testing and diagnosis procedures may be found in* CHILTON'S GUIDE TO FUEL INJECTION AND FEEDBACK CARBURETORS, *book No. 7488, available at your local retailer.*
The electronic fuel injection (EFI) system is an electronic type using various types of sensors to convert engine operating conditions into electronic signals. The generated information is fed to a control unit, where it is analyzed, then calculated electrical signals are sent to the various equipment, to control the idle speed, the timing and amount of fuel being injected into the engine.

Electrical Fuel Pump

The Stanza (1984-86) fuel pump is located under the vehicle in front of the fuel tank, the (1987-89) Stanza use in-tank fuel pump. The Pulsar (1984) Turbo and all other fuel injected Pulsar models (1987-88) use an in-tank type pump.
The fuel pumps are of a wet type, where the vane rollers are directly coupled to the motor, which is filled with fuel. A relief valve in the pump is designed to open, should a malfunction arise in the system.
NOTE: *Before disconnecting the fuel lines or any of the fuel system components, refer to Fuel Pressure Release procedures, in this section and release the fuel pressure.*

REMOVAL AND INSTALLATION

CAUTION: *Never smoke when working around gasoline! Avoid all sources of sparks or ignition. Gasoline vapors are EXTREMELY volatile!*

1984-86 Stanza

1. Disconnect the negative battery cable.
2. Raise and support the rear of the vehicle on jackstands.
3. Disconnect the electrical connector from the fuel pump.
4. Place fuel container under the fuel lines, then disconnect the fuel lines and drain the excess fuel into the container.
5. Remove the mounting braces and the fuel pump from the vehicle.
6. Install the vehicle fuel lines to the pump.
7. Install the mounting braces and mount pump to vehicle.

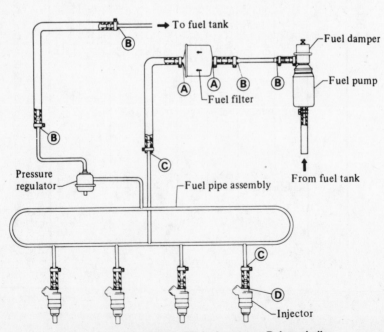

Description of the Stanza EFI fuel system—Pulsar similar

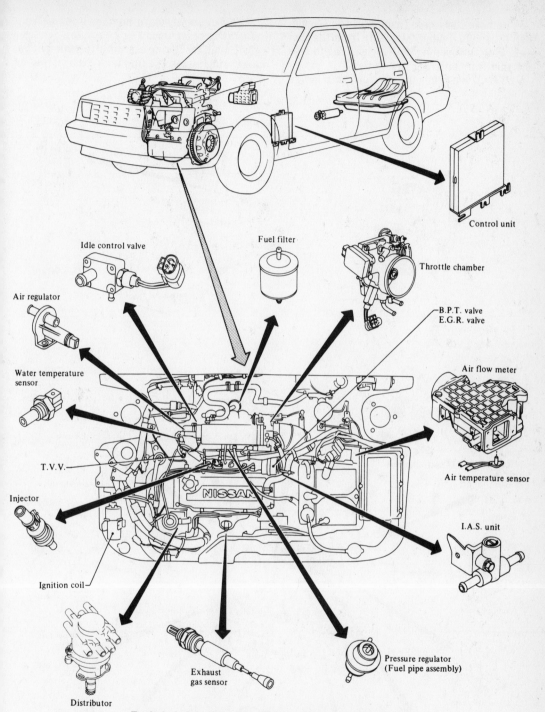

Idle control valve

Fuel filter

Control unit

Throttle chamber

Air regulator

B.P.T. valve
E.G.R. valve

Water temperature
sensor

Air flow meter

T.V.V.

Air temperature sensor

Injector

I.A.S. unit

Ignition coil

Distributor

Exhaust
gas sensor

Pressure regulator
(Fuel pipe assembly)

NISSAN

Exploded view of the EFI system—Stanza (1984 and later)

8. Connect fuel pump electrical connector.

9. Reconnect battery cable, start engine and check for leaks.

1987-88 Stanza
1984 Pulsar Turbo
1987-88 Pulsar

1. Disconnect the negative battery cable.
2. Open the trunk lid, disconnect the fuel gauge electrical connector and remove the fuel tank inspection cover.

NOTE: *If vehicle has no fuel tank inspection cover the fuel tank must be removed.*

3. Disconnect the fuel outlet and the return hoses.

4. Using a large brass drift pin and a hammer, drive the fuel tank locking ring in the counterclockwise direction.

5. Remove the locking ring and the O-ring, then lift the fuel pump assembly from the fuel tank. Plug the opening with a clean rag to prevent dirt from entering the system.

NOTE: *When removing the fuel tank gauge*

unit, be careful not to damage or deform it. Install a new O-ring.

6. Install fuel pump assembly in tank. With a new O-ring install the fuel tank locking ring in place.

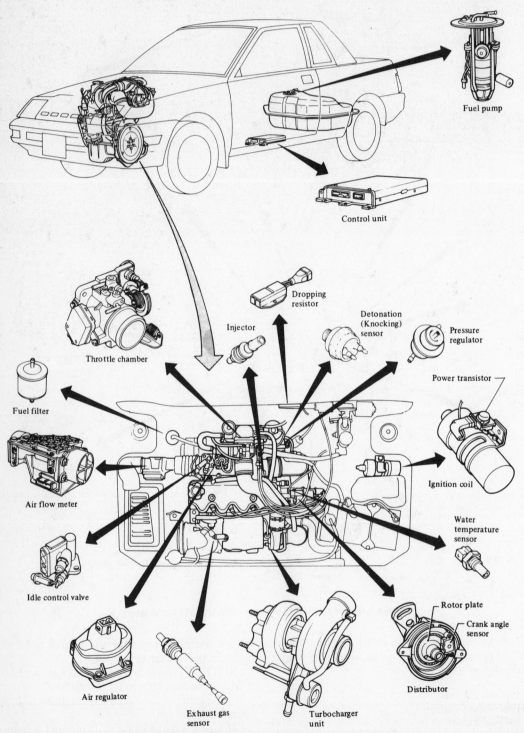

Fuel pump

Control unit

Throttle chamber

Injector

Dropping resistor

Detonation (Knocking) sensor

Pressure regulator

Power transistor

Fuel filter

Air flow meter

Ignition coil

Water temperature sensor

Idle control valve

Rotor plate

Crank angle sensor

Distributor

Air regulator

Exhaust gas sensor

Turbocharger unit

Exploded view of the Turbo EFI system—Pulsar (1984)

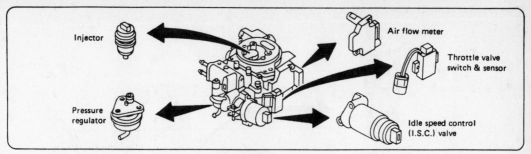

Throttle body assembly

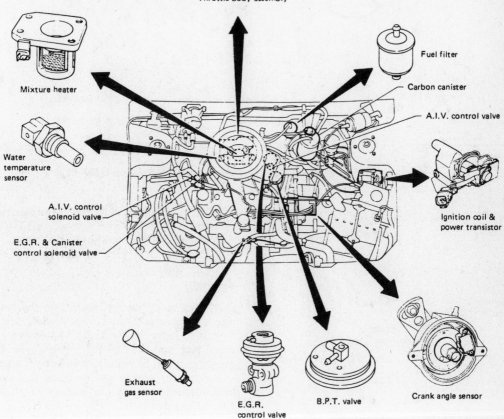

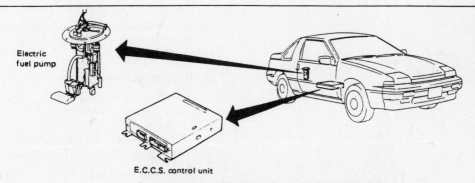

E.C.C.S. control unit

Exploded view of the EFI system—Pulsar (1987–88)

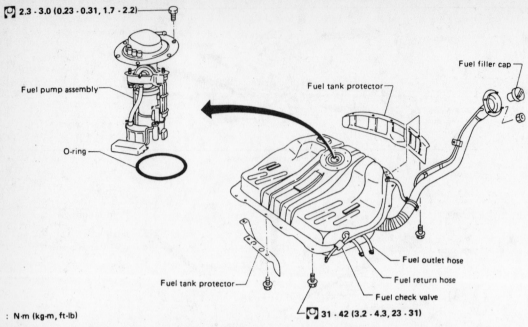

2.3 - 3.0 (0.23 - 0.31, 1.7 - 2.2)

Fuel pump assembly

Fuel filler cap

Fuel tank protector

O-ring

Fuel tank protector

Fuel outlet hose

Fuel return hose

Fuel check valve

: N·m (kg-m, ft-lb)

31 - 42 (3.2 - 4.3, 23 - 31)

In-tank fuel pump—Stanza (1987–88)—Pulsar turbo (1984)—Pulsar (1987–88)

Installing new O-ring in the fuel tank

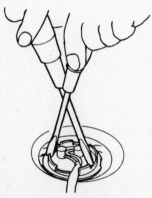

Remove locking ring on the fuel tank

7. Reconnect the fuel lines and the electrical connection.

8. Install the fuel tank inspection cover.

9. Connect battery cable, start engine and check for leaks.

TESTING

1. Disconnect the fuel hose from the metal pipe leading from the fuel filter, then install the Pressure Gauge tool J-25400-34 between the metal pipe and the fuel filter hose. Place the gauge, so it can be read from the driver's seat.

2. Start the engine and read the fuel pressure, it should be 30 psi (at idle) or 37 psi (engine accelerated).

NOTE: *If the reading is not correct, replace the pressure regulator and repeat the checking procedure. If the pressure is below specifications, check for clogged or deformed fuel lines; if necessary, replace the fuel pump or check valve.*

Fuel Pressure Regulator

The pressure regulator is located on the fuel return side of the fuel injection rail, under the fuel rail (Stanza EFI system) or next to the oil filter (Pulsar Turbo) and under the throttle body assembly on (Pulsar EFI models).

REMOVAL AND INSTALLATION

CAUTION: *Never smoke when working around gasoline! Avoid all sources of sparks or ignition. Gasoline vapors are EXTREMELY volatile!*

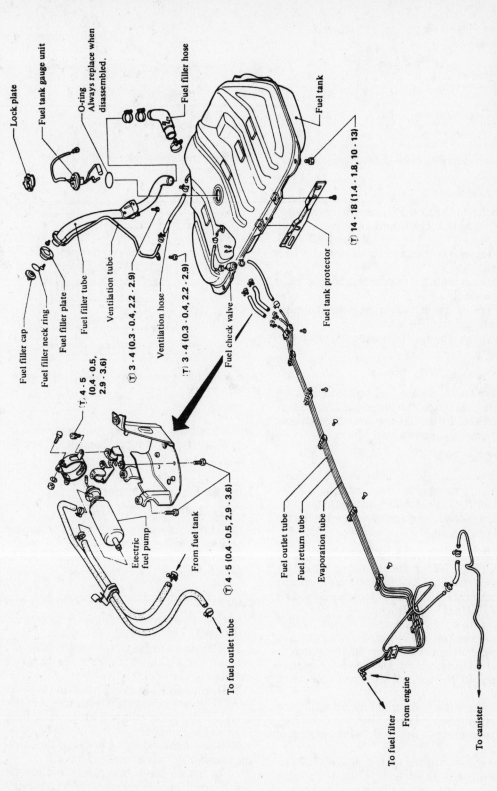

Lock plate

Fuel tank gauge unit

O-ring
Always replace when
disassembled.

Fuel filler hose

Fuel filler cap

Fuel filler neck ring

Fuel filler plate

Fuel filler tube

Ventilation tube

Ventilation hose

(T) 4 - 5
(0.4 - 0.5,
2.9 - 3.6)

(T) 3 - 4 (0.3 - 0.4, 2.2 - 2.9)

(T) 3 - 4 (0.3 - 0.4, 2.2 - 2.9)

Fuel check valve

Fuel tank

(T) 14 - 18 (1.4 - 1.8, 10 - 13)

Fuel tank protector

Fuel outlet tube

Fuel return tube

Evaporation tube

Electric
fuel pump

From fuel tank

(T) 4 - 5 (0.4 - 0.5, 2.9 - 3.6)

To fuel outlet tube

To fuel filter

From engine

To canister

τ : N·m (kg·m, ft-lb)

External fuel pump—Stanza (1984—86)

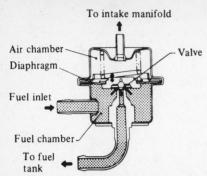

Cross-sectional view of the pressure regulator

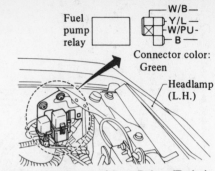

Location of fuel pump relay—Pulsar (Turbo)

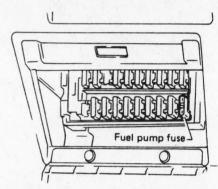

Removing fuel pump fuse—Stanza (1987)—other models similar

Stanza EFI System

1. Refer to the Fuel Pressure Release procedures, in this section and release the fuel pressure.
2. Remove the vacuum tubes and the EFI harness.
3. Remove the air regulator and the PCV valve assembly.
4. Remove the bolts retaining the fuel pipe assembly and the injectors.
5. Remove the fuel pipe assembly with the injectors.

Pulsar Turbo

To replace it, release fuel pressure, remove the fuel line clamps, the hoses and the mounting bracket. To install, use new hose clamps and reverse the removal procedures.

Pulsar EFI System

To replace it, release fuel pressure, remove the fuel line clamps, the hoses and the mounting screws from the throttle body assembly. To install, use new hose clamps and reverse the removal procedures.

FUEL PRESSURE RELEASE PROCEDURE

CAUTION: *Never smoke when working around gasoline! Avoid all sources of sparks or ignition. Gasoline vapors are EXTREMELY volatile!*

Any time the fuel system is being worked on, disconnect the negative battery cable, execept for those tests where battery voltage is required and always keep a dry chemical (Class B) fire extinguisher near the work area.

1. Remove the fuel pump fuse from the fuse block, fuel pump relay or disconnect the harness connector at the tank while engine is running.
2. It should run and then stall when the fuel in the lines is exhausted. When the engine stops, crank the starter for about 3 seconds to make sure all pressure in the fuel lines is released.

3. Install the fuel pump fuse, relay or harness connector after repair is made.

Throttle Body/Chamber
REMOVAL AND INSTALLATION

CAUTION: *Never smoke when working around gasoline! Avoid all sources of sparks or ignition. Gasoline vapors are EXTREMELY volatile!*

Stanza

NOTE: *The throttle chamber is located on the intake side of the intake plenum.*

1. Disconnect the negative battery cable and remove the intake duct from the throttle chamber.
2. Disconnect the vacuum hoses and the electrical harness connector from the throttle chamber. Disconnect the accelerator cable from the throttle chamber.
3. Remove the mounting bolts and the throttle chamber from the intake plenum.
4. To install, use a new gasket and reverse the removal procedures. Torque the throttle chamber bolts to 13-16 ft. lbs. Adjust the throttle cable if necessary.

Pulsar EFI

1. Release the fuel pump pressure and disconnect the negative battery cable.

2. Disconnect the vacuum hoses, fuel line and the electrical connections from the throttle body. Disconnect the accelerator cable from the throttle body.

3. Remove the mounting bolts and the throttle body from the intake manifold.

4. To install, use a new gasket and reverse

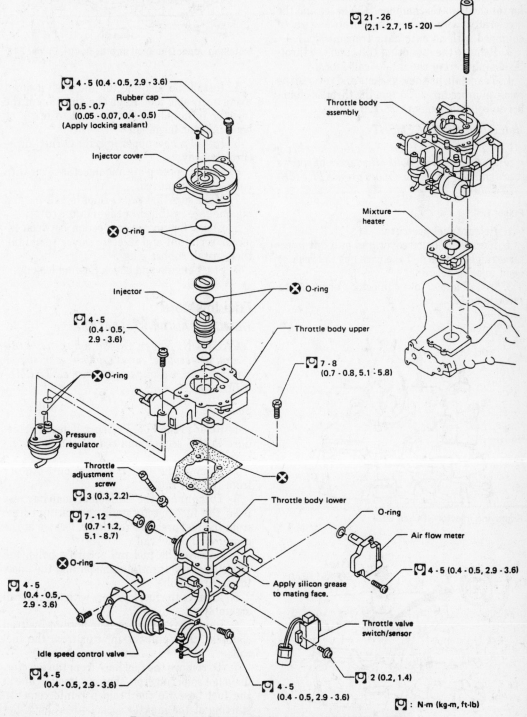

Exploded view of the throttle body assembly—Pulsar E16i

the removal procedures. Torque the throttle chamber bolts to 15-20 ft. lbs. Adjust the throttle cable if necessary.

Pulsar Turbo

1. Disconnect the air inlet pipe from the throttle chamber.
2. Disconnect the electrical harness connector (at the throttle chamber), the hoses and the accelerator wire and/or the throttle wire (if equipped with an automatic transmission).
3. Remove the mounting bolts and the throttle chamber from the intake collector.
4. To install, use new gaskets and reverse the removal procedures. Torque the throttle chamber-to-collector bolts to 78-120 in. lbs.

INJECTOR REPLACEMENT

CAUTION: *Never smoke when working around gasoline! Avoid all sources of sparks or ignition. Gasoline vapors are EXTREMELY volatile!*

Pulsar EFI

1. Release fuel pressure.
2. Remove injector cover and pull out injector straight upward. Take care not to break or bend injector terminal.
3. Install a new lower injector O-ring in the throttle body.

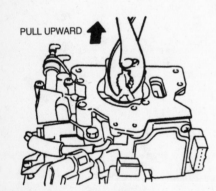

Removing injector—Pulsar E16i

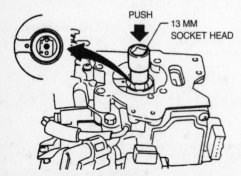

Installing injector—Pulsar E16i

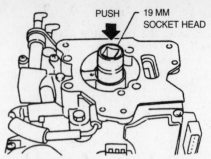

Installing upper O-ring on throttle body—Pulsar E16i

4. Install the fuel injector and push it down using a suitable tool. Align the direction of the injector terminals. Take care not to break or bend injector terminal.
5. Install a new upper injector O-ring in the throttle body.
6. Install upper plate and injector cover with rubber plug removed.
7. Make sure that two O-rings (small one and big one) are installed in the injector cover.
8. Check for proper connection between injector terminal and injector cover terminal, then install rubber plug.
9. Start engine and check for fuel leaks.

Fuel Injectors

REMOVAL AND INSTALLATION

CAUTION: *Never smoke when working around gasoline! Avoid all sources of sparks or ignition. Gasoline vapors are EXTREMELY volatile!*

Stanza

1. Refer to the Fuel Pressure Release Procedure in this section and reduce the fuel pressure to zero.
2. Remove the fuel inlet and outlet hoses from the fuel rail.
3. Disconnect the EFI electrical harness from the fuel injectors and the vacuum hose from the fuel pressure regulator, located at the center of the fuel rail.
4. Remove the fuel rail securing bolts, the collector at the throttle chamber and the injector securing bolts.
5. Remove the fuel injectors with the fuel rail assembly.
6. Remove the fuel injector hose-to-fuel rail clamp(s), then pull the injector from the fuel rail.
7. To remove the fuel hose from the injector, use a hot soldering iron, then cut (melt) a line in the fuel hose (to the braided reinforcement), starting at the injector socket to ¾" long. Remove the hose from the injector, by hand.

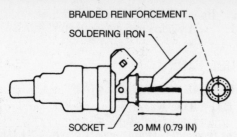

Removing fuel hose from injector—Stanza and Pulsar turbo

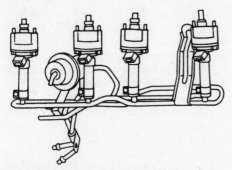

Fuel rail and pressure regulator—Stanza

NOTE: *DO NOT allow the soldering iron to cut all the way through the hose, nor touch the injector seat or damage the plastic socket connector.*

8. To install a new fuel hose, clean the injector tail section, wet the inside of the new hose with fuel, push the hose into the fuel injector hose socket (as far as it will go). Assemble the injector(s) onto the fuel rail.

9. Install the injectors with new O-rings and securing bolts.

10. Install the collector at the throttle chamber and the fuel rail securing bolts.

11. Connect the EFI electrical harness to the fuel injectors and the vacuum hose to the fuel pressure regulator.

12. Connect all the fuel lines.

13. Start engine and check for fuel leaks.

Pulsar Turbo

1. Refer to the Fuel Pressure Release procedure, in this section and lower the fuel pressure to zero.

2. Remove the air inlet pipe and the hose.

3. Disconnect the accelerator wire and (if equipped with an automatic transmission) the throttle wire.

4. Disconnect the throttle valve switch electrical harness connector, the mounting bolts and the throttle chamber.

5. Remove the PCV valve and the hose.

6. Loosen the clamps at both ends of the air pipe.

7. Disconnect the IVC and the air regulator harness connectors.

8. Remove the air pipe.

9. Disconnect the harness connectors from the injectors. Remove the fuel hoses. Remove the fuel rail mounting bolts and the fuel injector mounting screws.

10. Remove the fuel rail assembly by pulling out the fuel rail and the injectors.

11. Unfasten the fuel injector-to-fuel rail hose clamp and pull the injector from the fuel rail.

NOTE: *When disconnecting the fuel injector from the fuel rail, place a rag under it to prevent fuel splash.*

12. To remove the fuel hose from the injector, use a hot soldering iron, then cut (melt) a line in the fuel hose (to the braided reinforcement), starting at the injector socket to ¾" long (up the hose). Remove the hose from the injector, by hand.

NOTE: *DO NOT allow the soldering iron to cut all the way through the hose, nor touch the injector seat or damage the plastic socket connector.*

13. To install a new fuel hose, clean the injec-

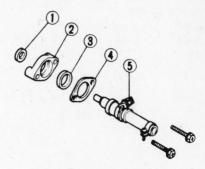

1   Injector lower rubber insulator
2   Injector lower holder
3   Injector upper rubber insulator
4   Injector upper holder
5   Injector

Injector—Pulsar turbo—others similar

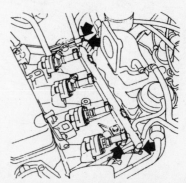

Removing fuel rail securing bolts—Pulsar turbo

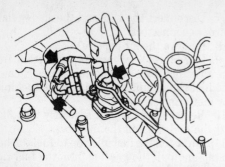

Removing I.C.V and air regulator harness connectors—Pulsar turbo

tor tail section, wet the inside of the new hose with fuel, push the hose into the fuel injector hose socket (as far as it will go). Assemble the injector(s) onto the fuel rail.

14. Install injectors on fuel rail.

15. Install fuel rail to engine. Always use new O-rings on injectors.

16. Install fuel lines to fuel rail and electrical connections to injectors.

17. Install the air pipe.

18. Reconnect the IVC and the air regulator harness connectors.

19. Install PCV valve and hose.

20. Install the throttle chamber and attaching parts.

21. Install the air inlet pipe and hose.

22. Start engine and check for fuel leaks.

FUEL TANK

REMOVAL AND INSTALLATION

CAUTION: *Never smoke when working around gasoline! Avoid all sources of sparks or ignition. Gasoline vapors are EXTREMELY volatile!*

F10

1. Disconnect the battery ground cable.

2. Drain the fuel into a suitable container.

3. Disconnect the filler hose, the air vent hose, fuel return hose, and fuel outlet hose.

4. Disconnect the wires from sending unit.

5. Remove the bolts securing the fuel tank and remove the tank.

6. Installation is in the reverse order of removal.

NOTE: *For the F10 Wagon, the removal procedure is the same as that for the sedan and hatchback. However, when removing the fuel tank bolts, it is easier if you start at the three bolts at the front of the tank.*

310

1. Disconnect the battery ground cable, remove the drain plug and drain the fuel.

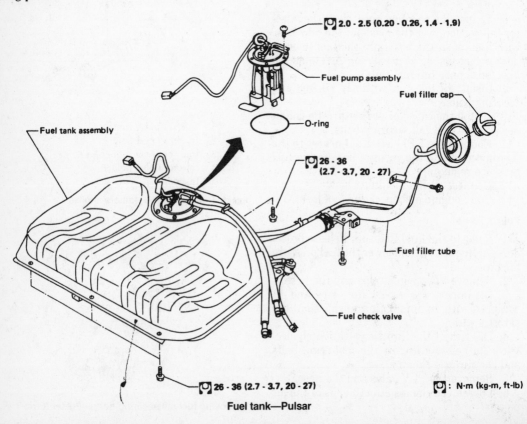

Fuel pump assembly

Fuel filler cap

O-ring

Fuel tank assembly

26 - 36 (2.7 - 3.7, 20 - 27)

Fuel filler tube

Fuel check valve

2.0 - 2.5 (0.20 - 0.26, 1.4 - 1.9)

26 - 36 (2.7 - 3.7, 20 - 27)

: N·m (kg-m, ft-lb)

Fuel tank—Pulsar

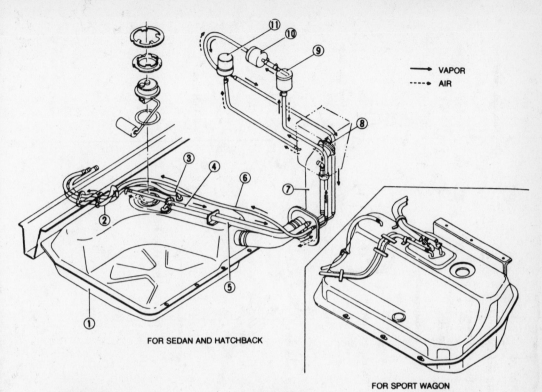

→ VAPOR
----→ AIR

FOR SEDAN AND HATCHBACK

FOR SPORT WAGON

1. Fuel tank
2. Fuel outlet hose
3. Fuel return hose
4. Evaporation hose to fuel tank

5. Air vent line
6. Evaporation hose to engine
7. Filler hose
8. Filler cap

9. Separator
10. Limit valve
11. Vent cleaner

F10 fuel tank

1. Fuel tank
2. Fuel suction hose
3. Fuel return hose
4. Evaporation hose
5. Vent tube
6. Filler hose
7. Filler tube
8. Filler cap
9. Fuel check valve
10. Breather tube

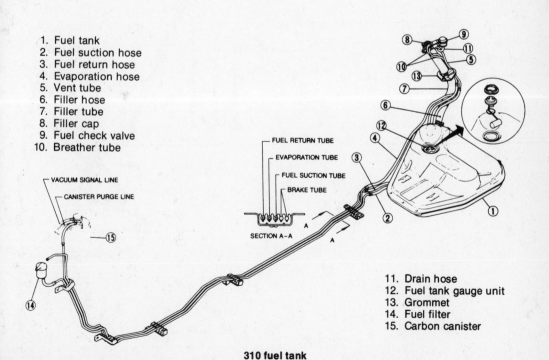

FUEL RETURN TUBE

EVAPORATION TUBE

FUEL SUCTION TUBE

BRAKE TUBE

VACUUM SIGNAL LINE

CANISTER PURGE LINE

SECTION A–A

11. Drain hose
12. Fuel tank gauge unit
13. Grommet
14. Fuel filter
15. Carbon canister

310 fuel tank

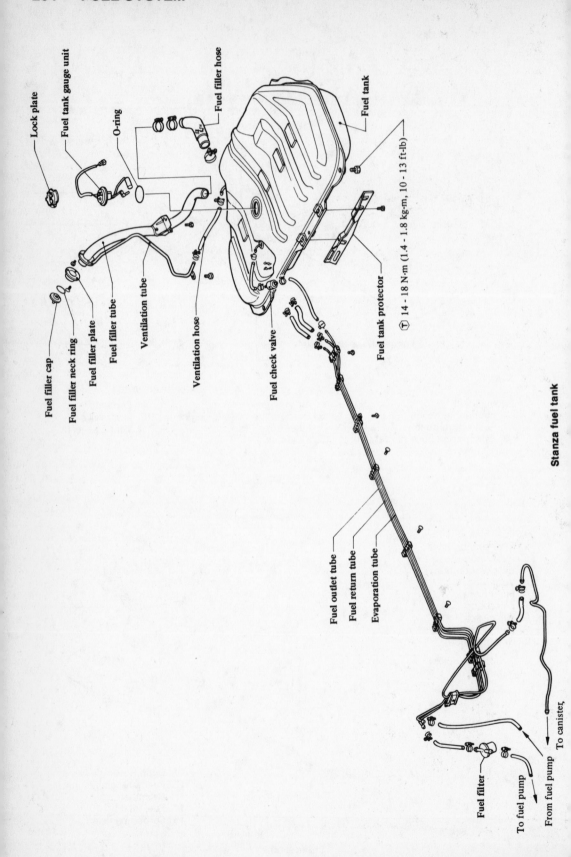

Lock plate

Fuel tank gauge unit

O-ring

Fuel filler hose

Fuel tank

Fuel filler cap

Fuel filler neck ring

Fuel filler plate

Fuel filler tube

Ventilation tube

Ventilation hose

Fuel check valve

Fuel tank protector

Ⓣ 14 - 18 N·m (1.4 - 1.8 kg-m, 10 - 13 ft-lb)

Fuel outlet tube

Fuel return tube

Evaporation tube

Fuel filter

To fuel pump

From fuel pump

To canister

Stanza fuel tank

2. Disconnect the filler tube and filler hose from the fuel tank. Disconnect the hoses attached to the fuel tank near the filler hose at the bottom front of the tank.

3. Loosen the tension on the parking brake and disconnect the wire on the fuel tank gauge unit.

4. Remove the retaining bolts and remove the tank by sliding it forward and down.

5. To install, reverse the removal procedures.

Pulsar and Stanza

1. Drain the fuel tank.
2. Remove the rear seat cushion.
3. Remove the inspection cover.

4. Disconnect the fuel gauge electrical harness connector.

5. Disconnect the fuel filler and the ventilation hoses. Disconnect the fuel outlet, return and evaporation hoses, at the front of the tank. Plug open fuel lines.

NOTE: *On the Stanza models, remove the tank protector.*

6. Remove the fuel tank mounting bolts and the tank from the vehicle.

7. Install the fuel tank to vehicle and torque the mounting bolts to 20-27 ft. lbs.

8. Reconnect all fuel lines, ventilation hoses and the electrical connection.

9. Install the inspection cover and rear seat cushion.

10. Start engine and check for fuel leaks.

Chassis Electrical

6

UNDERSTANDING AND TROUBLESHOOTING ELECTRICAL SYSTEMS

At the rate which both import and domestic manufacturers are incorporating electronic control systems into their production lines, it won't be long before every new vehicle is equipped with one or more on-board computer. These electronic components (with no moving parts) should theoretically last the life of the vehicle, provided nothing external happens to damage the circuits or memory chips.

While it is true that electronic components should never wear out, in the real world malfunctions do occur. It is also true that any computer-based system is extremely sensitive to electrical voltages and cannot tolerate careless or haphazard testing or service procedures. An inexperienced individual can literally do major damage looking for a minor problem by using the wrong kind of test equipment or connecting test leads or connectors with the ignition switch ON. When selecting test equipment, make sure the manufacturers instructions state that the tester is compatible with whatever type of electronic control system is being serviced. Read all instructions carefully and double check all test points before installing probes or making any test connections.

The following section outlines basic diagnosis techniques for dealing with computerized automotive control systems. Along with a general explanation of the various types of test equipment available to aid in servicing modern electronic automotive systems, basic repair techniques for wiring harnesses and connectors is given. Read the basic information before attempting any repairs or testing on any computerized system, to provide the background of information necessary to avoid the most common and obvious mistakes that can cost both time and money. Although the replacement and testing procedures are simple in themselves, the systems are not, and unless one has a thorough understanding of all components and their function within a particular computerized control system, the logical test sequence these systems demand cannot be followed. Minor malfunctions can make a big difference, so it is important to know how each component affects the operation of the overall electronic system to find the ultimate cause of a problem without replacing good components unnecessarily. It is not enough to use the correct test equipment; the test equipment must be used correctly.

Safety Precautions

CAUTION: *Whenever working on or around any computer based microprocessor control system, always observe these general precautions to prevent the possibility of personal injury or damage to electronic components.*

• Never install or remove battery cables with the key ON or the engine running. Jumper cables should be connected with the key OFF to avoid power surges that can damage electronic control units. Engines equipped with computer controlled systems should avoid both giving and getting jump starts due to the possibility of serious damage to components from arcing in the engine compartment when connections are made with the ignition ON.

• Always remove the battery cables before charging the battery. Never use a high output charger on an installed battery or attempt to use any type of "hot shot" (24 volt) starting aid.

• Exercise care when inserting test probes into connectors to insure good connections without damaging the connector or spreading the pins. Always probe connectors from the rear (wire) side, NOT the pin side, to avoid accidental shorting of terminals during test procedures.

• Never remove or attach wiring harness connectors with the ignition switch ON, especially to an electronic control unit.

• Do not drop any components during service procedures and never apply 12 volts directly to any component (like a solenoid or relay) unless instructed specifically to do so. Some component electrical windings are designed to safely handle only 4 or 5 volts and can be destroyed in seconds if 12 volts are applied directly to the connector.

• Remove the electronic control unit if the vehicle is to be placed in an environment where temperatures exceed approximately 176°F (80°C), such as a paint spray booth or when arc or gas welding near the control unit location in the car.

ORGANIZED TROUBLESHOOTING

When diagnosing a specific problem, organized troubleshooting is a must. The complexity of a modern automobile demands that you approach any problem in a logical, organized manner. There are certain troubleshooting techniques that are standard:

1. Establish when the problem occurs. Does the problem appear only under certain conditions? Were there any noises, odors, or other unusual symptoms?

2. Isolate the problem area. To do this, make some simple tests and observations; then eliminate the systems that are working properly. Check for obvious problems such as broken wires, dirty connections or split or disconnected vacuum hoses. Always check the obvious before assuming something complicated is the cause.

3. Test for problems systematically to determine the cause once the problem area is isolated. Are all the components functioning properly? Is there power going to electrical switches and motors? Is there vacuum at vacuum switches and/or actuators? Is there a mechanical problem such as bent linkage or loose mounting screws? Doing careful, systematic checks will often turn up most causes on the first inspection without wasting time checking components that have little or no relationship to the problem.

4. Test all repairs after the work is done to make sure that the problem is fixed. Some causes can be traced to more than one component, so a careful verification of repair work is important to pick up additional malfunctions that may cause a problem to reappear or a different problem to arise. A blown fuse, for example, is a simple problem that may require more than another fuse to repair. If you don't look for a problem that caused a fuse to blow, for example, a shorted wire may go undetected.

TEST EQUIPMENT

Jumper Wires

Jumper wires are simple, yet extremely valuable, pieces of test equipment. Jumper wires are merely wires that are used to bypass sections of a circuit. The simplest type of jumper wire is merely a length of multistrand wire with an alligator clip at each end. Jumper wires are usually fabricated from lengths of standard automotive wire and whatever type of connector (alligator clip, spade connector or pin connector) that is required for the particular vehicle being tested. The well equipped tool box will have several different styles of jumper wires in several different lengths. Some jumper wires are made with three or more terminals coming from a common splice for special purpose testing. In cramped, hard-to-reach areas it is advisable to have insulated boots over the jumper wire terminals in order to prevent accidental grounding, sparks, and possible fire, especially when testing fuel system components.

Jumper wires are used primarily to locate open electrical circuits, on either the ground (–) side of the circuit or on the hot (+) side. If an electrical component fails to operate, connect the jumper wire between the component and a good ground. If the component operates only with the jumper installed, the ground circuit is open. If the ground circuit is good, but the component does not operate, the circuit between the power feed and component is open. You can sometimes connect the jumper wire directly from the battery to the hot terminal of the component, but first make sure the component uses 12 volts in operation. Some electrical components, such as fuel injectors, are designed to operate on about 4 volts and running 12 volts directly to the injector terminals can burn out the wiring. By inserting an inline fuseholder between a set of test leads, a fused jumper wire can be used for bypassing open circuits. Use a 5 amp fuse to provide protection against voltage spikes. When in doubt, use a voltmeter to check the voltage input to the component and measure how much voltage is being applied normally. By moving the jumper wire successively back from the lamp toward the power source, you can isolate the area of the circuit where the open is located. When the component stops functioning, or the power is cut off, the open is in the segment of wire between the jumper and the point previously tested.

NOTE: *Never use jumpers made from wire that is of lighter gauge than used in the circuit under test. If the jumper wire is of too small gauge, it may overheat and possibly melt. Never use jumpers to bypass high resistance loads (such as motors) in a circuit. By-*

passing resistances, in effect, creates a short circuit which may, in turn, cause damage and fire. Never use a jumper for anything other than temporary bypassing of components in a circuit.

12 Volt Test Light

The 12 volt test light is used to check circuits and components while electrical current is flowing through them. It is used for voltage and ground tests. Twelve volt test lights come in different styles but all have three main parts; a ground clip, a probe, and a light. The most commonly used 12 volt test lights have pick-type probes. To use a 12 volt test light, connect the ground clip to a good ground and probe wherever necessary with the pick. The pick should be sharp so that it can penetrate wire insulation to make contact with the wire, without making a large hole in the insulation. The wrap-around light is handy in hard to reach areas or where it is difficult to support a wire to push a probe pick into it. To use the wrap around light, hook the wire to probed with the hook and pull the trigger. A small pick will be forced through the wire insulation into the wire core.

NOTE: *Do not use a test light to probe electronic ignition spark plug or coil wires. Never use a pick-type test light to probe wiring on computer controlled systems unless specifically instructed to do so. Any wire insulation that is pierced by the test light probe should be taped and sealed with silicone after testing.*

Like the jumper wire, the 12 volt test light is used to isolate opens in circuits. But, whereas the jumper wire is used to bypass the open to operate the load, the 12 volt test light is used to locate the presence of voltage in a circuit. If the test light glows, you know that there is power up to that point; if the 12 volt test light does not glow when its probe is inserted into the wire or connector, you know that there is an open circuit (no power). Move the test light in successive steps back toward the power source until the light in the handle does glow. When it does glow, the open is between the probe and point previously probed.

NOTE: *The test light does not detect that 12 volts (or any particular amount of voltage) is present; it only detects that some voltage is present. It is advisable before using the test light to touch its terminals across the battery posts to make sure the light is operating properly.*

Self-Powered Test Light

The self-powered test light usually contains a 1.5 volt penlight battery. One type of self-powered test light is similar in design to the 12 volt test light. This type has both the battery and the light in the handle and pick-type probe tip. The second type has the light toward the open tip, so that the light illuminates the contact point. The self-powered test light is dual purpose piece of test equipment. It can be used to test for either open or short circuits when power is isolated from the circuit (continuity test). A powered test light should not be used on any computer controlled system or component unless specifically instructed to do so. Many engine sensors can be destroyed by even this small amount of voltage applied directly to the terminals.

Open Circuit Testing

To use the self-powered test light to check for open circuits, first isolate the circuit from the vehicle's 12 volt power source by disconnecting the battery or wiring harness connector. Connect the test light ground clip to a good ground and probe sections of the circuit sequentially with the test light. (start from either end of the circuit). If the light is out, the open is between the probe and the circuit ground. If the light is on, the open is between the probe and end of the circuit toward the power source.

Short Circuit Testing

By isolating the circuit both from power and from ground, and using a self-powered test light, you can check for shorts to ground in the circuit. Isolate the circuit from power and ground. Connect the test light ground clip to a good ground and probe any easy-to-reach test point in the circuit. If the light comes on, there is a short somewhere in the circuit. To isolate the short, probe a test point at either end of isolated circuit (the light should be on). Leave the test light probe connected and open connectors, switches, remove parts, etc., sequentially, until the light goes out. When the light goes out, the short is between the last circuit component opened and the previous circuit opened.

NOTE: *The 1.5 volt battery in the test light does not provide much current. A weak battery may not provide enough power to illuminate the test light even when a complete circuit is made (especially if there are high resistances in the circuit). Always make sure that the test battery is strong. To check the battery, briefly touch the ground clip to the probe; if the light glows brightly the battery is strong enough for testing. Never use a self-powered test light to perform checks for opens or shorts when power is applied to the electrical system under test. The 12 volt vehicle power will quickly burn out the 1.5 volt light bulb in the test light.*

Voltmeter

A voltmeter is used to measure voltage at any point in a circuit, or to measure the voltage drop across any part of a circuit. It can also be used to check continuity in a wire or circuit by indicating current flow from one end to the other. Voltmeters usually have various scales on the meter dial and a selector switch to allow the selection of different voltages. The voltmeter has a positive and a negative lead. To avoid damage to the meter, always connect the negative lead to the negative (–) side of circuit (to ground or nearest the ground side of the circuit) and connect the positive lead to the positive (+) side of the circuit (to the power source or the nearest power source). Note that the negative voltmeter lead will always be black and that the positive voltmeter will always be some color other than black (usually red). Depending on how the voltmeter is connected into the circuit, it has several uses.

A voltmeter can be connected either in parallel or in series with a circuit and it has a very high resistance to current flow. When connected in parallel, only a small amount of current will flow through the voltmeter current path; the rest will flow through the normal circuit current path and the circuit will work normally. When the voltmeter is connected in series with a circuit, only a small amount of current can flow through the circuit. The circuit will not work properly, but the voltmeter reading will show if the circuit is complete or not.

Available Voltage Measurement

Set the voltmeter selector switch to the 20V position and connect the meter negative lead to the negative post of the battery. Connect the positive meter lead to the positive post of the battery and turn the ignition switch ON to provide a load. Read the voltage on the meter or digital display. A well charged battery should register over 12 volts. If the meter reads below 11.5 volts, the battery power may be insufficient to operate the electrical system properly. This test determines voltage available from the battery and should be the first step in any electrical trouble diagnosis procedure. Many electrical problems, especially on computer controlled systems, can be caused by a low state of charge in the battery. Excessive corrosion at the battery cable terminals can cause a poor contact that will prevent proper charging and full battery current flow.

Normal battery voltage is 12 volts when fully charged. When the battery is supplying current to one or more circuits it is said to be "under load". When everything is off the electrical system is under a "no-load" condition. A fully charged battery may show about 12.5 volts at no load; will drop to 12 volts under medium load; and will drop even lower under heavy load. If the battery is partially discharged the voltage decrease under heavy load may be excessive, even though the battery shows 12 volts or more at no load. When allowed to discharge further, the battery's available voltage under load will decrease more severely. For this reason, it is important that the battery be fully charged during all testing procedures to avoid errors in diagnosis and incorrect test results.

Voltage Drop

When current flows through a resistance, the voltage beyond the resistance is reduced (the larger the current, the greater the reduction in voltage). When no current is flowing, there is no voltage drop because there is no current flow. All points in the circuit which are connected to the power source are at the same voltage as the power source. The total voltage drop always equals the total source voltage. In a long circuit with many connectors, a series of small, unwanted voltage drops due to corrosion at the connectors can add up to a total loss of voltage which impairs the operation of the normal loads in the circuit.

INDIRECT COMPUTATION OF VOLTAGE DROPS

1. Set the voltmeter selector switch to the 20 volt position.
2. Connect the meter negative lead to a good ground.
3. Probe all resistances in the circuit with the positive meter lead.
4. Operate the circuit in all modes and observe the voltage readings.

DIRECT MEASUREMENT OF VOLTAGE DROPS

1. Set the voltmeter switch to the 20 volt position.
2. Connect the voltmeter negative lead to the ground side of the resistance load to be measured.
3. Connect the positive lead to the positive side of the resistance or load to be measured.
4. Read the voltage drop directly on the 20 volt scale.

Too high a voltage indicates too high a resistance. If, for example, a blower motor runs too slowly, you can determine if there is too high a resistance in the resistor pack. By taking voltage drop readings in all parts of the circuit, you can isolate the problem. Too low a voltage drop indicates too low a resistance. If, for example, a blower motor runs too fast in the MED and/or LOW position, the problem can be isolated in the resistor pack by taking voltage drop readings in all parts of the circuit to locate a possibly shorted resistor. The maximum allowable voltage drop under load is critical, especially if there is more than one high resistance problem in a circuit because all voltage drops are cumulative. A small drop is normal due to the resistance of the conductors.

HIGH RESISTANCE TESTING

1. Set the voltmeter selector switch to the 4 volt position.
2. Connect the voltmeter positive lead to the positive post of the battery.
3. Turn on the headlights and heater blower to provide a load.
4. Probe various points in the circuit with the negative voltmeter lead.
5. Read the voltage drop on the 4 volt scale. Some average maximum allowable voltage drops are:

FUSE PANEL – 7 volts
IGNITION SWITCH – 5volts
HEADLIGHT SWITCH – 7 volts
IGNITION COIL (+) – 5 volts
ANY OTHER LOAD – 1.3 volts
NOTE: *Voltage drops are all measured while a load is operating; without current flow, there will be no voltage drop.*

Ohmmeter

The ohmmeter is designed to read resistance (ohms) in a circuit or component. Although there are several different styles of ohmmeters, all will usually have a selector switch which permits the measurement of different ranges of resistance (usually the selector switch allows the multiplication of the meter reading by 10, 100, 1,000, and 10,000). A calibration knob allows the meter to be set at zero for accurate measurement. Since all ohmmeters are powered by an internal battery (usually 9 volts), the ohmmeter can be used as a self-powered test light. When the ohmmeter is connected, current from the ohmmeter flows through the circuit or component being tested. Since the ohmmeter's internal resistance and voltage are known values, the amount of current flow through the meter depends on the resistance of the circuit or component being tested.

The ohmmeter can be used to perform continuity test for opens or shorts (either by observation of the meter needle or as a self-powered test light), and to read actual resistance in a circuit. It should be noted that the ohmmeter is used to check the resistance of a component or wire while there is no voltage applied to the circuit. Current flow from an outside voltage source (such as the vehicle battery) can damage the ohmmeter, so the circuit or component should be isolated from the vehicle electrical system before any testing is done. Since the

ohmmeter uses its own voltage source, either lead can be connected to any test point.

NOTE: *When checking diodes or other solid state components, the ohmmeter leads can only be connected one way in order to measure current flow in a single direction. Make sure the positive (+) and negative (–) terminal connections are as described in the test procedures to verify the one-way diode operation.*

In using the meter for making continuity checks, do not be concerned with the actual resistance readings. Zero resistance, or any resistance readings, indicate continuity in the circuit. Infinite resistance indicates an open in the circuit. A high resistance reading where there should be none indicates a problem in the circuit. Checks for short circuits are made in the same manner as checks for open circuits except that the circuit must be isolated from both power and normal ground. Infinite resistance indicates no continuity to ground, while zero resistance indicates a dead short to ground.

RESISTANCE MEASUREMENT

The batteries in an ohmmeter will weaken with age and temperature, so the ohmmeter must be calibrated or "zeroed" before taking measurements. To zero the meter, place the selector switch in its lowest range and touch the two ohmmeter leads together. Turn the calibration knob until the meter needle is exactly on zero.

NOTE: *All analog (needle) type ohmmeters must be zeroed before use, but some digital ohmmeter models are automatically calibrated when the switch is turned on. Self-calibrating digital ohmmeters do not have an adjusting knob, but its a good idea to check for a zero readout before use by touching the leads together. All computer controlled systems require the use of a digital ohmmeter with at least 10 meagohms impedance for testing. Before any test procedures are attempted, make sure the ohmmeter used is compatible with the electrical system or damage to the onboard computer could result.*

To measure resistance, first isolate the circuit from the vehicle power source by disconnecting the battery cables or the harness connector. Make sure the key is OFF when disconnecting any components or the battery. Where necessary, also isolate at least one side of the circuit to be checked to avoid reading parallel resistances. Parallel circuit resistances will always give a lower reading than the actual resistance of either of the branches. When measuring the resistance of parallel circuits, the total resistance will always be lower than the smallest resistance in the circuit. Connect the meter leads to both sides of the circuit (wire or component) and read the actual measured ohms on the meter scale. Make sure the selector switch is set to the proper ohm scale for the circuit being tested to avoid misreading the ohmmeter test value.

NOTE: *Never use an ohmmeter with power applied to the circuit. Like the self-powered test light, the ohmmeter is designed to operate on its own power supply. The normal 12 volt automotive electrical system current could damage the meter!*

Ammeters

An ammeter measures the amount of current flowing through a circuit in units called amperes or amps. Amperes are units of electron flow which indicate how fast the electrons are flowing through the circuit. Since Ohms Law dictates that current flow in a circuit is equal to the circuit voltage divided by the total circuit resistance, increasing voltage also increases the current level (amps). Likewise, any decrease in resistance will increase the amount of amps in a circuit. At normal operating voltage, most circuits have a characteristic amount of amperes, called "current draw" which can be measured using an ammeter. By referring to a specified current draw rating, measuring the amperes, and comparing the two values, one can determine what is happening within the circuit to aid in diagnosis. An open circuit, for example, will not allow any current to flow so the ammeter reading will be zero. More current flows through a heavily loaded circuit or when the charging system is operating.

An ammeter is always connected in series with the circuit being tested. All of the current that normally flows through the circuit must also flow through the ammeter; if there is any other path for the current to follow, the ammeter reading will not be accurate. The ammeter itself has very little resistance to current flow and therefore will not affect the circuit, but it will measure current draw only when the circuit is closed and electricity is flowing. Excessive current draw can blow fuses and drain the battery, while a reduced current draw can cause motors to run slowly, lights to dim and other components to not operate properly. The ammeter can help diagnose these conditions by locating the cause of the high or low reading.

Multimeters

Different combinations of test meters can be built into a single unit designed for specific tests. Some of the more common combination test devices are known as Volt/Amp testers, Tach/Dwell meters, or Digital Multimeters. The Volt/Amp tester is used for charging system, starting system or battery tests and consists of a voltmeter, an ammeter and a variable resistance carbon pile. The voltmeter will usually have at least two ranges for use with 6, 12 and 24 volt systems. The ammeter also has more than one range for testing various levels of battery loads and starter current draw and the carbon pile can be adjusted to offer different amounts of resistance. The Volt/Amp tester has heavy leads to carry large amounts of current and many later models have an inductive ammeter pickup that clamps around the wire to simplify test connections. On some models, the ammeter also has a zero-center scale to allow testing of charging and starting systems without switching leads or polarity. A digital multimeter is a voltmeter, ammeter and ohmmeter combined in an instrument which gives a digital readout. These are often used when testing solid state circuits because of their high input impedance (usually 10 megohms or more).

The tach/dwell meter combines a tachometer and a dwell (cam angle) meter and is a specialized kind of voltmeter. The tachometer scale is marked to show engine speed in rpm and the dwell scale is marked to show degrees of distributor shaft rotation. In most electronic ignition systems, dwell is determined by the control unit, but the dwell meter can also be used to check the duty cycle (operation) of some electronic engine control systems. Some tach/dwell meters are powered by an internal battery, while others take their power from the car battery in use. The battery powered testers usually require calibration much like an ohmmeter before testing.

Special Test Equipment

A variety of diagnostic tools are available to help troubleshoot and repair computerized engine control systems. The most sophisticated of these devices are the console type engine analyzers that usually occupy a garage service bay, but there are several types of aftermarket electronic testers available that will allow quick circuit tests of the engine control system by plugging directly into a special connector located in the engine compartment or under the dashboard. Several tool and equipment manufacturers offer simple, hand held testers that measure various circuit voltage levels on command to check all system components for proper operation. Although these testers usually cost about $300–500, consider that the average computer control unit (or ECM) can cost just as much and the money saved by not replacing perfectly good sensors or components in an attempt to correct a problem could justify the purchase price of a special diagnostic tester the first time it's used.

These computerized testers can allow quick

and easy test measurements while the engine is operating or while the car is being driven. In addition, the on-board computer memory can be read to access any stored trouble codes; in effect allowing the computer to tell you where it hurts and aid trouble diagnosis by pinpointing exactly which circuit or component is malfunctioning. In the same manner, repairs can be tested to make sure the problem has been corrected. The biggest advantage these special testers have is their relatively easy hookups that minimize or eliminate the chances of making the wrong connections and getting false voltage readings or damaging the computer accidentally.

NOTE: *It should be remembered that these testers check voltage levels in circuits; they don't detect mechanical problems or failed components if the circuit voltage falls within the preprogrammed limits stored in the tester PROM unit. Also, most of the hand held testes are designed to work only on one or two systems made by a specific manufacturer.*

A variety of aftermarket testers are available to help diagnose different computerized control systems. Owatonna Tool Company (OTC), for example, markets a device called the OTC Monitor which plugs directly into the assembly line diagnostic link (ALDL). The OTC tester makes diagnosis a simple matter of pressing the correct buttons and, by changing the internal PROM or inserting a different diagnosis cartridge, it will work on any model from full size to subcompact, over a wide range of years. An adapter is supplied with the tester to allow connection to all types of ALDL links, regardless of the number of pin terminals used. By inserting an updated PROM into the OTC tester, it can be easily updated to diagnose any new modifications of computerized control systems.

Wiring Harnesses

The average automobile contains about ½ mile of wiring, with hundreds of individual connections. To protect the many wires from damage and to keep them from becoming a confusing tangle, they are organized into bundles, enclosed in plastic or taped together and called wire harnesses. Different wiring harnesses serve different parts of the vehicle. Individual wires are color coded to help trace them through a harness where sections are hidden from view.

A loose or corroded connection or a replacement wire that is too small for the circuit will add extra resistance and an additional voltage drop to the circuit. A ten percent voltage drop can result in slow or erratic motor operation, for example, even though the circuit is complete. Automotive wiring or circuit conductors can be in any one of three forms:

1. Single strand wire
2. Multistrand wire
3. Printed circuitry

Single strand wire has a solid metal core and is usually used inside such components as alternators, motors, relays and other devices. Multistrand wire has a core made of many small strands of wire twisted together into a single conductor. Most of the wiring in an automotive electrical system is made up of multistrand wire, either as a single conductor or grouped together in a harness. All wiring is color coded on the insulator, either as a solid color or as a colored wire with an identification stripe. A printed circuit is a thin film of copper or other conductor that is printed on an insulator backing. Occasionally, a printed circuit is sandwiched between two sheets of plastic for more protection and flexibility. A complete printed circuit, consisting of conductors, insulating material and connectors for lamps or other components is called a printed circuit board. Printed circuitry is used in place of individual wires or harnesses in places where space is limited, such as behind instrument panels.

Wire Gauge

Since computer controlled automotive electrical systems are very sensitive to changes in resistance, the selection of properly sized wires is critical when systems are repaired. The wire gauge number is an expression of the cross section area of the conductor. The most common system for expressing wire size is the American Wire Gauge (AWG) system.

Wire cross section area is measured in circular mils. A mil is $\frac{1}{1000}''$ (0.001''); a circular mil is the area of a circle one mil in diameter. For example, a conductor ¼'' in diameter is 0.250 in. or 250 mils. The circular mil cross section area of the wire is 250 squared (250^2) or 62,500 circular mils. Imported car models usually use metric wire gauge designations, which is simply the cross section area of the conductor in square millimeters (mm^2).

Gauge numbers are assigned to conductors of various cross section areas. As gauge number increases, area decreases and the conductor becomes smaller. A 5 gauge conductor is smaller than a 1 gauge conductor and a 10 gauge is smaller than a 5 gauge. As the cross section area of a conductor decreases, resistance increases and so does the gauge number. A conductor with a higher gauge number will carry less current than a conductor with a lower gauge number.

NOTE: *Gauge wire size refers to the size of*

the conductor, not the size of the complete wire. It is possible to have two wires of the same gauge with different diameters because one may have thicker insulation than the other.

12 volt automotive electrical systems generally use 10, 12, 14, 16 and 18 gauge wire. Main power distribution circuits and larger accessories usually use 10 and 12 gauge wire. Battery cables are usually 4 or 6 gauge, although 1 and 2 gauge wires are occasionally used. Wire length must also be considered when making repairs to a circuit. As conductor length increases, so does resistance. An 18 gauge wire, for example, can carry a 10 amp load for 10 feet without excessive voltage drop; however if a 15 foot wire is required for the same 10 amp load, it must be a 16 gauge wire.

An electrical schematic shows the electrical current paths when a circuit is operating properly. It is essential to understand how a circuit works before trying to figure out why it doesn't. Schematics break the entire electrical system down into individual circuits and show only one particular circuit. In a schematic, no attempt is made to represent wiring and components as they physically appear on the vehicle; switches and other components are shown as simply as possible. Face views of harness connectors show the cavity or terminal locations in all multi-pin connectors to help locate test points.

If you need to backprobe a connector while it is on the component, the order of the terminals must be mentally reversed. The wire color code can help in this situation, as well as a keyway, lock tab or other reference mark.

NOTE: *Wiring diagrams are not included in this book. As trucks have become more complex and available with longer option lists, wiring diagrams have grown in size and complexity. It has become almost impossible to provide a readable reproduction of a wiring diagram in a book this size. Information on ordering wiring diagrams from the vehicle manufacturer can be found in the owner's manual.*

WIRING REPAIR

Soldering is a quick, efficient method of joining metals permanently. Everyone who has the occasion to make wiring repairs should know how to solder. Electrical connections that are soldered are far less likely to come apart and will conduct electricity much better than connections that are only "pig-tailed" together. The most popular (and preferred) method of soldering is with an electrical soldering gun. Soldering irons are available in many sizes and wattage ratings. Irons with higher wattage ratings deliver higher temperatures and recover lost heat faster. A small soldering iron rated for no more than 50 watts is recommended, especially on electrical systems where excess heat can damage the components being soldered.

There are three ingredients necessary for successful soldering; proper flux, good solder and sufficient heat. A soldering flux is necessary to clean the metal of tarnish, prepare it for soldering and to enable the solder to spread into tiny crevices. When soldering, always use a resin flux or resin core solder which is non-corrosive and will not attract moisture once the job is finished. Other types of flux (acid core) will leave a residue that will attract moisture and cause the wires to corrode. Tin is a unique metal with a low melting point. In a molten state, it dissolves and alloys easily with many metals. Solder is made by mixing tin with lead. The most common proportions are 40/60, 50/50 and 60/40, with the percentage of tin listed first. Low priced solders usually contain less tin, making them very difficult for a beginner to use because more heat is required to melt the solder. A common solder is 40/60 which is well suited for all-around general use, but 60/40 melts easier, has more tin for a better joint and is preferred for electrical work.

Soldering Techniques

Successful soldering requires that the metals to be joined be heated to a temperature that will melt the solder – usually 360–460°F (182–238°C). Contrary to popular belief, the purpose of the soldering iron is not to melt the solder itself, but to heat the parts being soldered to a temperature high enough to melt the solder when it is touched to the work. Melting flux-cored solder on the soldering iron will usually destroy the effectiveness of the flux.

NOTE: *Soldering tips are made of copper for good heat conductivity, but must be "tinned" regularly for quick transference of heat to the project and to prevent the solder from sticking to the iron. To "tin" the iron, simply heat it and touch the flux-cored solder to the tip; the solder will flow over the hot tip. Wipe the excess off with a clean rag, but be careful as the iron will be hot.*

After some use, the tip may become pitted. If so, simply dress the tip smooth with a smooth file and "tin" the tip again. An old saying holds that "metals well cleaned are half soldered." Flux-cored solder will remove oxides but rust, bits of insulation and oil or grease must be removed with a wire brush or emery cloth. For maximum strength in soldered parts, the joint must start off clean and tight. Weak joints will result in gaps too wide for the solder to bridge.

If a separate soldering flux is used, it should be brushed or swabbed on only those areas that are to be soldered. Most solders contain a core of flux and separate fluxing is unnecessary. Hold the work to be soldered firmly. It is best to solder on a wooden board, because a metal vise will only rob the piece to be soldered of heat and make it difficult to melt the solder. Hold the soldering tip with the broadest face against the work to be soldered. Apply solder under the tip close to the work, using enough solder to give a heavy film between the iron and the piece being soldered, while moving slowly and making sure the solder melts properly. Keep the work level or the solder will run to the lowest part and favor the thicker parts, because these require more heat to melt the solder. If the soldering tip overheats (the solder coating on the face of the tip burns up), it should be retinned. Once the soldering is completed, let the soldered joint stand until cool. Tape and seal all soldered wire splices after the repair has cooled.

Wire Harness and Connectors

The on-board computer (ECM) wire harness electrically connects the control unit to the various solenoids, switches and sensors used by the control system. Most connectors in the engine compartment or otherwise exposed to the elements are protected against moisture and dirt which could create oxidation and deposits on the terminals. This protection is important because of the very low voltage and current levels used by the computer and sensors. All connectors have a lock which secures the male and female terminals together, with a secondary lock holding the seal and terminal into the connector. Both terminal locks must be released when disconnecting ECM connectors.

These special connectors are weather-proof and all repairs require the use of a special terminal and the tool required to service it. This tool is used to remove the pin and sleeve terminals. If removal is attempted with an ordinary pick, there is a good chance that the terminal will be bent or deformed. Unlike standard blade type terminals, these terminals cannot be straightened once they are bent. Make certain that the connectors are properly seated and all of the sealing rings in place when connecting leads. On some models, a hinge-type flap provides a backup or secondary locking feature for the terminals. Most secondary locks are used to improve the connector reliability by retaining the terminals if the small terminal lock tangs are not positioned properly.

Molded-on connectors require complete replacement of the connection. This means splicing a new connector assembly into the harness. All splices in on-board computer systems

should be soldered to insure proper contact. Use care when probing the connections or replacing terminals in them as it is possible to short between opposite terminals. If this happens to the wrong terminal pair, it is possible to damage certain components. Always use jumper wires between connectors for circuit checking and never probe through weatherproof seals.

Open circuits are often difficult to locate by sight because corrosion or terminal misalignment are hidden by the connectors. Merely wiggling a connector on a sensor or in the wiring harness may correct the open circuit condition. This should always be considered when an open circuit or a failed sensor is indicated. Intermittent problems may also be caused by oxidized or loose connections. When using a circuit tester for diagnosis, always probe connections from the wire side. Be careful not to damage sealed connectors with test probes.

All wiring harnesses should be replaced with identical parts, using the same gauge wire and connectors. When signal wires are spliced into a harness, use wire with high temperature insulation only. With the low voltage and current levels found in the system, it is important that the best possible connection at all wire splices be made by soldering the splices together. It is seldom necessary to replace a complete harness. If replacement is necessary, pay close attention to insure proper harness routing. Secure the harness with suitable plastic wire clamps to prevent vibrations from causing the harness to wear in spots or contact any hot components.

NOTE: *Weatherproof connectors cannot be replaced with standard connectors. Instructions are provided with replacement connector and terminal packages. Some wire harnesses have mounting indicators (usually pieces of colored tape) to mark where the harness is to be secured.*

In making wiring repairs, it's important that you always replace damaged wires with wires that are the same gauge as the wire being replaced. The heavier the wire, the smaller the gauge number. Wires are color-coded to aid in identification and whenever possible the same color coded wire should be used for replacement. A wire stripping and crimping tool is necessary to install solderless terminal connectors. Test all crimps by pulling on the wires; it should not be possible to pull the wires out of a good crimp.

Wires which are open, exposed or otherwise damaged are repaired by simple splicing. Where possible, if the wiring harness is accessible and the damaged place in the wire can be located, it is best to open the harness and check for all possible damage. In an inaccessible harness, the wire must be bypassed with a new insert, usually taped to the outside of the old harness.

When replacing fusible links, be sure to use fusible link wire, NOT ordinary automotive wire. Make sure the fusible segment is of the same gauge and construction as the one being replaced and double the stripped end when crimping the terminal connector for a good contact. The melted (open) fusible link segment of the wiring harness should be cut off as close to the harness as possible, then a new segment spliced in as described. In the case of a damaged fusible link that feeds two harness wires, the harness connections should be replaced with two fusible link wires so that each circuit will have its own separate protection.

NOTE: *Most of the problems caused in the wiring harness are due to bad ground connections. Always check all vehicle ground connections for corrosion or looseness before performing any power feed checks to eliminate the chance of a bad ground affecting the circuit.*

Repairing Hard Shell Connectors

Unlike molded connectors, the terminal contacts in hard shell connectors can be replaced. Weatherproof hard-shell connectors with the leads molded into the shell have non-replaceable terminal ends. Replacement usually involves the use of a special terminal removal tool that depress the locking tangs (barbs) on the connector terminal and allow the connector to be removed from the rear of the shell. The connector shell should be replaced if it shows any evidence of burning, melting, cracks, or breaks. Replace individual terminals that are burnt, corroded, distorted or loose.

NOTE: *The insulation crimp must be tight to prevent the insulation from sliding back on the wire when the wire is pulled. The insulation must be visibly compressed under the crimp tabs, and the ends of the crimp should be turned in for a firm grip on the insulation.*

The wire crimp must be made with all wire strands inside the crimp. The terminal must be fully compressed on the wire strands with the ends of the crimp tabs turned in to make a firm grip on the wire. Check all connections with an ohmmeter to insure a good contact. There should be no measurable resistance between the wire and the terminal when connected.

Mechanical Test Equipment

Vacuum Gauge

Most gauges are graduated in inches of mercury (in.Hg), although a device called a manometer reads vacuum in inches of water (in. H_2O). The normal vacuum reading usually varies between 18 and 22 in.Hg at sea level. To test engine vacuum, the vacuum gauge must be connected to a source of manifold vacuum. Many engines have a plug in the intake manifold which can be removed and replaced with an adapter fitting. Connect the vacuum gauge to the fitting with a suitable rubber hose or, if no manifold plug is available, connect the vacuum gauge to any device using manifold vacuum, such as EGR valves, etc. The vacuum gauge can be used to determine if enough vacuum is reaching a component to allow its actuation.

Hand Vacuum Pump

Small, hand-held vacuum pumps come in a variety of designs. Most have a built-in vacuum gauge and allow the component to be tested without removing it from the vehicle. Operate the pump lever or plunger to apply the correct amount of vacuum required for the test specified in the diagnosis routines. The level of vacuum in inches of Mercury (in.Hg) is indicated on the pump gauge. For some testing, an additional vacuum gauge may be necessary.

Intake manifold vacuum is used to operate various systems and devices on late model vehicles. To correctly diagnose and solve problems in vacuum control systems, a vacuum source is necessary for testing. In some cases, vacuum can be taken from the intake manifold when the engine is running, but vacuum is normally provided by a hand vacuum pump. These hand vacuum pumps have a built-in vacuum gauge that allow testing while the device is still attached to the component. For some tests, an additional vacuum gauge may be necessary.

HEATING AND AIR CONDITIONING

NOTE: *Refer to Chapter 1 for discharging, charging of the air conditioning system.*

Heater Assembly
REMOVAL AND INSTALLATION
F10

1. Disconnect the battery ground cable.
2. Drain the engine coolant and remove the heater hoses.

CAUTION: *When draining the coolant, keep in mind that cats and dogs are attracted by the ethylene glycol antifreeze, and are quite likely to drink any that is left in an uncovered container or in puddles on the ground. This will prove fatal in sufficient quantity. Always drain the coolant into a sealable container. Coolant should be reused unless it is contaminated or several years old.*

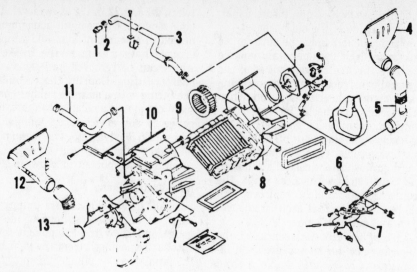

1. Connector
2. Clip
3. Heater hose (inlet)
4. Defroster nozzle (R.H.)
5. Defroster duct (R.H.)
6. Heater switch
7. Heater control
8. Heater case (R.H.)
9. Heater core
10. Heater case (L.H.)
11. Heater hose (outlet)
12. Defroster nozzle (L.H.)
13. Defroster duct (L.H.)

F10 heater assembly

3. Remove the defroster hoses from each side of the heater assembly.

4. Remove the cable retaining clamps, then the cables for the intake and the floor doors.

5. Disconnect the three pole connector.

6. Remove the four heater retaining screws and the heater.

7. Install the heater assembly with retaining screws in the vehicle. Reconnect all electrical connections.

8. Install heater cables and retaining clamps.

9. Install the defroster hoses to each side of the heater assembly.

10. Install heater hoses and refill the cooling system.

11. Connect battery cable, start engine and check system for proper operation.

310

1. Disconnect the negative battery terminal.

2. Set the temperature lever to the HOT position and drain the engine coolant.

CAUTION: *When draining the coolant, keep in mind that cats and dogs are attracted by the ethylene glycol antifreeze, and are quite likely to drink any that is left in an uncovered container or in puddles on the ground. This will prove fatal in sufficient quantity. Always drain the coolant into a sealable container. Coolant should be reused unless it is contaminated or several years old.*

3. Remove the instrument panel assembly. See the following section for instructions.

4. Disconnect the control cables, the control rod and the heater motor harness from the heater unit.

5. Disconnect the inlet and the outlet heater hoses from the engine compartment.

6. Remove the two lower and three upper bolts attaching the heater and blower units to the vehicle.

NOTE: The air conditioning unit is on the passenger's side of the vehicle. It does not have to be removed to remove the heater and blower units.

7. Remove the heater and blower units.

8. Install the heater and blower units with attaching bolts in the vehicle.

9. Install the heater hoses and refill the cooling system.

10. Connect the heater control cables, control rod and electrical connections.

11. Install the instrument panel assembly and connect the battery cable.

12. Start engine and check system for proper operation.

Stanza

Since the air conditioning evaporator core is mounted in the engine compartment on most models, no air conditioning interference is experienced when removing the heater core. When refilling the cooling system be sure to bleed the air from it, refer to Chapter 1.

1. Remove the instrument panel.

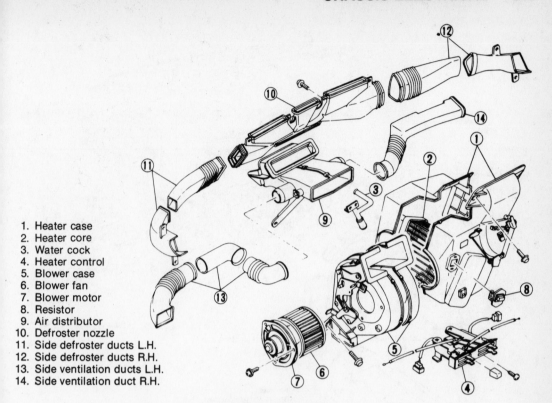

1. Heater case
2. Heater core
3. Water cock
4. Heater control
5. Blower case
6. Blower fan
7. Blower motor
8. Resistor
9. Air distributor
10. Defroster nozzle
11. Side defroster ducts L.H.
12. Side defroster ducts R.H.
13. Side ventilation ducts L.H.
14. Side ventilation duct R.H.

310 heater assembly

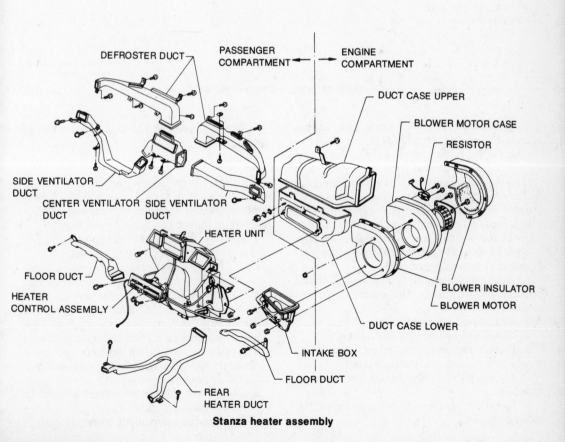

Stanza heater assembly

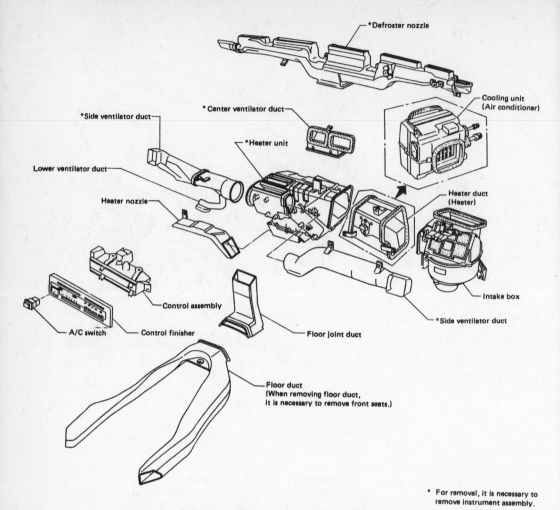

Heater assembly—Stanza (1987–88)

* For removal, it is necessary to remove instrument assembly.

2. Disconnect the heater hoses and vacuum tube in the engine compartment.

CAUTION: *When draining the coolant, keep in mind that cats and dogs are attracted by the ethylene glycol antifreeze, and are quite likely to drink any that is left in an uncovered container or in puddles on the ground. This will prove fatal in sufficient quantity. Always drain the coolant into a sealable container. Coolant should be reused unless it is contaminated or several years old.*

3. Disconnect the control lever and electrical connectors. Remove the heater control assembly.

4. Unbolt and remove the heater unit.

5. Install the heater unit in the vehicle.

6. Install the heater control assembly, control lever and electrical connections.

7. Connect the heater hoses and vacuum tube.

8. Install the instrument panel and refill the cooling system.

9. Start engine and check system for proper operation.

Pulsar

Since the air conditioning evaporator is located between the blower motor and the heater core, the heater core can be removed without disturbing the air conditioning evaporator.

1. Set the TEMP lever to the maximum HOT position and drain the engine coolant.

CAUTION: *When draining the coolant, keep in mind that cats and dogs are attracted by the ethylene glycol antifreeze, and are quite likely to drink any that is left in an uncovered container or in puddles on the ground. This will prove fatal in sufficient quantity. Always drain the coolant into a sealable container. Coolant should be reused unless it is contaminated or several years old.*

2. Disconnect the heater assembly hoses in the engine compartment.

3. Remove the instrument assembly.

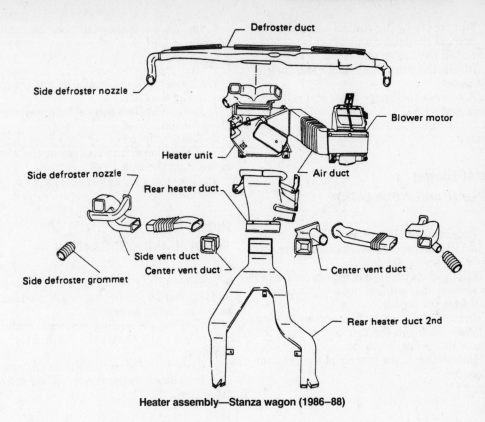

Defroster duct

Side defroster nozzle

Blower motor

Heater unit

Air duct

Side defroster nozzle

Rear heater duct

Side vent duct

Center vent duct

Center vent duct

Side defroster grommet

Rear heater duct 2nd

Heater assembly—Stanza wagon (1986–88)

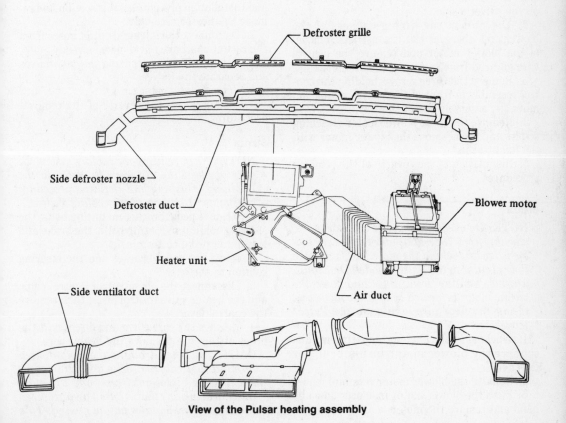

Defroster grille

Side defroster nozzle

Defroster duct

Blower motor

Heater unit

Air duct

Side ventilator duct

View of the Pulsar heating assembly

4. Remove the heater control assembly.

5. Remove the heater unit assembly.

6. Install the heater unit in the vehicle.

7. Install the control assembly and instrument panel.

8. Reconnect the heater hoses and refill the cooling system.

9. Start engine and check system for proper operation.

Heater Blower

REMOVAL AND INSTALLATION

F10

1. Refer to the Heater Assembly, Removal and Installation procedures, in this chapter and remove the heater assembly.

NOTE: *You may be able to remove the blower on some models without removing the heater unit from the vehicle.*

2. Remove the three or four screws holding the blower motor in the case and remove the motor with the fan attached.

3. Installation is the reverse of the removal procedures.

310

1. Disconnect the negative battery terminal and remove the instrument panel's lower cover on the driver's side.

2. Disconnect the wiring harness at the blower and wherever else it constricts removal of the blower motor and remove the control wire and rod from in front of the motor.

3. Remove the three screws holding the control assembly in front of the blower motor and move the assembly out of the way.

4. Remove the three blower motor attaching screws and then remove the blower motor with the fan attached.

5. Installation is the reverse of the removal procedures.

Stanza

NOTE: *On all Stanza models except wagons, starting from 1987 and later the blower motor is located behind the glove box, facing the floor similar to the Pulsar model. On Stanza wagons, starting from 1986 and later the blower motor is located behind the glove box, facing the floor also similar to the Pulsar model.*

1. Working in the engine compartment, disconnect the blower motor insulator upper fasteners.

2. Remove the blower motor retaining bolts.

3. Push the blower motor insulator down by hand and remove the motor.

4. Installation is the reverse of the removal procedures.

Pulsar

The blower motor is located behind the glove box, facing the floor.

1. Disconnect the electrical harness from the blower motor.

2. Remove the retaining bolts from the bottom of the blower unit and lower the blower motor from the case.

3. To install, reverse the removal procedures.

Heater Core

REMOVAL AND INSTALLATION

F10

1. Refer to the Heater Assembly, Removal and Installation procedures, this section and remove the heater assembly.

2. Remove the sealing material. Unfasten the seven clips that hold the heater case together.

3. Remove the heater core from the cases.

4. Installation is the reverse of the removal procedures.

310

1. Refer to the Heater Assembly, Removal and Installation procedures, this section and remove the heater assembly.

2. Disconnect the inlet and outlet hoses from the core if you have not done so already.

3. Remove the clips securing the case halves and separate the halves.

4. Remove the heater core.

5. Installation is the reverse of the removal procedures.

Stanza

NOTE: *When refilling the cooling system, be sure to bleed the air from it. Refer to the Draining, Flushing and Refilling procedure in Chapter 1 and bleed the cooling system.*

1. Remove pedal bracket mounting bolts, the steering column mounting bolts, the brake and the clutch pedal cotter pins.

2. Move the pedal bracket and the steering column to the left.

3. Disconnect the air mix door control cable and the heater valve control lever, then remove the control lever.

4. Remove the core cover and disconnect the hoses at the core. Remove the heater core.

CAUTION: *When draining the coolant, keep in mind that cats and dogs are attracted by the ethylene glycol antifreeze, and are quite likely to drink any that is left in an uncovered container or in puddles on the ground. This*

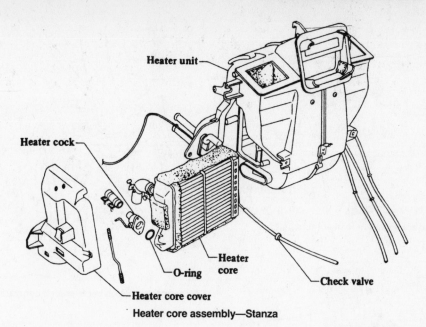

Heater unit

Heater cock

O-ring

Heater core cover

Heater core

Check valve

Heater core assembly—Stanza

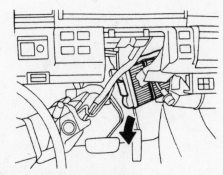

Removing heater core—Stanza

will prove fatal in sufficient quantity. Always drain the coolant into a sealable container. Coolant should be reused unless it is contaminated or several years old.

5. Installation is the reverse of the removal procedures.

Pulsar

1. Refer to the Heater Assembly, Removal and Installation procedures, in the section and remove the heater assembly from the vehicle.

2. Remove the heater assembly case bolts and separate the cases, then pull the heater core from the case.

3. To install, reverse the removal procedures. Refill the cooling system.

Heater Control Head
REMOVAL AND INSTALLATION
F10

1. Remove meter cover and disconnect three control cables.

2. Remove setting screws from rear side of heater control assembly.

3. Remove heater control head from vehicle.

4. To install reverse the removal procedures.

310

1. Remove center bezel and control cables from head assembly.

2. Remove screws securing control assembly to instrument panel.

3. Remove control assembly from the vehicle.

4. To install reverse the removal procedures.

Stanza And Pulsar

NOTE: *On Stanza models, remove cluster cover and instrument lower covers.*

1. Disconnect the negative battery cable.

2. Remove control cables by unfastening clamps at door levers.

3. Disconnect electrical connector and remove heater control head assembly mounting bolts. On Stanza models, remove ground wire from intake box if so equipped.

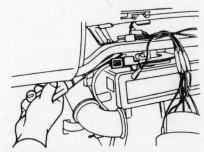

Heater control securing screws—F10

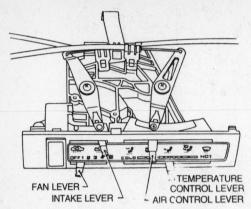

Heater control head—Pulsar—others similar

FAN LEVER
INTAKE LEVER
TEMPERATURE CONTROL LEVER
AIR CONTROL LEVER

Removing control cables at door levers

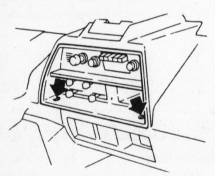

Mounting screws for heater control head—Pulsar

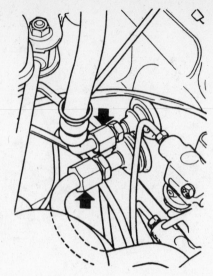

Disconnecting pipes in the engine compartment—F10

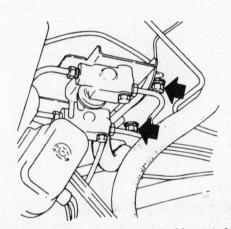

Removing 2 engine compartment attaching nuts for cooling unit—F10

4. Remove heater control head assembly.
5. To install reverse the removal procedures.

Evaporator Core/Cooling Unit

REMOVAL AND INSTALLATION

F10

NOTE: *Follow this procedure to remove auxiliary cooling fan from the cooling unit.*
1. Disconnect battery ground cable.
2. Discharge air conditioning system, refer to Chapter 1 for more details.
3. Disconnect low and high pressure pipes at connections in the engine compartment. Push two grommets out into the passenger compartment.
NOTE: *Be sure to use two wrenches when removing or connecting pipe joints. Always plug pipe openings immediately after pipe disconnection.*
4. Working inside the engine compartment, remove two cooling unit attaching nuts.
5. Remove console box.
6. Remove cooling unit attaching bolt and nut in the passenger compartment.
7. Remove cooling unit and bracket as an assembly.
8. Disconnect and mark all electrical connections from cooling unit.
9. Remove cooling unit from vehicle.
10. Remove all attaching parts from cooling unit.
11. Remove screws and springs securing upper case to lower case.
12. Separated case, remove auxiliary cooling fan, then remove evaporator.
13. Install evaporator and cooling fan in cooling unit case.

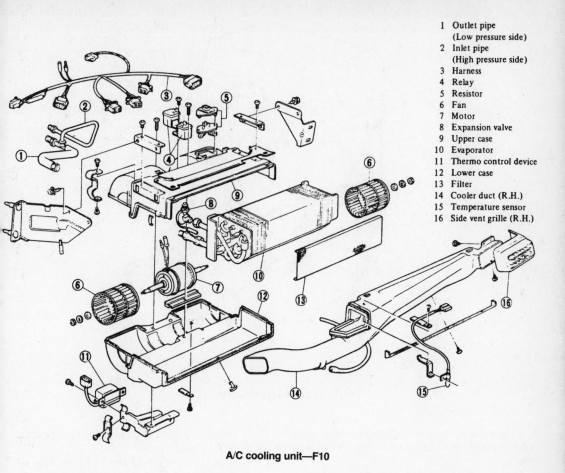

1   Outlet pipe
    (Low pressure side)
2   Inlet pipe
    (High pressure side)
3   Harness
4   Relay
5   Resistor
6   Fan
7   Motor
8   Expansion valve
9   Upper case
10 Evaporator
11 Thermo control device
12 Lower case
13 Filter
14 Cooler duct (R.H.)
15 Temperature sensor
16 Side vent grille (R.H.)

A/C cooling unit—F10

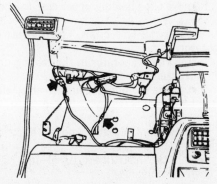

Removing electrical connections from cooling unit—F10

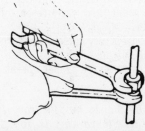

Using 2 wrenches to remove or install pipe joints

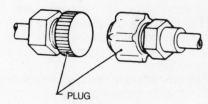

PLUG

Always plug A/C lines after disconnecting

14. Install the attaching parts on the cooling unit.

15. Install the cooling unit and bracket in the vehicle. Tighten all mounting bolts (inside passenger compartment and out in the engine compartment).

16. Connect all electrical connections and pressure pipes with new O-rings.

17. Install the console box.

18. Connect battery cable and charge the air conditioning system.

19. Check system for proper operation.

310

1. Disconnect battery ground cable.

2. Discharge air conditioning system, refer to Chapter 1 for more details.

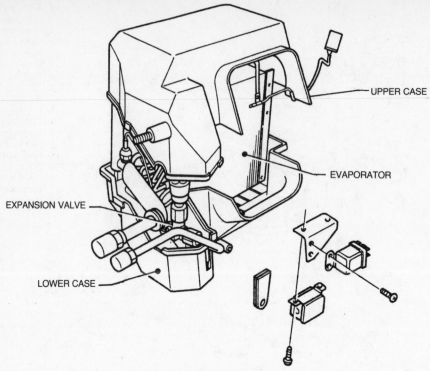

UPPER CASE

EVAPORATOR

EXPANSION VALVE

LOWER CASE

A/C cooling unit—310

3. Remove air cleaner, altitude compensator with bracket, and carburetor cooling fan with bracket.

4. Disconnect refrigerant lines from evaporator. Remove piping grommet and cover.

NOTE: *Be sure to use two wrenches when removing or connecting pipe joints. Always plug pipe openings immediately after pipe disconnection.*

5. Remove right side dash face finisher.

6. Remove instrument panel.

7. Disconnect all electrical connections.

8. Remove clip and disconnect control cable from air intake door shaft.

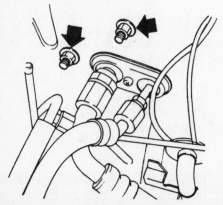

Removing mounting bolts on the cooling unit—310

9. Loosen band seal at joint of cooling unit and heating unit.

10. Remove mounting bolts and then remove cooling unit.

11. Remove clips holding upper case to lower case.

12. Separate the case, then remove evaporator.

13. Install the evaporator in the cooling unit case then assemble case.

14. Install the cooling unit in the vehicle and tighten band seal between cooling and heating unit.

15. Connect control cable and all electrical connections.

16. Install the instrument panel and right side dash face finisher.

17. Connect refrigerant lines to evaporator with new O-rings and install piping grommet and cover.

18. Install the air cleaner, altitude compensator with bracket, and carburetor cooling fan with bracket.

19. Connect battery cable and charge the air conditioning system.

20. Check system for proper operation.

Stanza

NOTE: *On Stanza models from 1987 and later and on Stanza wagons from 1986 and later the cooling unit which contains the*

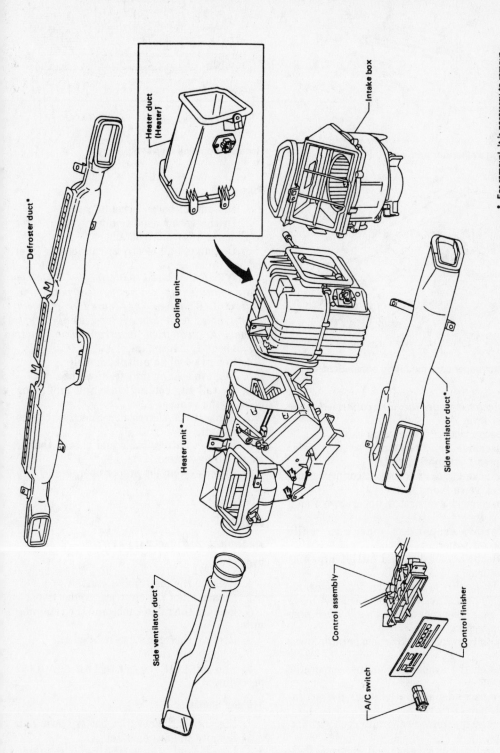

Heater duct
(Heater)

Intake box

• For removal, it is necessary to remove
instrument assembly.

Defroster duct*

Cooling unit

Heater unit*

Side ventilator duct*

Side ventilator duct*

Control assembly

Control finisher

A/C switch

Heater A/C unit assembly—Pulsar—Stanza (late model)

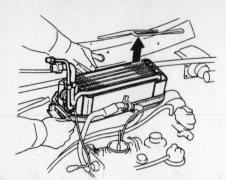

Removing evaporator from case—Stanza

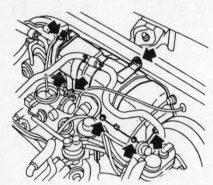

Evaporator upper case mounting bolts—Stanza

evaporator is under the dash connected to the heater unit.

1. Disconnect battery ground cable.
2. Discharge air conditioning system, refer to Chapter 1 for more details.
3. Remove air cleaner and disconnect vacuum check valve fixing bolt.
4. Disconnect evaporator upper case fixing bolts.
5. Remove evaporator upper case while scraping off sealer.
6. Disconnect inlet and outlet pipes at evaporator.
NOTE: *Be sure to use two wrenches when removing or connecting pipe joints. Always plug pipe openings immediately after pipe disconnection.*
7. Remove evaporator from evaporator lower case.
8. Install the evaporator in the evaporator lower case.
9. Connect inlet and outlet pipes at evaporator with new O-rings.
10. Install the upper evaporator case with fixing bolts.
11. Install the air cleaner and vacuum check valve fixing bolt.
12. Connect battery cable and charge the air conditioning system.
13. Check system for proper operation.

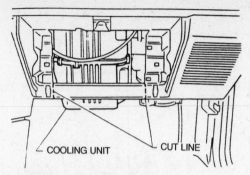

Removing cooling unit—Pulsar

Pulsar

1. Disconnect battery ground cable.
2. Discharge air conditioning system, refer to Chapter 1 for more details.
3. Disconnect all electrical connectors from cooling unit.
NOTE: *For vehicles with factory installed air conditioning, cut instrument panel and discard. Before cutting, cover blower motor vent holes with tape. After cutting, brush shavings away from the area around blower motor and remove tape.*
4. Remove cooling unit fixing bolts.
5. Remove cooling unit from vehicle.
6. Install the cooling unit and mounting bolts in the vehicle.
7. Connect all electrical connectors to the cooling unit.
8. Connect battery cable and charge the air conditioning system.
9. Check system for proper operation.

RADIO

REMOVAL AND INSTALLATION

F10

1. Remove the instrument cluster.
2. Detach all of the electrical connections.
3. Remove the radio knobs and the retaining nuts.
4. Remove the rear support bracket.
5. Remove the radio.
6. To install, reverse the removal procedures.

310 and Stanza

1. Disconnect the negative battery terminal.
2. Remove the center bezel.
3. Loosen and remove the radio retaining screws.
4. Remove the radio and disconnect the antenna feeder cable, the power lines and the speaker connections.

5. To install, reverse the removal procedures.

Pulsar

1. Remove the ash tray and the ash tray bracket.
2. Remove the radio mounting bolts.
3. Remove the instrument panel cover surrounding the radio.
4. Disconnect the electrical harness connector and the antenna plug from the radio.
5. To install, reverse the removal procedures.

WINDSHIELD WIPER

Blade and Arm
REMOVAL AND INSTALLATION
All Models

1. Pull the wiper arm up.
2. Push the lock pin, then remove the wiper blade.

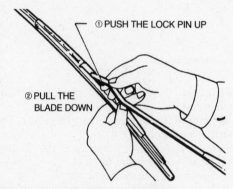

Removing wiper blades—all models

3. Insert the new wiper blade to the wiper arm until a click sounds.
4. Make sure the wiper blade contacts the glass. Otherwise, the arm may be damaged.
5. To remove the arm assembly lift the end of the wiper arm, which is spring loaded, at the base and remove the attaching nut. On early models just remove the attaching nut at the base of the wiper arm.

Motor and Linkage
REMOVAL AND INSTALLATION
F10

1. Disconnect the battery ground cable.
2. Lift the wiper arms, then remove the attaching nuts and the wiper arms.
3. Remove the meter cover.
4. Remove the glove box.
5. Remove the wiper motor attaching bolts.
6. Remove the ball joint connecting the motor shaft to the wiper link.
7. Remove the wiper motor from the dash panel after disconnecting the electrical harness.
8. Remove the wiper pivot bolts from under the dashboard and the linkage.
9. Install the linkage and pivot bolts.
10. Install the wiper motor and electrical connections.
11. Connect the ball joint from motor shaft to wiper link.
12. Install the glove box and meter cover.
13. Install the wiper arms and attaching nuts.
14. Connect the battery cable, check for proper operation.
NOTE: *Make sure you install the wiper arms in the correct positions by operating the sys-*

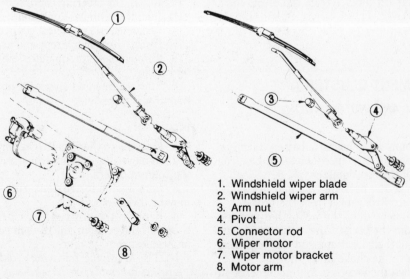

1. Windshield wiper blade
2. Windshield wiper arm
3. Arm nut
4. Pivot
5. Connector rod
6. Wiper motor
7. Wiper motor bracket
8. Motor arm

F10 wiper system

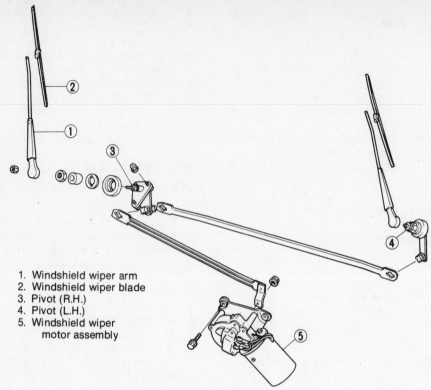

1. Windshield wiper arm
2. Windshield wiper blade
3. Pivot (R.H.)
4. Pivot (L.H.)
5. Windshield wiper
     motor assembly

310 and Stanza wiper system—Pulsar similar

tem (*without the arms*), *stopping it, then attach the arms.*

310, Pulsar and Stanza

1. Disconnect the negative battery terminal and remove the motor wiring connection.
2. Unbolt the motor from the body.
3. Disconnect the wiper linkage from the motor and remove the motor.
4. Disconnect linkage from the pivot.
5. To install, reverse the removal procedures.

INSTRUMENT CLUSTER

REMOVAL AND INSTALLATION

F10

1. Disconnect the negative battery terminal.
2. Disconnect the speedometer cable from the back of the speedometer.
3. Remove the package tray and disconnect the heater control cables from the heater.
4. Disconnect all of the wiring harness connectors from the back of the instrument panel after noting their locations and tagging them.
5. Remove the choke knob and nut.
6. Remove the steering column bracket installation bolts.

7. Loosen the instrument panel upper attaching screws.
8. Remove the bolts securing the sides of the instrument panel.
9. Remove the bolts attaching the instrument panel to the pedal bracket.
10. Remove the instrument panel.
11. Install the instrument panel with attaching bolts in the vehicle.
12. Install the steering column bracket.
13. Install the choke knob and nut.
14. Reconnect all electrical connections.
15. Install the package tray and heater cables.
16. Connect the speedometer cable and battery cable.
17. Start engine and check for proper operation of all components.

310

1. Disconnect the negative battery terminal.
2. Remove the steering wheel and the steering column covers.
3. Remove the instrument cluster lid by removing its screws.
4. Remove the instrument cluster screws, then pull the unit out and disconnect all wiring and cables from its rear.
NOTE: *Mark the wires to avoid confusion during assembly; be careful not to damage the printed circuit.*

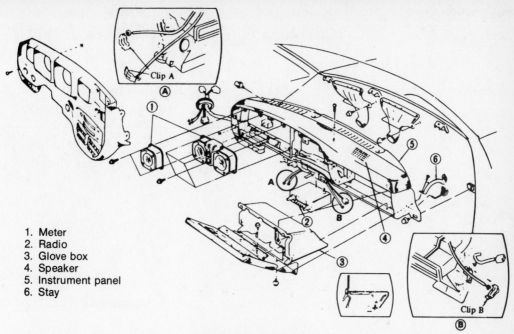

1. Meter
2. Radio
3. Glove box
4. Speaker
5. Instrument panel
6. Stay

F10 instrument panel

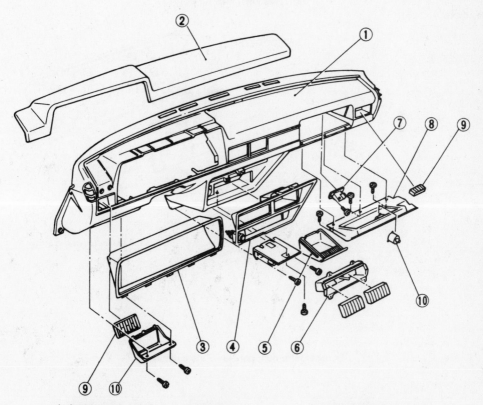

1. Instrument panel	5. Ash tray	9. Side ventilator case
2. Instrument pad	6. Center ventilator	10. Key lock
3. Cluster lid	7. Striker	11. Coin pocket
4. Center bezel	8. Glove lid	

310 instrument panel

SGL models

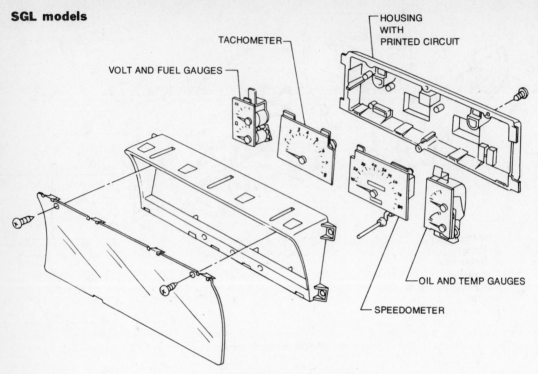

G models

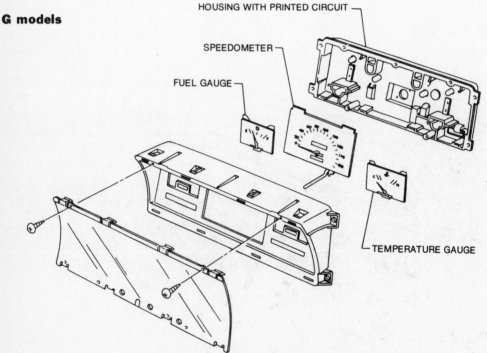

Stanza instrument panels—Pulsar similar

5. Remove the instrument cluster.

6. Install the instrument cluster and attaching screws.

7. Connect all electrical connections and and cables.

8. Install the steering wheel and the steering column covers.

9. Connect the battery cable.

10. Start engine and check for proper operation of all components.

Stanza

1. Disconnect the negative battery terminal.
2. Loosen the tilt adjusting lever and completely lower the steering column.
3. Remove the steering column cover.
4. Remove the mounting screws and slightly tilt the cluster lid forward, then release the lid from the front nails.
5. Remove the instrument cluster screws, pull the cluster forward, then disconnect the speedometer cable and the harness connectors.
6. Pull out the instrument cluster and remove it from the vehicle.
7. Install the instrument cluster and attaching screws.
8. Reconnect all electrical connections and speedometer cable.
9. Reconnect steering column and cover.
10. Connect the battery cable.
11. Start engine and check for proper operation of all components.

Pulsar

1. Disconnect the negative battery terminal.
2. Loosen the tilt adjusting lever and completely lower the steering column.
3. Remove the steering column cover.
4. Remove the mounting screws and the instrument cluster hood.
5. Remove the instrument cluster screws, pull the cluster forward, then disconnect the speedometer cable and the harness connectors.
6. Remove the instrument cluster from the vehicle.
7. Install the instrument cluster and attaching screws.
8. Reconnect all electrical connections and speedometer cable.
9. Reconnect steering column and cover.
10. Connect the battery cable.
11. Start engine and check for proper operation of all components.

Windshield Wiper Switch
REMOVAL AND INSTALLATION
F10

1. Disconnect the negative battery terminal.
2. Reach up under the left side of the dash and disconnect the electrical connector.
3. Disconnect the illumination fiberscope at the illumination lamp.
4. Remove the knob by pressing and turning it.
5. Remove the retaining nut on the meter cover.
6. Reach up under the instrument panel and remove the wiper switch.
7. Install the switch in the instrument panel with retaining nut.

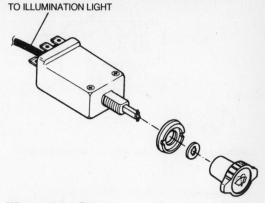

TO ILLUMINATION LIGHT

Wiper switch—F10

8. Install switch knob and connect the illumination fiberscope at the illumination lamp.
9. Reconnect electrical connector.
10. Reconnect the battery and check for proper operation.

310

1. Disconnect the negative battery cable.
2. Remove the horn pad, the steering wheel and the steering wheel cover.
3. Disconnect the electrical connectors from the combination switch.
4. Loosen the retaining screw and remove the combination switch assembly.
5. To install, reverse the removal procedures.

Pulsar (1983) and Stanza (1982-86)

1. Remove the steering wheel and the steering column cover.
2. Disconnect all of the combination switch wires.
3. Loosen the retaining screw and remove the combination switch wires.
4. To install, reverse the removal procedures.
NOTE: *On Stanza models (1987-88) the wiper switch can be removed from the combination switch on the steering column.*

Pulsar (1984-86)

The wiper switch can be removed without removing the combination switch from the steering column.

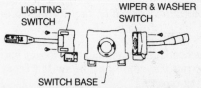

LIGHTING SWITCH

WIPER & WASHER SWITCH

SWITCH BASE

Removing wiper switch from combination switch

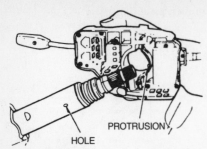

Removing combination switch from steering column

1. Remove the steering column cover.
2. Disconnect the wiper switch electrical connector.
3. Remove the wiper switch to combination switch retaining screws.
4. To install, reverse the removal procedures.
NOTE: *On the 1987-88 Pulsar models the wiper switch is located in the dash. To remove this switch disconnect the electrical connector and remove the retaining screw.*

Headlight Switch
REMOVAL AND INSTALLATION
F10
1. Disconnect the negative battery terminal.
2. Remove the steering column cover.
3. Disconnect the wiring harness connector.
4. Remove the ignition switch-to-steering column retaining screws and the switch assembly.
5. To install, reverse the removal procedures.

310, Stanza (1982-86) and Pulsar (1983)
1. Place the ignition switch in the **OFF** position and disconnect the negative battery terminal.
2. Remove the steering wheel and the steering column cover.
3. Disconnect the wiring harness from the combination switch.
4. Loosen the retaining screws and remove the combination switch.
5. To install, reverse the removal procedures.
NOTE: *On Stanza models (1987-88) the headlight switch can be removed from the combination switch on the steering column.*

Pulsar (1984-86)
The headlight switch can be removed without removing the combination switch from the steering column.
1. Remove the steering column cover.

2. Disconnect the headlight switch electrical connector.
3. Remove the headlight switch to combination switch retaining screws.
4. To install, reverse the removal procedures.
NOTE: *On the 1987-88 Pulsar models the headlight switch is located in the dash. To remove this switch disconnect the electrical connector and remove the retaining screw.*

Speedometer Cable
REPLACEMENT
1. Remove any lower dash covers that may be in the way and disconnect the speedometer cable from the back of the speedometer.
NOTE: *On some models it may be easier to remove the instrument cluster to gain access to the cable. On the Stanza and Pulsar, the cable connector-to-instrument cluster has a snap release; simply press on the connector tab to release it.*
2. Pull the cable from the cable housing. If the cable is broken, the other half of the cable will have to be removed from the transaxle end. Unscrew the retaining knob at the transaxle and remove the cable from the transaxle extension housing.
3. Lubricate the cable with graphite powder (sold as speedometer cable lubricant) and feed the cable into the housing. It is best to start at the speedometer end and feed the cable down towards the transaxle.
NOTE: *It is usually necessary to unscrew the transaxle connection and install the cable end to the gear, then reconnect the housing to the transaxle. Slip the cable end into the speedometer and reconnect the cable housing.*

Ignition Switch
Ignition switch removal and installation procedures are covered in Chapter 8; Suspension and Steering.

LIGHTING
Headlights
REMOVAL AND INSTALLATION
Except Pulsar Coupe
NOTE: *Many vehicles have radiator grilles which are unit constructed to also serve as headlight frames. In this case, it will be necessary to remove the grille to gain access to the headlights. If vehicle is equipped with COMPOSITE HEADLAMPS, it is advisable to take it to a dealer or a professional mechanic for replacement.*

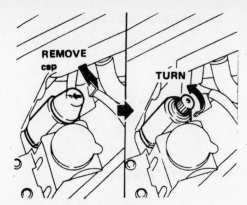

Manual operation of headlights

1. Remove the grille, if necessary.
2. Remove the headlight retaining ring screws. These are the three or four short screws in the assembly. There are also two longer screws at the top and side of the headlight which are used to aim the headlight. Do not tamper with these or the headlight will have to be re-aimed.
3. Remove the ring on round headlights by turning it clockwise.
4. Pull the headlight bulb from its socket and disconnect the electrical plug.
5. Connect the plug to the new bulb.
6. Position the headlight in the shell. Make sure that the word TOP is, indeed, at the top and that the knobs in the headlight lens engage the slots in the mounting shell.
7. Place the retaining ring over the bulb and install the screws.
8. Install the grille, if removed.

Pulsar Coupe

1. Turn on the retractable headlight switch, then after the headlights are open, disconnect the negative battery terminal.
2. Remove the screws and the clip, then headlight cover.
3. Remove the retaining ring cover.

4. Pull out the headlight, remove the rubber cap and the wiring connector. Remove the headlight.
5. To install, reverse the removal procedures.

MANUAL OPERATION OF HEADLIGHTS

1. Turn OFF both headlight switch and retractable headlight switch.
2. Disconnect the battery negative terminal.
3. Remove the motor shaft cap.
4. Turn the motor shaft counterclockwise by hand until the headlights are opened or closed.
5. Reinstall the motor shaft cap and connect the battery cable.

Signal And Marker Lights
REMOVAL AND INSTALLATION
Front Turn Signal And Parking Lights

1. Remove turn signal/parking light lens with retaining screws.
2. Slightly depress the bulb and turn it counterclockwise to release it.
3. To install the bulb carefully push down and turn bulb clockwise at the same time.
4. Install the turn signal/parking light lens with retaining screws.

Side Marker Lights

1. Remove side marker light lens with retaining screws.
2. Turn the bulb socket counterclockwise to release it from lens.
3. Pull bulb straight out.
4. To install bulb carefully push straight in.
5. Turn the bulb socket clockwise to install it in lens.
6. Install side marker light lens with retaining screws.

Rear Turn Signal, Brake And Parking Lights

1. Remove rear trim panel in rear of vehicle to gain access to the bulb socket.

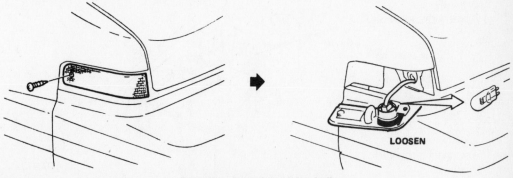

Removing front side marker bulb

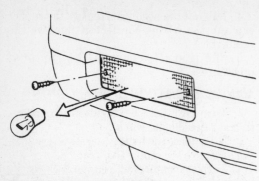

Removing front turn signal bulb

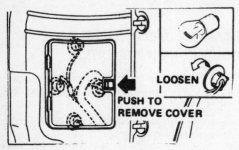

Removing trim panel—Stanza wagon—other models similar

2. Slightly depress the bulb and turn it counterclockwise to release it.

3. To install the bulb carefully push down and turn bulb clockwise at the same time.

4. Install trim panel.

CIRCUIT PROTECTION

Fuses

On all vehicles (except Stanza), the fuse block is located under the left side of the instrument panel. On the Stanza, the fuse block is located under the glove box, concealed by a protective cover; open the fuse block cover to expose the fuse block.

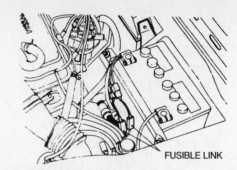

Fusible link—F10—others similar

REMOVAL AND INSTALLATION

The fuses can be easily inspected to see if they are blown. Simply pull the fuse from the block, inspect it and replace it with a new one, if necessary.

NOTE: *When replacing a blown fuse, be certain to replace it with one of the correct amperage.*

Fusible Links

A fusible link(s) is a protective device used in an electrical circuit. When current increases beyond a certain amperage, the fusible metal wire of the link melts, thus breaking the electrical circuit and preventing further damage to the other components and wiring. Whenever a fusible link is melted because of a short circuit,

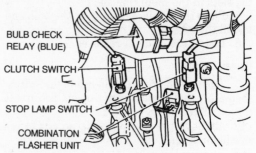

Flasher location—Stanza and Pulsar

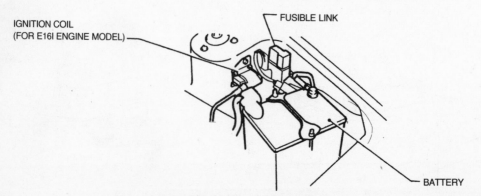

Fusible link—Pulsar—others similar

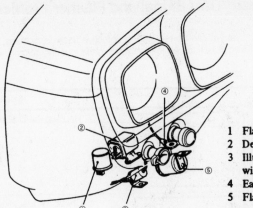

1 Flasher unit for hazard
2 Defogger relay
3 Illumination light for
  wiper and rear defogger
4 Earth point
5 Flasher unit for turn signal

Flasher location—F10

correct the cause before installing a new link.
Use the following chart to locate the fusible link(s).
All fusible links are the plug in kind. To replace them, simply unplug the bad link and insert the new one.

Circuit Breakers

Circuit breakers are also located in the fuse block. A circuit breaker is an electrical switch which breaks the circuit during an electrical overload. The circuit breaker will remain open until the short or overload condition in the circuit is corrected.

Flasher

To replace the flasher carefully pull it from the electrical connector. If necessary remove any component that restricts removal.

Fusible Links

Year	Model	Number	Color/Protects	Location
1976–78	F10	2	Red/N.A. Green/N.A.	At positive battery terminal
1979–81	310	4	1 Red/Fuse block 3 Green/Ignition, lights, fan	Mounted on fender well beside battery
1982	310 Stanza	4	1 Red/Fuse block, alternator, air conditioner relay 3 Green/Ignition switch, fan and defogger, lights, carburetor cooling fan (U.S. models)	Mounted on fender well beside battery
1983–88	Stanza Pulsar	—	—	Connected to the battery terminal

Fuse Box and Flasher Location

Year	Model	Fuse Box Location	Flasher Location
1976–78	F10	Below hood release knob	Under driver's side of dashboard ①
1979–82	310	Below hood release knob	Turn signal: Passenger side kick board Hazard: Driver's side of hood release
1982–86	Stanza	Under glove box	On the steering column support, behind the instrument panel
1983–88	Pulsar	Under dash next to driver's kick panel	On the steering column support behind the instrument panel

① Both the turn signal and the hazard flashers are side by side

Troubleshooting Basic Turn Signal and Flasher Problems

Most problems in the turn signals or flasher system, can be reduced to defective flashers or bulbs, which are easily replaced. Occasionally, problems in the turn signals are traced to the switch in the steering column, which will require professional service.

F = Front   R = Rear   ● = Lights off   ○ = Lights on

Problem		Solution
Turn signals light, but do not flash		• Replace the flasher
No turn signals light on either side		• Check the fuse. Replace if defective. • Check the flasher by substitution • Check for open circuit, short circuit or poor ground
Both turn signals on one side don't work		• Check for bad bulbs • Check for bad ground in both housings
One turn signal light on one side doesn't work		• Check and/or replace bulb • Check for corrosion in socket. Clean contacts. • Check for poor ground at socket
Turn signal flashes too fast or too slow		• Check any bulb on the side flashing too fast. A heavy-duty bulb is probably installed in place of a regular bulb. • Check the bulb flashing too slow. A standard bulb was probably installed in place of a heavy-duty bulb. • Check for loose connections or corrosion at the bulb socket
Indicator lights don't work in either direction		• Check if the turn signals are working • Check the dash indicator lights • Check the flasher by substitution
One indicator light doesn't light		• On systems with 1 dash indicator: See if the lights work on the same side. Often the filaments have been reversed in systems combining stoplights with taillights and turn signals. Check the flasher by substitution • On systems with 2 indicators: Check the bulbs on the same side Check the indicator light bulb Check the flasher by substitution

Troubleshooting Basic Lighting Problems

Problem	Cause	Solution
Lights		
One or more lights don't work, but others do	· Defective bulb(s) · Blown fuse(s) · Dirty fuse clips or light sockets · Poor ground circuit	· Replace bulb(s) · Replace fuse(s) · Clean connections · Run ground wire from light socket housing to car frame
Lights burn out quickly	· Incorrect voltage regulator setting or defective regulator · Poor battery/alternator connections	· Replace voltage regulator · Check battery/alternator connections
Lights go dim	· Low/discharged battery · Alternator not charging · Corroded sockets or connections · Low voltage output	· Check battery · Check drive belt tension; repair or replace alternator · Clean bulb and socket contacts and connections · Replace voltage regulator
Lights flicker	· Loose connection · Poor ground · Circuit breaker operating (short circuit)	· Tighten all connections · Run ground wire from light housing to car frame · Check connections and look for bare wires
Lights "flare"—Some flare is normal on acceleration—if excessive, see "Lights Burn Out Quickly"	· High voltage setting	· Replace voltage regulator
Lights glare—approaching drivers are blinded	· Lights adjusted too high · Rear springs or shocks sagging · Rear tires soft	· Have headlights aimed · Check rear springs/shocks · Check/correct rear tire pressure
Turn Signals		
Turn signals don't work in either direction	· Blown fuse · Defective flasher · Loose connection	· Replace fuse · Replace flasher · Check/tighten all connections
Right (or left) turn signal only won't work	· Bulb burned out · Right (or left) indicator bulb burned out · Short circuit	· Replace bulb · Check/replace indicator bulb · Check/repair wiring
Flasher rate too slow or too fast	· Incorrect wattage bulb · Incorrect flasher	· Flasher bulb · Replace flasher (use a variable load flasher if you pull a trailer)
Indicator lights do not flash (burn steadily)	· Burned out bulb · Defective flasher	· Replace bulb · Replace flasher
Indicator lights do not light at all	· Burned out indicator bulb · Defective flasher	· Replace indicator bulb · Replace flasher

Troubleshooting Basic Dash Gauge Problems

Problem	Cause	Solution
Coolant Temperature Gauge		
Gauge reads erratically or not at all	• Loose or dirty connections • Defective sending unit • Defective gauge	• Clean/tighten connections • Bi-metal gauge: remove the wire from the sending unit. Ground the wire for an instant. If the gauge registers, replace the sending unit. • Magnetic gauge: disconnect the wire at the sending unit. With ignition ON gauge should register COLD. Ground the wire; gauge should register HOT.
Ammeter Gauge—Turn Headlights ON (do not start engine). Note reaction		
Ammeter shows charge Ammeter shows discharge Ammeter does not move	• Connections reversed on gauge • Ammeter is OK • Loose connections or faulty wiring • Defective gauge	• Reinstall connections • Nothing • Check/correct wiring • Replace gauge
Oil Pressure Gauge		
Gauge does not register or is inaccurate	• On mechanical gauge, Bourdon tube may be bent or kinked • Low oil pressure • Defective gauge • Defective wiring • Defective sending unit	• Check tube for kinks or bends preventing oil from reaching the gauge • Remove sending unit. Idle the engine briefly. If no oil flows from sending unit hole, problem is in engine. • Remove the wire from the sending unit and ground it for an instant with the ignition ON. A good gauge will go to the top of the scale. • Check the wiring to the gauge. If it's OK and the gauge doesn't register when grounded, replace the gauge. • If the wiring is OK and the gauge functions when grounded, replace the sending unit
All Gauges		
All gauges do not operate All gauges read low or erratically All gauges pegged	• Blown fuse • Defective instrument regulator • Defective or dirty instrument voltage regulator • Loss of ground between instrument voltage regulator and car • Defective instrument regulator	• Replace fuse • Replace instrument voltage regulator • Clean contacts or replace • Check ground • Replace regulator
Warning Lights		
Light(s) do not come on when ignition is ON, but engine is not started Light comes on with engine running	• Defective bulb • Defective wire • Defective sending unit • Problem in individual system • Defective sending unit	• Replace bulb • Check wire from light to sending unit • Disconnect the wire from the sending unit and ground it. Replace the sending unit if the light comes on with the ignition ON. • Check system • Check sending unit (see above)

Troubleshooting the Heater

Problem	Cause	Solution
Blower motor will not turn at any speed	• Blown fuse • Loose connection • Defective ground • Faulty switch • Faulty motor • Faulty resistor	• Replace fuse • Inspect and tighten • Clean and tighten • Replace switch • Replace motor • Replace resistor
Blower motor turns at one speed only	• Faulty switch • Faulty resistor	• Replace switch • Replace resistor
Blower motor turns but does not circulate air	• Intake blocked • Fan not secured to the motor shaft	• Clean intake • Tighten security
Heater will not heat	• Coolant does not reach proper temperature • Heater core blocked internally • Heater core air-bound • Blend-air door not in proper position	• Check and replace thermostat if necessary • Flush or replace core if necessary • Purge air from core • Adjust cable
Heater will not defrost	• Control cable adjustment incorrect • Defroster hose damaged	• Adjust control cable • Replace defroster hose

Troubleshooting Basic Windshield Wiper Problems

Problem	Cause	Solution
Electric Wipers		
Wipers do not operate— Wiper motor heats up or hums	• Internal motor defect • Bent or damaged linkage • Arms improperly installed on linking pivots	• Replace motor • Repair or replace linkage • Position linkage in park and reinstall wiper arms
Wipers do not operate— No current to motor	• Fuse or circuit breaker blown • Loose, open or broken wiring • Defective switch • Defective or corroded terminals • No ground circuit for motor or switch	• Replace fuse or circuit breaker • Repair wiring and connections • Replace switch • Replace or clean terminals • Repair ground circuits
Wipers do not operate— Motor runs	• Linkage disconnected or broken	• Connect wiper linkage or replace broken linkage

Drive Train

7

UNDERSTANDING THE MANUAL TRANSMISSION

Because of the way an internal combustion engine breathes, it can produce torque, or twisting force, only within a narrow speed range. Most modern, overhead valve engines must turn at about 2,500 rpm to produce their peak torque. By 4,500 rpm they are producing so little torque that continued increases in engine speed produce no power increases.

The torque peak on overhead camshaft engines is, generally, much higher, but much narrower.

The manual transmission and clutch are employed to vary the relationship between engine speed and the speed of the wheels so that adequate engine power can be produced under all circumstances. The clutch allows engine torque to be applied to the transmission input shaft gradually, due to mechanical slippage. The car can, consequently, be started smoothly from a full stop.

The transmission changes the ratio between the rotating speeds of the engine and the wheels by the use of gears. 4-speed or 5-speed transmissions are most common. The lower gears allow full engine power to be applied to the wheels during acceleration at low speeds.

The clutch drive plate is a thin disc, the center of which is splined to the transmission input shaft. Both sides of the disc are covered with a layer of material which is similar to brake lining and which is capable of allowing slippage without roughness or excessive noise.

The clutch cover is bolted to the engine flywheel and incorporates a diaphragm spring which provides the pressure to engage the clutch. The cover also houses the pressure plate. The driven disc is sandwiched between the pressure plate and the smooth surface of the flywheel when the clutch pedal is released,

thus forcing it to turn at the same speed as the engine crankshaft.

The transmission contains a mainshaft which passes all the way through the transmission, from the clutch to the halfshafts. This shaft is separated at one point, so that front and rear portions can turn at different speeds.

Power is transmitted by a countershaft in the lower gears and reverse. The gears of the countershaft mesh with gears on the mainshaft, allowing power to be carried from one to the other. All the countershaft gears are integral with that shaft, while several of the mainshaft gears can either rotate independently of the shaft or be locked to it. Shifting from one gear to the next causes one of the gears to be freed from rotating with the shaft and locks another to it. Gears are locked and unlocked by internal dog clutches which slide between the center of the gear and the shaft. The forward gears usually employ synchronizers; friction members which smoothly bring gear and shaft to the same speed before the toothed dog clutches are engaged.

The clutch is operating properly if:

1. It will stall the engine when released with the vehicle held stationary.

2. The shift lever can be moved freely between 1st and reverse gears when the vehicle is stationary and the clutch disengaged.

A clutch pedal free-play adjustment is incorporated in the linkage. If there is about 1-2" (25-50mm) of motion before the pedal begins to release the clutch, it is adjusted properly. Inadequate free-play wears all parts of the clutch releasing mechanisms and may cause slippage. Excessive free-play may cause inadequate release and hard shifting of gears.

Some clutches use a hydraulic system in place of mechanical linkage. If the clutch fails to release, fill the clutch master cylinder with fluid to the proper level and pump the clutch pedal to fill the system with fluid. Bleed the system in the same way as a brake system. If leaks are located, tighten loose connections or overhaul the master or slave cylinder as necessary.

Front wheel drive cars do not have conventional rear axles or drive shafts. Instead, power is transmitted from the engine to a transaxle, or a combination of transmission and drive axle, in one unit. Both the transmission and drive axle accomplish the same function as their counterparts in a front engine/rear drive axle design. The difference is in the location of the components.

In place of a conventional driveshaft, a front-wheel-drive design uses two driveshafts, sometimes called halfshafts, which couple the drive axle portion of the transaxle to the wheels. Universal joints or constant velocity joints are used just as they would in a rear-wheel drive design.

MANUAL TRANSAXLE

Identification

The manual transaxle serial number label is attached on the clutch withdrawal lever or the upper part of the housing.

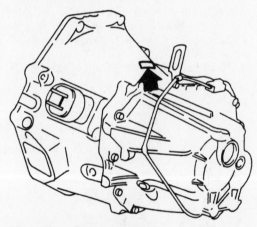

I.D. number—Stanza wagon

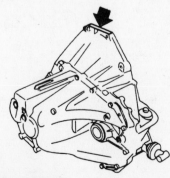

I.D. number—Stanza

I.D. number—Pulsar and 310

Adjustments
SHIFTER LINKAGE
F10
4-SPEED MODELS

1. The adjustment is made at the shift rods on the transaxle. Loosen the adjusting nuts marked No. 1 and No. 2 in the illustration.
2. Measure the clearance between the shift lever marked No. 3 in the illustration and the transaxle case. Make sure the shift lever is pushed completely into the transaxle case. The clearance is marked A in the illustration.
3. Place the transaxle in 4th gear. Shift lever No. 3 should now be fully downward.
4. Increase the initial clearance **A** by 8mm.
5. Push lever No. 4 fully upward. Now tighten nut No. 1 until it makes contact with trunnion No. 7. then back the nut off one full turn and tighten it with nut No. 2.

5-SPEED MODELS

1. Loosen locknuts Nos. 1, 2, 3 and 4.
2. Make sure shift lever No. 5 is pushed completely into the transaxle case, then move it back 8mm.
3. Place the car in 3rd gear.
4. Push select lever No. 6 fully down. Turn nut No. 3 until it comes into contact with trunnion No. 9. Back the nut off one or two turns and then tighten nut No. 3 with nut No. 4.
5. Shift the hand lever into Neutral, then adjust the dimension B of the hand lever assembly to 1.00-2.00mm and tighten the lock nut No. 1 with No. 2, securely.

310 Models
4-SPEED AND 5-SPEED MODELS

Adjustment can be made by adjusting the select lever.

1. Loosen the adjusting nuts at each end of the control rod lever near the bottom of the linkage.
2. Set the shift control lever in the Neutral position.
3. Fully push the shift lever (transaxle side)

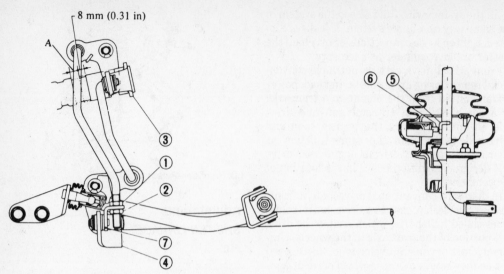

F10 4-speed linkage is adjusted in sequence at the numbered points

in the direction P1, as shown in the illustration. On the 4-speed transaxle, pull the lever back about 8mm. On the 5-speed, pull the shift lever back 11.5mm. With the select lever held in the above position, move the shift lever in direction P2, which engages the 3rd gear on the 4-speed transaxles and the 2nd gear on the 5-speed transaxles.

4. Push the control rod select lever as far as it will go in direction P3, then turn the upper adjusting nut until it touches the trunnion. Turn the nut a quarter turn more and lock the select lever with the other adjusting nut.

5. Operate the shift control lever to see if it shifts smoothly through the gears.

Pulsar and Stanza

NOTE: *On Pulsar models from 1983-86 adjustment is possible. On Pulsar models from 1987-88 no adjustment is possible. On Stanza models from 1982-86 adjustment is possible. On Stanza models from 1987-88 no adjustment is possible. On Stanza wagon no adjustment is possible.*

1. Raise and support the front of the vehicle on jackstands.

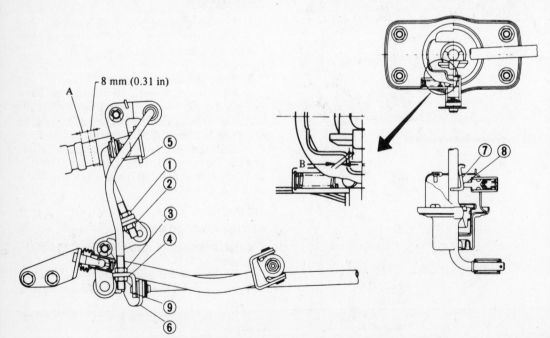

F10 5-speed linkage is adjusted in sequence at the numbered points

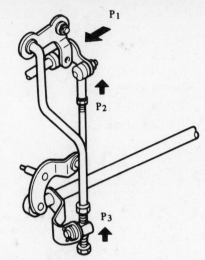

310 4-speed linkage

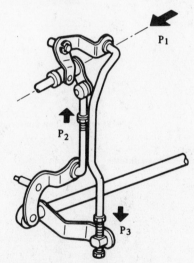

310 5-speed linkage

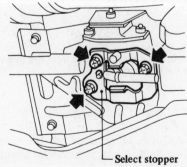

View of the select stopper plate—Stanza (Pulsar is similar)

2. Under the vehicle, at the shift control area, loosen the select stopper securing bolts.
3. Shift the gear selector into 1st gear.
4. Adjust the clearance between the control

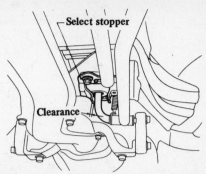

Adjusting the select stopper plate clearance—Stanza (Pulsar is similar)

lever and select stopper by sliding the select stopper so that the clearance is 1.00mm.
5. Torque the stopper securing bolts to 5.8-8.0 ft. lbs. (Stanza) or 2.3-3.7 ft. lbs. (Pulsar). Check that the control lever can be shifted without binding or dragging.

Back-Up Light Switch
REMOVAL AND INSTALLATION

1. Raise vehicle and support safely.
2. Disconnect the electrical connections.
3. Remove swith from transaxle housing, when removing place drain pan under transaxle to catch fluid.
4. To install reverse removal procedures.

Transaxle
REMOVAL AND INSTALLATION
F10 and 310 (1979-81)

1. Refer to the Engine, Removal and Installation procedures in Chapter 3, then remove the engine/transaxle assembly from the vehicle.
2. Remove the starter from the engine/transaxle assembly.
3. With the engine/transaxle assembly removed from the vehicle, remove the transaxle-to-engine bolts and separate transaxle from the engine.
NOTE: *The clutch assembly will remain attached to the engine.*
4. To install, reverse the removal procedures.
NOTE: *If the clutch has been removed, it will have to be re-aligned. When connecting the driveshafts, insert O-rings between the differential side flanges and the driveshafts.*

310 (1982), Pulsar and Stanza

1. Remove the battery.
NOTE: *On the Pulsar and the Stanza, remove the battery holding plate and the radiator reservoir.*

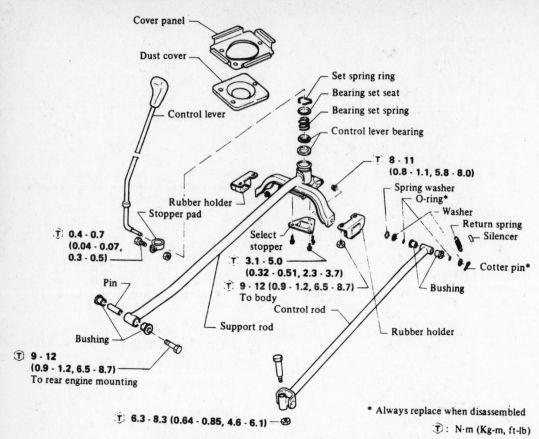

Cover panel

Dust cover

Control lever

Set spring ring

Bearing set seat

Bearing set spring

Control lever bearing

Ⓣ 8 - 11
(0.8 - 1.1, 5.8 - 8.0)

Spring washer

O-ring*

Washer

Return spring

Silencer

Cotter pin*

Bushing

Rubber holder

Rubber holder

Stopper pad

Ⓣ 0.4 - 0.7
(0.04 - 0.07,
0.3 - 0.5)

Select
stopper

Ⓣ 3.1 - 5.0
(0.32 - 0.51, 2.3 - 3.7)

Ⓣ 9 - 12 (0.9 - 1.2, 6.5 - 8.7)
To body

Pin

Bushing

Ⓣ 9 - 12
(0.9 - 1.2, 6.5 - 8.7)
To rear engine mounting

Support rod

Control rod

Ⓣ 6.3 - 8.3 (0.64 - 0.85, 4.6 - 6.1)

* Always replace when disassembled

Ⓣ : N·m (Kg-m, ft-lb)

Exploded view of gear control—Pulsar—Stanza similar

2. Drain the lubricant from the transaxle.
3. Remove the driveshafts from the transaxle.
NOTE: *Take care not to damage the seal lips. After the driveshafts are removed, insert a dummy shaft into each opening so that the side gears don't fall into the case.*
4. Remove the distributor, the air induction tube, the EGR tube and the exhaust manifold cover.
5. Remove the heater hose clamp.
6. Remove the clutch control cable from the lever.

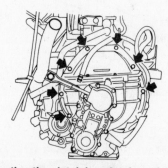

Separating the clutch housing from the engine on F10 and early 310 models

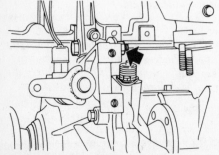

Removing the transmission mounting bracket on F10 and early 310 models

7. Disconnect the speedometer cable at the case.
8. Disconnect all wiring from the case. On the Pulsar and Stanza, remove the wheel well liner.
9. Separate the control and support rods from the case. On the Pulsar and Stanza, disconnect the exhaust pipe at the manifold.
10. Place a jackstand under the engine oil pan to take up the engine weight.
11. Take up the transaxle weight with a floor jack.

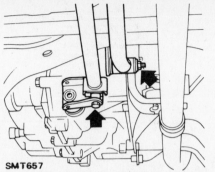

SMT657

Separating the control rod and the support rod on 1982 310

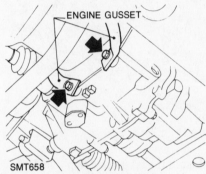

ENGINE GUSSET

SMT658

Engine gusset removal on 1982 310

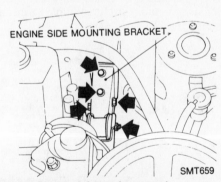

ENGINE SIDE MOUNTING BRACKET

SMT659

310 and Stanza right engine mount

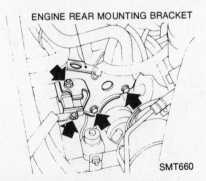

ENGINE REAR MOUNTING BRACKET

SMT660

310 and Stanza rear mounting bracket

12. Remove the engine gusset bolts. On the Pulsar and Stanza, remove the transmission protector.

13. On 5-speed models, remove the engine right side and rear mounting brackets and the starter.

14. Attach a shop crane to the transaxle at the clutch control cable bracket.

15. Unbolt the transaxle from the engine. On 5-speed models, pull the engine to the right and slide the transaxle away from the engine.

16. On the 310, lift the transaxle from the vehicle. On the Pulsar and Stanza, lower the transaxle from the vehicle.

17. Install the transaxle in the vehicle. Note the following points:

   a. Clean all mating surfaces.

   b. Apply EP chassis lube to the splines on the clutch disc and input shaft.

   c. Fill transaxle with 80W-90 gear oil. Apply sealant to the threads of the filler and drain plugs.

18. Install the driveshafts for the transaxle.

19. Install all brackets, protector and tighten engine gusset bolts.

20. Reconnect exhaust pipe at manifold on Pulsar and Stanza and starter if removed.

21. Install all wiring, cables and clamps and wheel well liner.

22. Install the distributor, the air induction tube, the EGR tube and the exhaust manifold cover.

23. Install the battery and any other components that were removed.

24. Road test for proper operation.

OVERHAUL
4- AND 5-SPEED TRANSAXLE
MODELS RN4F30A, RS5F30A AND RS5F31A

Transmission Case

DISASSEMBLY

1. Drain the oil from the transmission case.

2. Remove the mounting bolts, tap the case lightly with a rubber mallet and then lift off the transmission case.

NOTE: *When removing the transmission case, tilt it slightly to prevent interference from the 5th gear shift fork.*

3. Disconnect the back-up light switch and then remove the oil gutter.

4. Remove the input shaft bearing.

5. Remove the case cover, the mainshaft bearing adjusting shim and the spacer.

6. Remove the mainshaft bearing rear outer race and the differential side bearing outer race.

7. Draw out the reverse idler spacer.

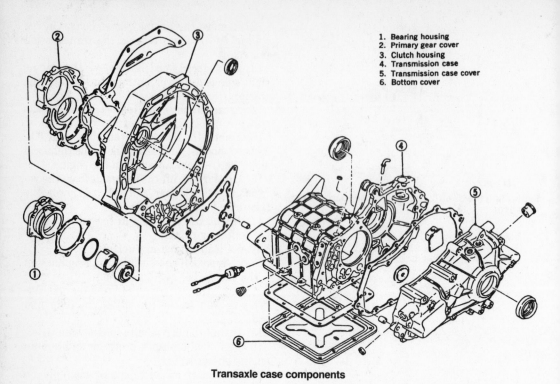

1. Bearing housing
2. Primary gear cover
3. Clutch housing
4. Transmission case
5. Transmission case cover
6. Bottom cover

Transaxle case components

ASSEMBLY

1. Press fit the differential side bearing outer race and the mainshaft rear bearing outer race.

2. Instal the input shaft needle bearing. Apply sealant to the welch plug and then install it on the transmission case.

3. Install the oil gutter. Apply sealant to the back-up light switch and install it.

4. If the transmission case has been replaced, adjust the differential side bearing and the mainshaft rotary frictional force by means of shims.

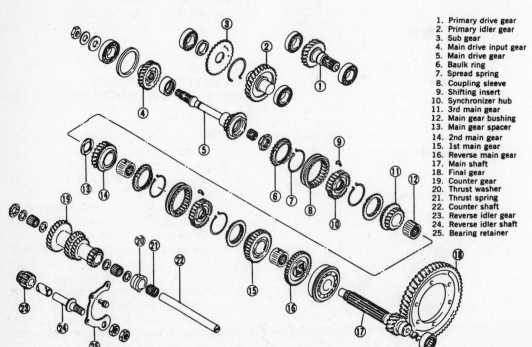

1. Primary drive gear
2. Primary idler gear
3. Sub gear
4. Main drive input gear
5. Main drive gear
6. Baulk ring
7. Spread spring
8. Coupling sleeve
9. Shifting insert
10. Synchronizer hub
11. 3rd main gear
12. Main gear bushing
13. Main gear spacer
14. 2nd main gear
15. 1st main gear
16. Reverse main gear
17. Main shaft
18. Final gear
19. Counter gear
20. Thrust washer
21. Thrust spring
22. Counter shaft
23. Reverse idler gear
24. Reverse idler shaft
25. Bearing retainer

4-speed gear components

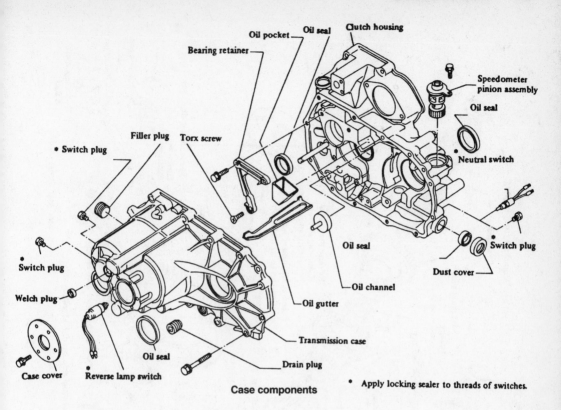

Case components   * Apply locking sealer to threads of switches.

5. Apply an even coating of sealant to the mating surfaces of the transmission case and the clutch housing. Mount the case on the clutch housing and tighten the mounting bolts to 12-15 ft. lbs.

6. Remove the transmission case cover. Clean the mating surfaces and apply sealant to the transmission case.

7. Install the case cover with the convex side facing outward. Tighten the mounting bolts to 4.6-6.1 ft. lbs.

8. Check that the gears move freely and then install the drain plug (with sealant) and fill with lubricant.

Clutch Housing

DISASSEMBLY

1. Drain the oil and then remove the transmission case.

2. Draw out the reverse idler spacer and fork shaft, then remove the 5th/3rd/4th shift fork.
NOTE: *Do not lose the shifter caps.*

3. Remove the control bracket with the 1st and 2nd gear shift fork.
NOTE: *Be careful not to lose the select check ball, spring and the shifter caps (5-speed only).*

On Stanza:

4. Remove the mainshaft and final drive assembly. Be sure to pull the mainshaft straight out.

5. Remove the bearing retainer securing bolts.

All other Models:

6. Remove the 3 screws and detach the bearing retainer. 1 of the screws is special torx type and should be removed using a special torx allen wrench.

7. Turn the clutch housing so that its side is facing down. Lightly tap the end of the input shaft (on the engine side) with a rubber mallet and then remove the input shaft along with the bearing retainer and reverse idler gear.
NOTE: *Don't remove the reverse idler shaft from the clutch housing because these fittings will be loose. Do not scratch the oil seal lip with the input shaft spline while removing the shaft.*

8. Remove the reverse idler gear and final drive assembly.

9. Remove the oil pocket, shift check ball springs and then the check ball plugs.

10. Drive the retaining pins out of the striking lever. Remove the striking rod, lever and interlock.

   a. Select a position where the pin doesn't interfere with the clutch housing when removing it.

   b. When removing the striking rod, be careful not to damage the oil seal lip. It may be a good idea to tape the edges of the striking rod when removing it.

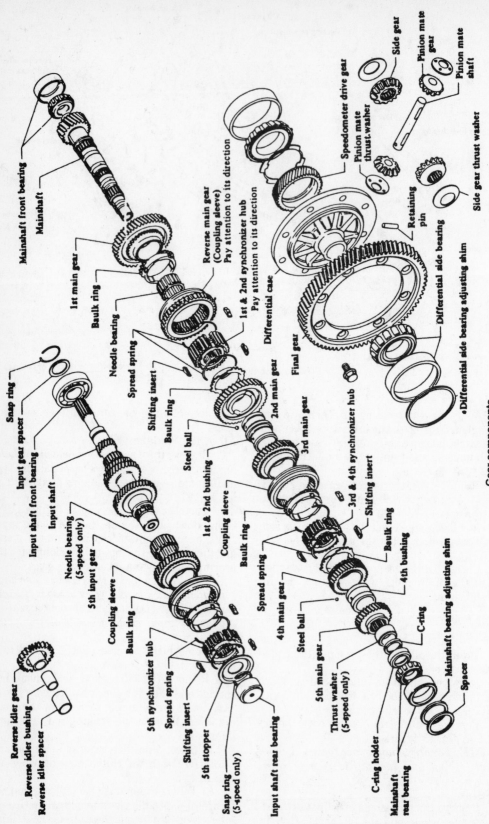

Gear components

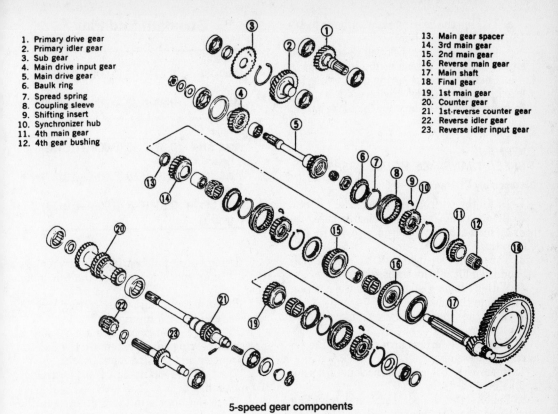

1. Primary drive gear
2. Primary idler gear
3. Sub gear
4. Main drive input gear
5. Main drive gear
6. Baulk ring
7. Spread spring
8. Coupling sleeve
9. Shifting insert
10. Synchronizer hub
11. 4th main gear
12. 4th gear bushing

13. Main gear spacer
14. 3rd main gear
15. 2nd main gear
16. Reverse main gear
17. Main shaft
18. Final gear
19. 1st main gear
20. Counter gear
21. 1st-reverse counter gear
22. Reverse idler gear
23. Reverse idler input gear

5-speed gear components

11. Remove the reverse and 5th gear check plug and then detach the check spring and balls. Remove the reverse and 5th gear check assembly.

12. Remove the clutch control shaft, release bearing and clutch lever.

13. Remove the mainshaft bearing outer race. Remove the differential side bearing outer race.

14. Remove the oil channel.

ASSEMBLY

1. Install a new oil channel so that the oil groove in the channel faces the oil pocket.

2. Install the mainshaft bearing and differential side bearing outer races.

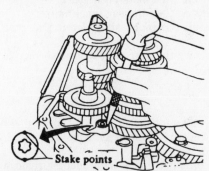

Stake the head of the Torx screw after installation

3. Install the clutch control shaft, release bearing and clutch lever.

4. Install the oil pocket.

NOTE: *Make sure that oil flows from the oil pocket to the oil channel.*

5. Install the reverse and 5th gear check assembly. The smaller check ball is inserted first and then the larger check ball.

NOTE: *When installing the clutch housing and reverse and 5th gear check assembly, it is necessary to adjust the reverse check force.*

a. Install a used check plug and tighten it to 14-18 ft. lbs.

b. Use a spring gauge to measure the spring check force (139-100 inch lbs. for the 4-speed; 195-239 inch lbs. for the 5-speed).

c. If the reverse check force is not within the above ranges, select another check plug of a different length until the specifications can be met.

6. Installation of the remaining components is the reverse order of removal. Please note the following:

   a. Follow all NOTES listed under the disassembly procedures.

   b. Apply a locking sealer to the threads of the torx screw and tighten it to 12-15 ft. lbs.(16.3-20.3 Nm). Use a punch and stake the head of the screw at two points.

c. Tighten the bearing retainer bolts to 12-15 ft. lbs.(16.3-20.3 Nm).

d. Coat the select check ball (5-speed) and shifter caps with grease before installing.

e. Coat the support spring with grease before installing it. This will prevent the spring from falling into the hole for the fork shaft in the clutch housing.

OVERHAUL
5-SPEED TRANSAXLE MODEL RS5F50A
Disassembly Of Transaxle

1. Drain the oil from the transaxle.
2. Before removing the transaxle case, remove the bolts and plugs shown in the illustration.
3. Tap on the case lightly with a rubber mallet and then lift off the transaxle case.
4. With a rubber mallet, remove the position switch from the case.
5. Mesh the 4th gear and then remove the reverse idler gear.
6. Remove the reverse arm shaft and the reverse level assembly.
7. Remove the 5th/reverse check plug, spring and ball.
8. Remove the stopper rings and retaining pins from the 5th/reverse and 3rd/4th fork rods.
9. Remove the 5th/reverse and 3rd/4th fork rods. Then remove the forks and brackets.
10. Remove both the input and mainshafts with the 1st/2nd fork and fork rod as a set.
11. Remove the final drive assembly.
12. Remove the reverse check assembly.
13. With a hammer and punch, remove the retaining pin and detach the selector.
14. To make it easier to remove the retaining pin which hods the striking lever to the striking rod, remove the drain plug.
15. With a hammer and punch remove the retaining pin and then withdraw the striking level and striking rod.

Gears and Shafts
END PLAY MEASUREMENT

Before disassembly of the input shaft or the main shaft, measure the gear and play to insure that it is within the specified limit.

- If the end play is not within the specified limit, disassemble and check the parts.
- Replace any worn or damaged parts.

Input Shaft

NOTE: *The following removal procedures require the use of a hydraulic press and various bearing adapter.*

1. Using a press and bearing adapter, remove the input shaft rear bearing.

Standard End Play

Position	mm (in)
Main 1st gear	0.23–0.43 (0.0091–0.0169)
Main 2nd gear	0.23–0.58 (0.0091–0.0228)
Input 3rd gear	0.23–0.43 (0.0091–0.0169)
Input 4th gear	0.25–0.55 (0.0098–0.0217)
Input 5th gear	0.23–0.48 (0.0091–0.0189)

2. Using a press and bearing adapter, remove the 5th gear synchronizer and the 5th input gear.
3. Remove the thrust washer ring, thrust washers and the 4th input gear.
4. Remove the snapring and then using a press and bearing adapter, remove the 3rd/4th synchronizer and the 3rd input gear.
5. Press off the input shaft front bearing.

To assemble:

6. Place the inserts in the 3 grooves on the coupling sleeve of the 3rd/4th synchronizer and the 5th synchronizer. Lubricate the 3rd input gear inner surface with gear oil, then install the 3rd input gear and 3rd bulk ring.
7. Press the 3rd/4th synchronizer hub together, pay attention to its direction.
8. Install the snapring of the proper thickness that will minimize the clearance of the groove in the input shaft. The allowable groove clearance should be 0-0.100mm.
9. Lubricate the 4th input gear with gear oil, then install the 4th input gear, thrust washers and thrust washer ring. The thrust washers should be selected to minimize clearance of the groove in the input shaft. The allowable groove clearance should be 0-0.06mm.
10. Lubricate the inner surface of 5th gear with gear oil, then install 5th gear.
11. Press on the 5th gear synchronizer.
12. Install the input shaft front and rear bearing.
13. Measure the gear endplay and correct as required.

Mainshaft

NOTE: *The following removal procedures require the use of a hydraulic press and various bearing adapters.*

1. Using a press and bearing adapter, remove the mainshaft rear bearing.
2. Remove the thrust washer and snapring.

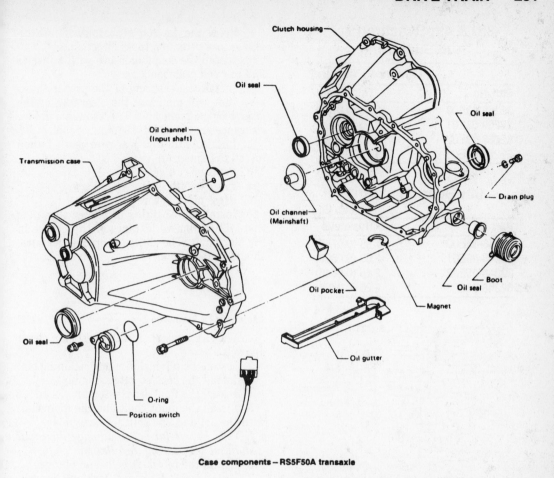

Case components – RS5F50A transaxle

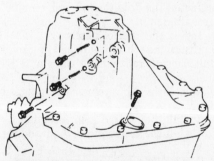

Remove these bolts before removing the case

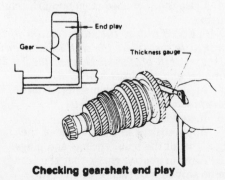

Checking gearshaft end play

3. Using a press and bearing adapter, remove the 5th and 4th main gears.

4. Using a press and bearing adapter, remove the 3rd and the 2nd main gears.

5. Remove the snapring and then using a press and bearing adapter, remove the 1st/2nd synchronizer and the 1st main gear.

6. Press off the mainshaft front bearing.

To Assemble:

7. Place the inserts in the 3 grooves on the coupling sleeve of the 1st/2nd synchronizer.

8. Lubricate the 1st gear inner surface with gear oil, then install the 1st gear and 1st baulk ring.

1st & 2nd Synchronizer Hub Snap Ring

	mm (in.)
Part No.	Thickness
32269-03E00	2.00 (0.0787)
32269-03E01	2.05 (0.0807)
32269-03E02	2.10 (0.0827)
32269-03E03	1.95 (0.0768)

3rd & 4th Synchronizer Hub Snap Ring

Thickness mm(in.)

Part No.	Thickness
32269-03E00	2.00 (0.0787)
32269-03E01	2.05 (0.0807)
32269-03E02	2.10 (0.0827)
32269-03E03	1.95 (0.0768)

5th Gear Snap Ring

mm (in.)

Part No.	Thickness
32348-05E00	1.95 (0.0768)
32348-05E01	2.05 (0.0807)
32348-05E02	2.15 (0.0846)
32348-05E03	2.25 (0.0886)

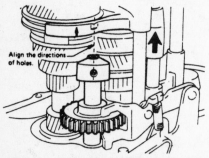

Instalation of the reverse idler gear shaft

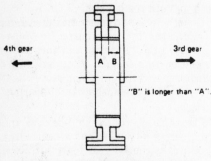

3rd/4th synchronizer hub assembly

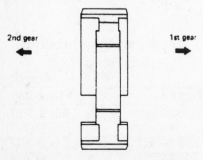

1st/2nd synchronizer hub assembly

9. Press the 1st/2nd synchronizer hub together, pay attention to its direction.

10. Install the coupling sleeve with 3 inserts and the 2nd gear baulk ring.

11. Install the snapring of the proper thickness that will minimize the clearance of the groove in the mainshaft. The allowable groove clearance should be 0-0.100mm.

12. Lubricate the 2nd gear with gear oil, then install the 2nd gear.

13. Press on 3rd gear.

14. Press on 4th gear.

15. Press on 5th gear.

16. Install the snapring of proper thickness that will minimize clearance of the groove in the mainshaft. The allowable groove clearance should be 0-0.15mm.

Assembly Of Transaxle

1. With a pin punch, install the striking lever and select lever.

2. Install the select shifter and retaining pin.

3. Install the reverse gate assembly.

4. Install the final drive assembly.

5. Install the input shaft and the mainshaft with the 1st and 2nd shift fork assembly.

NOTE: *Be careful not to damage the input shaft oil seal during installation.*

6. Install the interlock balls and plunger.

7. Install the 3rd/4th shift fork and bracket, then install the 3rd/4th shift rod, circular clip and retaining pin.

8. Install the interlock balls.

9. Install the 5th shift fork and bracket, then install the shift rod, circular clip and retaining pin.

10. Install the 5th/reverse check plug, spring and ball.

11. Install the reverse lever assembly.

12. Install the reverse arm shaft and retaining pin.

13. Mesh 4th gear. Then install the reverse idler gear and shaft, paying attention to the direction of the tapped hole.

14. Place the U-shaped magnet on the clutch housing.

NOTE: *To aid in the installation of the transaxle case, place the shift selector in the 1st/2nd shift bracket or between the 1st/2nd bracket and the 3rd/4th bracket.*

15. Apply sealant to the mating surface of the transmission case and install it.

16. Install the position switch.

17. Apply sealant to the threads of the check plugs. Install the balls, springs and plugs.

18. After assembly, check that the transaxle can be shifted into each gear smoothly.

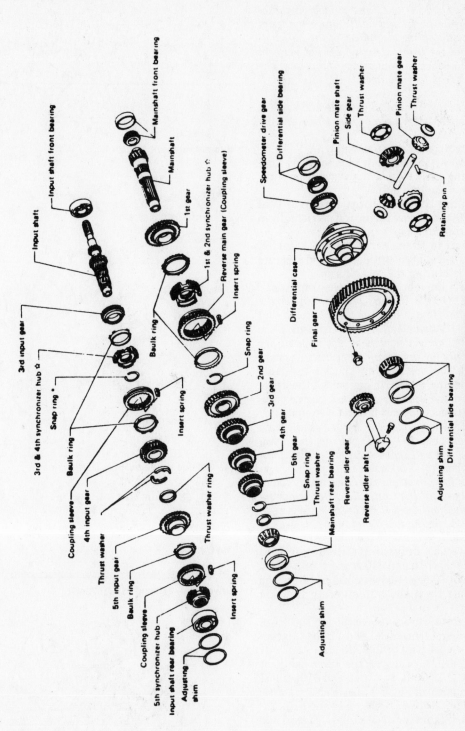

Input shaft front bearing

Input shaft

3rd input gear

3rd & 4th synchronizer hub ☆

Snap ring *

Coupling sleeve

Baulk ring

4th input gear

Thrust washer

5th synchronizer hub

Coupling sleeve

5th input gear

Baulk ring

Input shaft rear bearing

Adjusting shim

Insert spring

Thrust washer ring

Insert spring

Mainshaft front bearing

Mainshaft

1st gear

1st & 2nd synchronizer hub ☆
(Coupling sleeve)

Reverse main gear

Insert spring

Baulk ring

Snap ring

2nd gear

3rd gear

4th gear

5th gear

Snap ring

Thrust washer

Mainshaft rear bearing

Adjusting shim

Speedometer drive gear

Differential side bearing

Differential case

Final gear

Reverse idler gear

Reverse idler shaft

Adjusting shim

Differential side bearing

Pinion mate shaft

Thrust washer

Side gear

Pinion mate gear

Thrust washer

Retaining pin

Gear components — RS5F50A transaxle

Halfshaft

REMOVAL AND INSTALLATION

NOTE: *On 1987 and later models, installation of the halfshafts will require a special tool for the spline alignment of the halfshaft end and the transaxle case. Do not perform this procedure without access to this tool. The Kent Moore tool Number is J-34296 and J-34297*

1. Raise the front of the vehicle and support it on jackstands, then remove the wheel and the tire assembly.
2. Remove the caliper assembly.
3. Remove the cotter pin from the drive axle.
4. Using a bar to hold the wheel from turning, loosen the hub nut.
5. Using the Ball Joint Removal tool HT72520000, remove the tie rod ball joint from the steering knuckle.
6. Remove the control arm-to-steering knuckle, ball joint mounting nuts and separate the ball joint from the control arm.
7. Drain the lubricant from the transaxle.

NOTE: *On the 1976-81 models, remove the driveshaft flange bolts at the transaxle and remove the driveshaft from the transaxle. On the 1982 and later models, use a small pry bar to pry the driveshaft from the transaxle.*

8. Pull the hub/steering knuckle assembly away from the vehicle, to disconnect the driveshaft from the transaxle. Support engine properly and remove support bracket if so equipped.

NOTE: *When removing the driveshaft from the transaxle, DO NOT pull on the driveshaft, for it will separate at the sliding joint (damaging the boot), use a small pry bar to remove it from the transaxle. Be sure to replace the oil seal in the transaxle. After removing the driveshaft from the transaxle, be sure to install a holding tool to hold the side gear in place while the axle is removed.*

9. Use the driveshaft Remover tool ST35100000 (F10 and 310 models) or a wheel puller tool (Pulsar and Stanza), to press the driveshaft from the hub/steering knuckle assembly.
10. To install, use a new circlip (on the driveshaft), oil seal (transaxle) and torque the control arm-to-ball joint to 40-51 ft. lbs. (Stanza) or 40-47 ft. lbs. (All Others), the lower ball joint stud nut to 22-29 ft. lbs. (F10 and 310), 40-51 ft. lbs. (Stanza) or 25-36 ft. lbs. (Pulsar), the tie rod stud nut to 40-47 ft. lbs. (F10 and 310), 22-29 ft. lbs. (Stanza) or 22-36 ft. lbs. (Pulsar) and the hub nut to 145-203 ft. lbs. (Stanza) or 87-145 ft. lbs. (All Others).

NOTE: *When installing the driveshaft into the transaxle, use Oil Seal Protector tool KV38105500 or equivalent to protect the oil*

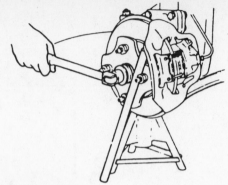

Hub nut removal

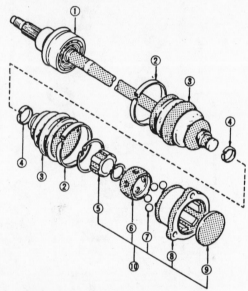

1. Outside joint assembly (Birfield joint)
2. Band
3. Dust cover
4. Band
5. Inner ring
6. Cage
7. Ball
8. Outer ring
9. Plug
10. Inside joint assembly (Double offset joint)

Drive axle—F10 and 310 (1976–81)

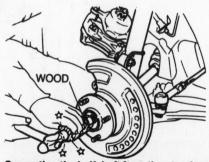

Separating the halfshaft from the steering knuckle

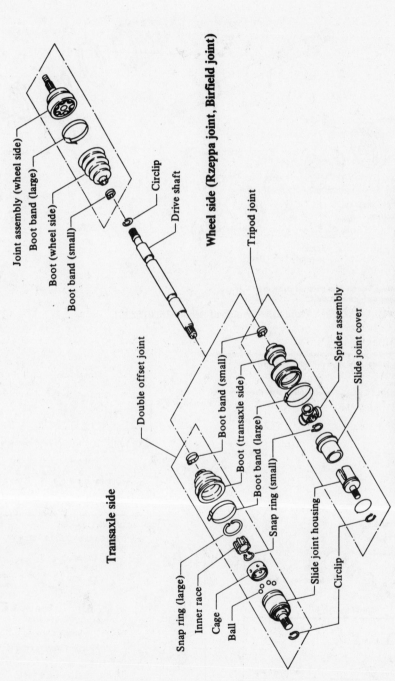

Joint assembly (wheel side)

Boot band (large)

Boot (wheel side)

Boot band (small)

Circlip

Drive shaft

Wheel side (Rzeppa joint, Birfield joint)

Tripod joint

Double offset joint

Boot band (small)

Boot (transaxle side)

Boot band (large)

Spider assembly

Slide joint cover

Snap ring (small)

Transaxle side

Snap ring (large)

Inner race

Cage

Ball

Slide joint housing

Circlip

Exploded view of the drive axle for Pulsar—Stanza is similar

Circular clip:
    Make sure circular clip is properly installed with side gear (transaxle side)
    and joint assembly (wheel side), and will not come out.
Drive shaft joint grease:
    Use NISSAN GENUINE GREASE or equivalent after every overhaul.

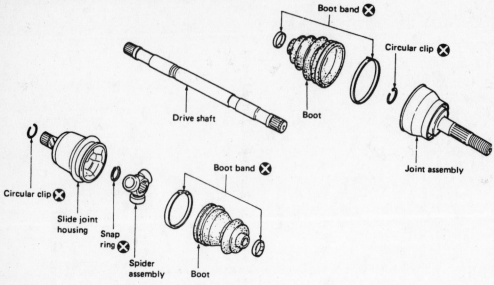

Be careful not to damage boots. Use suitable protector
or cloth during removal and installation.

Front axle drive shaft (Model ZF90T579C)

Circular clip:
    Make sure circular clip is properly meshed with side gear (transaxle side)
    and joint assembly (wheel side), and will not come out.

Drive shaft joint grease:
    Use NISSAN GENUINE GREASE or equivalent after every overhaul.

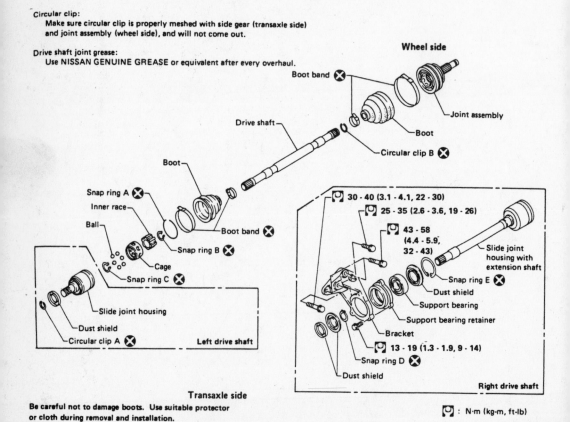

Be careful not to damage boots. Use suitable protector
or cloth during removal and installation.

Front axle drive shaft (Model BF86D586)

seal from damage; after installation, remove the tool.

11. Install new cotter pin in drive axle and mount the caliper assembly.

12. Install the wheel and tire assembly.

13. Road test for proper operation.

CV-JOINT OVERHAUL

Transaxle Side Joint

1. Remove boot bands.

2. Match mark slide joint housing and driveshaft and separate.

3. Match mark spider assembly and then remove snapring and spider assembly. DO NOT disassemble spider assembly.

NOTE: *Cover driveshaft serration with tape so not to damage the boot.*

4. Remove axle boot from driveshaft.

5. To install reverse the removal procedures.

NOTE: *Always use new snaprings and align all matchmarks. Pack driveshaft and boot assembly with grease.*

Wheel Side Joint

NOTE: *The joint on the wheel side cannot be disassembled.*

1. Match mark the driveshaft and the joint assembly.

2. Separate joint assembly with suitable tool.

3. Remove boot bands.

4. Install boot with new boot bands.

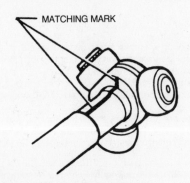

MATCHING MARK

Matchmark shaft and spider assembly

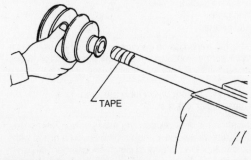

TAPE

Covering shaft serration with tape

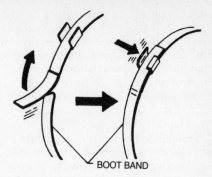

BOOT BAND

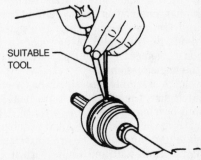

SUITABLE TOOL

Installing boot band

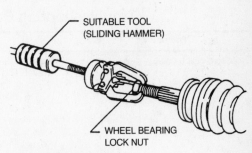

SUITABLE TOOL (SLIDING HAMMER)

WHEEL BEARING LOCK NUT

Separate wheel side joint

5. Align matchmarks lightly tap joint assembly onto the shaft.

6. Pack driveshaft with grease.

7. Lock both boot band clamps.

NOTE: *There are two different type (transaxle side) front axle joints used on Datsun/Nissan models.*

CLUTCH

Understanding the Clutch

The purpose of the clutch is to disconnect and connect engine power from the transmission. A car at rest requires a lot of engine torque to get all that weight moving. An internal combustion engine does not develop a high starting torque (unlike steam engines), so it must be allowed to operate without any load until it builds up enough torque to move the car. Torque increases with engine rpm. The clutch allows the engine to build up torque by physically disconnecting the engine from the transmission, relieving the engine of any load or resistance. The transfer of engine power to the transmission (the load) must be smooth and gradual; if it weren't, drive line components would wear out or break quickly. This gradual power transfer is made possible by gradually releasing the clutch pedal. The clutch disc and pressure plate are the connecting link between the engine and transmission. When the clutch pedal is released, the disc and plate contact each other (clutch engagement), physically joining the engine and transmission. When the pedal is pushed in, the disc and plate separate (the clutch is disengaged), disconnecting the engine from the transmission.

The clutch assembly consists of the flywheel, the clutch disc, the clutch pressure plate, the throwout bearing and fork, the actuating linkage and the pedal. The flywheel and clutch pressure plate (driving members) are connected to the engine crankshaft and rotate with it. The clutch disc is located between the flywheel and pressure plate, and splined to the transmission shaft. A driving member is one that is attached to the engine and transfers engine power to a driven member (clutch disc) on the transmission shaft. A driving member (pressure plate) rotates (drives) a driven member (clutch disc) on contact and, in so doing, turns the transmission shaft. There is a circular diaphragm spring within the pressure plate cover (transmission side). In a relaxed state (when the clutch pedal is fully released), this spring is convex; that is, it is dished outward toward the transmission. Pushing in the clutch pedal actuates an attached linkage rod. Connected to the other end of this rod is the throwout bearing fork. The throwout bearing is attached to the fork. When the clutch pedal is depressed, the clutch linkage pushes the fork and bearing forward to contact the diaphragm spring of the pressure plate. The outer edges of the spring are secured to the pressure plate and are pivoted on rings so that when the center of the spring is compressed by the throwout bearing, the outer edges bow outward and, by so doing, pull the pressure plate in

Troubleshooting Basic Clutch Problems

Problem	Cause
Excessive clutch noise	Throwout bearing noises are more audible at the lower end of pedal travel. The usual causes are: • Riding the clutch • Too little pedal free-play • Lack of bearing lubrication A bad clutch shaft pilot bearing will make a high pitched squeal, when the clutch is disengaged and the transmission is in gear or within the first 2" of pedal travel. The bearing must be replaced. Noise from the clutch linkage is a clicking or snapping that can be heard or felt as the pedal is moved completely up or down. This usually requires lubrication. Transmitted engine noises are amplified by the clutch housing and heard in the passenger compartment. They are usually the result of insufficient pedal free-play and can be changed by manipulating the clutch pedal.
Clutch slips (the car does not move as it should when the clutch is engaged)	This is usually most noticeable when pulling away from a standing start. A severe test is to start the engine, apply the brakes, shift into high gear and SLOWLY release the clutch pedal. A healthy clutch will stall the engine. If it slips it may be due to: • A worn pressure plate or clutch plate • Oil soaked clutch plate • Insufficient pedal free-play
Clutch drags or fails to release	The clutch disc and some transmission gears spin briefly after clutch disengagement. Under normal conditions in average temperatures, 3 seconds is maximum spin-time. Failure to release properly can be caused by: • Too light transmission lubricant or low lubricant level • Improperly adjusted clutch linkage
Low clutch life	Low clutch life is usually a result of poor driving habits or heavy duty use. Riding the clutch, pulling heavy loads, holding the car on a grade with the clutch instead of the brakes and rapid clutch engagement all contribute to low clutch life.

the same direction - away from the clutch disc. This action separates the disc from the plate, disengaging the clutch and allowing the transmission to be shifted into another gear. A coil type clutch return spring attached to the clutch pedal arm permits full release of the pedal. Releasing the pedal pulls the throwout bearing away from the diaphragm spring resulting in a reversal of spring position. As bearing pressure is gradually released from the spring center, the outer edges of the spring bow outward, pushing the pressure plate into closer contact with the clutch disc. As the disc and plate move closer together, friction between the two increases and slippage is reduced until, when full spring pressure is applied (by fully releasing the pedal), The speed of the disc and plate are the same. This stops all slipping, creating a direct connection between the plate and disc which results in the transfer of power from the engine to the transmission. The clutch disc is now rotating with the pressure plate at engine speed and, because it is splined to the transmission shaft, the shaft now turns at the same engine speed. Understanding clutch operation can be rather difficult at first; if you're still confused after reading this, consider the following analogy. The action of the diaphragm spring can be compared to that of an oil can bottom. The bottom of an oil can is shaped very much like the clutch diaphragm spring and pushing in on the can bottom and then releasing it produces a similar effect. As mentioned earlier, the clutch pedal return spring permits full release of the pedal and reduces linkage slack due to wear. As the linkage wears, clutch free-pedal travel will increase and free-travel will decrease as the clutch wears. Free-travel is actually throwout bearing lash.

The diaphragm spring type clutches used are available in two different designs: flat diaphragm springs or bent spring. The bent fingers are bent back to create a centrifugal boost ensuring quick re-engagement at higher engine speeds. This design enables pressure plate load to increase as the clutch disc wears and makes low pedal effort possible even with a heavy-duty clutch. The throwout bearing used with the bent finger design is 1¼" long and is shorter than the bearing used with the flat finger design. These bearings are not interchangeable. If the longer bearing is used with the bent finger clutch, free-pedal travel will not exist. This results in clutch slippage and rapid wear.

The transmission varies the gear ratio between the engine and drive wheels. It can be shifted to change engine speed as driving conditions and loads change. The transmission allows disengaging and reversing power from the engine to the wheels.

Clutch Specifications

Year	Model	Pedal Height Above Floor (in.)	Pedal Free-Play (in.)
1976–78	F10	6.9	0.23–0.55
1979–81	310	7.15	0.04–0.20
1982	310	7.27	0.43–0.83
1982	Stanza	6.00	0.43–0.63
1983–84	Stanza	6.05	0.43–0.63
1985–88	Stanza	6.20	0.47–0.67
1983–84	Pulsar	7.97	0.43–0.83
1985–88	Pulsar	8.33	0.49–0.69

CAUTION: *The clutch driven disc contains asbestos, which has been determined to be a cancer causing agent. Never clean clutch surface with compressed air! Avoid inhaling any dust from any clutch surface! When cleaning clutch surfaces, use a commercially available brake cleaning fluid.*

Adjustment

Refer to the Clutch Specifications Chart for clutch pedal height above floor and pedal free play.

The (1976-81) models have an hydraulically operated clutch. Pedal height is usually adjusted with a stopper limiting the upward travel of

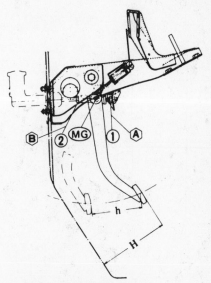

1. Adjust pedal height here
2. Adjust pedal free-play here
MG. Lubricate with multipurpose grease here
H. is pedal height
h. is free-play

Hydraulic clutch adjusting points

the pedal. Pedal free-play is adjusted at the clutch master cylinder pushrod. If the pushrod is nonadjustable, free-play is adjusted by placing shims between the master cylinder and the firewall. On a few models, pedal free play can also be adjusted at the operating (slave) cylin-

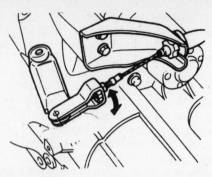

Clutch withdrawal lever adjustment—arrow shows locknut adjustment

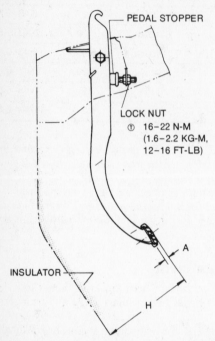

Stanza clutch pedal adjustment: H is the pedal height, A is the pedal free-play

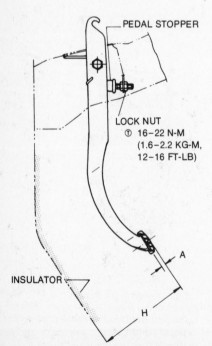

1982 310 clutch pedal adjustment: H is the pedal height, A is the pedal free-play

der pushrod. Pushrods are available in three lengths for the F10 and the 310.

The (1982 and later) models have a cable actuated mechanical clutch. The pedal height is adjusted at the clutch switch or the ASCD stop switch (both are located at the top of the clutch pedal). The free-play is adjusted at the cable bracket, located near the clutch release lever on the transaxle.

Driven Disc And Pressure Plate

REMOVAL AND INSTALLATION

F10 and 310 (1979-81)

NOTE: *The clutch/flywheel assembly can be serviced without disturbing any adjacent units. The clutch cover and the pressure plate are balanced as an assembly; if replacement of either part becomes necessary, replace both parts as an assembly.*

1. Disconnect the negative battery cable, the fresh air duct and the high tension coil between the ignition coil and the distributor.

2. Remove the fuel filter from the fuel filter bracket. Remove the clutch operating cylinder from the clutch housing.

3. On the right side wheel housing, remove the access hole cover protector and the dust cover. Working through the access hole, remove the E-clip (securing the withdrawal lever pin to the bearing housing) and the withdrawal lever.

4. Remove the bearing housing bolts and remove the primary drive gear assembly through the access hole.

5. At the upper section of the clutch housing, remove the bolts and the upper clutch housing section. By turning the flywheel with a pry bar, remove the clutch cover-to-flywheel bolts (loosen the bolts evenly).

6. Lift the clutch cover/disc assembly out through the clutch housing opening; the diaphragm spring can be removed at the same time.

7. Remove the strap holding the pressure

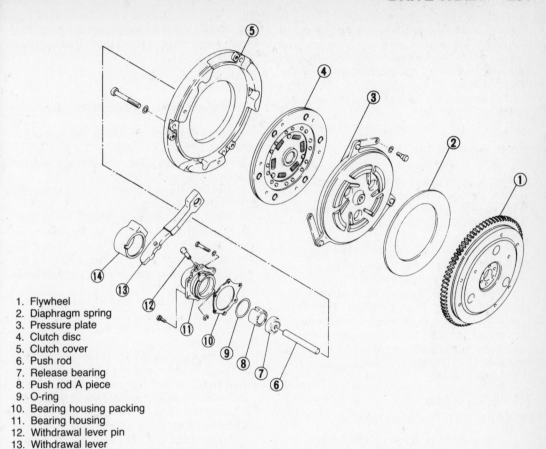

1. Flywheel
2. Diaphragm spring
3. Pressure plate
4. Clutch disc
5. Clutch cover
6. Push rod
7. Release bearing
8. Push rod A piece
9. O-ring
10. Bearing housing packing
11. Bearing housing
12. Withdrawal lever pin
13. Withdrawal lever
14. Dust cover

Exploded view of the clutch unit—A-series engine

plate to the clutch cover and remove the clutch from the center.

NOTE: *The strap must be replaced in the same position it had before removal. Mark the relative position before removal. Installing it out of position will cause an imbalance. If necessary, the clutch disc should be inspected and/or replaced at this time; the clutch lining wear limit is 0.30mm above the rivet heads.*

8. Install the clutch cover/disc assembly with

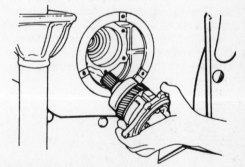

Removing the primary drive gear

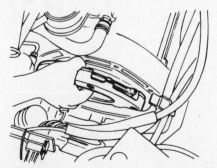

Removing the clutch cover assembly from the clutch housing—A-series engine

strap and torque the clutch cover-to-pressure plate bolts to 5-6 ft. lbs. (F10) or 7-9 ft. lbs. (310), the flywheel-to-crankshaft bolts to 58-65 ft. lbs., the clutch cover-to-flywheel bolts and the bearing housing-to-clutch housing bolts to 4.3-7.2 ft. lbs.

9. Install the primary drive gear assembly and bearing housing bolts.

10. Install withdrawl lever assembly and hole cover protector.

11. Install the fuel filter to the fuel filter

bracket. Install the clutch operating cylinder to the clutch housing.

12. Connect the fresh air duct and the high tension coil between the ignition coil and the distributor.

13. Reconnect the battery cable and make adjustments if necessary.

14. Road test vehicle for proper operation.

Pulsar, Stanza and 310 (1982)

1. Refer to the Manual Transaxle, Removal and Installation procedures, in this chapter and remove the transaxle from the vehicle.

2. Insert a clutch disc centering tool KV30101000 into the clutch disc hub for support.

3. Loosen the pressure plate bolts evenly, a little at a time to prevent distortion.

4. Remove the clutch assembly.

5. Installation is the reverse of removal. Apply a light coating of chassis lube to the clutch disc splines and the input shaft. Use a centering tool to aid installation. Torque the pressure plate bolts in a criss-cross pattern, a little at a time each to 12-15 ft. lbs. (310) or 16-22 ft. lbs. (Pulsar and Stanza).

Master Cylinder

REMOVAL AND INSTALLATION

1. Disconnect the clutch pedal arm from the pushrod.

2. Disconnect the clutch hydraulic line from the master cylinder.

NOTE: *Take precautions to keep brake fluid from coming in contact with any painted surfaces.*

3. Remove the nuts attaching the master cylinder and remove the master cylinder and pushrod toward the engine compartment side.

4. Install the master cylinder in the reverse order of removal and bleed the clutch hydraulic system.

OVERHAUL

1. Remove the master cylinder from the vehicle.

2. Drain the clutch fluid from the master cylinder reservoir.

3. Remove the boot, the circlip and the pushrod.

4. Remove the stopper, the piston, the cup and the return spring.

5. Clean all of the parts in clean brake fluid.

6. Check the master cylinder and piston for wear, corrosion and scores, then replace the parts as necessary. Light scoring and glaze can be removed with crocus cloth soaked in brake fluid.

7. Generally, the cup seal should be replaced each time the master cylinder is disassembled. Check the cup and replace it, if it is worn, fatigued or damaged.

8. Check the clutch fluid reservoir, the filler cap, the dust cover and the pipe for distortion and damage, replace the parts as necessary.

9. Lubricate the new parts with clean brake fluid.

10. Reassemble the master cylinder parts in the reverse order of disassembly, taking note of the following:

   a. Reinstall the cup seal carefully to prevent damaging the lipped portions.

   b. Adjust the height of the clutch pedal after installing the master cylinder in position on the vehicle.

   c. Fill the master cylinder and clutch fluid reservoir, then bleed the clutch hydraulic system.

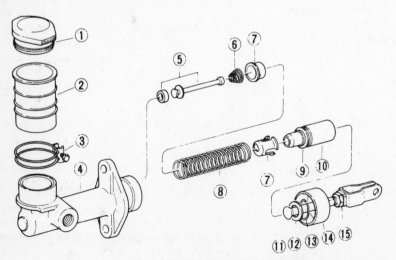

1. Reservoir cap
2. Reservoir
3. Reservoir band
4. Cylinder body
5. Valve assembly
6. Valve spring
7. Spring seat
8. Return spring
9. Piston cup
10. Piston
11. Push rod
12. Stopper
13. Stopper ring
14. Dust cover
15. Nut

Typical master cylinder

Slave Cylinder

REMOVAL AND INSTALLATION

1. Remove the slave cylinder attaching bolts and the pushrod from the shaft fork.

2. Disconnect the flexible fluid hose from the slave cylinder and remove the unit from the vehicle.

3. Install the slave cylinder in the reverse order of removal and bleed the clutch hydraulic system.

OVERHAUL

1. Remove the slave cylinder from the vehicle.

2. Remove the pushrod and the boot.

3. Force out the piston by blowing compressed air into the slave cylinder at the hose connection.

NOTE: *Be careful not to apply excess air pressure to avoid possible injury.*

4. Clean all of the parts in clean brake fluid.

5. Check and replace the slave cylinder bore and piston if wear or severe scoring exists. Light scoring and glaze can be removed with crocus cloth soaked in brake fluid.

6. Normally, the piston cup should be replaced when the slave cylinder is disassembled. Check the piston cup and replace it, if it is found to be worn, fatigued or scored.

7. Replace the rubber boot, if it is cracked or broken.

8. Lubricate all parts with clean brake fluid

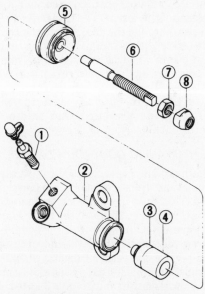

1. Bleeder screw	5. Dust cover
2. Cylinder body	6. Push rod
3. Piston cup	7. Lock nut
4. Piston	8. Push nut

Typical slave cylinder

and assemble in reverse of disassembly. Bleed the system.

AUTOMATIC TRANSAXLE

Understanding Automatic Transmissions

The automatic transmission allows engine torque and power to be transmitted to the drive wheels within a narrow range of engine operating speeds. The transmission will allow the engine to turn fast enough to produce plenty of power and torque at very low speeds, while keeping it at a sensible rpm at high vehicle speeds. The transmission performs this job entirely without driver assistance. The transmission uses a light fluid as the medium for the transmission of power. This fluid also works in the operation of various hydraulic control circuits and as a lubricant. Because the transmission fluid performs all of these three functions, trouble within the unit can easily travel from one part to another. For this reason, and because of the complexity and unusual operating principles of the transmission, a very sound understanding of the basic principles of operation will simplify troubleshooting.

THE TORQUE CONVERTER

The torque converter replaces the conventional clutch. It has three functions:

1. It allows the engine to idle with the vehicle at a standstill, even with the transmission in gear.

2. It allows the transmission to shift from range to range smoothly, without requiring that the driver close the throttle during the shift.

3. It multiplies engine torque to an increasing extent as vehicle speed drops and throttle opening is increased. This has the effect of making the transmission more responsive and reduces the amount of shifting required.

The torque converter is a metal case which is shaped like a sphere that has been flattened on opposite sides. It is bolted to the rear end of the engine's crankshaft. Generally, the entire metal case rotates at engine speed and serves as the engine's flywheel.

The case contains three sets of blades. One set is attached directly to the case. This set forms the torus or pump. Another set is directly connected to the output shaft, and forms the turbine. The third set is mounted on a hub which, in turn, is mounted on a stationary shaft through a one-way clutch. This third set is known as the stator.

A pump, which is driven by the converter hub

at engine speed, keeps the torque converter full of transmission fluid at all times. Fluid flows continuously through the unit to provide cooling.

Under low speed acceleration, the torque converter functions as follows:

The torus is turning faster than the turbine. It picks up fluid at the center of the converter and, through centrifugal force, slings it outward. Since the outer edge of the converter moves faster than the portions at the center, the fluid picks up speed.

The fluid then enters the outer edge of the turbine blades. It then travels back toward the center of the converter case along the turbine blades. In impinging upon the turbine blades, the fluid loses the energy picked up in the torus.

If the fluid were now to immediately be returned directly into the torus, both halves of the converter would have to turn at approximately the same speed at all times, and torque input and output would both be the same.

In flowing through the torus and turbine, the fluid picks up two types of flow, or flow in two separate directions. It flows through the turbine blades, and it spins with the engine. The stator, whose blades are stationary when the vehicle is being accelerated at low speeds, converts one type of flow into another. Instead of allowing the fluid to flow straight back into the torus, the stator's curved blades turn the fluid almost 90° toward the direction of rotation of the engine. Thus the fluid does not flow as fast toward the torus, but is already spinning when the torus picks it up. This has the effect of allowing the torus to turn much faster than the turbine. This difference in speed may be compared to the difference in speed between the smaller and larger gears in any gear train. The result is that engine power output is higher, and engine torque is multiplied.

As the speed of the turbine increases, the fluid spins faster and faster in the direction of engine rotation. As a result, the ability of the stator to redirect the fluid flow is reduced. Under cruising conditions, the stator is eventually forced to rotate on its one-way clutch in the direction of engine rotation. Under these conditions, the torque converter begins to behave almost like a solid shaft, with the torus and turbine speeds being almost equal.

THE PLANETARY GEARBOX

The ability of the torque converter to multiply engine torque is limited. Also, the unit tends to be more efficient when the turbine is rotating at relatively high speeds. Therefore, a planetary gearbox is used to carry the power output of the turbine to the halfshafts.

Planetary gears function very similarly to conventional transmission gears. However, their construction is different in that three elements make up one gear system, and, in that all three elements are different from one another. The three elements are: an outer gear that is shaped like a hoop, with teeth cut into the inner surface; a sun gear, mounted on a shaft and located at the very center of the outer gear; and a set of three planet gears, held by pins in a ringlike planet carrier, meshing with both the sun gear and the outer gear. Either the outer gear or the sun gear may be held stationary, providing more than one possible torque multiplication factor for each set of gears. Also, if all three gears are forced to rotate at the same speed, the gearset forms, in effect, a solid shaft.

Most modern automatics use the planetary gears to provide either a single reduction ratio of about 1.8:1, or two reduction gears: a low of about 2.5:1, and an intermediate of about 1.5:1. Bands and clutches are used to hold various portions of the gearsets to the transmission case or to the shaft on which they are mounted. Shifting is accomplished, then, by changing the portion of each planetary gearset which is held to the transmission case or to the shaft.

THE SERVOS AND ACCUMULATORS

The servos are hydraulic pistons and cylinders. They resemble the hydraulic actuators used on many familiar machines, such as bulldozers. Hydraulic fluid enters the cylinder, under pressure, and forces the piston to move to engage the band or clutches.

The accumulators are used to cushion the engagement of the servos. The transmission fluid must pass through the accumulator on the way to the servo. The accumulator housing contains a thin piston which is sprung away from the discharge passage of the accumulator. When fluid passes through the accumulator on the way to the servo, it must move the piston against spring pressure, and this action smooths out the action of the servo.

THE HYDRAULIC CONTROL SYSTEM

The hydraulic pressure used to operate the servos comes from the main transmission oil pump. This fluid is channeled to the various servos through the shift valves. There is generally a manual shift valve which is operated by the transmission selector lever and an automatic shift valve for each automatic upshift the transmission provides: i.e., 2-speed automatics have a low/high shift valve, while 3-speeds have a 1-2 valve, and a 2-3 valve.

There are two pressures which effect the operation of these valves. One is the governor pressure which is affected by vehicle speed. The other is the modulator pressure which is affected by intake manifold vacuum or throttle position. Governor pressure rises with an increase in vehicle speed, and modulator pressure rises as the throttle is opened wider. By responding to these two pressures, the shift valves cause the upshift points to be delayed with increased throttle opening to make the best use of the engine's power output.

Most transmissions also make use of an auxiliary circuit for downshifting. This circuit may be actuated by the throttle linkage or the vacuum line which actuates the modulator, or by a cable or solenoid. It applies pressure to a special downshift surface on the shift valve or valves.

The transmission modulator also governs the line pressure, used to actuate the servos. In this way, the clutches and bands will be actuated with a force matching the torque output of the engine.

The automatic transaxle is available on all 1982 and later models.

Identification

The automatic transaxle serial number label is attached to the upper part of the housing on the Pulsar model and to upper portion of the oil pan on all Stanza models.

AUTOMATIC TRANSAXLE NUMBER

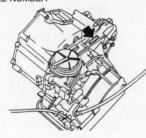

I.D. number—Pulsar

AUTOMATIC TRANSAXLE NUMBER

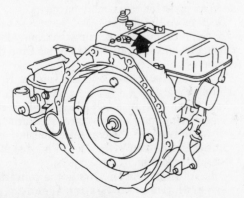

I.D. number—Stanza wagon

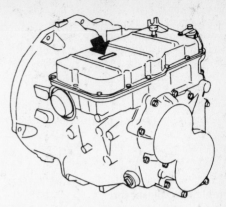

AUTOMATIC TRANSAXLE

I.D. number—Stanza

Fluid Pan

REMOVAL AND INSTALLATION

1. Raise and support the vehicle on jackstands.
2. Place a container under the transaxle to catch the oil when the pan is removed.
3. Remove the transaxle pan bolts.
NOTE: *If the pan sticks, bump it with a soft hammer to break it loose.*
4. Using a putty knife, clean the gasket mounting surfaces.
5. To install, use a new gasket, sealant and reverse the removal procedures. Torque the oil pan bolts to 3.6-5.1 ft. lbs. Refill the transaxle.

FILTER SERVICE

1. Refer to the Oil Pan, Removal and Installation procedures, in this chapter and remove the oil pan.
2. Remove the control valve body, oil strainer plate bolts and the plate.
NOTE: *If the separator plate shows signs of scratches or damage, replace it.*
3. To install, reverse the removal procedures.

Adjustments

THROTTLE WIRE

The throttle wire is adjusted by means of double nuts on the carburetor side.

1. Loosen the adjusting nuts at the carburetor throttle wire bracket.
2. With the throttle fully opened, turn the threaded shaft inward as far as it will go and tighten the 1st nut against the bracket.
3. Back off the 1st nut 1-1½ turns and tighten the 2nd nut against the bracket.
4. The throttle wire stroke between the threaded shaft and the cam should be 27.5-31.5mm.

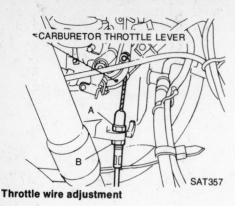

Throttle wire adjustment

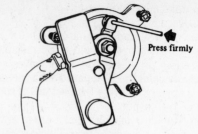

Adjusting the inhibitor switch

CONTROL CABLE

1. Place the control lever in Park.
2. Connect the control cable end to the lever in the transaxle unit and tighten the cable bolt securing.
3. Move the lever to the No. 1 position. Make sure that the lever works smoothly and quietly.
4. Place the control lever in Park.
5. Make sure that the lever locks in Park. Remove the cable adjusting outer nut and loosen the inner nut. Connect the control cable to the trunnion and install the outer nut.
6. Pull on the cable a couple of times, then tighten the outer nut until it just contacts the bracket. Tighten the inner nut securely. The length of the cable between the inner end of the rubber boot and the outer end of the rod should be 120.5mm.

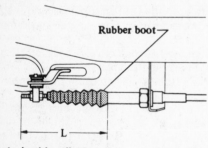

Control cable adjustment

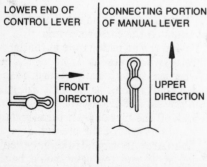

Correct positioning of the control lever cotter pin

7. Check all parts to ensure smooth working order. Check the cable spring cotter pin to make sure that it is assembled as shown.

INHIBITOR SWITCH

The inhibitor switch allows the back-up lights to work when the transaxle is placed in Reverse range and acts as a Neutral switch, by allowing the current to pass to the starter when the transaxle is placed in Neutral or Park.

1. Raise and support the vehicle on jackstands.
2. Loosen the inhibitor switch adjusting screws. Place the select lever in the Neutral position.
3. Using a 2.5mm diameter pin, place the pin into the adjustment holes on both the inhibitor switch and the switch lever (the switch lever should be as near vertical position as possible).
4. Tighten the adjusting screws to 1.4-1.9 ft. lbs. Check the switch for continuity.

Transaxle

REMOVAL AND INSTALLATION

310 (1982)

1. Refer to the Engine, Removal and Installation procedures in Chapter 3, then remove the engine and transaxle as an assembly.
2. Remove the converter housing dust cover.
3. Unbolt the flex plate from the converter.
4. Make two chalk marks on the converter and flex plate for reassembly purposes.
5. Remove the starter.
6. Remove the bolts securing the transaxle to the engine and separate the transaxle from the engine.
7. Install the transaxle in the vehicle. Note the following:

   a. Align the previously made chalk marks when installing the converter. Measure the distance between the transaxle housing end face and the converter face. The distance should be 22mm.

   b. After installation, rotate the converter several times to ensure freedom of movement.

c. Connect all wires and adjust all linkage points as previously described.
8. Install engine assembly.
9. Road test for proper operation.

Pulsar and Stanza

1. Disconnect the negative battery terminal.
2. Raise and support the front of the vehicle on jackstands.
   NOTE: *On Stanza wagon models, remove air cleaner and airflow meter and disconnect the front exhaust pipe.*
3. Remove the left front wheel assembly and the left front fender protector. Drain the transaxle fluid.
4. Disconnect the drive axles, the speedometer cable, the throttle wire from the carburetor throttle lever.
5. Remove the control cable from the rear of the transaxle, then the oil level gauge tube.
6. Place a floor jack under the transaxle and a support under the engine.
7. Disconnect and plug the oil cooler hoses from the tubes. Remove the torque converter-to-drive plate bolts.
   NOTE: *When removing the torque converter-to-drive plate bolts, turn the crankshaft for access to the bolts and place alignment marks on the converter-to-drive plate for alignment purposes.*
8. Remove the engine mount securing bolts and the starter motor.
9. Remove the transaxle-to-engine bolts, pull the transaxle away from the engine and lower it from the vehicle.
10. Install the engine/transaxle assembly in vehicle. Measure the distance between the torque converter and the transaxle housing, it should be more than 22mm. Torque the converter-to-drive plate bolts to 36-51 ft. lbs., the converter housing-to-engine to 12-16 ft. lbs.
11. Install the control cable to the rear of the transaxle, then the oil level gauge tube.
12. Connect the drive axles, the speedometer cable, the throttle wire to the carburetor throttle lever.
13. Install all securing bolts and brackets.
14. Install the left front wheel assembly and the left front fender protector. Refill the transaxle fluid.
15. Connect battery cable and road test for proper operation.

Halfshafts
REMOVAL AND INSTALLATION

Refer to the Manual Transaxle procedures with this exception, insert a dowel or equivalent through the right side halfshaft hole and use a small mallet to tap the left halfshaft out of the

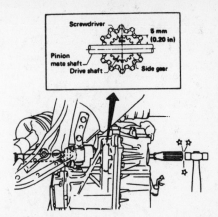

Removing the left halfshaft on models with a automatic transaxle

transaxle case. Withdraw the shaft from the steering knuckle and remove it. Be careful not to damage the pinion mating shaft and the side gear while tapping the left halfshaft out of the transaxle case.

OVERHAUL

Refer to the Manual Transaxle section procedures above.

TRANSFER CASE
REMOVAL AND INSTALLATION

1. Drain the gear oil from the transaxle and the transfer case.
2. Disconnect and remove the forward exhaust pipe.
3. Using chalk or paint, matchmark the flanges on the driveshaft and then unbolt and remove the driveshaft from the transfer case.
4. Unbolt and remove the transfer control actuator from the side of the transfer case.
5. Disconnect and remove the right side halfshaft.
6. Unscrew and withdraw the speedometer pinion gear from the transfer case. Position it out of the way and secure it with wire.
7. Unbolt and remove the front, rear and side transfer case gussets (support members).
8. Use an hydraulic floor jack and a block of wood to support the transfer case, remove the transfer case-to-transaxle mounting bolts and then remove the case itself. Be careful when moving it while supported on the jack.
9. Install the transfer case in the vehicle. Tighten the transfer case-to-transaxle mounting bolts and the transfer case gusset mounting bolts to 22-30 ft. lbs. (30-40 Nm).
10. Be sure to use a multi-purpose grease to lubricate all oil seal surfaces prior to reinstallation.

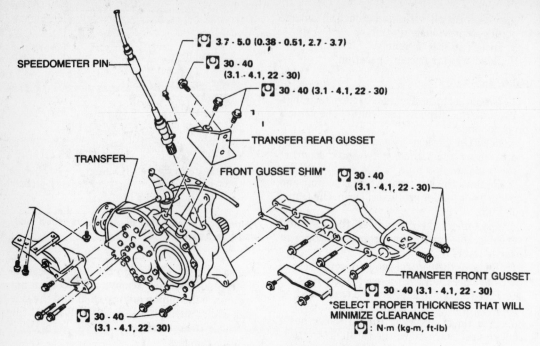

SPEEDOMETER PIN

3.7 - 5.0 (0.38 - 0.51, 2.7 - 3.7)

30 - 40 (3.1 - 4.1, 22 - 30)

30 - 40 (3.1 - 4.1, 22 - 30)

TRANSFER REAR GUSSET

TRANSFER

FRONT GUSSET SHIM*

30 - 40 (3.1 - 4.1, 22 - 30)

TRANSFER FRONT GUSSET

30 - 40 (3.1 - 4.1, 22 - 30)

*SELECT PROPER THICKNESS THAT WILL MINIMIZE CLEARANCE

: N·m (kg-m, ft-lb)

30 - 40 (3.1 - 4.1, 22 - 30)

Transfer case removal—Stanza wagon 4wd

11. Install the speedometer pinion gear.
12. Install the halfshaft.
13. Connect the transfer control actuator to the side of the transfer case.
14. Install the driveshaft to the transfer case.

15. Install the forward exhaust pipe.
16. Refill all fluid levels, the transfer case and the transaxle use different types and weights of lubricant then road test for proper operation.

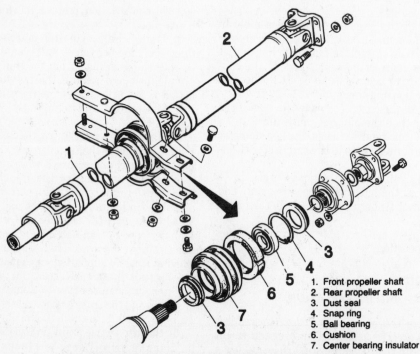

1. Front propeller shaft
2. Rear propeller shaft
3. Dust seal
4. Snap ring
5. Ball bearing
6. Cushion
7. Center bearing insulator

Two piece driveshaft with center bearing and three U-joints

DRIVELINE

Front Driveshaft And U-Joints
REMOVAL AND INSTALLATION

These models use a driveshaft with 3 U-joints and a center support bearing. The driveshaft is balanced as an assembly. It is not recommended that it be disassembled.

1. Mark the relationship of the driveshaft flange to the differential flange.
2. Unbolt the center bearing bracket.
3. Unbolt the driveshaft flange from the differential flange.

Troubleshooting Basic Driveshaft and Rear Axle Problems

When abnormal vibrations or noises are detected in the driveshaft area, this chart can be used to help diagnose possible causes. Remember that other components such as wheels, tires, rear axle and suspension can also produce similar conditions.

BASIC DRIVESHAFT PROBLEMS

Problem	Cause	Solution
Shudder as car accelerates from stop or low speed	• Loose U-joint • Defective center bearing	• Replace U-joint • Replace center bearing
Loud clunk in driveshaft when shifting gears	• Worn U-joints	• Replace U-joints
Roughness or vibration at any speed	• Out-of-balance, bent or dented driveshaft • Worn U-joints • U-joint clamp bolts loose	• Balance or replace driveshaft • Replace U-joints • Tighten U-joint clamp bolts
Squeaking noise at low speeds	• Lack of U-joint lubrication	• Lubricate U-joint; if problem persists, replace U-joint
Knock or clicking noise	• U-joint or driveshaft hitting frame tunnel • Worn CV joint	• Correct overloaded condition • Replace CV joint

BASIC REAR AXLE PROBLEMS

First, determine when the noise is most noticeable.

Drive Noise: Produced under vehicle acceleration.

Coast Noise: Produced while the car coasts with a closed throttle.

Float Noise: Occurs while maintaining constant car speed (just enough to keep speed constant) on a level road.

Road Noise

Brick or rough surfaced concrete roads produce noises that seem to come from the rear axle. Road noise is usually identical in Drive or Coast and driving on a different type of road will tell whether the road is the problem.

Tire Noise

Tire noises are often mistaken for rear axle problems. Snow treads or unevenly worn tires produce vibrations seeming to originate elsewhere. **Temporarily** inflating the tires to 40 lbs will significantly alter tire noise, but will have no effect on rear axle noises (which normally cease below about 30 mph).

Engine/Transmission Noise

Determine at what speed the noise is most pronounced, then stop the car in a quiet place. With the transmission in Neutral, run the engine through speeds corresponding to road speeds where the noise was noticed. Noises produced with the car standing still are coming from the engine or transmission.

Front Wheel Bearings

While holding the car speed steady, lightly apply the footbrake; this will often decease bearing noise, as some of the load is taken from the bearing.

Rear Axle Noises

Eliminating other possible sources can narrow the cause to the rear axle, which normally produces noise from worn gears or bearings. Gear noises tend to peak in a narrow speed range, while bearing noises will usually vary in pitch with engine speeds.

NOISE DIAGNOSIS

The Noise Is	Most Probably Produced By
· Identical under Drive or Coast	· Road surface, tires or front wheel bearings
· Different depending on road surface	· Road surface or tires
· Lower as the car speed is lowered	· Tires
· Similar with car standing or moving	· Engine or transmission
· A vibration	· Unbalanced tires, rear wheel bearing, unbalanced driveshaft or worn U-joint
· A knock or click about every 2 tire revolutions	· Rear wheel bearing
· Most pronounced on turns	· Damaged differential gears
· A steady low-pitched whirring or scraping, starting at low speeds	· Damaged or worn pinion bearing
· A chattering vibration on turns	· Wrong differential lubricant or worn clutch plates (limited slip rear axle)
· Noticed only in Drive, Coast or Float conditions	· Worn ring gear and/or pinion gear

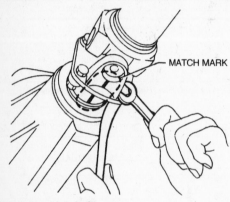

— MATCH MARK

Removing driveshaft

4. Pull the driveshaft back under the rear axle.

5. On installation, align the marks made in Step 1. Torque the flange bolts to 17-24 ft. lbs. Center bearing bracket both torque is 26-35 ft. lbs.

Center Bearing

REMOVAL AND INSTALLATION

The center bearing is a sealed unit which must be replaced as an assembly if defective.

1. Remove the driveshaft.

2. Paint a matchmark across where the flanges behind the center yoke are joined. This is for assembly purposes. If you don't paint or somehow mark the relationship between the 2 shafts, they may be out of balance when you put them back together.

3. Remove the bolts and separate the shafts. Make a matchmark on the front driveshaft half which lines up with the mark on the flange half.

4. Devise a way to hold the driveshaft while unbolting the companion flange from the front driveshaft. Do not place the front driveshaft tube in a vise. The best way is to grip the flange

while loosening the nut. It is going to require some strength to remove.

5. Press the companion flange off the front driveshaft and press the center bearing from its mount.

6. The new bearing is already lubricated. Install it into the mount, making sure that the seals and so on are facing the same way as when removed.

7. Slide the companion flange onto the front driveshaft, aligning the marks made during removal. Install the washer and locknut. If the washer and locknut are separate pieces, tighten them to 145-175 ft. lbs. If they are a unit, tighten it to 180-217 ft. lbs. Check that the bearing rotates freely around the driveshaft. Stake the nut.

8. Connect the companion flange to the other half of the driveshaft, aligning the marks made during removal. Tighten the bolts securely.

9. Install the driveshaft.

FINAL DRIVE UNIT

Differential Carrier

REMOVAL AND INSTALLATION

Stanza 4-Wheel Drive Wagon

1. Jack up the rear of the vehicle and drain the oil from the differential. Support with jackstands. Position the floor jack underneath the differential unit.

2. Disconnect the brake hydraulic lines and the parking brake cable.

3. Disconnect the sway bar from the control arms on either sides.

4. Remove the rear exhaust tube.

5. Disconnect the driveshaft and the rear axle shafts.

6. Remove the rear shock absorbers from the control arms.

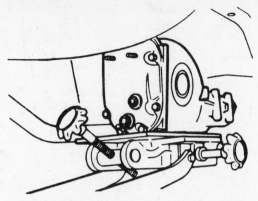

Lowering differential carrier assembly out of vehicle

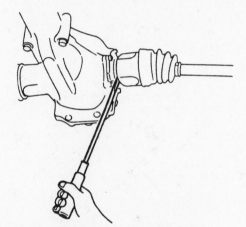

Removing rear halfshaft from backing plate

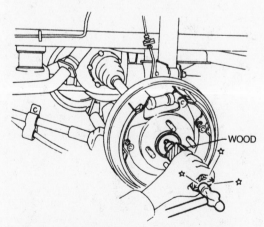

Removing rear halfshaft from differential carrier

7. Unbolt the differential unit from the chassis, at the differential mounting insulator.

8. Lower the rear assembly out of the car using the floor jack. It is best to have at least one other person helping to balance the assembly.

9. Install the differential unit to the chassis. Torque the rear cover-to-insulator nuts to 72-

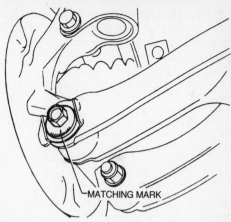

—MATCHING MARK

Matchmark the toe adjustment bolt to the transverse link

87 ft. lbs.; the mounting insulator-to-chassis bolts to 22-29 ft. lbs.; the driveshaft-to-flange bolts to 43-51 ft. lbs. Torque the strut nuts to 51-65 ft. lbs.; and the sway bar-to-control arm nuts to 12-15 ft. lbs.

10. Reconnect the rear exhaust tube.

11. Connect the brake hydraulic lines and the parking brake cable.

12. Bleed the brake system.

13. Road test for proper operation.

Rear Halfshafts

REMOVAL AND INSTALLATION

Stanza 4-Wheel Drive Wagon

1. Raise the rear of the vehicle and support it with jackstands.

2. Remove the wheel and tire assembly.

3. Pull out the wheel bearing cotter pin and then remove the adjusting cap and insulator.

4. Set the parking brake and then remove the wheel bearing lock nut.

5. Disconnect and plug the hydraulic brake lines. Disconnect the parking brake cable.

6. Using a block of wood and a small mallet, carefully tap the halfshaft out of the knuckle/backing plate assembly.

7. Unbolt the radius rod and the transverse link at the wheel end.

NOTE: *Before removing the transverse link mounting bolt, matchmark the toe-in adjusting plate to the link.*

8. Using a suitable pry bar, carefully remove the halfshaft from the final drive.

9. On installation , position the halfshaft into the knuckle and then insert it into the final drive; makeing sure the serrations are properly aligned.

10. Push the shaft into the final drive and then press-fit the circlip on the halfshaft into the groove on the side gear.

11. After insertion, pull the halfshaft by hand to be certain that it is properly seated in the side gear and will not come out.

12. Connect the radius rod and the transverse link at the wheel end.

13. Install the knuckle/backing plate assembly.

14. Connect the hydraulic brake lines and the parking brake cable.

15. Install wheel bearing lock nut, insulator, adjusting cap and cotter pin.

16. Install the wheel and tire assembly.

17. Bleed the brake system.

18. Road test for proper operation.

Suspension and Steering

FRONT SUSPENSION

The independent front suspension system on all models covered uses MacPherson struts. Each strut combines the function of coil spring and shock absorber. The spindle is mounted to the lower part of the strut which has a single ball joint. No upper suspension arm is required in this design. The spindle and lower suspension transverse link (control arm) are located fore and aft by the tension rods to the front part of the chassis on most models. A cross-chassis sway bar is used on all models.

Troubleshooting Basic Steering and Suspension Problems

Problem	Cause	Solution
Hard steering (steering wheel is hard to turn)	• Low or uneven tire pressure • Loose power steering pump drive belt • Low or incorrect power steering fluid • Incorrect front end alignment • Defective power steering pump • Bent or poorly lubricated front end parts	• Inflate tires to correct pressure • Adjust belt • Add fluid as necessary • Have front end alignment checked/adjusted • Check pump • Lubricate and/or replace defective parts
Loose steering (too much play in the steering wheel)	• Loose wheel bearings • Loose or worn steering linkage • Faulty shocks • Worn ball joints	• Adjust wheel bearings • Replace worn parts • Replace shocks • Replace ball joints
Car veers or wanders (car pulls to one side with hands off the steering wheel)	• Incorrect tire pressure • Improper front end alignment • Loose wheel bearings • Loose or bent front end components • Faulty shocks	• Inflate tires to correct pressure • Have front end alignment checked/adjusted • Adjust wheel bearings • Replace worn components • Replace shocks
Wheel oscillation or vibration transmitted through steering wheel	• Improper tire pressures • Tires out of balance • Loose wheel bearings • Improper front end alignment • Worn or bent front end components	• Inflate tires to correct pressure • Have tires balanced • Adjust wheel bearings • Have front end alignment checked/adjusted • Replace worn parts
Uneven tire wear	• Incorrect tire pressure • Front end out of alignment • Tires out of balance	• Inflate tires to correct pressure • Have front end alignment checked/adjusted • Have tires balanced

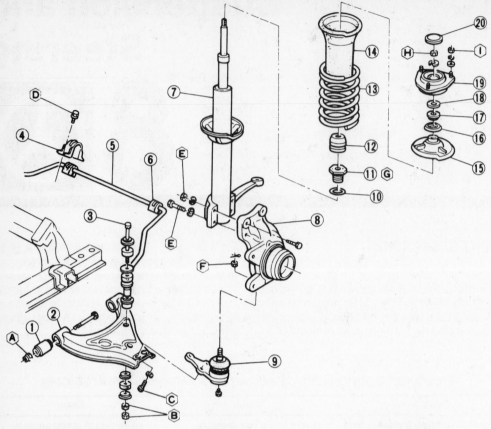

1. Transverse link bushing
2. Transverse link
3. Connecting bolt
4. Stabilizer bracket
5. Stabilizer
6. Stabilizer bushing
7. Strut
8. Knuckle
9. Ball joint
10. O-ring
11. Gland packing assembly
12. Bound bumper
13. Coil spring
14. Dust cover
15. Spring seat
16. Grease seal
17. Thrust seat
18. Thrust plate
19. Mount insulator
20. Insulator cap

F10, 310 front suspension

MacPherson Strut

REMOVAL AND INSTALLATION

F10 and 310

1. Raise the vehicle and support it on jackstands. Remove the wheel.

2. Disconnect and plug the brake hose.

3. Using the Ball Joint Puller tool HT72520000, disconnect the tie rod from the strut.

4. Place a jackstand under the control arm to support it.

5. Remove the steering knuckle-to-strut mounting bolts and separate the strut from the steering knuckle.

6. Open the hood and remove the strut-to-body nuts.

7. Remove the strut assembly from the vehicle.

8. Install the strut assembly on the vehicle

and torque the strut-to-body bolts to 11-17 ft. lbs., the strut-to-steering knuckle to 24-33 ft. lbs. and the tie rod ball joint-to-strut to 40-47 ft. lbs.

NOTE: *The self-locking nuts holding the top of the strut must be replaced.*

9. Bleed the brakes.

10. Install the wheel.

Stanza and Pulsar

1. Raise and support the vehicle on jackstands.

2. Remove the wheel.

3. Detach the brake tube from the strut.

4. Support the transverse link with a jackstand.

5. Detach the steering knuckle from the strut.

6. Loosen, but do not remove, the strut piston rod locknut.

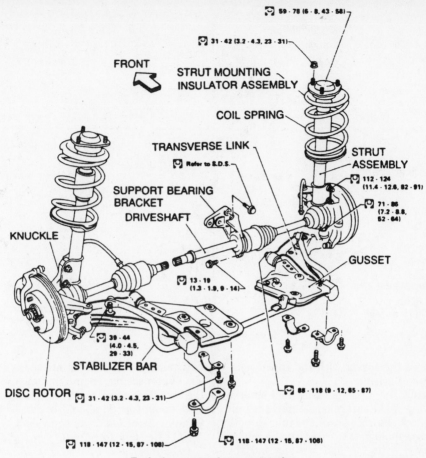

59 - 78 (6 - 8, 43 - 58)

31 - 42 (3.2 - 4.3, 23 - 31)

FRONT

STRUT MOUNTING
INSULATOR ASSEMBLY

COIL SPRING

TRANSVERSE LINK

Refer to S.D.S.

STRUT
ASSEMBLY

SUPPORT BEARING
BRACKET

112 - 124
(11.4 - 12.6, 82 - 91)

DRIVESHAFT

71 - 86
(7.2 - 8.8,
52 - 64)

KNUCKLE

GUSSET

13 - 19
(1.3 - 1.9, 9 - 14)

39 - 44
(4.0 - 4.5,
29 - 33)

STABILIZER BAR

88 - 118 (9 - 12, 65 - 87)

DISC ROTOR   31 - 42 (3.2 - 4.3, 23 - 31)

118 - 147 (12 - 15, 87 - 108)

118 - 147 (12 - 15, 87 - 108)

Typical strut-type front suspension

7. Support the strut and remove the three upper attaching nuts. Remove the strut from the vehicle.

8. Install the strut assembly on the vehicle and torque the strut-to-body nuts to 23-31 ft. lbs., the piston rod locknut to 43-54 ft. lbs. and the strut-to-knuckle bolts to 56-80 ft. lbs. (Stanza) or 72-87 ft. lbs. (Pulsar).

9. If brake line was removed bleed brakes and install the wheel.

OVERHAUL

CAUTION: *The coil springs are under considerable tension and can exert enough force to cause serious injury. Disassemble the struts only if the proper tools are available and use extreme caution.*

The coil springs on all models must be removed with the aid of a coil spring compressor. If you don't have one, don't try to improvise by using something else: you could risk injury. The coil spring compressor is Special Tool ST35652001 or variations of that number. Basically, they are all the same tool. These are the recommended compressors, although they are

probably not the only spring compressors which will work. Always follow manufacturer's instructions when operating a spring compressor. You can now buy cartridge type shock absorbers for some models: installation procedures are not the same as those given here. In this case, follow the instructions that come with the shock absorbers.

To remove the coil spring, you must first remove the strut assembly from the vehicle. See above for procedures.

1. Secure the strut assembly in a vise.

2. Attach the spring compressor to the spring, leaving the top few coils free.

3. Remove the dust cap from the top of the strut to expose the center nut, if a dust cap is provided.

4. Compress the spring just far enough to permit the strut insulator to be turned by hand. Remove the self-locking center nut.

5. Take out the strut insulator, strut bearing, oil seal, upper spring seat and bound bumper rubber from the top of the strut. Note their sequence of removal and be sure to assemble them in the same order.

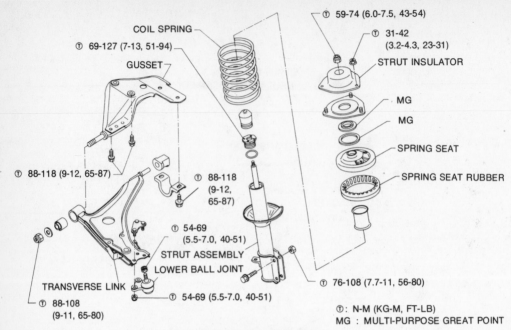

① 59-74 (6.0-7.5, 43-54)

① 31-42 (3.2-4.3, 23-31)

STRUT INSULATOR

COIL SPRING

① 69-127 (7-13, 51-94)

GUSSET

MG

MG

SPRING SEAT

SPRING SEAT RUBBER

① 88-118 (9-12, 65-87)

① 88-118 (9-12, 65-87)

① 54-69 (5.5-7.0, 40-51)

STRUT ASSEMBLY

LOWER BALL JOINT

TRANSVERSE LINK

① 88-108 (9-11, 65-80)

① 54-69 (5.5-7.0, 40-51)

① 76-108 (7.7-11, 56-80)

①: N-M (KG-M, FT-LB)
MG : MULTI-PURPOSE GREAT POINT

Stanza front suspension

6. Remove the spring with the spring compressor still attached.

Reassembly the strut assembly and observe the following. Make sure you assemble the unit with the shock absorber piston rod fully extended. When assembling, take care that the rubber spring seats, both top and bottom and the spring are positioned in their grooves before releasing the spring.

7. To remove the shock absorber: Remove the dust cap (if equipped) and push the piston rod down until it bottoms. With the piston in this position, loosen and remove the gland packing shock absorber retainer. This calls for the Special Tool ST35500001, but you should be able to loosen it either with a pipe wrench or by tapping it around with a drift.

NOTE: *If the gland tube is dirty, clean it before removing it to prevent dirt from contaminating the fluid inside the strut tube.*

8. Remove the O-ring from the top of the piston guide and lift out the piston rod together with the cylinder. Drain all of the fluid from the strut and shock components into a suitable container. Clean all parts.

NOTE: *The piston rod, piston rod guide and cylinder are a matched set: single parts of this shock assembly should not be exchanged with parts of other assemblies.*

Assembly the shock absorber into the assembly with the following notes:

After installing the cylinder and piston rod assembly (the shock absorber kit) in the outer casing, remove the piston rod guide (if equipped) from the cylinder and pour the cor-

rect amount of new fluid into the cylinder and strut outer casing. To find this amount, consult the instructions with your shock absorber kit. The amount of oil should be listed. Use only Genuine Strut Oil or its equivalent.

NOTE: *It is important that the correct amount of fluid be poured into the strut to assure correct shock absorber damping force.*

Install the O-ring, fluid and any other cylinder components. Fit the gland packing and tighten it after greasing the gland packing-to-piston rod mating surfaces.

NOTE: *When tightening the gland packing, extend the piston rod about 3-5 inches from the end of the outer casing to expel most of the air from the strut.*

After the kit is installed, bleed the air from the system in the following manner: hold the strut with its bottom end facing down. Pull the piston rod out as far as it will go. Turn the strut upside down and push the piston in as far as it will go. Repeat this procedure several times until an equal pressure is felt on both the pullout and the push in strokes of the piston rods. The remaining assembly is the reverse of disassembly.

Lower Ball Joint
INSPECTION

The lower ball joint should be replaced when play becomes excessive. The manufacturer does not publish specifications on just what constitutes excessive play, relying instead on a method of determining the force (in inch pounds) required to keep the ball joint turning. This method is not very helpful to the backyard mechanic since it involves removing the ball joint, which is what we are trying to avoid in the first place. An effective way to determine ball joint play is to jack up the car until the wheel is just a couple of inches off the ground and the ball joint is unloaded (meaning you can't jack directly underneath the ball joint). Place a long bar under the tire and move the wheel and tire assembly up and down. Keep one hand on top of the tire while you are doing this. If there is over ¼" of play at the top of the tire, the ball joint is probably bad. This is assuming that the wheel bearings are in good shape and properly adjusted. As a double check on this, have someone watch the ball joint while you move the tire up and down with the bar. If you can see considerable play, besides feeling play at the top of the wheel, the ball joint needs replacing.

REMOVAL AND INSTALLATION

F10

1. Raise the vehicle and support it on jackstands. Remove the wheel.
2. Remove the ball stud-to-steering knuckle nut and force out the stud with a ball joint fork, being careful not to damage the ball joint dust cover.
3. Remove the ball joint bolts and the ball joint.
4. Install the ball joint in the control arm and tighten the ball stud-to-steering knuckle nut to 22-29 ft. lbs. and the ball joint-to-control arm bolts to 40-47 ft. lbs.
5. Install the wheel.

310, Pulsar and Stanza

NOTE: *On most late model vehicles, the transverse link (lower control arm) must be removed and then the ball joint must be pressed out. The ball joint should be greased every 30,000 miles. There is a plugged hole in the bottom of the joint for installation of a grease fitting.*

Ball joint removal

1. Refer to the Drive Axle, Removal and Installation procedures, in Chapter 7 and remove the drive axle.
2. Remove the ball joint-to-control arm nut. Using the Ball Joint Remover tool HT72520000, separate the ball joint from the control arm.
3. Remove the other ball joint bolts from the control arm and the ball joint from the vehicle.
4. Install the ball joint in the control arm and tighten the ball stud attaching nut (from ball joint-to-steering knuckle) to 22-29 ft. lbs. (310), 25-36 ft. lbs. (Pulsar) or 40-51 ft. lbs. (Stanza) and the ball joint to transverse link bolts to 40-47 ft. lbs. (310 and Pulsar) or 40-51 ft. lbs. (Stanza).
5. Install the drive axle.

Lower Control Arm (Transverse Link)
REMOVAL AND INSTALLATION

F10 and 310

NOTE: *Always use a new nut when installing the ball joint to the control arm.*
1. Raise and support the car on jackstands.
2. Remove the wheel.
3. Unbolt the control arm from the ball joint.
4. Remove the stabilizer link-to-control arm nut and separate the link from the arm.
5. Unbolt the control arm-to-subframe bolts and remove the control arm from the vehicle.
6. Install lower control arm on the vehicle and torque the control arm-to-sub frame bolts to 42-51 ft. lbs., the ball joint-to-control arm

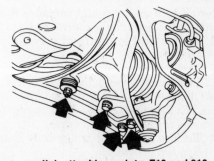

Transverse link attaching points, F10 and 310

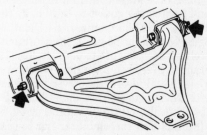

Unbolting transverse link from sub frame on F10 and 310

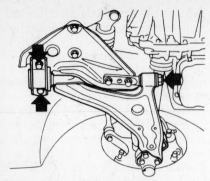

Removing Stanza transverse link

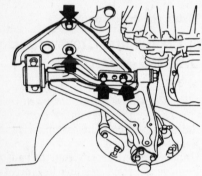

Removing Stanza gusset

nut to 40-47 ft. lbs. and the stabilizer link-to-control arm nut to 70-100 in. lbs.

7. Install the wheel.

1983-86 Pulsar
Stanza

NOTE: *Always use a new nut when installing the ball joint to the control arm.*

1. Raise and support the vehicle on jackstands.

2. Remove the wheel.

3. Remove the lower ball joint bolts from the control arm.

NOTE: *If equipped with a stabilizer bar, disconnect it from the control arm.*

4. Remove the control arm-to-body bolts.

5. Remove the gusset.

6. Remove the control arm from the vehicle.

7. Install the lower control arm on the vehicle and tighten the gusset-to-body bolts to 65-87 ft. lbs. (1982-86 Stanza), 87-108 ft. lbs. (1987-88 Stanza) or 65-80 ft. lbs. (Pulsar); the control arm securing nut to 65-80 ft. lbs. (1982-86 Stanza), 87-108 ft. lbs. (1987-88 Stanza) or 72-87 ft. lbs. (Pulsar); the lower ball joint-to-control arm nuts to 40-51 ft. lbs. (1982-86 Stanza), 56-80 ft. lbs. (1987-88 Stanza) or 40-47 ft. lbs. (Pulsar) and the stabilizer bar-to-control arm to 80-100 in. lbs. (2wd Stanza and Pulsar) or 12-16 ft. lbs. (4wd Stanza).

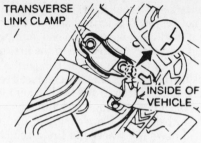

Transverse link clamp positioning

8. Reconnect the stabilizer if so equipped to the control arm.

9. Install the wheel.

NOTE: *When installing the link, tighten the nut securing the link spindle to the gusset. Final tightening should be made with the weight of the car on the wheels.*

1987-88 Pulsar

NOTE: *A ball joint removal tool will be required for this operation.*

1. Raise the vehicle and support it with safety stands. Remove the wheel.

2. Remove the wheel bearing locknut.

3. Remove the tie rod ball joint with a puller.

4. Remove the lower strut-to-knuckle mounting bolts and separate the strut from the knuckle.

5. Separate the outer end of the halfshaft from the steering knuckle by carefully tapping it with a rubber mallet.

NOTE: *Be sure to cover the CV-joints with a shop rag.*

6. Using a ball joint removal tool, separate the lower ball joint stud from the steering knuckle.

7. Unbolt and remove the transverse link and ball joint as an assembly.

8. Install the lower control arm to the vehicle.

9. Reconnect the ball joint and halfshaft.

10. Connect the strut to the knuckle.

11. Install the tie rod ball joint.

12. Tighten the wheel bearing lock nut.

13. Install the wheel and make sure the tab on the transverse link clamp is pointing in the proper direction. Final tightening of all bolts should take place with the weight of the vehicle on the wheels. Check wheel alignment.

Stabilizer Bar
REMOVAL AND INSTALLATION
Pulsar and Stanza Wagon

1. Disconnect the parking brake cable at the equalizer on the Stanza wagon.

2. On the Stanza wagon (4wd), remove the

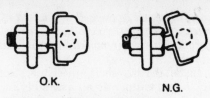

OK. N.G.

Ball joint socket positioning

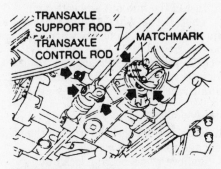

Removing the stabilizer bar on the Stanza wagon (4wd)

5. Remove the stabilizer bar-to-transverse link (lower, control arm) mounting bolts.

6. Remove the 4 stabilizer bar bracket mounting bolts and then pull the bar out, around the link and exhaust pipe.

7. Install the stabilizer bar and mounting brackets. Never fully tighten the mounting bolts unless the car is resting on the ground with normal weight upon the wheels. On the 1987-88 Pulsar, be sure the stabilzer bar ball joint socket is properly positioned.

8. Install the driveshaft to the transfer case if it was removed.

9. Reconnect the front exhaust pipe at the manifold.

10. Connect the parking brake cables and install any other bolts that were removed.

11. Final tightening of all bolts should take place with the weight of the vehicle on the wheels.

Front Axle Hub, Knuckle And Bearing

REMOVAL AND INSTALLATION

F10 And 310

NOTE: *Nissan recommends that the hub, caliper, knuckle and the halfshaft be removed as one assembly.*

1. Raise and support the front of the vehicle safely and remove the wheels.

mounting nuts for the transaxle support rod and the transaxle control rod.

3. Disconnect the front exhaust pipe at the manifold and position it out of the way.

4. On the Stanza wagon (4wd), matchmark the flanges and then separate the driveshaft from the transfer case.

1. Driveshaft
2. Strut assembly
3. Grease seal
4. Inner sheel bearing
5. Knuckle
6. Spacer
7. Outer wheel bearing
8. Grease seal
9. Rotor
10. Wheel hub
11. Hub nut
12. Ball joint
13. Transverse link assembly

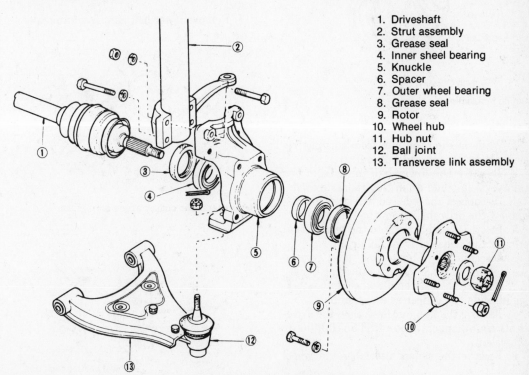

F10, 310 front hub and knuckle

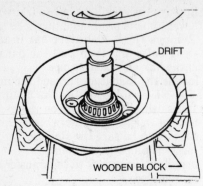

Separating wheel hub from disc using press

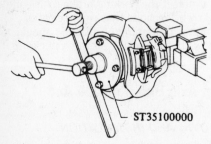

Removing driveshaft from hub using special tool

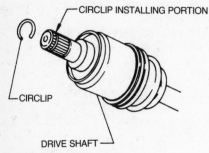

Circlip installation

2. While holding the hub from turning, remove the cotter pin and hub nut.

3. Remove the lower ball joint from the transverse link and drain the transaxle fluid.

4. Disconnect the side rod ball stud and disconnect the driveshaft from the transaxle.

5. Insert a suitable rod into the transaxle to prevent the side gear from falling off.

6. Disconnect the brake line, then remove the steering knuckle-to-strut attaching bolts.

7. Remove the driveshaft, wheel hub, steering knuckle and caliper as an assembly.

8. Remove the hub nut first, then the driveshaft using special tool #ST35100000 or equivalent.

9. Remove the caliper assembly and wheel hub.

NOTE: *To replace the wheel bearings and*

races they must be pressed in and out of the knuckle assembly. To pack the wheel bearings they will have to be removed from the knuckle assembly.

10. Install the driveshaft, wheel hub, steering knuckle and caliper as an assembly in the vehicle.

11. Connect the brake line and lower ball joint.

12. Install the hub nut and cotter pin.

13. Install the wheels, bleed brakes and torque hub nut to 145 ft. lbs. when the vehicle is on the ground.

NOTE: *When the driveshaft is drawn out from the transaxle, circlip should be replaced with a new one even if it appears good.*

Pulsar And Stanza

1. Raise and support the front of the vehicle safely and remove the wheels.

2. Remove wheel bearing lock nut.

3. Remove brake cliper assembly. Make sure not to twist the brake hose.

4. Remove tie rod ball joint.

NOTE: *Cover axle boots with waste cloth or equivalent so as not to damage them when removing driveshaft. Make a matching mark on strut housing and ajusting pin before removing them.*

5. Separate halfshaft from the knuckle by slightly tapping it.

6. Mark and remove the strut mounting bolts.

7. Remove lower ball joint from knuckle.

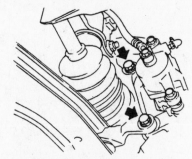

Removing brake caliper assembly—Pulsar

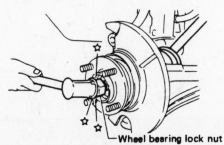

Removing halfshaft from knuckle

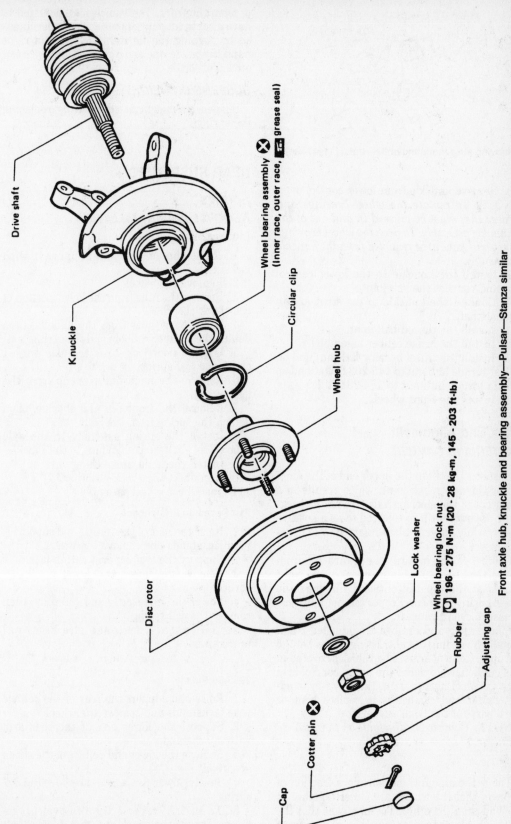

Drive shaft

Knuckle

Wheel bearing assembly ⊗ (Inner race, outer race, ⬛ grease seal)

Circular clip

Wheel hub

Disc rotor

Lock washer

Wheel bearing lock nut
⬕ 196 - 275 N·m (20 - 28 kg-m, 145 - 203 ft-lb)

Rubber

Adjusting cap

Cotter pin ⊗

Cap

Front axle hub, knuckle and bearing assembly—Pulsar—Stanza similar

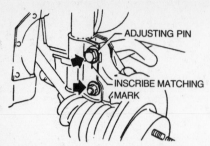

ADJUSTING PIN

INSCRIBE MATCHING MARK

Removing strut mounting bolts—Pulsar (1987–88)

8. Remove knuckle from lower control arm.
NOTE: *To replace the wheel bearings and races they must be pressed in and out of the knuckle assembly. To pack the wheel bearings they will have to be removed from the knuckle assembly.*
9. Install the knuckle to the lower control arm and connect the ball joint.
10. Connect the knuckle to the strut and to the halfshaft.
11. Install the tie rod ball joint.
12. Install the brake caliper assembly.
13. Install the wheel bearing lock nut and on Pulsar torque hub nut to 145-203 ft. lbs. and on Stanza torque hub nut to 174-231 ft. lbs.
14. Install the front wheels.

Front End Alignment

CASTER AND CAMBER

Caster is the tilt of the upper end of the kingpin or the upper ball joint, which results in a slight tilt of the steering axis forward or backward. Rearward tilt is referred to as a positive caster, while forward tilt is referred to as negative caster.

Camber is the inward or outward tilt from the vertical (measured in degrees) of the front wheels at the top. An outward tilt gives the wheel positive camber. Proper camber is critical to assure even tire wear.

Since caster and camber are adjusted traditionally by adding or subtracting shims behind the upper control arms. The vehicles covered in this guide have replaced the upper control arm with the MacPherson strut, the only way to adjust caster and camber is to replace bent or worn parts of the front suspension.

NOTE: *Camber is adjustable on the 1987-88 Pulsar.*

TOE

Toe is the amount, measure in a fraction of an inch, that the wheels are closer together at one end than the other. Toe-in means that the front wheels are closer together at the front than the rear; toe-out means the rears are closer than the front. The vehicles are adjusted to have a slight amount of toe-in. Toe-in is adjusted by turning the tie rod, which has a right hand thread on one end and a left hand thread on the other.

SUSPENSION HEIGHT

Suspension height is adjusted by replacing the springs.

REAR SUSPENSION

Springs

REMOVAL AND INSTALLATION

F10 Station Wagon

1. Raise the vehicle and support it with jackstands.
2. Remove the wheel.
3. Remove the nuts from the lower portion of the shock absorber.
4. Remove the nuts from the U-bolts, then detach the bumper rubbers and the spring seat.
5. Using a floor jack, raise the axle until it clears the leaf spring.
6. Remove the hand brake clamp from the leaf spring.
7. Remove the front pin and shackle, then detach the spring from the body.
8. Install the spring assembly to the axle tube with U-bolts and align pins in the shackle.
9. Install the hand brake clamp.
10. Reconnect the shock absorber.
11. Install the wheel assembly.

F10 Sedan and Hatchback

1. Raise the rear of the vehicle and support it with jackstands and remove the wheel.
2. Support the trailing arm with a jack.
3. Remove the upper and lower shock absorber nuts.
4. Lower the jack slowly and carefully, then remove the coil spring.
5. To install, reverse the removal procedures.

310
1983-86 Pulsar

1. Raise and support the rear of the vehicle with jackstands and remove the wheel.
2. Support the lower end of the rear arm with a jackstand.
3. Remove the lower end bolt from the shock absorber.
4. Slowly, lower the jack and remove the coil spring.
5. To install, reverse the removal procedures. Torque the shock absorber's lower bolt to 51-65 ft. lbs.

Wheel Alignment Specifications

Year	Model	Caster		Camber			Steering Axle Inclination (deg)	Wheel Pivot Ratio (deg)	
		Range (deg)	Preferred Setting (deg)	Range (deg)	Preferred Setting (deg)	Toe-In (in.)		Inner Wheel	Outer Wheel
1976–78	F10	20'P–1°50'P	1°05'P	50'P–2°20'P	1°35'P	①	9°15'–10°45'	36°30'–39°30'	31°–34°
1979–82	310	25'P–1°55'P	1°10'P	15'P–1°45'P	1°P	0–0.08	11°10'–12°30'	36°30'–39°30'	29°30'–32°30' ②
1982–84	Stanza	40'P–2°10'P	1°25'P	45'N–45'P	0	0–0.08	13°40'–15°10'	36°–40°	30°–34°
1985–88	Stanza	40'P–2°10'P	25'P	25'N–1°05'P	20'N	0–0.08	13°40'–15°10'	36°–40°	30°–34°
1983	Pulsar	45'P–2°15'P	1°30'P	35'N–1°05'P	15'P	0–0.08	12°10'–13°40'	40°–44°	31°–35°
1984	Pulsar	45'P–2°15'P	1°30'P	35'N–1°05'P	15'P	0–0.08	12°10'–13°40'	40°30'–43°30'	31°30'–34°30'
1985–88	Pulsar	45'P–2°15'P	1°30'P	25'N–1°05'P	20'P	0.12–0.20	12°10'–13°40'	③ ⑤	④ ⑥

① 0–0.79 Radial tires
  0.20–0.28 Bias tires
② Power Steering: 28°30'–31°30'
③ M/T and A/T (power steering): 40°30'–43°30'
④ M/T and A/T (without power steering): 31°30'–34°30'
⑤ A/T (manual steering): 37°30'–40°30'
⑥ A/T (manual steering): 29°30'–32°30'

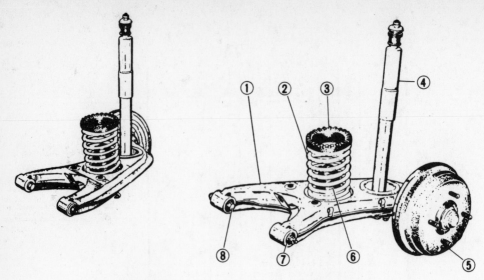

1. Rear arm
2. Coil spring
3. Rubber seat
4. Shock absorber

5. Drum
6. Bumper
7. Bushing
8. Rear arm bolt

F10 sedan and hatchback rear suspension

Shock Absorber

REMOVAL AND INSTALLATION

F10 and 310

1. Open the trunk and remove the cover panel to expose the shock mounts. Pry off the mount covers (if equipped). On leaf spring models, jack up the rear of the vehicle and support the rear axle on stands.

2. Remove the two nuts holding the top of the shock absorber. Unbolt the bottom of the shock absorber.

3. Remove the shock absorber.

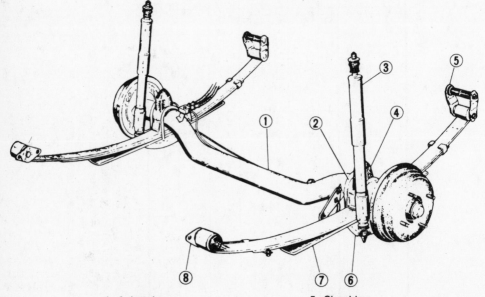

1. Axle tube
2. U-bolt
3. Shock absorber
4. Bumper rubber

5. Shackle
6. Spring seat
7. Leaf spring
8. Front pin

F10 station wagon rear suspension

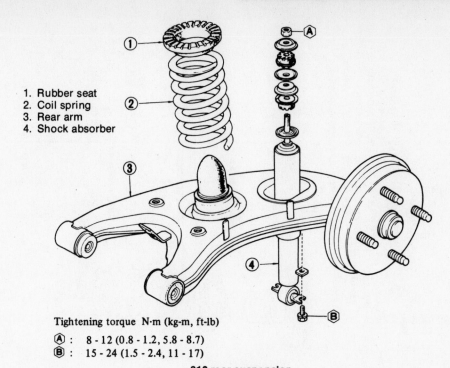

1. Rubber seat
2. Coil spring
3. Rear arm
4. Shock absorber

Tightening torque N·m (kg-m, ft-lb)

Ⓐ : 8 - 12 (0.8 - 1.2, 5.8 - 8.7)
Ⓑ : 15 - 24 (1.5 - 2.4, 11 - 17)

310 rear suspension

4. To install, reverse the removal procedures.

1983-86 Pulsar
Stanza 2WD Wagon

1. Raise and support the rear of the vehicle on jackstands.
2. Remove the upper nut and the lower mounting bolt form the shock absorber.
3. Remove the shock absorber from the vehicle.
4. To install, reverse the removal procedures. Torque the upper shock absorber nut to 78-104 in. lbs. and the lower shock absorber bolt to 51-65 ft. lbs.

TESTING

Shock absorbers require replacement if the vehicle fails to recover quickly (after a large bump is encountered), if there is a tendency for the vehicle to sway or if the suspension is overly susceptible to vibration.

A good way to test the shocks is to apply downward pressure to one corner of the vehicle until it is moving up and down for almost the full suspension travel, then release it and watch the recovery. If the vehicle bounces slightly about one more time and then comes to rest, the shocks are serviceable. If the vehicle goes on bouncing, the shocks require replacement.

MacPherson Struts

REMOVAL AND INSTALLATION

1987-88 Pulsar
1982-86 Stanza except Wagon

1. Raise and support the rear of the vehicle on jackstands.
2. Remove the wheel.
3. Disconnect the brake tube and parking brake cable.
4. If necessary, remove the brake assembly and wheel bearing.
5. Disconnect the parallel links and radius rod from the strut or knuckle.
6. Support the strut with a jackstand.
7. Remove the strut upper end nuts and then remove the strut from the vehicle.
8. Install the strut assembly to the vehicle and tighten the strut-to-parallel link nuts to 65-87 ft. lbs., the strut-to-radius rod nuts to 54-69 ft. lbs. and the strut-to-body nuts to 23-31 ft. lbs. On the Pulsar tighten the radius rod-to-knuckle nuts to 43-61 ft. lbs., the strut-to-knuckle and parallel link-to-knuckle bolts to 72-87 ft. lbs. and the strut-to-body nuts to 18-22 ft. lbs.
9. Reconnect the brake tube and parking brake cable.
10. Install the wheel.

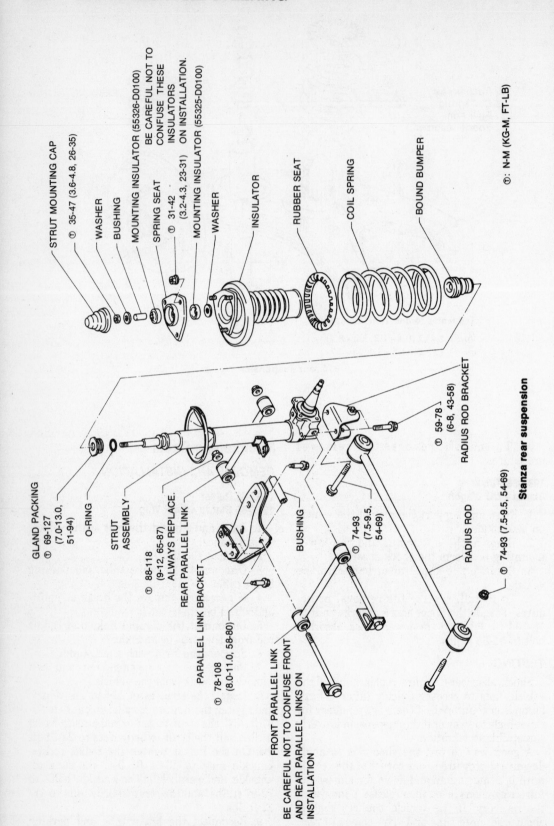

STRUT MOUNTING CAP

Ⓣ 35-47 (3.6-4.8, 26-35)

WASHER

BUSHING

MOUNTING INSULATOR (55326-D0100)

SPRING SEAT

Ⓣ 31-42 (3.2-4.3, 23-31)

MOUNTING INSULATOR (55325-D0100)

WASHER

INSULATOR

RUBBER SEAT

COIL SPRING

BOUND BUMPER

BE CAREFUL NOT TO CONFUSE THESE INSULATORS ON INSTALLATION.

Ⓣ: N-M (KG-M, FT-LB)

GLAND PACKING

Ⓣ 69-127 (7.0-13.0, 51-94)

O-RING

STRUT ASSEMBLY

Ⓣ 88-118 (9-12, 65-87) ALWAYS REPLACE.

REAR PARALLEL LINK

PARALLEL LINK BRACKET

Ⓣ 78-108 (8.0-11.0, 58-80)

FRONT PARALLEL LINK
BE CAREFUL NOT TO CONFUSE FRONT AND REAR PARALLEL LINKS ON INSTALLATION

BUSHING

Ⓣ 74-93 (7.5-9.5, 54-69)

RADIUS ROD

Ⓣ 74-93 (7.5-9.5, 54-69)

RADIUS ROD BRACKET

Ⓣ 59-78 (6-8, 43-58)

Stanza rear suspension

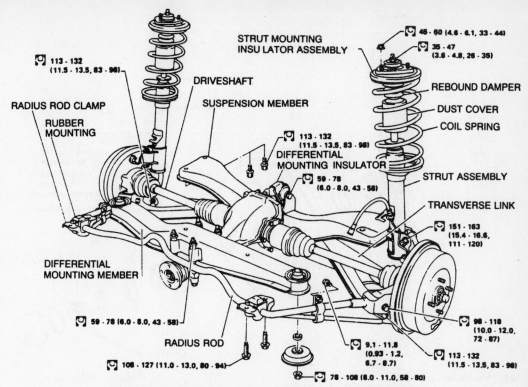

Typical MacPherson strut rear suspension—Stanza 4WD wagon

1987-88 Stanza except Wagon

1. Remove wheel and unclip the rear brake line at the strut. Unbolt and remove the brake assembly, wheel bearings and backing plate. Position the brake caliper out of the way and suspend it so as not to stress the brake line.
2. Remove the radius rod mounting bolt, radius rod mounting bracket.
3. Remove the 2 parallel link mounting bolts.
4. Remove the rear seat and parcel shelf.
5. Position a floor jack under the strut and raise it just enought to support the strut.
6. Remove the 3 upper strut mounting nuts and then lift out the strut.
7. Install the strut assembly in the vehicle. Tighten all bolts sufficiently to safely support the vehicle and then lower the car to the ground so it rests on its own weight. Tighten the upper strut mounting nuts to 23-31 ft. lbs., the radius rod bracket bolts to 43-58 ft. lbs. and the parallel link mounting bolts to 65-87 ft. lbs.
8. Install the brake caliper.
9. Install the backing plate, brake assembly and wheel bearings.
10. Install the wheel.

Stanza 4WD Wagon

1. Block the front wheels.
2. Raise and support the rear of the vehicle with jackstands.
3. Position a floor jack under the transverse

link on the side of the strut to be removed. Raise it just enough to support the strut.
4. Open the rear of the car and remove the 3 nuts that attach the top of the strut to the body.
5. Remove the wheel.
6. Remove the brake line from its bracket and position it out of the way.
7. Remove the 2 lower strut-to-knuckle mounting bolts.
8. Carefully lower the floor jack and remove the strut.
9. Install the strut assembly in the vehicle. Final tightening of the strut mounting bolts should take place with the wheels on the ground and the vehicle unladen. Tighten the upper strut-to-body nuts to 33-40 ft. lbs. (45-60 Nm). Tighten the lower strut-to-knuckle bolts to 111-120 ft. lbs. (151-163 Nm).
10. Connect the brake line.
11. Install the wheel.

OVERHAUL

Refer to Front Suspension section MacPherson Struts.

Rear Wheel Bearings

REMOVAL AND INSTALLATION

F10 and 310
Pulsar and Stanza (2WD)

1. Raise and support the vehicle safely.
2. Remove the rear wheels.

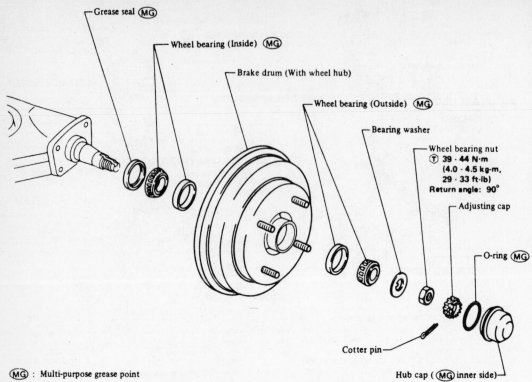

Wheel bearing installation—Pulsar (1983–86)

MG : Multi-purpose grease point

CAUTION:
- Tighten wheel bearing lock nut to the specified torque.
- Preload adjustment of wheel bearing not necessary.
- Axial end play: 0.05 mm (0.0020 in) or less

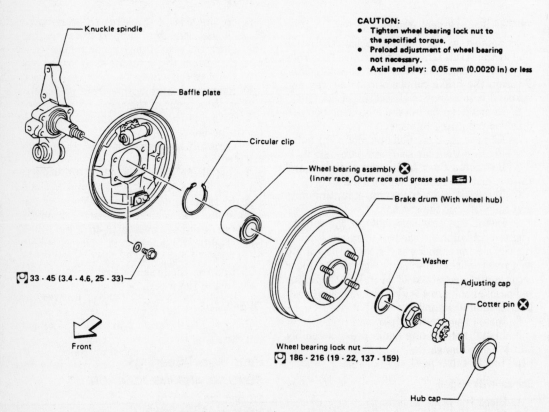

Wheel bearing installation—Pulsar (1987–88)

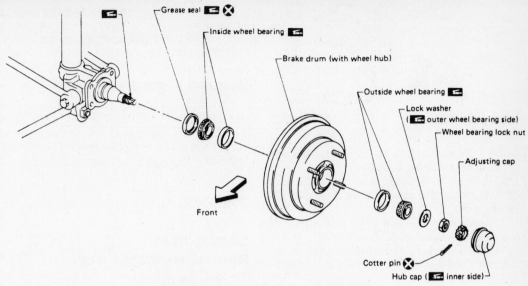

Rear wheel bearing installation—Stanza 2 WD

3. Work off center hub cap by using thin tool. If necessary tap around it with a soft hammer while removing.

4. Pry off cotter pin and take out adjusting cap and wheel bearing lock nut.

NOTE: *During removal, be careful to avoid damaging O ring in dust cap on 310 model.*

5. Remove drum with bearing inside.

NOTE: *On Pulsar models, a circular clip holds inner wheel bearing in brake hub.*

6. Remove bearing from drum using long brass drift pin or equivalent.

7. Install the inner bearing assembly in the brake drum and install the drum on the vehicle.

NOTE: *The rear wheel bearings must be adjusted after installation, if one piece bearing is used just the torque wheel bearing lock nut.*

8. Install the outer bearing assembly, wheel bearing lock nut, adjusting cap and cotter pin.

9. Install the center cap and the wheel assembly. To remove the wheel bearing races knock them out of the brake drum using a suitable brass punch.

ADJUSTMENT

1. Raise the rear of the vehicle and support it on jackstands.

2. Remove the wheel.

3. Remove the bearing dust cap with a pair of channel locks pliers.

4. Remove the cotter pin and retaining nut cap (if equipped), dispose of the cotter pin.

5. Tighten the wheel bearing nut to 18-22 ft. lbs. (F10) or to 29-33 ft. lbs. (all other models).

6. Rotate the drum back and forth a few revolutions to snug down the bearing.

7. On the F10, loosen the nut until it can be

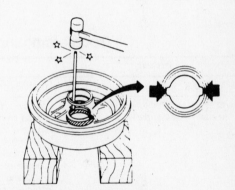

Removing wheel bearing race from drum

turned by hand, then tighten it with a hand held socket as far as it will go.

8. On the 310, Pulsar and Stanza, after turning the wheel, recheck the torque of the nut, then loosen it 90° from its position.

9. Install the retaining nut cap (if equipped). Align the cotter pin holes in the nut or nut cap with the hole in the spindle by turning the nut clockwise on the F10. On the 310, Pulsar and Stanza tighten the nut no more than 15° to align the holes.

10. Install the cotter pin, bend up its ends and install the dust cap.

Stanza (4WD)

1. Raise and support the vehicle safely.

2. Remove wheel bearing lock nut while depressing brake pedal.

3. Disconnect brake hydraulic line and parking brake cable.

4. Separate driveshaft from knuckle by slightly tapping it with suitable tool. Cover axle

Packing wheel bearing

boots with waste cloth so as not to damage them when removing driveshaft.

5. Remove all knuckle retaining bolts and nuts. Make a match mark before removing adjusting pin.

6. Remove knuckle and inner and outer circular clips. Remove wheel bearings.

NOTE: *To remove the wheel bearing races knock them out of the knuckle using a suitable brass punch.*

7. Install the knuckle with wheel bearings to the driveshaft.

8. Connect brake hydraulic line and parking brake cable.

9. Install the wheel bearing lock nut.

10. Bleed brakes.

Rear End Alignment

The camber is preset at the factory and cannot be adjusted; if the camber alignment is not within specifications, check the associated parts, then repair or replace them. The only adjustments that can be performed is toe-in.

STEERING

Steering Wheel

REMOVAL AND INSTALLATION

1. Position the wheels in the straight ahead direction. The steering wheel should be right side up and level.

Troubleshooting the Steering Column

Problem	Cause	Solution
Will not lock	• Lockbolt spring broken or defective	• Replace lock bolt spring
High effort (required to turn ignition key and lock cylinder)	• Lock cylinder defective	• Replace lock cylinder
	• Ignition switch defective	• Replace ignition switch
	• Rack preload spring broken or deformed	• Replace preload spring
	• Burr on lock sector, lock rack, housing, support or remote rod coupling	• Remove burr
	• Bent sector shaft	• Replace shaft
	• Defective lock rack	• Replace lock rack
	• Remote rod bent, deformed	• Replace rod
	• Ignition switch mounting bracket bent	• Straighten or replace
	• Distorted coupling slot in lock rack (tilt column)	• Replace lock rack
Will stick in "start"	• Remote rod deformed	• Straighten or replace
	• Ignition switch mounting bracket bent	• Straighten or replace
Key cannot be removed in "off-lock"	• Ignition switch is not adjusted correctly	• Adjust switch
	• Defective lock cylinder	• Replace lock cylinder
Lock cylinder can be removed without depressing retainer	• Lock cylinder with defective retainer	• Replace lock cylinder
	• Burr over retainer slot in housing cover or on cylinder retainer	• Remove burr
High effort on lock cylinder between "off" and "off-lock"	• Distorted lock rack	• Replace lock rack
	• Burr on tang of shift gate (automatic column)	• Remove burr
	• Gearshift linkage not adjusted	• Adjust linkage
Noise in column	• One click when in "off-lock" position and the steering wheel is moved (all except automatic column)	• Normal—lock bolt is seating
	• Coupling bolts not tightened	• Tighten pinch bolts

Troubleshooting the Steering Column (cont.)

Problem	Cause	Solution
Noise in column (cont.)	• Lack of grease on bearings or bearing surfaces	• Lubricate with chassis grease
	• Upper shaft bearing worn or broken	• Replace bearing assembly
	• Lower shaft bearing worn or broken	• Replace bearing. Check shaft and replace if scored.
	• Column not correctly aligned	• Align column
	• Coupling pulled apart	• Replace coupling
	• Broken coupling lower joint	• Repair or replace joint and align column
	• Steering shaft snap ring not seated	• Replace ring. Check for proper seating in groove.
	• Shroud loose on shift bowl. Housing loose on jacket—will be noticed with ignition in "off-lock" and when torque is applied to steering wheel.	• Position shroud over lugs on shift bowl. Tighten mounting screws.
High steering shaft effort	• Column misaligned	• Align column
	• Defective upper or lower bearing	• Replace as required
	• Tight steering shaft universal joint	• Repair or replace
	• Flash on I.D. of shift tube at plastic joint (tilt column only)	• Replace shift tube
	• Upper or lower bearing seized	• Replace bearings
Lash in mounted column assembly	• Column mounting bracket bolts loose	• Tighten bolts
	• Broken weld nuts on column jacket	• Replace column jacket
	• Column capsule bracket sheared	• Replace bracket assembly
	• Column bracket to column jacket mounting bolts loose	• Tighten to specified torque
	• Loose lock shoes in housing (tilt column only)	• Replace shoes
	• Loose pivot pins (tilt column only)	• Replace pivot pins and support
	• Loose lock shoe pin (tilt column only)	• Replace pin and housing
	• Loose support screws (tilt column only)	• Tighten screws
Housing loose (tilt column only)	• Excessive clearance between holes in support or housing and pivot pin diameters	• Replace pivot pins and support
	• Housing support-screws loose	• Tighten screws
Steering wheel loose—every other tilt position (tilt column only)	• Loose fit between lock shoe and lock shoe pivot pin	• Replace lock shoes and pivot pin
Steering column not locking in any tilt position (tilt column only)	• Lock shoe seized on pivot pin	• Replace lock shoes and pin
	• Lock shoe grooves have burrs or are filled with foreign material	• Clean or replace lock shoes
	• Lock shoe springs weak or broken	• Replace springs
Noise when tilting column (tilt column only)	• Upper tilt bumpers worn	• Replace tilt bumper
	• Tilt spring rubbing in housing	• Lubricate with chassis grease
One click when in "off-lock" position and the steering wheel is moved	• Seating of lock bolt	• None. Click is normal characteristic sound produced by lock bolt as it seats.
High shift effort (automatic and tilt column only)	• Column not correctly aligned	• Align column
	• Lower bearing not aligned correctly	• Assemble correctly
	• Lack of grease on seal or lower bearing areas	• Lubricate with chassis grease
Improper transmission shifting—automatic and tilt column only	• Sheared shift tube joint	• Replace shift tube
	• Improper transmission gearshift linkage adjustment	• Adjust linkage
	• Loose lower shift lever	• Replace shift tube

Troubleshooting the Turn Signal Switch

Problem	Cause	Solution
Turn signal will not cancel	• Loose switch mounting screws • Switch or anchor bosses broken • Broken, missing or out of position detent, or cancelling spring	• Tighten screws • Replace switch • Reposition springs or replace switch as required
Turn signal difficult to operate	• Turn signal lever loose • Switch yoke broken or distorted • Loose or misplaced springs • Foreign parts and/or materials in switch • Switch mounted loosely	• Tighten mounting screws • Replace switch • Reposition springs or replace switch • Remove foreign parts and/or material • Tighten mounting screws
Turn signal will not indicate lane change	• Broken lane change pressure pad or spring hanger • Broken, missing or misplaced lane change spring • Jammed wires	• Replace switch • Replace or reposition as required • Loosen mounting screws, reposition wires and retighten screws
Turn signal will not stay in turn position	• Foreign material or loose parts impeding movement of switch yoke • Defective switch	• Remove material and/or parts • Replace switch
Hazard switch cannot be pulled out	• Foreign material between hazard support cancelling leg and yoke	• Remove foreign material. No foreign material impeding function of hazard switch—replace turn signal switch.
No turn signal lights	• Inoperative turn signal flasher • Defective or blown fuse • Loose chassis to column harness connector • Disconnect column to chassis connector. Connect new switch to chassis and operate switch by hand. If vehicle lights now operate normally, signal switch is inoperative • If vehicle lights do not operate, check chassis wiring for opens, grounds, etc.	• Replace turn signal flasher • Replace fuse • Connect securely • Replace signal switch • Repair chassis wiring as required
Instrument panel turn indicator lights on but not flashing	• Burned out or damaged front or rear turn signal bulb • If vehicle lights do not operate, check light sockets for high resistance connections, the chassis wiring for opens, grounds, etc. • Inoperative flasher • Loose chassis to column harness connection • Inoperative turn signal switch • To determine if turn signal switch is defective, substitute new switch into circuit and operate switch by hand. If the vehicle's lights operate normally, signal switch is inoperative.	• Replace bulb • Repair chassis wiring as required • Replace flasher • Connect securely • Replace turn signal switch • Replace turn signal switch
Stop light not on when turn indicated	• Loose column to chassis connection • Disconnect column to chassis connector. Connect new switch into system without removing old.	• Connect securely • Replace signal switch

Troubleshooting the Turn Signal Switch (cont.)

Problem	Cause	Solution
Stop light not on when turn indicated (cont.)	Operate switch by hand. If brake lights work with switch in the turn position, signal switch is defective.	
	• If brake lights do not work, check connector to stop light sockets for grounds, opens, etc.	• Repair connector to stop light circuits using service manual as guide
Turn indicator panel lights not flashing	• Burned out bulbs • High resistance to ground at bulb socket • Opens, ground in wiring harness from front turn signal bulb socket to indicator lights	• Replace bulbs • Replace socket • Locate and repair as required
Turn signal lights flash very slowly	• High resistance ground at light sockets • Incorrect capacity turn signal flasher or bulb • If flashing rate is still extremely slow, check chassis wiring harness from the connector to light sockets for high resistance • Loose chassis to column harness connection • Disconnect column to chassis connector. Connect new switch into system without removing old. Operate switch by hand. If flashing occurs at normal rate, the signal switch is defective.	• Repair high resistance grounds at light sockets • Replace turn signal flasher or bulb • Locate and repair as required • Connect securely • Replace turn signal switch
Hazard signal lights will not flash—turn signal functions normally	• Blow fuse • Inoperative hazard warning flasher • Loose chassis-to-column harness connection • Disconnect column to chassis connector. Connect new switch into system without removing old. Depress the hazard warning lights. If they now work normally, turn signal switch is defective. • If lights do not flash, check wiring harness "K" lead for open between hazard flasher and connector. If open, fuse block is defective	• Replace fuse • Replace hazard warning flasher in fuse panel • Conect securely • Replace turn signal switch • Repair or replace brown wire or connector as required

Troubleshooting the Ignition Switch

Problem	Cause	Solution
Ignition switch electrically inoperative	• Loose or defective switch connector • Feed wire open (fusible link) • Defective ignition switch	• Tighten or replace connector • Repair or replace • Replace ignition switch
Engine will not crank	• Ignition switch not adjusted properly	• Adjust switch
Ignition switch wil not actuate mechanically	• Defective ignition switch • Defective lock sector • Defective remote rod	• Replace switch • Replace lock sector • Replace remote rod
Ignition switch cannot be adjusted correctly	• Remote rod deformed	• Repair, straighten or replace

Troubleshooting the Manual Steering Gear

Problem	Cause	Solution
Hard or erratic steering	• Incorrect tire pressure	• Inflate tires to recommended pressures
	• Insufficient or incorrect lubrication	• Lubricate as required (refer to Maintenance Section)
	• Suspension, or steering linkage parts damaged or misaligned	• Repair or replace parts as necessary
	• Improper front wheel alignment	• Adjust incorrect wheel alignment angles
	• Incorrect steering gear adjustment	• Adjust steering gear
	• Sagging springs	• Replace springs
Play or looseness in steering	• Steering wheel loose	• Inspect shaft spines and repair as necessary. Tighten attaching nut and stake in place.
	• Steering linkage or attaching parts loose or worn	• Tighten, adjust, or replace faulty components
	• Pitman arm loose	• Inspect shaft splines and repair as necessary. Tighten attaching nut and stake in place
	• Steering gear attaching bolts loose	• Tighten bolts
	• Loose or worn wheel bearings	• Adjust or replace bearings
	• Steering gear adjustment incorrect or parts badly worn	• Adjust gear or replace defective parts
Wheel shimmy or tramp	• Improper tire pressure	• Inflate tires to recommended pressures
	• Wheels, tires, or brake rotors out-of-balance or out-of-round	• Inspect and replace or balance parts
	• Inoperative, worn, or loose shock absorbers or mounting parts	• Repair or replace shocks or mountings
	• Loose or worn steering or suspension parts	• Tighten or replace as necessary
	• Loose or worn wheel bearings	• Adjust or replace bearings
	• Incorrect steering gear adjustments	• Adjust steering gear
	• Incorrect front wheel alignment	• Correct front wheel alignment
Tire wear	• Improper tire pressure	• Inflate tires to recommended pressures
	• Failure to rotate tires	• Rotate tires
	• Brakes grabbing	• Adjust or repair brakes
	• Incorrect front wheel alignment	• Align incorrect angles
	• Broken or damaged steering and suspension parts	• Repair or replace defective parts
	• Wheel runout	• Replace faulty wheel
	• Excessive speed on turns	• Make driver aware of conditions
Vehicle leads to one side	• Improper tire pressures	• Inflate tires to recommended pressures
	• Front tires with uneven tread depth, wear pattern, or different cord design (i.e., one bias ply and one belted or radial tire on front wheels)	• Install tires of same cord construction and reasonably even tread depth, design, and wear pattern
	• Incorrect front wheel alignment	• Align incorrect angles
	• Brakes dragging	• Adjust or repair brakes
	• Pulling due to uneven tire construction	• Replace faulty tire

Troubleshooting the Power Steering Gear

Problem	Cause	Solution
Hissing noise in steering gear	• There is some noise in all power steering systems. One of the most common is a hissing sound most evident at standstill parking. There is no relationship between this noise and performance of the steering. Hiss may be expected when steering wheel is at end of travel or when slowly turning at standstill.	• Slight hiss is normal and in no way affects steering. Do not replace valve unless hiss is extremely objectionable. A replacement valve will also exhibit slight noise and is not always a cure. Investigate clearance around flexible coupling rivets. Be sure steering shaft and gear are aligned so flexible coupling rotates in a flat plane and is not distorted as shaft rotates. Any metal-to-metal contacts through flexible coupling will transmit valve hiss into passenger compartment through the steering column.
Rattle or chuckle noise in steering gear	• Gear loose on frame	• Check gear-to-frame mounting screws. Tighten screws to 88 N·m (65 foot pounds) torque.
	• Steering linkage looseness	• Check linkage pivot points for wear. Replace if necessary.
	• Pressure hose touching other parts of car	• Adjust hose position. Do not bend tubing by hand.
	• Loose pitman shaft over center adjustment	• Adjust to specifications
	NOTE: A slight rattle may occur on turns because of increased clearance off the "high point." This is normal and clearance must not be reduced below specified limits to eliminate this slight rattle.	
	• Loose pitman arm	• Tighten pitman arm nut to specifications
Squawk noise in steering gear when turning or recovering from a turn	• Damper O-ring on valve spool cut	• Replace damper O-ring
Poor return of steering wheel to center	• Tires not properly inflated	• Inflate to specified pressure
	• Lack of lubrication in linkage and ball joints	• Lube linkage and ball joints
	• Lower coupling flange rubbing against steering gear adjuster plug	• Loosen pinch bolt and assemble properly
	• Steering gear to column misalignment	• Align steering column
	• Improper front wheel alignment	• Check and adjust as necessary
	• Steering linkage binding	• Replace pivots
	• Ball joints binding	• Replace ball joints
	• Steering wheel rubbing against housing	• Align housing
	• Tight or frozen steering shaft bearings	• Replace bearings
	• Sticking or plugged valve spool	• Remove and clean or replace valve
	• Steering gear adjustments over specifications	• Check adjustment with gear out of car. Adjust as required.
	• Kink in return hose	• Replace hose
Car leads to one side or the other (keep in mind road condition and wind. Test car in both directions on flat road)	• Front end misaligned	• Adjust to specifications
	• Unbalanced steering gear valve	• Replace valve
	NOTE: If this is cause, steering effort will be very light in direction of lead and normal or heavier in opposite direction	

Troubleshooting the Power Steering Gear (cont.)

Problem	Cause	Solution
Momentary increase in effort when turning wheel fast to right or left	• Low oil level • Pump belt slipping • High internal leakage	• Add power steering fluid as required • Tighten or replace belt • Check pump pressure. (See pressure test)
Steering wheel surges or jerks when turning with engine running especially during parking	• Low oil level • Loose pump belt • Steering linkage hitting engine oil pan at full turn • Insufficient pump pressure • Pump flow control valve sticking	• Fill as required • Adjust tension to specification • Correct clearance • Check pump pressure. (See pressure test). Replace relief valve if defective. • Inspect for varnish or damage, replace if necessary
Excessive wheel kickback or loose steering	• Air in system • Steering gear loose on frame • Steering linkage joints worn enough to be loose • Worn poppet valve • Loose thrust bearing preload adjustment • Excessive overcenter lash	• Add oil to pump reservoir and bleed by operating steering. Check hose connectors for proper torque and adjust as required. • Tighten attaching screws to specified torque • Replace loose pivots • Replace poppet valve • Adjust to specification with gear out of vehicle • Adjust to specification with gear out of car
Hard steering or lack of assist	• Loose pump belt • Low oil level **NOTE:** Low oil level will also result in excessive pump noise • Steering gear to column misalignment • Lower coupling flange rubbing against steering gear adjuster plug • Tires not properly inflated	• Adjust belt tension to specification • Fill to proper level. If excessively low, check all lines and joints for evidence of external leakage. Tighten loose connectors. • Align steering column • Loosen pinch bolt and assemble properly • Inflate to recommended pressure
Foamy milky power steering fluid, low fluid level and possible low pressure	• Air in the fluid, and loss of fluid due to internal pump leakage causing overflow	• Check for leak and correct. Bleed system. Extremely cold temperatures will cause system aeration should the oil level be low. If oil level is correct and pump still foams, remove pump from vehicle and separate reservoir from housing. Check welsh plug and housing for cracks. If plug is loose or housing is cracked, replace housing.
Low pressure due to steering pump	• Flow control valve stuck or inoperative • Pressure plate not flat against cam ring	• Remove burrs or dirt or replace. Flush system. • Correct
Low pressure due to steering gear	• Pressure loss in cylinder due to worn piston ring or badly worn housing bore • Leakage at valve rings, valve body-to-worm seal	• Remove gear from car for disassembly and inspection of ring and housing bore • Remove gear from car for disassembly and replace seals

Troubleshooting the Power Steering Pump

Problem	Cause	Solution
Chirp noise in steering pump	• Loose belt	• Adjust belt tension to specification
Belt squeal (particularly noticeable at full wheel travel and stand still parking)	• Loose belt	• Adjust belt tension to specification
Growl noise in steering pump	• Excessive back pressure in hoses or steering gear caused by restriction	• Locate restriction and correct. Replace part if necessary.
Growl noise in steering pump (particularly noticeable at stand still parking)	• Scored pressure plates, thrust plate or rotor • Extreme wear of cam ring	• Replace parts and flush system • Replace parts
Groan noise in steering pump	• Low oil level • Air in the oil. Poor pressure hose connection.	• Fill reservoir to proper level • Tighten connector to specified torque. Bleed system by operating steering from right to left—full turn.
Rattle noise in steering pump	• Vanes not installed properly • Vanes sticking in rotor slots	• Install properly • Free up by removing burrs, varnish, or dirt
Swish noise in steering pump	• Defective flow control valve	• Replace part
Whine noise in steering pump	• Pump shaft bearing scored	• Replace housing and shaft. Flush system.
Hard steering or lack of assist	• Loose pump belt • Low oil level in reservoir **NOTE:** Low oil level will also result in excessive pump noise • Steering gear to column misalignment • Lower coupling flange rubbing against steering gear adjuster plug • Tires not properly inflated	• Adjust belt tension to specification • Fill to proper level. If excessively low, check all lines and joints for evidence of external leakage. Tighten loose connectors. • Align steering column • Loosen pinch bolt and assemble properly • Inflate to recommended pressure
Foaming milky power steering fluid, low fluid level and possible low pressure	• Air in the fluid, and loss of fluid due to internal pump leakage causing overflow	• Check for leaks and correct. Bleed system. Extremely cold temperatures will cause system aeration should the oil level be low. If oil level is correct and pump still foams, remove pump from vehicle and separate reservoir from body. Check welsh plug and body for cracks. If plug is loose or body is cracked, replace body.
Low pump pressure	• Flow control valve stuck or inoperative • Pressure plate not flat against cam ring	• Remove burrs or dirt or replace. Flush system. • Correct
Momentary increase in effort when turning wheel fast to right or left	• Low oil level in pump • Pump belt slipping • High internal leakage	• Add power steering fluid as required • Tighten or replace belt • Check pump pressure. (See pressure test)
Steering wheel surges or jerks when turning with engine running especially during parking	• Low oil level • Loose pump belt • Steering linkage hitting engine oil pan at full turn • Insufficient pump pressure	• Fill as required • Adjust tension to specification • Correct clearance • Check pump pressure. (See pressure test). Replace flow control valve if defective.

Troubleshooting the Power Steering Pump (cont.)

Problem	Cause	Solution
Steering wheel surges or jerks when turning with engine running especially during parking (cont.)	• Sticking flow control valve	• Inspect for varnish or damage, replace if necessary
Excessive wheel kickback or loose steering	• Air in system	• Add oil to pump reservoir and bleed by operating steering. Check hose connectors for proper torque and adjust as required.
Low pump pressure	• Extreme wear of cam ring • Scored pressure plate, thrust plate, or rotor • Vanes not installed properly • Vanes sticking in rotor slots • Cracked or broken thrust or pressure plate	• Replace parts. Flush system. • Replace parts. Flush system. • Install properly • Freeup by removing burrs, varnish, or dirt • Replace part

2. Disconnect the battery ground cable.

3. Some models have countersunk screws on the back of the steering wheel, remove the screws and pull off the horn pad.

NOTE: *Some models have a horn wire running from the pad to the steering wheel; disconnect it.*

4. Remove the rest of the horn switching mechanism, noting the relative location of the parts. Remove the mechanism only if it hinders subsequent wheel removal procedures.

5. Matchmark the top of the steering column shaft and the steering wheel flange.

6. Remove the attaching nut. Using the Steering Wheel Remover tool ST27180001, pull the steering wheel from the steering column.

NOTE: *Do not strike the shaft with a hammer, which may cause the column to collapse.*

7. Install the steering wheel in the reverse order of removal, aligning the punch marks; DO NOT drive or hammer the wheel.

8. Tighten the steering wheel nut to 14-18 ft. lbs. (F10), 22-25 ft. lbs. (310), 29-40 ft. lbs. (Pulsar) and 27-38 ft. lbs. (Stanza).

9. Reinstall the horn button, pad or ring.

Use a puller to remove the steering wheel

Turn Signal Switch
REMOVAL AND INSTALLATION

On some later models, the turn signal switch is part of a combination switch. The whole unit is removed together.

1984 and Later, except Pulsar
1987-88 Stanza

1. Refer to the Steering Wheel, Removal and Installation procedures, in this section and remove the steering wheel.

2. Remove the steering column cover(s).

3. Disconnect the electrical connectors from the switch.

4. Remove the retaining screws and the switch from the steering column.

5. To install, reverse the removal procedures.

NOTE: *Many models have turn signal switches that have a tab which must fit into a hole in the steering shaft in order for the system to return the switch to the neutral position after the turn has been made. Be sure to align the tab and the hole when installing.*

1984 and Later Pulsar

1. Disconnect the negative battery terminal.

2. Remove the steering column covers.

3. Disconnect the electrical connector from the turn signal side of the combination switch.

4. Remove the retaining screws and separate the turn signal switch from the combination switch.

5. To install, reverse the removal procedures.

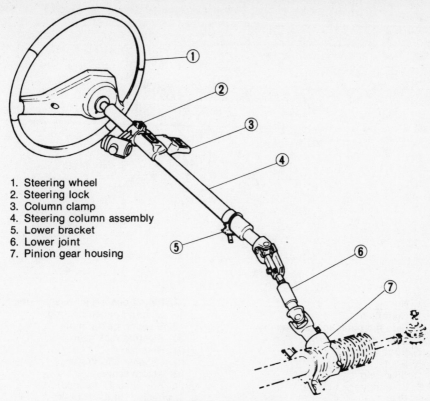

1. Steering wheel
2. Steering lock
3. Column clamp
4. Steering column assembly
5. Lower bracket
6. Lower joint
7. Pinion gear housing

F10 and 310 steering column

Steering Lock/Ignition Lock
REMOVAL AND INSTALLATION

The steering lock/ignition switch assembly is attached to the steering column by special screws whose heads shear off on installation. The screws must be drilled out to remove the assembly.

1. Refer to the Steering Wheel, Removal and Installation procedures, in this section and remove the steering wheel.

2. Remove the steering column cover(s).

3. Using a drill, drill out the self-shear type screws of the steering lock retainer.

NOTE: *The F10 models use only 2 self-shearing screws to hold the steering lock onto the steering column. All other models use 2 self-shearing screws and 2 regular screws.*

4. Remove the screws and the steering lock from the steering column.

5. To install, use new self-shearing screws and reverse the removal procedures. Torque the self-shearing type screws until the heads break off.

Tie Rod Ends (Steering Side Rods)
REMOVAL AND INSTALLATION

1. Raise the front of the vehicle and support it on jackstands. Remove the wheel.

2. Locate the faulty tie rod end. It will have a lot of play in it and the dust cover will probably be ripped.

3. Remove the cotter pin and the tie rod ball joint stud nut. Note the position of the steering linkage.

4. Loosen the tie rod-to-steering gear locknut.

5. Using the Ball Joint Remover tool HT72520000, remove the tie rod ball joint from the strut or the steering knuckle.

6. Loosen the locknut and remove the tie rod end from the tie rod, counting the number of turns it takes to completely free it.

7. Install the new tie rod end, turning it in exactly as far as you screwed out the old one. Make sure it is correctly positioned in relationship to the steering linkage.

8. Fit the ball joint and nut, tighten them and install a new cotter pin. Torque the ball

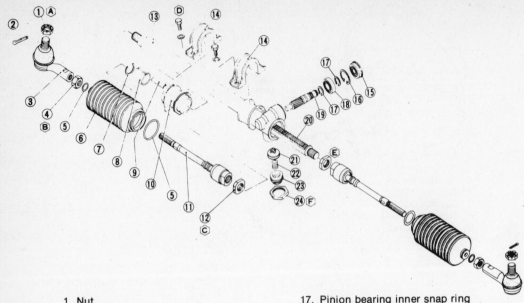

1. Nut
2. Cotter pin
3. Side rod outer socket assembly
4. Lock nut
5. Boot clamp
6. Boot
7. Snap ring
8. Steering rack bushing
9. Plate
10. Steering gear mount
11. Side rod inner socket assembly
12. Lock nut
13. Steering gear housing assembly
14. Steering clamp
15. Oil seal
16. Pinion bearing outer snap ring

17. Pinion bearing inner snap ring
18. Steering pinion bearing
19. Steering gear pinion
20. Steering rack gear
21. Retainer
22. Retainer spring
23. Adjust screw
24. Adjust screw lock nut

Tightening torque:N-m (kg-m, ft-lb)
Ⓐ 54-64 (5.5-6.5, 40-47)
Ⓑ 37-46 (3.8-4.7, 27-34)
Ⓒ 78-98 (8-10, 58-72)
Ⓓ 22-33 (2.2-3.4, 16-25)
Ⓔ 78-98 (8-10, 58-72)
Ⓕ 39-59 (4-6, 29-43)

F10 and 310 manual steering gear

joint stud nut to 40-47 ft. lbs. (F10 and 310), 22-29 ft. lbs. (Stanza) or 22-36 ft. lbs. (Pulsar) and the ball joint-to-tie rod end locknut to 27-34 ft. lbs.

NOTE: *Before finally tightening the tie rod lock nut or clamp, adjust the toe-in of the vehicle. See section under Front Suspension.*

Manual Steering Gear

REMOVAL AND INSTALLATION

F10 and 310

1. Raise and support the car on jackstands.
2. Remove the steering joint cover and remove the steering column-to-lower joint bolts.
3. Remove the lower joint-to-steering pinion gear bolt and disconnect the joint from the gear.
4. Remove the tie rod ball stud nuts.
5. Using the Ball Joint Remover tool HT72520000, remove the tie rod ball studs.
6. Unclamp and remove the steering gear.
7. Install the steering gear assembly to the

vehicle. Torque the tie rod-to-knuckle arm nut to 40-47 ft. lbs., the steering gear-to-frame clamp bolts to 16-25 ft. lbs., the lower joint-to-pinion gear bolt to 17-22 ft. lbs. and the lower joint-to-steering column bolt to 17-22 ft. lbs.
8. Check the wheel alignment.

Pulsar and Stanza

1. Raise and support the car on jackstands.
2. Using the Ball Joint Remover tool HT72520000, remove the tie rod from the knuckle.
3. Loosen, but do not remove, the steering gear mounting bolts.
4. Remove the steering column lower joint.
5. Unbolt and remove the gear.
6. Install the steering gear assembly to the vehicle. Torque the tie rod-to-steering knuckle nut to 22-29 ft. lbs. (Stanza) or 26-35 ft. lbs. (Pulsar), the steering gear-to-frame clamp bolts to 43-58 ft. lbs., the lower joint-to-pinion gear bolt to 23-31 ft. lbs. (Stanza) or 22-29 ft. lbs.

(Pulsar) and the lower joint-to-steering column bolt to 23-31 ft. lbs. (Stanza) or 22-29 ft. lbs. (Pulsar).

NOTE: *When installing the lower steering joint to the steering gear, make sure that the wheels are aligned with the vehicle and the steering joint slot is aligned with the steering gear cap or spacer mark.*

Power Steering Gear

REMOVAL AND INSTALLATION

310

1. Raise and support the front of the car on jackstands.
2. Remove the lower joint cover and loosen, but do not remove the bolts attaching the lower joint at the column.
3. Unbolt the lower joint from the steering pinion gear.
4. Using the Ball Joint Remover tool HT72520000, remove the tie rod from the knuckle.
5. Disconnect the hoses at the gear.
6. Unbolt and remove the gear linkage.
7. Install the power steering gear assembly to the vehicle. Torque the side rod-to-knuckle arm nut to 40-47 ft. lbs., the steering gear clamp bolts to 16-25 ft. lbs., the steering gear-to-sub frame bolts to 16-25 ft. lbs., the lower joint-to-pinion gear bolt to 17-22 ft. lbs., the lower joint-to-steering column bolt to 17-22 ft.

lbs. and the power steering hoses-to-steering gear to 36-51 ft. lbs.

8. Bleed the power steering system and check the wheel alignment.

Pulsar

1. Raise and support the car on jackstands.
2. Disconnect the hose clamp and hose at the steering gear. Disconnect the flare nut and the tube at the steering gear, then drain the fluid from the gear.
3. Using the Ball Joint Remover tool HT72520000, remove the tie rod from the knuckle.
4. Place a floor jack under the transaxle and support it.
5. Remove the exhaust tube and the the rear engine mount.
6. Remove the steering column lower joint.
7. Unbolt and remove the steering gear unit and the linkage.
8. Install the power steering gear assembly to the vehicle. Torque the tie rod-to-steering knuckle nut to 26-36 ft. lbs., the steering gear-to-frame clamp bolts to 43-58 ft. lbs., the lower joint-to-pinion gear bolt to 22-29 ft. lbs., the lower joint-to-steering column bolt to 22-29 ft. lbs., the low pressure hose clip bolt to 9-17 inch lbs. and the high pressure hose-to-gear to 11-18 ft. lbs.
9. Bleed the power steering system and check the wheel alignment.

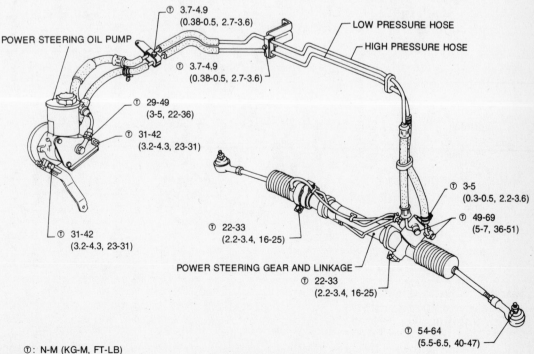

310 power steering gear

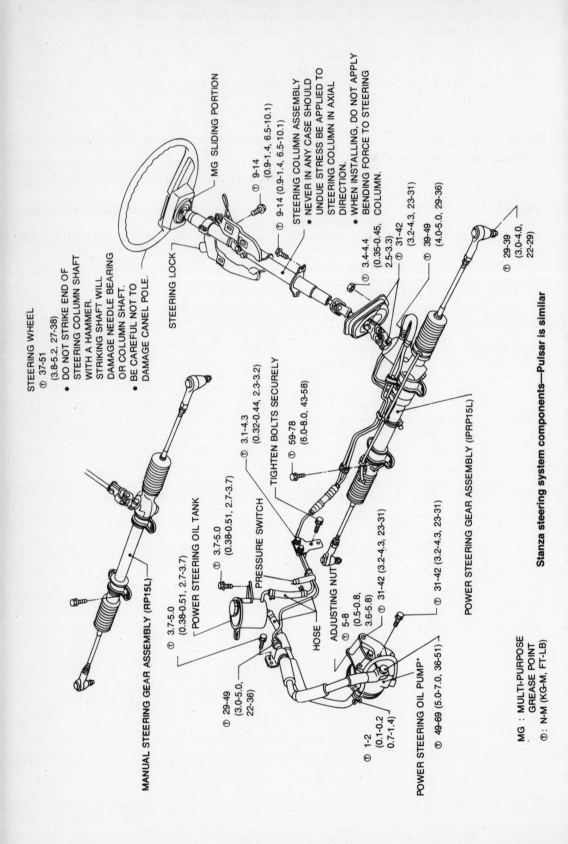

STEERING WHEEL
Ⓣ 37-51
(3.8-5.2, 27-38)
- DO NOT STRIKE END OF STEERING COLUMN SHAFT WITH A HAMMER. STRIKING SHAFT WILL DAMAGE NEEDLE BEARING OR COLUMN SHAFT.
- BE CAREFUL NOT TO DAMAGE CANEL POLE.

STEERING LOCK

MG SLIDING PORTION

Ⓣ 9-14
(0.9-1.4, 6.5-10.1)

Ⓣ 9-14 (0.9-1.4, 6.5-10.1)

STEERING COLUMN ASSEMBLY
- NEVER IN ANY CASE SHOULD UNDUE STRESS BE APPLIED TO STEERING COLUMN IN AXIAL DIRECTION.
- WHEN INSTALLING, DO NOT APPLY BENDING FORCE TO STEERING COLUMN.

Ⓣ 3.4-4.4
(0.35-0.45, 2.5-3.3)

Ⓣ 31-42 (3.2-4.3, 23-31)

Ⓣ 39-49 (4.0-5.0, 29-36)

Ⓣ 29-39 (3.0-4.0, 22-29)

MANUAL STEERING GEAR ASSEMBLY (RP15L)

Ⓣ 3.7-5.0 (0.38-0.51, 2.7-3.7)

POWER STEERING OIL TANK

Ⓣ 3.7-5.0 (0.38-0.51, 2.7-3.7)

Ⓣ 3.1-4.3 (0.32-0.44, 2.3-3.2)

PRESSURE SWITCH

TIGHTEN BOLTS SECURELY

Ⓣ 59-78 (6.0-8.0, 43-58)

HOSE

ADJUSTING NUT

Ⓣ 5-8 (0.5-0.8, 3.6-5.8)

Ⓣ 31-42 (3.2-4.3, 23-31)

POWER STEERING GEAR ASSEMBLY (IPRP15L)

Ⓣ 29-49 (3.0-5.0, 22-36)

Ⓣ 1-2 (0.1-0.2 0.7-1.4)

POWER STEERING OIL PUMP*

Ⓣ 49-69 (5.0-7.0, 36-51)

MG : MULTI-PURPOSE GREASE POINT
Ⓣ : N-M (KG-M, FT-LB)

Stanza steering system components—Pulsar is similar

NOTE: *When installing the lower steering joint to the steering gear, make sure that the wheels are aligned with the vehicle and the steering joint slot is aligned with the steering gear cap or spacer mark.*

Stanza

1. Raise and support the car on jackstands.
2. Disconnect the hose clamp and hose at the steering gear. Disconnect the flare nut and the tube at the steering gear, then drain the fluid from the gear.
3. Using the Ball Joint Remover tool HT72520000, remove the tie rod from the knuckle.
4. Loosen, but do not remove, the steering gear mounting bolts.
5. Remove the steering column lower joint.
6. Unbolt and remove the steering gear.
7. Install the power steering gear assembly to the vehicle. Torque the tie rod-to-steering knuckle nut to 22-29 ft. lbs., the steering gear-to-frame clamp bolts to 43-58 ft. lbs., the lower joint-to-pinion gear bolt to 23-31 ft. lbs., the lower joint-to-steering column bolt to 23-31 ft. lbs., the low pressure hose clip bolt to 9-17 inch lbs. and the high pressure hose-to-gear to 29-36 ft. lbs.
8. Bleed the power steering system and check the wheel alignment.
NOTE: *When installing the lower steering joint to the steering gear, make sure that the wheels are aligned with the vehicle and the steering joint slot is aligned with the steering gear cap or spacer mark.*

Power Steering Pump
REMOVAL AND INSTALLATION

1. Remove the hoses at the pump and plug and openings shut to prevent contamination. Position the disconnected lines in a raised attitude to prevent leakage.
2. Loosen the power steering pump drive belt adjuster and the drive belt.
3. Loosen the retaining bolts, then remove the braces and the pump from the vehicle.
4. To install, reverse the removal procedures. Adjust the belt tension and bleed the power steering system.

BLEEDING THE POWER STEERING SYSTEM

1. Fill the pump reservoir and allow to remain undisturbed for a few minutes.
2. Raise the car until the front wheels are clear of the ground.
3. With the engine off, quickly turn the wheels right and left several times, lightly contacting the stops.
4. Add fluid if necessary.
5. Start the engine and let it idle until it reaches operating temperatures.
6. Repeat Steps 3 and 4 with the engine idling.
NOTE: *Do not allow the steering linkage to contact the stops for any longer than 15 seconds, with the engine running.*
7. Stop the engine, lower the car until the wheels just touch the ground. Start the engine, allow it to idle and turn the wheels back and forth several times. Check the fluid level and refill if necessary.

Brakes

9

BASIC OPERATING PRINCIPLES

Hydraulic systems are used to actuate the brakes of all automobiles. The system transports the power required to force the frictional surfaces of the braking system together from the pedal to the individual brake units at each wheel. A hydraulic system is used for two reasons.

First, fluid under pressure can be carried to all parts of an automobile by small pipes and flexible hoses without taking up a significant amount of room or posing routing problems.

Second, a great mechanical advantage can be given to the brake pedal end of the system, and the foot pressure required to actuate the brakes can be reduced by making the surface area of the master cylinder pistons smaller than that of any of the pistons in the wheel cylinders or calipers.

The master cylinder consists of a fluid reservoir and a double cylinder and piston assembly. Double type master cylinders are designed to separate the front and rear braking systems hydraulically in case of a leak.

Steel lines carry the brake fluid to a point on the vehicle's frame near each of the vehicle's wheels. The fluid is then carried to the calipers and wheel cylinders by flexible tubes in order to allow for suspension and steering movements.

In drum brake systems, each wheel cylinder contains two pistons, one at either end, which push outward in opposite directions.

In disc brake systems, the cylinders are part of the calipers. One cylinder in each caliper is used to force the brake pads against the disc.

All pistons employ some type of seal, usually made of rubber, to minimize fluid leakage. A rubber dust boot seals the outer end of the cylinder against dust and dirt. The boot fits around the outer end of the piston on disc brake calipers, and around the brake actuating rod on wheel cylinders.

The hydraulic system operates as follows: When at rest, the entire system, from the piston(s) in the master cylinder to those in the wheel cylinders or calipers, is full of brake fluid. Upon application of the brake pedal, fluid trapped in front of the master cylinder piston(s) is forced through the lines to the wheel cylinders. Here, it forces the pistons outward, in the case of drum brakes, and inward toward the disc, in the case of disc brakes. The motion of the pistons is opposed by return springs mounted outside the cylinders in drum brakes, and by spring seals, in disc brakes.

Upon release of the brake pedal, a spring located inside the master cylinder immediately returns the master cylinder pistons to the normal position. The pistons contain check valves and the master cylinder has compensating ports drilled in it. These are uncovered as the pistons reach their normal position. The piston check valves allow fluid to flow toward the wheel cylinders or calipers as the pistons withdraw. Then, as the return springs force the brake pads or shoes into the released position, the excess fluid reservoir through the compensating ports. It is during the time the pedal is in the released position that any fluid that has leaked out of the system will be replaced through the compensating ports.

Dual circuit master cylinders employ two pistons, located one behind the other, in the same cylinder. The primary piston is actuated directly by mechanical linkage from the brake pedal through the power booster. The secondary piston is actuated by fluid trapped between the two pistons. If a leak develops in front of the secondary piston, it moves forward until it bottoms against the front of the master cylinder, and the fluid trapped between the pistons will operate the rear brakes. If the rear brakes develop a leak, the primary piston will move forward until direct contact with the secondary piston takes place, and it will force the secondary piston to actuate the front brakes. In either case, the brake pedal moves farther when the brakes are applied, and less braking power is available.

All dual circuit systems use a switch to warn the driver when only half of the brake system is operational. This switch is located in a valve body which is mounted on the firewall or the frame below the master cylinder. A hydraulic piston receives pressure from both circuits, each circuit's pressure being applied to one end of the piston. When the pressures are in balance, the piston remains stationary. When one circuit has a leak, however, the greater pressure in that circuit during application of the brakes will push the piston to one side, closing the switch and activating the brake warning light.

In disc brake systems, this valve body also contains a metering valve and, in some cases, a proportioning valve. The metering valve keeps pressure from traveling to the disc brakes on the front wheels until the brake shoes on the rear wheels have contacted the drums, ensuring that the front brakes will never be used alone. The proportioning valve controls the pressure to the rear brakes to lessen the chance of rear wheel lock-up during very hard braking.

Warning lights may be tested by depressing the brake pedal and holding it while opening one of the wheel cylinder bleeder screws. If this does not cause the light to go on, substitute a new lamp, make continuity checks, and, finally, replace the switch as necessary.

The hydraulic system may be checked for leaks by applying pressure to the pedal gradually and steadily. If the pedal sinks very slowly to the floor, the system has a leak. This is not to be confused with a springy or spongy feel due to the compression of air within the lines. If the system leaks, there will be a gradual change in the position of the pedal with a constant pressure.

Check for leaks along all lines and at wheel cylinders. If no external leaks are apparent, the problem is inside the master cylinder.

Disc Brakes
BASIC OPERATING PRINCIPLES

Instead of the traditional expanding brakes that press outward against a circular drum, disc brake systems utilize a disc (rotor) with brake pads positioned on either side of it. Braking effect is achieved in a manner similar to the way you would squeeze a spinning phonograph record between your fingers. The disc (rotor) is a casting with cooling fins between the two braking surfaces. This enables air to circulate between the braking surfaces making them less

sensitive to heat buildup and more resistant to fade. Dirt and water do not affect braking action since contaminants are thrown off by the centrifugal action of the rotor or scraped off the by the pads. Also, the equal clamping action of the two brake pads tends to ensure uniform, straight line stops. Disc brakes are inherently self-adjusting.

There are three general types of disc brake:
1. A fixed caliper.
2. A floating caliper.
3. A sliding caliper.

The fixed caliper design uses two pistons mounted on either side of the rotor (in each side of the caliper). The caliper is mounted rigidly and does not move.

The sliding and floating designs are quite similar. In fact, these two types are often lumped together. In both designs, the pad on the inside of the rotor is moved into contact with the rotor by hydraulic force. The caliper, which is not held in a fixed position, moves slightly, bringing the outside pad into contact with the rotor. There are various methods of attaching floating calipers. Some pivot at the bottom or top, and some slide on mounting bolts. In any event, the end result is the same.

All the cars covered in this book employ the sliding caliper design.

Drum Brakes
BASIC OPERATING PRINCIPLES

Drum brakes employ two brake shoes mounted on a stationary backing plate. These shoes are positioned inside a circular drum which rotates with the wheel assembly. The shoes are held in place by springs. This allows them to slide toward the drums (when they are applied) while keeping the linings and drums in alignment. The shoes are actuated by a wheel cylinder which is mounted at the top of the backing plate. When the brakes are applied, hydraulic pressure forces the wheel cylinder's actuating links outward. Since these links bear directly against the top of the brake shoes, the tops of the shoes are then forced against the inner side of the drum. This action forces the bottoms of the two shoes to contact the brake drum by rotating the entire assembly slightly (known as servo action). When pressure within the wheel cylinder is relaxed, return springs pull the shoes back away from the drum.

Most modern drum brakes are designed to self-adjust themselves during application when the vehicle is moving in reverse. This motion causes both shoes to rotate very slightly with the drum, rocking an adjusting lever, thereby causing rotation of the adjusting screw.

Troubleshooting the Brake System

Problem	Cause	Solution
Low brake pedal (excessive pedal travel required for braking action.)	• Excessive clearance between rear linings and drums caused by inoperative automatic adjusters	• Make 10 to 15 alternate forward and reverse brake stops to adjust brakes. If brake pedal does not come up, repair or replace adjuster parts as necessary.
	• Worn rear brakelining	• Inspect and replace lining if worn beyond minimum thickness specification
	• Bent, distorted brakeshoes, front or rear	• Replace brakeshoes in axle sets
	• Air in hydraulic system	• Remove air from system. Refer to Brake Bleeding.
Low brake pedal (pedal may go to floor with steady pressure applied.)	• Fluid leak in hydraulic system	• Fill master cylinder to fill line; have helper apply brakes and check calipers, wheel cylinders, differential valve tubes, hoses and fittings for leaks. Repair or replace as necessary.
	• Air in hydraulic system	• Remove air from system. Refer to Brake Bleeding.
	• Incorrect or non-recommended brake fluid (fluid evaporates at below normal temp).	• Flush hydraulic system with clean brake fluid. Refill with correct-type fluid.
	• Master cylinder piston seals worn, or master cylinder bore is scored, worn or corroded	• Repair or replace master cylinder
Low brake pedal (pedal goes to floor on first application—o.k. on subsequent applications.)	• Disc brake pads sticking on abutment surfaces of anchor plate. Caused by a build-up of dirt, rust, or corrosion on abutment surfaces	• Clean abutment surfaces
Fading brake pedal (pedal height decreases with steady pressure applied.)	• Fluid leak in hydraulic system	• Fill master cylinder reservoirs to fill mark, have helper apply brakes, check calipers, wheel cylinders, differential valve, tubes, hoses, and fittings for fluid leaks. Repair or replace parts as necessary.
	• Master cylinder piston seals worn, or master cylinder bore is scored, worn or corroded	• Repair or replace master cylinder
Decreasing brake pedal travel (pedal travel required for braking action decreases and may be accompanied by a hard pedal.)	• Caliper or wheel cylinder pistons sticking or seized	• Repair or replace the calipers, or wheel cylinders
	• Master cylinder compensator ports blocked (preventing fluid return to reservoirs) or pistons sticking or seized in master cylinder bore	• Repair or replace the master cylinder
	• Power brake unit binding internally	• Test unit according to the following procedure: (a) Shift transmission into neutral and start engine (b) Increase engine speed to 1500 rpm, close throttle and fully depress brake pedal (c) Slow release brake pedal and stop engine (d) Have helper remove vacuum check valve and hose from power unit. Observe for backward movement of brake pedal. (e) If the pedal moves backward, the power unit has an internal bind—replace power unit

Troubleshooting the Brake System (cont.)

Problem	Cause	Solution
Spongy brake pedal (pedal has abnormally soft, springy, spongy feel when depressed.)	• Air in hydraulic system	• Remove air from system. Refer to Brake Bleeding.
	• Brakeshoes bent or distorted	• Replace brakeshoes
	• Brakelining not yet seated with drums and rotors	• Burnish brakes
	• Rear drum brakes not properly adjusted	• Adjust brakes
Hard brake pedal (excessive pedal pressure required to stop vehicle. May be accompanied by brake fade.)	• Loose or leaking power brake unit vacuum hose	• Tighten connections or replace leaking hose
	• Incorrect or poor quality brakelining	• Replace with lining in axle sets
	• Bent, broken, distorted brakeshoes	• Replace brakeshoes
	• Calipers binding or dragging on mounting pins. Rear brakeshoes dragging on support plate.	• Replace mounting pins and bushings. Clean rust or burrs from rear brake support plate ledges and lubricate ledges with molydisulfide grease. **NOTE:** If ledges are deeply grooved or scored, do not attempt to sand or grind them smooth—replace support plate.
	• Caliper, wheel cylinder, or master cylinder pistons sticking or seized	• Repair or replace parts as necessary
	• Power brake unit vacuum check valve malfunction	• Test valve according to the following procedure: (a) Start engine, increase engine speed to 1500 rpm, close throttle and immediately stop engine (b) Wait at least 90 seconds then depress brake pedal (c) If brakes are not vacuum assisted for 2 or more applications, check valve is faulty
	• Power brake unit has internal bind	• Test unit according to the following procedure: (a) With engine stopped, apply brakes several times to exhaust all vacuum in system (b) Shift transmission into neutral, depress brake pedal and start engine (c) If pedal height decreases with foot pressure and less pressure is required to hold pedal in applied position, power unit vacuum system is operating normally. Test power unit. If power unit exhibits a bind condition, replace the power unit.
	• Master cylinder compensator ports (at bottom of reservoirs) blocked by dirt, scale, rust, or have small burrs (blocked ports prevent fluid return to reservoirs).	• Repair or replace master cylinder **CAUTION:** Do not attempt to clean blocked ports with wire, pencils, or similar implements. Use compressed air only.
	• Brake hoses, tubes, fittings clogged or restricted	• Use compressed air to check or unclog parts. Replace any damaged parts.
	• Brake fluid contaminated with improper fluids (motor oil, transmission fluid, causing rubber components to swell and stick in bores	• Replace all rubber components, combination valve and hoses. Flush entire brake system with DOT 3 brake fluid or equivalent.
	• Low engine vacuum	• Adjust or repair engine

Troubleshooting the Brake System (cont.)

Problem	Cause	Solution
Grabbing brakes (severe reaction to brake pedal pressure.)	• Brakelining(s) contaminated by grease or brake fluid	• Determine and correct cause of contamination and replace brakeshoes in axle sets
	• Parking brake cables incorrectly adjusted or seized	• Adjust cables. Replace seized cables.
	• Incorrect brakelining or lining loose on brakeshoes	• Replace brakeshoes in axle sets
	• Caliper anchor plate bolts loose	• Tighten bolts
	• Rear brakeshoes binding on support plate ledges	• Clean and lubricate ledges. Replace support plate(s) if ledges are deeply grooved. Do not attempt to smooth ledges by grinding.
	• Incorrect or missing power brake reaction disc	• Install correct disc
	• Rear brake support plates loose	• Tighten mounting bolts
Dragging brakes (slow or incomplete release of brakes)	• Brake pedal binding at pivot	• Loosen and lubricate
	• Power brake unit has internal bind	• Inspect for internal bind. Replace unit if internal bind exists.
	• Parking brake cables incorrectly adjusted or seized	• Adjust cables. Replace seized cables.
	• Rear brakeshoe return springs weak or broken	• Replace return springs. Replace brakeshoe if necessary in axle sets.
	• Automatic adjusters malfunctioning	• Repair or replace adjuster parts as required
	• Caliper, wheel cylinder or master cylinder pistons sticking or seized	• Repair or replace parts as necessary
	• Master cylinder compensating ports blocked (fluid does not return to reservoirs).	• Use compressed air to clear ports. Do not use wire, pencils, or similar objects to open blocked ports.
Vehicle moves to one side when brakes are applied	• Incorrect front tire pressure	• Inflate to recommended cold (reduced load) inflation pressure
	• Worn or damaged wheel bearings	• Replace worn or damaged bearings
	• Brakelining on one side contaminated	• Determine and correct cause of contamination and replace brakelining in axle sets
	• Brakeshoes on one side bent, distorted, or lining loose on shoe	• Replace brakeshoes in axle sets
	• Support plate bent or loose on one side	• Tighten or replace support plate
	• Brakelining not yet seated with drums or rotors	• Burnish brakelining
	• Caliper anchor plate loose on one side	• Tighten anchor plate bolts
	• Caliper piston sticking or seized	• Repair or replace caliper
	• Brakelinings water soaked	• Drive vehicle with brakes lightly applied to dry linings
	• Loose suspension component attaching or mounting bolts	• Tighten suspension bolts. Replace worn suspension components.
	• Brake combination valve failure	• Replace combination valve
Chatter or shudder when brakes are applied (pedal pulsation and roughness may also occur.)	• Brakeshoes distorted, bent, contaminated, or worn	• Replace brakeshoes in axle sets
	• Caliper anchor plate or support plate loose	• Tighten mounting bolts
	• Excessive thickness variation of rotor(s)	• Refinish or replace rotors in axle sets
Noisy brakes (squealing, clicking, scraping sound when brakes are applied.)	• Bent, broken, distorted brakeshoes	• Replace brakeshoes in axle sets
	• Excessive rust on outer edge of rotor braking surface	• Remove rust

Troubleshooting the Brake System (cont.)

Problem	Cause	Solution
Noisy brakes (squealing, clicking, scraping sound when brakes are applied.) (cont.)	• Brakelining worn out—shoes contacting drum of rotor	• Replace brakeshoes and lining in axle sets. Refinish or replace drums or rotors.
	• Broken or loose holdown or return springs	• Replace parts as necessary
	• Rough or dry drum brake support plate ledges	• Lubricate support plate ledges
	• Cracked, grooved, or scored rotor(s) or drum(s)	• Replace rotor(s) or drum(s). Replace brakeshoes and lining in axle sets if necessary.
	• Incorrect brakelining and/or shoes (front or rear).	• Install specified shoe and lining assemblies
Pulsating brake pedal	• Out of round drums or excessive lateral runout in disc brake rotor(s)	• Refinish or replace drums, re-index rotors or replace

Power Boosters

Power brakes operate just as non-power brake systems except in the actuation of the master cylinder pistons. A vacuum diaphragm is located on the front of the master cylinder and assists the driver in applying the brakes, reducing both the effort and travel he must put into moving the brake pedal.

The vacuum diaphragm housing is connected to the intake manifold by a vacuum hose. A check valve is placed at the point where the hose enters the diaphragm housing, so that during periods of low manifold vacuum brake assist vacuum will not be lost.

Depressing the brake pedal closes off the vacuum source and allows atmospheric pressure to enter on one side of the diaphragm. This causes the master cylinder pistons to move and apply the brakes. When the brake pedal is released, vacuum is applied to both sides of the diaphragm, and return springs return the diaphragm and master cylinder pistons to the released position. If the vacuum fails, the brake pedal rod will butt against the end of the master cylinder actuating rod, and direct mechanical application will occur as the pedal is depressed.

The hydraulic and mechanical problems that apply to conventional brake systems also apply to power brakes, and should be checked for if the tests below do not reveal the problem.

Test for a system vacuum leak as described below:

1. Operate the engine at idle without touching the brake pedal for at least one minute.
2. Turn off the engine, and wait one minute.
3. Test for the presence of assist vacuum by depressing the brake pedal and releasing it several times. Light application will produce less and less pedal travel, if vacuum was present. If there is no vacuum, air is leaking into the system somewhere.

Test for system operation as follows:

1. Pump the brake pedal (with engine off) until the supply vacuum is entirely gone.
2. Put a light, steady pressure on the pedal.
3. Start the engine, and operate it at idle. If the system is operating, the brake pedal should fall toward the floor if constant pressure is maintained on the pedal.

Power brake systems may be tested for hydraulic leaks just as ordinary systems are tested.

BRAKE SYSTEM

Adjustments
DRUM BRAKES

1. Raise and support the rear of the vehicle on jackstands.
2. Remove the rubber cover from the backing plate.
3. Insert a brake adjusting tool through the hole in the brake backing plate. Turn the toothed adjusting nut to spread the brake shoes, making contact with the brake drum.

NOTE: *When adjusting the brake shoes, turn the wheel until considerable drag is felt. If necessary, hit the brake drum with a rubber hammer to align the shoes with the drum.*

4. When considerable drag is felt, back off the adjusting nut a few notches, so that the correct clearance is maintained between the brake drum and the brake shoes. Make sure that the wheel rotates freely.

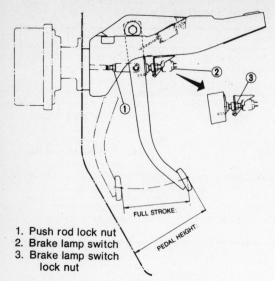

1. Push rod lock nut
2. Brake lamp switch
3. Brake lamp switch lock nut

Typical brake pedal adjustment—F10 model

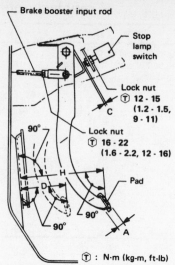

⊤ : N·m (kg-m, ft-lb)

Pedal adjustments for the Pulsar (1985 and later)

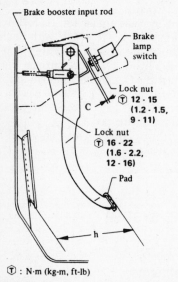

⊤ : N·m (kg-m, ft-lb)

Pedal adjustments for the Pulsar (1983–84)—310 and Stanza are similar

BRAKE PEDAL HEIGHT ADJUSTMENT

Before adjusting the pedal, make sure that the wheel brakes are correctly adjusted. Adjust the pedal height with the input rod, attached to the top of the brake pedal. Pedal height (floorboard to pedal pad) should be 178mm (F10), 184mm (310), 152mm (Stanza) and 200mm (Pulsar).

Brake Light Switch

REMOVAL AND INSTALLATION

1. Disconnect the negative battery cable.
2. Disconnect the wiring connector at the switch.

3. Remove the switch lock nut.
4. Remove the switch.
5. Install the switch and adjust it so the brake lights are not on unless the brake pedal is depressed.

ADJUSTMENT

Adjust the clearance between the brake pedal and the stop lamp switch or the ASCD switch, by loosening the locknut and adjusting the switch. The clearance should be approximately 1.0-5.0mm for 310, 0-1.0mm for Pulsar and Stanza (1982-84) or 0.30-1.00mm for Stanza (1985 and later).

NOTE: *On the F10 models, the stop light switch is adjusted so that the switch is not activated when the brake pedal is relaxed.*

Master Cylinder

WARNING: *Clean, high quality brake fluid is essential to the safe and proper operation of the brake system. You should always buy the highest quality brake fluid that is available. If the brake fluid becomes contaminated, drain and flush the system and fill the master cylinder with new fluid.*

Never reuse any brake fluid. Any brake fluid that is removed from the system should be discarded.

REMOVAL AND INSTALLATION

1. Clean the outside of the master cylinder thoroughly, particularly around the cap and fluid lines. Disconnect the fluid lines and cap them to exclude dirt.
2. If equipped with a fluid level sensor, disconnect the wiring harness from the master cylinder.

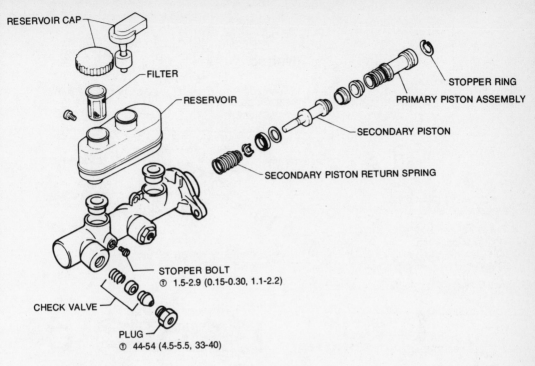

310 master cylinder

3. Disconnect the brake fluid tubes, then plug the openings to prevent dirt from entering the system.

4. Remove the mounting bolts at the firewall or the brake booster (if equipped) and remove the master cylinder from the vehicle.

5. Install the master cylinder to the vehicle. Connect all brake lines and fluid level sensor

1. Reservoir cap
2. Filter
3. Reservoir tank assembly
4. Stopper ring
5. Stopper
6. Primary piston assembly
7. Primary return spring
8. Secondary piston assembly
9. Stopper screw
10. Secondary return spring
11. Plug
12. Check valve

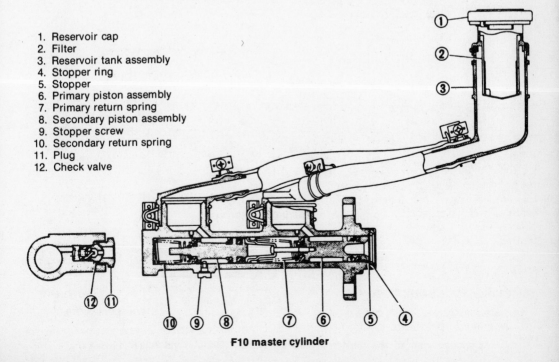

F10 master cylinder

Nabco

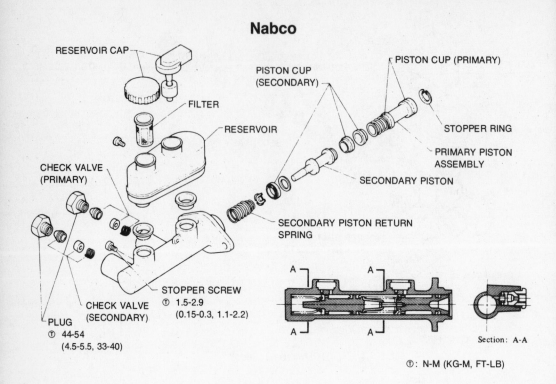

RESERVOIR CAP

FILTER

RESERVOIR

PISTON CUP (SECONDARY)

PISTON CUP (PRIMARY)

STOPPER RING

PRIMARY PISTON ASSEMBLY

SECONDARY PISTON

CHECK VALVE (PRIMARY)

SECONDARY PISTON RETURN SPRING

CHECK VALVE (SECONDARY)

STOPPER SCREW
Ⓣ 1.5-2.9
(0.15-0.3, 1.1-2.2)

PLUG
Ⓣ 44-54
(4.5-5.5, 33-40)

A   A

A   A

Section: A-A

Ⓣ: N-M (KG-M, FT-LB)

Tokico

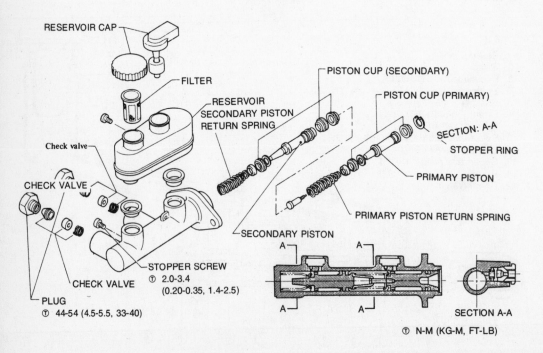

RESERVOIR CAP

FILTER

RESERVOIR

SECONDARY PISTON
RETURN SPRING

PISTON CUP (SECONDARY)

PISTON CUP (PRIMARY)

SECTION: A-A

STOPPER RING

PRIMARY PISTON

PRIMARY PISTON RETURN SPRING

Check valve

CHECK VALVE

CHECK VALVE

SECONDARY PISTON

STOPPER SCREW
Ⓣ 2.0-3.4
(0.20-0.35, 1.4-2.5)

PLUG
Ⓣ 44-54 (4.5-5.5, 33-40)

A   A

A   A

SECTION A-A

Ⓣ N-M (KG-M, FT-LB)

Exploded view of the master cylinders—Stanza (1982–83) and Pulsar (1983–84)

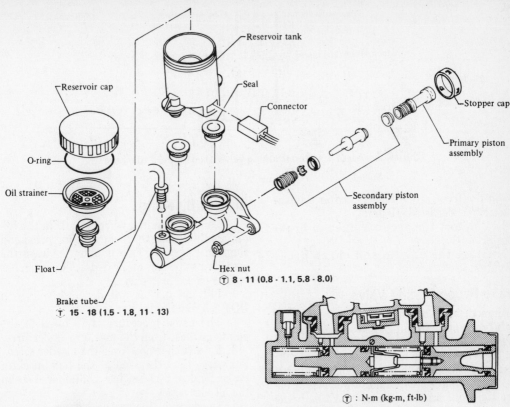

Exploded view of master cylinder used on Stanza (1984 and later) and Pulsar

wiring is so equipped. Refill the reservoir with brake fluid and bleed the system.

NOTE: *Ordinary brake fluid will boil and cause brake failure under the high temperatures developed in disc brake systems; use DOT 3 brake fluid in the brake systems.*

OVERHAUL

NOTE: *Master cylinders are supplied to the manufacturer by two suppliers: Nabco and Tokico. Parts between these manufacturers are not interchangeable. Be sure you obtain the correct rebuilding kit for your master cylinder.*

The master cylinder can be disassembled using the illustrations as a guide. Clean all of the parts in clean brake fluid. Replace the cylinder or piston (as necessary), if the clearance between the two exceeds 0.15mm. Lubricate all of the parts with clean brake fluid on assembly.

NOTE: *Master cylinder rebuilding kits, containing all the wearing parts, are available to simplify the overhaul.*

Power Booster

REMOVAL AND INSTALLATION

1. Remove the master cylinder mounting nuts and pull the master cylinder assembly

(brake lines connected) away from the power booster.

2. Detach the vacuum lines from the booster.

3. Detach the booster pushrod at the pedal clevis.

4. Unbolt the booster from under the dash and lift it out of the engine compartment.

5. Install the brake booster to the vehicle. Torque the master cylinder-to-booster nuts to 6-8 ft. lbs.; the booster-to-firewall nuts to 6-8 ft. lbs. Adjust the length of the pushrod so that the distance between the pushrod clevis hole and the rear face of the booster is 130mm (310 and Stanza) or 150mm (Pulsar). On the F10 models, measure the length of the pushrod at the front of the power booster; the distance be-

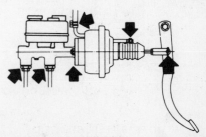

Power booster attaching points

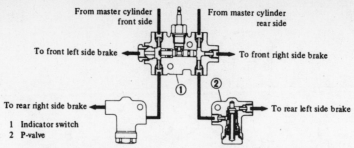

From master cylinder front side

From master cylinder rear side

To front left side brake

To front right side brake

To rear right side brake

To rear left side brake

1 Indicator switch
2 P-valve

Cut-away view of the proportioning valve used on the F10 model

tween the front of the power booster and the master cylinder is 9.6-10.0mm.

6. Connect the vacuum lines to brake booster.

7. Start the engine and check brake operation.

Brake Proportioning Valve

All models covered in this guide are equipped with brake proportioning valves of several different types. The valves all do the same job, which is to separate the front and rear brake lines, allowing them to function independently and preventing the rear brakes from locking before the front brakes. Damage, such as brake line leakage, in either the front or the rear brake system will not affect the normal operation of the unaffected system. If, in the event of a panic stop, the rear brakes lock up before the front brakes, it could mean the proportioning valve is defective. In that case, replace the entire proportioning valve.

REMOVAL AND INSTALLATION

1. Remove the brake line tubes from the proportioning valve, then plug the openings to prevent dirt from entering the system.

2. Remove the mounting bolt(s) and the valve from the vehicle.

3. To install, reverse the removal procedures. Refill the master cylinder reservoir and bleed the brake system.

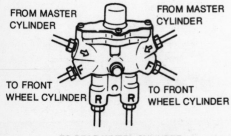

FROM MASTER CYLINDER

FROM MASTER CYLINDER

TO FRONT WHEEL CYLINDER

TO FRONT WHEEL CYLINDER

TO REAR WHEEL CYLINDER

Proportioning valve—310, Stanza and Pulsar

System Bleeding

Bleeding is required whenever air in the hydraulic fluid causes a spongy feeling pedal and sluggish response. This is almost always the case after some part of the hydraulic system has been repaired or replaced.

1. Fill the master cylinder reservoir with DOT 3 brake fluid.

2. The usual procedure is to bleed at the points farthest from the master cylinder first.

3. Fit a rubber hose over the bleeder screw. Submerge the other end of the hole in clean brake fluid in a clear glass container. Loosen the bleeder screw.

4. Slowly pump the brake pedal several times until fluid free of bubbles is discharged. An assistant is required to pump the pedal.

5. On the last pumping stroke, hold the pedal down and tighten the bleeder screw. Check the fluid level periodically during the bleeding operation.

NOTE: *Bleed the front brakes in the same way as the rear brakes.*

6. Check that the brake pedal is now firm. If not, repeat the bleeding operation.

FRONT DISC BRAKES

CAUTION: *Brake shoes contain asbestos, which has been determined to be a cancer causing agent. Never clean brake surfaces with compressed air! Avoid inhaling any dust from any brake surfaces! When cleaning brake surfaces, use a commercially available brake cleaning fluid.*

Brake Pads
INSPECTION

You should be able to check the pad lining thickness without removing the pads. Check the Brake Specifications Chart at the end of this chapter to find the manufacturer's pad wear limit. However, this measurement may disagree with your state inspection laws. When

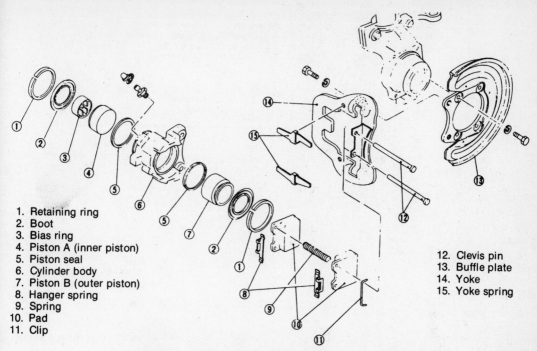

1. Retaining ring
2. Boot
3. Bias ring
4. Piston A (inner piston)
5. Piston seal
6. Cylinder body
7. Piston B (outer piston)
8. Hanger spring
9. Spring
10. Pad
11. Clip

12. Clevis pin
13. Buffle plate
14. Yoke
15. Yoke spring

Exploded view of the 310 front disc brakes—F10 is similar

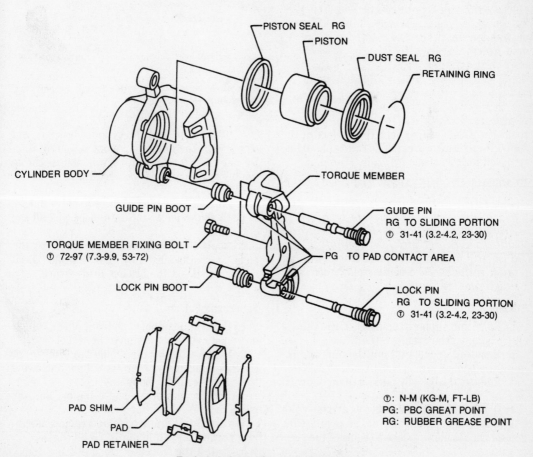

PISTON SEAL RG

PISTON

DUST SEAL RG

RETAINING RING

CYLINDER BODY

TORQUE MEMBER

GUIDE PIN BOOT

GUIDE PIN
RG TO SLIDING PORTION
Ⓣ 31-41 (3.2-4.2, 23-30)

TORQUE MEMBER FIXING BOLT
Ⓣ 72-97 (7.3-9.9, 53-72)

PG TO PAD CONTACT AREA

LOCK PIN BOOT

LOCK PIN
RG TO SLIDING PORTION
Ⓣ 31-41 (3.2-4.2, 23-30)

PAD SHIM

PAD

PAD RETAINER

Ⓣ: N-M (KG-M, FT-LB)
PG: PBC GREAT POINT
RG: RUBBER GREASE POINT

Exploded view of Stanza front brakes

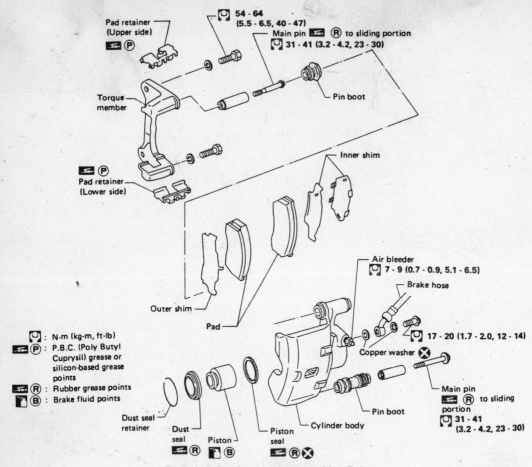

Exploded view front brake assembly—Pulsar

replacing pads, always check the surface of the rotors for scoring or wear. The rotors should be removed for resurfacing if badly scored.

REMOVAL AND INSTALLATION

CAUTION: *Brake shoes contain asbestos, which has been determined to be a cancer causing agent. Never clean the brake surfaces with compressed air! Avoid inhaling any dust from any brake surface! When cleaning brake surfaces, use a commercially available brake cleaning fluid.*

F10 and 310

1. Raise and support the front of the vehicle on jackstands, then remove the wheels.

2. Remove the clip, pull out the pins and remove the pad springs.

3. Remove the pads by pulling them out with pliers.

4. To install, first lightly coat the yoke groove and the end surface of the piston with grease. Do not allow grease to contact the pads or rotor.

5. Open the bleeder screw slightly and push

the outer piston into the cylinder until its end aligns with the end of the boot retaining ring. Do not push too far, which will require disassembly of the caliper to correct it. Install the inner pad.

6. Pull the yoke toward the outside of the car to push the inner piston into place. Install the outer pad.

7. Apply the brakes a few times to seat the pads. Check the master cylinder and add fluid if necessary. Bleed the brakes, if necessary.

Stanza and Pulsar

1. Raise and support the front of the vehicle on jackstands, then remove the wheels.

2. Remove the bottom guide pin (Stanza) or the lock pin (Pulsar) from the caliper and swing the caliper cylinder body upward.

3. Remove the brake pad retainers and the pads.

4. Install the brake pads and caliper assembly. Torque the guide pin to 23-30 ft. lbs.

5. Install the wheels.

6. Apply the brakes a few times to seat the

pads. Check the master cylinder and add fluid if necessary. Bleed the brakes, if necessary.

Brake Calipers

REMOVAL AND INSTALLATION

CAUTION: *Brake shoes contain asbestos, which has been determined to be a cancer causing agent. Never clean the brake surfaces with compressed air! Avoid inhaling any dust from any brake surface! When cleaning brake surfaces, use a commercially available brake cleaning fluid.*

F10

1. Refer to the Disc Brake Pads, Removal and Installation procedures, in this section and remove the brake pads.
2. Disconnect and plug the brake tube from the caliper assembly.
3. Remove the caliper-to-steering knuckle mounting bolts, then remove the caliper from the vehicle.
4. Install the brake caliper to the steering knuckle.
5. Install the brake pads.
6. Bleed the brake system.

310

1. Refer to the Disc Brake Pads, Removal and Installation procedures, in this section and remove the brake pads.
2. Disconnect and plug the brake tube from the caliper assembly.
3. Remove the steering knuckle arm-to-strut assembly nut(s) and separate the assembly.
4. Remove the caliper-to-steering knuckle spindle mounting bolts, then remove the caliper from the strut.
5. Install the brake caliper to the vehicle.
6. Install the brake pads.
7. Bleed the brake system.

Stanza and Pulsar

1. Raise and support the vehicle on jackstands, then remove the wheels.
2. Disconnect and plug the brake tube at the brake hose connection.
3. Remove the torque member-to-steering knuckle mounting bolts, then remove the caliper assembly from the vehicle.
4. Install the brake caliper to the vehicle.
5. Install the brake pads.
6. Bleed the brake system.

OVERHAUL

F10 and 310

1. Refer to the Caliper, Removal and Installation procedures, in this section and remove the cylinder body from the caliper assembly.

2. Loosen the bleeder screw and press the pistons into the center of their bores.
3. While holding the yoke, gently tap on the inboard piston side of the caliper to separate the yoke from the caliper.
4. Remove the bias ring from primary piston. Remove the retaining rings and boots from both pistons. GRADUALLY, feed compressed air into the cylinder (through the brake tube) to force out the pistons. Remove the piston seal from the cylinder carefully with the fingers, so as not to mar the cylinder wall.
5. Remove the yoke springs from the yoke.
6. Wash all parts with clean brake fluid.
7. If the piston or cylinder is badly worn or scored, replace both. The piston surface is plated and must not be polished with emery paper. Replace all seals.

NOTE *The rotor can be removed and machined if scored, but final thickness must be at least 8.4mm. Runout must not exceed 0.025mm.*

8. Lubricate the cylinder bore with clean brake fluid and install the piston seal.
9. Insert the bias ring into primary piston so that the rounded ring portion comes to the bottom of the piston. Primary piston has a small depression inside, while secondary does not.
10. Lubricate the pistons with clean brake fluid and insert into the cylinder. Install the boot and retaining ring. The yoke groove of the bias ring of primary piston must align with the yoke groove of the cylinder.
11. Install the yoke springs to the yoke so the projecting portion faces to the disc (rotor).
12. Lubricate the sliding portion of the cylinder and yoke. Assemble the cylinder and yoke by tapping the yoke lightly.
13. Replace the caliper assembly and pads. Torque the caliper mounting bolts to 40-47 ft. lbs., the disc rotor bolts to 18-25 ft. lbs. and the strut bolt torque is 33-44 ft. lbs. Bleed the system of air.

Stanza and Pulsar

1. Refer to the Caliper, Removal and Installation procedures, in this section and remove the cylinder body and the torque member from the steering knuckle.
2. Remove the brake tube from the cylinder body.
3. Using compressed air, GRADUALLY, force the piston and the dust seal out of the cylinder body.

CAUTION: *Place a piece of wood in the jaws of the caliper to catch the piston, in case it leaves the caliper too fast.*

4. Remove the piston seal.
5. Clean all of the parts in clean brake fluid.

Check and/or replace any damaged parts. Lubricate all of the new parts with brake fluid.

6. Install piston and all new seals in the caliper assembly.

7. Install the caliper assembly to the vehicle.

Brake Disc
REMOVAL AND INSTALLATION

CAUTION: *Brake shoes contain asbestos, which has been determined to be a cancer causing agent. Never clean the brake surfaces with compressed air! Avoid inhaling any dust from any brake surface! When cleaning brake surfaces, use a commercially available brake cleaning fluid.*

1. Refer to the Caliper, Removal and Installation procedures, in this section and remove the caliper and the yoke (F10 and 310) or the cylinder body and the torque member (Stanza and Pulsar) from the steering knuckle.

NOTE: *Do not disconnect the brake tube (if possible), support the assembly on a wire.*

2. Remove the grease cap, the cotter pin, the adjusting cap, the wheel bearing locknut and the thrust washer from the drive shaft.

3. Using Wheel Hub Remover tool ST35100000 (F10 and 310) or tools KV40101000 and ST36230000 (Stanza and Pulsar), press the wheel hub/disc assembly from the steering knuckle.

4. Remove the disc-to-wheel hub bolts and separate the disc from the wheel hub.

5. Install wheel hub/disc assembly to the vehicle. Torque the disc-to-wheel hub bolts to 28-38 ft. lbs. (Stanza) or 18-25 ft. lbs. (F10, 310 and Pulsar) and the hub nut to 145-203 ft. lbs. (Stanza) or 87-145 ft. lbs. (F10, 310 and Pulsar).

6. Install the caliper assembly and any other components to the vehicle.

7. Bleed brake system if necessary.

INSPECTION

1. Check the disc for cracks and/or chips, if necessary, replace the disc.

2. Using a dial indicator, check the runout of the disc, it should be less than 0.15mm (F10), 0.13mm (310), 0.076mm (Stanza and Pulsar); if greater than the maximum, replace the disc.

3. Using a dial indicator, check the parallelism of the disc, it should be less than 0.03mm, if greater than the maximum, replace the disc.

4. Using a micrometer, check the thickness of the disc; it should be greater than 8.6mm (F10 and 310), 16.0mm (Stanza) or 10.0mm (Pulsar), if not, replace the disc.

REAR DRUM BRAKES

CAUTION: *Brake shoes contain asbestos, which has been determined to be a cancer causing agent. Never clean brake surfaces with compressed air! Avoid inhaling any dust from any brake surfaces! When cleaning brake surfaces, use a commercially available brake cleaning fluid.*

Brake Drum
REMOVAL AND INSTALLATION

CAUTION: *Brake shoes contain asbestos, which has been determined to be a cancer causing agent. Never clean the brake surfaces with compressed air! Avoid inhaling any dust from any brake surface! When cleaning brake surfaces, use a commercially available brake cleaning fluid.*

NOTE: *For rear wheel bearing procedures refer to Chapter 8.*

1. Raise the rear of the vehicle and support it on jackstands.

2. Remove the wheels.

3. Release the parking brake.

4. Remove the grease cap, the cotter pin and the wheel bearing castle nut (F10 and 310) or the adjusting cap and the wheel bearing nut (Pulsar and Stanza).

5. Pull off the drum, taking care not to drop the tapered bearing.

6. Install the drum assembly to the vehicle. Adjust the wheel bearing and torque the nut to 30 ft. lbs.

7. Install the wheels.

INSPECTION

After removing the brake drum, wipe out the accumulated dust with a damp cloth.

CAUTION: *DO NOT blow the brake dust out of the drums with compressed air or lung power. Brake linings contain asbestos, a known cancer causing substance. Dispose of the cloth after use.*

Inspect the drum for cracks, deep grooves, roughness, scoring or out-of-roundness. Replace any brake drum which is cracked.

Smooth any slight scores by polishing the friction surface with the fine emery cloth. Heavy or extensive scoring will cause excessive brake lining wear and should be removed from the brake drum through resurfacing.

Brake Shoes
REMOVAL AND INSTALLATION

CAUTION: *Brake shoes contain asbestos, which has been determined to be a cancer causing agent. Never clean the brake surfaces*

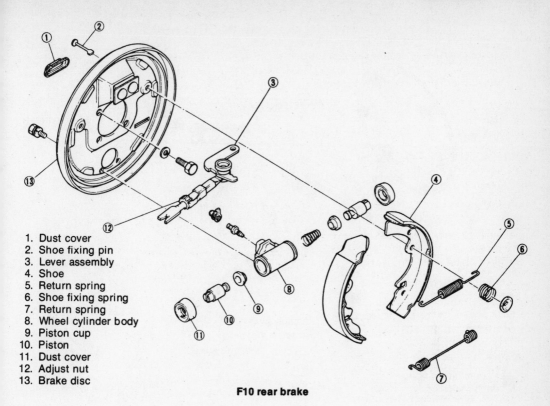

1. Dust cover
2. Shoe fixing pin
3. Lever assembly
4. Shoe
5. Return spring
6. Shoe fixing spring
7. Return spring
8. Wheel cylinder body
9. Piston cup
10. Piston
11. Dust cover
12. Adjust nut
13. Brake disc

F10 rear brake

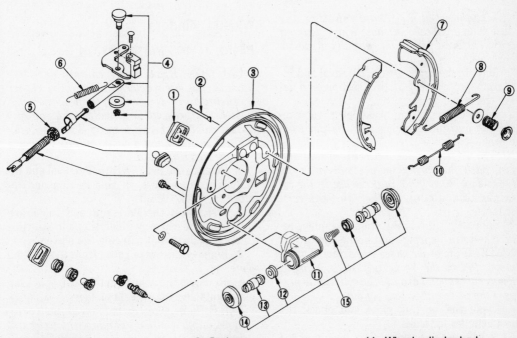

1. Dust cover
2. Shoe fixing pin
3. Back plate
4. Adjuster assembly
5. Adjusting nut

6. Spring
7. Shoe
8. Return spring
9. Shoe fixing spring
10. Return spring

11. Wheel cylinder body
12. Piston cup
13. Piston
14. Dust cover
15. Wheel cylinder assembly

310 rear brake

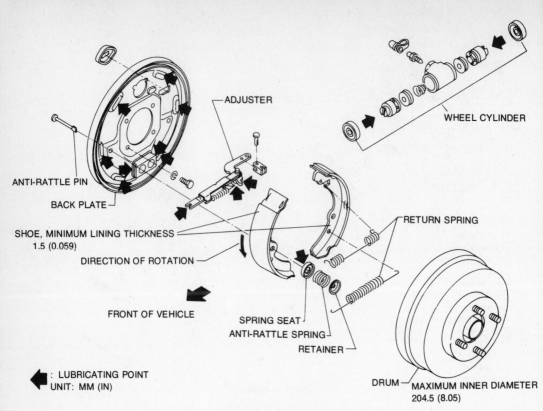

ADJUSTER

WHEEL CYLINDER

ANTI-RATTLE PIN

BACK PLATE

SHOE, MINIMUM LINING THICKNESS
1.5 (0.059)

DIRECTION OF ROTATION

RETURN SPRING

FRONT OF VEHICLE

SPRING SEAT
ANTI-RATTLE SPRING
RETAINER

◀ : LUBRICATING POINT
UNIT: MM (IN)

DRUM — MAXIMUM INNER DIAMETER
204.5 (8.05)

Stanza rear brake

with compressed air! Avoid inhaling any dust from any brake surface! When cleaning brake surfaces, use a commercially available brake cleaning fluid.

1. Refer to the Brake Drum, Removal and Installation procedures, in this section and remove the brake drum.

2. Release the parking brake lever, then remove the anti-rattle spring and the pin from the brake shoes.

NOTE: *To remove the anti-rattle spring and pin, push the spring/pin assembly into the brake shoe, turn it 90° and release it; the retainer cap, spring, washer and pin will separate.*

3. Supporting the brake shoe assembly, remove the return springs and brake shoes.

NOTE: *If the brake shoes are difficult to remove, loosen the brake adjusters. Place a heavy rubber band around the cylinder to prevent the piston from coming out.*

4. Clean the backing plate and check the wheel cylinder for leaks.

5. Lubricate the backing plate pads and the screw adjusters with lithium base grease. Install the brake shoes and springs.

6. Install the drum assembly.

7. Adjust brakes and bleed system if necessary.

Wheel Cylinders

REMOVAL AND INSTALLATION

CAUTION: *Brake shoes contain asbestos, which has been determined to be a cancer causing agent. Never clean the brake surfaces with compressed air! Avoid inhaling any dust from any brake surface! When cleaning brake surfaces, use a commercially available brake cleaning fluid.*

1. Refer to the Brake Drum, Removal and Installation procedures, in this section and remove the brake drum.

2. Disconnect the flare nut and the brake tube from the wheel cylinder, then plug the line to prevent dirt from entering the system.

3. Remove the brake shoes from the backing plate.

4. Remove the wheel cylinder-to-backing plate bolts and the wheel cylinders.

NOTE: *If the wheel cylinder is difficult to remove, bump it with a soft hammer to release it from the backing plate.*

5. Install the wheel cylinder assembly to the backing plate.

6. Connect all brake lines and install the brake drum.

7. Bleed the brake system.

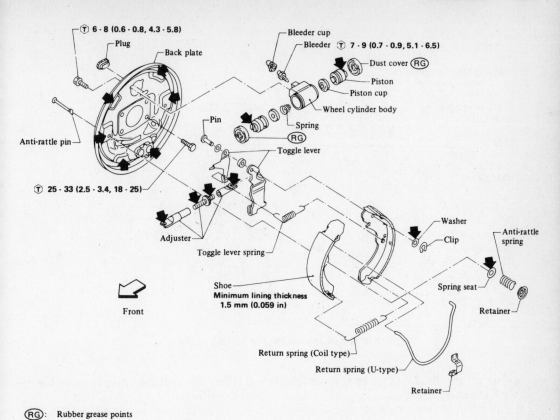

6 - 8 (0.6 - 0.8, 4.3 - 5.8)
Plug
Back plate
Bleeder cup
Bleeder   7 - 9 (0.7 - 0.9, 5.1 - 6.5)
Dust cover (RG)
Piston
Piston cup
Wheel cylinder body
Anti-rattle pin
Pin
Spring
(RG)
Toggle lever
25 - 33 (2.5 - 3.4, 18 - 25)
Adjuster
Toggle lever spring
Washer
Clip
Anti-rattle spring
Shoe
Minimum lining thickness
1.5 mm (0.059 in)
Spring seat
Retainer
Front
Return spring (Coil type)
Return spring (U-type)
Retainer

(RG):   Rubber grease points
:   Lubricating point
(T) :   N·m (kg-m, ft-lb)

Exploded view of the Pulsar rear brake assembly

PARKING BRAKE

Cables

REMOVAL AND INSTALLATION

Rear Cable

F10 AND 310

1. Raise and support the rear of the vehicle on jackstands.
2. Place the parking brake lever in the released position.
3. Loosen the adjuster locknut and separate the rear cable from the adjuster.
4. Remove the parking brake clevis pin (at each rear wheel) from the rear end of the rear cable.
5. Remove the lock plate and the clamps retaining the rear cable to the vehicle, then remove the rear cable.
6. Install the parking brake cable and clamps to the vehicle at the adjuster. Connect the brake cable at the rear wheels. Adjust the parking brake cable.

STANZA

1. Raise and support the rear of the vehicle on jackstands.

2. Place the parking brake lever in the released position.
3. At the equalizer, loosen the adjusting nut, then remove the locking plate and the rear cable from it.
4. At both rear wheels, disconnect the rear cable clevis pin from the toggle lever.
5. Remove all of the rear cable fixing bracket screws and pull the cable from the vehicle.
6. Install the parking brake cable and clamps to the vehicle at the equalizer. Connect the brake cable at the rear wheels. Adjust the parking brake cable.

PULSAR

1. Refer to the Brake Drum, Removal and Installation procedures, in this section and remove the brake drum.
2. At the cable adjuster, loosen the adjusting nut, then separate the rear cable from the adjuster.
3. Remove the brake shoes from the backing plate, then separate the rear cable from the toggle lever.
4. Pull the cable through the backing plate and remove it from the vehicle.

1. Warning lamp switch
2. Hand brake lever
3. Front cable
4. Cable supporter
5. Lock nut
6. Clevis
7. Adjuster
8. Return spring
9. Equalizer
10. Rear cable

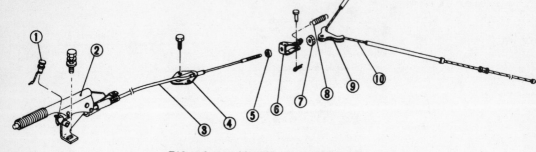

F10 sedan and hatchback parking brake

5. Install the brake cable to the vehicle through the backing plate.

6. Install the brake shoes with cable attached and drum.

7. Connect the brake cable at the adjuster.

8. Adjust the parking brake cable.

Front Cable

1. Raise and support the rear of the vehicle on jackstands.

2. Place the parking brake lever in the released position.

3. On the Pulsar, separate the front cable from the rear cable at the equalizer. On the Stanza, disconnect the front cable from the equalizer lever by removing the clevis pin.

4. Remove the center console.

5. Disconnect the parking brake lamp switch harness connector, then remove the seat belt anchor bolts.

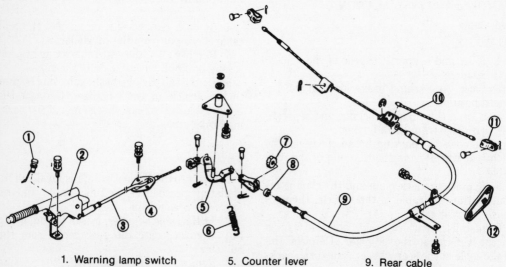

1. Warning lamp switch
2. Hand brake lever
3. Front cable
4. Cable supporter
5. Counter lever
6. Return spring
7. Adjuster
8. Lock nut
9. Rear cable
10. Equalizer
11. Clevis
12. Wire bracket

F10 station wagon parking brake

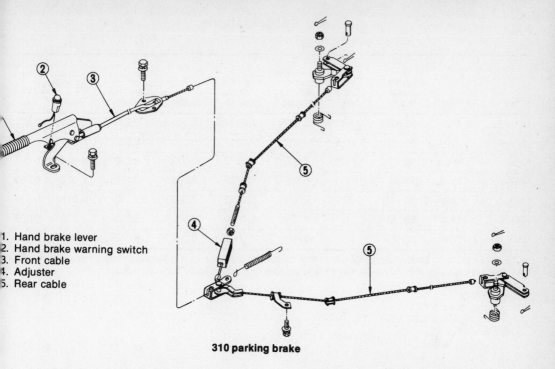

1. Hand brake lever
2. Hand brake warning switch
3. Front cable
4. Adjuster
5. Rear cable

310 parking brake

6. Remove the control lever mounting bolts and the front cable bracket mounting screws.

7. If necessary, separate the front cable from the parking brake control lever by breaking the pin.

NOTE: *If the pin must be broken to separate the front cable from the control lever, be sure to use a new pin in the installation procedures.*

8. Install the control lever/front cable assem-

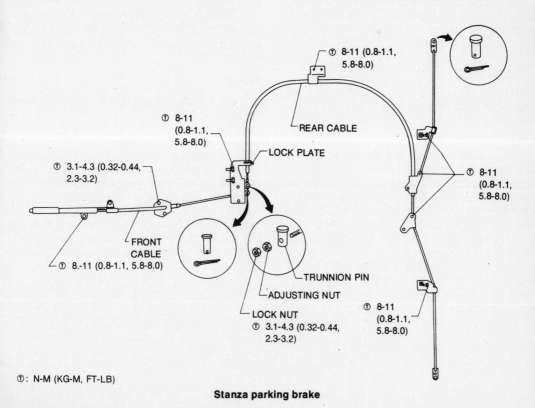

ⓣ 8-11 (0.8-1.1, 5.8-8.0)

ⓣ 8-11 (0.8-1.1, 5.8-8.0)

REAR CABLE

LOCK PLATE

ⓣ 3.1-4.3 (0.32-0.44, 2.3-3.2)

ⓣ 8-11 (0.8-1.1, 5.8-8.0)

FRONT CABLE
ⓣ 8.-11 (0.8-1.1, 5.8-8.0)

TRUNNION PIN

ADJUSTING NUT

LOCK NUT
ⓣ 3.1-4.3 (0.32-0.44, 2.3-3.2)

ⓣ 8-11 (0.8-1.1, 5.8-8.0)

ⓣ : N-M (KG-M, FT-LB)

Stanza parking brake

Brake Specifications

All measurements given are in inches unless noted

Year	Model	Lug Nut Torque (ft. lbs.)	Master Cylinder Bore	Brake Disc		Drum		Minimum Lining Thickness	
				Minimum Thickness	Maximum Run-Out	Diameter	Max. Wear Limit	Front	Rear
1977–78	F10	58–65	0.750	0.339	0.0059	8.000	8.050	0.063	0.039
1979–82	310	58–72	0.8125	0.339	0.0047	8.000	8.050	0.079	0.059
1982	Stanza	58–72	0.8125	0.630	0.0059	8.000	8.050	0.080	0.059
1983–88	Stanza	58–72	0.8125	0.630	0.0028	8.000	8.050	0.079	0.059
1983	Pulsar	58–72	①	0.394	0.0028	7.090	7.130	0.079	0.059
1984	Pulsar	58–72	②	0.394	0.0028	8.000	8.050	0.079	0.059
1985–88	Pulsar	58–72	①	0.394	0.0028	8.000	8.050	0.079	0.059

NOTE: Minimum lining thickness is as recommended by the manufacturer. Due to variation in state inspection regulations, the minimum allowable thickness may be different than recommended by the manufacturer.

① Small: 0.750
   Large: 0.9375
② Non Turbo; Small: 0.750
               Large: 0.9375
   Turbo; Small: 0.8125
           Large: 1.000

bly in through the driver's compartment with a new pin if necessary.

9. Connect the parking brake lamp switch harness connector and the seat belt anchor bolts.

10. Install the center console.

11. Connect the rear end of brake cable to the attaching point.

12. Adjust the parking brake cable.

ADJUSTMENT

Handbrake adjustments are generally not needed, unless the cables have stretched.

F10, 310 and Pulsar

There is an adjusting nut on the cable under the car, usually at the end of the front cable and near the point at which the two cables from the rear wheels come together (the equalizer). Some models also have a turnbuckle in the rear cable to compensate for cable stretching.

1. Adjust the rear brakes with the parking brake fully released.

2. Apply the hand brake lever so that it is 5-6 notches (F10-Sedan and Hatchback), 6-8 notches (F10 Sport Wagon), 7-8 notches (310) or 6-7 notches (Pulsar) from its fully released position.

3. Adjust the parking brake turnbuckle, locknuts or equalizer so that the rear brakes are locked.

4. Release the parking brake. The wheels should turn freely. If not, loosen the parking brake adjuster until the wheels turn with no drag.

Stanza

1. Make sure that the rear brakes are in good condition.

2. Carefully remove the dust boot from around the parking brake lever.

3. The adjustment is made by determining the amount of force needed to pull up on the lever. A force of 44 lbs. should be needed to raise the lever 7-8 notches or clicks.

4. To adjust the pull, raise and support the vehicle on jackstands. There are two nuts on the handbrake clevis rod. Loosen the locknut and turn the adjusting nut to establish the correct pull.

5. Tighten the adjuster locknut.

CHILTON'S
AUTO BODY REPAIR TIPS

Tools and Materials • Step-by-Step Illustrated Procedures
How To Repair Dents, Scratches and Rust Holes
Spray Painting and Refinishing Tips

With a little practice, basic body repair procedures can be mastered by any do-it-yourself mechanic. The step-by-step repairs shown here can be applied to almost any type of auto body repair.

TOOLS & MATERIALS

You may already have basic tools, such as hammers and electric drills. Other tools unique to body repair — body hammers, grinding attachments, sanding blocks, dent puller, half-round plastic file and plastic spreaders — are relatively inexpensive and can be obtained wherever auto parts or auto body repair parts are sold. Portable air compressors and paint spray guns can be purchased or rented.

Auto Body Repair Kits

The best and most often used products are available to the do-it-yourselfer in kit form, from major manufacturers of auto body repair products. The same manufacturers also merchandise the individual products for use by pros.

Kits are available to make a wide variety of repairs, including holes, dents and scratches and fiberglass, and offer the advantage of buying the materials you'll need for the job. There is little waste or chance of materials going bad from not being used. Many kits may also contain basic body-working tools such as body files, sanding blocks and spreaders. Check the contents of the kit before buying your tools.

BODY REPAIR TIPS

Safety

Many of the products associated with auto body repair and refinishing contain toxic chemicals. Read all labels before opening containers and store them in a safe place and manner.

• Wear eye protection (safety goggles) when using power tools or when performing any operation that involves the removal of any type of material.

• Wear lung protection (disposable mask or respirator) when grinding, sanding or painting.

Sanding

1 Sand off paint before using a dent puller. When using a non-adhesive sanding disc, cover the back of the disc with an overlapping layer or two of masking tape and trim the edges. The disc will last considerably longer.

2 Use the circular motion of the sanding disc to grind *into* the edge of the repair. Grinding or sanding away from the jagged edge will only tear the sandpaper.

3 Use the palm of your hand flat on the panel to detect high and low spots. Do not use your fingertips. Slide your hand slowly back and forth.

WORKING WITH BODY FILLER

Mixing The Filler

Cleanliness and proper mixing and application are extremely important. Use a clean piece of plastic or glass or a disposable artist's palette to mix body filler.

1 Allow plenty of time and follow directions. No useful purpose will be served by adding more hardener to make it cure (set-up) faster. Less hardener means more curing time, but the mixture dries harder; more hardener means less curing time but a softer mixture.

2 Both the hardener and the filler should be thoroughly kneaded or stirred before mixing. Hardener should be a solid paste and dispense like thin toothpaste. Body filler should be smooth, and free of lumps or thick spots.

Getting the proper amount of hardener in the filler is the trickiest part of preparing the filler. Use the same amount of hardener in cold or warm weather. For contour filler (thick coats), a bead of hardener twice the diameter of the filler is about right. There's about a 15% margin on either side, but, if in doubt use less hardener.

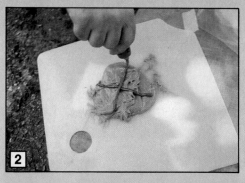

3 Mix the body filler and hardener by wiping across the mixing surface, picking the mixture up and wiping it again. Colder weather requires longer mixing times. Do not mix in a circular motion; this will trap air bubbles which will become holes in the cured filler.

Applying The Filler

1 For best results, filler should not be applied over ¼" thick.

Apply the filler in several coats. Build it up to above the level of the repair surface so that it can be sanded or grated down.

The first coat of filler must be pressed on with a firm wiping motion.

Apply the filler in one direction only. Working the filler back and forth will either pull it off the metal or trap air bubbles.

REPAIRING DENTS

Before you start, take a few minutes to study the damaged area. Try to visualize the shape of the panel before it was damaged. If the damage is on the left fender, look at the right fender and use it as a guide. If there is access to the panel from behind, you can reshape it with a body hammer. If not, you'll have to use a dent puller. Go slowly and work the metal a little at a time. Get the panel as straight as possible before applying filler.

1 This dent is typical of one that can be pulled out or hammered out from behind. Remove the headlight cover, headlight assembly and turn signal housing.

2 Drill a series of holes ½ the size of the end of the dent puller along the stress line. Make some trial pulls and assess the results. If necessary, drill more holes and try again. Do not hurry.

3 If possible, use a body hammer and block to shape the metal back to its original contours. Get the metal back as close to its original shape as possible. Don't depend on body filler to fill dents.

4 Using an 80-grit grinding disc on an electric drill, grind the paint from the surrounding area down to bare metal. Use a new grinding pad to prevent heat buildup that will warp metal.

5 The area should look like this when you're finished grinding. Knock the drill holes in and tape over small openings to keep plastic filler out.

6 Mix the body filler (see Body Repair Tips). Spread the body filler evenly over the entire area (see Body Repair Tips). Be sure to cover the area completely.

7 Let the body filler dry until the surface can just be scratched with your fingernail. Knock the high spots from the body filler with a body file ("Cheesegrater"). Check frequently with the palm of your hand for high and low spots.

8 Check to be sure that trim pieces that will be installed later will fit exactly. Sand the area with 40-grit paper.

9 If you wind up with low spots, you may have to apply another layer of filler.

10 Knock the high spots off with 40-grit paper. When you are satisfied with the contours of the repair, apply a thin coat of filler to cover pin holes and scratches.

11 Block sand the area with 40-grit paper to a smooth finish. Pay particular attention to body lines and ridges that must be well-defined.

12 Sand the area with 400 paper and then finish with a scuff pad. The finished repair is ready for priming and painting (see Painting Tips).

Materials and photos courtesy of Ritt Jones Auto Body, Prospect Park, PA.

REPAIRING RUST HOLES

There are many ways to repair rust holes. The fiberglass cloth kit shown here is one of the most cost efficient for the owner because it provides a strong repair that resists cracking and moisture and is relatively easy to use. It can be used on large and small holes (with or without backing) and can be applied over contoured areas. Remember, however, that short of replacing an entire panel, no repair is a guarantee that the rust will not return.

1 Remove any trim that will be in the way. Clean away all loose debris. Cut away all the rusted metal. But be sure to leave enough metal to retain the contour or body shape.

2 Grind away all traces of rust with a 24-grit grinding disc. Be sure to grind back 3-4 inches from the edge of the hole down to bare metal and be sure all traces of paint, primer and rust are removed.

3 Block sand the area with 80 or 100 grit sandpaper to get a clear, shiny surface and feathered paint edge. Tap the edges of the hole inward with a ball peen hammer.

4 If you are going to use release film, cut a piece about 2-3″ larger than the area you have sanded. Place the film over the repair and mark the sanded area on the film. Avoid any unnecessary wrinkling of the film.

5 Cut 2 pieces of fiberglass matte to match the shape of the repair. One piece should be about 1″ smaller than the sanded area and the second piece should be 1″ smaller than the first. Mix enough filler and hardener to saturate the fiberglass material (see Body Repair Tips).

6 Lay the release sheet on a flat surface and spread an even layer of filler, large enough to cover the repair. Lay the smaller piece of fiberglass cloth in the center of the sheet and spread another layer of filler over the fiberglass cloth. Repeat the operation for the larger piece of cloth.

7 Place the repair material over the repair area, with the release film facing outward. Use a spreader and work from the center outward to smooth the material, following the body contours. Be sure to remove all air bubbles.

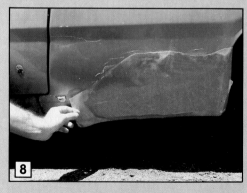

8 Wait until the repair has dried tack-free and peel off the release sheet. The ideal working temperature is 60°-90° F. Cooler or warmer temperatures or high humidity may require additional curing time. Wait longer, if in doubt.

9 Sand and feather-edge the entire area. The initial sanding can be done with a sanding disc on an electric drill if care is used. Finish the sanding with a block sander. Low spots can be filled with body filler; this may require several applications.

10 When the filler can just be scratched with a fingernail, knock the high spots down with a body file and smooth the entire area with 80-grit. Feather the filled areas into the surrounding areas.

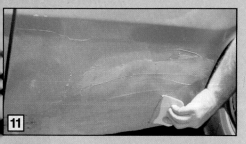

11 When the area is sanded smooth, mix some topcoat and hardener and apply it directly with a spreader. This will give a smooth finish and prevent the glass matte from showing through the paint.

12 Block sand the topcoat smooth with finishing sandpaper (200 grit), and 400 grit. The repair is ready for masking, priming and painting (see Painting Tips).

Materials and photos courtesy Marson Corporation, Chelsea, Massachusetts

PAINTING TIPS

Preparation

1 SANDING — Use a 400 or 600 grit wet or dry sandpaper. Wet-sand the area with a 1/4 sheet of sandpaper soaked in clean water. Keep the paper wet while sanding. Sand the area until the repaired area tapers into the original finish.

2 CLEANING — Wash the area to be painted thoroughly with water and a clean rag. Rinse it thoroughly and wipe the surface dry until you're sure it's completely free of dirt, dust, fingerprints, wax, detergent or other foreign matter.

3 MASKING — Protect any areas you don't want to overspray by covering them with masking tape and newspaper. Be careful not get fingerprints on the area to be painted.

4 PRIMING — All exposed metal should be primed before painting. Primer protects the metal and provides an excellent surface for paint adhesion. When the primer is dry, wet-sand the area again with 600 grit wet-sandpaper. Clean the area again after sanding.

Painting Techniques

P aint applied from either a spray gun or a spray can (for small areas) will provide good results. Experiment on an old piece of metal to get the right combination before you begin painting.

SPRAYING VISCOSITY (SPRAY GUN ONLY) — Paint should be thinned to spraying viscosity according to the directions on the can. Use only the recommended thinner or reducer and the same amount of reduction regardless of temperature.

AIR PRESSURE (SPRAY GUN ONLY) — This is extremely important. Be sure you are using the proper recommended pressure.

TEMPERATURE — The surface to be painted should be approximately the same temperature as the surrounding air. Applying warm paint to a cold surface, or vice versa, will completely upset the paint characteristics.

THICKNESS — Spray with smooth strokes. In general, the thicker the coat of paint, the longer the drying time. Apply several thin coats about 30 seconds apart. The paint should remain wet long enough to flow out and no longer; heavier coats will only produce sags or wrinkles. Spray a light (fog) coat, followed by heavier color coats.

DISTANCE — The ideal spraying distance is 8″-12″ from the gun or can to the surface. Shorter distances will produce ripples, while greater distances will result in orange peel, dry film and poor color match and loss of material due to overspray.

OVERLAPPING — The gun or can should be kept at right angles to the surface at all times. Work to a wet edge at an even speed, using a 50% overlap and direct the center of the spray at the lower or nearest edge of the previous stroke.

RUBBING OUT (BLENDING) FRESH PAINT — Let the paint dry thoroughly. Runs or imperfections can be sanded out, primed and repainted.

Don't be in too big a hurry to remove the masking. This only produces paint ridges. When the finish has dried for at least a week, apply a small amount of fine grade rubbing compound with a clean, wet cloth. Use lots of water and blend the new paint with the surrounding area.

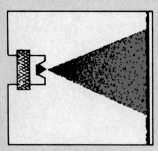

WRONG

Thin coat. Stroke too fast, not enough overlap, gun too far away.

CORRECT

Medium coat. Proper distance, good stroke, proper overlap.

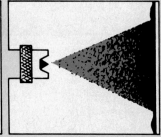

WRONG

Heavy coat. Stroke too slow, too much overlap, gun too close.

10 Body

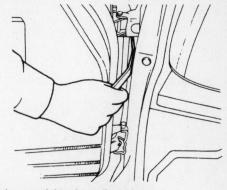

EXTERIOR

Doors

REMOVAL AND INSTALLATION

Front and Rear

1. Place a jack or stand beneath the door to support its weight.
   NOTE: *Place a rag at lower edge of the door and jack or stand to prevent damage to painted surface.*
2. Remove door without hinge.
3. Remove the door hinge.
4. Installation is in the reverse order of removal.
   NOTE: *When installing hinge, coat the hinge link with recommended multipurpose grease.*

ADJUSTMENT

Front and Rear

Proper door alignment can be obtained by adjusting the door hinge and door lock striker. The door hinge and striker can be moved up and down fore and aft in enlarged holes by loosening the attaching bolts.
   NOTE: *The door should be adjusted for an even and parallel fit for the door opening and surrounding body panels.*

Using special tool to adjust hinge

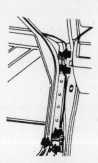

Removing mounting bolts from door

Hood

REMOVAL AND INSTALLATION

1. Open the hood and protect the body with covers to protect the painted surfaces.
2. Mark the hood hinge locations on the hood for proper reinstallation.
3. Holding both sides of the hood, unscrew the bolts securing the hinge to the hood. This operation requires a helper.
4. Installation is the reverse of removal.

ALIGNMENT

The hood can be adjusted with bolts attaching the hood to the hood hinges, hood lock

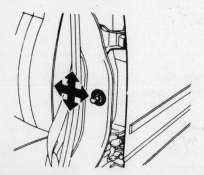

Adjusting door striker

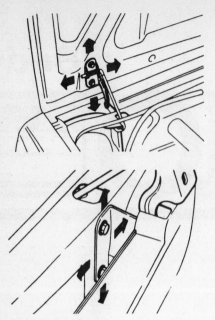

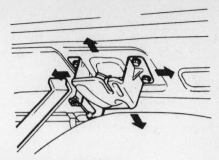

Adjusting hood at hood lock

Adjusting hood at hinges

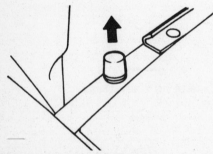

Adjusting hood at bumper rubber

mechanism and hood bumpers. Adjust the hood for an even fit between the front fenders.

1. Adjust the hood fore and aft by loosening the bolts attaching the hood to the hinge and repositioning hood.

2. Loosen the hood bumper lock nuts and lower bumpers until they do not contact the front of the hood when the hood is closed.

3. Set the striker at the center of the hood lock, and tighten the hood lock securing bolts temporarily.

4. Raise the two hood bumpers until the hood is flush with the fenders.

5. Tighten the hood lock securing bolts after the proper adjustment has been obtained.

Trunklid

REMOVAL AND INSTALLATION

1. Open the trunk lid and position a cloth or cushion to protect the painted areas.

2. Mark the trunk lid hinge locations or trunk lid for proper reinstallation.

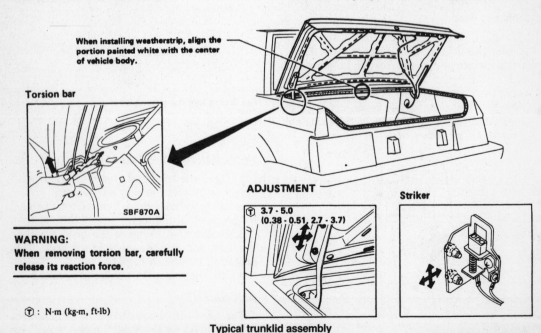

When installing weatherstrip, align the portion painted white with the center of vehicle body.

Torsion bar

SBF870A

WARNING:
When removing torsion bar, carefully release its reaction force.

ⓣ : N·m (kg-m, ft-lb)

ADJUSTMENT

ⓣ 3.7 - 5.0
(0.38 - 0.51, 2.7 - 3.7)

Striker

Typical trunklid assembly

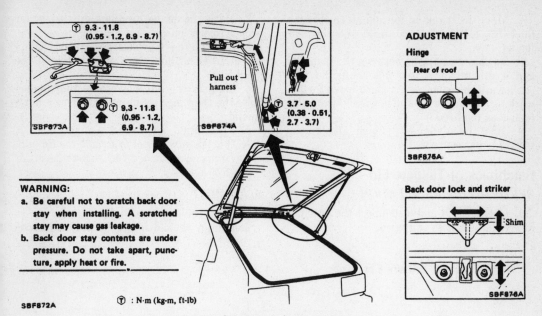

Typical hatchback assembly

3. Support the trunk lid by hand and remove the bolts attaching the trunk lid to the hinge. Then remove the trunk lid.

4. Installation is the reverse of removal.

ALIGNMENT

1. Loosen the trunk lid hinge attaching bolts until they are just loose enough to move the trunk lid.

1. Lock
2. Bumper rubber
3. Tailgate
4. Tailgate stay
5. Lock cylinder
6. Retaining clip
7. Striker catcher
8. Shim
9. Striker
10. Wedge bumper
11. Back door hinge

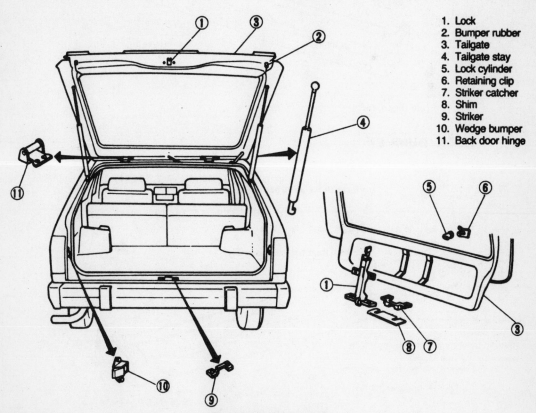

Typical tailgate assembly

2. Move the trunk lid for and aft to obtain a flush fit between the trunk lid and the rear fender.

3. To obtain a snug fit between the trunk lid and weatherstrip, loosen the trunk lid lock striker attaching bolts enough to move the lid, working the striker up and down and from side to side as required.

4. After the adjustment is made tighten the striker bolts securely.

Hatchback or Tailgate Lid
REMOVAL AND INSTALLATION

1. Open the lid and disconnect the rear defogger harness if so equipped.

2. Mark the hinge locations on the lid for proper relocation.

3. Position rags between the roof and the upper end of the lid to prevent scratching the paint.

4. Support the lid and remove the support bolts the the hinge retaining bolts and remove the lid.

5. Installation is the reverse of removal.
NOTE: *Be careful not to scratch the lift support rods. A scratched rod may cause oil or gas leakaged*

ALIGNMENT

1. Open the hatchback lid.
2. Loosen the lid hinge to body attaching

FRONT BUMPER

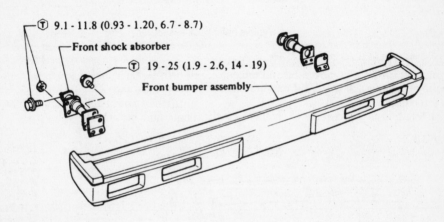

$\widehat{T}$ 9.1 - 11.8 (0.93 - 1.20, 6.7 - 8.7)

Front shock absorber

$\widehat{T}$ 19 - 25 (1.9 - 2.6, 14 - 19)

Front bumper assembly

$\widehat{T}$: N·m (kg-m, ft-lb)

REAR BUMPER

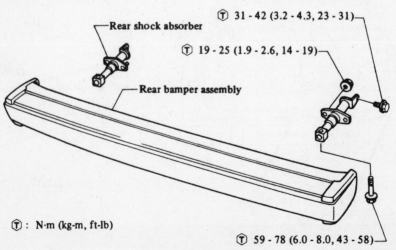

$\widehat{T}$ 31 - 42 (3.2 - 4.3, 23 - 31)

Rear shock absorber

$\widehat{T}$ 19 - 25 (1.9 - 2.6, 14 - 19)

Rear bamper assembly

$\widehat{T}$: N·m (kg-m, ft-lb)

$\widehat{T}$ 59 - 78 (6.0 - 8.0, 43 - 58)

Typical bumper assembly

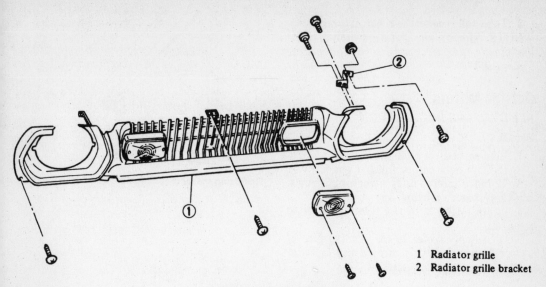

1 Radiator grille
2 Radiator grille bracket

Removing radiator grille bolts

bolts until they are just loose enough to move the lid.

3. Move the lid up and down to obtain a flush fit between the lid and the roof.

4. After adjustment is completed tighten the hinge attaching bolts securely.

Bumpers

REMOVAL AND INSTALLATION

Front and Rear

1. Disconnect all electrical connectors at bumper assembly if so equipped.

2. Remove bumper mounting bolts and bumper assembly.

3. Remove shock absorbers from bumper.
CAUTION: *The shock absorber is filled with a high pressure gas and should not be diassembled, drilled or exposed to an open flame.*

4. Install shock absorbers and bumper in reverse order of removal.

Grille

REMOVAL AND INSTALLATION

1. Remove radiator grille bracket bolts.
NOTE: *Early models use clips to hold the radiator grille assembly to the vehicle.*

2. Remove radiator grille from the vehicle.

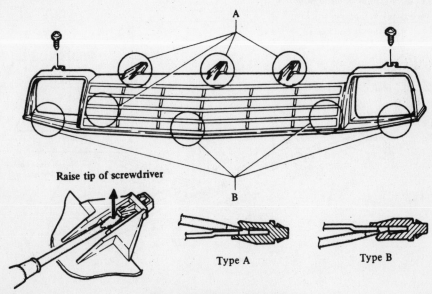

Raise tip of screwdriver

A

B

Type A   Type B

Removing radiator grille clips

3. To install reverse the removal procedures.
NOTE: *The radiator grille assembly is made of plastic, thus never use excessive force to remove it.*

Outside Mirrors

REMOVAL AND INSTALLATION

Manual

1. Remove control knob handle.
2. Remove door corner finisher panel.
3. **Remove mirror body attaching screws,** and then remove mirror body
4. Installation is in the reverse order of removal.
NOTE: *Apply sealer to the rear surface of door corner finisher panel during installation to prevent water leak.*

Power

1. Remove door corner finisher panel.
2. Remove mirror body attaching screws, and then remove mirror body

Removing mirror mounting screws

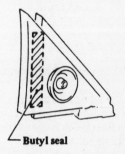

Apply sealer to rear surface of finisher panel

3. Disconnect the electrical connection.
NOTE: *It may be necessary to remove the door trim panel to gain access to the electrical connection.*
4. Installation is in the reverse order of removal.

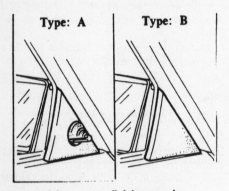

Two types of door corner finisher panels

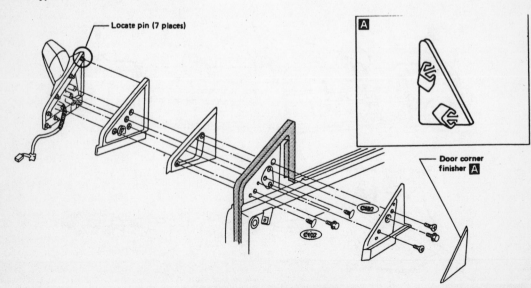

Typical power mirror installation

Antenna

REMOVAL AND INSTALLATION

Fender Mounted

1. Remove antenna mounting nut.
2. Disconnect the antenna lead at the radio.
3. Remove antenna from vehicle.
4. Installation is in the reverse order of removal.

INTERIOR

Door Panel, Glass and Regulator

REMOVAL AND INSTALLATION

Front and Rear

1. Remove the regulator handle by pushing the set pin spring.
2. Remove the arm rest, door inside handle escutcheon and door lock.
3. Remove the door finisher and sealing screen.

Rear

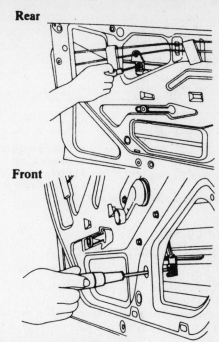

Front

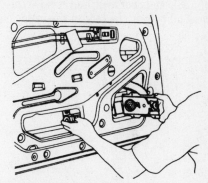

Removing glass attaching bolts

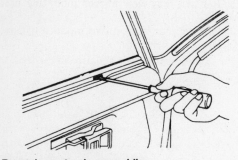

Removing outer door moulding

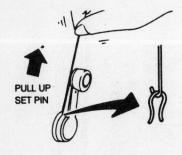

Removing regulator from door

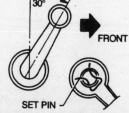

PULL UP SET PIN

30°

FRONT

SET PIN

Regulator handle and set pin removal and installation

4. On some models it may be necessary to remove the outer door moulding.
5. Lower the door glass with the regulator handle until the regulator-to-glass attaching bolts appear at the access holes in the door inside panel.
6. Raise the door glass and draw it upwards.
7. Remove the regulator attaching bolts and remove the regulator assembly through the large access hole in ther door panel.
8. Install the window regulator assembly in the door.
9. Connect all mounting bolts and check for proper operation.
10. Adjust the window if necessary and install the door trim panel.
11. Install all the attaching components to the door panel.
12. Install the window regulator handle.

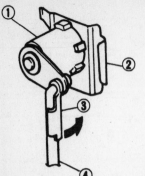

1. Door lock cylinder
2. Retaining clip
3. Resin clip
4. Lock cylinder rod

Removing the lock cylinder rod

Door Locks

REMOVAL AND INSTALLATION

1. Remove the door panel and sealing screen.
2. Remove the lock cylinder from the rod by turning the resin clip.
3. Loosen the nuts attaching the outside door handle and remove the outside door handle.
4. Remove the screws retaining the inside door handle and door lock, and remove the door lock assembly from the hole in the inside of the door.

5. Remove the lock cylinder by removing the retaining clip.
6. Install the lock cylinder and clip to the door.
7. Install the door lock assembly and handles.
8. Install door panel and all attaching parts.

Electrical Window Motor

REMOVAL AND INSTALLATION

1. Remove the door panel and sealing screen.
2. Remove the power widow motor mounting bolts
3. Remove all electrical connections and cable connection.
4. Remove the power window motor from the vehicle
5. Installation is in the reverse order of removal.

Inside Rear View Mirror

REMOVAL AND INSTALLATION

1. Remove rear view mirror mounting bolt cover.
2. Remove rear view mirror mounting bolts.
3. Remove mirror.

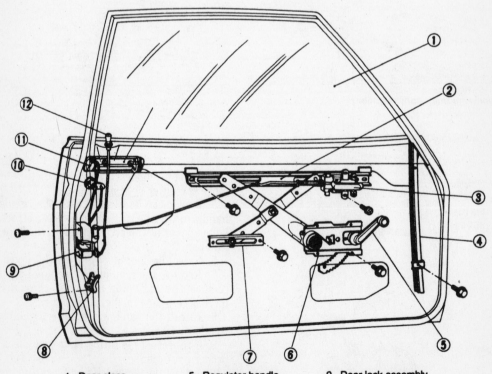

1. Door glass
2. Guide channel A
3. Inside door handle
4. Front lower sash
5. Regulator handle
6. Regulator assembly
7. Guide channel B
8. Glass lower guide
9. Door lock assembly
10. Door lock cylinder
11. Outside door handle
12. Inside door lock knob

Typical front door assembly—early models

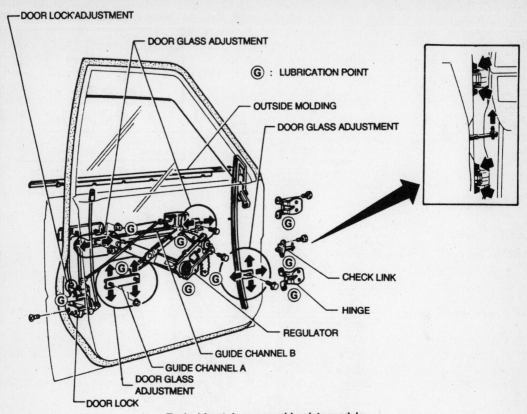

DOOR LOCK ADJUSTMENT

DOOR GLASS ADJUSTMENT

G : LUBRICATION POINT

OUTSIDE MOLDING

DOOR GLASS ADJUSTMENT

CHECK LINK

HINGE

REGULATOR

GUIDE CHANNEL B

GUIDE CHANNEL A

DOOR GLASS
ADJUSTMENT

DOOR LOCK

Typical front door assembly—late models

1. Door glass
2. Inside door lock knob
3. Inside door handle
4. Guide channel A
5. Regulator handle
6. Regulator assembly
7. Lower sash
8. Center sash
9. Door lock assembly
10. Outside door handle

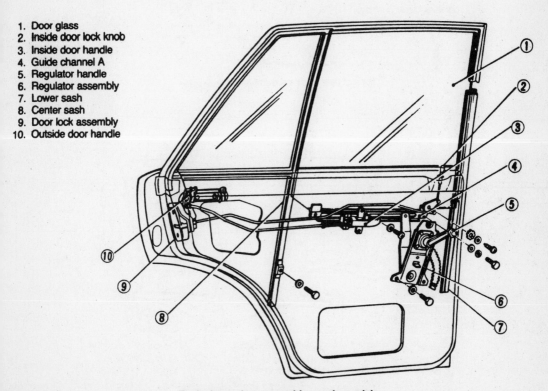

Typical rear door assembly—early models

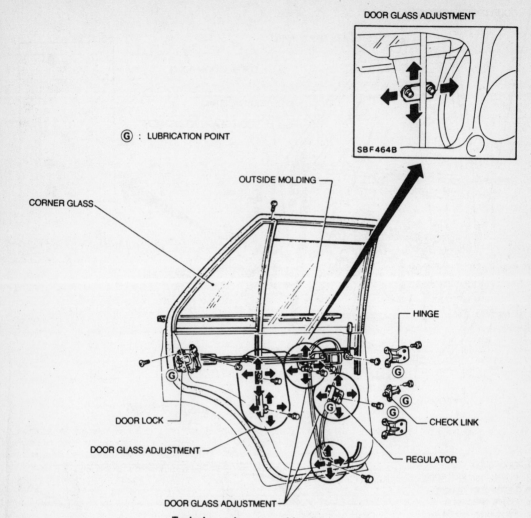

DOOR GLASS ADJUSTMENT

SBF464B

Ⓖ : LUBRICATION POINT

CORNER GLASS

OUTSIDE MOLDING

HINGE

Ⓖ

DOOR LOCK

DOOR GLASS ADJUSTMENT

CHECK LINK

REGULATOR

DOOR GLASS ADJUSTMENT

Typical rear door assembly—late models

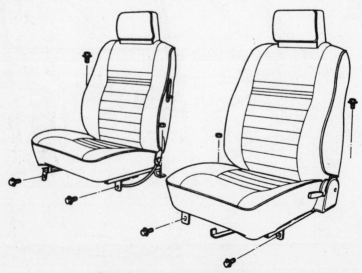

Typical front seat mounting bolts

Typical rear seat mounting bolts

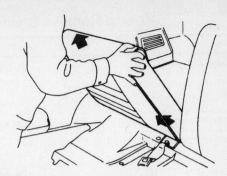

Removing rear seat—early models

4. Installation is in the reverse order of removal.

Seats

REMOVAL AND INSTALLATION

Front

1. Remove front seat mounting bolts
2. Remove front seat assembly.
3. Installation is in the reverse order of removal.

Rear

1. Remove rear seat cushion mounting bolts.
2. Remove screw attaching luggage floor carpet.
3. Remove rear seat back by tilting forward and pulling straight up.
NOTE: *On hatchback models the rear seat back is remove similar as above.*

How to Remove Stains from Fabric Interior

For rest results, spots and stains should be removed as soon as possible. Never use gasoline, lacquer thinner, acetone, nail polish remover or bleach. Use a 3' x 3" piece of cheesecloth. Squeeze most of the liquid from the fabric and wipe the stained fabric from the outside of the stain toward the center with a lifting motion. Turn the cheesecloth as soon as one side becomes soiled. When using water to remove a stain, be sure to wash the entire section after the spot has been removed to avoid water stains. Encrusted spots can be broken up with a dull knife and vacuumed before removing the stain.

Type of Stain	How to Remove It
Surface spots	Brush the spots out with a small hand brush or use a commercial preparation such as K2R to lift the stain.
Mildew	Clean around the mildew with warm suds. Rinse in cold water and soak the mildew area in a solution of 1 part table salt and 2 parts water. Wash with upholstery cleaner.
Water stains	Water stains in fabric materials can be removed with a solution made from 1 cup of table salt dissolved in 1 quart of water. Vigorously scrub the solution into the stain and rinse with clear water. Water stains in nylon or other synthetic fabrics should be removed with a commercial type spot remover.
Chewing gum, tar, crayons, shoe polish (greasy stains)	Do not use a cleaner that will soften gum or tar. Harden the deposit with an ice cube and scrape away as much as possible with a dull knife. Moisten the remainder with cleaning fluid and scrub clean.
Ice cream, candy	Most candy has a sugar base and can be removed with a cloth wrung out in warm water. Oily candy, after cleaning with warm water, should be cleaned with upholstery cleaner. Rinse with warm water and clean the remainder with cleaning fluid.
Wine, alcohol, egg, milk, soft drink (non-greasy stains)	Do not use soap. Scrub the stain with a cloth wrung out in warm water. Remove the remainder with cleaning fluid.
Grease, oil, lipstick, butter and related stains	Use a spot remover to avoid leaving a ring. Work from the outisde of the stain to the center and dry with a clean cloth when the spot is gone.

How to Remove Stains from Fabric Interior (cont.)

Type of Stain	How to Remove It
Headliners (cloth)	Mix a solution of warm water and foam upholstery cleaner to give thick suds. Use only foam—liquid may streak or spot. Clean the entire headliner in one operation using a circular motion with a natural sponge.
Headliner (vinyl)	Use a vinyl cleaner with a sponge and wipe clean with a dry cloth.
Seats and door panels	Mix 1 pint upholstery cleaner in 1 gallon of water. Do not soak the fabric around the buttons.
Leather or vinyl fabric	Use a multi-purpose cleaner full strength and a stiff brush. Let stand 2 minutes and scrub thoroughly. Wipe with a clean, soft rag.
Nylon or synthetic fabrics	For normal stains, use the same procedures you would for washing cloth upholstery. If the fabric is extremely dirty, use a multi-purpose cleaner full strength with a stiff scrub brush. Scrub thoroughly in all directions and wipe with a cotton towel or soft rag.

Mechanic's Data

11

TAX
10.16mm
1":254mm
Liter
Parts
Overhaul

General Conversion Table

Multiply By	To Convert	To	
		LENGTH	
2.54	Inches	Centimeters	.3937
25.4	Inches	Millimeters	.03937
30.48	Feet	Centimeters	.0328
.304	Feet	Meters	3.28
.914	Yards	Meters	1.094
1.609	Miles	Kilometers	.621
		VOLUME	
.473	Pints	Liters	2.11
.946	Quarts	Liters	1.06
3.785	Gallons	Liters	.264
.016	Cubic inches	Liters	61.02
16.39	Cubic inches	Cubic cms.	.061
28.3	Cubic feet	Liters	.0353
		MASS (Weight)	
28.35	Ounces	Grams	.035
.4536	Pounds	Kilograms	2.20
—	To obtain	From	Multiply by

Multiply By	To Convert	To	
		AREA	
.645	Square inches	Square cms.	.155
.836	Square yds.	Square meters	1.196
		FORCE	
4.448	Pounds	Newtons	.225
.138	Ft./lbs.	Kilogram/meters	7.23
1.36	Ft./lbs.	Newton-meters	.737
.112	In./lbs.	Newton-meters	8.844
		PRESSURE	
.068	Psi	Atmospheres	14.7
6.89	Psi	Kilopascals	.145
		OTHER	
1.104	Horsepower (DIN)	Horsepower (SAE)	.9861
.746	Horsepower (SAE)	Kilowatts (KW)	1.34
1.60	Mph	Km/h	.625
.425	Mpg	Km/1	2.35
—	To obtain	From	Multiply by

Tap Drill Sizes

National Coarse or U.S.S.

Screw & Tap Size	Threads Per Inch	Use Drill Number
No. 5	40	39
No. 6	32	36
No. 8	32	29
No. 10	24	25
No. 12	24	17
1/4	20	8
5/16	18	F
3/8	16	5/16
7/16	14	U
1/2	13	27/64
9/16	12	31/64
5/8	11	17/32
3/4	10	21/32
7/8	9	49/64

National Coarse or U.S.S.

Screw & Tap Size	Threads Per Inch	Use Drill Number
1	8	7/8
1 1/8	7	63/64
1 1/4	7	1 7/64
1 1/2	6	1 11/32

National Fine or S.A.E.

Screw & Tap Size	Threads Per Inch	Use Drill Number
No. 5	44	37
No. 6	40	33
No. 8	36	29
No. 10	32	21

National Fine or S.A.E.

Screw & Tap Size	Threads Per Inch	Use Drill Number
No. 12	28	15
1/4	28	3
6/16	24	1
3/8	24	Q
7/16	20	W
1/2	20	29/64
9/16	18	33/64
5/8	18	37/64
3/4	16	11/16
7/8	14	13/16
1 1/8	12	1 3/64
1 1/4	12	1 11/64
1 1/2	12	1 27/64

Drill Sizes In Decimal Equivalents

Inch	Decimal	Wire & Letter	mm
1/64	.0156		.39
	.0157		.4
	.0160	78	
	.0165		.42
	.0173		.44
	.0177		.45
	.0180	77	
	.0181		.46
	.0189		.48
	.0197		.5
	.0200	76	
	.0210	75	
	.0217		.55
	.0225	74	
	.0236		.6
	.0240	73	
	.0250	72	
	.0256		.65
	.0260	71	
	.0276		.7
	.0280	70	
	.0292	69	
	.0295		.75
	.0310	68	
1/32	.0312		.79
	.0315		.8
	.0320	67	
	.0330	66	
	.0335		.85
	.0350	65	
	.0354		.9
	.0360	64	
	.0370	63	
	.0374		.95
	.0380	62	
	.0390	61	
	.0394		1.0
	.0400	60	
	.0410	59	
	.0413		1.05
	.0420	58	
	.0430	57	
	.0433		1.1
	.0453		1.15
	.0465	56	
3/64	.0469		1.19
	.0472		1.2
	.0492		1.25
	.0512		1.3
	.0520	55	
	.0531		1.35
	.0550	54	
	.0551		1.4
	.0571		1.45
	.0591		1.5
	.0595	53	
	.0610		1.55
1/16	.0625		1.59
	.0630		1.6
	.0635	52	
	.0650		1.65
	.0669		1.7
	.0670	51	
	.0689		1.75
	.0700	50	
	.0709		1.8
	.0728		1.85
	.0730	49	
	.0748		1.9
	.0760	48	
	.0768		1.95
5/64	.0781		
	.0785	47	1.98
	.0787		2.0
	.0807		2.05
	.0810	46	
	.0820	45	
	.0827		2.1
	.0846		2.15
	.0860	44	
	.0866		2.2
	.0886		2.25
	.0890	43	
	.0906		2.3
	.0925		2.35
	.0935	42	
3/32	.0938		2.38
	.0945		2.4
	.0960	41	
	.0965		2.45
	.0980	40	
	.0981		2.5
	.0995	39	
	.1015	38	
	.1024		2.6
	.1040	37	
	.1063		2.7
	.1065	36	
	.1083		2.75
7/64	.1094		2.77
	.1100	35	
	.1102		2.8
	.1110	34	
	.1130	33	
	.1142		2.9
	.1160	32	
	.1181		3.0
	.1200	31	
	.1220		3.1
1/8	.1250		3.17
	.1260		3.2
	.1280		3.25
	.1285	30	
	.1299		3.3
	.1339		3.4
	.1360	29	
	.1378		3.5
	.1405	28	
9/64	.1406		3.57
	.1417		3.6
	.1440	27	
	.1457		3.7
	.1470	26	
	.1476		3.75
	.1495	25	
	.1496		3.8
	.1520	24	
	.1535		3.9
	.1540	23	
5/32	.1562		3.96
	.1570	22	
	.1575		4.0
	.1590	21	
	.1610	20	
	.1614		4.1
	.1654		4.2
	.1660	19	
	.1673		4.25
	.1693		4.3
	.1695	18	
11/64	.1719		4.36
	.1730	17	
	.1732		4.4
	.1770	16	
	.1772		4.5
	.1800	15	
	.1811		4.6
	.1820	14	
	.1850	13	
	.1850		4.7
	.1870		4.75
3/16	.1875		4.76
	.1890		4.8
	.1890	12	
	.1910	11	
	.1929		4.9
	.1935	10	
	.1960	9	
	.1969		5.0
	.1990	8	
	.2008		5.1
	.2010	7	
13/64	.2031		5.16
	.2040	6	
	.2047		5.2
	.2055	5	
	.2067		5.25
	.2087		5.3
	.2090	4	
	.2126		5.4
	.2130	3	
	.2165		5.5
7/32	.2188		5.55
	.2205		5.6
	.2210	2	
	.2244		5.7
	.2264		5.75
	.2280	1	
	.2283		5.8
	.2323		5.9
	.2340	A	
15/64	.2344		5.95
	.2362		6.0
	.2380	B	
	.2402		6.1
	.2420	C	
	.2441		6.2
	.2460	D	
	.2461		6.25
	.2480		6.3
1/4	.2500	E	6.35
	.2520		6.
	.2559		6.5
	.2570	F	
	.2598		6.6
	.2610	G	
	.2638		6.7
17/64	.2656		6.74
	.2657		6.75
	.2660	H	
	.2677		6.8
	.2717		6.9
	.2720	I	
	.2756		7.0
	.2770	J	
	.2795		7.1
	.2810	K	
9/32	.2812		7.14
	.2835		7.2
	.2854		7.25
	.2874		7.3
	.2900	L	
	.2913		7.4
	.2950	M	
	.2953		7.5
19/64	.2969		7.54
	.2992		7.6
	.3020	N	
	.3031		7.7
	.3051		7.75
	.3071		7.8
	.3110		7.9
5/16	.3125		7.93
	.3150		8.0
	.3160	O	
	.3189		8.1
	.3228		8.2
	.3230	P	
	.3248		8.25
	.3268		8.3
21/64	.3281		8.33
	.3307		8.4
	.3320	Q	
	.3346		8.5
	.3386		8.6
	.3390	R	
	.3425		8.7
11/32	.3438		8.73
	.3445		8.75
	.3465		8.8
	.3480	S	
	.3504		8.9
	.3543		9.0
	.3580	T	
	.3583		9.1
23/64	.3594		9.12
	.3622		9.2
	.3642		9.25
	.3661		9.3
	.3680	U	
	.3701		9.4
	.3740		9.5
3/8	.3750		9.52
	.3770	V	
	.3780		9.6
	.3819		9.7
	.3839		9.75
	.3858		9.8
	.3860	W	
	.3898		9.9
25/64	.3906		9.92
	.3937		10.0
	.3970	X	
	.4040	Y	
13/32	.4062		10.31
	.4130	Z	
	.4134		10.5
27/64	.4219		10.71
	.4331		11.0
7/16	.4375		11.11
	.4528		11.5
29/64	.4531		11.51
15/32	.4688		11.90
	.4724		12.0
31/64	.4844		12.30
	.4921		12.5
1/2	.5000		12.70
	.5118		13.0
33/64	.5156		13.09
17/32	.5312		13.49
	.5315		13.5
35/64	.5469		13.89
	.5512		14.0
9/16	.5625		14.28
	.5709		14.5
37/64	.5781		14.68
	.5906		15.0
19/32	.5938		15.08
39/64	.6094		15.47
	.6102		15.5
5/8	.6250		15.87
	.6299		16.0
41/64	.6406		16.27
	.6496		16.5
21/32	.6562		16.66
	.6693		17.0
43/64	.6719		17.06
11/16	.6875		17.46
	.6890		17.5
45/64	.7031		17.85
	.7087		18.0
23/32	.7188		18.25
	.7283		18.5
47/64	.7344		18.65
	.7480		19.0
3/4	.7500		19.05
49/64	.7656		19.44
	.7677		19.5
25/32	.7812		19.84
	.7874		20.0
51/64	.7969		20.24
	.8071		20.5
13/16	.8125		20.63
	.8268		21.0
53/64	.8281		21.03
27/32	.8438		21.43
	.8465		21.5
55/64	.8594		21.82
	.8661		22.0
7/8	.8750		22.22
	.8858		22.5
57/64	.8906		22.62
	.9055		23.0
29/32	.9062		23.01
59/64	.9219		23.41
	.9252		23.5
15/16	.9375		23.81
	.9449		24.0
61/64	.9531		24.2
	.9646		24.5
31/32	.9688		24.6
	.9843		25.0
63/64	.9844		25.0
1	1.0000		25.4

GLOSSARY OF TERMS

AIR/FUEL RATIO: The ratio of air to gasoline by weight in the fuel mixture drawn into the engine.

AIR INJECTION: One method of reducing harmful exhaust emissions by injecting air into each of the exhaust ports of an engine. The fresh air entering the hot exhaust manifold causes any remaining fuel to be burned before it can exit the tailpipe.

ALTERNATOR: A device used for converting mechanical energy into electrical energy.

AMMETER: An instrument, calibrated in amperes, used to measure the flow of an electrical current in a circuit. Ammeters are always connected in series with the circuit being tested.

AMPERE: The rate of flow of electrical current present when one volt of electrical pressure is applied against one ohm of electrical resistance.

ANALOG COMPUTER: Any microprocessor that uses similar (analogous) electrical signals to make its calculations.

ARMATURE: A laminated, soft iron core wrapped by a wire that converts electrical energy to mechanical energy as in a motor or relay. When rotated in a magnetic field, it changes mechanical energy into electrical energy as in a generator.

ATMOSPHERIC PRESSURE: The pressure on the Earth's surface caused by the weight of the air in the atmosphere. At sea level, this pressure is 14.7 psi at 32°F (101 kPa at 0°C).

ATOMIZATION: The breaking down of a liquid into a fine mist that can be suspended in air.

AXIAL PLAY: Movement parallel to a shaft or bearing bore.

BACKFIRE: The sudden combustion of gases in the intake or exhaust system that results in a loud explosion.

BACKLASH: The clearance or play between two parts, such as meshed gears.

BACKPRESSURE: Restrictions in the exhaust system that slow the exit of exhaust gases from the combustion chamber.

BAKELITE: A heat resistant, plastic insulator material commonly used in printed circuit boards and transistorized components.

BALL BEARING: A bearing made up of hardened inner and outer races between which hardened steel ball roll.

BALLAST RESISTOR: A resistor in the primary ignition circuit that lowers voltage after the engine is started to reduce wear on ignition components.

BEARING: A friction reducing, supportive device usually located between a stationary part and a moving part.

BIMETAL TEMPERATURE SENSOR: Any sensor or switch made of two dissimilar types of metal that bend when heated or cooled due to the different expansion rates of the alloys. These types of sensors usually function as an on/off switch.

BLOWBY: Combustion gases, composed of water vapor and unburned fuel, that leak past the piston rings into the crankcase during normal engine operation. These gases are removed by the PCV system to prevent the build-up of harmful acids in the crankcase.

BRAKE PAD: A brake shoe and lining assembly used with disc brakes.

BRAKE SHOE: The backing for the brake lining. The term is, however, usually applied to the assembly of the brake backing and lining.

BUSHING: A liner, usually removable, for a bearing; an anti-friction liner used in place of a bearing.

BYPASS: System used to bypass ballast resistor during engine cranking to increase voltage supplied to the coil.

CALIPER: A hydraulically activated device in a disc brake system, which is mounted straddling the brake rotor (disc). The caliper contains at least one piston and two brake pads. Hydraulic pressure on the piston(s) forces the pads against the rotor.

CAMSHAFT: A shaft in the engine on which are the lobes (cams) which operate the valves. The camshaft is driven by the crankshaft, via a belt, chain or gears, at one half the crankshaft speed.

CAPACITOR: A device which stores an electrical charge.

CARBON MONOXIDE (CO): a colorless, odorless gas given off as a normal byproduct of combustion. It is poisonous and extremely dangerous in confined areas, building up slowly to toxic levels without warning if adequate ventilation is not available.

CARBURETOR: A device, usually mounted on the intake manifold of an engine, which mixes the air and fuel in the proper proportion to allow even combustion.

CATALYTIC CONVERTER: A device installed in the exhaust system, like a muffler, that converts harmful byproducts of combustion into carbon dioxide and water vapor by means of a heat-producing chemical reaction.

CENTRIFUGAL ADVANCE: A mechanical method of advancing the spark timing by using flyweights in the distributor that react to centrifugal force generated by the distributor shaft rotation.

CHECK VALVE: Any one-way valve installed to permit the flow of air, fuel or vacuum in one direction only.

CHOKE: A device, usually a moveable valve, placed in the intake path of a carburetor to restrict the flow of air.

CIRCUIT: Any unbroken path through which an electrical current can flow. Also used to describe fuel flow in some instances.

CIRCUIT BREAKER: A switch which protects an electrical circuit from overload by opening the circuit when the current flow exceeds a predetermined level. Some circuit breakers must be reset manually, while other reset automatically

COIL (IGNITION): A transformer in the ignition circuit which steps of the voltage provided to the spark plugs.

COMBINATION MANIFOLD: An assembly which includes both the intake and exhaust manifolds in one casting.

COMBINATION VALVE: A device used in some fuel systems that routes fuel vapors to a charcoal storage canister instead of venting them into the atmosphere. The valve relieves fuel tank pressure and allows fresh air into the tank as fuel level drops to prevent a vapor lock situation.

COMPRESSION RATIO: The comparison of the total volume of the cylinder and combustion chamber with the piston at BDC and the piston at TDC.

CONDENSER: 1. An electrical device which acts to store an electrical charge, preventing voltage surges.
2. A radiator-like device in the air conditioning system in which refrigerant gas condenses into a liquid, giving off heat.

CONDUCTOR: Any material through which an electrical current can be transmitted easily.

CONTINUITY: Continuous or complete circuit. Can be checked with an ohmmeter.

COUNTERSHAFT: An intermediate shaft which is rotated by a mainshaft and transmits, in turn, that rotation to a working part.

CRANKCASE: The lower part of an engine in which the crankshaft and related parts operate.

CRANKSHAFT: The main driving shaft of an engine which receives reciprocating motion from the pistons and converts it to rotary motion.

CYLINDER: In an engine, the round hole in the engine block in which the piston(s) ride.

CYLINDER BLOCK: The main structural member of an engine in which is found the cylinders, crankshaft and other principal parts.

CYLINDER HEAD: The detachable portion of the engine, fastened, usually, to the top of the cylinder block, containing all or most of the combustion chambers. On overhead valve engines, it contains the valves and their operating parts. On overhead cam engines, it contains the camshaft as well.

DEAD CENTER: The extreme top or bottom of the piston stroke.

DETONATION: An unwanted explosion of the air fuel mixture in the combustion chamber caused by excess heat and compression, advanced timing, or an overly lean mixture. Also referred to as "ping".

DIAPHRAGM: A thin, flexible wall separating two cavities, such as in a vacuum advance unit.

DIESELING: A condition in which hot spots in the combustion chamber cause the engine to run on after the key is turned off.

DIFFERENTIAL: A geared assembly which allows the transmission of motion between drive axles, giving one axle the ability to turn faster than the other.

DIODE: An electrical device that will allow current to flow in one direction only.

DISC BRAKE: A hydraulic braking assembly consisting of a brake disc, or rotor, mounted on an axle, and a caliper assembly containing, usually two brake pads which are activated by hydraulic pressure. The pads are forced against the sides of the disc, creating friction which slows the vehicle.

DISTRIBUTOR: A mechanically driven device on an engine which is responsible for electrically firing the spark plug at a predetermined point of the piston stroke.

DOWEL PIN: A pin, inserted in mating holes in two different parts allowing those parts to maintain a fixed relationship.

DRUM BRAKE: A braking system which consists of two brake shoes and one or two wheel cylinders, mounted on a fixed backing plate, and a brake drum, mounted on an axle, which revolves around the assembly. Hydraulic action applied to the wheel cylinders forces the shoes outward against the drum, creating friction and slowing the vehicle.

DWELL: The rate, measured in degrees of shaft rotation, at which an electrical circuit cycles on and off.

ELECTRONIC CONTROL UNIT (ECU): Ignition module, module, amplifier or igniter. See Module for definition.

ELECTRONIC IGNITION: A system in which the timing and firing of the spark plugs is controlled by an electronic control unit, usually called a module. These systems have not points or condenser.

ENDPLAY: The measured amount of axial movement in a shaft.

ENGINE: A device that converts heat into mechanical energy.

EXHAUST MANIFOLD: A set of cast passages or pipes which conduct exhaust gases from the engine.

FEELER GAUGE: A blade, usually metal, of precisely predetermined thickness, used to measure the clearance between two parts. These blades usually are available in sets of assorted thicknesses.

F-Head: An engine configuration in which the intake valves are in the cylinder head, while the camshaft and exhaust valves are located in the cylinder block. The camshaft operates the intake valves via lifters and pushrods, while it operates the exhaust valves directly.

FIRING ORDER: The order in which combustion occurs in the cylinders of an engine. Also the order in which spark is distributed to the plugs by the distributor.

FLATHEAD: An engine configuration in which the camshaft and all the valves are located in the cylinder block.

FLOODING: The presence of too much fuel in the intake manifold and combustion chamber which prevents the air/fuel mixture from firing, thereby causing a no-start situation.

FLYWHEEL: A disc shaped part bolted to the rear end of the crankshaft. Around the outer perimeter is affixed the ring gear. The starter drive engages the ring gear, turning the flywheel, which rotates the crankshaft, imparting the initial starting motion to the engine.

FOOT POUND (ft.lb. or sometimes, ft. lbs.): The amount of energy or work needed to raise an item weighing one pound, a distance of one foot.

FUSE: A protective device in a circuit which prevents circuit overload by breaking the circuit when a specific amperage is present. The device is constructed around a strip or wire of a lower amperage rating than the circuit it is designed to protect. When an amperage higher than that stamped on the fuse is present in the circuit, the strip or wire melts, opening the circuit.

GEAR RATIO: The ratio between the number of teeth on meshing gears.

GENERATOR: A device which converts mechanical energy into electrical energy.

HEAT RANGE: The measure of a spark plug's ability to dissipate heat from its firing end. The higher the heat range, the hotter the plug fires.

HUB: The center part of a wheel or gear.

HYDROCARBON (HC): Any chemical compound made up of hydrogen and carbon. A major pollutant formed by the engine as a byproduct of combustion.

HYDROMETER: An instrument used to measure the specific gravity of a solution.

INCH POUND (in.lb. or sometimes, in. lbs.): One twelfth of a foot pound.

INDUCTION: A means of transferring electrical energy in the form of a magnetic field. Principle used in the ignition coil to increase voltage.

INJECTION PUMP: A device, usually mechanically operated, which meters and delivers fuel under pressure to the fuel injector.

INJECTOR: A device which receives metered fuel under relatively low pressure and is activated to inject the fuel into the engine under relatively high pressure at a predetermined time.

INPUT SHAFT: The shaft to which torque is applied, usually carrying the driving gear or gears.

INTAKE MANIFOLD: A casting of passages or pipes used to conduct air or a fuel/air mixture to the cylinders.

JOURNAL: The bearing surface within which a shaft operates.

KEY: A small block usually fitted in a notch between a shaft and a hub to prevent slippage of the two parts.

MANIFOLD: A casting of passages or set of pipes which connect the cylinders to an inlet or outlet source.

MANIFOLD VACUUM: Low pressure in an engine intake manifold formed just below the throttle plates. Manifold vacuum is highest at idle and drops under acceleration.

MASTER CYLINDER: The primary fluid pressurizing device in a hydraulic system. In automotive use, it is found in brake and hydraulic clutch systems and is pedal activated, either directly or, in a power brake system, through the power booster.

MODULE: Electronic control unit, amplifier or igniter of solid state or integrated design which controls the current flow in the ignition primary circuit based on input from the pick-up coil. When the module opens the primary circuit, the high secondary voltage is induced in the coil.

NEEDLE BEARING: A bearing which consists of a number (usually a large number) of long, thin rollers.

OHM: (Ω) The unit used to measure the resistance of conductor to electrical flow. One ohm is the amount of resistance that limits current flow to one ampere in a circuit with one volt of pressure.

OHMMETER: An instrument used for measuring the resistance, in ohms, in an electrical circuit.

OUTPUT SHAFT: The shaft which transmits torque from a device, such as a transmission.

OVERDRIVE: A gear assembly which produces more shaft revolutions than that transmitted to it.

OVERHEAD CAMSHAFT (OHC): An engine configuration in which the camshaft is mounted on top of the cylinder head and operates the valve either directly or by means of rocker arms.

OVERHEAD VALVE (OHV): An engine configuration in which all of the valves are located in the cylinder head and the camshaft is located in the cylinder block. The camshaft operates the valves via lifters and pushrods.

OXIDES OF NITROGEN (NOx): Chemical compounds of nitrogen produced as a byproduct of combustion. They combine with hydrocarbons to produce smog.

OXYGEN SENSOR: Used with the feedback system to sense the presence of oxygen in the exhaust gas and signal the computer which can reference the voltage signal to an air/fuel ratio.

PINION: The smaller of two meshing gears.

PISTON RING: An open ended ring which fits into a groove on the outer diameter of the piston. Its chief function is to form a seal between the piston and cylinder wall. Most automotive pistons have three rings: two for compression sealing; one for oil sealing.

PRELOAD: A predetermined load placed on a bearing during assembly or by adjustment.

PRIMARY CIRCUIT: Is the low voltage side of the ignition system which consists of the ignition switch, ballast resistor or resistance wire, bypass, coil, electronic control unit and pick-up coil as well as the connecting wires and harnesses.

PRESS FIT: The mating of two parts under pressure, due to the inner diameter of one being smaller than the outer diameter of the other, or vice versa; an interference fit.

RACE: The surface on the inner or outer ring of a bearing on which the balls, needles or rollers move.

REGULATOR: A device which maintains the amperage and/or voltage levels of a circuit at predetermined values.

RELAY: A switch which automatically opens and/or closes a circuit.

RESISTANCE: The opposition to the flow of current through a circuit or electrical device, and is measured in ohms. Resistance is equal to the voltage divided by the amperage.

RESISTOR: A device, usually made of wire, which offers a preset amount of resistance in an electrical circuit.

RING GEAR: The name given to a ring-shaped gear attached to a differential case, or affixed to a flywheel or as part a planetary gear set.

ROLLER BEARING: A bearing made up of hardened inner and outer races between which hardened steel rollers move.

ROTOR: 1. The disc-shaped part of a disc brake assembly, upon which the brake pads bear; also called, brake disc.
2. The device mounted atop the distributor shaft, which passes current to the distributor cap tower contacts.

SECONDARY CIRCUIT: The high voltage side of the ignition system, usually above 20,000 volts. The secondary includes the ignition coil, coil wire, distributor cap and rotor, spark plug wires and spark plugs.

SENDING UNIT: A mechanical, electrical, hydraulic or electromagnetic device which transmits information to a gauge.

SENSOR: Any device designed to measure engine operating conditions or ambient pressures and temperatures. Usually electronic in nature and designed to send a voltage signal to an on-board computer, some sensors may operate as a simple on/off switch or they may provide a variable voltage signal (like a potentiometer) as conditions or measured parameters change.

SHIM: Spacers of precise, predetermined thickness used between parts to establish a proper working relationship.

SLAVE CYLINDER: In automotive use, a device in the hydraulic clutch system which is activated by hydraulic force, disengaging the clutch.

SOLENOID: A coil used to produce a magnetic field, the effect of which is produce work.

SPARK PLUG: A device screwed into the combustion chamber of a spark ignition engine. The basic construction is a conductive core inside of a ceramic insulator, mounted in an outer conductive base. An electrical charge from the spark plug wire travels along the conductive core and jumps a preset air gap to a grounding point or points at the end of the conductive base. The resultant spark ignites the fuel/air mixture in the combustion chamber.

SPLINES: Ridges machined or cast onto the outer diameter of a shaft or inner diameter of a bore to enable parts to mate without rotation.

TACHOMETER: A device used to measure the rotary speed of an engine, shaft, gear, etc., usually in rotations per minute.

THERMOSTAT: A valve, located in the cooling system of an engine, which is closed when cold and opens gradually in response to engine heating, controlling the temperature of the coolant and rate of coolant flow.

TOP DEAD CENTER (TDC): The point at which the piston reaches the top of its travel on the compression stroke.

TORQUE: The twisting force applied to an object.

TORQUE CONVERTER: A turbine used to transmit power from a driving member to a driven member via hydraulic action, providing changes in drive ratio and torque. In automotive use, it links the driveplate at the rear of the engine to the automatic transmission.

TRANSDUCER: A device used to change a force into an electrical signal.

TRANSISTOR: A semi-conductor component which can be actuated by a small voltage to perform an electrical switching function.

TUNE-UP: A regular maintenance function, usually associated with the replacement and adjustment of parts and components in the electrical and fuel systems of a vehicle for the purpose of attaining optimum performance.

TURBOCHARGER: An exhaust driven pump which compresses intake air and forces it into the combustion chambers at higher than atmospheric pressures. The increased air pressure allows more fuel to be burned and results in increased horsepower being produced.

VACUUM ADVANCE: A device which advances the ignition timing in response to increased engine vacuum.

VACUUM GAUGE: An instrument used to measure the presence of vacuum in a chamber.

VALVE: A device which control the pressure, direction of flow or rate of flow of a liquid or gas.

VALVE CLEARANCE: The measured gap between the end of the valve stem and the rocker arm, cam lobe or follower that activates the valve.

VISCOSITY: The rating of a liquid's internal resistance to flow.

VOLTMETER: An instrument used for measuring electrical force in units called volts. Voltmeters are always connected parallel with the circuit being tested.

WHEEL CYLINDER: Found in the automotive drum brake assembly, it is a device, actuated by hydraulic pressure, which, through internal pistons, pushes the brake shoes outward against the drums.

ABBREVIATIONS AND SYMBOLS

A: Ampere

AC: Alternating current

A/C: Air conditioning

A-h: Ampere hour

AT: Automatic transmission

ATDC: After top dead center

μA: Microampere

bbl: Barrel

BDC: Bottom dead center

bhp: Brake horsepower

BTDC: Before top dead center

BTU: British thermal unit

C: Celsius (Centigrade)

CCA: Cold cranking amps

cd: Candela

cm^2: Square centimeter

cm^3, cc: Cubic centimeter

CO: Carbon monoxide

CO_2: Carbon dioxide

cu.in., in^3: Cubic inch

CV: Constant velocity

Cyl.: Cylinder

DC: Direct current

ECM: Electronic control module

EFE: Early fuel evaporation

EFI: Electronic fuel injection

EGR: Exhaust gas recirculation

Exh.: Exhaust

F: Fahrenheit

F: Farad

pF: Picofarad

μF: Microfarad

FI: Fuel injection

ft.lb., ft. lb., ft. lbs.: foot pound(s)

gal: Gallon

g: Gram

HC: Hydrocarbon

HEI: High energy ignition

HO: High output

hp: Horsepower

Hyd.: Hydraulic

Hz: Hertz

ID: Inside diameter

in.lb.; in. lb.; in. lbs: inch pound(s)

Int.: Intake

K: Kelvin

kg: Kilogram

kHz: Kilohertz

km: Kilometer

km/h: Kilometers per hour

kΩ: Kilohm

kPa: Kilopascal

kV: Kilovolt

kW: Kilowatt

l: Liter

l/s: Liters per second

m: Meter

mA: Milliampere

mg: Milligram

mHz: Megahertz

mm: Millimeter

mm^2: Square millimeter

m^3: Cubic meter

MΩ: Megohm

m/s: Meters per second

MT: Manual transmission

mV: Millivolt

μm: Micrometer

N: Newton

N-m: Newton meter

NOx: Nitrous oxide

OD: Outside diameter

OHC: Over head camshaft

OHV: Over head valve

Ω: Ohm

PCV: Positive crankcase ventilation

psi: Pounds per square inch

pts: Pints

qts: Quarts

rpm: Rotations per minute

rps: Rotations per second

R-12: A refrigerant gas (Freon)

SAE: Society of Automotive Engineers

SO$_2$: Sulfur dioxide

T: Ton

t: Megagram

TBI: Throttle Body Injection

TPS: Throttle Position Sensor

V: 1. Volt; 2. Venturi

μV: Microvolt

W: Watt

x: Infinity

<: Less than

>: Greater than

Index

Power brake booster, 309, 313, 314
Power seat motor, 335
Power steering gear
    Removal and installation, 301-303
    Troubleshooting, 295-297
Power steering pump, 30
    Removal and installation, 303
    Troubleshooting, 295-297, 298
Preventive Maintenance Charts, 160
Pushing, 33

Q

Quick Reference Specifications, check description
    charts

R

Radiator, 29, 116-1119
Radiator cap, 29
Radio, 226, 227
Rear axle
    Axle shaft, 271
    Axle shaft bearing, 30, 31, 287-289
    Removal and installation, 269-271
Rear brakes, 309-320
Rear bumper, 329
Rear main oil seal, 144
Rear suspension
    Control arms, 284-287
    Shock absorbers, 284, 285
    Springs, 282
    Sway bar, 287
    Troubleshooting, 273
Rear wheel bearings, 31, 287-289
Regulator
    Operation, 331
    Removal and installation, 75, 76
    Testing and adjustment, 75, 77
Reluctor, 52, 53
Rings, 144
Rocker arms or shaft, 100-102
Rotor (Brake disc), 318
Routine maintenance, 6

S

Safety notice, iv, 3, 206
Seats, 335
Serial number location, 6, 7
Shock absorbers, 274, 284-287
Slave cylinder, 99, 263
Solenoid, 77-85, 86
Spark plugs, 37, 41
Spark plug wires, 44
Spark plug switching control, 152
Special tools, 3, 147, 207, 215
Specifications Charts
    Alternator and regulator, 77
    Brakes, 324
    Camshaft, 96
    Capacities, 24
    Carburetor, 189-191

Crankshaft and connecting rod, 96
Fastener markings and torque standards, 98
Fuses and Circuit Breakers, 235
General engine, 94
Light bulbs, 160, 232
Piston and ring, 97
Preventive Maintenance, 6-12
Starter, 87, 88
Torque, 98
Tune-up, 42, 43
Valves, 95
Wheel alignment, 283
Speedometer cable, 232
Spindles, 279
Springs, 282
Stabilizer bar, 278
Stain removal, 335, 336
Starter
    Drive replacement, 80
    Overhaul, 79
    Removal and installation, 78-85
    Solenoid or relay replacement, 77-85, 86
    Specifications, 87, 88
    Troubleshooting, 87
Steering column, 290
Steering gear
    Manual, 300, 301
    Power, 301-303
Steering knuckles, 279
    Tie rod ends, 298, 300
Steering lock, 299
Steering wheel, 290
Striker plate, 325, 333, 334
Stripped threads, 88
Suspension, 273-290, 299
Switches
    Back-up light, 243, 266
    Headlight, 232
    Ignition switch, 232
    Multi-function switch, 298
    Windshield wiper, 231

T

Tailgate, 327, 328
Tailgate lock, 328
Tailpipe, 150
Thermostat, 102
Throttle body, 60, 198-200
Tie rod ends, 299, 300
Timing (ignition), 44, 54
    Point type systems, 44, 45
    Electronic systems, 48-54
Timing belt, 131-136
Timing chain and gears, 131-136
Timing gear cover, 131-136
Tires
    Description, 23
    Rotation, 20, 21
    Troubleshooting, 21, 22
    Wear problems, 21
Toe-in, 282, 290
Tools, 2, 4, 147, 207, 215

Chilton's Repair & Tune-Up Guides

The Complete line covers domestic cars, imports, trucks, vans, RV's and 4-wheel drive vehicles.

RTUG Title	Part No.	RTUG Title	Part No.
AMC 1975-82	7199	**Corvair 1960-69**	6691
Covers all U.S. and Canadian models		Covers all U.S. and Canadian models	
Aspen/Volare 1976-80	6637	**Corvette 1953-62**	6576
Covers all U.S. and Canadian models		Covers all U.S. and Canadian models	
Audi 1970-73	5902	**Corvette 1963-84**	6843
Covers all U.S. and Canadian models.		Covers all U.S. and Canadian models	
Audi 4000/5000 1978-81	7028	**Cutlass 1970-85**	6933
Covers all U.S. and Canadian models including turbocharged and diesel engines		Covers all U.S. and Canadian models	
Barracuda/Challenger 1965-72	5807	**Dart/Demon 1968-76**	6324
Covers all U.S. and Canadian models		Covers all U.S. and Canadian models	
Blazer/Jimmy 1969-82	6931	**Datsun 1961-72**	5790
Covers all U.S. and Canadian 2- and 4-wheel drive models, including diesel engines		Covers all U.S. and Canadian models of Nissan Patrol; 1500, 1600 and 2000 sports cars; Pick-Ups; 410, 411, 510, 1200 and 240Z	
BMW 1970-82	6844		
Covers U.S. and Canadian models		**Datsun 1973-80 Spanish**	7083
Buick/Olds/Pontiac 1975-85	7308	**Datsun/Nissan F-10, 310, Stanza, Pulsar 1977-86**	7196
Covers all U.S. and Canadian full size rear wheel drive models		Covers all U.S. and Canadian models	
Cadillac 1967-84	7462	**Datsun/Nissan Pick-Ups 1970-84**	6816
Covers all U.S. and Canadian rear wheel drive models		Covers all U.S and Canadian models	
Camaro 1967-81	6735	**Datsun/Nissan Z & ZX 1970-86**	6932
Covers all U.S. and Canadian models		Covers all U.S. and Canadian models	
Camaro 1982-85	7317	**Datsun/Nissan 1200, 210, Sentra 1973-86**	7197
Covers all U.S. and Canadian models		Covers all U.S. and Canadian models	
Capri 1970-77	6695	**Datsun/Nissan 200SX, 510, 610, 710, 810, Maxima 1973-84**	7170
Covers all U.S. and Canadian models		Covers all U.S. and Canadian models	
Caravan/Voyager 1984-85	7482	**Dodge 1968-77**	6554
Covers all U.S. and Canadian models		Covers all U.S. and Canadian models	
Century/Regal 1975-85	7307	**Dodge Charger 1967-70**	6486
Covers all U.S. and Canadian rear wheel drive models, including turbocharged engines		Covers all U.S. and Canadian models	
		Dodge/Plymouth Trucks 1967-84	7459
Champ/Arrow/Sapporo 1978-83	7041	Covers all $^1/_2$, $^3/_4$, and 1 ton 2- and 4-wheel drive U.S. and Canadian models, including diesel engines	
Covers all U.S. and Canadian models			
Chevette/1000 1976-86	6836	**Dodge/Plymouth Vans 1967-84**	6934
Covers all U.S. and Canadian models		Covers all $^1/_2$, $^3/_4$, and 1 ton U.S. and Canadian models of vans, cutaways and motor home chassis	
Chevrolet 1968-85	7135		
Covers all U.S. and Canadian models		**D-50/Arrow Pick-Up 1979-81**	7032
Chevrolet 1968-79 Spanish	7082	Covers all U.S. and Canadian models	
Chevrolet/GMC Pick-Ups 1970-82 Spanish	7468	**Fairlane/Torino 1962-75**	6320
		Covers all U.S. and Canadian models	
Chevrolet/GMC Pick-Ups and Suburban 1970-86	6936	**Fairmont/Zephyr 1978-83**	6965
Covers all U.S. and Canadian $^1/_2$, $^3/_4$ and 1 ton models, including 4-wheel drive and diesel engines		Covers all U.S. and Canadian models	
		Fiat 1969-81	7042
Chevrolet LUV 1972-81	6815	**Fiesta 1978-80**	6846
Covers all U.S. and Canadian models		Covers all U.S. and Canadian models	
Chevrolet Mid-Size 1964-86	6840	**Firebird 1967-81**	5996
Covers all U.S. and Canadian models of 1964-77 Chevelle, Malibu and Malibu SS; 1974-77 Laguna; 1978-85 Malibu; 1970-86 Monte Carlo; 1964-84 El Camino, including diesel engines		Covers all U.S. and Canadian models	
		Firebird 1982-85	7345
		Covers all U.S. and Canadian models	
		Ford 1968-79 Spanish	7084
Chevrolet Nova 1986	7658	**Ford Bronco 1966-83**	7140
Covers all U.S. and Canadian models		Covers all U.S. and Canadian models	
Chevy/GMC Vans 1967-84	6930	**Ford Bronco II 1984**	7408
Covers all U.S. and Canadian models of $^1/_2$, $^3/_4$, and 1 ton vans, cutaways, and motor home chassis, including diesel engines		Covers all U.S. and Canadian models	
		Ford Courier 1972-82	6983
		Covers all U.S. and Canadian models	
Chevy S-10 Blazer/GMC S-15 Jimmy 1982-85	7383	**Ford/Mercury Front Wheel Drive 1981-85**	7055
Covers all U.S. and Canadian models		Covers all U.S. and Canadian models Escort, EXP, Tempo, Lynx, LN-7 and Topaz	
Chevy S-10/GMC S-15 Pick-Ups 1982-85	7310	**Ford/Mercury/Lincoln 1968-85**	6842
Covers all U.S. and Canadian models		Covers all U.S. and Canadian models of FORD Country Sedan, Country Squire, Crown Victoria, Custom, Custom 500, Galaxie 500, LTD through 1982, Ranch Wagon, and XL; MERCURY Colony Park, Commuter, Marquis through 1982, Gran Marquis, Monterey and Park Lane; LINCOLN Continental and Towne Car	
Chevy II/Nova 1962-79	6841		
Covers all U.S. and Canadian models			
Chrysler K- and E-Car 1981-85	7163		
Covers all U.S. and Canadian front wheel drive models			
Colt/Challenger/Vista/Conquest 1971-85	7037		
Covers all U.S. and Canadian models			
Corolla/Carina/Tercel/Starlet 1970-85	7036	**Ford/Mercury/Lincoln Mid-Size 1971-85**	6696
Covers all U.S. and Canadian models		Covers all U.S. and Canadian models of FORD Elite, 1983-85 LTD, 1977-79 LTD II, Ranchero, Torino, Gran Torino, 1977-85 Thunderbird; MERCURY 1972-85 Cougar,	
Corona/Cressida/Crown/Mk.II/Camry/Van 1970-84	7044		
Covers all U.S. and Canadian models			

continued on next page

RTUG Title	Part No.
1983-85 Marquis, Montego, 1980-85 XR-7; LINCOLN 1982-85 Continental, 1984-85 Mark VII, 1978-80 Versailles	
Ford Pick-Ups 1965-86	6913
Covers all $^1/_2$, $^3/_4$ and 1 ton, 2- and 4-wheel drive U.S. and Canadian pick-up, chassis cab and camper models, including diesel engines	
Ford Pick-Ups 1965-82 Spanish	7469
Ford Ranger 1983-84	7338
Covers all U.S. and Canadian models	
Ford Vans 1961-86	6849
Covers all U.S. and Canadian $^1/_2$, $^3/_4$ and 1 ton van and cutaway chassis models, including diesel engines	
GM A-Body 1982-85	7309
Covers all front wheel drive U.S. and Canadian models of BUICK Century, CHEVROLET Celebrity, OLDSMOBILE Cutlass Ciera and PONTIAC 6000	
GM C-Body 1985	7587
Covers all front wheel drive U.S. and Canadian models of BUICK Electra Park Avenue and Electra T-Type, CADILLAC Fleetwood and deVille, OLDSMOBILE 98 Regency and Regency Brougham	
GM J-Car 1982-85	7059
Covers all U.S. and Canadian models of BUICK Skyhawk, CHEVROLET Cavalier, CADILLAC Cimarron, OLDSMOBILE Firenza and PONTIAC 2000 and Sunbird	
GM N-Body 1985-86	7657
Covers all U.S. and Canadian models of front wheel drive BUICK Somerset and Skylark, OLDSMOBILE Calais, and PONTIAC Grand Am	
GM X-Body 1980-85	7049
Covers all U.S. and Canadian models of BUICK Skylark, CHEVROLET Citation, OLDSMOBILE Omega and PONTIAC Phoenix	
GM Subcompact 1971-80	6935
Covers all U.S. and Canadian models of BUICK Skyhawk (1975-80), CHEVROLET Vega and Monza, OLDSMOBILE Starfire, and PONTIAC Astre and 1975-80 Sunbird	
Granada/Monarch 1975-82	6937
Covers all U.S. and Canadian models	
Honda 1973-84	6980
Covers all U.S. and Canadian models	
International Scout 1967-73	5912
Covers all U.S. and Canadian models	
Jeep 1945-87	6817
Covers all U.S. and Canadian CJ-2A, CJ-3A, CJ-3B, CJ-5, CJ-6, CJ-7, Scrambler and Wrangler models	
Jeep Wagoneer, Commando, Cherokee, Truck 1957-86	6739
Covers all U.S. and Canadian models of Wagoneer, Cherokee, Grand Wagoneer, Jeepster, Jeepster Commando, J-100, J-200, J-300, J-10, J20, FC-150 and FC-170	
Laser/Daytona 1984-85	7563
Covers all U.S. and Canadian models	
Maverick/Comet 1970-77	6634
Covers all U.S. and Canadian models	
Mazda 1971-84	6981
Covers all U.S. and Canadian models of RX-2, RX-3, RX-4, 808, 1300, 1600, Cosmo, GLC and 626	
Mazda Pick-Ups 1972-86	7659
Covers all U.S. and Canadian models	
Mercedes-Benz 1959-70	6065
Covers all U.S. and Canadian models	
Mercedes-Benz 1968-73	5907
Covers all U.S. and Canadian models	

RTUG Title	Part No.
Mercedes-Benz 1974-84	6809
Covers all U.S. and Canadian models	
Mitsubishi, Cordia, Tredia, Starion, Galant 1983-85	7583
Covers all U.S. and Canadian models	
MG 1961-81	6780
Covers all U.S. and Canadian models	
Mustang/Capri/Merkur 1979-85	6963
Covers all U.S. and Canadian models	
Mustang/Cougar 1965-73	6542
Covers all U.S. and Canadian models	
Mustang II 1974-78	6812
Covers all U.S. and Canadian models	
Omni/Horizon/Rampage 1978-84	6845
Covers all U.S. and Canadian models of DODGE omni, Miser, 024, Charger 2.2; PLYMOUTH Horizon, Miser, TC3, TC3 Tourismo; Rampage	
Opel 1971-75	6575
Covers all U.S. and Canadian models	
Peugeot 1970-74	5982
Covers all U.S. and Canadian models	
Pinto/Bobcat 1971-80	7027
Covers all U.S. and Canadian models	
Plymouth 1968-76	6552
Covers all U.S. and Canadian models	
Pontiac Fiero 1984-85	7571
Covers all U.S. and Canadian models	
Pontiac Mid-Size 1974-83	7346
Covers all U.S. and Canadian models of Ventura, Grand Am, LeMans, Grand LeMans, GTO, Phoenix, and Grand Prix	
Porsche 924/928 1976-81	7046
Covers all U.S. and Canadian models	
Renault 1975-85	7165
Covers all U.S. and Canadian models	
Roadrunner/Satellite/Belvedere/GTX 1968-73	5821
Covers all U.S. and Canadian models	
RX-7 1979-81	7031
Covers all U.S. and Canadian models	
SAAB 99 1969-75	5988
Covers all U.S. and Canadian models	
SAAB 900 1979-85	7572
Covers all U.S. and Canadian models	
Snowmobiles 1976-80	6978
Covers Arctic Cat, John Deere, Kawasaki, Polaris, Ski-Doo and Yamaha	
Subaru 1970-84	6982
Covers all U.S. and Canadian models	
Tempest/GTO/LeMans 1968-73	5905
Covers all U.S. and Canadian models	
Toyota 1966-70	5795
Covers all U.S. and Canadian models of Corona, MkII, Corolla, Crown, Land Cruiser, Stout and Hi-Lux	
Toyota 1970-79 Spanish	7467
Toyota Celica/Supra 1971-85	7043
Covers all U.S. and Canadian models	
Toyota Trucks 1970-85	7035
Covers all U.S. and Canadian models of pick-ups, Land Cruiser and 4Runner	
Valiant/Duster 1968-76	6326
Covers all U.S. and Canadian models	
Volvo 1956-69	6529
Covers all U.S. and Canadian models	
Volvo 1970-83	7040
Covers all U.S. and Canadian models	
VW Front Wheel Drive 1974-85	6962
Covers all U.S. and Canadian models	
VW 1949-71	5796
Covers all U.S. and Canadian models	
VW 1970-79 Spanish	7061
VW 1970-81	6837
Covers all U.S. and Canadian Beetles, Karmann Ghia, Fastback, Squareback, Vans, 411 and 412	

Chilton's Repair Manuals are available at your local retailer or by mailing a check or money order for **$15.95** per book plus **$3.50** for 1st book and **$.50** for each additional book to cover postage and handling to:

Chilton Book Company
Dept. DM
Radnor, PA 19089

NOTE: When ordering be sure to include your name & address, book part No. & title.